MW01268725

small arms survey 2009

shadows of war

THE GRADUATE INSTITUTE | GENEVA
INSTITUT DE HAUTES ÉTUDES INTERNATIONALES ET DU DÉVELOPPEMENT
GRADUATE INSTITUTE OF INTERNATIONAL AND DEVELOPMENT STUDIES

CAMBRIDGE UNIVERSITY PRESS

Cambridge, New York, Melbourne, Madrid, Cape Town, Singapore, São Paulo, Delhi

Cambridge University Press
The Edinburgh Building, Cambridge CB2 8RU, UK

Published in the United States of America by Cambridge University Press, New York

www.cambridge.org
Information on this title: www.cambridge.org/9780521706568

© Small Arms Survey, Graduate Institute of International
and Development Studies, Geneva 2009

This publication is in copyright. Subject to statutory exception
and to the provisions of relevant collective licensing agreements,
no reproduction of any part may take place without the written
permission of Cambridge University Press.

First published 2009

Printed in the United Kingdom at the University Press, Cambridge

A catalogue record for this publication is available from the British Library

Library of Congress Cataloguing in Publication data

ISBN 978-0-521-88041-1 hardback
ISBN 978-0-521-70656-8 paperback

Cambridge University Press has no responsibility for the persistence or
accuracy of URLs for external or third-party Internet websites referred to in
this publication, and does not guarantee that any content on such websites is,
or will remain, accurate or appropriate.

FOREWORD

What I have learnt from a number of peace processes is that to overcome animosity and apprehension, the parties need to have a sustained, long-term commitment to peace. Peace agreements deserve to be celebrated; rejecting violence gives hope for the future. Yet experience shows that an agreement is only the beginning of a long and arduous road towards sustained peace. Building peace must involve all in the community. Support from the international community can play a crucial role in this process.

The commitment of the parties to a settlement is almost always challenged by a range of threats in the post-conflict period. Typically, they emerge from economic, governance, and security sector problems prevailing in war-torn societies. After armed conflict, public infrastructure is often ruined, state finances depleted, large numbers of people and entire communities displaced, and poverty aggravated. Institutions and agencies of the state must be rebuilt from the ground up. The scale of the challenge is not made any easier by the fact that the ethnic, political, or economic reasons for the conflict often remain unresolved.

The *Small Arms Survey 2009: Shadows of War* makes it clear that armed violence in the post-war period is particularly detrimental to any peace-building effort. Violence and insecurity can be worse than in wartime. Violence can inexplicably multiply and assume new forms, thus jeopardizing recovery. Consequently, managing armed violence is a priority concern for post-conflict societies and the multilateral and bilateral agencies working to support them.

If it takes into account the lessons available, the international community is increasingly better placed to respond to post-war violence. Disarmament, demobilization, and reintegration do not amount to a panacea, but increasingly integrated, flexible, and synergetic approaches need to be developed. Preventing violence and reforming the state security sector are recognized as essential elements of successful peace processes. Combining formal and informal measures of stabilization and 'second-generation' measures gives reason for hope, as highlighted in the pages of this volume.

Any armed conflict causes immense human suffering and should be brought to an end without delay. Achieving this in a sustainable way is a precondition for early recovery. This requires constant reassessment of the knowledge base and the tools available to assist war-affected societies in securing lasting peace and security. By providing informed reflection on recent developments in post-conflict security promotion, the *Small Arms Survey* makes a valuable contribution to this end.

—Martti Ahtisaari

Former President of Finland

2008 Nobel Peace Prize laureate

CONTENTS

ABOUT THE SMALL ARMS SURVEY

The Small Arms Survey is an independent research project located at the Graduate Institute of International and Development Studies in Geneva, Switzerland. Established in 1999, the project is supported by the Swiss Federal Department of Foreign Affairs, and by sustained contributions from the Governments of Belgium, Canada, Finland, Germany, the Netherlands, Norway, Sweden, and the United Kingdom. The Survey is also grateful for past and current project support received from the Governments of Australia, Denmark, France, New Zealand, Spain, and the United States, as well as from different United Nations agencies, programmes, and institutes.

The objectives of the Small Arms Survey are: to be the principal source of public information on all aspects of small arms and armed violence; to serve as a resource centre for governments, policy-makers, researchers, and activists; to monitor national and international initiatives (governmental and nongovernmental) on small arms; to support efforts to address the effects of small arms proliferation and misuse; and to act as a clearinghouse for the sharing of information and the dissemination of best practices. The Survey also sponsors field research and information-gathering efforts, especially in affected states and regions. The project has an international staff with expertise in security studies, political science, law, economics, development studies, and sociology, and collaborates with a network of researchers, partner institutions, non-governmental organizations, and governments in more than 50 countries.

NOTES TO READERS

Abbreviations: Lists of abbreviations can be found at the end of each chapter.

Chapter cross-referencing: Chapter cross-references appear capitalized in brackets throughout the text. For example, in Chapter 8 on reintegration of former combatants in Aceh: 'As in other post-war contexts, these acts of violence differed in nature from those of the war era (POST-CONFLICT SECURITY).'

Exchange rates: All monetary values are expressed in current US dollars (USD). When other currencies are also cited, unless otherwise indicated, they are converted to USD using the 365-day average exchange rate for the period 1 September 2007 to 31 August 2008.

Small Arms Survey: The plain text—Small Arms Survey—is used to indicate the overall project and its activities, while the italicized version—*Small Arms Survey*—refers to the publication. The *Survey,* appearing italicized, refers generally to past and future editions.

Web site: For more detailed information and current developments on small arms issues, readers are invited to visit the Small Arms Survey Web site at www.smallarmssurvey.org

Small Arms Survey
Graduate Institute of International and Development Studies
47 Avenue Blanc, 1202 Geneva, Switzerland

t +41 22 908 5777
f +41 22 732 2738
e sas@smallarmssurvey.org
w www.smallarmssurvey.org

ACKNOWLEDGEMENTS

This is the ninth edition of the *Small Arms Survey*. Like previous editions, it is a collective product of the staff of the Small Arms Survey project, based at the Graduate Institute of International and Development Studies in Geneva, Switzerland, with support from partners. Numerous researchers in Geneva and around the world have contributed to this volume, and it has benefited from the input and advice of government officials, advocates, experts, and colleagues from the small arms research community and beyond.

The principal chapter authors were assisted by in-house and external contributors who are acknowledged in the relevant chapters. In addition, detailed reviews of the chapters were provided by: Bradford Adams, Edward Aspinall, Dainius Baublys, Jurgen Brauer, Mark Bromley, Silvia Cattaneo, Christina Clark-Kazak, Helen Close, Neil Corney, John Darby, Owen Greene, Gavin Hales, Peter Hall, Paul Holtom, Michael Hasenau, Tracy Hite, David Huxford, Richard Jones, Mark Knight, Andrew Leigh, Roy Licklider, Neda Mansouri, Gary Milante, Ananda Millard, Luke Mullany, Robin Poulton, Daniël Prins, Hameed Quraishi, Hans Risser, Les Roberts, Mark Sedra, Susan Shepler, Clare da Silva, Michael Spagat, Rachel Stohl, Cordula Strocka, Yuhki Tajima, Alex de Waal, and Siemon Wezeman.

Eric G. Berman, Keith Krause, Emile LeBrun, and Glenn McDonald were responsible for the overall planning and organization of this edition. Alessandra Allen managed the editing and production of the *Survey* with the help of Tania Inowlocki. Tania Inowlocki, Michael James, and Alex Potter copy-edited the book; Jillian Luff produced the maps; Richard Jones provided the layout and design; Donald Strachan proofread the *Survey*; and Margaret Binns compiled the index. John Haslam, Carrie Cheek, and Alison Powell of Cambridge University Press provided support throughout the production of the *Survey*. Richard Abott, Ivanka Barzashka, Sahar Hasan, Sarah Hoban, Jasna Lazarevic, Emilia Richard, Savannah de Tessières, and Bilyana Tsvetkova assisted with fact-checking. Yuliya Fruman helped with photo research. David Olivier, Benjamin Pougnier, and Carole Touraine provided administrative support.

The project also benefited from the support of the Graduate Institute of International and Development Studies, in particular Philippe Burrin, Oliver Jütersonke, and Monique Nendaz.

We are extremely grateful to the Swiss government—especially the Department for Foreign Affairs and the Swiss Development Cooperation—for its generous financial and overall support of the Small Arms Survey project, in particular Rita Adam, Serge Bavaud, Siro Beltrametti, Erwin Bollinger, Jean-François Cuénod, Thomas Greminger, Cristina Hoyos, Peter Maurer, Jürg Streuli, Anton Thalmann, and Reto Wollenmann. Financial support for the project was also provided by the Governments of Australia, Belgium, Canada, Denmark, Finland, Germany, the Netherlands, Norway, Spain, Sweden, and the United Kingdom.

In addition, during 2008 the project received financial support for various projects from within the framework of the European Cooperation in the field of Scientific and Technical Research (COST), the Francophonie, the Norwegian Institute of International Affairs (NUPI), the Organisation for Economic Co-operation and Development, the UN Children's Fund, the UN Development Programme, the UN Institute for Disarmament Research, UN Office for the Coordination of Humanitarian Affairs, the UN Office on Drugs and Crime, and the World Bank. The project further benefits from the support of international agencies, including the International Committee of the Red Cross, the UN Office for Disarmament Affairs, the UN High Commissioner for Refugees, and the World Health Organization.

In Geneva, the project has received support and expert advice from: David Atwood, Peter Batchelor, Robin Coupland, Paul Eavis, Gillian Frost, Magnus Hellgren, Hannu Himanen, Patrick Mc Carthy, Jennifer Milliken, and Tarja Pesämaa.

Beyond Geneva, we also received support from a number of colleagues. In addition to those mentioned above, and in specific chapters, we would like to thank: Michael Cassandra, Dalius Čekuolis, Gugulethu Dube, George Fuchs, Debarati Guha-Sapir, Steven Malby, Mary May, Yeshua Moser-Puangsuwan, and Jorge Restrepo.

Our sincere thanks go out to many other individuals (who remain unnamed) for their continuing support of the project. Our apologies to anyone we have failed to mention.

—Keith Krause, Programme Director
Eric G. Berman, Managing Director

Small Arms Survey 2009

Editors	Eric G. Berman, Keith Krause, Emile LeBrun, and Glenn McDonald
Coordinator	Glenn McDonald
Publications Manager	Alessandra Allen
Designer	Richard Jones, Exile: Design & Editorial Services
Cartographer	Jillian Luff, MAP*grafix*
Copy-editors	Tania Inowlocki, Michael James, and Alex Potter
Proofreader	Donald Strachan

Principal chapter authors

Introduction	Glenn McDonald and Emile LeBrun
Chapter 1	Pablo Dreyfus, Jasna Lazarevic, Nic Marsh, and Matt Schroeder
Chapter 2	Sarah Parker
Chapter 3	James Bevan
Chapter 4	James Bevan, Glenn McDonald, and Sarah Parker
Chapter 5	Aaron Karp
Chapter 6	Jonah Leff and Helen Moestue
Chapter 7	Robert Muggah
Chapter 8	Patrick Barron
Chapter 9	Michael Bhatia, Emile LeBrun, Robert Muggah, and Mark Sedra
Chapter 10	Royce Hutson and Athena Kolbe

A fireman takes cover during a confrontation between militant supporters of toppled president Jean-Bertrand Aristide and the police in Posmarchan, Haiti, June 2005. © Ramon Espinosa/AP Photo

Introduction

INTRODUCTION

The end of armed conflict does not always—or even typically—bring an end to pervasive armed violence. Peace agreements are signed, fighting forces disbanded, many of their weapons recovered and destroyed; nevertheless, guns continue to kill and injure large numbers of people. Parts of a country that were formerly insulated from the impacts of war may suddenly be transformed into killing fields. The civil war in Guatemala ended in 1996, but violence in the country, now at critical levels, has expanded to affect the entire society. The Democratic Republic of the Congo saw its violent death rates drop after the formal end of war in 2002, yet overall mortality has remained exceptionally high, with hundreds of thousands of people dying from easily treatable illnesses, such as malaria, diarrhoea, pneumonia, and malnutrition—delayed, indirect consequences of war. In case after case, the much heralded 'peace dividend' is suppressed by the aftershocks of armed conflict.

Post-conflict violence is frequently fuelled by many of the same political, economic, and communal factors that give rise to war in the first place. Fragile state structures exacerbate the problem—for example, by enabling former warlords to seek new revenue streams through organized criminal violence. An abundance of (unregulated) small arms and light weapons, coupled with an increased social acceptance of armed violence, add to the mix. A shifting constellation of state agents and armed groups prey on these vulnerabilities. Among war's many shadows is the very real risk that the society will return to full-scale armed conflict.

Given the extent to which post-war violence can undermine community security and socio-economic development, curtailing it is an obvious priority for affected states as well as the donor governments and international agencies that have invested heavily in the promotion of peace and state reconstruction. For this reason, the disarmament, demobilization, and reintegration (DDR) of ex-combatants has been a staple of international peace-building for at least two decades. Much work has been done to distil and refine good DDR practices; the most prominent of these contributions is the United Nations' set of Integrated DDR Standards (IDDRS), developed in 2006. Yet documents such as the IDDRS reflect a set of assumptions that may not apply in all contexts. Moreover, if the state cannot provide security for all of its citizens, weapons management programmes will have limited feasibility and reach.

The *Small Arms Survey 2009: Shadows of War* explores some of the many challenges facing countries emerging from war. It reviews how affected states, UN agencies, and donor governments respond to these problems, not only through DDR and other conventional programmes, but also using approaches that focus on identifying and counteracting risk factors for armed violence in the post-war period. 'Interim stabilization' measures, designed to create space before more formal, large-scale security promotion activities take place, are undertaken during the sensitive period coinciding with or immediately after the end of armed conflict. 'Second-generation' interventions accompany or follow DDR and security sector reform (SSR), addressing specific security challenges, often at the local level.

Other tools remain underutilized. The tracing of weapons and ammunition can help detect illicit trafficking and weak stockpile security, crucial findings in fragile post-conflict environments, where even a small number of arms can undermine security gains. For this reason, controlling arms flows and stockpiles will remain a priority for many post-war societies. At the same time, policy-makers are expanding their focus beyond the tools of armed violence in an attempt to shape not only weapons availability, but also the conditions that foster weapons misuse.

Chapter highlights

Four chapters in the *Small Arms Survey 2009* are devoted to the book's principal theme of post-conflict violence and security promotion. A chapter on post-conflict security, outlining the key challenges in this area, is followed by three case studies. A chapter on DDR in Aceh raises important questions about the application of the reintegration model to middle-income countries. Afghanistan serves as a vivid illustration of the difficulty inherent in building security while simultaneously creating a new state; it also exemplifies why the 'post-conflict' label may not always be appropriate after the formal end of a war. The thematic section ends with a chapter that explores perceptions of security in Southern Lebanon following the 2006 Hizbollah–Israel war. In an environment where the root causes of political violence endure, the population is cautious about government gun control yet surprisingly supportive of state security institutions.

This year's second theme, arms transfers, is addressed in the volume's three opening chapters. While the fate of the Arms Trade Treaty process was unclear at the time of writing, this edition's comprehensive review of export controls identifies some important control gaps and troubling differences in licensing practices among the world's major exporting states. In the chapter on authorized small arms transfers, new sources of data—and the expansion and refinement of existing sources—have allowed for a more precise estimate of the scale of the global firearms trade. The third chapter in the transfers section emphasizes the potential value of tracing weapons and ammunition in conflict and post-conflict settings, though it notes that, despite modest resource implications, the international community has yet to embrace this measure.

Additional chapters in the 2009 edition focus on small arms measures and impacts. The UN update chapter analyses developments at the United Nations in 2008, a year that opened up new possibilities for the *Programme of Action* and finally brought ammunition into the global arms control picture. A review of state-sponsored disarmament, weapons collection, and destruction concludes that these activities are most effective when accepted as legitimate. An overview of the impacts of small arms on children and youth rounds out the volume.

Transfers section

Chapter 1 (Authorized transfers): New sources of data—and the expansion and refinement of existing sources—are resulting in greater understanding of the international trade in small arms and light weapons. As in previous years, the transfers chapter uses customs data compiled by the UN (UN Comtrade) as the basis for its analysis of the global authorized trade but, in part of the chapter, supplements it with information from other sources including the UN Register of Conventional Arms and national reporting.

Using UN Comtrade data, the chapter identifies a 28 per cent increase in the value of worldwide transfers of small arms and light weapons from 2000 to 2006. Using multiple data sources for 53 exporting countries, it estimates the value of documented firearms transfers at approximately USD 1.58 billion in 2006. This figure includes USD 140 million in firearms transfers that were not captured by customs data. This study is the first phase of a multi-year project aimed at developing a more precise estimate of the global trade in small arms and light weapons, including their parts, accessories, and ammunition.

Definition of small arms and light weapons

The Small Arms Survey uses the term 'small arms and light weapons' to cover both military-style small arms and light weapons as well as commercial firearms (handguns and long guns). It largely follows the definition used in the Report of the UN Panel of Governmental Experts on Small Arms (UN doc. A/52/298):

Small arms: revolvers and self-loading pistols, rifles and carbines, sub-machine guns, assault rifles, and light machine guns.

Light weapons: heavy machine guns, grenade launchers, portable anti-tank and anti-aircraft guns, recoilless rifles, portable anti-tank missile and rocket launchers, portable anti-aircraft missile launchers, and mortars of under 100 mm calibre.

Chapter 2 (Export controls): This chapter provides an overview of the export controls of the world's major exporting states. It compares the legislative and administrative frameworks governing the licensing of military small arms exports and explores the associated decision-making process, including the government agencies involved in licensing decisions and the criteria they apply.

Strong export controls are a vital tool in the fight against diversion and illicit trafficking. This chapter highlights the diversity among states' export control arrangements and exposes some of the gaps in the implementation of their international and regional arms transfer commitments. The most glaring weaknesses seem to affect post-shipment controls—and end-use monitoring in particular—making it difficult for states to determine whether their export control systems are effective in preventing the diversion of weapons to unauthorized end users and end uses.

Chapter 3 (Conflict tracing): The international community has come to recognize that the ability to trace weapons—from their place of manufacture to their use in the world's conflicts of concern—is an important component of efforts to control illicit small arms proliferation. Despite more than a decade of attention to small arms identification and tracing, however, the international community has yet to make full use of these significant tools in conflict and post-conflict contexts. Efforts to control illicit trafficking need to be founded on firm evidence if they are to be successful. To this end, this chapter explores the processes and competencies required to identify weapons and track their transfer routes. It is intended to serve as a practical guide to the tracing of small arms, light weapons, and their ammunition, one that could facilitate the development of more effective tracing by states and organizations working in conflict and post-conflict societies.

Spotlight issues

Chapter 4 (UN update): The UN update chapter reviews three main developments at the United Nations in 2008: the Third Biennial Meeting for the *UN Programme of Action* (BMS3), an experts' report on ammunition stockpiles, and initial discussions of a possible Arms Trade Treaty. Although the BMS3 outcome and *Ammunition Report* offer a wealth of possibilities for international small arms work over the coming years, the chapter stresses that, for the moment, these remain possibilities, not realities.

The documents agreed in 2008, coupled with earlier ones on weapons tracing and brokering, help establish a set of benchmarks for implementation in the areas they cover. This should facilitate the evaluation of progress in the implementation of the *Programme of Action* and other instruments, especially if accompanied by more systematic and rigorous reporting, including an analysis of reporting. Fundamentally, the production of new documents, important as they might be, is only progress on paper. Eight years after the adoption of the *UN Programme of Action*, the priority remains implementation.

Chapter 5 (Disarmament): Small arms and light weapons disarmament measures are becoming routine and widespread. This chapter provides an empirical review of their contribution to conflict and violence abatement. It focuses on systematic weapons collection and destruction among civilians, the state, and non-state combatants. The data and case studies show that, whether they are a cause of change or a correlate, collection and disarmament activities are usually associated with reduced armed violence and enhanced political stability. The prospects for further small arms collection and disarmament are considerable. At least 40 per cent of state arsenals—some 76 million small arms—appear to be surplus to requirements and highly suitable for destruction. Collection and destruction seem readily feasible for approximately 20 per cent of all civilian firearms—another 120 million or more. The experiences recounted in this chapter indicate that disarmament is neither a universal antidote for armed violence and political instability, nor, when undertaken with public consent, a threat to liberty or security.

Chapter 6 (Children and youth): Those seeking to understand and mitigate the impacts of armed violence increasingly recognize children and youth as a distinct stakeholder group. It is widely understood that male adolescents and young men are disproportionately the direct victims (as well as perpetrators) of armed violence. An expanding body of research is also highlighting the specific—and often long-lasting—effects of such violence on broader groups of children and youth. This chapter shows that while the direct impacts of armed violence are highly visible and measurable, the indirect impacts, including disrupted schooling, disease, and malnutrition, affect many others. Despite their vulnerabilities, it also appears that, as a group, children and youth demonstrate enormous resilience to the effects of armed violence. Further study is needed, however, to understand how these coping mechanisms function and how they can be strengthened.

Post-conflict section

Chapter 7 (Post-conflict security): Armed violence can persist long after the formal end of war. Managing such violence is essential to the long-term recovery of affected societies, yet conventional approaches to post-conflict security promotion, such as DDR and SSR, are often unable to meet these security needs. This chapter reviews the factors that influence the distribution and intensity of post-conflict armed violence, including the persistence of wartime patronage networks and changing motivations of violence entrepreneurs. It also examines some of the new strategies that seek to address the risks and dynamics of post-conflict violence. These include the deployment of interim stabilization measures in the period before DDR and SSR can get under way and second-generation interventions, which typically target key security challenges. In contrast to many of the larger, more conventional programmes, these measures are tailored to the local context and based on identified needs and risk factors.

Chapter 8 (Aceh): The transition from secessionist conflict to peace in Aceh, Indonesia, has been hailed as a model. Following the 2005 peace agreement between the Free Aceh Movement and the government, disarmament proceeded smoothly, former rebels became legitimate political figures, and security gains were realized. Yet the reintegration of former combatants has not proceeded effectively, and peace dividends are unequally distributed across communities.

Based on surveys of ex-combatants and civilians, conflict monitoring, and poverty assessments conducted over three years, the chapter finds that reintegration programmes have failed, in part because of false assumptions about ex-combatants and their relations to the community. Orthodox DDR theory presupposes low levels of social cohesion between ex-combatants and civilians and, moreover, assumes that the former will face economic disadvantage upon their return to civilian life; yet neither assumption held true in Aceh. Cash distributions without technical assistance or monitoring, and the absence of long-term assistance to conflict-affected areas, are other key reasons for the disappointing reintegration outcomes.

Chapter 9 (Afghanistan): Since the overthrow of the Taliban regime in late 2001, the international community has supported efforts to build an effective security sector, facilitate the development of a nationally representative government, and reduce the widespread influence and authority of armed groups in Afghanistan. These activities have involved the disarmament, demobilization, and reintegration of the Afghan Military Forces (AMF) and follow-on measures targeting AMF and other groups that were missed during DDR.

Three years after the DDR effort ended, some important gains have been realized, including the disarmament and demobilization of some 63,000 AMF and the collection of approximately 100,000 weapons and 30,000 tons of ammunition. The disbandment of illegal armed groups project has also reduced the numbers of warlords, drug lords, and other illegal armed group leaders in the government. But the persistence of commander–militiamen linkages and continuing—even growing—insecurity in the country have demonstrated the limits of what can be achieved when state-building, peace-building, counter-insurgency, and counter-narcotics operations coincide.

Chapter 10 (Southern Lebanon): The Lebanon chapter presents the results of a household survey conducted in the south of the country in March–May 2008, nearly two years after the Hizbollah–Israel war. It supports independent reports of some 1,000 deaths and widespread property damage in the south as a result of the 2006 war and helps shed light on attitudes towards arms and security in the region.

Although Southern Lebanon has long been characterized as a Hizbollah stronghold, its people appear to have more confidence in state security institutions than previously believed. The study reveals strong support for the Lebanese army and police, but also points to the limits of public confidence in state security providers. While significant numbers of southerners back government regulation of civilian gun ownership and the banning of non-state armed groups, many others oppose such measures. Continuing tensions, both within the country and with Israel, are a likely source of caution on weapons issues.

Conclusion

The shadows of war are many and overlapping. In some countries, the conflict–post-conflict distinction has lost its meaning. In others, the risk of a return to war persists because the motivations for conflict remain, as do the means. It is unreasonable to expect a country emerging from many years of war to make a smooth and painless transition to peace. This edition highlights the numerous hazards this transition entails, as well as some of the measures—whether well-established or less conventional—designed to put war-torn societies on a path to sustainable peace.

In this volume, the Small Arms Survey continues its exploration of the causes, consequences, and correctives to the problem of armed violence, with a particular focus on small arms and light weapons proliferation. The 2010 edition of the *Survey* will continue to investigate these issues with a special emphasis on weapons use and armed violence perpetrated by urban gangs and other groups, including some of the interventions now being deployed to address this problem of growing concern.

—Glenn McDonald and Emile LeBrun
Editors

Visitors inspect assault rifles and guns during a defence f
in Belgrade, Serbia, June 2007. © Srdjan Ilic/AP Pho

Sifting the Sources

AUTHORIZED SMALL ARMS TRANSFERS

1

INTRODUCTION

For years, spotty and imperfect information from governments precluded a firm estimate of the global authorized trade in small arms and light weapons, and their parts, accessories, and ammunition. The *Small Arms Survey 2006* advanced a figure of around USD 4 billion, based on available customs data amounting to roughly half of this figure, but underlined its tentative nature (Small Arms Survey, 2006, pp. 66–67). Nonetheless, new sources of data—and the expansion and refinement of existing sources—are resulting in greater international understanding of the trade in small arms and light weapons.

According to customs data reported to the UN Commodity Trade Statistics Database (UN Comtrade),[1] in 2006 firearms accounted for approximately USD 1.44 billion of the USD 2.97 billion in transfers of small arms, light weapons, and their parts, accessories, and ammunition. This chapter assesses the former figure through an in-depth analysis of data on the three main categories of firearms: sporting and hunting shotguns and rifles, pistols and revolvers, and military firearms. A 53-country comparison of data from UN Comtrade with data from other sources—including the UN Register of Conventional Arms (UN Register) and national and regional arms transfer reports[2]—reveals an estimated USD 140 million in additional firearms transfers not captured in customs data. Based on this combined data, the Small Arms Survey estimates that the documented global authorized trade in firearms was worth approximately USD 1.58 billion in 2006.[3] The undocumented trade, which remains prevalent despite greater reporting on firearms transfers, is likely to be at least USD 100 million (see Box 1.3). Assuming that the trade in light weapons—along with parts, accessories, and ammunition for small arms and light weapons—is also under-reported in UN Comtrade, the actual value of the trade in small arms and light weapons almost certainly exceeds the previous USD 4 billion estimate. Over the next few years, the Small Arms Survey will attempt to deal with this issue more definitively by systematically analysing the trade in light weapons, as well as parts, accessories, and ammunition for small arms and light weapons. By the end of this process, the Survey will have comprehensively reassessed the entire global trade and will be able to provide a more refined analysis.

Major findings of this chapter include the following:

- A comprehensive survey of data on firearms transfers from 53 important exporting countries reveals that the authorized trade in firearms worldwide was at least USD 1.58 billion in 2006.
- Existing data suggests that the previous estimate of USD 4 billion for the global authorized trade in small arms and light weapons and their parts, accessories, and ammunition is a significant underestimate.
- According to available customs data, the authorized trade in small arms and light weapons, and their parts, accessories, and ammunition increased by approximately increased by approximately 28 per cent from 2000 to 2006 after adjusting for inflation.

- While many countries have improved their reporting of small arms and light weapons transfers, a number of others remain selective in the information that they provide, issue misleading information, or do not report on such transfers at all.
- Suspected or known significant exporters of small arms that report little or no information on their firearms exports include Belarus, Iran, Israel, North Korea, and South Africa. Other exporters, including China, Pakistan, Singapore, and the Russian Federation, provide some data on exports of sporting shotguns and rifles, but little or no data on their military firearms exports.

The authorized trade in firearms worldwide was at least USD 1.58 billion in 2006.

- In 2006 the top exporters of small arms and light weapons (those with an annual export value of at least USD 100 million), according to available customs data, were (in descending order) the United States, Italy, Germany, Brazil, Austria, and Belgium. We believe that China and the Russian Federation also merit 'top' exporter status, although customs data alone does not support this. The top importers of small arms and light weapons for that year (those with an annual import value of at least USD 100 million), according to customs data, were (in descending order) the United States, France, Japan, Canada, South Korea, Germany, and Australia.[4]
- The exports of no more than 20 countries account for 80 per cent of the trade in small arms and light weapons.
- The 2009 Transparency Barometer identifies Switzerland, the United Kingdom, Germany, Norway, the Netherlands, Serbia,[5] and the United States as the most transparent of the major small arms and light weapons exporters. The least transparent major exporters are Iran and North Korea, both scoring zero.
- The United States imports most of the world's exported handguns and many of the world's exported sporting and hunting shotguns and rifles. In 2006 handgun sales to the United States accounted for 59 per cent of the major exporters' sales, and US imports of sporting and hunting shotguns and rifles accounted for 42 per cent.
- Most of the reported trade in sporting and hunting shotguns and rifles occurs among wealthy Western countries, which are both major exporters and importers.

The chapter begins with a brief overview of terms and definitions in the section entitled 'Framing the issues'. The next section, 'Global trends, 2000–06', provides a brief analysis of recent trends in the authorized trade in small arms and light weapons and their parts, accessories, and ammunition, as revealed by customs data reported to UN Comtrade. The focus of the chapter then narrows to an analysis of the authorized trade in firearms, while drawing on data from several additional sources, including the UN Register and various national and regional reports. The section entitled 'Charting a new approach' looks at recent changes to the various data sources and what they reveal (and do not reveal) about the global trade in firearms. It also summarizes the results of a 53-country assessment of data on firearms transfers from multiple sources. The next section, 'Analysis of firearms transfers in 2006', gives a category-by-category analysis of firearms transfers in 2006. The Small Arms Trade Transparency Barometer 2009 concludes the chapter.

FRAMING THE ISSUE: KEY TERMS AND CONCEPTS

This section provides summaries and definitions for several key terms and references used repeatedly in the chapter.[6] For the purposes of this chapter, the terms 'small arms' and 'light weapons' are used slightly differently than in the 1997 *Report of the Panel of Governmental Experts on Small Arms* (UNGA, 1997).[7] The term 'small arms and light weapons' is used here to refer not only to the items individually categorized as 'small arms' and 'light weapons' by the UN Panel, but also small arms ammunition, missiles and shells for light weapons, landmines, grenades, and parts and accessories, which the UN Panel places in a separate category. Explosives, which the UN Panel included in the same category as ammunition, are excluded.

In the context of this chapter, 'firearms' refers to the following items:

- pistols and revolvers;
- sporting rifles and shotguns; and
- military firearms, including light machine guns; heavy machine guns with a calibre of 14.5 mm or less; sub-machine guns, assault rifles, and non-automatic military rifles; military shotguns; and anti-materiel rifles with a calibre of 14.5 mm or less.

The term 'firearms' is used instead of 'small arms', because heavy machine guns, which are defined as 'light weapons' by the UN Panel, are included in the same category as other military firearms in some of the sources reviewed for this chapter.[8] It is therefore often impossible to disaggregate these weapons from the other types of firearms categorized by the UN Panel as 'small arms'.

The chapter focuses exclusively on authorized transfers. In the context of this chapter, authorized transfers means international transfers that are authorized by the importing, exporting, or transit states. Such shipments will often—but not always—require an export licence or authorization and other forms of documentation. The term

Box 1.1 International transfers

Most existing sources of information on international arms transfers focus on commercial exports and, to a lesser extent, government-to-government transfers. Almost all of the data that the chapter uses reflects cases involving a change in ownership between countries. Nevertheless, it also includes transfers without a change of ownership despite the movement of weapons across international borders (e.g. point 3.1, below). Available data sources, especially UN Comtrade, do not always distinguish between the two cases. The sources used in the chapter include the following types of international transfers:

1. Sales

1.1. Commercial sales: sales by either private or state-owned manufacturers or dealers to private or state buyers with the purpose of making a profit.

1.2. Government-to-government sales: sales of arms negotiated by a state, or sales of weapons owned by a state, to a state institution in another country for use by state institutions in national defence, law enforcement, or security activities.

1.3. Trials and sampling: small arms and light weapons sent abroad for trials and sampling to facilitate a possible commercial or government-to-government deal.

2. International assistance and training

2.1. Assistance: small arms and light weapons sent by a government to another government without involving a sale and with the purpose of assisting the armed or security forces of the recipient country.

2.2. Training: small arms and light weapons sent to an ally or a friendly country for use as part of a training programme or in military exercises.

3. Other kinds of transfers

3.1. Peacekeeping operations: small arms and light weapons sent by one state to its peacekeeping forces deployed abroad.

3.2. Repairs: small arms and light weapons sent abroad for repairs.

3.3. Surplus disposal: returning old weapons (without involving a sale) to the original manufacturer or exporting state. For example, a manufacturer may receive old weapons as part of a deal to supply new ones.

3.4. Returning leased or lent weapons to the leasing or lending country.

3.5. Intra-governmental transfers: weapons sent by a government institution to its agents abroad for purposes other than peacekeeping, including training.

3.6. Transfers by individuals: arms owned by civilians that accompany, or are sent to, a person who has travelled internationally. An example is of people taking their own sporting guns on safari or hunting holidays.

'authorized' is used instead of 'legal', because transfers authorized by governments are not necessarily 'legal' in that a fully licensed arms transfer could still violate international law.

UN Comtrade

Much of the data used in this chapter comes from UN Comtrade, the database administered by the UN Statistics Division. UN member states send to UN Comtrade data derived from customs authorities that summarizes the annual movement of goods across borders. UN Comtrade is a rich data source on the trade in small arms and light weapons. In 2006, for example, some 17,500 records containing information on transfers of small arms, light weapons, and their parts, accessories, and ammunition were reported by 126 countries. Far more data is available via UN Comtrade than from either national reports on arms exports or the UN Register. In addition, UN Comtrade uses standardized categories developed by the World Customs Organization (WCO) for all goods. This means that, unlike information from other data sources, reports from UN Comtrade can be compared and aggregated with ease.

Nevertheless, UN Comtrade does pose some challenges for researchers. Some major exporters, such as South Africa, do not report any transfers of small arms and light weapons. More countries are partial reporters. For example, China and the Russian Federation report transfers of sporting shotguns and rifles, but withhold information on handguns and military small arms and light weapons. Similarly, Austria, Belgium, and Brazil do not report their exports of pistols and revolvers to UN Comtrade. UN Comtrade also provides little information on imports of weapons by states in sub-Saharan Africa. Furthermore, the customs categories are not always very specific. In some cases, several types of weapon or ammunition are combined. Lastly, UN Comtrade merely records the movement of goods across borders; it does not specify the identity of the end users; whether they were located in the importing country; or if the transfer was a permanent export or some other kind of transaction, such as the return of equipment for repair. UN Comtrade is a useful source of data, but it does not cover all transfers and, where possible, it should be corroborated with other data sources.

China and Russia withhold information on transfers of military small arms and light weapons.

Firearms are reported to UN Comtrade by national customs agencies under the following codes (930190 was introduced in 2002):

1) military firearms: 930190;
2) pistols and revolvers: 930200;
3) sporting and hunting shotguns: 930320; and
4) sporting and hunting rifles: 930330.

These codes follow international standards set by the World Customs Organization, referred to as 'Harmonized System' or 'HS'. According to the WCO, the HS is composed of approximately 5,000 commodity groups, each of which is identified by a six-digit code. The codes are arranged in a logical structure and defined by detailed rules and classifications of goods. The Harmonized System is used by over 200 countries as the basis of their customs tariffs international trade statistics. Over 98 per cent of international trade in goods is classified by Harmonized System, which is governed by 'The International Convention on the Harmonized Commodity Description and Coding System' (WCO, n.d., p. 1).[9]

It is important to clarify that some countries produce and export civilian versions of assault rifles, anti-materiel rifles, and military shotguns that are sold in civilian markets in countries in which the possession of these weapons by private users is lawful. In some cases, the 'commercial' versions of these firearms are declared as 'sporting rifles' or 'sporting shotguns'. Therefore, for the purposes of this chapter, the terms 'sporting rifle' and 'military weapon' do not refer to the specific technical characteristics of the weapons, but to what the exporting country declares them to be.

GLOBAL TRENDS, 2000-06

This section charts trends in the global market for small arms, light weapons, and their parts, accessories, and ammunition. Unlike the two sections that follow, this section is based solely on trade data supplied by the UN Comtrade database.[10] The figures presented here do not show a complete picture of the trends in world trade, because some countries have not reported data. All figures in this section have been adjusted for inflation, and are presented in constant 2006 US dollars (USD). The section covers the time period 2000–06, which corresponds with the first year that the Small Arms Survey assessed the global trade in small arms and light weapons using trade data (2000) and the most recent year for which comprehensive data is available (2006).

It is important to note that, compared to other sections in this chapter, this section covers different weapons types and uses only one data source. It is therefore to be expected that the figures in this section will differ from those in other sections.

After correcting for inflation, there was an absolute increase of some USD 653 million in the value of the global trade in small arms, light weapons, and their parts, accessories, and ammunition from 2000 to 2006. According to UN Comtrade data, between 2000 and 2006 the value of global transfers of small arms and light weapons rose from USD 2.31 billion in 2000 to USD 2.97 billion in 2006. This increase of USD 653 million was a rise of 28 per cent over the seven-year period. This increase was not uniform. As shown in Figure 1.1, the value of the identified trade was largely static until 2004, when it rose to almost USD 3 billion, a figure that it reached again in 2006.

Figure 1.1 **The value of the global trade in small arms and light weapons, and their parts, accessories, and ammunition (USD*), 2000-06**

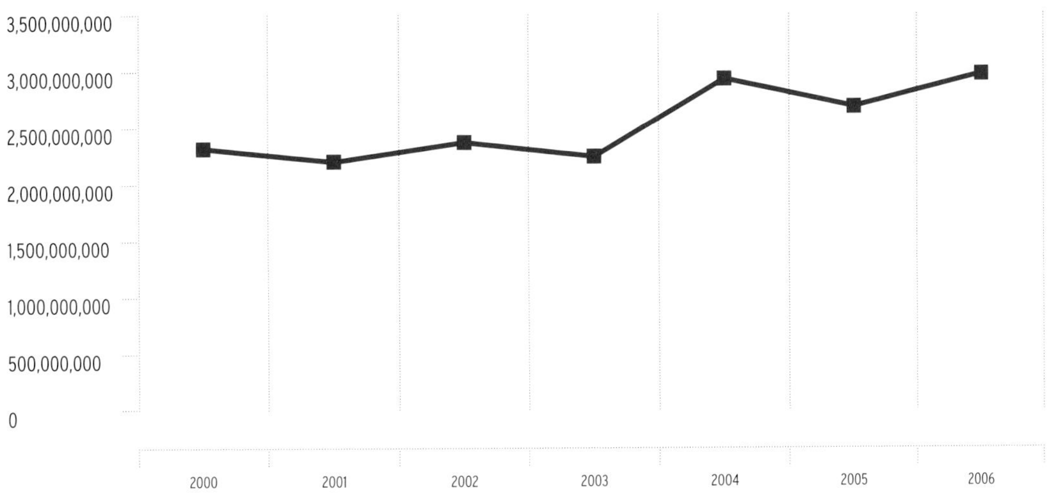

* All USD values have been adjusted for inflation and are expressed in constant 2006 USD.

Sources: UN Comtrade (n.d.); NISAT (n.d.)

Previous editions of the *Small Arms Survey* (Small Arms Survey, 2003; 2004) have highlighted the global distribution of the production of small arms, light weapons, and their parts, accessories, and ammunition, which, as of 2003, were produced in over 90 countries. Nevertheless, analysis of UN Comtrade data from 2000 to 2006 indicates that the top 15 exporters accounted for 83 per cent of all exports over the seven-year period. The United States is consistently the largest exporter, and it alone accounted for 22 per cent of all exports in the period 2000–06. The next 14 largest exporters were, in descending order, Italy, Germany, Belgium, Brazil, Austria, the United Kingdom, Japan, Canada, Switzerland, Spain, the Russian Federation, the Czech Republic, France, and Turkey. While use of additional data sources described in the following two sections of this chapter[11] increases our estimates of some countries' exports, it is highly likely that between 2000 and 2006 some 80 per cent of world exports of small arms, light weapons, and their parts, accessories, and ammunition were concentrated among less than 20 exporters.

The top 15 importers accounted for 67 per cent of all imports, and the United States alone was responsible for, on average, 27 per cent of all imports of small arms, light weapons, and their parts, accessories, and ammunition. Indeed, the USD 653 million increase in the value of the estimated global trade can be explained in part by imports into the United States, which rose by a total of USD 291 million over the seven-year period. Increased demand by the United States accounted for 48 per cent of the increase in all imports. The next 14 largest importing countries (in descending order of average annual imports) were Saudi Arabia, Cyprus, Germany, France, the United Kingdom, Canada, South Korea, Australia, Italy, Japan, Spain, the Netherlands, Greece, and Belgium.

Table 1.1 Trends in small arms transfers reported to UN Comtrade, 2000-06

	2000 value (USD thousands)	2006 value (USD thousands)	Absolute growth, 2000-06 (USD thousands)	Relative growth (%)
Military small arms & light weapons	527,710	375,493	-152,216	-29
Pistols & revolvers	265,604	427,550	161,946	61
Sporting shotguns	282,848	458,414	175,566	62
Sporting rifles	182,487	304,316	121,829	67
Parts & accessories for pistols or revolvers	60,164	120,765	60,600	101
Shotgun barrels	39,087	47,549	8,463	22
Parts & accessories for rifles or shotguns	155,096	223,266	68,170	44
Shotgun cartridges	249,927	275,239	25,312	10
Small-calibre ammunition (<14.5 mm)	551,550	734,840	183,290	33
Total	**2,314,472**	**2,967,433**	**652,960**	**28**

Note: All USD values have been adjusted for inflation and are expressed in constant 2006 USD; all figures have been rounded, which explains differences in totals.

Sources: UN Comtrade (n.d.); NISAT (n.d.)

The top 15 importers had a smaller share of the total compared to the exporters for two reasons. Firstly, the only barriers to becoming a significant importing state are demand, financial resources, and the willingness of others to sell to you. Becoming a major exporter, however, requires the development of significant production capacity or the possession of large stocks of surplus weapons. Secondly, individual countries frequently made significant imports over a few years, but not over the entire seven-year period. Such large 'one-off' purchases may be explained by procurement cycles.

It should be noted that the USD 653 million increase in the value of the global trade is not explained by an increase in reporters to UN Comtrade. The number of countries reporting to UN Comtrade did grow over the seven-year period, but the vast majority of increases in global transfers have been made by exporters and importers whose reporting practices have not changed. As this section highlights, the global trade in small arms and light weapons is dominated by a small number of countries; in general, the new reporters contributed only marginally to the global total. The two countries whose improved reporting coincided with the largest increases in exports over the period 2000–06 were Romania and Serbia and Montenegro.[12] Nevertheless, the absolute increases in exports for each country only amounted to 5.3 per cent and 1.8 per cent of the global increase, respectively.

Nor is the increase in the value of the global trade explained by a rise in exports of military small arms and light weapons destined for Iraq or Afghanistan, or to peacekeeping forces worldwide (see Box 1.4). In fact, these weapons, which include equipment such as assault rifles, sub-machine guns, rocket launchers, and mortars, showed considerable volatility. As Table 1.1 shows, the seven-year period ended with a 29 per cent decrease in military small arms and light weapons exports reported to UN Comtrade.[13]

Figure 1.2 **Changes in the value of the trade in four categories of small arms and light weapons (USD*), 2000-06**

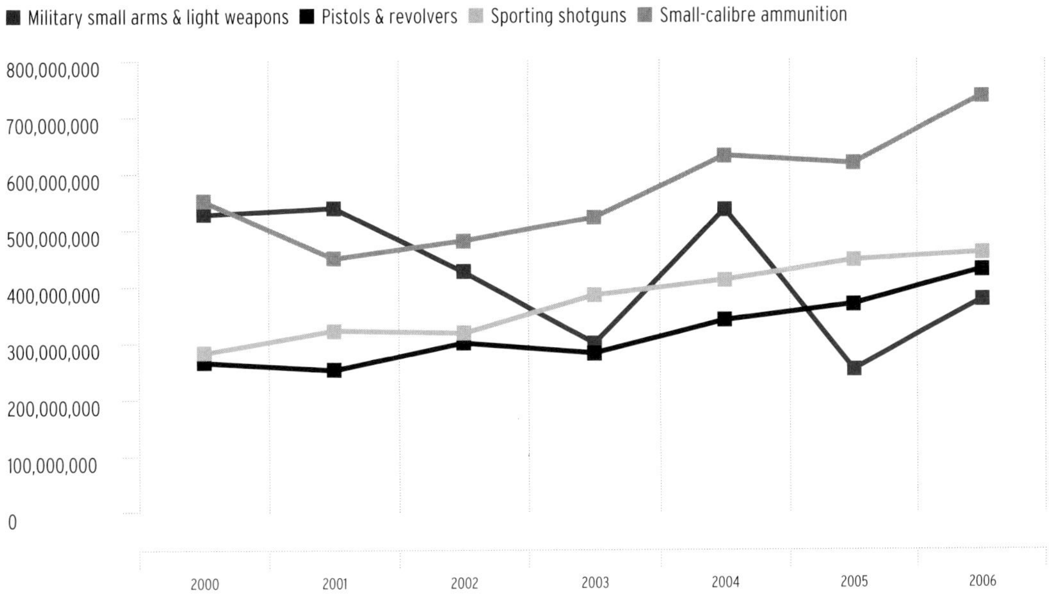

Military small arms & light weapons; Pistols & revolvers; Sporting shotguns; Small-calibre ammunition

800,000,000
700,000,000
600,000,000
500,000,000
400,000,000
300,000,000
200,000,000
100,000,000
0

2000 2001 2002 2003 2004 2005 2006

* All USD values have been adjusted for inflation and are expressed in constant 2006 USD.

Sources: UN Comtrade (n.d.); NISAT (n.d.)

The three largest absolute increases in the trade in small arms and light weapons reported to UN Comtrade were, in descending order, small-calibre ammunition, sporting and hunting shotguns, and pistols and revolvers. These three categories are examined in greater detail in the remainder of this section, along with military small arms and light weapons (which showed the greatest volatility).

Figure 1.2 highlights the fact that changes in these sectors were not uniform. Military weapons in particular experienced very wide year-on-year variations. Exports of military weapons have varied dramatically, starting the period at USD 528 million and ending at USD 375 million in 2006, i.e. USD 152 million lower than in 2000.

The value of the trade in ammunition, and pistols and revolvers, also rose and fell during the period, but much less dramatically. Measured in total value, small arms ammunition exports in 2000 were the largest category in every year but 2001 (when they were second to military small arms and light weapons). Initially, exports declined, but bounced back in 2001 and steadily increased throughout the rest of the period, ending with a total value of USD 735 million in 2006. Small-calibre ammunition was also the category that increased in value most in absolute terms, from USD 552 million in 2000 to USD 735 million in 2006.

Small-calibre ammunition

The highest growth sector was small-calibre (<14.5 mm) ammunition. The value of small-calibre ammunition transfers reported to UN Comtrade increased by USD 183 million, or 33 per cent, between 2000 and 2006. The ten largest exporters of small-calibre ammunition over this period on average are given in Table 1.2. These ten countries accounted for 70 per cent of all exports from 2000 to 2006, during which there was an absolute increase in global exports of USD 183 million. Fifty-five countries increased their exports between 2000 and 2007, and the aggregated value of this rise was USD 304 million. These increases were partially offset by decreases in 38 countries, the aggregated value of which was USD 121 million. Such mixed fortunes are reflected in the record of the ten largest exporters, as shown in Table 1.3.

Table 1.2 Ten largest exporters of small-calibre ammunition, 2000-06

Exporter	Average exports, 2000-06 (USD thousands)	% of all exports in this category, 2000-06
United States	158,885	28
Germany	43,790	8
Switzerland	35,384	6
Canada	28,145	5
United Kingdom	26,267	5
Russian Federation	25,097	4
Norway	22,050	4
Sweden	21,942	4
Czech Republic	19,149	3
South Korea	18,358	3

Note: All USD values have been adjusted for inflation and are expressed in constant 2006 USD; all figures have been rounded.

Table 1.3 Change in exports among the ten largest exporters of small-calibre ammunition, 2000-06

Exporter	Absolute change in exports, 2000-06 (USD thousands)	Relative change (%)
United States	88,228	61
Germany	30,992	138
Canada	30,055	184
Switzerland	21,339	94
Norway	8,224	104
South Korea	-3,612	-18
Sweden	-7,356	-29
Czech Republic	-12,461	-42
Russian Federation	-25,288	-44
United Kingdom	-30,855	-55

Note: All USD values have been adjusted for inflation and are expressed in constant 2006 USD; all figures have been rounded.

Table 1.4 Ten largest increases in small-calibre ammunition exports, 2000-06

Exporter	Absolute change in exports, 2000-06 (USD thousands)	Relative change (%)
United States	88,228	61
Germany	30,992	138
Canada	30,055	184
Switzerland	21,339	94
Serbia & Montenegro	19,906	2,304
Brazil	16,389	166
France	11,289	94
Finland	9,607	93
Norway	8,224	104
Austria	7,706	148

Note: All USD values have been adjusted for inflation and are expressed in constant 2006 USD; all figures have been rounded.

The ten countries with the largest absolute increases in small-calibre ammunition exports between 2000–06 are given in Table 1.4. These ten countries accounted for 80 per cent of the total USD 304 million aggregated increase in small-calibre ammunition exports. The ten countries experiencing the largest decreases are given in Table 1.5.

Table 1.5 Ten largest decreases in small-calibre ammunition exports, 2000-06

Exporter	Absolute change in exports, 2000-06 (USD thousands)	Relative change (%)
Portugal	-3,475	-99
South Korea	-3,612	-18
Iran	-4,124	-100
Greece	-5,084	-91
Netherlands	-6,204	-95
Sweden	-7,356	-29
Czech Republic	-12,461	-42
South Africa	-12,482	-82
Russian Federation	-25,288	-44
United Kingdom	-30,855	-55

Note: All USD values have been adjusted for inflation and are expressed in constant 2006 USD; all figures have been rounded.

Table 1.6 Ten largest importers of small-calibre ammunition, 2000-06

Importer	Average imports, 2000-06 (USD thousands)	% of all imports in this category, 2000-06
United States	96,996	17
Germany	42,626	7
Australia	28,954	5
Netherlands	24,843	4
Canada	22,937	4
France	21,568	4
United Kingdom	19,417	3
South Korea	18,540	3
Israel	17,671	3
Switzerland	16,302	3

Note: All USD values have been adjusted for inflation and are expressed in constant 2006 USD; all figures have been rounded.

The ten largest importers of small-calibre ammunition in the period 2000–06 are given in Table 1.6. These ten countries accounted for 54 per cent of all imports. The countries with the largest increases in imports are given in Table 1.7. The rise in Egypt's imports is particularly striking. Starting with a value of USD 0.484 million in 2000, imports of small arms ammunition by Egypt steadily increased to USD 51.7 million by 2006.

Table 1.7 **Ten countries with the largest absolute rise in imports of small-calibre ammunition, 2000-06**

Importer	Absolute change in imports, 2000-06 (USD thousands)	Relative change (%)
United States	61,789	84
Egypt	51,177	10,563
Netherlands	43,461	333
Australia	38,390	131
France	24,945	203
Israel	18,637	167
Cyprus	13,984	3,386
Denmark	13,026	370
Canada	10,194	43
Switzerland	10,188	91

Note: All USD values have been adjusted for inflation and are expressed in constant 2006 USD; all figures have been rounded.

The global market in small-calibre ammunition is dominated by a small number of exporters and importers, but not to the same extent as for sporting shotguns, pistols, and revolvers. Purchasers of small-calibre ammunition include ministries of defence, police and law enforcement agencies, and private individuals. While civilian demand is likely to vary according to local levels of income, laws, and culture, the demand by governments is likely to vary less among countries. Regardless of their location and nationality, armed uniformed personnel need to be supplied with ammunition.

The large absolute increase in imports by the United States may well be associated with widely reported difficulties in meeting the ammunition requirements of troops stationed in Iraq and Afghanistan from domestic production and stockpiles (see Government Accountability Office, 2005). UN Comtrade data sheds little light on this issue, since it only identifies the importing country, not the recipient.

Sporting shotguns

The trade in sporting shotguns increased steadily from 2000 to 2006. Exports were 62 per cent higher in 2006 than in 2000. The ten largest exporters on average of sporting shotguns over this period are given in Table 1.8. These ten countries accounted for 93 per cent of all identified transfers of sporting shotguns in the period 2000–06.

Of the categories of small arms and light weapons assessed in this chapter, sporting shotguns experienced the second-highest absolute growth in the value of transfers reported to UN Comtrade, increasing by USD 176 million from 2000 to 2006. Absolute increases in exports were identified in 64 countries, with an aggregated absolute rise of USD 187 million. These increases were offset slightly by declines by 42 countries, which totalled USD 11.5 million. Among the ten largest exporters, all but one experienced rises in the value of their exports (see Table 1.9).

Table 1.8 Ten largest exporters of sporting shotguns, 2000-06

Exporter	Average exports, 2000-06 (USD thousands)	% of all exports in this category, 2000-06
Italy	189,920	51
Turkey	24,434	7
Russian Federation	20,544	5
Germany	19,723	5
United States	18,788	5
Belgium	17,669	5
Japan	16,590	4
Spain	14,801	4
United Kingdom	14,030	4
Brazil	12,345	3

Note: All USD values have been adjusted for inflation and are expressed in constant 2006 USD; all figures have been rounded.

Table 1.9 Change in exports among the ten largest exporters of sporting shotguns, 2000-06

Exporter	Absolute change in exports, 2000-06 (USD thousands)	Relative change (%)
Italy	94,727	74
Turkey	34,175	382
Russian Federation	10,336	69
Germany	9,432	55
United States	-3,736	-17
Belgium	7,299	54
Japan	930	5
Spain	2,897	24
United Kingdom	1,660	11
Brazil	11,263	144

Note: All USD values have been adjusted for inflation and are expressed in constant 2006 USD; all figures have been rounded.

The United States had the largest absolute decrease in exports. The second-largest decline was experienced by Portugal, a country just outside the top ten exporters. Exports from Portugal fell by USD 3.2 million between 2000 and 2006.

The largest importers comprised a similar group of countries to the exporters (see Table 1.10). These ten countries accounted for 77 per cent of global imports. The United States held a dominant position over the period, with an average of almost half of all imports.

Table 1.10 Ten largest importers of sporting shotguns, 2000-06

Importer	Average imports, 2000-06 (USD thousands)	% of all imports in this category, 2000-06
United States	169,201	45
United Kingdom	28,471	8
France	21,209	6
Belgium	13,642	4
Spain	12,751	3
Germany	11,915	3
Russian Federation	9,239	2
Greece	7,514	2
Canada	7,124	2
Portugal	6,878	2

Note: All USD values have been adjusted for inflation and are expressed in constant 2006 USD; all figures have been rounded.

Table 1.11 The ten fastest-growing importers of sporting shotguns, 2000-06

Importer	Absolute increase in imports, 2000-06 (USD thousands)	Relative change (%)
United States	69,870	52
United Kingdom	21,692	146
Spain	12,616	278
Russian Federation	12,145	383
France	10,801	73
Germany	8,986	131
Canada	5,642	105
Ukraine	4,891	218
Denmark	3,805	251
Australia	3,519	129

Note: All USD values have been adjusted for inflation and are expressed in constant 2006 USD; all figures have been rounded.

The countries with the largest absolute increases in imports of sporting shotguns from 2000 to 2006 are given in Table 1.11. The absolute increases in imports of sporting shotguns by these ten countries accounted for USD 154 million, or 89 per cent of the total global increase of USD 176 million. The import activity of the United States, which accounted for 40 per cent of the total absolute increase, is particularly noteworthy. Not only was it the largest importer of sporting shotguns in 2000, but imports by the United States grew by 52 per cent over the seven years studied. This growth could explain why US exports fell while those of other major exporters' rose. It may be that, as sales increased in the US domestic market, US firms concentrated on supplying consumers at home. For more information on the dominance of the United States and Western Europe in the demand for sporting firearms, see the section entitled 'Analysis of firearms transfers in 2006'.

Pistols and revolvers

The international trade in pistols and revolvers shows similar characteristics to that of sporting shotguns, since the sector is dominated by a few countries and has seen an overall increase in transfers. Over the period 2000–06 transfers of pistols and revolvers reported to UN Comtrade increased by USD 162 million, or 61 per cent. The ten countries with the largest average exports over the period are given in Table 1.12.

Table 1.12 Ten largest exporters of pistols and revolvers, 2000-06

Exporter	Average exports, 2000-06 (USD thousands)	% of all exports in this category, 2000-06
Austria	81,133	25
Germany	63,943	20
Brazil	37,323	12
United States	28,895	9
Italy	27,871	9
Czech Republic	14,541	5
Croatia	10,388	3
Canada	7,391	2
Israel	6,984	2
Argentina	6,415	2

Note: All USD values have been adjusted for inflation and are expressed in constant 2006 USD; all figures have been rounded.

Table 1.13 Change in exports among the ten largest exporters of pistols and revolvers, 2000-06

Exporter	Absolute change in exports, 2000-06 (USD thousands)	Relative change (%)
Austria	47,852	70
Germany	46,819	112
Croatia	25,960	2,282
Italy	17,958	78
Brazil	11,078	30
Czech Republic	6,126	61
Argentina	5,534	146
Israel	255	3
Canada	-1,500	-18
United States	-5,803	-16

Note: All USD values have been adjusted for inflation and are expressed in constant 2006 USD; all figures have been rounded.

These ten countries accounted for 89 per cent of all global exports of pistols and revolvers over the seven years studied in this chapter. All but two of them experienced an increase in exports over the period 2000–06 (see Table 1.13).

The importance of the US pistol market is illustrated by the case of Croatia, which dramatically increased its exports over the seven-year period. In 2000 exports of pistols and revolvers from Croatia were worth just USD 1.1 million. By 2006 they had increased to USD 27 million, 98 per cent of which were to the United States. This case suggests that a country can become a major global player just by developing an export market in the United States. This dependence on the United States as an importer is reflected, to a lesser extent, in all the other exporters, only three of which exported less than half of their exports to the United States (see Table 1.14).

Table 1.14 Dependence on exports to the United States, 2006

Exporter	Proportion of exports sent to the United States (%)
Croatia	98
Canada	96
Brazil	86
Austria	75
Israel	68
Argentina	68
Italy	44
Germany	38
Czech Republic	32

Table 1.15 Ten largest increases in pistol and revolver exports, 2000-06

Exporter	Absolute change in exports, 2000-06 (USD thousands)	Relative change (%)
Austria	47,852	70
Germany	46,819	112
Croatia	25,960	2,282
Italy	17,958	78
Brazil	11,078	30
Czech Republic	6,126	61
Belgium	5,817	195
Argentina	5,534	146
Poland	3,061	4,103
China	2,202	144

Note: All USD values have been adjusted for inflation and are expressed in constant 2006 USD; all figures have been rounded.

From 2000 to 2006, 58 countries saw an increase in their exports of pistols and revolvers, and the aggregated increase in all exports was USD 181 million. This was offset by declines in 49 countries, the total value of which was USD 19 million. The countries with the largest absolute increases in exports are given in Table 1.15.

As noted above, the United States is clearly the world's largest importer of pistols and revolvers, accounting for 54 per cent of all imports. No other country imports more than 4 per cent of the global total (see Table 1.16). These ten countries received 73 per cent of all imports of pistols and revolvers over the period 2000–06. As well as being the largest market, the United States was also the location of the greatest absolute growth in imports (see Table 1.17).

Table 1.16 Ten largest importers of pistols and revolvers, 2000-06

Importer	Average imports, 2000-06 (USD thousands)	% of all imports in this category, 2000-06
United States	173,209	54
France	12,537	4
Thailand	7,836	2
Germany	7,713	2
Spain	6,729	2
Italy	5,500	2
Belgium	5,440	2
Canada	5,346	2
Mexico	4,892	2
Philippines	4,575	1

Note: All USD values have been adjusted for inflation and are expressed in constant 2006 USD; all figures have been rounded.

Table 1.17 Ten countries with the largest absolute rise in imports of pistols and revolvers, 2000-06

Importer	Absolute change in imports, 2000-06 (USD thousands)	Relative change (%)
United States	99,986	69
France	27,327	1,954
Saudi Arabia	12,448	6,937
Thailand	8,477	124
Canada	7,346	454
Spain	5,068	148
Philippines	3,348	172
South Africa	2,809	663
Iraq*	2,761	n/a
Brazil	2,124	724

* The dramatic increase by Iraq is largely explained by the lifting of the UN arms embargo that was in place until 2003.

Note: All USD values have been adjusted for inflation and are expressed in constant 2006 USD; all figures have been rounded.

Military small arms and light weapons

Between 2000 and 2006 the trade in military small arms and light weapons reported to UN Comtrade declined from USD 528 million to USD 375 million, an absolute decline of USD 152 million, or 29 per cent. The ten largest exporters are given in Table 1.18.

In this section, 'military small arms and light weapons' refers to small arms designed to military specifications, including automatic rifles and carbines, sub-machine guns, and combat shotguns; and to light weapons such as grenade launchers, rocket launchers, and heavy machine guns. The data used to compile these numbers was reported

Table 1.18 Ten largest exporters of military small arms and light weapons, 2000-06

Exporter	Average exports, 2000-06 (USD thousands)	% of all exports in this category, 2000-06
United States	228,512	54
Belgium	27,136	6
France	22,651	5
Germany	16,213	4
United Kingdom	13,651	3
China	10,148	2
Norway	9,520	2
Italy	9,331	2
Canada	8,857	2
Switzerland	6,945	2

Note: All USD values have been adjusted for inflation and are expressed in constant 2006 USD; all figures have been rounded.

Table 1.19 Ten largest absolute decreases in exports of military small arms and light weapons, 2000-06

Exporter	Absolute change in exports, 2000-06 (USD thousands)	Relative change (%)
United States	-173,630	-48
France	-26,742	-87
Italy	-18,219	-55
United Kingdom	-16,887	-74
Belgium	-13,751	-70
Canada	-13,245	-76
Saudi Arabia	-5,493	-95
Sweden	-2,077	-34
Georgia	-1,180	-100
Slovakia	-1,111	-100

Note: All USD values have been adjusted for inflation and are expressed in constant 2006 USD; all figures have been rounded.

under UN Comtrade codes 930100 (mainly before 2002), and 930190 and 930120 (mainly after 2002). Note that in UN Comtrade code 930100, data on transfers of artillery systems and other large conventional weapons is combined with data on military small arms and light weapons. All known transfers of artillery were compared to the data used to produce this section, and any transactions that could have comprised heavy artillery were removed. Nevertheless, some countries are not sufficiently transparent to allow one to distinguish between military small arms and light weapons and conventional weapons. Consequently, a small percentage of the data in this section may reflect transfers of items other than small arms and light weapons.

Thirty-eight countries' exports of military small arms and light weapons decreased between 2000 and 2006. The aggregated value of these decreases was USD 277 million. The ten exporters experiencing the largest absolute decreases are given in Table 1.19.

Exports of over USD 1 million were recorded for Slovakia and Georgia in 2000, but by 2006 their identified exports had dropped to zero. Similarly, in 2000 Saudi Arabia exported USD 5 million in military small arms and light weapons, after which it exported either nothing or less than USD 500,000 per year. In 2000 the United States dominated the international trade in military small arms and light weapons, accounting for 68 per cent of all exports. By 2006 the United States' dominance had waned slightly, its share of the world export market in military small arms and light weapons declining to 49 per cent.

These decreases were partially offset by increases in exports from 47 countries totalling USD 125 million. The ten countries with the largest absolute increase in exports are given in Table 1.20. The relatively large increases by Bangladesh and Thailand occurred because they exported no military small arms and light weapons in 2000, but in 2006 they both made a single large transfer to one country. It is likely that they will return to being minimal exporters in future years. The context of the Bangladesh transfer is explained in greater detail in Box 1.4. It is also important to note that, of the ten countries identified below, only Serbia and Montenegro, Thailand, Spain, and Poland report their exports of military small arms and light weapons to UN Comtrade. The large relative increase by Serbia and Montenegro is partly explained by it starting to report data to UN Comtrade during the period studied. The figures

Table 1.20 Ten largest absolute increases in exports of military small arms and light weapons, 2000–06

Exporter	Absolute change in exports, 2000–06 (USD thousands)	Relative change (%)
China	20,092	1,815
Germany	15,551	333
Israel	11,613	611
South Africa	11,078	1,148
Russian Federation	11,061	592
Serbia & Montenegro	9,787	751,021
Bangladesh	8,733	n/a
Thailand	7,928	n/a
Spain	6,163	659
Poland	4,865	310

Note: All USD values have been adjusted for inflation and are expressed in constant 2006 USD; all figures have been rounded.

Table 1.21 Ten largest importers of military small arms and light weapons, 2000-06

Importer	Average imports, 2000-06 (USD thousands)	% of all imports in this category, 2000-06
Cyprus*	106,998	20
South Korea	48,487	9
Japan	38,904	7
Greece	34,847	6
Saudi Arabia	34,303	6
United States	26,981	5
Netherlands	17,928	3
Turkey	14,928	3
Egypt	13,992	3
Australia	13,436	2

* The peculiarity of Cyprus being the largest importer was noted in previous editions of the Small Arms Survey (Small Arms Survey, 2003, pp. 104-05; 2004, p. 108).

Note: All USD values have been adjusted for inflation and are expressed in constant 2006 USD; all figures have been rounded.

for the other countries are based on 'mirror data' (i.e. reports by countries importing their exports) and therefore are likely to be underestimates.

The main importers of military small arms and light weapons during 2000–06 are given in Table 1.21. The high volatility of this sector is explained by three factors. The first is the cyclical nature of the military procurement process. Governments purchase large quantities of weapons infrequently. For example, a country may re-equip all its soldiers with a new model of assault rifle and then place no additional large orders for that type of gun for decades.[14] Secondly, as noted above, many of the largest exporters have not reported their data to UN Comtrade, and the figures are calculated from mirror data. We therefore have a much narrower view of the trade than we do with, for example, sporting shotguns, which are widely reported. Thirdly, the customs codes for military small arms and light weapons were changed in 2002. This transition means that the data from before and after this date are not completely comparable, although there is a large degree of overlap.

Summary

A large proportion of the discussion on the global trade in small arms and light weapons is actually a discussion of the United States. It is by far the largest importer of pistols and revolvers, sporting shotguns, and small-calibre ammunition. Furthermore, increases in demand in the United States explain almost half of the global rise in exports of small arms, light weapons, and their parts, accessories, and ammunition. Of the four sectors analysed here, the only one in which the United States was not both the largest exporter and importer was military small arms and light weapons. While dominant in military exports, the United States was the sixth-largest importer in this category. After the United States, and depending on the type of weapons, another 15–20 countries account for most imports and exports. Most transfers of pistols and revolvers, small-calibre ammunition, and sporting shotguns, for example, were between developed countries. In all, the major exporters are responsible for some 83 per cent of all exports reported to UN Comtrade between 2000 and 2006. Production of small arms and light weapons has been globalized, but a handful of countries still control most of the trade.

CHARTING A NEW APPROACH

In 2006, using data sources that were improving in terms of quantity and quality, but still deficient in key ways, the Small Arms Survey reiterated its earlier USD 4 billion estimate of the annual value of the global authorized trade in small arms and light weapons, and their parts, accessories, and ammunition (Small Arms Survey, 2006, pp. 66–67). Three years later, is there enough additional data to measure this trade more accurately? This section launches a multi-year exploration of this question that will culminate in a revised dollar value estimate for the entire global authorized trade in small arms and light weapons. The trade in firearms was assessed this year and will be followed by a similar assessment of parts and accessories, ammunition, and light weapons in subsequent years.[15]

As part of this year's assessment, the authors compiled data on firearms exports from 53 countries in 2006. This data was drawn from multiple sources, including new ones, such as information on small arms transfers submitted to the UN Register. Below is a brief assessment of the data itself, followed by an analysis of what the data says about the global trade in firearms. Note that this and the next section of the chapter[16] focus solely on firearms (see the introduction for a definition of this term), and therefore the values do not include other types of light weapons, parts, accessories, or ammunition unless otherwise indicated.

Much of the global trade in small arms remains difficult to ascertain.

Changes to the data and reporting since 2001

The quantity and, to a lesser extent, clarity and utility of data on firearms transfers has increased notably since the first edition of the *Small Arms Survey* in 2001. New sources of data shed light on previously unreported arms transfers and clarify data in existing sources that is ambiguous or incomplete. Particularly noteworthy is the background information on firearms transfers submitted to the UN Register. In 2006 these submissions revealed new information or additional details about the export of military firearms from 35 of the 53 countries surveyed for this chapter (UNDDA, 2006).[17] New national reporting by major exporters of firearms like Bulgaria and Ukraine has also resulted in the release of large quantities of useful data.[18]

The expansion and refinement of existing data sources has also improved public understanding of the firearms trade. Changes to the way in which countries report on arms exports to UN Comtrade have made this data more useful. As part of a package of amendments to the Harmonized Commodity Description and Coding Systems enacted in 2002, the WCO created new sub-headings for HS code number 930100, 'military weapons'. The new sub-headings effectively disaggregate data on the disparate collection of weapons lumped together under the old code, allowing researchers to distinguish transfers of military firearms (930190) from transfers of artillery, rocket launchers, torpedo tubes, and other weapons. The adoption of these sub-headings has been rapid and widespread. By 2006 only seven countries still reported under the old 930100 code.

Also indicative of the trend towards more and better data are improvements to the report on arms exports published as part of the *Annual Report According to Operative Provision 8 of the European Union Code of Conduct on Arms Exports* (EU Report),[19] a key source of data on European arms exports (e.g. see CoEU, 2007; 2008). When the EU first published the report in 1999, data on conventional arms transfers was limited to the total value of arms exports and the number of arms export licences issued by each EU member state. In contrast, the 2007 report contains a detailed breakdown of exports by Military List category to each recipient, including data on both actual deliveries of weapons and licences issued.[20]

Despite these improvements, much of the global trade in firearms remains difficult to ascertain. Several major small arms producers report only on certain categories of firearms. Of the 53 countries surveyed for this chapter, seven provided data to UN Comtrade on exports of sporting and hunting firearms, but little or no official data on handguns or military firearms. These countries include the Russian Federation and China—two of the largest exporters of firearms in the world. Other countries provide even less information: six of the countries surveyed provided no data on firearms exports at all in 2006. Mirror data from importing countries filled in some of the resulting gaps, but many large arms transfers undoubtedly went unreported.[21]

Among countries that do report on firearms exports through one or more of the reporting mechanisms surveyed for this chapter, the scope, clarity, and specificity of this data varies significantly. Some data sources are remarkably detailed, listing not only the type, quantity, value, and recipient of transferred firearms, but also the purpose of the transfer (e.g. 'for re-export to India') and the mode and date of delivery (UNDDA, 2006, p. 26). New Zealand's submission to the UN Register for 2007, for example, identifies the importing country, make, model, and serial number of each exported firearm (New Zealand, 2008). Other reports reveal little about the reporter's export and import activity. Japan's submission to the UN Register for 2006, for example, aggregates all data on procurement, including domestic procurement (UNDDA, 2006, p. 21). This data reveals little about Japan's suppliers and their export activity.

The lack of compatibility between data sources is another significant barrier to fully understanding the firearms trade. Some sources, such as the EU Report, provide only the values of transfers, while others, including

Box 1.2 US arms exports and the mysterious 9301909090 transfers to Japan

Even data from the most transparent countries often suffers from ambiguity, imprecision, and opacity. The United States, which is often identified by the Small Arms Survey as one of the most transparent small arms exporters in the world (see Transparency Barometer), is a good example. The US government publishes several different publicly available reports on arms transfers; disaggregates customs data on firearms transfers into ten-digit commodity codes; and helps private researchers to clarify ambiguities in data sources and reconcile seemingly contradictory data.

Despite this openness, ambiguities in data classification, importer sensitivities, and a patchwork approach to national reporting on arms transfers preclude a definitive accounting of US firearms exports. The effect of these limitations on clarity and transparency is readily apparent in the case of arms exports to Japan in 2006. Of the USD 245 million in exports reported by US exporters under the four main customs categories used for firearms in 2006, Japan was identified as the importing country of nearly 38 per cent (USD 92 million). Of that total, more than 98 per cent (USD 90 million) was filed under an obscure sub-category of 'military weapons' ambiguously labelled 'other' weapons (commodity code 9301909090) (US Census Bureau, 2008). What is meant by 'other' is not clear, and exporters have shipped items other than firearms under this sub-heading in the past.[22] The primary US national report, the Section 655 report, provides little clarification, because data on government-to-government military sales to Japan is redacted and information on commercial sales is limited to licensing data. Since US licences are good for four years and not every licence results in a transfer, the licensing data is of limited utility.

A month-long inquiry by the US Census Bureau into the USD 90 million in exports of 'other' weapons to Japan revealed that 57 per cent (USD 51,653,899) were categorized incorrectly. Exports valued at USD 34,643,080 were subsequently recategorized as parts and accessories for unspecified 'other' military weapons, and the remaining USD 17,010,819 in exports was recategorized as 'parts for guided missiles'.[23] These corrections alone resulted in a downward revision of the estimated value of US firearms exports in 2006 by more than 20 per cent.

This case illustrates both the shortcomings of existing data on firearms transfers and the difficulty of confirming and corroborating this data. Few governments publish data that is detailed enough to spot such anomalies, and fewer still would respond expeditiously to outside requests to investigate them. Even in countries like the United States, where such inquiries are possible, investigating each ambiguously categorized transfer in this way is not feasible. Thus, even in the most transparent countries, analysing the firearms trade is a difficult task and systematically confirming each transfer is nearly impossible.

the UN Register, only indicate the number of units transferred. As a result, combining and reconciling these data sources is difficult. Furthermore, financial data often reveals very little about the nature and size of the export, yet it remains the most commonly reported data on firearms transfers.

Compounding this problem is inconsistent and misleading data. A particularly nettlesome inconsistency is the apparent submission to the UN Register of licensing data by some countries and delivery data by others. Despite guidelines from the UN to 'report only those transfers which they consider to have been effected during that reporting year' (UNDDA, 2007, p. 5), 6 of the 13 respondents to a survey conducted by the Stockholm International Peace Research Institute (SIPRI) indicated that their submissions to the UN Register for 2006 were based on licensing data, which may or may not reflect actual exports (Holtom, 2008, p. 26). Another problem is the miscategorization of exports in customs data. As documented by the Small Arms Survey, Brazil routinely reports exports of pistols as sporting and hunting rifles in its customs data (Small Arms Survey, 2007, pp. 95–96).

A lack of transparency in reporting facilitates the concealment of arms sales to abusive regimes.

Thus, despite significant improvements in the quantity and quality of data on small arms transfers, much of the trade remains opaque. This opacity not only hinders attempts to measure the global trade in firearms, but also facilitates the concealment of arms sales to abusive or aggressive regimes; impedes efforts to prevent excessive accumulation of weapons; and hinders the proper operation of multilateral agreements, which depend on detailed, accurate information on arms transfers to monitor compliance by member states.

Revising the global estimate for authorized firearms transfers

To convert the expanding pool of data on firearms transfers into knowledge about the overall trade, the authors collated and analysed data on 53 countries. Forty-six of the countries were selected based on their status as the largest exporters of small arms and light weapons in 2006, as revealed in UN Comtrade data.[24] Seven additional countries were selected either because they have significant export potential (owing to large surplus small arms holdings, or latent or nascent production capacity) or because they are suspected of significant export activity, but publish little or no data on their arms exports.[25] Together, these countries account for approximately 99 per cent of small arms and light weapons transfers recorded in UN Comtrade (in dollar value terms). The majority of data collected for this study came from the following sources: UN Comtrade (n.d.), the UN Register, the EU Report (CoEU, 2007), national arms export reports, the NISAT Database on Small Arms Transfers (NISAT, n.d.), and other regional and country-specific sources, including field research conducted by country experts.[26]

For each of the 53 countries, data on exports of military firearms,[27] pistols and revolvers, and sporting and hunting shotguns and rifles was collected from each of the aforementioned data sources. Individual spreadsheets were then created for each country and populated with the data, which was then compared. Often, two or more sources reported different values for the same exports. In those cases, the data that was the most detailed or specific, or from the source considered most reliable, was selected.[28]

When data on the quantity (units) of exported small arms was provided, but not the value of the export, the unit data was converted into a dollar value by multiplying the number of units by an average per unit price calculated from data on past exports of the same or comparable firearms from the country in question. When data on export values from previous years was not available or not available in sufficient quantity from a given country, a global average unit price—calculated from seven years of export data on exports of the same or comparable firearms collected from various countries[29]—was used. In cases where data on transfers of different types of firearms was aggregated under a single munitions category, the data was used only when more detailed or specific corresponding data

Table 1.22 **Estimated* small arms exports from 53 countries, aggregated by category, 2006**

Category	UN Comtrade total (USD)**	Revised estimate (USD)**	% difference
Military firearms	244 million	321 million	32
Pistols & revolvers	428 million	430 million	<1
Sporting rifles & shotguns	756 million	779 million	3
Firearms (unspecified)	n/a	39 million	n/a
Total	**1,428 million**	**1,568 million**	**10**

* It is important to stress that these values are only estimates. As explained in Box 1.2, data limitations preclude definitive assessments of even the most transparent countries.

** Totals are rounded to the nearest million.

was not included in other sources. The estimated value of these transfers was a small percentage of the global total (see 'Firearms (unspecified)' in Table 1.22).

For each country, the data selected from the various sources was then added together to come up with estimated dollar value totals for each category of firearms (i.e. military firearms, pistols and revolvers, and sporting and hunting shotguns and rifles). The category totals for each country were then added together to derive estimated global totals for each category. These totals are provided in Table 1.22. The first estimate, presented in the column entitled 'UN Comtrade total', is composed solely of data from UN Comtrade. The second column, labelled 'Revised estimate', contains the totals derived from the abovementioned methodology and sources. Compiling and juxtaposing the totals from the two sets of data in this way highlights the differences between the historic source of data (UN Comtrade) and the new and expanded sources of data, as reflected in the revised estimate. It also underscores the fact that the two figures are estimates, not definitive calculations.[30]

Figure 1.3 **Difference between UN Comtrade data and combined data sources (%)**

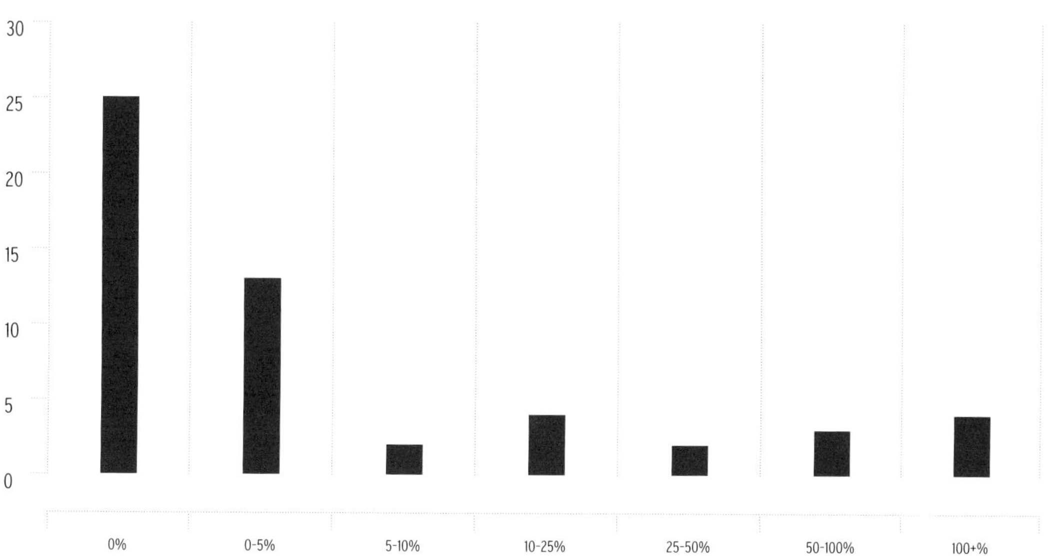

As Table 1.22 shows, the data sources reviewed for this chapter contained records of approximately USD 1.57 billion in firearms transfers for the 53 countries surveyed. Roughly 9 per cent of this total, or USD 140 million, reflects transfers in excess of what was reported to UN Comtrade. The non-UN Comtrade data sources were particularly rich in data on military firearms, as evidenced by the 32 per cent upward revision in the global estimate for transfers in this category. The differences between the estimated totals for transfers of handguns and sporting shotguns and rifles were less dramatic at the global level, but significant differences were apparent at the country level.

Our findings also varied significantly from country to country, as illustrated in Figure 1.3. In 25 of the 53 countries analysed there was no difference between the dollar value total calculated using data from UN Comtrade and the total derived from all sources. Modest differences (less than 5 per cent) were apparent in the totals for 13 of the countries, and in 2 other cases the difference was between 5 and 10 per cent. In 13 of the 53 countries analysed, the difference between the revised estimate and the UN Comtrade total was more significant, i.e. greater than 10 per cent. In 4 of these countries, the difference between the revised estimate and the UN Comtrade total exceeded 100 per cent.

Public understanding of firearms exports from many countries remains extremely limited.

Cumulatively, the additional data collected for the countries in which the difference was 10 per cent or greater reflects dozens of arms transfers consisting of thousands of weapons not reported to UN Comtrade. Data on Hungary alone reveals additional transfers of 24,280 sub-machine guns, 2,736 light machine guns, 136 heavy machine guns, and 175 pistols. This case also illustrates the importance of unit data. Ageing and surplus weapons are often given away or sold for a fraction of their original cost. Therefore, data on the value of these transfers is rarely a good indicator of their significance from a security or foreign policy perspective.

Our research also generated more detailed information on arms transfers reported to UN Comtrade. This information revealed more precisely the types of exported firearms and, in some cases, facilitated the identification and correction of errors. Data on US military firearms obtained from the US Census Bureau is a good example. Unlike the data in UN Comtrade, which is lumped together in a single six-digit commodity category labelled 'military weapons' that includes all military firearms and unspecified 'infantry support weapons', the data from the Census Bureau is broken down into four (4) ten-digit sub-categories: 'military rifles' (9301903000), 'military shotguns' (9301906000), 'machine guns, military' (9301909030), and 'other' military weapons (9301909090). This data indicates that, of the roughly 75,000[31] 'military weapons' aggregated under the six-digit category in UN Comtrade, 29 per cent were military rifles, 14 per cent were military shotguns, and 45 per cent were machine guns. The remaining units were listed by exporters as 'other' weapons. An analysis by the Small Arms Survey of the disaggregated data in the 'other' category led to the discovery and correction of a USD 50 million error in the data on exports to Japan (see Box 1.2). This discovery would not have been possible without the disaggregated data.

As noted above, our research yielded little or no additional data on nearly 65 per cent of the countries studied.[32] Sources other than UN Comtrade contained negligible additional data on 9 countries and no additional data on 25 other countries. The latter group includes several countries that report little or no data to UN Comtrade, including Iran and North Korea, both of which are believed to be producers and exporters of small arms. These gaps in data are explained by several factors, including the voluntary nature of the reporting mechanisms and non- or partial reporting of mirror data by importing states. Thus, despite the proliferation of data in recent years, public understanding of firearms exports from many countries remains extremely limited.

Box 1.3 Assessing the undocumented trade

Given the lack of data on firearms transfers from several known or suspected exporting states, the undocumented trade in firearms is probably significant. Determining the full extent of this trade is not possible with any specificity. However, some sense of the export activity not currently caught in existing data sources can be garnered indirectly, through such sources as information on firearms production, political-military relationships, media accounts of recent transfers, and mirror data from importing states. Using this information, we estimate the undocumented trade in firearms to be at least USD 100 million. This is a conservative estimate, and is arrived at very differently from the other estimates provided in this chapter, which are grounded in extensive–if imperfect–data. We provide a brief explanation of our estimates below, by firearm category.[33]

Military firearms

We estimate that the highest level of undocumented trade involves firearms made to military specifications. Prior behaviour, the size of the national firearms industry, press reports of alleged deals, fieldwork, or a combination of these suggests that certain countries were major exporters in 2006, even though available data appears incomplete. China is probably the country with the largest quantity of undocumented exports, given numerous, but often vague, reports of exports of Chinese military firearms to states in Africa and Asia. Other countries that appear to have significant levels of undocumented transfers are Israel, Singapore, and Taiwan. Countries with somewhat smaller levels of estimated undocumented transfers are Belarus, Iran, North Korea, Pakistan, and South Africa. As fieldwork indicated that the Russian Federation's only significant export was to Venezuela, a country for which we have import data, it was considered not to have significant undocumented exports in 2006.

Anchored outside Durban harbour, the Chinese container vessel An Yue Jiang carries a cargo of weapons destined for Zimbabwe, April 2008. © AP Photo

Revolvers and pistols

UN Comtrade and other sources provide considerable data on transfers from the 11 top exporters of pistols and revolvers. However, there are countries that produce pistols that do not report consistently to UN Comtrade and for which there appears to be inadequate mirror data. These are China, the Russian Federation, and South Africa. The undocumented trade in pistols and revolvers from these states could be significant, given (1) their production capacity, including the production of export models; (2) extensive military cooperation and defence trade agreements with countries in Africa, Asia, and Latin America that under-report firearms imports to UN Comtrade; and (3) an absence of mirror data from the United States, which is transparent and imports 56 per cent of the pistols exported by the 53 countries surveyed in this chapter.

Sporting and hunting rifles and shotguns

The value of undocumented transfers of sporting and hunting rifles and shotguns appears to be minimal. Since most countries in the world report on transfers of sporting rifles and shotguns to UN Comtrade, we can be fairly certain that nearly all of the major exporters can be identified–at least by using the data that importers provide to UN Comtrade. Of the 17 countries identified through UN Comtrade as exporting 1 per cent or more of the USD 779 million in documented transfers of sporting and hunting shotguns and rifles, there is robust information available for all of them but Ukraine, and its exports are included in its national report (Pyadushkin, 2008).[34] Nonetheless, there is at least one country suspected of exporting sporting and hunting rifles for which we have no UN Comtrade data: Belarus. While Belarus does not appear to be a major producer of firearms, it may have a large surplus of Soviet and pre-Soviet-period firearms available for export.

ANALYSIS OF FIREARMS TRANSFERS IN 2006

Military firearms

In 2006 the 53 countries analysed in this section exported at least 500,000 military firearms worth an estimated USD 321 million. These transfers accounted for 20 per cent of the value of authorized transfers of all firearms during that year. As some countries reported little or no information on the number of arms exported, the above tally is an underestimate.

This section examines the trade in firearms made to military specifications: automatic rifles and carbines; sniper rifles; light, sub-, general purpose, and heavy machine guns; and 'combat' shotguns.[35] Heavy machine guns, due to their lack of portability by one person, are normally categorized as light weapons. They are included here because, in practice, exporters often place heavy machine guns in the same category as military small arms, often making it impossible to disaggregate data on heavy machine guns from other small arms.

It is important to note that this section examines different categories of weapons to those analysed in the section entitled 'Global trends, 2000–06'. In the latter section, the category 'military small arms and light weapons' included all types of light weapons, including rocket launchers and grenade launchers. In the present section, the term 'military

Figure 1.4 **Proportion of identified global trade in military firearms (%), 2006**

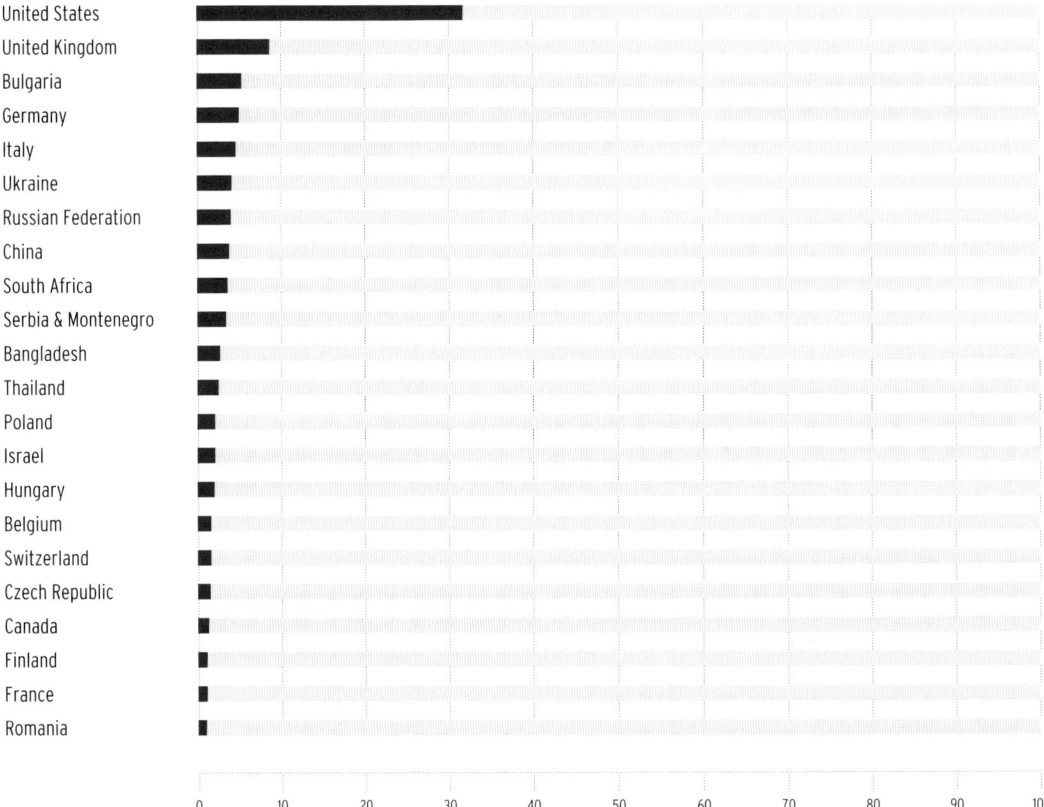

Note: This figure only includes those countries with 1 per cent or more of global transfers, so the percentages for the individual countries will not total 100 per cent.

Sources: UN Comtrade (n.d.); national arms export reports; CoEU (2007); UNDDA (2006); NISAT (n.d.)

Iraqi soldiers hold new rifles distributed by US forces at Camp Taji in north Baghdad, May 2007. © Ceerwin Aziz/AFP

firearms' is used and it only includes the previously mentioned firearms. As a result, the figures in the two sections are often very different.

The present section reiterates some of the findings in the section entitled 'Global trends, 2000–06'.[36] While a diversification of production capacity is clearly reflected in the 2006 data, this section also suggests that, in practice, the trade in military firearms is dominated by the United States and a small number of other countries. Of those countries whose transfers of military firearms is documented, only 22 had exports that totalled 1 per cent or more of the total global trade carried out by the 53 countries. Of these, three had 5–10 per cent, and the United States accounted for almost a third of all identified transfers with 32 per cent.

Table 1.23 summarizes the available data on exports of military firearms for all countries with more than 1 per cent of global exports. This data was drawn from several data sources, including UN Comtrade, national arms export reports, the EU Report, the UN Register, field research, and the NISAT database. Despite the wide array of sources used, the figures for four countries in the table—the Russian Federation, Israel, South Africa, and China—are likely to be significant underestimates, because these countries withhold data on exports of military firearms. Data on these countries' exports is therefore largely limited to 'mirror data' (i.e. data submitted by importing countries). Conversely, two countries, Bangladesh and Thailand, are unlikely to be included in subsequent years' tallies of the top exporters. In both cases, their inclusion is explained by a single large transfer—from Bangladesh to Côte d'Ivoire and from Thailand to Singapore.

Table 1.23 Countries with 1% or more of global transfers, 2006

Country (in descending order of value of transfers)*	Number of identified military firearms (may not include all transfers)	% of all military firearms transfers	% of all small arms transfers	Top five partners (exports >USD 100,000)
United States	• Machine guns: 31,928 • Military rifles & carbines: 26,129 • Unspecified: 13,124 • Combat shotguns: 7,830 Total: 79,011	31.8	6.5	Japan Colombia Netherlands Bahrain Egypt
United Kingdom	• Sniper rifles: 15,273 • Sub-machine guns: 1,356 • Assault rifles: 12,909 • General purpose machine guns: 466 • Semi-automatic rifles: 207 • Heavy machine guns: 33 • Light machine guns: 115 • Rifles & carbines: 13 • Automatic rifles: 21 • Unspecified: 1 Total: 30,394	8.7	1.8	Afghanistan Turkey Saudi Arabia Brazil Pakistan
Bulgaria	• Light machine guns: 2 (Limited available data on quantities)	5.3	1.1	Iraq
Germany	• Unspecified: 19,453 • Assault rifles: 1,482 • Sub-machine guns: 440 Total: 21,375	5.0	1.0	Saudi Arabia United States Latvia Switzerland Malaysia
Italy	• Unspecified: 2,498 Total: 2,498	4.6	0.9	Switzerland Mexico United States
Ukraine	• Assault rifles & sub-machine guns: 152,502 • Unspecified: 17,217 • Light machine guns: 799 • Heavy machine guns: 13 Total: 170,531	4.1	0.8	Libya Georgia[37] Azerbaijan Chad United States
Russian Federation	• Unspecified: 48,187 Total: 48,187	4.0	0.8	Venezuela United States
China	• Unspecified: 24,555 • Rifles & carbines: 390 • Sub-machine guns: 118 Total: 25,063	3.7	0.8	Ethiopia Tanzania Madagascar

South Africa	• Unspecified: 2 (Limited available data on quantities)	3.6	0.7	Colombia Saudi Arabia
Serbia & Montenegro	• Unspecified: 12,466 Total: 12,466	3.4	0.7	Burma/Myanmar Cameroon Iraq Armenia Greece
Bangladesh	Data on quantities not available	2.7	0.6	Côte d'Ivoire
Thailand	• Unspecified: 8,817 Total: 8,817	2.5	0.5	Singapore
Poland	• Unspecified: 7,163 • Heavy machine guns: 345 • Assault rifles: 22 Total: 7,530	2.1	0.4	Jamaica Iraq India Bulgaria Jordan
Israel	• Unspecified: 9,133 • Assault rifles: 200 • Rifles & carbines: 2 Total: 9,335	2.1	0.4	Colombia Trinidad & Tobago United States Cameroon Australia
Hungary	• Sub-machine guns: 24,280 • Unspecified: 5,437 • Light machine guns: 2,736 • Heavy machine guns: 136 Total: 32,589	2.0	0.4	Afghanistan United States Romania Iraq
Belgium	• Unspecified: 3,307 • Rifles & carbines: 344 • Light machine guns: 60 • Heavy machine guns: 1 Total: 3,712	1.6	0.3	Switzerland Mexico United States Canada Germany
Switzerland	• Unspecified: 6,848 Total: 6,848	1.6	0.3	Egypt Germany France Italy Singapore
Czech Republic	• Rifles & carbines: 3,855 • Sub-machine guns: 196 • Heavy machine guns: 159 • Assault rifles: 30 • Light machine guns: 19 Total: 4,259	1.5	0.3	Georgia Bosnia & Herzegovina Canada

Canada	• Unspecified: 2,452 Total: 2,452	1.3	0.3	United Kingdom United States Netherlands Denmark Sweden
Finland	• Unspecified: 1,234 • Sniper rifles: 20 Total: 1,254	1.1	0.2	Estonia Sweden United States Germany Italy
France	• Unspecified: 14 • Machine guns: 4 (Limited available data on quantities)	1.1	0.2	Colombia Australia Senegal
Romania	• Unspecified: 4,259 Total: 4,259	1.0	0.2	Germany Afghanistan Iraq Maldive Islands

* The countries are ranked in descending order according to the financial value of their transfers. Proportions of the trade in military firearms and all small arms are similarly calculated by the value of transfers.

Sources: UN Comtrade (n.d.); national arms export reports; CoEU (2007); UNDDA (2006); NISAT (n.d.); US Census Bureau (2008)

Figure 1.5 **Number of military firearms exported during 2006**

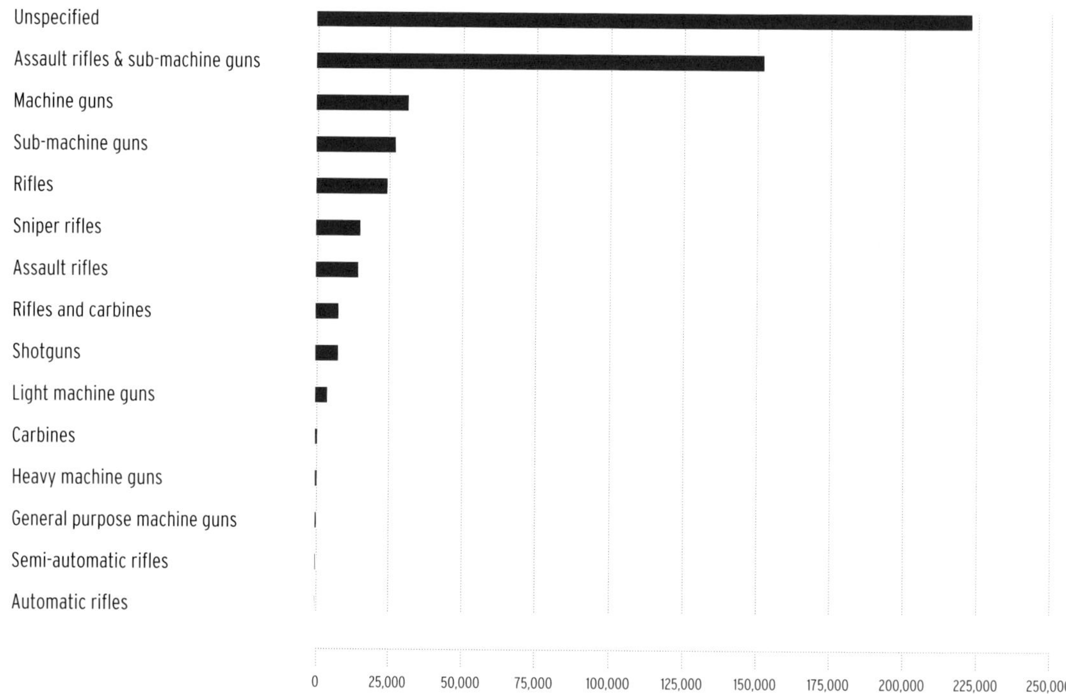

Sources: UN Comtrade (n.d.); national arms export reports; CoEU (2007); UNDDA (2006); field research; NISAT (n.d.)

As mentioned in the section entitled 'Charting a new approach', this chapter draws heavily on a detailed study of the transfers by the top 53 exporters. Based on this study, we estimate that at least 500,000 military firearms were transferred by the 53 countries in 2006. As this figure was generated from several different data sources covering exports and imports, and many countries did not report the number of units they transferred, it is an incomplete and provisional tally of the military firearms exported during 2006. Of these weapons, 44 per cent were not identified by specific type of firearms (e.g. 'rifle'). Instead, they are described in more generic terms, such as 'smooth-bore weapons with a calibre of less than 20 mm, other arms and automatic weapons with a calibre of 12.5 mm or less' (described in Table 1.23 and Figure 1.5 as 'unspecified'). The other 56 per cent of the firearms were identified by specific type. A summary of data on these firearms is provided in Figure 1.5. Note that the designations provided in Table 1.23 and Figure 1.5 come directly from the various data sources, which do not use consistent classifications. For example, firearms labelled as 'machine guns' by one country are disaggregated into 'sub-machine guns', 'light machine guns', and 'heavy machine guns' by others.

The types of firearms exported, as presented in Table 1.23 and Figure 1.5, reflect exporters for which data was available. Several made significant transfers to Iraq and Afghanistan, including a Hungarian export of 21,480 sub-machine guns to Afghanistan and 11,026 assault rifles from the United Kingdom. If countries such as China, Israel, the Russian Federation, or

Box 1.4 **Transfers to peacekeeping forces**

One important type of transfer of military small arms and light weapons is to forces deployed on international operations that include armed peacekeepers. These missions can be mandated by the UN Security Council, and operate under the auspices of regional organisations (such as the EU and the African Union) or as part of a bilateral agreement between two governments.

Arms transfers to peacekeeping forces are an interesting subgroup of the transfers analysed in this chapter. Sometimes arms and associated parts and ammunition are transported with military forces as they are being deployed, and then return with them. In other cases, a government may transfer weapons to a mission staffed by other nationalities, perhaps as part of a military aid package. While peacekeeping operations are frequently established in areas under UN arms embargoes, such transfers are lawful, as most embargo resolutions exclude transfers of arms for peacekeeping forces.

Some data sources highlight transfers to peacekeeping forces, while others, including UN Comtrade, do not. In addition, transfers to peacekeepers may be made concomitantly with transfers to a foreign government. It is therefore impossible to consistently disaggregate transfers to peacekeeping operations from other types of transfers of small arms and light weapons, thus precluding the development of an accurate estimate of their value.

Nevertheless, there are several recent examples of transfers that are almost certainly related to peacekeeping. One transfer mentioned in this chapter is that of USD 8,733,369 worth of military firearms (UN Comtrade code 930190) from Bangladesh to Côte d'Ivoire in 2006. In 2006 Bangladesh stationed 3,400 soldiers, 250 police, and 25 military observers in Côte d'Ivoire as part of the UN Operation in Côte d'Ivoire (UNOCI, 2006). The Government of Bangladesh did not provide the authors with specific information on this export, but a Bangladeshi army officer confirmed that the only circumstances in which such arms transfers take place is to peacekeeping operations.[38]

The EU Report includes information on 'Exports By EU Member States and Acceding Countries to United Nations-Mandated Or Other International Missions in 2006' (CoEU, 2007, table A.11). These exports included both transfers to national troops stationed abroad (e.g. Hungary) and transfers to international missions or organizations, such as the Austrian export of pistols and components to the International Criminal Tribunal for Rwanda. These transfers are highlighted in Table 1.24.

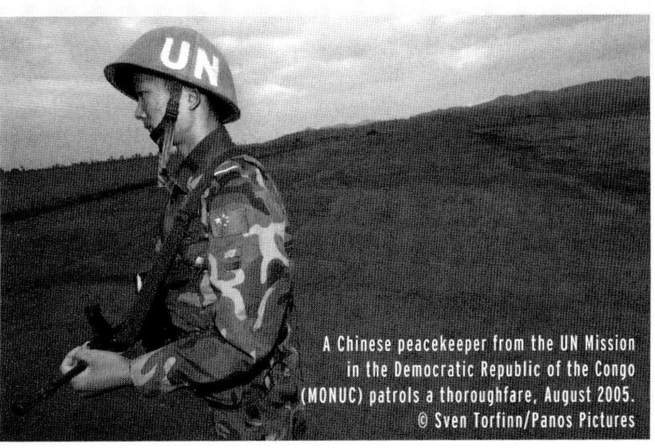

A Chinese peacekeeper from the UN Mission in the Democratic Republic of the Congo (MONUC) patrols a thoroughfare, August 2005. © Sven Torfinn/Panos Pictures

Table 1.24 EU member states' exports to international missions, 2006

Exporting country	Destination country	Recipient	Weapon type (only small arms and light weapons shown)
Austria	Democratic Republic of the Congo (DRC)	UN Mission in the Democratic Republic of the Congo (MONUC)	Pistols and components
	Iraq	Multinational Force*	Pistols and components
	Kuwait	UN Assistance Mission for Iraq (UNAMI)	Pistols and components
	Lebanon	UN Economic and Social Commission for Western Asia; UN International Independent Investigation Commission	Pistols and components
	Liberia	UN Mission in Liberia (UNMIL)	Pistols and components
	Serbia & Montenegro	UN Mission in Kosovo (UNMIK)	Components (for small arms and light weapons)
	Tanzania	International Criminal Tribunal for Rwanda (Security Unit)	Pistols and components
Hungary	Cyprus	UN Peacekeeping Force in Cyprus	7.62 PKMSZ machine gun; 7.62 mm AK63/D AMMSZ sub-machine gun; 9 mm P9RC revolver**; ammunition for pistols
	Georgia	UN Observer Mission in Georgia	Training ammunition; revolvers; pistols
	Israel	Multinational Force and Observers Sinai	9 mm P9RC pistol**
	Lebanon	UN Interim Force in Lebanon (UNIFIL)	9 mm 96M P9RC PA pistol** & ammunition
Germany	Burundi	UN Operation in Burundi Movement Control Logistic Base	Parts for pistols
	DRC	MONUC Logistic Base	Semi-automatic smooth-bore guns; parts for sub-machine guns; ammunition for guns; ammunition for hunting guns; ammunition for pistols
	Republic of Congo	MONUC chief procurement officer	Sub-machine guns; parts for sub-machine guns
	Kuwait	Administrative officer, UNAMI Movement Control	Parts for sub-machine guns
	Liberia	UNMIL Receiving and Inspection Unit	Parts for sub-machine guns

Greece	Afghanistan	International Security Assistance Force (ISAF)	Ammunition; weapon sight
	Bosnia & Herzegovina	EU Force (EUFOR) Operation Althea	Pistol
	DRC	EUFOR in the Democratic Republic of the Congo (EUFOR RD Congo)	Assault rifle; pistol
	Macedonia	UNMIK	Ammunition
Portugal	Afghanistan	ISAF	Small arms & light weapons; ammunition
	DRC	EUFOR RD Congo	Small arms & light weapons; ammunition;
	Gabon	Support for EUFOR RD Congo	Small arms & light weapons; ammunition
	Lebanon	UNIFIL	Small arms & light weapons; ammunition
United Kingdom	Haiti	EU***	Revolvers (15); shotguns (6); semi-automatic pistols (8); components for semi-automatic pistols; sub-machine guns (6); small arms ammunition; sporting gun ammunition

* The Multinational Force in Iraq was authorized by UN Security Council Resolution 1511 of 2003.

** This information was taken directly from the EU Report, hence the discrepancies in the way in which what appears to be the same type of weapon is named/categorized.

*** Taken directly from the EU Report.

Source: CoEU (2007)

South Africa were also to report their exports of military firearms, the ratios in Figure 1.5 would probably be significantly different.

Of the ten largest exporters of military firearms, the export values of four—Hungary, the United Kingdom, Bulgaria, and Ukraine—increased by over USD 5 million when data from sources other than UN Comtrade was considered. The United Kingdom is most striking. It has been described as a mid-level producer (see Small Arms Survey, 2003, pp. 64–65), and thus it is noteworthy that data sources other than UN Comtrade suggest that it ranked among the largest exporters of military firearms in the world during 2006.

Pistols and revolvers

Background: pistols and revolvers: weapons of two worlds

Due to existing national regulations and controls, in most parts of the world military firearms (sub-machine guns, automatic rifles, military shotguns, machine guns, and anti-materiel rifles) are mainly legally sold to military forces, law enforcement agencies, and very specific (and smaller) civilian markets, such as collectors and museums. Similarly, the authorized production and trade of sporting and hunting rifles and shotguns address the demand of specific groups of civilian users, such as hunters and sporting shooters and inhabitants of isolated rural areas. Long-barrelled guns are poorly suited to urban environments, where they cannot be carried without causing alarm (Small Arms Survey, 2007, pp. 63–64). In contrast, pistols and revolvers, commonly referred to as side arms or handguns, differ from other types of firearms in that there is roughly equal demand for them in military, law enforcement, and civilian markets. Small, easy to use, conceal, and carry, and very effective at close range, handguns are effective weapons for personal defence in urban environments and for close-range engagements by military and law enforcement users (Small Arms Survey, 2007, pp. 63–64; Forecast International, 2007a, pp. 15–17).

With the exception of the small and highly specialized niche market for high-precision sporting shooting pistols, handguns are generally produced for both civilian and military/law enforcement markets. Some manufacturers have developed less powerful versions of some high-calibre models in order to avoid national legal restrictions regarding magazine capacity or calibre.[39] A small number of models were designed specifically for military use, such as fully automatic versions of semi-automatic pistols or extremely powerful (and rare) calibres such as the FN Five-SeveN (5.7 mm).

In military/law enforcement markets, the demand for handguns is steady and largely determined by purchase cycles related to the renewal/modernization of ageing weapons,[40] or the adoption of a new standardized calibre deemed more effective for law enforcement, such as the .40 S&W calibre, which has significant stopping power.

Pistols and revolvers account for 27 per cent of all firearms exported in 2006.

Most of the 650 million firearms in civilian hands are estimated to be handguns, ownership of which is largely concentrated in urban markets of developed countries. The demand for these weapons is driven by factors such as income distribution, culture, the (real or perceived) need for security (Small Arms Survey, 2007, pp. 57–64), and the restrictiveness and effectiveness of domestic firearms regulations. In wealthier markets, it is more likely that demand will reflect the latest 'fashions' in handgun technology, including new calibres and models incorporating new technologies (Small Arms Survey, 2007, pp. 57–65; 2005, pp. 22–23).

Exports of pistols and revolvers, 2006

In 2006 the total estimated value of exported pistols and revolvers for the 53 countries surveyed was approximately USD 430 million. That is less than 1 per cent higher than the total reported to UN Comtrade (approximately USD 428 million). The difference stems mainly from exports that are not declared in UN Comtrade by either importing or exporting countries, but are either declared by the exporting country or by importing countries in the UN Register. The largest transfers of pistols and revolvers that were not recorded in UN Comtrade were exports from Austria (3,784 units in imports declared to the UN Register by Lithuania, Greece, and Hungary). These totals include 592 units reported by Greece, 3,111 units reported by Lithuania, and 81 units reported by Hungary.

Pistols and revolvers account for 27 per cent of all firearms exported in 2006, according to existing data sources. The largest exporters (with 1 per cent or more of global transfers) were Austria, Germany, Brazil, Italy, the United States, Croatia, the Czech Republic, Argentina, Belgium, Israel, and Canada, as shown in Table 1.25.

As shown in Table 1.25, the largest importer of pistols and revolvers is the United States, the main commercial market for firearms in the world and a country where the civilian population holds about 270 million of the 650 million firearms estimated to be in civilian hands worldwide (Small Arms Survey, 2007, p. 39). In fact, the United States received 59 per cent of handguns, in dollar value terms, exported from the countries in Table 1.25. An exception to this reliance on the US market seems to be Germany, which exported nearly as many handguns (in dollar value terms) to France as to the United States in 2006. This may be related to the fact that the SIG SAUER SP 2022 pistol has been the standard service weapon in France since 2003, with orders of over 250,000 pistols. These pistols were

Table 1.25 Countries with 1% or more of global transfers of pistols and revolvers, 2006

Exporter	Number of identified pistols & revolvers (may not include all transfers)	% of all pistols & revolvers transfers by value	% of all firearms transfers by value	Top five partners by value (in order of importance)
Austria	410,702	27.31	7.48	United States Saudi Arabia Thailand Brazil Italy
Germany	288,579	20.61	5.65	United States France Spain Sweden Switzerland
Brazil	278,262	11.10	3.04	United States Philippines Germany Honduras Ecuador
Italy	145,741	9.52	2.61	United States Argentina Spain Mexico South Africa
United States	94,867	7.14	1.95	Canada Thailand Belgium Germany Japan
Croatia	143,432	6.31	1.73	United States Dominican Republic Canada Thailand Bosnia & Herzegovina
Czech Republic	35,363	3.64	1.24	United States Thailand Egypt Colombia Germany
Argentina	88,895	2.17	0.59	United States Nicaragua Guatemala Costa Rica Dominican Republic

▶▶

Belgium	17,886	2.05	0.56	United States Pakistan Italy Australia Luxemburg
Israel	72,205	1.93	0.53	United States Colombia Guatemala Germany Barbados
Canada	12,993	1.65	0.45	United States Norway Italy Philippines France
Total units	**1,588,925**			

made in Germany, since SIG SAUER is a Swiss–German industrial conglomerate that includes J.P. Sauer & Sohn and Blaser, Gmbh. in Germany and Swiss Arms AG in Switzerland, and that manufactures weapons in both countries (SIG SAUER, 2008).

The leading pistols exporter in the world is Austria, which produces probably the most innovative design of the last three decades: polymer-made pistols, pioneered by the Austrian company Glock in the 1980s. Glock's early adoption of this technology explains, in part, Austria's dominant position in the market in 2006. Germany (Walther, H&K, Sauer), Italy (Beretta), the United States (Colt, Ruger, Smith & Wesson, etc.), the Czech Republic, and Belgium are historically large exporters of pistols that continue to command a large share of the global market today. Other major exporters of pistols and revolvers are Brazil, Argentina, Croatia, and Israel, each of which captured a significant share of the US market during the 1990s and the beginning of the current decade through aggressive marketing strategies and high-quality products. The fruits of these efforts are reflected in the data from 2006. Eighty-six per cent of Brazil's USD 48 million in exports of pistols and revolvers, and 68 per cent of Argentina's exports, went to the United States. Croatia is an even starker case, with more than 98 per cent of its revenue from handgun exports (USD 27 million) generated through sales to the United States. In the case of Brazil (Taurus, Imbel) and Argentina (Bersa), penetration of the US market was made possible through the production of reliable, high-quality handguns that cost less than similar US-made products (Small Arms Survey, 2004, pp. 16–26; Dreyfus, Lessing, and Purcena, 2005).

Through the production of reliable and robust models such as the Israeli Military Industries' Jericho and Desert Eagle series (Forecast International, 2007b, pp. 8–9), Israel has also established itself as a major player in the US market. In 2006 Israel exported nearly USD 6 million worth of pistols and revolvers to the United States (NISAT, n.d.). Israel also exports significant quantities of pistols and revolvers (close to USD 1 million in 2006) to Colombia and Guatemala, two traditional customers of Israeli military equipment (Small Arms Survey, 2004, p. 23; Klare and Andersen, 1996, pp. 1–16; Beit-Hallahmi, 1987, pp. 79–84)). Croatia won its access to the US market through production cooperation agreements with US-based companies such as Springfield Armory, which markets Hrvatski Samokres (commonly known as HS) pistols to US civilians (Small Arms Survey, 2003, p. 45).

Brazil, Austria, Belgium, and the 'invisible pistols'

As in past years, the only available data on handgun transfers from Austria, Brazil, and Belgium in 2006 was mirror data from importers. This is because these countries do not report their exports of these products to UN Comtrade. Moreover, there is strong evidence that Brazil reports its pistols under category 930330 (sporting and hunting rifles) (Small Arms Survey, 2007, pp. 94–97; En la Mira, 2007; 2008).

Officials of the Directorate of Controlled Products of the Brazilian Army, the office in charge of authorizing production, imports, and exports of arms, admitted during a Hearing Commission of the Brazilian Congress (which was active from March 2005 to November 2006) that specific pistols and revolvers categories are not published or communicated to open sources (such as UN Comtrade) for national security reasons. According to these officials, the values and quantities of exports of pistols and revolvers are not reported in order to protect information considered by Brazil to be strategic (Brazil, 2006, p. 439).

It is, however, possible to identify the destination of Austrian, Brazilian, and Belgian pistols by looking at the import data provided by their main importers, particularly the United States. Of these three countries, Brazil is the only one in which, after empirical tests, there is evidence that the pistols are more likely reported under another category of firearms, in this case sporting rifles (Small Arms Survey, 2007, pp. 94–97; 2006, p. 75; En la Mira, 2007; 2008). The data from Belgium and Austria does not follow a similar pattern.

Sporting and hunting shotguns and rifles

Background: an exclusive, lucrative, and blurred market

In general, sporting and hunting weapons are produced for a small and very demanding market sector that requires precise, accurate, and long-lasting weapons that have a high production cost. There is, however, a market for cheaper mass-produced products. Prices in this market range from USD 64,600 for a UK-made Holland and Holland Deluxe Hammerless Double shotgun to a KBI M-1500 SC .22 calibre rifle worth USD 200 made in the United States (Carpentieri, 2003, pp. 474, 485).

A hunting firearm on display during the fourth annual trade fair for US products and services in Beirut, Lebanon, October 2008. © Jamal Saidi/Reuters

This market is composed of the following types of products:

1) precision shooting rifles (labour-intensive production; very expensive);
2) high-calibre bolt-action precision hunting rifles (labour-intensive production; very expensive);
3) repeating and semi-automatic small-calibre rifles (mass-produced; generally low priced);
4) semi-automatic versions of automatic military rifles (e.g. the AR-15 rifle by Pac-West Arms) (mass-produced; moderately priced);
5) civilian versions of military anti-materiel sniper rifles (e.g. Barrett .50 rifles) (labour-intensive production; expensive);
6) hand-made, single shot, single- or double-barrelled rifles and shotguns (i.e. some Holland and Holland models) (labour-intensive production; very expensive);

7) mass-produced single shot and repeating shotguns (low to moderately priced)
8) semi-automatic shotguns (i.e. Franchi SPA 12) (mass-produced, but sophisticated and expensive); and
9) 50-year-old+ surplus military bolt-action rifles for use as hunting rifles (inexpensive to moderately priced, depending on the condition of the weapons).

Box 1.5 The risks of exporting 'human-hunting' sporting rifles

Domestic sales of semi-automatic 'sporting' rifles in the United States and their export to countries with weak controls and regulations can facilitate access to high-firepower weaponry by criminal and illegal armed groups. In 2007 the US Bureau of Alcohol, Tobacco, Firearms and Explosives (ATF) traced about 3,000 US-made small arms seized by the police in operations against drug traffickers in the State of Rio de Janeiro, Brazil, between 1998 and 2003. A total of 856 of the traced weapons had information about the first purchaser of the weapon. Twenty-three per cent of these 856 weapons were assault rifles. Thirty-four per cent of these weapons had been purchased directly from gun shops in the United States, mainly in the state of Florida (Werneck, 2007). The ATF also traced US semi-automatic assault rifles (mainly Colt and Ruger) seized in Rio de Janeiro that were originally exported to gun shops (for civilian consumption) in Paraguay (Werneck, 2007). The seizures of these weapons coincided with a period of increasing exports of sporting rifles to Paraguay in the mid-1990s. This diversion of weapons through Paraguay led the US government to establish a ban on firearms exports to that country in 1996 (Dreyfus, Marsh, and De Sousa Nascimento, 2006, p. 21).

The production of labour-intensive, expensive hunting weapons is concentrated in European countries (including Eastern Europe and the Russian Federation). These industries are descended from ancient small arms manufacturing traditions (e.g. firms such as Holland and Holland in the United Kingdom and Beretta in Italy) and are based in countries with historically strong (although waning) hunting traditions, particularly in countries like Austria, Germany, Italy, France, and Spain. There are also highly respected manufacturers of these types of weapons in the United States (such as Marlin).

The production of civilian versions of assault rifles and high-calibre sniper rifles is mainly concentrated in the United States, where the country's gun culture embraces (and permissive regulations facilitate) the ownership of semi-automatic assault rifles and sniper rifles by civilians. This market has grown since the US assault weapons ban expired in 2004.

Simple and inexpensive hunting weapons are primarily produced in the United States and in countries outside Europe, such as Brazil and the Philippines. The export of surplus bolt-action rifles is currently a lucrative market for Ukraine, a country that is 'disposing' of numerous surplus weapons by selling some of them. Bolt-action rifles such as pre-Second World War and Second World War Mosin-Nagant rifles, or even Mauser 98K carbines captured from the enemy during the war, are being sold as sporting rifles, mainly to collectors and hunters in the United States. These exports posed an interesting dilemma for the authors of this chapter, as these weapons were originally made to military specifications, but are currently purchased by collectors, hunters, or sports shooters. As their military role is now obsolete and their use is for civilian recreation, and based on a background information paper produced for this chapter (Pyadushkin, 2008), they are classified here as sporting rifles.

Exports of sporting and hunting shotguns and rifles, 2006

Based on data compiled on the 53 countries surveyed for this chapter, the total value of sporting and hunting shotguns and rifles exported in 2006 was USD 779 million. This estimate is 3 per cent higher than the total value of transfers reported to UN Comtrade (USD 756 million). The difference between the UN Comtrade total and our estimate is largely explained by transfers reported by exporters and importers to the UN Register or in national reports that are not reflected in UN Comtrade data. Exports from Ukraine (USD 13.5 million) account for most of this difference.[41]

Table 1.26 **Countries with 1% or more of global transfers of sporting and hunting shotguns and rifles, 2006**

Exporter	Number of identified firearms (may not include all transfers)	% of all shotguns & rifles transfers by value	% of all firearms transfers by value	Five top destination countries for shotguns by value	Five top destination countries for rifles by value
Italy	Shotguns: 310,065 Rifles: 34,962	32.22	16.01	United States United Kingdom France Spain Russian Federation	United States France United Kingdom Spain Russian Federation
Germany	Shotguns: 58,304 Rifles: 145,997	9.63	4.78	United States Russian Federation Ukraine Austria Kazakhstan	United States Russian Federation France Spain Italy
United States	Shotguns: 82,001 Rifles: 144,989	7.77	3.86	Canada Italy New Zealand United Kingdom Thailand	Canada Australia New Zealand United Kingdom France
Belgium	Shotguns: 21,646 Rifles: 49,433	6.27	3.11	United Kingdom France Italy Denmark Spain	United States France Italy Spain Germany
Turkey	Shotguns: 204,976 Rifles: 39,758	6.04	3.00	United States France Germany Italy Egypt	United States United Kingdom New Zealand Argentina Mexico
Japan	Shotguns: 32,879 Rifles: 75,463	5.04	2.50	Belgium United States Australia Canada Denmark	United States Canada France Belgium Greece
United Kingdom	Shotguns: 1,237 Rifles: 205,140	4.71	2.34	United States France Jordan Finland Germany	United States Switzerland Germany Qatar Russian Federation
Brazil	Shotguns: 145,771 Rifles: 116,026	4.40	2.19	United States Botswana Canada Australia Argentina	United States Philippines Indonesia Honduras Dominican Republic

▶▶

Russian Federation	Shotguns: Rifles:	155,089 50,338	3.88	1.93	United States Cyprus Germany Ukraine France	Germany United States Ukraine Cyprus Kazakhstan
Finland	Shotguns: Rifles:	504 53,501	3.06	1.52	Austria Lithuania Estonia Czech Republic Italy	United States Canada Australia Sweden United Kingdom
Czech Republic	Shotguns: Rifles:	3,100 68,790	2.51	1.25	Thailand Slovakia Lithuania Poland Bosnia & Herzegovina	United States United Kingdom France Australia Thailand
Spain	Shotguns: Rifles:	34,503 7,269	2.13	1.06	United States United Kingdom Portugal France Norway	France Denmark United States Greece Portugal
Canada	Shotguns: Rifles:	4,308 185,480	2.10	1.04	Pakistan United Kingdom Iceland United States Germany	United States New Zealand United Kingdom Greenland Russian Federation
Ukraine	Shotguns: Rifles:	35 147,153	1.73	0.86	Germany Vietnam	United States United Kingdom Germany Czech Republic Georgia
Austria	Shotguns: Rifles:	2,839 34,304	1.52	0.76	Saudi Arabia Switzerland Bulgaria United States Slovenia	Russian Federation Germany United States United Kingdom France
Portugal	Shotguns: Rifles:	11,228 10,702	1.25	0.62	Belgium France Spain United States Germany	Belgium United States Sweden Spain Japan
China	Shotguns: Rifles:	57,841 30,156	1.11	0.55	United States Germany Lebanon Argentina Canada	United States Germany New Zealand France Cambodia
Total units		**2,525,787**				

The research conducted for this chapter also reveals that sporting and hunting shotguns and rifles accounted for 50 per cent of all firearms exported in 2006 by value, at least among the 53 countries surveyed. The leading exporters (with 1 per cent or more of global transfers) of sporting and hunting shotguns and rifles are Italy, Germany, the United States, Belgium, Turkey, Japan, the United Kingdom, Brazil, the Russian Federation, Finland, the Czech Republic, Spain, Canada, Ukraine, Austria, Portugal, and China, as shown in Table 1.26.

As with handguns, the largest market for sporting shotguns and rifles in 2006 was the United States, which imported approximately 42 per cent of the exports from the countries listed in Table 1.26. Regarding the non-US export market, as Table 1.26 shows, most of the exports of sporting shotguns and rifles originating in Western Europe went to other Western European countries, indicating a flow of very expensive weapons among wealthy developed countries. In fact, Western European countries imported 22 per cent of the transfers of sporting and hunting shotguns and rifles originating in the countries listed in Table 1.26. Similarly, most non-European purchasers of high-value European or US-made shotguns and rifles are also wealthy developed countries such as Australia, New Zealand, and Japan.

Outside the Western world and other developed countries, Kazakhstan and Botswana were also important destinations for sporting and hunting rifles in 2006. These exports are probably related to 'hunting vacations' and the safari business, as these countries are major hunting destinations. In this regard, export statistics may include weapons accompanying their owners on trips abroad or temporarily imported by safari and hunting expedition companies during the hunting season, in addition to permanent commercial exports. The Middle East, particularly the Arab Emirates, was also an important destination outside the Western world. Among the countries listed in Table 1.26, Brazil is the leading non-European exporter, exporting hunting shotguns to Botswana and rifles to the Philippines, Indonesia, Honduras, the Dominican Republic, and the United States in 2006. This data is consistent with the characteristics of Brazil's sporting rifle industry. The Brazilian companies CBC (Companhia Brasileira de Cartuchos) and Rossi have lines of inexpensive, mass-produced .22 LR hunting rifles and carbines that have secured a place in the United States, but also in less exclusive and demanding markets in developing countries.

Sporting and hunting shotguns and rifles accounted for half of all firearms exported in 2006.

THE 2009 TRANSPARENCY BAROMETER

The Small Arms Trade Transparency Barometer was introduced in the *Small Arms Survey 2004* in order to assess countries' transparency in reporting on their small arms and light weapons exports. Points are awarded for timeliness, access and consistency, clarity, comprehensiveness, and deliveries, as well as licences granted and refused. The Barometer examines those countries claiming—or believed—to have exported USD 10 million or more of small arms, light weapons, and their parts, accessories, and ammunition during at least one calendar year between 2001 and 2007.

The Barometer has undergone several significant changes since its introduction. Initially, it included only countries believed to have reached the USD 10 million threshold for the year being reviewed. The timeliness of submissions was not originally evaluated.

The 2009 Barometer contains several additional changes to reflect best practices and encourage the use of important new reporting tools. The overall points distribution system has been maintained, but greater emphasis is placed on consistent, more recent, and more frequent reporting.[42] It also gives full value for 'nil' reporting (i.e. if a country indicates that it did not export a particular type of small arm or light weapon in the year under review). The Barometer now assesses and encourages states to use the UN Register of Conventional Arms, which is increasingly used to cover small arms-related activity.[43] Additionally, the 2009 Barometer reflects specific characteristics of national reporting practices.[44]

As no further changes to the system are envisaged for the foreseeable future, the Survey will retroactively rescore all previous Barometers against the new criteria to allow for comparability and to establish trends. A complete presentation of the scoring system can be found on the Small Arms Survey Web site.[45]

As a rule, the 2009 Barometer assesses national transparency in small arms export activity for 2007, based on reporting in 2008. Three main sources are used: (1) national arms export reports; (2) the UN Register; and (3) UN Comtrade. National reporting includes information that states provide to the EU.[46] Should other regional organizations make information on the international arms transfers of their members *publicly* available, it would also be evaluated and scored for the Barometer. The Barometer also assesses national reports that other institutes routinely make available electronically and free of charge.[47]

Box 1.6 **US scoring**

Since the Barometer's inception in 2004, the United States has consistently achieved the highest score. This year, however, it has dropped to 16.50 points, placing it together with the Netherlands and Serbia in fifth place.

The Barometer has expanded in scope and now examines information given on temporary exports, end users, re-exports, intangible transfers, and transit/trans-shipments. It also asks countries to provide information on their arms export legislation, including its implementation, and other measures and commitments. States are, in essence, now required to provide more information. In the US case, this has resulted in the loss of several points.

Through UN Comtrade and in its national report, the United States provides very detailed information on its permanent transfers of small arms, associated components, and ammunition, as well as intangible transfers. It does not, however, give information on temporary exports, brokering agents, end users, or the transit/trans-shipment of small arms. While the United States publishes the text of all its arms export legislation on its Web site, it does not provide a link to this information in its national report, as required by the Barometer.

As its name indicates, the Transparency Barometer is designed to measure—and promote—*transparency*. It can also be used to highlight trends in national reporting. Yet it does not assess the accuracy of the data that states provide.

Forty-five countries' reporting practices were assessed in this edition: the 40 countries covered last year, plus 'newcomers' Argentina, Cyprus, Denmark, Hungary, and Taiwan—all believed to have exported at least USD 10 million worth of relevant materiel in 2007. The three most transparent countries are Switzerland, the United Kingdom, and Germany. The least transparent were North Korea and Iran, both scoring zero. The average score decreased almost 8 per cent (from 12.26 to 11.29), but some countries' scores changed considerably more than this average. Not including the five states new to the index, the greatest change in both absolute and percentage terms was Romania, whose score rose 7.25 points (or 85 per cent) from last year. The change in the US score, a reduction of just over 21 per cent, is also noteworthy. Washington's 4.5 point reduction results in the loss of the number one spot that it has held since the Barometer's creation in 2004 (see Box 1.6). Four states—Bosnia and Herzegovina, Finland, France, and Italy—lost at least 17 per cent of their points under the revised scoring system and were replaced in this year's top ten by Denmark, the Netherlands, Romania, Serbia,[48] and Sweden. More than half the countries reviewed this year received less than half the maximum number of points on offer (i.e. less than 12.5 out of 25), suggesting that despite some progress, states can do much more to improve their reporting.

Table 1.27 **Small Arms Trade Transparency Barometer 2009, covering major exporters***

	Total (25 max.)	Export report (year covered)**/ EU Report***	UN Comtrade**	UN Register**	Timeliness (1.5 max.)	Access and consistency (2 max.)	Clarity (5 max.)	Comprehen-siveness (6.5 max.)	Deliveries (4 max.)	Licences granted (4 max.)	Licences refused (2 max.)
Switzerland	21.00	X (07)	X	X	1.50	1.50	4.50	5.25	3.00	3.50	1.75
United Kingdom	18.50	X (07)/EU Report	X	X	1.50	2.00	4.00	4.75	3.00	2.50	0.75
Germany[1]	18.00	X (06)/EU Report	X	X	1.50	1.50	3.50	4.00	3.00	3.50	1.00
Norway	16.75	X (07)	X	X	1.50	1.50	4.25	3.25	3.00	2.50	0.75
Netherlands	16.50	X (07)/EU Report	X	X	1.50	2.00	3.00	3.75	3.00	2.00	1.25
Serbia[2]	16.50	X (05–06)	X	X	1.50	0.50	3.25	3.75	3.50	2.50	1.50
United States[3]	16.50	X (07)	X	X	1.50	1.50	3.00	4.50	3.00	3.00	0.00
Denmark	15.75	X (06)/EU Report	X	X	1.50	1.50	3.75	4.00	2.00	2.00	1.00
Romania	15.75	X (07)/EU Report	X	X	1.50	0.50	2.50	4.25	3.00	3.00	1.00
Slovakia	15.50	X (07)/EU Report	X	X	1.50	1.50	3.00	3.00	3.00	2.00	1.50
Sweden	15.50	X (07)/EU Report	X	X	1.50	1.50	3.50	3.75	3.00	2.00	0.25
Italy	15.00	X (07)/EU Report	X	X	1.50	1.50	3.50	3.75	3.00	1.50	0.25
France[4]	14.75	X (07)/EU Report	X	X	1.50	1.50	3.75	3.25	3.00	1.50	0.25
Finland	14.50	X (06)/EU Report	X	X	1.50	1.50	2.75	3.50	3.00	2.00	0.25
Spain[5]	14.25	X (07)/EU Report	X	X	1.50	1.50	2.25	3.25	3.50	2.00	0.25
Belgium	13.25	X (07)/EU Report	X	X	1.50	2.00	2.50	2.50	3.00	1.50	0.25
Bosnia & Herzegovina[6]	13.00	X (06)	X	X	1.50	1.00	2.50	2.50	3.00	1.50	1.00
Poland[7]	13.00	EU Report	X	X	1.50	1.00	2.00	3.75	3.00	1.50	0.25
Czech Republic	12.75	X (07)/EU Report	X	X	1.50	1.00	2.25	3.25	3.00	1.50	0.25
Portugal[8]	12.75	X (06)/EU Report	X	X	1.50	1.50	2.75	2.25	3.00	1.50	0.25

▶▶

Austria[9]	12.00	X (07)/EU Report	X	X	1.50	1.50	2.75	1.50	3.00	1.50	0.25
Canada[10]	11.75	X (03-05)	X	X	1.50	1.50	2.25	3.50	3.00	0.00	0.00
Croatia	11.00	–	X	X	1.50	1.00	1.50	3.50	3.50	0.00	0.00
Australia	10.25	–	X	X	1.50	1.00	1.50	3.25	3.00	0.00	0.00
Cyprus[11]	10.25	EU Report	X	X	1.50	1.00	1.50	2.25	3.00	1.00	0.00
Hungary[12]	10.25	EU Report	X	X	1.50	1.50	1.75	1.75	2.00	1.50	0.25
Pakistan	10.00	–	X	X	1.50	1.00	1.50	3.00	3.00	0.00	0.00
Thailand	10.00	–	X	–	1.50	0.50	1.50	3.50	3.00	0.00	0.00
South Korea	9.75	–	X	X	1.50	1.00	1.50	2.75	3.00	0.00	0.00
Japan	9.50	–	X	X	1.50	1.00	1.25	2.75	3.00	0.00	0.00
Turkey	9.50	–	X	X	1.50	1.00	1.25	2.75	3.00	0.00	0.00
Brazil	9.00	–	X	X	1.50	1.00	1.00	2.50	3.00	0.00	0.00
Argentina	8.75	–	X	X	1.50	0.50	1.50	2.25	3.00	0.00	0.00
Mexico	8.75	–	X	X	1.50	0.50	1.00	2.75	3.00	0.00	0.00
Saudi Arabia	8.75	–	X	–	1.50	0.50	1.50	2.25	3.00	0.00	0.00
Ukraine	8.00	X (07)	–	X	1.50	1.50	1.00	2.00	2.00	0.00	0.00
Bulgaria	7.50	X (07)/EU Report	–	X	1.50	1.50	1.50	0.00	1.50	1.50	0.00
China	7.50	–	X	X	1.50	0.50	1.00	1.50	3.00	0.00	0.00
Singapore	6.50	–	X	X	1.50	1.00	1.00	1.00	2.00	0.00	0.00
Taiwan[13]	6.25	–	X	–	1.50	0.50	1.00	1.25	2.00	0.00	0.00
Israel	6.00	–	X	X (06)	1.50	0.50	0.50	1.50	2.00	0.00	0.00
Russian Federation	5.50	–	X	X	1.50	1.00	0.50	0.50	2.00	0.00	0.00
South Africa[14]	2.00	X (03-04)	–	X	1.50	0.50	0.00	0.00	0.00	0.00	0.00
Iran	0.00	–	–	–	0.00	0.00	0.00	0.00	0.00	0.00	0.00
North Korea	0.00	–	–	–	0.00	0.00	0.00	0.00	0.00	0.00	0.00

* Major exporters are those countries that export–or are believed to export–at least USD 10 million worth of small arms, light weapons, their ammunition, and associated components annually. The 2009 Barometer includes all countries that were among the major exporters at least once in their reporting covering the years 2001-07. For major exporters in 2005, see Annexe 4.1 of Small Arms Survey (2008), <http://www.smallarmssurvey.org/files/sas/publications/year_b_pdf/2008/CH4%20Transfer%20diversion%20annexes.pdf>; for those in 2004, see Annexe 3.1 of Small Arms Survey (2007), <http://www.smallarmssurvey.org/files/sas/publications/year_b_pdf/2007/CH3-Transfers_Annexe_3.pdf>; for those in 2003, see Small Arms Survey (2006, pp. 68-74); for those in 2002, see Small Arms Survey (2005, pp. 102-5); and for those in 2001, see Small Arms Survey (2004, pp. 103-6).

** X indicates that a report was issued.

*** The Barometer analysed the tenth annual EU Report (CoEU, 2008), reporting on EU member states' activities in 2007.

Scoring system

The scoring system for the 2009 Barometer has changed from 2008. The new system provides more comprehensive, nuanced, and consistent thresholds for the various categories. The Barometer's seven categories assess timeliness, access, and consistency in reporting (categories i-ii, discussed below); its clarity and comprehensiveness (iii-iv); and the level of detail provided on actual deliveries, licences granted, and licences refused (v-vii).

(i) Timeliness (1.5 points max.): The first category awards points for the timeliness (promptness) of reports and of the data they contain.

(ii) Access and consistency (2.0 points max.): This second category reviews the accessibility of the information that states provide, its frequency, and the use of multiple reporting instruments.

(iii) Clarity (5 points max.): The main purpose of this third category is to analyse the extent to which information on small arms and light weapons transfers, including their ammunition, can be distinguished from conventional arms transfers. It also evaluates the information that countries provide on relevant legislation, including its implementation; measures to prevent diversion; and international, regional, and sub-regional commitments relating to the control of small arms transfers. Finally, it grants points for data on aggregated totals of deliveries and licences granted/refused, as well as information on brokers.

(iv) Comprehensiveness (6.5 points max.): The fourth category examines the level of detail provided on weapons types (e.g. (un-)guided light weapons, sporting and hunting guns, pistols and revolvers, military firearms, small arms ammunition, and ammunition larger than 12.7 mm). It also evaluates reporting of different types of transfers (e.g. permanent re-exports and transit/trans-shipment activities).

(v) Deliveries (4 points max.): The fifth category awards points for information shared on actual deliveries; end users; and the types, values, and quantities of delivered weapons.

(vi) Licences granted (4 points max.): The sixth category awards points for information shared on licence recipients; end users; and the types, values, and quantities of approved transactions.

(vii) Licences refused (2 points max.): The seventh category considers whether or not the country identified countries that were refused licences; gave an explanation of such refusals; and provided information on the types, value, and quantity of weapons for which licences were refused.

For more detailed information on the scoring guidelines, visit the Small Arms Survey Web page:
<http://www.smallarmssurvey.org/files/portal/issueareas/transfers/baro.html>.

Explanatory notes

Note A: The Barometer is based on each country's most recent arms exports report made publicly available from 1 January 2007 to 31 December 2008.

Note B: The Barometer takes into account country reporting to the UN Register from 1 January 2007 to 20 January 2009. Reporting to UN Comtrade for 2007 is considered up to 23 January 2009.

Note C: The fact that the Barometer is based on three sources–national arms export reports, customs data made available to the UN, and reporting to the UN Register–works to the advantage of states that publish data in all three outlets. Points awarded from each of the three sources are added up. There is, however, no double counting. If countries provide the same information to two or more different sources, they are awarded the same number of points that they would have received had they provided the information to a single source.

Note D: Where governments indicate that they do not export, or have not exported, a particular type or particular types of small arms or light weapons during the applicable reporting period ('nil reporting'), this can be considered complete information for the purpose of attributing points under relevant categories of the Barometer.

Country-specific notes

[1] Germany published a national arms export report in 2007 that was limited to data from 2006. It did issue a national report for its arms exports activities in 2007. This report was published in January 2009 (after the cut-off date of 31 December 2008) and could therefore not be evaluated for the 2009 scoring. Germany is therefore evaluated with data from 2006 for its national report and 2007 data for the EU Report. Germany's reporting to the UN Register does not contain actual deliveries, but licences issued. This information was scored accordingly.

[2] Serbia published a national arms export report in 2007 that was limited to data from 2005-06. The country, separated from Montenegro as of 3 June 2006, is evaluated on a 24.5 points scale because it cannot get all the points rewarded under 'Access and consistency'.

[3] The US report is divided into several documents. For the purposes of the Barometer, the US annual report refers to the State Department report pursuant to section 655 on direct commercial sales and the report on foreign military sales, which is prepared by the US Department of Defense (US, 2008a).

[4] France's 2007 report has changed in format, resulting in it being much less detailed than the previous national report. France therefore loses several points.

[5] Spain makes public its report on small arms and light weapons exports to the Organization for Security and Co-operation in Europe (OSCE) as an annexe to its arms export report. The report contains information on licences granted and actual deliveries. It covers only OSCE states and a very limited number of transactions. Spain is therefore granted only half of the points for providing information on the intended country of import and types and quantities of weapons or ammunition exported.

[6] Bosnia and Herzegovina published a national arms export report in 2007 that was limited to data from 2006.

[7] Poland is one of the three EU member states under review that do not produce a national report, but the country reports to the EU Report.

[8] Portugal published a national arms export report in 2008 that included data from 2006. The country's data in its national report (2006) does not correspond with the data evaluated in the EU Report (2007).

[9] Austria's national report does not contain information on its small arms exports, but the country appends to the report its reporting to the EU Report.

[10] Canada published a national arms export report in 2007 that was limited to data from 2003-05. Canada has not been granted a point under 'Deliveries', although the Canadian annual report states that the majority of exports are for private end use. For a point to be awarded under this category, more detailed information needs to be provided.

[11] Cyprus is one of the three EU member states under review that do not produce a national report, but the country does report to the EU Report.

[12] Hungary is one of the three EU member states under review that do not produce a national report, but the country does report to the EU Report.

[13] Taiwan's score has been evaluated on the basis of data it submits to UN Comtrade, as published by the International Trade Centre (ITC) in its Trade Map database (ITC, 2008).

[14] South Africa published a national arms export report in 2007 that was limited to data from 2003-04. The country does not define the abbreviations of military categories 'A', 'B', 'C', and 'D' used in its national report. Efforts to obtain a definition from South African authorities were not successful before the printing of the *Small Arms Survey 2009*.

Sources

Austria (2007); Belgium (2008a; 2008b; 2008c; 2008d); Bosnia and Herzegovina (2007); Bulgaria (2008); Canada (2007); CoEU (2008); Czech Republic (2008); Denmark (2007); Finland (2007); France (2008); Germany (2007); Italy (2008); ITC (2008); Netherlands (2008); Norway (2008); Portugal (2007); Romania (2008); Serbia (2007); Slovakia (2008); South Africa (2007); Spain (2008); Sweden (2008); Switzerland (2008); Ukraine (2008); UN Comtrade (n.d.); UK (2008); US (2008a; 2008b)

CONCLUSION

As has been demonstrated throughout this chapter, the global trade in small arms and light weapons—and our understanding of this trade—has increased significantly in recent years. After adjusting for inflation, small arms and light weapons transfers reported to UN Comtrade increased by 28 per cent from 2000 to 2006, totalling just under USD 3 billion in 2006. The value of firearms exports alone, as reported to UN Comtrade, was nearly USD 1.44 billion. Our 53-country assessment of other data sources suggests that this data under-represents the actual trade in firearms by at least USD 140 million, which increases the estimated total for the documented trade in firearms to USD 1.58 billion. While the USD 140 million difference between the UN Comtrade total and the Small Arms Survey's revised estimate is relatively minor in dollar value terms, it represents tens of thousands of weapons, including sniper rifles, machine guns, and assault rifles—the weapons of choice for many violent extremist groups and criminals. Our assessment also revealed several persistent data gaps that, if filled, would probably add at least USD 100 million—representing the transfer of thousands of weapons—to the current estimate of approximately USD 1.58 billion.

These data gaps, and the inherent differences among the markets for small arms, light weapons, parts, accessories, and ammunition, preclude a definitive assessment of the broader trade. Nonetheless, some tentative conclusions about the value of small arms and light weapons trade can be drawn from our findings. Assuming that light weapons[49] are under-reported to UN Comtrade to the same extent as military firearms, and given the high unit cost of the guided missiles fired by some light weapons,[50] the total figure for small arms and light weapons transfers would probably increase by hundreds of millions or billions of dollars if these transfers were included.[51] A clearer picture of the entire trade in small arms and light weapons will emerge over the next few years as the Small Arms Survey systematically assesses the trade in ammunition, parts and accessories, and light weapons.

Regarding the relevance of our findings to small arms control initiatives, the gaps in the data—including the shortage of specific data on the number and type of firearms transferred—uncovered during our survey are more revealing than the additional data it yielded. Data on several producers and exporters remains incomplete at best and non-existent at worst. Systematic monitoring of these countries' exports is extremely difficult. It may be possible for national intelligence agencies to track shipments from some of these countries, but few, if any, intelligence agencies have the mandate and resources to systematically track and evaluate all such transfers. Irresponsible transfers are occasionally exposed by enterprising journalists or as the result of chance events, but these transfers are the rare exceptions; it is likely that most dubious small arms transfers receive little or no international scrutiny. Recent improvements in data on the small arms trade suggest a growing international willingness to expose this trade to more scrutiny, but this sentiment is far from universal. ■

LIST OF ABBREVIATIONS

ATF	US Bureau of Alcohol, Tobacco, Firearms and Explosives
EU	European Union
EUFOR	EU Force
EUFOR RD Congo	EU Force in the Democratic Republic of the Congo
EUR	euro
EU Report	*Annual Report According to Operative Provision 8 of the European Union Code of Conduct on Arms Exports*
DRC	Democratic Republic of the Congo
HS	Harmonized System (of the World Customs Organization)
ISAF	International Security Assistance Force
ITC	International Trade Centre
MONUC	UN Mission in the Democratic Republic of the Congo
OSCE	Organization for Security and Co-operation in Europe
SIPRI	Stockholm International Peace Research Institute
UN	United Nations
UNAMI	UN Assistance Mission for Iraq
UN Comtrade	UN Commodity Trade Statistics Database
UNIFIL	UN Interim Force in Lebanon
UNMIK	UN Mission in Kosovo
UNMIL	UN Mission in Liberia
UN Panel	UN Panel of Governmental Experts on Small Arms
UN Comtrade	UN Commodity Trade Statistics Database
US	United States
USD	US dollar
WCO	World Customs Organization

ENDNOTES

1 The UN Comtrade database is available, free of charge, at <http://comtrade.un.org/db/>.

2 A more complete list of the data sources used in this report is included in Annexe 1.3.

3 This figure includes the USD 1,568 million in transfers documented as part of our 53-country study (see Table 1.22), plus USD 10 million in transfers reflected in UN Comtrade data for the countries not included in the 53-country study.

4 For additional information, see the online Annexes to this chapter on exporter and importer tables for 2006.

5 The Federal Republic of Yugoslavia ceased to exist on 4 February 2003 and was replaced by the union between Serbia and Montenegro. This union ended on 3 June 2006 (i.e. near the end of the period under analysis), and Montenegro became an independent state. For stylistic reasons,

the name Serbia and Montenegro is used throughout this chapter, except for the discussion of the Transparency Barometer, which reflects countries' reporting for 2007, i.e. after the break-up of the union, where the name Serbia is used.

6 Additional information is provided in Annexe 1.3.

7 The UN Panel's definition of small arms includes 'revolvers and self-loading pistols; rifles and carbines; sub-machine-guns; assault rifles; [and] light machine-guns'. Light weapons, as defined by the UN Panel, are 'heavy machine-guns; hand-held under-barrel and mounted grenade launchers; portable anti-aircraft guns; portable anti-tank guns; recoilless rifles; portable launchers of anti-tank missile and rocket systems; portable launchers of anti-aircraft missile systems; [and] mortars of calibres of less than 100 mm'. Ammunition is combined with explosives in a separate category consisting of 'cartridges (rounds) for small arms; shells and missiles for light weapons; mobile containers with missiles or shells for single-action anti-aircraft and anti-tank systems; anti-personnel and anti-tank hand grenades; landmines; [and] explosives' (UNGA, 1997).

8 For example, 14.5 mm machine guns and anti-materiel rifles are presumably included in UN Comtrade category 930190.

9 The International Convention on the Harmonized Commodity Description and Coding System has been in force since 1 January 1988 (WCO, n.d.). See <http://www.wcoomd.org/home_wco_topics_hsoverviewboxes_hsharmonizedsystem.htm> for more information.

10 Data from UN Comtrade was downloaded on 27 August 2008. Data submitted to UN Comtrade can be revised by the reporting countries, so subsequent access to UN Comtrade may produce different figures.

11 Entitled 'Charting a new approach' and 'Analysis of firearms transfers in 2006'.

12 Serbia and Montenegro did not start reporting on all categories of small arms and light weapons until 2004, and Romania did not report to UN Comtrade before 2006.

13 It is possible that exports to Iraq, Afghanistan, and peacekeeping forces deployed in other countries were responsible for the rise in exports of small-calibre ammunition.

14 For more information on cyclical procurement, see Small Arms Survey (2006, ch. 1).

15 It should be noted that, for the purposes of monitoring and detecting problematic arms transfers, data on the quantity, type, and intended end users of exported firearms is often more useful than data on the value of the transfer. The former type of data is still the rare exception, however, and while data on the values of transfers is an imperfect substitute, it does provide information on the origins and destinations of exported firearms, the types of firearms being transferred, the market shares of individual exporting countries, and trends in firearms transfers over time.

16 Entitled 'Analysis of firearms transfers in 2006'.

17 The agency's name was changed from the UN Department of Disarmament Affairs (UNDDA) to the UN Office for Disarmament Affairs (UNODA) in 2007.

18 The national reports for both countries are available on the Small Arms Survey's *National Arms Export Reports* Web page, available at <http://hei.unige.ch/sas/files/portal/issueareas/transfers/transam.html#be>.

19 Also known as the Consolidated EU Report.

20 Whereas the 1999 EU Report stated only that Austria issued 1,605 arms export licences with a combined value of EUR 208,741,703, the 2007 report reveals that Austria issued, *inter alia*, one licence for the export to Afghanistan of 'smooth-bore weapons with a calibre of less than 20 mm, other arms and automatic weapons with a calibre of 12.7 mm (calibre 0,50 inches) or less' and/or accessories or components valued at EUR 51,185. The report also indicates that Austria exported EUR 51,185 worth of items from this category to Afghanistan in 2006 (CoEU, 2007, p. 9).

21 In the context of this chapter, 'mirror data' is defined as data on arms transfers from a specific exporter that is reported by the importing country. Often, mirror data is the only data available for exports from non-transparent countries. For example, mirror data from 17 countries reveals that in 2006 China exported USD 3.7 million worth of pistols and revolvers. Since China does not provide export data on pistols and revolvers to UN Comtrade, the mirror data from importers of Chinese weapons is the only data available.

22 An example of an export categorized under 9301909090 that is not a firearm is the Silent Guardian™ Protection System, a five-ton device that directs a beam of energy at the skin of its target, causing an 'intolerable heating sensation' (Raytheon, 2006) (correspondence with US State Department official, 21 October 2008).

23 Letter from Paul E. Herrick, Chief, Commodity Analysis Branch, Foreign Trade Division, US Census Bureau to author Matthew Schroeder, 24 December 2008.

24 The threshold for inclusion in the list of the 46 countries is USD 4 million or more in small arms and light weapons exports, as documented in UN Comtrade, in 2006. It should be noted that not all of these countries are major producers. For more information on firearms production, see Small Arms Survey (2001–04; 2007).

25 The list of countries differs slightly from the Small Arms Survey's list of major exporters (i.e. exporters who have exported—or are suspected of exporting—USD 10 million or more in a given year). Eight of the 53 countries assessed as part of this year's study are not among the major exporters listed in the Transparency Barometer in recent years, and one country included in the Transparency Barometer, Saudi Arabia, was not included in the list of 53 countries.

26 For a more complete list of sources, see Annexe 1.3.

27 Prior to 2002 trade data on military firearms was combined with data on artillery, rocket launchers, grenade launchers, and other weapons in a single commodity category (930100). The standard international customs categories reported to UN Comtrade were comprehensively revised in 2002, during which category 930100 was replaced with four sub-categories, including the one currently used for military firearms (930190). The other sub-categories were 'self-propelled [military weapons]', including anti-aircraft guns, anti-tank guns, howitzers, and mortars (930111); 'other' non-self-propelled artillery, including fixed artillery and artillery mounted on railway trucks (930119); and rocket launchers; flame-throwers; grenade launchers; torpedo tubes and similar projectors (930120). Note that a handful of countries continue to report under the pre-2002 nomenclature. Data from category 930100 was not used if the more specific information was available from another source, or if other sources indicated that the transfer included artillery. Category 930100 data was not used in the section entitled 'Analysis of firearms transfers in 2006'. It was used in the section entitled 'Framing the issues', but before using 930100 data, the authors consulted SIPRI records on transfers of artillery, and any transfers that corresponded with a reported transfer of artillery were deleted from the dataset.

28 For a detailed explanation of how the reliability of the data sources used in this chapter was evaluated, see Annexe 1.3.

29 For a detailed explanation of how the global average unit prices were calculated, see Annexe 1.3.

30 For a more detailed explanation of the methodology used in this section, see Annexe 1.3.

31 This total reflects a 33 per cent downward revision in the number of units recorded in US customs data (from 110,403 units to the current total of 74,089 units) in December 2008. The revision was prompted by the discovery of a reporting error regarding arms exports to Japan (see Box 1.2).

32 By 'little or no additional data', we are referring to countries in which the difference between the total value of firearms transfers recorded in UN Comtrade and those recorded in all assessed data sources was less than 1 per cent.

33 For more information, see Annexe 1.3.

34 Note: Ukraine does not produce sporting rifles, but exports old, surplus bolt-action rifles.

35 'Combat' shotguns are made to military specifications, and some are, for example, capable of fully automatic fire. A sniper rifle is a high-precision rifle that is used against a single target, often at long range, without using automatic fire. Such rifles can be designed to be used against personnel or matériel. A carbine is a lighter and shorter version of a rifle. It is easier to carry, but usually has reduced range compared to a rifle.

36 The chapter also substantiates the finding in previous editions of the Small Arms Survey yearbook (Small Arms Survey, 2003; 2004), i.e. that production of small arms and light weapons is located in over 90 countries.

37 For a detailed discussion of recent transfers of small arms and light weapons to Georgia, see Annexe 1.4.

38 Private communication, 5 January 2009.

39 In many countries in Latin America, for example, the types of handguns that civilians can possess are limited by the calibre of the weapon. In the 1980s and 1990s the civilian markets for .380 (9 mm short) calibre pistols expanded as the use of the 9 mm Luger and .45 became restricted to civilian users.

40 For example, since the late 1990s, the Brazilian state law enforcement forces have slowly been shifting from .38 revolvers to .40 S&W Taurus pistols. Similarly, the French national police force shifted from .38 Manurhin revolvers to SIG SAUER P2022 German-made pistols in 2003.

41 The above information on Ukraine was provided to field researcher Maxim Pyadushkin by the State Service of Export Control of Ukraine (Pyadushkin, 2008). According to the data, Ukraine exported a total of 147,135 units. No data on the value of the shipments was provided, so a deflated average unit price was calculated from observations of sporting rifle transfers in the period 2000–06 (NISAT, n.d.).

42 The revised Transparency Barometer, for example, awards points for reporting more than once a year.

43 In 2003 the UN formally expanded the UN Register's seven categories of conventional weapon systems to include man-portable air-defence systems and several light weapons (such as mortars, as well as recoilless rifles and guns that fired munitions of at least 75 mm in diameter). That same year it introduced voluntary reporting for international small arms and light weapons transfers. The new tool has garnered a growing number of adherents: 48 states submitted background information on international transfers of small arms and light weapons for 2007 to the UN Register (Holtom, 2009), compared with 36 submissions for 2006 and only five for 2005 (Holtom, 2008).

44 For instance, in previous editions of the Barometer, Belgium was not granted any points for regional reporting on arms exports. With the revised system, the Survey can analyse all three regional reports issued by Belgian regional authorities and the report by the Belgian Parliament on activities of the Belgian military and police. The new scoring system also takes account of the fact that Taiwan, although not a UN member (and therefore not able to report to the UN Register), can provide customs data (taken into account in this edition) and issue a national report.

45 <http://www.smallarmssurvey.org/files/portal/issueareas/transfers/baro.html>

46 EU member states report on their exports of military goods under the EU's *Annual Report According to Operative Provision 8 of the European Union Code of Conduct on Arms Exports* (e.g. CoEU, 2007; 2008). The first EU Report was published in 1999, and since then all member states have contributed to it. Data provided by 19 EU member states (Austria, Belgium, Bulgaria, Cyprus, the Czech Republic, Denmark, Finland, France, Germany, Hungary, Italy, the Netherlands, Poland, Portugal, Romania, Slovakia, Spain, Sweden, and the United Kingdom) is reflected in the 2009 scores.

47 Such institutes include the Federation of American Scientists (<http://www.fas.org>), the Groupe de Recherche et d'Information sur la Paix et la Sécurité (<http://www.grip.org>), the South Eastern and Eastern European Clearinghouse for the Control of Small Arms and Light Weapons (<http://www.seesac.org>), and the Stockholm International Peace Research Institute (<http://www.sipri.org>).

48 For the use of the name Serbia here, as opposed to the name Serbia and Montenegro used elsewhere in this chapter, see note 5, above.

49 While it is possible that transfers of small arms parts, accessories, and ammunition are also under-represented in UN Comtrade, the high number of countries that reported on these transfers in 2006 suggests that UN Comtrade is capturing most of them. The number of countries that reported on both categories of small arms ammunition (930630 and 930621), for example, was roughly equal to the number of countries that reported on pistol transfers.

50 Customs data on man-portable guided missiles is nearly impossible to disaggregate from data on other weapons, as the missiles are included in category 930690, which also includes large-calibre ammunition, bombs, and missiles classed as major conventional weapons.

51 Anecdotal information on recent sales of guided missiles suggests that even a few large sales could push the global dollar value total for light weapons ammunition into the billions. A single transfer of 2,675 Spike guided anti-tank missiles and 264 launchers in 2003, for example, was valued at USD 512 million (Small Arms Survey, 2008, p. 20).

ANNEXES

Online at ‹http://www.smallarmssurvey.org/files/sas/publications/yearb2009.html›

Annexe 1.1 Annual authorized small arms and light weapons exports for major exporters (yearly sales of more than USD 10 million), 2006

This annexe provides UN Comtrade data on transfers of small arms and light weapons from major exporters in 2006.

Annexe 1.2 Annual authorized small arms and light weapons imports for major importers (yearly imports of more than USD 10 million), 2006

This annexe provides UN Comtrade data on transfers of small arms and light weapons from major importers in 2006.

Annexe 1.3 Methodology

This annexe provides a detailed summary of the methodology used in Chapter 1, 'Sifting the Sources: Authorized Small Arms Transfers'.

Annexe 1.4 'Small Arms and Light Weapons Transfers to Georgia'

This annexe provides a detailed overview of data on transfers of small arms and light weapons to Georgia during the period 2001–07.

BIBLIOGRAPHY

Austria. 2007. *Österreichische Exportkontrolle für Konventionelle Militärgüter: Politische und Rechtliche Rahmenbedingungen*. Vienna: Federal Ministry of Foreign Affairs. Web edition. Accessed 22 February 2009. <http://www.bmeia.gv.at/fileadmin/user_upload/bmeia/media/2-Aussenpolitik_Zentrale/4586_detailbericht_exportkontrolle_konventionelle_waffen.pdf>

Batchelor, Peter. 2003. 'Workshops and Factories: Products and Producers.' In Small Arms Survey, 2003, pp. 9–56.

Beit-Hallahmi, Benjamin. 1987. *The Israeli Connection: Who Israel Arms and Why*. London: I. B. Tauris.

Belgium. 2008a. *Rapport au Parlement sur l'application de la Loi du 5 Aout 1991 Relative à l'importation, à l'exportation et au Transit d'armes, de Munitions et de Matériel devant Servir Spécialement à un Usage Militaire et à la Technologie y Afférente du 1er Janvier 2007 au 31 Décembre 2007*. Brussels: Belgian Parliament.

—. 2008b. *Rapport au parlement Wallon sur l'application de la Loi du 5 Aout 1991, Modifiée par les Lois du 25 et du 26 Mars 2003 Relatives à l'importation, à l'exportation et au Transit d'armes, de Mentions et de Matériel devant Servir Spécialement à un Usage Militaire et de la Technologie y Afférente.* Namur: Wallonian Parliament. Web edition. Accessed 22 February 2009. <http://gov.wallonie.be/IMG/pdf/Rapport_2007.pdf>

—. 2008c. *Vierde Jaarklijks Verslag en Negende Halfjaarlijks Verslag van de Vlaamse Regering aan het Vlaams Parlement over de Verstrekte en Geweigerde Vergunningen voor Wapens, Munitie en Speciaal voor Militair Gebruik of voor Ordehandha Ving Dienstig Materieel en Daaraan Verbonden Technologie.* Brussels: Flemish Parliament. Web edition. Accessed 22 February 2009. <http://www.grip.org/research/bd/trf/rap_gov_be/2007VL.pdf>

—. 2008d. *Rapport du Gouvernement de la Région de Bruxelles-Capitale au Parlement de la Région de Bruxelles-Capitale Concernant l'application de la Loi du 5 Aout 1991, Telle que Modifiée, Relative à l'importation, à l'exportation, au Transit et à la Lutte Contre le Trafic d'armes, de Munitions et de Matériel devant Servir Spécialement à un Usage Militaire ou de Maintien de l'ordre et de la Technologie y Afférente.* Période du 1er Janvier 2007 au 31 Décembre 2007. Brussels: Brussels-Capital Parliament.

Bosnia and Herzegovina. 2007. *Annual Arms Exports and Imports Report: Information on Licences Issued for Brokering of Arms, Military Equipment and Dual-use Products in 2006.* Sarajevo: Ministry of Foreign Trade and Economic Relations. June.

Brazil. Câmara dos Deputados. 2006. *Relatório da Comissão Parlamentar de Inquérito Destinada a Investigar as Organizações Criminosas do Tráfico de Armas, Brasília, Câmara dos Deputados.* Accessed January 2007. <http://apache.camara.gov.br/portal/arquivos/Camara/internet/comissoes/temporarias/cpi/cpiarmas/Relatorio%20Final%20Aprovado.pdf>

Bulgaria. 2008. *Report on the Implementation of the Law on the Foreign Trade in Military Equipment and Dual Use Goods and Technologies.* Sofia: Ministry of the Economy and Energy. Web edition. Accessed 22 February 2009. <http://www.mee.government.bg/bids.html?id=214823>

Canada. 2007. *Report on Exports of Military Goods from Canada 2003–2005.* Ottawa: Foreign Affairs and International Trade Canada. Web edition. Accessed 22 February 2009. <http://www.international.gc.ca/eicb/military/miliexport07-en.asp>

Carpentieri, Stephen, ed. 2003. *Gun Trader's Guide,* 26th edn. Accokeek: Stoeger.

CoEU (Council of the European Union). 2007. *Ninth Annual Report According to Operative Provision 8 of the European Union Code of Conduct on Arms Exports. Official Journal of the European Union,* C 253, Vol. 50. 26 October. Web edition. <http://eur-lex.europa.eu/LexUriServ/LexUriServ.do?uri=OJ:C:2007:253:0001:0332:EN:PDF>

—. 2008. *Tenth Annual Report According to Operative Provision 8 of the European Union Code of Conduct on Arms Exports. Official Journal of the European Union,* C 300. 22 November. Web edition. Accessed 22 February 2009. <http://eur-lex.europa.eu/LexUriServ/LexUriServ.do?uri=OJ:C:2008:300:0001:0374:EN:PDF>

Czech Republic. 2008. *Annual Report on the Czech Republic's Control of the Export of Military Equipment and Small Arms for Civilian Use, 2007.* Prague: Ministry of Foreign Affairs.

Denmark. 2007. *Udførsel af våben og produkter med dobbelt anvendelse fra Danmark 2006.* Copenhagen: Ministry of Foreign Affairs. Web edition. Accessed 11 March 2009. <http://www.um.dk/da/menu/Udenrigspolitik/FredSikkerhedOgInternationalRetsorden/NedrustningIkkespredningOgEksportkontrol/Eksportkontrol/Udfoerselsrapporter/>

Dreyfus, Pablo, Benjamin Lessing, and Julio César Purcena. 2005. 'A Indústria Brasileira de armas leves e de pequeno porte.' In Rubem César Fernandes, ed. *Brasil: as armas e as vítimas.* Rio de Janeiro: 7 Letras, pp. 64–125.

Dreyfus, Pablo, Nicholas Marsh, and Marcelo de Sousa Nascimento. 2006. *Tracking the Guns: International Diversion of Small Arms to Illicit Markets in Rio de Janeiro.* Rio de Janeiro and Oslo: Viva Rio and PRIO. <http://www.comunidadesegura.org/?q=en/node/32137>

En la Mira: The Latin American Small Arms Watch. 2007. 'An Evaluation of the Balance of Trade: Exports and Imports of Small Arms and Light Weapons, Parts and Ammunition in Latin America and the Caribbean, 2000–2005.' *En la Mira: The Latin American Small Arms Watch,* No.12. <http://www.comunidadesegura.org/files/active/0/relatorio_ingles_final1.pdf>

—. 2008. 'The Balance in Balance: Exports and Imports of Small Arms and Light Weapons (SALW), Parts and Ammunition in Latin America and the Caribbean 2000–2006.' *En la Mira: The Latin American Small Arms Watch,* No. 23. <http://www.comunidadesegura.org/?q=en/node/40470>

Finland. 2007. *National Report of Finland for 2006.* Helsinki: Ministry of Defence.

Forecast International. 2007a. 'Europe.' In *Ordnance & Munitions Forecast: Military Sidearms.* Newtown: Forecast International.

—. 2007b. 'International.' In *Ordnance & Munitions Forecast: Military Sidearms.* Newtown: Forecast International.

France. 2008. *Les Exportations d'armement de la France en 2007.* Rapport au parlement. Paris: Ministry of Defence. Web edition. Accessed 22 February 2009. <http://www.defense.gouv.fr/defense/enjeux_defense/defense_au_parlement/rapports_d_activite/rapport_au_parlement_sur_les_exportations_d_armement_2007>

Germany. 2007. *Bericht der Bundesregierung über ihre Exportpolitik für Konventionelle Rüstungsgüter im Jahre 2006 (Rüstungsexportbericht 2006).* Berlin: Federal Ministry of Economics and Labour. Web edition. Accessed 22 February 2009. <http://www.bmwi.de/BMWi/Navigation/Service/publikationen,did=223654.html>

Government Accountability Office. 2005. *DOD Meeting Small and Medium Calibre Ammunition Needs, but Additional Actions Are Necessary*. GAO-05-687. Washington, DC: Government Accountability Office.

Holtom, Paul. 2008. *Transparency in Transfers of Small Arms and Light Weapons: Reports to the United Nations Register of Conventional Arms, 2003–2006*. SIPRI Policy Paper No. 22. Stockholm: Elanders. July.

—. 2009. *Reporting Transfers of Small Arms and Light Weapons to the United Nations Register of Conventional Arms, 2007*. Stockholm: SIPRI. February.

Human Rights Watch. 2008. *Up in Flames: Humanitarian Law Violations and Civilian Victims in the Conflict over South Ossetia*. <http://www.hrw.org/en/reports/2009/01/22/flames-0>

Italy. 2008. *Relazione—Relative all'anno 2007—sulle Operationi Autorizzate e Svolte per il Controllo dell'esportazione, Importazione e Transito dei Materiali di Armamento Nonchè dell'esportazione e del Transito dei Prodotti ad alta Tecnologia*. Doc. LXVII, N.1. Rome: Italian Government. Web edition. Accessed 22 February 2009. <http://www.senato.it/leg/16/BGT/Schede/docnonleg/15805.htm>

ITC (International Trade Centre). 2008. *Trade Map: Trade Statistics for International Business Development*. Database. Geneva: ITC. Web edition. Accessed 22 February 2009. <http://www.trademap.org/index.aspx?ReturnUrl=%2fProduct_SelCountry_TS.aspx>

Klare, Michael and David Andersen. 1996. *A Scourge of Guns: The Diffusion of Small Arms and Light Weapons in Latin America*. Washington, DC: Federation of American Scientists.

Netherlands, The. 2008. *Annual Report on The Netherlands Arms Export Policy 2007*. The Hague: Ministry of Economic Affairs and Ministry of Foreign Affairs. 9 September. Web edition. Accessed 22 February 2009. <http://www.ez.nl/content.jsp?objectid=147591&rid=147549>

New Zealand. 2008. *Information on International Transfers of Small Arms and Light Weapons Provided to the UN Register of Conventional Weapons*. 30 May. <http://disarmament.un.org/UN_REGISTER.nsf>

NISAT (Norwegian Initiative on Small Arms Transfers). n.d. NISAT Small Arms Trade Database. Researcher's Database. Accessed 27 August 2008. <http://www.prio.no/NISAT/Small-Arms-Trade-Database/>

Norway. 2008. *Eksport av Forsvarsmateriell fra Noreg i 2007: Eksportkontroll og Internasjonalt Ikkje-spreiingssamarbeid*. Oslo: Ministry of Foreign Affairs. Web edition. Accessed 22 February 2009. <http://www.regjeringen.no/nn/dep/ud/Dokument/Proposisjonar-og-meldingar/Stortingsmeldingar.html?id=866>

Portugal. 2007. *Anuário estatístico da defesa nacional*. Lisbon: Ministry of Defence. Web edition. Accessed 22 February 2009. <http://www.mdn.gov.pt/mdn/pt/Defesa/Publicacoes/>

Pyadushkin, Maxim. 2008. *Ukraine: Selling the Soviet Legacy or Smart Surplus Management*. Unpublished Small Arms Survey background paper.

Raytheon. 2006. 'Silent Guardian™ Protection System: Less-than-Lethal Directed Energy Protection.' <http://www.raytheon.com/capabilities/rtnwcm/groups/rms/documents/content/rtn_rms_ps_silent_guardian_ds.pdf>

Romania. 2008. *Arms Export Controls: Annual Report January–December 2007*. Bucharest: National Agency for Export Controls, Conventional Arms Division. September.

Serbia. 2007. *Annual Report on the Realization of Foreign Trade Transfers of Controlled Goods for 2005 and 2006*. Belgrade: Ministry of the Economy and Regional Development.

SIG SAUER. 2008. Web site. <http://www.sigsauer.de/index.php?id=614&lang=en>

Slovakia. 2008. *Vyrocna Sprava o Obchode s Vojenskym Materialom za Rok 2007*. Bratislava: Ministry of the Economy. Web edition. Accessed 22 February 2009. <http://www.economy.gov.sk/files/licencie/sprava2007.doc>

Small Arms Survey. 2001. *Small Arms Survey 2001: Profiling the Problem*. Oxford: Oxford University Press.

—. 2002. *Small Arms Survey 2002: Counting the Human Cost*. Oxford: Oxford University Press.

—. 2003. *Small Arms Survey 2003: Development Denied*. Oxford: Oxford University Press.

—. 2004. *Small Arms Survey 2004: Rights at Risk*. Oxford: Oxford University Press.

—. 2005. *Small Arms Survey 2005: Weapons at War*. Oxford: Oxford University Press.

—. 2006. *Small Arms Survey 2006: Unfinished Business*. Oxford: Oxford University Press.

—. 2007. *Small Arms Survey 2007: Guns and the City*. Cambridge: Cambridge University Press.

—. 2008. *Small Arms Survey 2008: Risk and Resilience*. Cambridge: Cambridge University Press.

South Africa. 2007. *2003 and 2004 National Conventional Arms Control Committee's (NCACC) Annual Report(s)*. Pretoria: NCACC.

Spain. 2008. *Spanish Export Statistics Regarding Defence Material, other Material and Dual-use Items and Technologies, 2007*. Madrid: Ministry of Industry, Tourism and Trade. Web edition. Accessed 22 February 2009. <http://www.comercio.es/NR/rdonlyres/28015A5E-2BD4-488F-BF98-14BD1478901A/0/SPANISHSTATISTICSDMOMDU2007.pdf>

Sweden. 2008. *Strategic Export Controls: Military Equipment and Dual-use Products*. Stockholm: National Inspectorate of Strategic Products. Web edition. Accessed 22 February 2009. <http://www.isp.se/sa/node.asp?node=528>

Switzerland. 2008. *Die Exportkontrolle im Bereich Small Arms and Light Weapons (SALW) unter der Kriegsmaterialgesetzgebung: Jahresbericht 2007.* Bern: Swiss State Secretariat for Economic Affairs. December. Web edition. Accessed 22 February 2009. <http://www.seco.admin.ch/themen/00513/00600/00614/00618/index.html?lang=de>

UK (United Kingdom). 2008. *United Kingdom Strategic Export Controls.* London: Foreign and Commonwealth Office. July. Web edition. Accessed 22 February 2009. <http://www.fco.gov.uk/en/about-the-fco/publications/publications/annual-reports/export-controls1>

Ukraine. State Service of Export Control of Ukraine. 2007. *Information on the Volume of International Transfers of Weapons Performed by Ukraine during 2006.* 27 September. <http://www.sipri.org/contents/armstrad/atlinks_gov.html#UKR>

—. 2008. *Information on the Scope of International Weapons Programmes in Ukraine.* Kiev: State Service of Export Control of Ukraine. Web edition. Accessed 22 February 2009. <http://www.dsecu.gov.ua/control/uk/publish/article?art_id=41896&cat_id=41879&search_param=%E7%E4%B3%E9%F1%ED%E5%ED%E8%F5&searchPublishing=1>

UN Comtrade (UN Commodity Trade Statistics Database). n.d. Database. Accessed 27 August 2008. <http://comtrade.un.org/db/>

UNDDA (UN Department of Disarmament Affairs). 2006. *United Nations Register of Conventional Weapons: International Transfers of Small Arms and Light Weapons.* <http://disarmament.un.org/cab/register.html>

—. 2007. *United Nations Register of Conventional Arms: Guidelines for Reporting International Transfers: Questions & Answers.* <http://disarmament.un.org/cab/register_files/Q&A%20booklet%20English.pdf>

UNGA (UN General Assembly). 1997. *Report of the Panel of Governmental Experts on Small Arms.* A/52/298 of 27 August. New York: UN.

UNOCI (UN Operation in Côte d'Ivoire). 2006. 'Your Interaction with Ivorians Is Critical to UNOCI's Success, PDSRSG Tells Bangladeshi Peacekeepers.' ONUCI-232. Press release.

UNODA (UN Office for Disarmament Affairs). 2006. *International Transfers of Small Arms and Light Weapons: Calendar Year 2006.* <http://disarmament.un.org/cab/register_files/SALW2006booklet.doc>

US (United States). 2008a. *Report by the Department of State Pursuant to Section 655 of the Foreign Assistance Act of 1961, as Amended.* Washington, DC: US Department of State and Department of Defense. Web edition. Accessed 22 February 2009. <http://www.pmddtc.state.gov/reports/documents/rpt655_FY07.pdf>

—. 2008b. *DSCA Security Assistance Sales: Detailed Deliveries for Fiscal Year 2007.* 'Fiscal Year 2007 "Section 655" Report.' Made available by the Federation of American Scientists. Web edition. Accessed 22 February 2009. <http://fas.org/programs/ssp/asmp/factsandfigures/government_data/section655_FY2007.html>

US Census Bureau. 2008. *U.S. Exports of Firearms by Country, Monthly January through December.* Unpublished report prepared by the US Census Bureau for the Small Arms Survey. 29 September.

Werneck, Antônio. 2007. 'A conexão Flórida: armas compradas nos EUA por brasileiros terminam nas mãos do tráfico do Rio.' *O Globo* (Rio de Janeiro). 12 August, p. 20.

WCO (World Customs Organization). n.d. *General Information: The Harmonized Commodity Description and Coding System.* <http://www.wcoomd.org/files/1.%20Public%20files/PDFandDocuments/Conventions/Hsconve21.pdf>

—. 2008. 'List of Countries, Territories or Customs or Economic Unions Applying the HS.' October. <http://www.wcoomd.org/files/1.%20Public%20files/PDFandDocuments/Harmonized%20System/HS-Eng_20081029.pdf>

ACKNOWLEDGEMENTS

Principal authors

Authorized transfers: Pablo Dreyfus (Viva Rio), Nicolas Marsh (PRIO) and Matt Schroeder (FAS)

Small Arms Trade Transparency Barometer: Jasna Lazarevic

Contributors

Authorized transfers: Kristina Aronson, Philip Gounev, and Maxim Pyadushkin; Marcelo de Sousa Nascimento (ISER); Natasha Leite de Moura and Júlio Cesar Purcena (Viva Rio)

Small Arms Trade Transparency Barometer: Helen Close

French EUFOR soldiers in Abeche, Chad, June 2008.
© Issouf Sanogo/AFP

Devils in Diversity

EXPORT CONTROLS FOR MILITARY SMALL ARMS

2

INTRODUCTION

Rigorous export controls are an essential tool in the fight against the illicit small arms trade. Under the United Nations *Programme of Action* on small arms, states have committed themselves to establishing effective export control systems and to assessing applications for export authorizations according to strict national regulations and procedures that are consistent with their existing responsibilities under relevant international law (UNGA, 2001, para. II.11). Many states claim to have developed strong, effective systems. It is clear, however, that legally traded weapons continue to reach the illicit market. Panels appointed to monitor UN Security Council arms embargoes regularly uncover violations, while expert groups continue to urge states to ensure their national systems and internal controls are at the highest possible standard (UNGA, 2008, para. 29). This begs the question: how well are states currently regulating small arms exports? What more needs to be done?

This chapter compares the export control systems in 26 states that have been consistently classified as 'major exporters' by the Small Arms Survey (TRANSFERS).[1] Its principal conclusions include the following:

- All the major exporters have export controls and licensing procedures in place, but these vary considerably in terms of procedure and content.
- Many states regulate the export of military and non-military small arms under separate mechanisms, but different countries do not categorize the same weapons in the same way.
- States apply varying levels of scrutiny to export decisions depending on the nature of and reason for the export.
- Many states require non-re-export undertakings as part of the licensing process, but there are indications that states seldom follow up on these.
- The decision to establish a 'common market' in the European Union for defence-related goods raises a number of concerns regarding the possible re-export and ultimate end use of such goods.

This chapter focuses on legislation and regulations governing the permanent export of *military* small arms. It does not analyse the licensing systems for non-military exports, except to the extent that they are governed by the same law as military exports. Nor does it analyse other components of transfer control systems, such as the regulation of import, transit, trans-shipment, or brokering.

The first section of this chapter provides an overview of the nature and purpose of export controls. It explains what is meant by the term 'export' and reviews the principal types of small arms and light weapons affected by export controls. The chapter then compares export licensing processes in the selected countries, with a focus on pre-licensing requirements, exceptions to licensing requirements, the types of licenses granted, and diversion-prevention mechanisms. The final section reviews the government ministries that are involved in decisions to export small arms, as well as the criteria that are applied to such decisions. Throughout, the chapter highlights the wide variations in national export control systems, identifying specific strengths and weaknesses.

OVERVIEW

This section introduces the basic concepts that will underpin the review of national export controls in the rest of the chapter. It outlines the various components of these systems and addresses such basic questions as the purpose and scope of export controls. It situates national controls against the backdrop of states' international commitments and examines the types of weapons covered by the systems under review.

What are export controls?

Export controls comprise the laws, regulations, and administrative procedures that a country uses to regulate the export of strategic goods, including military equipment. They seek to control: the destination of the strategic goods; the person or entity that ultimately takes control of and uses the goods (end user); and their ultimate use (end use). In most states, the export of strategic goods requires the permission of the government, obtained through a licensing process. Governments decide whether to authorize exports on the basis of applicable national legislation and policy.

There is no single model for an export control system; however, any export control system needs to have certain features to be effective, as identified in the *Handbook of Best Practices on Small Arms and Light Weapons* of the Organization for Security and Co-operation in Europe (OSCE). These include a legal basis, an export policy, a decision-making mechanism, and an enforcement mechanism (OSCE, 2003, part V, p. 2). Additionally, there should be effective oversight and scrutiny of the export control regime ensuring some minimum degree of transparency and allowing other branches of government (typically parliaments) to monitor national export policies.

Various multilateral arrangements attempt to regulate the export of arms, including small arms.[2] The nature and scope of these arrangements vary. Some, such as the UN *Firearms Protocol*, the *Convention against the Illicit Manufacturing of and Trafficking in Firearms, Ammunition, Explosives, and Other Related Materials* (CIFTA), and the *Protocol* of the Southern African Development Community (SADC), are legally binding; some, such as the 1996 *Disarmament Commission Guidelines*, establish non-binding guidelines; and others, such as the *Model Regulations* of the Organization of American States, serve as templates. Some instruments cover all conventional weapons, such as the Wassenaar Arrangement and the European Union (EU) *Code of Conduct*;[3] others cover small arms and light weapons only, such as the UN *Programme of Action*, the OSCE *Document on Small Arms*, and the Wassenaar *Best Practice Guidelines for Exports of Small Arms and Light Weapons*. Levels of regional activity and participation in the various instruments also vary. Table 2.1 contains a list of the instruments affecting small arms transfers to

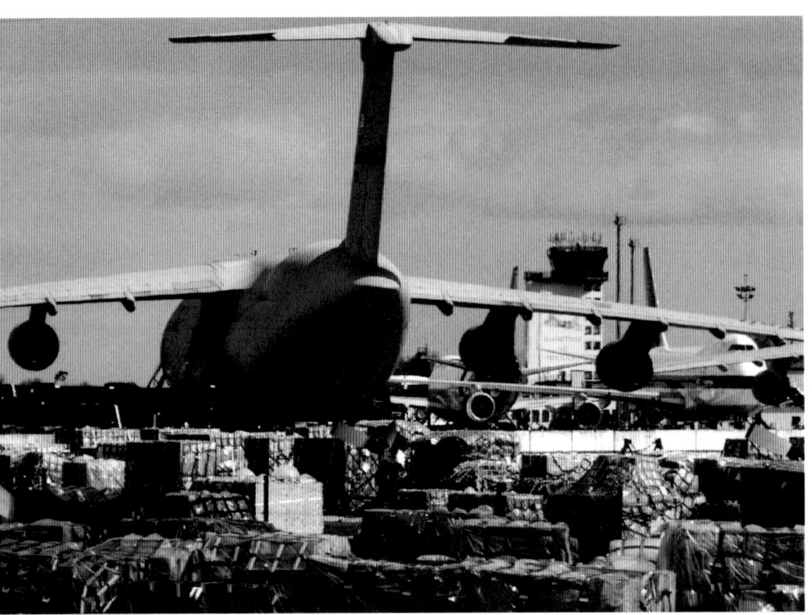

Supplies ready to be transported to the Gulf region from the US military base at Ramstein, Germany, April 2003. © Alexander Heimann/AFP

Table 2.1 **Small arms transfer instruments applicable to major exporting states**

	Legally binding												
Instrument	CIFTA (1997)		UN Firearms Protocol (2001)		SADC Protocol (2001)	OSCE Principles Governing Conventional Arms Transfers (1993)	Disarmament Commission Guidelines (1996)	EU Code of Conduct (1998)[4]	Letter of Intent (1998)	OAS Model Regulations (1998)	OSCE Document on Small Arms (2000)	UN Programme of Action (2001)	Wassenaar 'Best Practice Guidelines' (2002)
	Signed	Ratified	Signed	Ratified									
Austria			■			■	■	■			■	■	■
Belgium				■		■	■	■			■	■	■
Brazil		■		■			■			■		■	
Bulgaria				■		■	■	■			■	■	■
Canada	■		■			■	■			■	■	■	■
China			■				■					■	
Czech Republic						■	■	■			■	■	■
Finland			■			■	■	■			■	■	■
France						■	■	■	■		■	■	■
Germany			■			■	■	■	■		■	■	■
Israel							■					■	
Italy				■		■	■	■	■		■	■	■
Japan			■				■					■	■
Norway				■		■	■				■	■	■
Portugal			■			■	■	■			■	■	■
Republic of Korea			■				■					■	■
Romania				■		■	■	■			■	■	■
Russian Federation						■	■				■	■	■
Singapore							■					■	
South Africa				■	■		■					■	■
Spain				■		■	■	■	■		■	■	■
Sweden			■			■	■	■	■		■	■	■
Switzerland						■	■				■	■	■
Turkey				■		■	■	○			■	■	■
United Kingdom			■			■	■	■	■		■	■	■
United States	■					■	■			■	■	■	■

Notes: Shaded type indicates that instruments serve to guide states in deciding whether to grant an export licence (see 'Licensing criteria', below).

○ Candidate country

Box 2.1 Glossary of export control terms

Actors

Consignee (also known as the 'foreign consignee'): The consignee is a recipient of the exported goods. The goods may remain with the consignee (in which case the consignee is the end user), or they may be forwarded on to the end user. There may be several intermediate consignees who assist in effecting delivery to the end user, who is the ultimate consignee.

End user (also known as the 'ultimate consignee'): The person or entity in the importing state that ultimately receives and uses the exported items.

Exporting state (or 'country of origin'): The country from where the arms are exported; responsible for authorizing the export (granting the export licence).

Foreign intermediate parties: Entities involved in the transaction, such as freight forwarders, customs brokers, agents or representatives, and arms brokers.

Importing state (or 'country of final destination' or 'final destination country' or 'recipient country'): The country where the end user is located.

Activities

End use: Normally the licence application or associated documentation indicates how the end user (or 'ultimate consignee') intends to use the items being exported.

Export: The physical movement of goods from one state to another.

Re-export (or 're-transfer'): Generally, the export of goods that have been imported from another country (the 'country of origin'). In some jurisdictions, goods in transit are considered 're-exports' (or 'exports') when they leave the territory of the transit state.

Transfer: A transfer of arms, like an export, involves the physical movement of goods. However, technically the term 'transfer' is broader than the term 'export' because it covers not only the movement of goods from one state to another (i.e. international transfer), but also the movement of goods *within* a country.

Transit/trans-shipment: The transit of arms involves their movement from State A (exporting state) through State B (transit state) to State C (importing state), where (in contrast to trans-shipment) there is no change in the mode of transport. The arms may be deemed 'exports' and in some cases 're-exports' by the transit state when they leave its territory.

Documents

End-user certificate: An end-user certificate (EUC) is a document provided by the end user in the importing country. Practice varies, but generally the EUC contains details of the goods being exported, their value and quantity, and the parties involved in the transaction, notably the end user. It may also specify the end use of the goods and contain an undertaking on the part of the end user not to re-export the goods without the approval of or notification to the exporting state.

International import certificate: An international import certificate (IIC) is issued by the government of the importing state. It indicates that the latter is aware of and has no objections to the import of specified items and quantities of controlled goods. The importer obtains the IIC and provides it to the exporter, who in turn attaches it to their application for an export licence if required.

Delivery verification certificate: A delivery verification certificate (DVC) is a certificate provided by the government of the importing state that confirms the controlled goods have been delivered or have arrived in the importing state. The importer applies for the DVC and is required to provide evidence that the delivery has taken place, such as a bill of lading, airway bill, or a form endorsed by the customs authority of the importing state. Once obtained, the importer provides the DVC to the exporter. If the exporting state requires a DVC, it will generally appear as a condition on the face of the export licence, and the exporter will be expected to provide the DVC within a certain timeframe following shipment of the goods (e.g. 90 days in the United States[5]).

which major exporting states are parties or in which they are participants. In addition, there are international legal norms that apply to arms transfers, including UN Security Council arms embargoes prohibiting transfers to certain states or groups (Small Arms Survey, 2007, p. 130–32).[6]

Box 2.1 provides an overview of the terms commonly used to describe the actors involved in an export and their transactions. Additionally, there are two other conceptual issues that warrant analysis before embarking on a comparison of states' export controls: what is an 'export'? And what types of small arms are subject to export controls?

What is an export?

In simple terms, an export involves the physical movement of goods from one country (the 'exporting country') to another country (the 'importing country', 'recipient country', or 'country of destination'). Small arms may be exported in a variety of circumstances:

- **Permanent exports.** Permanent exports of small arms can occur through:
  - *Commercial sales:* a manufacturer in the exporting state sells its small arms to an entity in a foreign country. That entity could be a government or a firearms dealer in the importing state.
  - *Government-to-government sales:* the government of the exporting state sells small arms to the government of the importing state for use by its defence or police forces. These arms may be procured from the surplus stocks of the exporting government; they may be produced by a state-owned company; or the exporting government may procure them on behalf of the importing government from a private arms manufacturing company operating in the exporting state.
  - *Government donation:* the exporting government may give the arms to another government free of charge as part of a military assistance project.

Members of the US military deliver weapons and ammunition to the Salah Ad Din Provincial Police Headquarters in Tikrit, Iraq, February 2004. © Stan Honda/AFP

- **Temporary exports.** Small arms may be moved to another country on a temporary basis. These include military small arms that accompany the defence forces of an exporting state on a temporary peacekeeping assignment and are later returned to the exporting country, or weapons that are exported to another country for repairs or for display in trade fairs. Since ownership of these arms does not pass to the recipient country, such exports are not considered to be international transfers (TRANSFERS).[7] Temporary exports also occur when individuals take their firearms on hunting expeditions in a foreign country.
- **Transit.** The arms are transported from State A ('exporting state'), through State B ('transit state'), to State C ('importing state').

States regulate these transactions in a variety of ways, with some providing exemptions from licensing requirements for certain transactions, especially temporary exports by their own armed forces or transfers to allies. In other words, states apply varying levels of scrutiny to export decisions depending on the nature of and reason for the export.

Types of small arms subject to export controls

The states reviewed for this chapter are classified by the Small Arms Survey as 'major exporters' based on the total value of *all* of their small arms exports, with no differentiation made as to whether they export military small arms, non-military small arms, or both. Given the chapter's focus on export control systems for *military* small arms, a few of the major exporters are thus less relevant for this review. Some of these countries predominantly and, in some cases, exclusively, export non-military firearms. In certain cases, this is a matter of policy. For example, **Japan** states that the export of 'arms' has been banned since 1976 (Japan METI, 2002), but excludes from this category 'hunting guns and sport guns' (Japan, 2008). Other countries, such as **Norway**, no longer produce military small arms although they do produce ammunition for such weapons (Weidacher, 2005, p. 59; Norway, 2008, p. 3).

States apply varying levels of scrutiny to export decisions.

Many states regulate the export of military equipment or so-called 'war material'[8] under a legislative and administrative framework that is distinct from the one governing the export of commodities without strategic applications. Small arms straddle both categories since they can be used for both military and non-military purposes. Accordingly, in many jurisdictions, separate legislation and procedures govern the export of military small arms vs. non-military small arms. Moreover, since not all states use the same classification system, certain arms may be considered *military* arms in one state and *non-military* arms in another.

Separate regulation of the export of military and non-military small arms is consistent with the fact that export control regimes, such as the Wassenaar Arrangement and the EU *Code of Conduct,* were established to govern the export of *military* equipment, including small arms for military use. This focus is reflected in the control lists associated with these regimes: the Wassenaar Munitions List and the EU Common Military List (WA, 2008; EU, 2008b). Both control lists cover the same broad range of conventional arms and dual-use equipment, including most small arms, all light weapons, and their ammunition (see Box 2.2). Small arms that are not covered include: (1) smoothbore weapons used for hunting or sporting purposes that are not specially designed for military use and are not fully automatic (most types of shotgun); and (2) weapons using non-centre fire cased ammunition and that are not fully automatic, such as modern pistols and rifles primarily designed for sport shooting.[9]

As illustrated by Table 2.1 many of the major exporters are members of the EU and/or participate in the Wassenaar Arrangement. Not surprisingly, most have harmonized their national control lists with the EU Common Military List or the

Box 2.2 Small arms-related categories in the Wassenaar Munitions List and EU Common Military List

ML1[10] Smooth-bore weapons with a calibre of less than 20 mm, other arms and automatic weapons with a calibre of 12.7 mm (calibre 0.5 in.) or less and accessories, as follows, and specially designed components therefor:

a. Rifles, carbines, revolvers, pistols, machine pistols, and machine guns;

b. Smooth-bore weapons, as follows:

  1. Smooth-bore weapons specially designed for military use;
  2. Other smooth-bore weapons, as follows:
     a. Of the fully automatic type;
     b. Of the semi-automatic or pump-action type;

c. Weapons using caseless ammunition;

d. Silencers, special gun-mountings, clips, weapons sights, and flash suppressers for arms controlled by sub-items ML1.a., ML1.b., or ML1.c.

(The notes to ML1 state: 'ML1 does not control smooth-bore weapons used for hunting or sporting purposes.')

ML2 Smooth-bore weapons with a calibre of 20 mm or more, other weapons or armament with a calibre greater than 12.7 mm (calibre 0.50 in.), projectors and accessories, as follows, and specially designed components therefor:

a. Guns, howitzers, cannon, mortars, anti-tank weapons, projectile launchers, military flame throwers, rifles, recoilless rifles, smooth-bore weapons, and signature reduction devices therefor;

b. Military smoke, gas and pyrotechnic projectors or generators;

c. Weapons sights.

Source: WA (2008)

Wassenaar Munitions List (which are equivalent) or are in the process of doing so.[11] Even some states that do *not* participate in either arrangement have adopted one of these lists. For example, **Israel** and **Singapore** have harmonized their control lists with the Wassenaar Munitions List even though they do not participate in the arrangement (Israel, 2007;[12] Singapore, 2007, sch., part I, div. 2).

Some states, such as **South Africa** and **Spain**, have simply annexed one of the lists in their entirety to the relevant regulations (South Africa, 2004; Spain, 2007b). Others have adapted the Wassenaar Munitions List slightly, with most countries—such as the **Czech Republic** and **Switzerland**—expressly excluding weapons for hunting and sporting purposes or, as is the case for **Sweden**, emphasizing that only small arms designed or adapted for combat purposes are covered by the control list (Czech Republic, 1994b, annexe; Switzerland, 1998, annexe 1). In other words, it is clear from their control lists that their export controls governing the export of strategic and military equipment are only intended to regulate the export of *military* small arms, while non-military exports are subject to a different regulatory regime.

Yet some states, such as **Canada** and the **United Kingdom**, use adapted versions of the Wassenaar Munitions List that do not exclude hunting and sporting or non-military weapons (Canada, 2006, p. 49; UK, 2009). Accordingly, the same controls apply to exports of military and non-military small arms, although the range of exclusions and exceptions to the licensing of non-military exports is correspondingly larger. This means that the same licensing authority regulates the export of military and non-military small arms and that they are subject to the same foreign policy considerations and transfer criteria. In contrast, **Finland** includes some items from the Wassenaar list but excludes 'non-automatic rifles, carbines, revolvers and pistols and smooth-bore weapons', which it classifies as civilian firearms, whose export is licensed under a separate regime (Finland, 2008).

It is common for one licensing authority to authorize exports of military small arms, and for a different government agency to approve the export of non-military arms. For example, in both **Finland** and **Portugal**, the Ministry of Defence has primary responsibility for licensing exports of military small arms, but the Ministry of Interior is responsible for licensing exports of non-military arms. In the **Republic of Korea** and **South Africa**, the national police service makes the decision to license exports of non-military small arms, and different agencies authorize military exports (see Table 2.3). If, however, a proposed export involves more than ten firearms or 20,000 rounds of ammunition, the National Commissioner of the South African Police Service must submit the licensing application to the interagency committee charged with licensing military exports—the National Conventional Arms Control Committee (NCACC)—for consideration (South Africa, 2004, sec. 7). In other countries, certain transactions of non-military small arms are also subject to the same scrutiny as military exports.

In **Sweden**, military equipment has been divided into two separate categories for the purpose of export controls: military equipment for combat purposes (MEC) and other military equipment (OME). Barrelled weapons with a calibre of less than 20 mm are classified as MEC if they are 'designed for combat', while those 'designed for hunting and sport purposes' are classified as OME. Barrel weapons over 20 mm calibre are classified as OME if they are 'designed for the launching of non-destructive ammunition' (Sweden, 1992b, annexe). The same licensing authority controls the export of both categories, but different export criteria are applied (see below).[13]

Exports of non-military small arms are also at risk of diversion and misuse.

The question of whether states subject their exports of non-military small arms to the same scrutiny and foreign policy considerations as their exports of military small arms is important since exports of non-military small arms are also at risk of diversion to and misuse by unauthorized end users (Small Arms Survey, 2008, ch. 2).[14] It is difficult to quantify the scale or proportion of non-military arms exports relative to military small arms exports, largely due to the lack of comprehensive data on the small arms trade. However, United Nations Commodity Trade Statistics Database (UN Comtrade) data suggests that in 2006, for example, sporting and hunting shotguns and rifles accounted for almost half (49 per cent) of all firearms exported that year (TRANSFERS). To this figure must be added handguns, which remain in wide demand among civilians.

Source of exported arms

The small arms that states export may be new weapons produced by the arms industry (state- or privately owned), or they may be sourced from surplus stockpiles belonging to the state.[15]

Industry. The size and nature of the arms industry in each of the major exporters varies. In the **Russian Federation**, for example, the industry consists of one wholly state-owned corporation, Rostekhnologii (Pyadushkin, 2008). In **Romania**, the core of the arms industry also remains state-owned, with the two principal companies being RomArm and the trade company RomTehnica; however, the government has encouraged limited privatization and the creation of joint ventures with foreign partners (Wood, 2007, p. 12).

Brazil's arms industry is made up of both state-owned and private companies. Indeed, the industry in Brazil is dominated by two private companies—Forjas Taurus S.A. and the Companhia Brasileira de Cartuchos—and a public company—IMBEL—administered by the Ministry of Defence (Dreyfus, Lessing, and Purcena, 2005, p. 50). **France** also has both private and state-owned corporations, with the retention of one state-owned corporation, Nexter (formerly GIAT Industries) (Elluin, 2008). Other states have privatized the industry completely, such that there are no state-owned entities engaged in production (e.g. **Austria** and the **United Kingdom**).

State stockpiles and surplus. Some of the major exporting states, such as **Norway** and **Portugal**,[16] no longer produce military small arms (Weidacher, 2005, pp. 59–61 ; Portugal, 2008, p. 2; Teixeira, 2007). Consequently, exports of military small arms from these countries consist of transfers of surplus stocks, transfers to peacekeeping and defence forces or weapons in transit.

Indeed, despite the presumption in favour of the destruction of surplus stocks in the *Programme of Action*, the OSCE *Document on Small Arms*, and a European Council Joint Action of 2002, many of the major exporters indicate in their national reports on *Programme of Action* implementation that they still export their surplus small arms to other states.[17] This is the case for: **Canada**, the **Czech Republic**, **Finland**, **Germany**, **Israel**, **Portugal**, and the **Russian Federation** (Cattaneo and Parker, 2008, p. 83). Other states also export their surplus small arms—including the **United Kingdom** (UK, 2008b, sec. 4.1) and the **United States** (US, 2005b, sec. 516)—although they may not mention this in their national reports.

The Wassenaar *Best Practices for Disposal of Surplus/Demilitarised Military Equipment* stipulate that surplus military equipment, including small arms and light weapons, should remain subject to the same export controls as new equipment (WA, 2000).[18] Similarly, the OSCE *Document on Small Arms and Light Weapons*—while expressing a preference for the destruction of surplus arms—notes that: 'if their disposal is to be effected by export from the territory of a participating State, such an export will only take place in accordance with the export criteria' set out in the document (OSCE, 2000, sec. IV.C.1). **Israel** asserts that the export of surplus small arms and light weapons 'is followed by the exact same stringent export control and authorization procedures, including marketing and export licenses' that govern the export of new firearms (Israel, 2008). However, as discussed below, some states exempt exports by state agencies from export licensing and authorization procedures; presumably this includes exports of state surplus.

Many major exporters export their surplus small arms instead of destroying them.

THE LICENSING PROCESS

In general terms, the process for authorizing arms exports is virtually the same in all states under review. Prospective exporters must obtain an export licence. A designated government ministry or department decides whether to grant the licence in consultation with other ministries, based on the country's legislation and specific political and security considerations.

However, the question of *what* arms are subject to control, *how* the licensing process operates, *who* makes the decision, and *how* that decision is made (including the criteria that are considered) varies from state to state. Table 2.2 provides a comparative overview of the major elements of the licensing process.

Pre-licensing requirements

In many states, companies or persons wishing to export arms must complete certain administrative steps before they can apply for a licence to export a specific shipment. In some states, they are simply required to register themselves on a national register by lodging certain information regarding their activities and operations. In other states, they must seek prior authorization before entering into contractual negotiations for a specific transfer or some other form of preliminary licence. Some states require both registration and another form of authorization before an export licence can be sought. In most cases, registration or authorization is valid for a limited time, and thereafter must be renewed (see Table 2.2). In some states, such as **Spain**, however, once a company is registered to trade in military equipment, there is no need to reregister.

State agents such as the police and defence agencies are generally not required to register or seek any special authorization to export arms. In some states, state agents are also exempted from having to obtain an export licence, as is discussed below.

Table 2.2 Overview of pre-licensing and licensing systems of major exporters

State	Pre-licensing				Types of licences						Licensing requirements			
	Registration	Transaction authorization	Requirements for exporter	Duration of exporter's pre-licensing authorization	Required	Exceptions	Individual	General	Global	Duration	EUC	No re-transfer	Import certificate	DVC
Austria	■		Licence to trade.		■		■	■			■	■	■	■
Belgium	■	■	Accreditation as an 'arms dealer' and 'preliminary licence'.	Registration and accreditation: indefinite.	■	■	■			1 year.	■	■	■	■
Brazil		■	Authorization to initiate preliminary negotiations.	2 years.	■		■				■	■	■	
Bulgaria	■	■	'Activities authorization' required.	First authorization: 1 year; subsequent authorizations issued for 3 years.	■	■	■			Up to one year and may be prolonged only once for up to 6 months.	■	■	■	■
Canada	■			5 years.	■	■	■	■		Individual licences are issued for a single shipment. The export becomes invalid after the first shipment is made even if the shipment is only a partial one.	■	■	■	
China	■	■	Authorization to engage in military export activities.		■		■				■	■		

▶▶

Czech Republic		■	Trading permit for military equipment.	5 years.	■	■	■				■			
Finland					■	■	■				■	■	■	■
France		■	Authorization to trade and consent to negotiate a contract.	5 years.	■	■	■		■	Individual: 2 years; global: 1 year.	■	■	■	■
Germany			No pre-licensing requirement unless licensed production agreement is involved that requires the export of military equipment.		■	■	■			1 year and can be extended for 1 additional year.	■	■	■	■
Israel	■	■	Applicant must obtain a defence marketing licence before a defence export licence will be granted.		■		■				■	■	■	
Italy	■	■	Authorization to initiate contractual negotiations.	3 years.	■	■	■		■	Individual: 18 months; global: 3 years.	■	■	■	■
Norway					■	■	■				■	■	■	
Portugal	n/a[a]				■		■				■	■	■	
Republic of Korea		■	Preliminary permit to negotiate.		■		■				■	■	■	
Romania		■	Prior authorization.	1 year.	■	■	■		■	Individual: 1 year; global licences for military transfers are available under the Romanian system, but it is not clear that these would cover small arms transfers.	■	■	■	■

Russian Federation		■	General permit to export weapons.		■		■				■	■		
Singapore	■				■		■			Tier 1: 1 month (renewable up to 3 months if shipment has not been effected); Tier 2: 3 years; Tier 3: 3 years.	■		■	
South Africa	■				■	b	■				■	■		■
Spain	■	■	Preliminary agreement required if contract requires long period of execution.	Up to 3 years.	■	■	■	■	■	6 months (individual); 3 years (global).	■	■		■
Sweden		■	Manufacturers and suppliers must notify the Swedish Inspectorate of Strategic Products (ISP) prior to submitting a tender or entering an agreement to supply military equipment to an overseas buyer. ISP may prohibit the activity. Notification is not required if foreign consignee has been approved in past 3 years.		■	■	■	■	■	General licences may be provided to allow for temporary exports for the purposes of repair, replacement, or demonstration with respect to certain equipment controlled under Wassenaar; global licences may also be granted but only for products with civil end use.	■	■		
Switzerland		■	An initial licence to trade in war material.	An initial licence to trade in war material will be withdrawn if it has not been used for 3 years.	■		■			1 year and may be extended up to 6 months.	■	■	■	c
Turkey	■				■		■				■	■		
United Kingdom	No				■		■	■	■		■	No		
United States	■			2 years.	■	■	■			4 years.	■	■	■	■

Country	Record-keeping: duration	Penalties for exporting without a licence	
		Fine[d]	Imprisonment
Austria	Licensee: 3 years.	Up to 360 units of net daily income.	Up to 2 years.
Belgium		EUR 1,000-1,000,000 **(USD 1,400-1,400,000)**.	Up to 5 years (penalties are doubled in case of a second conviction).
Brazil		n/a	4 to 8 years.
Bulgaria	Licencee must keep a separate register for the transactions concluded and keep the commercial and shipping documents and info relating to the transactions for at least 10 years.	A fine of BGN 5,000-50,000 **(USD 3,500-35,000)** for natural persons and company officials; a property sanction of BGN 25,000-250,000 **(USD 17,400-174,000)** for legal persons and sole proprietors; a fine or a property sanction of BGN 50,000-500,000 **(USD 35,000-350,000)** for repeated infringement.	1 to 6 years; extended to 2-8 years if the act is committed by an official or for a second time; where it involves a large amount, increase to 3-10 years; and where for a particularly large amount and the case has been especially grave: 5-15 years.
Canada	All those registered must keep and maintain records of transactions during the period of registration and for a period of 5 years after the day on which the person ceases to be registered.	Offence punishable on summary conviction: fine up to CAD 25,000 **(USD 21,000)**; indictable offence: court has discretion to set fine.	Offence punishable on summary conviction: up to 12 months; indictable offence: up to 10 years.
China	China reports that since 2006, all companies are required to register detailed information on small arms exports with the competent authority. These records are retained on a long-term basis by the authority.	CNY 100,000-500,000 **(USD 15,000-73,000)**.	Depends on whether the offence violates criminal law.
Czech Republic		Up to CZK 5 million **(USD 260,000)**. If the violation has caused damage to the Czech Republic or important policy, commercial, or security interests, the fine my be up to CZK 30 million **(USD 1.6 million)**.	1-8 years; 3-10 years if in collusion with an organized group; if committed during state emergency; repeat offence; if the person has 'gained considerable benefit' from the act, or if it has caused great damage.
Finland		Minimum penalty is a fine (not specified).	Maximum penalty is 4 years; Penal Code also contains provisions concerning forfeiture of the economic benefit produced by the crime.

France	Licensee: records must be kept (duration unspecified).	EUR 100,000 **(USD 140,000)**; increased to EUR 500,000 **(USD 700,000)** when the offence is committed by an organized gang.	7 years (increased to 10 years when the offence is committed by an organized gang).
Germany		Fine (not specified).	Up to 5 years; up to 10 years for serious cases.
Israel	Licensee: 10 years from date of completion of the defence export.	30 times greater than fine set out in the Criminal Code; 50 times greater if 'severe circumstances' apply (e.g. exporting to the enemy).	3 years (5 years if 'severe circumstances' apply, e.g. exporting to the enemy).
Italy	Licensee: 5 years (10 years for some information, e.g. details acquired from carriers and transport agents on the transport route and arrangements).	EUR 2,500–250,000 **(USD 3,400–340,000)**.	3-13 years.
Norway	Licensee: at least 10 years after expiry of the licence.	Fine can be imposed, size depends on discretion of judge (and degree of violation).	Prison sentence may be imposed, term depends on discretion of judge (and degree of violation). Intentional violation: up to 5 years; negligent violation of regulations: up to 2 years.
Portugal[e]		A company involved in the unlawful possession or sale of forbidden firearms (including military firearms) could be fined EUR 12,000–7,200,000 **(USD 16,000–9,800,000)**.	Imprisonment from 2 to 10 years, in ordinary cases, but could be aggravated to 4 to 12 years if: a) the offender is a police officer; b) the weapons were destined for use by criminal gangs or criminal organizations; or c) if this constitutes the seller's livelihood or main income.
Republic of Korea		Fine of less than KRW 50 million **(USD 38,000)**.	Maximum of 10 years.
Romania			2-7 years.
Russia	Not specified, but must submit quarterly reports to the Federal Service on Military-Technical Cooperation.	Up to RUB 1 million **(USD 34,000)** or an annual income for 5 years as a possible supplement to a prison sentence (plus termination of permit to export weapons for a company).	3-12 years (for a private person).
Singapore	Licensee: 5 years from end of calendar year in which authorized transaction took place.	Fine not exceeding SGD 100,000 **(USD 67,000)** or 3 times the value of the goods (SGD 200,000; **USD 135,000**), or 4 times value for a second or subsequent conviction.	Imprisonment not exceeding 2 years (and/or fine); 3 years for a second or subsequent conviction.

South Africa	Not specified. Regulations merely stipulate that a person trading in conventional arms must keep full records and permits of all trade activities.	Fine.	Maximum 25 years (and/or fine). Seizure and disposal of the goods is also possible.
Spain	Licensee: 4 years following date of expiration of authorization.	Smuggling (export without a permit) is punishable by a short-term prison sentence and a fine ranging from twice to four times the value of the goods.	Smuggling (export without a permit) is punishable by a short-term prison sentence.
Sweden	5 years.	If the offence is deemed 'petty' a fine (unspecified) will be imposed.	Grave smuggling: imprisonment for 6 months to 6 years; gross negligence: fine (unspecified) or imprisonment for up to 2 years.
Switzerland	Licensee: at least 10 years.	Wilfully: up to CHF 1 million **(USD 900,000)** or term of imprisonment; serious cases: penal servitude up to 10 years and fine up to CHF 5 million **(USD 4,500,000)**; and negligence: imprisonment up to 6 months or fine up to CHF 100,000 **(USD 90,000)**.	
Turkey	Exporters provide information on exports to the Ministry of National Defence every 3 months. The Ministry keeps export records for 5 years.	Fine.	1-5 years imprisonment. Ministry of Defence reserves the right to apply to the Court of Justice with a request for closure of enterprises that are deemed to be unfit for functioning in this sector.
United Kingdom	Licensee: 3 years.	On summary conviction: fine is the prescribed sum or 3 times the value of the goods, whichever is greater; conviction on indictment, to a penalty of any amount.	Summary conviction: up to 6 months; conviction on indictment: up to 10 years.
United States	5 years from expiration of licence or date of transaction.	No more than USD 1 million.	Not more than 10 years.

Notes: This table collects information from legislation and other publicly available sources, including national reports on implementation. Blank cells reflect gaps in information deriving from those sources. In practice, however, states may include elements in their export controls that are not reflected in their national legislation or other publicly available sources.

* Although Japan is one of the countries reviewed, it does not form part of this table on licensing systems for military small arms exports because of Japan's declared policy of not exporting arms other than hunting and sport guns (Japan, 2008).

[a] In Portugal, the commercial manufacture and export of military small arms is prohibited, but exports of surplus military small arms may take place subject to a permit issued by the Ministry of Defence (Teixeira, 2007; Portugal, 2008).

[b] The National Conventional Arms Control Amendment Bill includes a proposed amendment that would exempt the South African Police Service or the South African National Defence Force from the provisions of the National Conventional Arms Control Act in cases of an emergency or special operations (South Africa, 2008, art. 25A).

[c] In Switzerland, the EUC must include a pledge that the Swiss authorities have the right to verify the end use and end-use location of any supplied item at any time on their demand. Although no delivery verification certificate, as such, is required, the Federal Office of the Police Central Office for combating illegal transactions in war material is responsible for the monitoring of the arrival of deliveries (Liatowitsch, 2008).

[d] The financial penalties were converted from the national currency to US dollars using currency conversion rates as of 8 January 2009. These amounts have been rounded.

[e] Portugal prohibits the export of military small arms (which are included in the category of 'class A' weapons, whose possession, use, and transfer are forbidden). The penalties described here apply to the unlawful possession or transfer of prohibited firearms (including 'class A' weapons) in a domestic setting.

Source: Parker (2009)

In some cases, the precondition to the issuance of a licence takes the form of an authorization to initiate and conduct contractual negotiations to export arms. For example, in **Brazil**, when a commercial opportunity appears, companies must ask the Ministry of Foreign Affairs for authorization to initiate preliminary negotiations. If the ministry has no objections then negotiations are authorized for a period of two years. In **France** an exporter must go through several preliminary steps before an export licence may be sought: authorization to trade (valid for up to five years) must first be obtained from the Ministry of Defence. Once a potential commercial opportunity has been identified, the exporter must then seek two preliminary agreements from the prime minister: one at the 'negotiating phase' to negotiate the contract and a second at the 'signature phase' (Aubin and Idiart, 2007, p. 139).

In **Belgium**, in addition to being included on the national database of registered exporters, anyone wanting to export small arms must obtain two kinds of accreditation before applying for an export licence. The first one is an accreditation as an 'arms dealer' issued by the governor of the province where the company is located;[19] the second is a preliminary licence issued by the minister of justice (called 'licence of integrity') as a proof of integrity (Moreau, 2008).

In **Switzerland**, in addition to an 'initial licence', any individual or entity wishing to trade in war material (including military small arms) but not manufacturing such weapons must obtain a 'trading licence' before applying for an export licence (Switzerland, 1996b, art. 16a). In the **United States**, in addition to a requirement that exporters be registered before receiving an export licence, prior approval of or prior notification to the Directorate of Defense Trade Controls is needed before making certain proposals to a foreign person if the proposal involves the sale of 'significant military equipment' (defined as including small arms and light weapons) valued at USD 14 million or more for use by the armed forces of a country other than a NATO member or Australia, New Zealand, or Japan (US, 2007, sec. 126.8).

Pre-licensing registration offers an additional layer of scrutiny.

The number of individuals and companies authorized to trade in military equipment varies considerably among the major exporters. The **Czech Republic**, for example, reports that as of the end of 2007, 155 business entities held trading permits for military equipment (Czech Republic, 2007a, p. 5); data for 2006 indicates that in the **United States**, more than 5,000 entities were registered to manufacture, export, or broker defence articles or services (US, 2006). In both cases the number of entities authorized to export small arms is not specified. **China**, on the other hand, reported in 2008 that only 10 companies were authorized to engage in arms export activities and only four of these were authorized to *export* small arms (China, 2008, p. 10).

There are obvious benefits associated with a pre-licensing registration system. It offers an additional layer of scrutiny, providing an opportunity to vet potential exporters before they apply for a licence and to inform traders about applicable legislation. Depending on the country, the registration or authorization process may also provide information on the legal status of the exporter, the nature of its business activities, and details of any foreign ownership. In many states registration also entails reporting and record-keeping obligations beyond those required as part of the licensing process, thus bolstering existing checks and balances.

The **United Kingdom**, however—after considering the possible introduction of pre-licensing registration in 2007—remains 'unconvinced' that such a system adds anything to the licensing process. In the British case, exporters must provide full details of the proposed transaction as part of their licence application, and licences may be revoked or refused by the government at that stage (UKBERR, 2007, p. 38).

Interestingly, **France** is examining the possibility of moving to single prior approval by merging its 'negotiating' and 'sale' steps (France, 2007, p. 10). This is seen as a way of reducing administrative burdens and taking account of the fact that, due to the changing nature of the arms industry—which increasingly involves subcontracting to

Box 2.3 **Free trade in arms within Europe?**

On 16 December 2008, the European Parliament and the Council of the European Union adopted a directive that allows the free movement of defence products, including small arms and light weapons, among EU member states. At this writing, the directive was set to enter into force 20 days after its publication in the *Official Journal of the European Union* in the first half of 2009 (EC, 2008, art. 18).

The European Commission proposed the directive to simplify transfers of defence-related products within the European Community in December 2007, following the publication of a study on obstacles to intra-community transfers in 2005 and a consultation process involving the public and member states in 2006 and 2007 (EC, 2007c). Carried out by Unisys on behalf of the European Commission to assess obstacles to intra-community transfers, the study concludes that the diverse licensing requirements of EU countries impose a significant administrative burden on companies and 'appear to be out of proportion with actual control needs', especially in the light of the fact that 'license applications for intra-community transfers are almost never rejected' (Unisys, 2005, p. 5).

The Commission cited this finding in its explanatory memorandum to the proposed directive and noted that the aim of the directive was to reduce the obstacles to the circulation of defence-related products created by the patchwork of licensing schemes and to diminish the resulting distortions in competition (EC, 2007a, p. 2). The broader aim is to increase the competitiveness of the European defence industry and make it economically more efficient. The concern is that if better cooperation and integration are not promoted in Europe's defence industry, it will cease to be competitive on the world market, which will not only have economic costs, but will also hamper the pursuit of the European security and defence policy (EC, 2007b, p. 6).

The directive seeks to achieve these objectives using a twin-track approach. First, in order to simplify intra-community transfers, it encourages the use of general and global licences for transfers of defence products, envisaging only exceptional use of an individual licence, specifically:

a. where the request for a licence is limited to one transfer;
b. where it is necessary for the protection of essential security interests, or the protection of public policy;
c. where it is necessary for compliance with international obligations and commitments of Member States;
d. where a Member State has serious reasons to believe the supplier will not be able to comply with all the terms and conditions necessary to grant it a global licence (EC, 2008, art. 7).

Second, in order to harmonize EU transfer policies, the directive requires states to establish general licensing systems for transfers to the armed forces of EU member states and to *certified companies* in other EU countries (as well as in cases where items are being transferred for exhibitions or repairs in another member state) (EC, 2008, art. 5). Member states will be responsible for certifying recipients of defence-related products within their territories. This certification establishes that the company in question can be relied on to observe any export limitations imposed as part of the transfer licence, that is, limitations on the ability to export the goods to a country that is outside the European Community (EC, 2008, art. 9).

As noted, part of the reasoning behind the decision to simplify intra-Community transfers is the claim that licensing requirements appear to create a disproportionate administrative burden compared to the actual control needs. The evidence given to support this conclusion is the fact that no intra-community transfer of defence equipment has been denied since 2003, as reported in the impact assessment that accompanied the proposed directive (EC, 2007b, p. 15). However, the impact assessment only includes data for 2003, 2004, and 2005. Subsequent annual reports on the EU *Code of Conduct* indicate there have been at least 3 denials of intra-community export licences since 2003, and at least one of these pertained to small arms (EU, 2007; 2008a).

The impact assessment also notes that all the 15 denials registered in 2003 concerned exports to three Baltic states that were not yet EU members, and rather dismissively claims that the refusals were primarily linked to a lack of awareness of the legislation in the new member states and a 'lack of established trust concerning the actual enforcement of re-exportation controls by these new occasional buyers' (EC, 2007b, p. 15). Most importantly, the report notes that the 'categories where refusals occurred (small, light arms) concerned *equipment with a potentially higher risks* (sic) *of uncontrolled dissemination (re-export)*' (EC, 2007b, p. 15, emphasis added).

The European Union has grown considerably in recent years, with ten new member states admitted in 2004 and two in 2007.[20] Three candidate countries are awaiting admission: Croatia, the former Yugoslav Republic of Macedonia, and Turkey. Many of these new and candidate countries are exporters of small arms and other conventional weapons. Clearly, whatever the sophistication of their export control systems, these states do not have the same experience as older EU members in implementing the EU *Code of Conduct*. This, plus the acknowledged risk of diversion for small arms exports, raises questions about the desirability of the proposed market liberalization (Saferworld, 2006, para. 12(v)).

subsidiaries in other countries and increased cooperation—'growing interdependence among control systems is unavoidable' (France, 2007, p. 9). This emphasis on the need for increased overall efficiency among European partners is shared by other states and underpins a proposal to allow the free movement of defence products within the European Union (see Box 2.3).

Exceptions to the licensing requirement

As noted, all the major exporters of small arms require a licence to export military small arms. There are a range of exceptions to this requirement that are dependent on the nature of the exporter, the end user, and the end use.

Nature of exporter

Exceptions to licensing requirements depend on the exporter, end user, and end use.

Government exports. Many states expressly exempt arms exports by their own state agencies from relevant export controls. In some cases, an exemption is granted for government-to-government sales. **Israel** exempts state exports of defence equipment to another state from the provisions of its export control laws and subjects them to a separate procedure (Israel, 2007, sec. 47(b)). **Spain** exempts 'exports or concessions between governments for the purposes of military aid, under the terms of international agreements' from export controls (Spain, 1990, sec. 9(b)). **Norway** exempts exports by the Norwegian defence authorities if the recipient is a defence authority in a NATO or EU member state (Norway, 2007, sec. 3(i)), while the **United States** exempts exports related to its foreign assistance or government sales programmes and subjects them to a separate process (US, 2007, sec. 126.6).[21]

Nature of the end use and end user

Peacekeeping and humanitarian activities. In some instances the exemption for government exports is limited to temporary exports conducted for a specific purpose. For example, many states exempt from regulation or automatically grant authorization to exports of military equipment destined for use by their own or other armed forces in operations overseas, such as peacekeeping operations, humanitarian activities, and other international exercises authorized by the UN or regional organizations such as the OSCE. **Bulgaria**, the **Czech Republic**, **Finland**, **Italy**, and **Spain** fall into that category.[22]

Participants in export control regimes and regional arrangements. Some states waive the requirement for an export licence if the recipient country is a member of a particular export control regime or regional arrangement. For example, transfers to NATO members are entirely exempt from the licensing regime in **Romania** and **Finland** (Wood, 2007, pp. 9, 21; Finland, 1990, art. 3).

Other states grant something akin to preferential treatment in such circumstances. If prospective recipients are members of international export control regimes and 'conduct a responsible export policy', **Finland** does not seek foreign and security policy advice when making a licensing decision (Finland, 2008). Similarly, in **Germany**, exports of war weapons and other military equipment to NATO and EU member states as well as 'NATO equivalent countries' such as Australia, Japan, New Zealand, and Switzerland are not subject to restrictions 'unless in specific cases this is warranted on particular political grounds' (Germany, 2008). **Canada** also reports that it has a fast-track procedure for most members of NATO and the Organisation for Economic Co-operation and Development (OECD), where there are fewer *prima facie* concerns about export control regimes and the risk of diversion (Canada, 2008).

Other states, such as **Sweden**, seem to take a more general approach, noting that:

> *There are no foreign policy obstacles in relation to co-operation with or exports to the Nordic countries and traditionally neutral countries in Europe. . . . As co-operation with other countries within the European*

Community expands, the same principles for overseas co-operation and exports should be applied where these countries are concerned. (Sweden, n.d.a)

Such preferential treatment is common among EU member states, and in fact the complete removal of restrictions on exports between EU members is under consideration (see Box 2.3).

Country lists. Some states keep lists of countries to which preferential treatment is given in the context of arms exports. This either involves an expedited process or no licence requirement at all. For example, arms transfers between Benelux countries (**Belgium**, the **Netherlands**, and **Luxembourg**) do not require a licence. In the **Russian Federation**, the Ministry of Foreign Affairs prepares a list of states to which military items may be transferred, while transfers to all other states are subject to a presidential decree (Russian Federation, 2007, p. 12). In **Switzerland**, a pre-licensing 'trading licence' is not required if the transaction involves one of 25 specifically listed countries (Switzerland, 1998, annexe 2).[23] In **Canada**, a permit to export arms to the United States is only required if it involves prohibited firearms (such as sawn-off shotguns and automatic firearms). In fact, Canada only allows these firearms to be exported to countries it lists in its Automatic Firearms Control List (Canada, 2006, p. xix).

At the same time, many states keep lists of countries to which exports of arms or military equipment are banned. These correspond with arms embargoes imposed by the UN Security Council or regional bodies such as the EU or the OSCE; they may be included in an annexe or schedule to states' legislation or posted on government Web sites.[24]

Types of licences

Some states only issue individual licences for small arms exports.

States issue three main types of export licences: individual, general, and global.

Individual licence: An individual licence authorizes the shipment of specified goods to a specified consignee or end user. It is a single, one-off authorization that may lapse after a specified period of time or when a specified quantity or value of goods has been delivered.

General licence: Offering a simplified procedure, a general licence can take one of several forms. It is a broad grant of authority to all exporters for certain categories of goods to almost all destinations. If a general licence has been granted with respect to a certain item, exporters do not need to apply for a licence to export that item, but they will usually need to register with the relevant authority to indicate that they will be using the general licence. General licences remain in force until they are revoked by the relevant authority.

Global licence: A global licence is granted to a specific exporter and allows for the export of an unlimited quantity of goods to one or several destinations, consignees, or end users. This is a more flexible means of licensing and is often used as a means of preventing an undue administrative burden for the exporter if an unusually large number of licences would otherwise be required. A global licence will be granted for a specific period of time.

All of the major exporters of small arms issue individual licences for the export of small arms and light weapons, and some stipulate that they *only* issue individual licences for small arms exports (e.g. **Czech Republic**, **Finland**, **Germany**, **Norway**, and **Turkey**).[25] Few of the states reviewed permit the use of general licences for exports of military equipment, including small arms. For example, the **United Kingdom** grants Open General Export Licences (OGELs), which allow an exporter to export specified items without having to apply for an individual licence, provided the exporter has registered to use the open licence and that conditions of the licence are met.[26]

At this writing, the United Kingdom appears to be the only state offering a general licence for military small arms. This OGEL covers small arms and other defence equipment being transferred to certain countries as part of a UK

Government Defence Contract.[27] The United Kingdom also has an OGEL that allows an individual who holds a firearms certificate to export up to six rifles, smooth-bore weapons, and related ammunition for sporting purposes from the United Kingdom to Uganda or Tanzania, provided that the person returns the firearms to the United Kingdom within three months.[28]

Global licences for exports of military equipment are generally only issued for the export of dual-use goods. However, six states—**France**, **Germany**, **Italy**, **Spain**, **Sweden**, and the **United Kingdom**—signed a letter of intent in 1998 and a follow-up Framework Agreement (FA) in 2000 that established a framework for cooperation regarding the production and export of military equipment. Global project licences (GPLs) were introduced as part of this framework. These simplify the arrangements for licensing military goods and technologies between FA states that are collaborating in defence projects. Each FA state issues its own GPL that permits multiple exports of specified goods and technology needed for a project or intended for the armed forces of another FA state. In practice, these have not been extensively utilized by FA partners.

The system for strategic goods control in **Singapore** establishes three 'tiers' of licences or permits for exporting strategic goods, including military small arms (Singapore, 2008). Tier 1 permits are equivalent to individual licences in that they authorize single, one-off transactions; Tier 2 permits allow the export of a specific product to multiple destinations or multiple products to a single end user; and Tier 3 permits allow multiple products to be exported to

Box 2.4 Tracker: software for processing, recording, and monitoring export licences

The United States has developed software that allows licensing bodies to process export licence applications. The so-called 'Tracker' system acts as a central location for governments to input, process, track, review, and approve or reject licence applications. It also facilitates electronic submission and monitoring of licence applications by applicants.

The software aims to increase the efficiency of pre-licence review, licensing, and post-licence procedures by:

- Storing information about organizations, individuals, products, and locations involved in exports and allowing searches to be conducted in any field;
- Providing secure information exchange for departments engaged in the licensing decision;
- Supporting enforcement activities by providing customs officers at remote sites with access to licence data. Photographs of suspicious items can be uploaded into Tracker at the customs point and reviewed by technical experts at other locations;
- Assisting with generating reports to satisfy domestic and international reporting requirements. For example, data from Tracker can be exported into other reporting software.[29] Accordingly, it is hoped the Tracker system will reduce administrative burdens and promote national reporting (e.g. under the UN Register of Conventional Arms and the EU *Code of Conduct*).

New developments

- An Internal Compliance Program is being integrated to help the industry develop internal procedures to ensure compliance with export legislation;
- A tool that provides automatic feedback on end users of potential concern is being incorporated;
- A Licensing Officer Information System that provides a training tool for licensing officers is being incorporated; and
- A search tool called the Product Identification Search Engine (PISE) is being introduced; it links items on the country's National Control List with images and descriptions of the items.[30]

Who has it?

The US State Department's Export Control and Related Border Security (EXBS) programme has been working in cooperation with other governments to improve strategic trade control systems; it has shared the Tracker system software with more than 20 countries. Map 2.1 shows the countries where the Tracker system has been deployed or is being implemented, and where information sharing is taking place.

Map 2.1 **Countries using the Tracker system software**

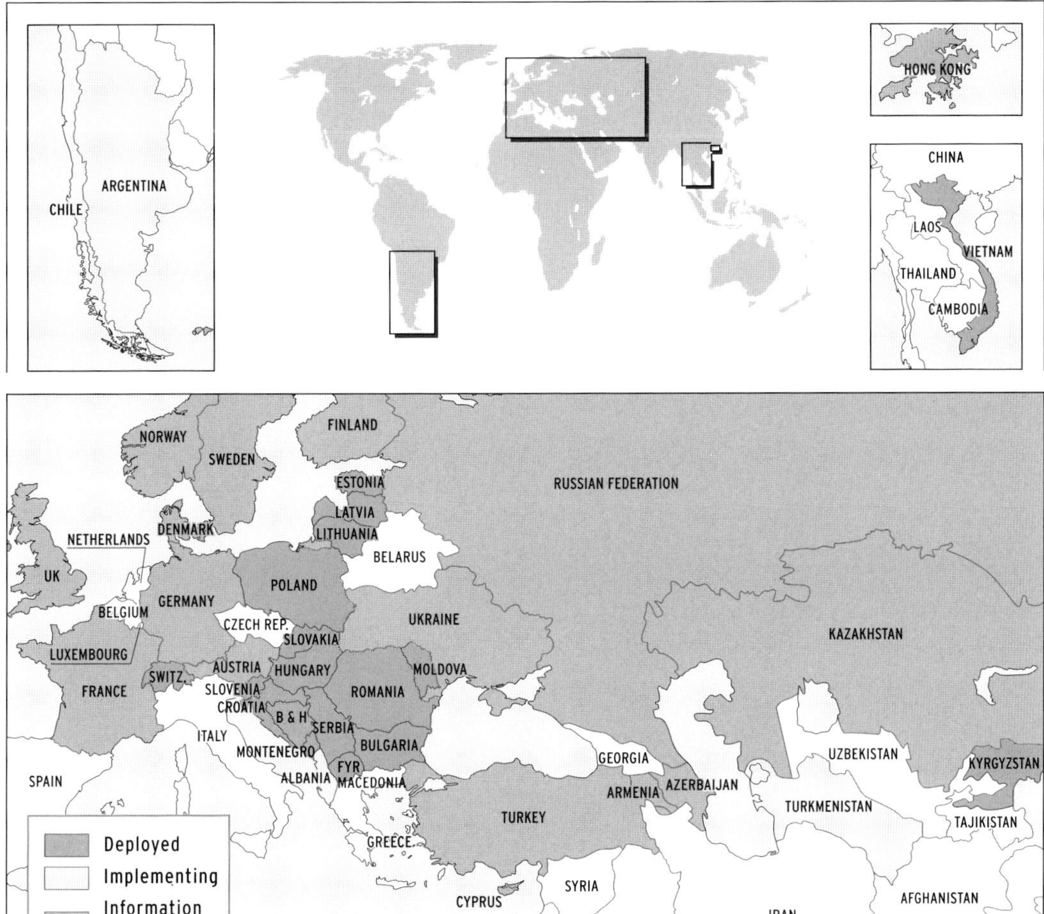

Source: www.trackernet.org

pre-approved destinations. Eligibility for Tier 2 and 3 permits depends on the nature of the goods being exported (for instance, goods intended or likely to be used for weapons of mass destruction can only be exported under Tier 1 permits) as well as the exporter's compliance record with Singapore Customs and implementation of an effective internal (export control) compliance programme. Internal compliance programmes must include such elements as record-keeping, audits, and end-user screening (to ensure exports are to known legitimate customers or end users).

Licensing bodies in more than 20 countries currently use the US software 'Tracker' in processing export licence applications (see Box 2.4).

Licensing requirements

End-user certification

As part of the licensing process, applicants are normally required to provide the relevant licensing authority with documentation, such as an end-user certificate (EUC), identifying the goods to be exported, the recipient country, the end user, the end use, and, in some cases, the value of the goods and the identity of other parties involved in the transaction. As illustrated by Table 2.2, all the major exporting states include the provision of an EUC as part of the licensing application (with the exception of **Japan**, which has a declared policy of not exporting military small arms). Some states insist on an EUC for *all* exports, while others *may* request an EUC depending on the circumstances. In some cases, for example, an import certificate provided by the recipient state may be provided in lieu of an EUC if the recipient state is an EU member state, NATO ally, or other 'friendly' country.

Given the risks of diversion, it is important that the exporting state obtain some kind of confirmation that the importing state is aware of and authorizes the weapons transfer (Small Arms Survey, 2008, chs. 4–5). Good practice dictates that states verify the information contained in EUCs when considering licence applications, ensuring, in particular, that recipient state authorizations are genuine (OSCE, 2004, para. 3). While some states say they conduct such verification through their local embassies in recipient states, for example, it is unclear to what extent small arms exporters, as a whole, do so (Small Arms Survey, 2008, p. 172).

Additional information—such as a commitment by the final consignee to provide a delivery verification certificate (DVC)—may also be included in an EUC (OSCE, 2004, para. 1). Table 2.2 indicates which major exporters seek the provision of DVCs as part of export licensing. While checks applied at the licensing stage offer exporting states the most cost-effective means of preventing arms diversion, post-shipment verification is also useful in deterring unauthorized changes in end user or end use, and in bolstering the assessment of diversion risks prior to export (Small Arms Survey, 2008, pp. 173–76). In this spirit, the OSCE *Document on Small Arms* suggests that states conduct physical inspections of shipments at the point of delivery to ensure the arms have been delivered securely, as a means of preventing illegal diversion (OSCE, 2000, sec. III.6). The European Parliament has echoed this recommendation by issuing a 'demand to set up a transfer verification and post-export monitoring system that should include systematic physical inspections at points of transfer and of stockpiles by the competent national authorities' (EU, 2004).

It is unclear to what extent small arms exporters conduct verification.

Some states, such as **Bulgaria** and the **United States**, specifically make reference to physical inspections as part of their delivery controls (Bulgaria, 2007a, art. 71.6; USDoS, 2008, p. 7). Other states, such as Ukraine, include ambiguous provisions in their laws that might include physical checks: 'the duly authorized state export control body . . . shall be entitled to conduct . . . verification of delivery or end-use of goods at any stage of the international transfer and after actual delivery to the end-user' (Ukraine, 2003, art. 19). In practice, however, it seems that few states other than the United States conduct significant physical and post-delivery checks (Macalesher and Parker, 2007, p. 23; Small Arms Survey, 2008, pp. 171–73).

Re-export provisions

Re-export (or re-transfer) notification requirements are another important means of preventing diversion.[31] The *Programme of Action,* the Wassenaar *Best Practice Guidelines for Exports of Small Arms and Light Weapons,* and the OSCE *Document on Small Arms* all encourage states to notify the original exporting state before they re-export imported weapons (UNGA, 2001, para. II.13; WA, 2002, para. I.3; OSCE, 2000, sec. III, (2)(B)(5)). These instruments, however, fall short of best practice as they fail to stipulate that the original exporting state *consent* to the re-export, requiring merely that it be notified. Nevertheless, in practice states often require that their written authorization be obtained before any re-export.

As indicated in Table 2.2, at least 22 of the major exporters reviewed have restrictions on the re-export of arms. These usually take the form of a requirement that a clause be included in the sales contract that the importer and/

or end user will not re-export the arms without the prior written consent of the exporting state, as is the case in **Bulgaria** and the **United States** (Bulgaria, 2007a, art.70(1); US, 2007, sec. 123.9(b)); or the inclusion of an undertaking in the end-user certificate that the arms will not be re-exported without the authorization of the exporting state (e.g. **Brazil**, **France**, **Germany**, **Italy**, **Romania**, the **Russian Federation**, **South Africa**, **Spain**).[32] Re-export provisions are not automatic; typically they *may* be required depending on the circumstances of the transaction and the identity of the end user.

In some cases, as in **Bulgaria** and **Romania**, the undertaking not to re-export has to be made by the importer or end user (Bulgaria, 2007a, art. 70(1); Wood, 2007, p. 24). In **Canada** the export licence applicant must submit a declaration that, to the best of the applicant's knowledge, the goods will enter into the economy of the recipient country and will not be trans-shipped or diverted from that country (Canada, 2001, sec. 3(2)(a)). In other cases, as in **Switzerland**, the recipient state undertakes not to authorize the re-export of the arms without the consent of the original exporting country (Switzerland, 1996b, art. 18). In the case of **France** the end user and the government of the recipient country may be required to declare that they will not re-export or authorize a re-export (respectively) without the prior written approval of the French government (France, n.d.).

Post-shipment controls are essential tools in the diversion-prevention arsenal.

In almost all cases where prior consent is required in advance of re-export, it is the consent of the original exporting state that is meant. **Bulgarian** regulations, however, provide that the consent to re-export may be given by the national competent authority of the recipient state if it is a Wassenaar member (Bulgaria, 2007a, art. 70(1)).[33] Clearly, this removes any control the original exporting country may have over the final destination of the small arms. In theory, participating states in the Wassenaar Arrangement may apply the same criteria to exports of small arms, but in practice their assessment of the risks involved in a particular export will often differ.

Once the original exporting state has surrendered physical control of the arms, it is difficult to monitor their use and any subsequent transfer. Costs are one factor, problems in securing cooperation from recipient governments another. Nevertheless, post-shipment controls, including the selective use of end-use monitoring, constitute essential—and cost-effective—tools in the diversion-prevention arsenal.[34]

Problems associated with the extraterritorial application of laws, and the fact that the original exporter surrenders legal ownership of the weapons it exports, mean that non-re-export clauses have a political rather than a legal effect. The strongest response to a breach of such provisions is to refuse future exports to the offending state. Such is the response adopted by **Sweden** and **Germany**, which do not allow future exports of military equipment to states that have permitted or failed to prevent the re-export of military arms in breach of previous undertakings (Sweden, n.d.a; Germany, 2000, para. IV). Unauthorized re-transfer will also, in many cases, lead exporting states to conclude that the recipient presents an unacceptably high risk of diversion for any future arms transfers.

In principle, the onus is on the recipient state to notify the original exporting country that it is contemplating a re-export of arms. Some insight into the question of whether any of the major exporters do this can be gleaned from their national reports. **Norway** comments that it has 'no experience with such cases' (Norway, 2008). **Sweden** notes that it depends on the type of small arms. So, for example, if hunting rifles were involved, it would not usually notify the original exporting state unless the exporting state required it, but if man-portable air defence systems, or MANPADS, were to be re-exported, the original exporting state would be notified for approval (Sweden, 2008).

Other states, such as **Austria** and **Germany**, note that it depends on the re-export clauses in the original documentation (Klob, 2007; Germany, 2008). **Switzerland** indicates that the federal law on war material 'does not expressly require Switzerland to notify the original exporting State when re-exporting [small arms and light weapons]'. However, the federal law on the control of dual-use and specific military goods, which include some light weapons, 'stipulates that there must be consultation with the original exporting State if the latter insists on its formal consent in all cases of re-exporting. Consequently the export permit may be denied in the absence of approval by the original exporting State' (Switzerland, 2005). **Israel**, for its part, notes that the re-export of surplus small arms and light weapons that are of foreign origin 'will require re-export approval by the country of origin, as appropriate' (Israel, 2008).

The **Bulgarian** regulations provide that, where an export licence application pertains to the re-export of arms, the applicant must submit a licence for re-export issued by the original exporting state or, where the original exporting state does not issue such licences, the foreign forwarder must issue a statement certifying that no prohibition on re-export has been imposed (Bulgaria, 2007b, art. 6). In other words, the onus is on the exporting company rather than on the licensing authority to confirm that re-export authorization is not required.

It is difficult to get a clear picture of how and indeed whether exporting states monitor end use with a view to identifying unauthorized re-transfer. It is clear, however, that states do seriously consider the risk that arms might be re-exported when making a licensing decision. Concern that equipment might be diverted within the buyer country or re-exported under undesirable conditions—Criterion 7 of the EU *Code of Conduct*—was the reason EU member states most often gave for refusing an export licence for small arms in 2007. Figure 2.1 shows that Criterion 7 was invoked 73 times out of a total of 160 reasons provided (46 per cent).[35]

Figure 2.1 **Frequency with which EU member states cite EU Code of Conduct criteria to refuse export licences, 2007 (n=160)**

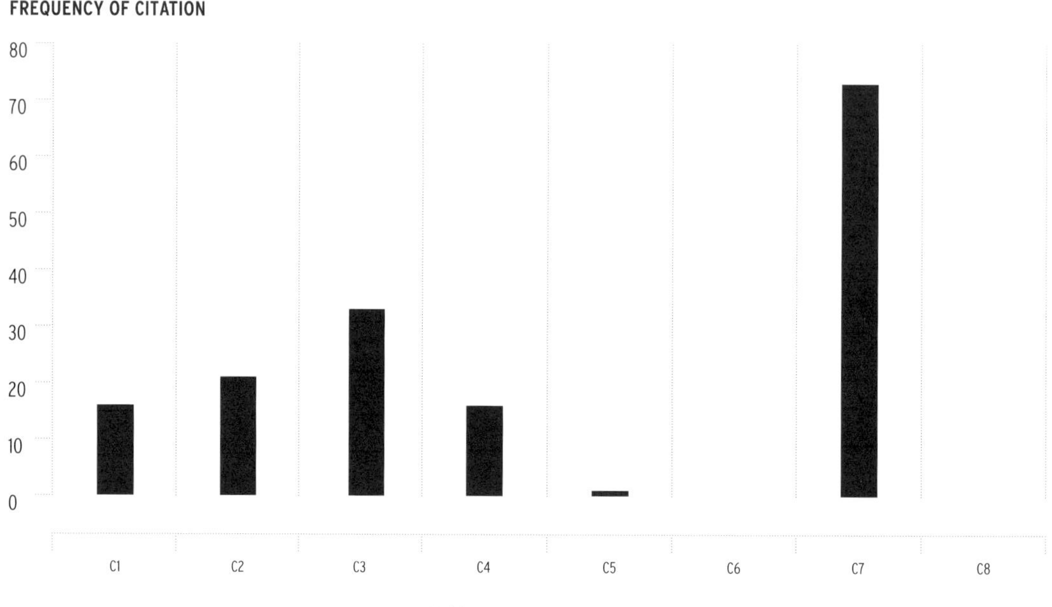

Legend: C1=respect for international commitments of EU member states; C2=respect for human rights in the country of final destination; C3=the internal situation of the country of final destination; C4=preservation of regional peace, security, and stability; C5=the national security of the member states and of territories whose external relations are the responsibility of a member state; C6=the behaviour of the buyer country with regard to the international community (especially its attitude towards terrorism); C7=concern that equipment might be diverted within the buyer country or re-exported under undesirable conditions; C8=compatibility of the export with the technical and economic capacity of the recipient country.

In fact, the consultation carried out by the European Commission as part of the preparations for the directive on intra-community transfers reveals that 'the main justification for applying export control systems to the transfer of defence-related products to other Member States was the *risk of re-exportation* outside the Community after the transfer to another Member State' (EC, 2006, p. 6, emphasis in original). The directive acknowledges that there is a risk that less stringent controls and a reduction in the number of individual licences in favour of general licences may weaken re-export controls. To compensate for this, the proposal notes the need to create conditions for mutual confidence and trust through the inclusion of guarantees that ensure that defence-related products are not exported to third countries in violation of transfer restrictions (EC, 2008, recital 29).

Indeed Article 10 of the directive on intra-community transfers of defence-related products provides that member states must ensure that, if recipients of defence-related products are attempting to export items originally transferred from another member state, the recipients have respected any export limitations attached to them; if the consent of the originating member state is required but has not been obtained, the member state shall consult the originating member state (see Box 2.3). The directive does not, however, incorporate a proposed amendment to Article 10 stipulating that if the consent of the originating member state is not obtained, the export shall not take place (EP, 2008, amend. 18). Nor did the directive incorporate the suggestion that member states should establish, *as a criminal offence,* the re-export to third countries of defence-related products in breach of conditions attached to their use (EP, 2008, amend. 23).

The re-transfer of arms within the recipient state warrants attention.

As discussed earlier, despite the presumption in favour of destruction, some states continue to sell their surplus small arms. One way an exporting state can ensure its weapons are not re-exported is to review the importing state's policy with regard to surplus. If the original exporter only transfers military small arms to states that *destroy* surplus as a matter of national policy, this can help ensure the arms are not re-exported.

Indeed, the *User's Guide* to the EU *Code of Conduct* suggests posing the following question when assessing the risk that arms might be diverted or re-exported to unauthorized end users (Criterion 7): 'Does the country of stated end use have any history of diversion of arms, including the re-export of surplus equipment to countries of concern?' (EU, 2006, p. 48). Moreover, the version of the *Code* adopted as the Common Position in December 2008 contains an amended version of Criterion 7 that calls on states to consider 'the record of the recipient country in respecting any re-export provision or consent to re-export' (EU, 2008c).

Another consideration often overlooked in the context of re-exports is the issue of re-transfers *within* the recipient state. Non-re-export undertakings tend to focus on the re-sale of arms to other *states,* but the re-transfer of arms within the recipient state may also warrant attention—in particular, the possible transfer of military small arms to the civilian population.

Enforcement

The enforcement of export control violations involves several agencies. Generally, customs authorities have responsibility for inspecting export shipments and detecting licence violations or attempts to export without a licence (smuggling). When violations are detected, customs and police authorities will be involved in an investigation, which may lead to civil or criminal prosecution. It is beyond the scope of this chapter to explore the specific powers granted to enforcement agencies in the states under review, or to compare the number of licence violations or prosecutions that take place in each state, but a comparison of administrative and criminal penalties linked to export control offences shows they vary considerably in terms of type and scale (see Table 2.2).

Administrative penalties include fines, confiscation of the goods to be exported, and/or revocation of licences or trading permits. The amount of administrative fines varies considerably among the states reviewed. Some countries use a formula to calculate the fine based on the value of the goods (e.g. **Japan**, **Singapore**, **Spain**, **United Kingdom**[36]); others, such as **Austria** and the **Russian Federation**, base the fine on the income of the offender (Klob, 2007; Pyadushkin, 2008). Other states prescribe a set fine, with minimums ranging from EUR 1,000 (USD 1,355) in **Belgium** to CHF five million (USD 4.5 million) in **Switzerland** (Moreau, 2008; Switzerland, 1996b, art. 33(2)). In some states, aggravating factors may serve to increase the fine imposed. For example, in **France**, the fine will be increased from EUR 100,000 (USD 135,000) to EUR 500,000 (USD 680,000) if the offence is committed by an organized gang (Elluin, 2008). In **Israel**, the fine imposed will be 50 times greater in 'severe circumstances', such as if the end-user is an enemy of the state (Israel, 2007, sec. 33(1)).

The decision to export military equipment involves economic, defence, security, and foreign policy considerations.

With respect to sentencing, among the states reviewed imprisonment for exporting without a licence ranges from 6 months (e.g. **Sweden**, **Switzerland**, the **United Kingdom**) to 25 years (**South Africa**).[37] Again, aggravating factors may serve to increase the sentence in a few cases: if it involves an intentional as opposed to a negligent violation (e.g. **Norway**, **Sweden**, **Switzerland**); if the offence has been committed for a second time (e.g. **Belgium**, **Bulgaria**, **Singapore**); or if the violation has caused damage to foreign policy, commercial, or security interests of the state (**Czech Republic**).[38]

LICENSING AUTHORITY: WHO DECIDES?

Each of the major exporters has appointed a particular department or ministry to manage the export licensing process, although in most cases the actual decision to grant an export licence involves consultation across a number of agencies. As indicated in Table 2.3, most export control authorities are located in the Ministry of Economy and/or Trade or its equivalent, while consultations with the Ministries of Foreign Affairs, Defence, or the Interior form part of the decision-making process.

This reveals two important points. First, it highlights the fact that the decision to export military equipment, including small arms, is a complex one that involves economic, defence, security, and foreign policy considerations, hence the need for interagency consultation. Second, and perhaps more surprising, given that the central organ responsible for export licensing in most of the major exporters is the Ministry of Economy and/or Trade, it may be inferred that states see this process primarily as an economic issue.

The influence of the representatives of different ministries during the interagency consultancy process varies. For example, in **Bosnia and Herzegovina**, while the Ministry of Foreign Trade and Economic Relations is the main agency responsible for licensing decisions, the Ministries of Foreign Affairs, Defence, and Security must all give their consent to a licence, and accordingly each has the power to veto a licensing decision.[39] In contrast, in **Romania**, although licence applications are submitted to the Inter-Ministerial Council for Export Control for review, decisions do not have to be made on the basis of consensus, and the president of the National Agency for Export Controls (ANCEX) has the final say (Wood, 2007, p. 16). As Saferworld points out, the power held by the president of ANCEX in the licensing process is of concern, not only because it diminishes interagency cooperation, but also because the president of ANCEX is appointed directly by the Romanian prime minister, which could allow the latter to unduly influence the final decision (Wood, 2007, p. 16).

The **Bulgarian** system seems to have found a middle ground whereby licensing decisions are adopted by a two-thirds majority of all Inter-Ministerial Commission members when representatives of all ministries and agencies represented on the Commission are in attendance. If not all representatives are present, decisions must be unanimous (Bulgaria, 2007a, art. 30(7)). In **Israel**, if the representative of the Ministry of Foreign Affairs participating in an advisory committee on a commercial export licence makes a recommendation or reservation that is not accepted by the committee, the matter is put to senior members of the Ministries of Defense and Foreign Affairs for their joint deliberation. If a conclusion still cannot be reached, the matter is resolved by the subcommittee of the Ministerial Committee for National Security, which is responsible for considering government-to-government exports (Israel, 2007, secs. 24, 47(c)). In **Sweden**, the Export Control Council, composed of representatives of all parliamentary parties, assists the director-general in interpreting and applying the export control guidelines in place. The Council has an advisory role only, and it is ultimately up to the director-general to decide whether to grant an export licence (Sweden, 2007, p. 20; 2008, p. 15).

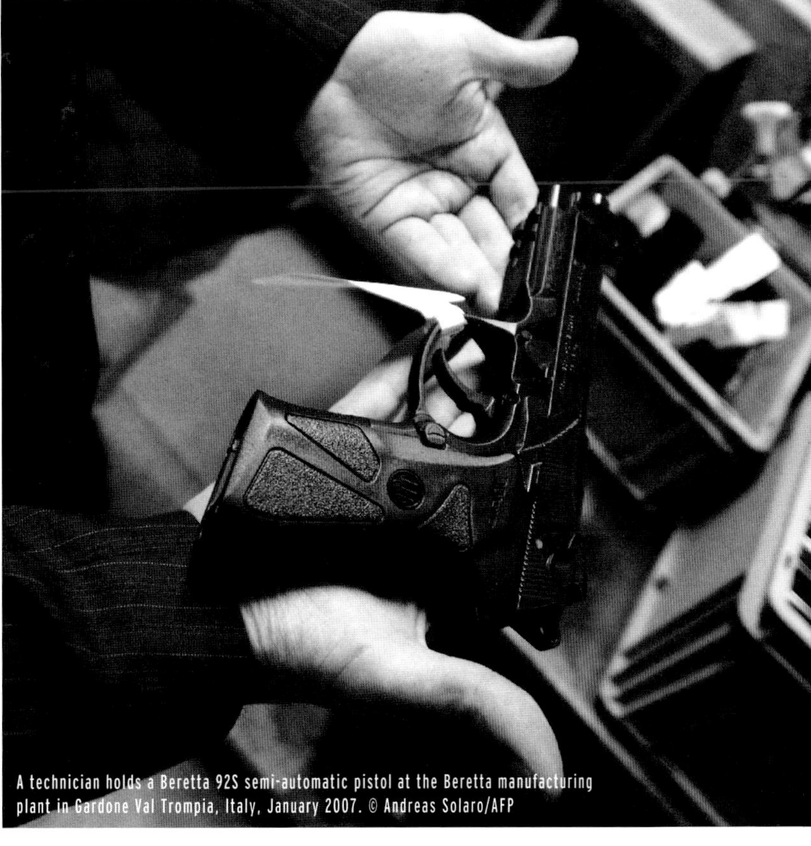

A technician holds a Beretta 92S semi-automatic pistol at the Beretta manufacturing plant in Gardone Val Trompia, Italy, January 2007. © Andreas Solaro/AFP

The use of interagency consultation in the licensing process helps ensure that all state interests are reflected and represented. Generally speaking, the Ministry of Foreign Affairs will offer guidance based on the country's international export control commitments (e.g. the EU *Code of Conduct* or the OSCE *Document on Small Arms*), while the Ministry of Defence will advise on the security aspects of the proposed trade. Of course, while such a process helps bring all government perspectives into the licensing mix, it will not prevent a single interest (e.g. economic) from overriding others (e.g. security or human rights concerns) if decision-making power is concentrated in a single department.

In addition to the competing *national* interests represented by the different agencies and ministries involved in an export licensing decision, the *personal* interests of representatives may also influence the decision. For this reason, **South African** legislation stipulates that any member of the licensing committee or any other person involved in the decision-making process who has a financial or other interest that might conflict with relevant professional duties must disclose that interest and may not take part in the decision (South Africa, 2002, sec. 25). A failure to disclose such an interest may lead to a fine or imprisonment of up to ten years (sec. 24(2)(c)).

Table 2.3 **Overview of licensing agencies and interagency consultations**

Country	Licensing agency	Ministry of Foreign Affairs	Ministry of Economy	Ministry of (Industry and) Trade	Ministry of Interior	Ministry of Defence	Other ministries consulted
Austria*	Items under the War Material Act: Ministry of the Interior.	C			**L**		
	Items under the Foreign Trade Act: Ministry of Economics and Labour.	C	**L**				
Belgium**	Federal: Ministry of Economy.	C	**L**			C	
	Wallonia: Economy and Employment Department.	C	**L**			C	Ministry of Justice, Customs Service, and semi-public organization Wallonie-Bruxelles International, which manages the international relations of the Walloon Region and the French-speaking Community.
	Brussels Capital Region: International Relations Department.	**L**				C	Ministry of Justice and Customs Service.
	Flanders: Flemish Ministry of Economy, Business, Science, Innovation and Foreign Trade.	C	**L**			C	Ministry of Justice and Customs Service.
Brazil	Ministry of Defence.	C	C			**L**	Ministry of Development, Industry, and Foreign Trade, Ministry of Science and Technology.
Bulgaria	Export Control and Weapons of Mass Destruction Non-Proliferation Interministerial Commission, within the Ministry of Economy and Energy.	C	**L**		C	C	
Canada	Ministry of Foreign Affairs.	**L**		C		C	May consult: Industry Canada, the Royal Canadian Mounted Police, the Canadian Security and Intelligence Service, the Communications Security Establishment, Customs and Excise.
China	State Administration for Science, Technology and Industry for National Defence, within the Ministry of Industry and Information Technology.						'Relevant departments of the State Council' and the Central Military Commission (China, 2002, art. 14).
Czech Republic	Ministry of Industry and Trade.	C		**L**	C	C	

▶▶

Finland	Ministry of Defence.	c			c	L	National Board of Customs and the Security Police.
France	Director-general of Customs acting in the name of the Minister of the Economy, Finance and Industry, after approval of the Ministries of Defence and Foreign Affairs and transmission to the National Defence General Secretariat acting on behalf of the prime minister.	c	**L**			c	
Germany	Federal Ministry of Economics and Technology (for 'war weapons').	c	**L**		c	c	
Israel	Commercial sales: director-general or head of the Defence Export Control Division, Ministry of Defence.	c				**L**	Advisory Committee (incl. employees of the Ministries of Defence and Foreign Affairs and defence forces plus Ministry of Industry, Trade and Labor if dual-use item is involved).
	Government-to-government exports: Ministry of Defence.	c	c			**L**	Must be submitted for approval to sub-committee of the Ministerial Committee for National Security (chaired by the prime minister and including the ministers of Foreign Affairs, Justice, and Finance).
Italy	Ministry of Foreign Affairs: Armaments Authorization Unit.	**L**	c		c	c	Environment, Industry, Foreign Trade, and Finance.
Japan	Minister of Economy, Trade and Industry.	c	**L**				
Norway	Ministry of Foreign Affairs.	**L**				c	
Portugal	Ministry of Defence.	c				**L**	
Republic of Korea	Defence Acquisition Program Administration, reports to Ministry of National Defence.	c				**L**	National Intelligence Service.
Romania	National Agency for Export Controls (ANCEX), activities coordinated by Ministry of Foreign Affairs.	**L**	c		c	c	Ministry of Administration and Interior, National Customs Authority, Romanian Intelligence Service, and the Foreign Intelligence Service.
Russian Federation	Federal Service on Military-Technical Cooperation with Foreign States, operating under the authority of the Ministry of Defence.					**L**	President (the Ministry of Foreign Affairs may also be involved, but this is unclear).

Singapore	Singapore Customs, Strategic Goods Control Branch.						Unknown.
South Africa	National Conventional Arms Control Committee (NCACC).	***		***		***	South African Police Service, National Intelligence Agency, and South African Secret Service.
Spain	Inter-Ministerial Regulatory Board on Foreign Trade in Defence or Dual-Use Items, attached to the Ministry of Industry, Tourism and Trade.	c		**L**	c	c	National Centre for Intelligence, Department of Customs and Excise Duties of the National Tax Administration Agency.
Sweden	MEC and OME destined for non-OECD countries: National Inspectorate of Strategic Products, answers to Ministry for Foreign Affairs. OME destined for OECD countries: Swedish Police Service.	c				c	Export Control Council (11 members of parliament representing all parties).
Switzerland	State Secretariat for Economic Affairs, within the Federal Department of Economic Affairs.	c	**L**				
Turkey	Ministry of National Defence.	c				**L**	Turkish General Staff.
United Kingdom	Export Control Organisation, Department for Business, Enterprise and Regulatory Reform (BERR).	c		**L**		c	Department for International Development may be consulted if application is to developing countries eligible for concessional loans from the World Bank International Development Association.
United States	Government-to-government sales: Defense Security Cooperation Agency, Department of Defense.					**L**	Department of State; approval of Congress is also required for certain exports.
	Commercial sales: Directorate of Defense Trade Controls, within the Bureau of Political-Military Affairs in the Department of State.					c	Approval of Congress is also required for certain exports, including firearms valued at USD 1 million or more.

Notes:

c: The ministry in question is consulted or participates in the interagency decision-making process.

L: The ministry in question is the lead agency responsible for processing the licensing application and, in some instances, the ultimate decision-maker.

* The Austrian legislation distinguishes between war material (governed by the War Material Act) and all other military items on the EU Common Military List that fall under the Foreign Trade Act.

** Under the Special Act of 12 August 2003, the three regions of Belgium (Brussels Capital, Flanders, and Wallonia) were given jurisdiction over the import, export, and transit of arms, munitions, and equipment intended for military use or law enforcement and associated technology as well as dual-use items and technology. Each region has created an Arms Unit to exercise these powers. Note that the Belgian federal authority (Ministry of Economy) retains authority for export licences issued to the Belgian armed forces and federal police; it is also responsible for combating illicit arms trafficking.

*** The NCACC consists of ministers and deputy ministers appointed by the president (South Africa, 2002, sec. 5). In practice, it includes the ministers for Foreign Affairs, Defence, and Trade and Industry, although ministers who do not have a line-function interest in the trade in conventional arms are also included. The composition of the NCACC in 2003, for example, included the ministers for the Intelligence Services; Transport; Housing; Health; and Science and Technology (South Africa, 2003, p. 2).

LICENSING CRITERIA: TO SELL OR NOT TO SELL?

Fundamental to any export control system are the principles or criteria states apply when authorizing an export.

In addition to general considerations of international and regional peace and security, and national interests as a whole, the issues states consider in deciding whether to permit the export of small arms can be broadly categorized as follows:

- *Considerations based on existing international and regional commitments:* whether the proposed export would be contrary to applicable regional instruments, the UN Charter, arms embargoes, or other existing legal and political commitments;
- *Considerations based on the likely user of the arms:* whether the arms to be exported might be used by terrorists, criminals, or insurgent groups, or diverted to such groups;
- *Considerations based on the likely use of the arms:* whether the arms to be exported might be used to commit human rights violations, violations of international humanitarian law (IHL), or acts of genocide;
- *Considerations based on the likely impact of the arms transfer:* whether the proposed export might contribute to regional or internal instability, exacerbate an existing conflict, or undermine sustainable development; and
- *Considerations based on other features of the recipient country:* such as their record of compliance with international obligations or their legitimate defence needs.

These categories are derived from the instruments shaded in red in Table 2.1; these contain principles or guidelines that states have agreed to take into account when deciding whether to grant an export licence. All of the instruments in Table 2.1 that contain detailed transfer criteria are politically rather than legally binding, except the EU *Code of Conduct,* which became legally binding in December 2008. Regardless of whether these undertakings are legal or political in nature, states have committed themselves to fulfilling them.

Transfer criteria are not always specified in main legal instruments.

The OSCE *Document on Small Arms,* the EU *Code of Conduct,* and the Wassenaar *Best Practice Guidelines for Exports of Small Arms and Light Weapons* are of particular relevance to this chapter since they contain extensive, similar lists of export criteria to be applied to the export of military small arms. All but three—**Brazil**, **China**, and **Israel**—of the major exporters under review participate in at least one agreement. According to the tenth annual report on the EU *Code of Conduct,* **Canada** and **Norway** have also aligned themselves with the EU *Code of Conduct* (EU, 2008a, p. 2).

In some cases, details of the transfer criteria applied by states to export licensing decisions are reflected in their national legislation; examples include **China**, the **Republic of Korea**, **South Africa**, and **Switzerland**.[40] Some EU member states have incorporated the EU *Code of Conduct* in their national legislation; these include **Belgium**, **Bulgaria**, **Italy**, and **Spain**.[41] However, transfer criteria are not always specified in main legal instruments and often appear in guidelines or policy documents instructing government agencies as to how they should decide on licence applications. For example, **Finland** has established a set of guidelines that specifically refer to and annexe the EU *Code of Conduct* and the OSCE *Principles Governing Arms Transfers* (Finland, 1995, sec. 1(2.2)).

Table 2.4 provides an overview of the different transfer criteria applied by states. The list of criteria is based on the EU *Code of Conduct* and is supplemented by additional criteria derived from the OSCE *Document on Small Arms* and the Wassenaar *Best Practice Guidelines for Exports of Small Arms and Light Weapons.* The list is by no means exhaustive and states do of course apply other criteria to their export licensing decisions that are not reflected in the table. A distinction has been made between the criteria each country has committed to by virtue of its participation in

Table 2.4 **Overview of transfer criteria**

Country		Transfer contravenes international commitments (e.g. embargoes)	Risk arms may contribute to destabilizing accumulation of arms	Risk the transfer may prolong existing tensions or conflicts	Risk transfer might support terrorism	Risk transfer might facilitate organized crime	Risk transfer might be used for internal repression	Risk of diversion or re-export	Recipient's compliance with international commitments	Recipient's respect for IHL	Recipient's legitimate defence and security needs	Recipient's respect for human rights
Austria	*Control system*	x	x	x	x	x	x	x	x	x	x	x
	Commitment	x	x	x	x	x	x	x	x	x	x	x
Belgium	*Control system*	x	x	x	x	x	x	x	x	x	x	x
	Commitment	x	x	x	x	x	x	x	x	x	x	x
Brazil	*Control system*											
	Commitment		x								x	
Bulgaria	*Control system*	x		x	x	x	x	x	x	x	x	x
	Commitment	x	x	x	x	x	x	x	x	x	x	x
Canada	*Control system*	x		x				x				x[a]
	Commitment	x	x	x	x	x	x	x	x	x	x	x
China	*Control system*										x[b]	
	Commitment		x								x	

▸▸

Czech Republic	*Control system*	x	x	x	x	x	x	x	x	x	x	x
	Commitment	x	x	x	x	x	x	x	x	x	x	x
Finland	*Control system*	x	x	x	x	x	x	x	x	x	x	x
	Commitment	x	x	x	x	x	x	x	x	x	x	x
France	*Control system*	x	x	x	x	x	x	x	x	x	x	x
	Commitment	x	x	x	x	x	x	x	x	x	x	x
Germany	*Control system*	x	x	x	x	x	x	x	x	x	x	x
	Commitment	x	x	x	x	x	x	x	x	x	x	x
Israel	*Control system*	x			x	x						
	Commitment		x								x	
Italy	*Control system*	x	x	x	x	x	x	x	x	x	x	x
	Commitment	x	x	x	x	x	x	x	x	x	x	x
Japan[c]	*Control system*	x		x								
	Commitment	x	x	x	x	x	x	x	x	x	x	x
Norway	*Control system*	x	x	x	x				x	x		x
	Commitment	x	x	x	x	x	x	x	x	x	x	x
Portugal	*Control system*	x	x	x	x	x	x	x	x	x	x	x
	Commitment	x	x	x	x	x	x	x	x	x	x	x
Republic of Korea	*Control system*	x	x		x							x
	Commitment	x	x	x	x	x	x	x	x	x	x	x
Romania	*Control system*	x	x	x	x	x	x	x	x	x	x	x
	Commitment	x	x	x	x	x	x	x	x	x	x	x

Russian Federation	*Control system*	X	X					X	X			X
	Commitment	X	X	X	X	X	X	X	X	X	X	X
Singapore	*Control system*											
	Commitment		X								X	
South Africa	*Control system*	X	X	X	X	X	X				X	X
	Commitment	X	X	X	X	X	X	X	X	X	X	X
Spain	*Control system*	X	X	X	X	X	X	X	X	X	X	X
	Commitment	X	X	X	X	X	X	X	X	X	X	X
Sweden	*Control system (for MEC)*	X	X	X	X	X	X	X	X	X	X	X
	Control system (for OME)[d]			X								X
	Commitment	X	X	X	X	X	X	X	X	X	X	X
Switzerland	*Control system*	X	X	X	X	X	X	X	X		X	X
	Commitment	X	X	X	X	X	X	X	X	X	X	X
Turkey	*Control system*	X										
	Commitment	X	X	X	X	X	X	X	X	X	X	X
United Kingdom	*Control system*	X	X[e]	X	X	X	X	X	X	X	X	X
	Commitment	X	X	X	X	X	X	X	X	X	X	X
United States	*Control system*	X	X[f]	X	X				X		X	X
	Commitment	X	X	X	X	X	X	X	X	X	X	X

Notes:

Grey shading indicates the information was sourced from a state's national report on Programme of Action implementation.

[a] There is a caveat: 'unless it can be demonstrated that there is no reasonable risk that the goods might be used against the civilian population' (Canada, 2007c, p. 2).

[b] Translation of the relevant text: 'conduciveness to the capability for just self-defence of the recipient country' (China, 2002, art. 5(1)).

[c] The criteria marked are those applied by the METI to its strategic exports, although it is acknowledged Japan has a declared policy of not exporting arms other than hunting and sport guns (Japan, 2008).

[d] The Guidelines state that a licence should be granted for the export of equipment classified as OME on condition that the recipient state is not engaged in armed conflict; has no internal armed disturbances; and has no extensive and serious infringements of human rights (Sweden, n.d.a).

[e] The relevant text reads: 'the need not to introduce into the region new capabilities' (UK, 2000).

[f] The relevant text states that it 'would contribute to an arms race' (US DoS, n.d.)

Source: Parker (2009)

a relevant instrument or arrangement (reflected in the row marked 'Commitment') and the criteria incorporated by each country in its export controls system according to publicly available sources (reflected in the row marked 'Control system'). Information is derived from a variety of sources, including states' national legislation, their national reports, and policy statements reflected in annual reports and government Web sites. Grey shading indicates the information was sourced from a state's national report on *Programme of Action* implementation. In these reports, many EU states indicate that they apply the EU *Code of Conduct* to their export licensing decisions.

In their national reports on *Programme of Action* implementation, their annual reports on arms transfers, and on the Web sites of relevant agencies, some states indicate that they apply the EU *Code of Conduct* to their export licensing decisions; these states include **Austria**, the **Czech Republic**, **France**, **Germany**, **Portugal**, **Romania**, **Sweden**, and the **United Kingdom**.[42] Relatively few countries, however, expressly mention their commitment to the OSCE or Wassenaar criteria governing small arms exports. While quite similar, they are not identical. One undertaking that does not appear in the EU *Code of Conduct* but is reflected in the OSCE and Wassenaar documents is that states should take into account the stockpile management and security procedures of a potential recipient country (OSCE, 2000, sec. III.1 (A)(2)(c); WA, 2002, sec. II.1).[43] Only a few of the major exporters reviewed—e.g. **Belgium**, **Italy**, and **Norway**—make express reference in their licensing principles to the need to consider whether the recipient has stockpile security sufficient to prevent theft, loss, diversion, or unauthorized transfers (Moreau, 2008; Fallani, 2007; Leonhardsen, 2007).

States have incorporated numerous other criteria in their licensing systems that are not reflected in Table 2.4. For example, in addition to the regional stability and legitimate defence needs principles, **China** has adopted a third principle: no interference in the internal affairs of the recipient country (China, 2002, art. 5). This reflects the principle of non-intervention in the internal affairs of another state enshrined in the UN Charter (UN, 1945, art. 2(7)). **Austria**, **Finland**, and **Norway** also consider whether the recipient is in breach of a ceasefire agreement (Klob, 2007; Kotiaho, 2008; Leonhardsen, 2007); the **Republic of Korea** takes into account whether the transfer involves a 'high possibility of causing diplomatic friction' (Republic of Korea, 2008, p. 16); and **Belgium** and **Switzerland** consider whether child soldiers are used in the recipient's army (Moreau, 2008; Switzerland, 1998, art. 5(b)).

Only a few major exporters consider the status of stockpile security in the recipient country.

In addition to understanding what criteria states have incorporated in their export control systems, it is also worth exploring the challenges of practical implementation. The EU *Code of Conduct* provides some elaboration of its criteria. For example, under Criterion 8 (technical and economic capacity of the recipient country), the *Code* stipulates that 'States will take into account, in the light of information from relevant sources such as UNDP, World Bank, IMF and OECD reports, whether the proposed export would seriously hamper the sustainable development of the recipient country.' Further practical guidance is provided in the *User's Guide to the EU Code of Conduct on Arms Exports* (EU, 2006). The Wassenaar Arrangement has also developed guidelines to assist states in evaluating the risks associated with a potential export (WA, 1998).

Many governments utilize national intelligence sources to inform their arms licensing decisions. This information is sometimes shared between friendly governments. States may also make use of numerous non-governmental tools and information sources, including the media, reports by non-governmental organizations and human rights agencies, as well as data sets such as the Cingranelli–Richards Human Rights Data Set, the Universal Human Rights Index, the World Bank's Worldwide Governance Indicators, the Ibrahim Index of African Governance, and the Countries at the Crossroads Survey.[44] Box 2.5 describes one such tool. The International Committee of the Red Cross has also produced a set of guidelines to assist states in their assessment of a recipient state's compliance with international humanitarian law (ICRC, 2007).

Box 2.5 Practical tools for assessing export criteria

In **Germany**, the Federal Ministry for Economic Development and Cooperation funds a project run by the Bonn International Center for Conversion designed to provide information on the extent to which potential recipients of German arms exports meet EU *Code of Conduct* criteria. The project Web site hosts a database that measures 170 countries against the following seven criteria, based on the EU *Code*: international or regional arms embargoes, respect for human rights, good governance, internal conflict, membership in human rights and arms control conventions, arms export controls, and the danger of disproportionate military capacities impairing development.

For each criterion, each country is classified as either 'green', 'yellow', or 'red' with each colour indicating the respective degree of correspondence, and an explanation of how the evaluation was made. See Figure 2.2 for an example for a sample recipient.

Figure 2.2 Evaluation of sample country's compliance with EU Code of Conduct criteria

1. International or Regional Arms Embargoes

show details

2. Adherence to Human Rights

show details

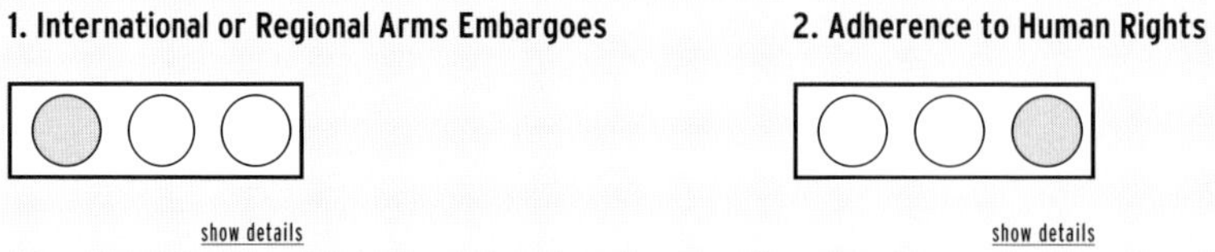

Source: BICC (n.d.)

Despite an abundance of practical tools, which could, in theory, facilitate a more harmonized approach to arms transfer licensing, different states do make varying decisions regarding the risks inherent in a particular transaction, even when applying the same criteria. This is well illustrated by the incident involving the export of rifles by Austria to Iran in 2004. Austria approved the sale of 800 Steyr .50 HS rifles after it concluded in 2004 that they would be used by Iran to fight narcotics smugglers. Approval was granted despite concerns raised by the United States and the United Kingdom that the weapons might end up in the hands of insurgents. Indeed, in 2007, US troops recovered more than 100 of the rifles in the hands of insurgents in Iraq (IHT, 2007).

This case highlights the fact that different states may approach the same decision differently, depending on their assessment of the circumstances. The incident also illustrates another difficulty associated with licensing decisions: circumstances may change. It is reported that in defending the approval of sale, the Austrian Foreign Ministry spokeswoman Astrid Harz noted that the proposal was assessed very carefully and that the situation in Iraq and the region in 2003–04—when the decision was made—was very different from the situation in 2007, when the weapons were discovered in Iraq (IHT, 2007; *Daily Telegraph*, 2007).

A similar response was put forward by China following media reports of the shipment of arms from China to Zimbabwe in April 2008, at a time of heightened political tensions due to upcoming national elections. Foreign Ministry spokeswoman Jiang Yu stated that the shipment 'was perfectly normal trade in military goods between China and Zimbabwe', adding that 'the contract for the shipment was signed last year and was unrelated to the recent changes in Zimbabwe's domestic situation' (*China Daily*, 2008). While circumstances can change unpredictably, overtaking initial licensing decisions, it may be convincingly argued, in these cases, that the deterioration was foreseeable and—along with existing red flags—should have been factored into the licensing decision.

CONCLUSION

This chapter has reviewed national export controls in the world's major exporting states with a view to comparing and, to some extent, evaluating these systems. The chapter's first observation is one of sheer diversity. States employ a dizzying array of policies and procedures in an effort to ensure their arms exports serve national policy goals and, no less important, that once authorized for shipment abroad, the weapons reach their intended end users and are used according to the terms of the corresponding licensing agreement.

The chapter's second observation is that existing control measures are of varying quality. The basic components of export control systems appear to be in place in virtually all of the world's major small arms exporters (such as pre-licensing requirements, interagency decision-making, end-user certification, and sanctions). But the effectiveness of those components varies. Some states easily meet accepted standards of best practice, while others appear to fall short; yet more detailed information is required for a definitive assessment of national export controls. More often than not, given resource and space limitations, the chapter stops at an assessment of national practices. The extent to which states implement their legislation remains, in most cases, undisclosed.

Awareness of the need to maintain robust, effective export controls is increasing among states, which has resulted in a growing list of regional and international commitments on small arms transfers, together with a growing recognition of the relevance of existing legal norms in this area. The chapter makes an initial assessment of the degree to which states have translated international and regional commitments into legislative form. While this is a crucial step towards full compliance with such norms, it is only an initial step and not one that all states have taken.

In diversity lies danger. As the chapter indicates, there are many control gaps among the world's major exporting states. These extend to all aspects of national export controls but appear particularly acute once weapons leave the national territory. Gaps also exist between the licensing criteria states have incorporated in their legislation or policy guidance and the practical application of such criteria to specific cases. As illustrated, different states can reach very different conclusions in the same case. Clearly, there is much work to do, at the international level, to ensure that national control systems complement, rather than contradict, one another. ■

LIST OF ABBREVIATIONS

ANCEX National Agency for Export Controls (Romania)

CIFTA Convention against the Illicit Manufacturing of and Trafficking in Firearms, Ammunition, Explosives, and Other Related Materials

DVC Delivery Verification Certificate

EU European Union

EUC End-user certificate

FA Framework Agreement (France, Germany, Italy, Spain, Sweden, and the UK)

GPL Global project licence

IIC International import certificate

IHL International humanitarian law

MEC Military equipment for combat purposes (Sweden)

NCACC National Conventional Arms Control Committee (South Africa)

OAS Organization of American States

OECD Organisation for Economic Co-operation and Development

OGEL Open general export licence (UK)

OME	Other military equipment (vs. MEC, Sweden)
OSCE	Organization for Security and Co-operation in Europe
PISE	Product Identification Search Engine
SADC	Southern African Development Community
SEESAC	South Eastern and Eastern Europe Clearinghouse for the Control of Small Arms and Light Weapons
UN	United Nations

ENDNOTES

1 The 26 states reviewed in this chapter have been classified by the Small Arms Survey as major exporters of small arms and light weapons for at least four of the past five years (since 2004). That is, their annual exports have exceeded USD 10 million. Note: Mexico also qualifies in this category, but more research is necessary to assess its status with respect to transfer controls.

2 For a detailed list of regional and multilateral instruments affecting small arms transfers, see Parker (2008).

3 Although the EU *Code of Conduct* was transformed into a legally binding Common Position in December 2008, references throughout this chapter are to the EU *Code of Conduct* rather than the *Common Position*. Since research for the chapter was completed before the adoption of the *Common Position*, it reflects the situation as it existed under the EU *Code*. See EU (1998).

4 The EU *Code of Conduct* became a legally binding Common Position in December 2008. See endnote 3.

5 See US (1997, part 748.13).

6 For online details of current UN Security Council arms embargoes, see UNSC Sanctions Committees (n.d.).

7 The *Report of the Governmental Technical Experts on the Register of Conventional Arms* states, 'Since the supply of equipment by a State to units of its armed forces stationed abroad does not involve transfer of national title and control, such supply is not considered an international transfer.' See UNGA (1992, paras. 10–12).

8 Also referred to as 'war materiel'.

9 See WA (2008, notes to sec. ML1) and EU (1998, Op. Provision 1; 2008b, notes to sec. ML1).

10 In the Wassenaar Munitions List, items are categorized numerically as 'Munitions List 1' (ML1), 'Munitions List 2' (ML2), and so forth. They are similarly identified in the EU Common Military List.

11 France is in the process of repealing the order of 20 November 1991 establishing its list of war materiel and related materials, and integrating the EU Common Military List (Elluin, 2008).

12 Under the *Defense Export Control Law, 5766-2007*, 'defense equipment' is defined to include 'combat equipment', which in turn is defined to cover 'equipment included in the Munitions List of the Wassenaar Arrangement, as periodically updated' (Israel, 2007, ch. B).

13 With regard to the export of hunting and sporting rifles, however, Sweden's National Inspectorate of Strategic Products (ISP) handles exports to states that are not members of the Organisation for Economic Co-operation and Development (OECD) while the Swedish Police Service handles exports to other OECD states.

14 In the *Programme of Action*, states have undertaken to assess export applications 'according to strict national regulations and procedures that cover *all* small arms and light weapons' (UNGA, 2001, para. II.11, emphasis added).

15 In some jurisdictions arms that are transiting the state may be considered 'exports' when they leave the territory of the state. However, some states expressly exclude goods in transit from the definition of 'export' (e.g. Singapore).

16 In addition, the commercial export of military small arms is prohibited (Teixeira, 2007).

17 See UNGA (2001, para. II.18), OSCE (2000, sect. IV.C.1), and EU (2002, art. 4(c)).

18 The Wassenaar *Best Practices for Disposal of Surplus/Demilitarised Military Equipment* (agreed at the plenary in December 2000), provides a list of best practices for disposal of surplus military equipment (items that may or may not have been demilitarized) drawn from the responses provided by participating states on this subject. These practices are those actually followed or aspired to by Wassenaar Arrangement participating states and are illustrative of effective export control over surplus/demilitarized military equipment.

19 Belgium is composed of three regions: Brussels Capital, Flanders, and Wallonia. Flanders and Wallonia are each subdivided into five provinces.

20 Cyprus, the Czech Republic, Estonia, Hungary, Latvia, Lithuania, Malta, Poland, Slovakia, and Slovenia were admitted in 2004; Bulgaria and Romania joined in 2007.

21 See also Small Arms Survey (2008, p. 166).

22 Bulgaria (2007a, art. 3); Czech Republic (1994a, art. 3); Finland (2008b, p. 12); Italy (2007); Spain (2004a, ch. 1, sec. 1, art. 2(2)(d)(5)); Switzerland (1997, art. 13(f)); US (2007, sec. 126.4).

23 The 25 countries are: Argentina, Australia, Austria, Belgium, Canada, the Czech Republic, Denmark, Finland, France, Germany, Greece, Hungary, Ireland, Italy, Japan, Luxembourg, New Zealand, the Netherlands, Norway, Poland, Portugal, Sweden, Spain, the United Kingdom, and the United States.

24 For example, the Swedish Inspectorate of Strategic Products hosts a site listing all UN, OSCE, and EU arms embargoes in force (Sweden, n.d.a); in the United Kingdom, the Department for Business Enterprise and Regulatory Reform maintains a site detailing arms embargoes in place and other restrictions (UKBERR, n.d.a.).

25 Czech Republic (2007b, p. 4); Finland (2008); Germany (2008); Norway (Leonhardsen, 2007); Turkey (2008, p. 9).

26 See UKBERR (n.d.b).

27 For further details, including a full list of destination countries to which the open licence applies, see UKBERR (2008).

28 For a full list of the conditions attached, see UKBERR (2004).

29 Such reporting software includes the Annual Arms Report CD produced by the South Eastern and Eastern Europe Clearinghouse for the Control of Small Arms and Light Weapons (SEESAC). Designed for use in the western Balkans, it provides templates for reporting arms sales.

30 The United Kingdom uses PISE for its 'Goods Checker', a Web-based tool that helps exporters determine whether their goods, software, or technology is controlled by UK or EU strategic export control legislation. See UKBERR (n.d.c).

31 See Small Arms Survey (2008, ch. 5).

32 Dreyfus and Perez (2007); Elluin (2008); Germany (2008); Fallani (2007); Romania (Wood, 2007, p. 24); Russian Federation (2007, p. 13); South Africa (2002, sec. 17(c)); Spain (2004a, ch. 2, sec. 1, art. 23(1)(c)).

33 This is also in line with the OSCE *Standard Elements* (OSCE, 2004, para. 1).

34 See Small Arms Survey (2008, chs. 4–5).

35 See EU (2008a). These findings are based on the approximate number of times each criterion was invoked as the basis for a refusal. Sometimes more than one criterion is invoked for a refusal. Accordingly, the number of times criteria were invoked exceeds the total number of refusals made. The calculation includes licence refusals for categories ML1 and ML2 of the EU Common Military List. If export refusals for ML3 (ammunition) are also included, Criterion 7 was invoked in 89 out of 206 cases (43 per cent).

36 Japan (1997, art. 69-6(1)); Singapore (2003, sec. 5(6)(a)); Spain (2004b, p. 8), UK (1979, sec. 68(3)).

37 Sweden (2000, sec. 5); Switzerland (1996b, art. 33(3)); UK (1979, sec. 68(3)); South Africa (2002, s. 24(2).

38 Norway (1987, para. 5); Sweden (2000, sec. 7); Switzerland (1996b, art. 33(3)); Moreau (2008); Bulgaria (2002); Singapore (2003, sec. 5(6)(b)); Czech Republic (1994a, art. 25(2)).

39 Although Bosnia and Herzegovina falls outside the sample of exporting states under review (it has only been classified as a major exporter twice in the last five years), it is referred to here because the veto power granted to each agency involved in the inter-agency consultancy process is an unusual feature (SEESAC, 2006, p. 22).

40 China (2002, art. 5); Republic of Korea (2008, p. 16); South Africa (2002, sec.15); Switzerland (1998, art. 5).

41 Moreau (2008); Bulgaria (2001, art. 5); Fallani (2007); Spain (2004a, art. 8).

42 Austria (2007b); Czech Republic (2007b, p. 11); France (2007, p. 5); Germany (2008, p. 24); Romania (2005b, p. 10); Sweden (2008, p. 14); and UK (2008a).

43 Consideration of the recipient country's stockpile management is not mentioned within the EU *Code of Conduct* criteria; however, according to the *User's Guide,* one of the elements to consider when formulating a judgement regarding the recipient's ability to exert effective export controls under Criterion 7 is: 'Is stockpile management and security of sufficient standard?' (EU, 2006, sec. 3.4.3, p. 48).

44 For details on these data sets, see CIRI (n.d.); UN (n.d.); World Bank (n.d.); Mo Ibrahim Foundation (n.d.); and Freedom House (n.d.).

BIBLIOGRAPHY

Aubin, Yann and Arnaud Idiart. 2007. *Export Control Law and Regulations Handbook: A Practical Guide to Military and Dual-Use Goods Trade Restrictions and Compliance.* The Hague: Kluwer Law International.

Austria. 2006. *National Report on the Implementation of the UN Small Arms Programme of Action.* <http://disarmament.un.org/cab/nationalreports/2006/austria.pdf>

—. 2007. *National Report on the Implementation of the UN Small Arms Programme of Action.* <http://www.un-casa.org/CASACountryProfile/PoANationalReports/2007@12@Austria%202007.doc>

BICC (Bonn International Center for Conversion). n.d. 'Sicherheit, Rüstung und Entwicklung in Empfängerländern deutscher Rüstungsexporte (Security, Armaments, and Development in Recipient Countries of German Arms Exports).' <http://www.bicc.de/ruestungsexport/>

Brazil. 2008. *National Report on the Implementation of the UN Small Arms Programme of Action.* <http://www.un-casa.org/CASACountryProfile/PoANationalReports/2008@27@Brazil%20Report.pdf>

Bulgaria. 2001. *Decree of the Council of Ministers No. 91/2001.* As amended 29 April 2008.

—. 2002. *National Report on the Implementation of the UN Small Arms Programme of Action.* <http://disarmament.un.org/CAB/nationalreports/2002/bulgaria.pdf>

—. 2006. *National Report on the Implementation of the UN Small Arms Programme of Action.* <http://www.un-casa.org/CASACountryProfile/PoANationalReports/2006@30@Bulgaria.pdf>

—. 2007a. *Law on Export Control of Arms and Dual-use Items and Technologies.* Unofficial translation by Ministry of Economy and Energy. <http://www.mi.government.bg/eng/ind/earms.html>

—. 2007b. *Regulation on Implementation of the Law on Export Control of Arms and Dual-use Items and Technologies.* Unofficial translation by Ministry of Economy and Energy. <http://www.mi.government.bg/eng/ind/earms.html>

Canada. 2001. *Controlled Goods Regulations* (SOR/2001-32). As of February 2009. <http://laws.justice.gc.ca/en/ShowFullDoc/cr/SOR-2001-32///en>

—. 2006. *A Guide to Canada's Export Controls.* June. <http://www.international.gc.ca/controls-controles/assets/pdfs/military/documents/exportcontrols-en.pdf>

—. 2007a. *Export and Import Permits Act.* R.S., 1985, c. E-19, August. <http://laws.justice.gc.ca/en/ShowFullDoc/cs/E-19///en>

—. 2007b. *Export Permits Regulations.* SOR/97-204, August. <http://laws.justice.gc.ca/en/ShowFullDoc/cr/SOR-97-204///en>

—. 2007c. *Report on Exports of Military Goods from Canada: 2003–2005.* Ottawa: Department of Foreign Affairs and International Trade Canada/ Export Controls Division of the Export and Import Controls Bureau. <http://www.international.gc.ca/controls-controles/assets/pdfs/military/documents/Military_Report2007-en.pdf>

—. 2008. *National Report on the Implementation of the UN Small Arms Programme of Action.* <http://www.un-casa.org/CASACountryProfile/PoANationalReports/2008@35@Canada%202008.pdf>

Cattaneo, Silvia and Sarah Parker. 2008. *Implementing the United Nations Programme of Action on Small Arms and Light Weapons: Analysis of the National Reports Submitted by States from 2002 to 2008.* Geneva: United Nations Institute for Disarmament Research.

China. 2002. *Regulations of the People's Republic of China on Administration of Arms Export (Arms Export Regulations).* October. <http://www.gov.cn/english/laws/2005-07/25/content_16975.htm>

—. 2008. *National Report on the Implementation of the UN Small Arms Programme of Action.* <http://www.un-casa.org/CASACountryProfile/PoANationalReports/2008@42@China_E%202008.pdf>

China Daily. 2008. 'Shipment of Arms Normal Trade: FM.' 23 April. <http://www.chinadaily.com.cn/cndy/2008-04/23/content_6636859.htm>

CIRI (Cingranelli–Richards Human Rights Dataset). n.d. CIRI Human Rights Data Project. <http://ciri.binghamton.edu>

Czech Republic. 1994a. *Act No. 38/1994 Coll. to Regulate Trade in Military Equipment with Foreign Countries.* Updated to 2004. Unofficial English translation provided by Ministry of Industry and Trade. <http://download.mpo.cz/get/26807/40199/476706/priloha002.doc>

—. 1994b. *Decree of the Ministry of Industry and Trade No. 89/1994 Coll. Implementing Certain Provisions of Act No. 38/1994 Coll.* Unofficial English translation provided by Ministry of Industry and Trade. <http://download.mpo.cz/get/26807/40199/476707/priloha001.doc>

—. 2005a. *Act No. 228/2005 on Control of Trade in Products Whose Possession Is Regulated in the Czech Republic for Security Reasons.* Unofficial English translation provided by Ministry of Industry and Trade.

—. 2005b. *Government Regulation No. 230/2005 Laying Down a List of Products, Conditions Subject to Which Imports or Exports or Transport of Listed Products May Be Carried Out.* Unofficial English translation provided by Ministry of Industry and Trade.

—. 2007a. *Annual Report of the Czech Republic's Control of the Export of Military Equipment and Small Arms for Civilian Use: 2007.* Prague: Ministry of Foreign Affairs.

—. 2007b. *National Report on the Implementation of the UN Small Arms Programme of Action.* <http://www.un-casa.org/CASACountryProfile/PoANationalReports/2007@53@Czech%20Republic%20>

Daily Telegraph (United Kingdom). 2007. 'We Are Not Responsible for Rifles, says Austria.' 14 February <http://www.telegraph.co.uk/news/worldnews/1542670/We-are-not-responsible-for-rifles%2C-says-Austria.html>

Dreyfus, Pablo, Benjamin Lessing, and Júlio César Purcena. 2005. 'The Brazilian Small Arms Industry: Legal Production and Trade.' In Rubem César Fernandes, ed. *Brazil: The Arms and the Victims.* Rio de Janeiro: 7 Letras/ISER. <http://www.smallarmssurvey.org/files/portal/issueareas/transfers/transfers_pdf/2005_Dreyfus_et_al.pdf>

— and Rebeca Perez. 2007. *Firearms Legislation Project: Questionnaire (Brazil).* Unpublished background paper. Geneva: Small Arms Survey.

EC (Commission of the European Communities). 2006. *Consultation Paper on the Intra-Community Circulation of Products for the Defence of Member States*. Brussels: EC. 21 March.

—. 2007a. *Proposal for a Directive of the European Parliament and of the Council on Simplifying Terms and Conditions of Transfers of Defence-related Products within the Community*. Document COM(2007) 765 final, 2007/0279 (COD). Brussels: EC. 5 December.

—. 2007b. *Accompanying Document to the Proposal for a Directive of the European Parliament and of the Council on Simplifying Terms and Conditions of Transfers of Defence-related Products within the Community: Impact Assessment*. Document COM(2007) 765 final, SEC(2007) 1594. Brussels: EC. 5 December.

—. 2007c. *Directive of the European Parliament and of the Council on Simplifying the Terms and Conditions of Transfers of Defence-related Products within the Community*. Brussels: EC. 12 May. <http://eur-lex.europa.eu/LexUriServ/LexUriServ.do?uri=CELEX:52007PC0765:EN:NOT>

—. 2008. *Position of the European Parliament Adopted at First Reading on 16 December 2008 with a View to the Adoption of Directive 2009/.../EC of the European Parliament and of the Council on Simplifying Terms and Conditions of Transfers of Defence-related Products within the Community*. Adopted 16 December. <http://www.europarl.europa.eu/sides/getDoc.do;jsessionid=FE68FF66A91E1C70835139583754912б.node1?pubRef=-//EP//TEXT+TA+P6-TA-2008-0603+0+DOC+XML+V0//EN#BKMD-29>

Elluin, Aymeric. 2008. *Firearms Legislation Project: Questionnaire (France)*. Unpublished background paper. Geneva: Small Arms Survey.

EP (European Parliament). 2008. *Draft Report on the Proposal for a Directive of the European Parliament and the Council on Simplifying Terms and Conditions of Transfers of Defence-related Products within the Community*. Committee on the Internal Market and Consumer Protection. 19 June.

EU (European Union). 1998. *European Union Code of Conduct on Arms Exports*. 5 June. <consilium.europa.eu/uedocs/cmsUpload/08675r2en8.pdf>

—. 2002. 'Council Joint Action of 12 July 2002 on the European Union's Contribution to Combating the Destabilising Accumulation and Spread of Small Arms and Light Weapons and Repealing Joint Action 1999/34/CFSP.' *Official Journal of the European Communities*. 2002/589/CFSP. Notice No. L 191/1. 12 July.

—. 2004. Resolution on the Council's Fifth Annual Report according to Operative Provision 8 of the European Union Code of Conduct on Arms Exports. INI/2004/2103, para. 18.

—. 2006. *User's Guide to the EU Code of Conduct on Arms Exports*. 20 June. <http://register.consilium.europa.eu/pdf/en/06/st10/st10713.en06.pdf>

—. 2007. 'Ninth Annual Report According to Operative Provision 8 of the European Union Code of Conduct on Arms Exports.' *Official Journal of the European Union*. Notice No. 2007/C 253/01. 26 October.

—. 2008a. 'Tenth Annual Report According to Operative Provision 8 of the European Union Code of Conduct on Arms Exports.' *Official Journal of the European Union*. Notice No. 2008/C 300/01. 22 November.

—. 2008b. *Common Military List of the European Union*. 10 March. 18 April. <http://eur-lex.europa.eu/LexUriServ/LexUriServ.do?uri=OJ:C:2008:098:0001:0032:EN:PDF>

—. 2008c. 'Council Common Position 2008/944/CFSP of 8 December 2008 Defining Common Rules Governing Control of Exports of Military Technology and Equipment.' *Official Journal of the European Union*. Notice No. L 335/99. 13 December.

Fallani, Fulvia. 2007. *Firearms Legislation Project: Questionnaire (Italy)*. Unpublished background paper. Geneva: Small Arms Survey.

Finland. 1990. *Act on the Export and Transit of Defence Materiel* (242/1990; amendments up to 900/2002 included) (unofficial translation). <http://www.finlex.fi/fi/laki/kaannokset/1990/en19900242.pdf>

—. 1995. *Decision of the Council of State on the General Guidelines for the Export and Transit of Defence Materiel* (474/1995).

—. 2008. *National Report on the Implementation of the UN Small Arms Programme of Action*. <http://www.un-casa.org/CASACountryProfile/PoANationalReports/2008@66@Finland%202008.pdf>

France. 2007. *Report of the French Parliament Regarding Defence Equipment Exports in 2006*. Paris: Ministry of Defence. December.

—. n.d. *End-use Certificate* (sample end-use certificates). Sec. B.6. <http://www.defense.gouv.fr/das/content/download/47263/469227/file/memento_2005_memento_2005.pdf>

Freedom House. n.d. Countries at the Crossroads Survey. <http://www.freedomhouse.org/template.cfm?page=139&edition=8>

Germany. 2000. *Politische Grundsätze der Bundesregierung für den Export von Kriegswaffen und sonstigen Rüstungsgütern* (Political Principles of the Federal Government for the Export of War Weapons and Other Military Equipment). 19 January. <http://www.ausfuhrkontrolle.info/ausfuhrkontrolle/de/krwaffkontrg/bekanntmachungen/grundsatz_politisch.pdf>

—. 2002. *Act Implementing Article 26(2) of the Basic Law (War Weapons Control Act)*. As amended by art. 3 of the law of 11 October, *Federal Law Gazette*, I, p. 3970. Official translation. <http://www.bafa.de/bafa/en/export_control/legislation/export_control_cwc_p_war_weapons_control_act.pdf>

—. 2007. *BAFA Export Controls: Brief Outline*. Federal Office of Economics and Export Control. March. <http://www.bafa.de/bafa/en/export_control/publications/export_control_brief_outline.pdf>

—. 2008. *National Report on the Implementation of the UN Small Arms Programme of Action*. 14 March. <http://www.un-casa.org/CASACountryProfile/PoANationalReports/2008@73@Germany%202008.pdf>

ICRC (International Committee of the Red Cross). 2007. *Arms Transfer Decisions: Applying International Humanitarian Law Criteria*. Geneva: ICRC. <http://www.icrc.org/Web/Eng/siteeng0.nsf/html/p0916>

IHT (*International Herald Tribune*). 2007. 'Austrian Rifles Supplied to Iran Have Found Their Way to Iraqi Insurgents.' 13 February. <http://www.iht.com/articles/ap/2007/02/13/europe/EU-GEN-Britain-Austria-Iraq-Rifles.php>

Israel. 2007. *Defense Export Control Law, 5766-2007*. Unofficial translation, Office of the General Counsel, Ministry of Defence. October.

—. 2008. *National Report on the Implementation of the UN Small Arms Programme of Action*. <http://www.un-casa.org/CASACountryProfile/PoANationalReports/2008@95@Israel(E).pdf>

Italy. 2003. *National Report on the Implementation of the UN Small Arms Programme of Action*. <http://disarmament.un.org/cab/nationalreports/2002/italy.pdf>

Japan. 1997. *Foreign Exchange and Foreign Trade Control Law (Law no. 228 of December 1949)*, as amended 1997. Unofficial translation. <http://www.japanlaw.info/forex/law/JS.htm>

—. 2006. *Export Trade Control Order* (Order no. 378 of December 1949, as amended by Cabinet Order no. 304 of 2006). Unofficial translation available at <http://www.asianlii.org/jp/legis/laws/etco1949con378od11949475>

—. 2008. *National Report on the Implementation of the UN Small Arms Programme of Action*. March. <http://www.un-casa.org/CASACountryProfile/PoANationalReports/2008@98@Japan.pdf>

Japan METI (Ministry of Economy, Trade, and Industry). 2002. *Japan's Policies on the Control of Arms Exports*. <http://www.meti.go.jp/policy/anpo/kanri/top-page/top/japan's-policies-on.htm>

Japan MFA (Japan Ministry of Foreign Affairs). n.d. *Japan's Policies on the Control of Arms Exports*. <http://www.mofa.go.jp/policy/un/disarmament/policy/index.html>

Klob, Bernhard. 2007. *Firearms Legislation Project: Questionnaire (Austria)*. Unpublished background paper. Geneva: Small Arms Survey.

Kotiaho, Paavo. 2008. *Firearms Legislation Project: Questionnaire (Finland)*. Unpublished background paper. Geneva: Small Arms Survey.

Laist, Elkana. 2007. *Firearms Legislation Project: Questionnaire (Israel)*. Unpublished background paper. Geneva: Small Arms Survey.

Lee, Sun Goo. *Firearms Legislation Project: Questionnaire (Republic of Korea)*. Unpublished background paper. Geneva: Small Arms Survey.

Leonhardsen, Erlend. 2007. *Firearms Legislation Project: Questionnaire (Norway)*. Unpublished background paper. Geneva: Small Arms Survey.

Liatowitsch, Mischa. 2008. *Firearms Legislation Project: Questionnaire (Switzerland)*. Unpublished background paper. Geneva: Small Arms Survey.

Macalesher, Jacqueline and Robert Parker. 2007. *Bulgaria's Arms Transfer Control System at EU Accession: An Analysis*. London: Saferworld.

Mo Ibrahim Foundation. n.d. Ibrahim Index of African Governance. <http://www.moibrahimfoundation.org/the-index.asp>

Moreau, Virginie. 2008. *Firearms Legislation Project: Questionnaire (Belgium)*. Unpublished background paper. Geneva: Small Arms Survey.

Norway. 1987. Act of 18 December 1987 nr. 93 on Control of Export of Strategic Goods, Services and Technology. Unofficial translation.

—. 1989. Ministry of Foreign Affairs Ordinance of 10 January 1989 to Implement Export Regulations for Strategic Goods, Services and Technology. Unofficial translation.

—. 2007. *Regulations to the Implementation of Control of the Export of Strategic Goods, Services and Technology*. Unofficial translation provided by the Ministry of Foreign Affairs. <http://www.ub.uio.no/ujur/ulovdata/for-19890110-051-eng.pdf>

—. 2008. *National Report on the Implementation of the UN Small Arms Programme of Action*. <http://www.un-casa.org/CASACountryProfile/PoANationalReports/2008@148@Norway%202008.doc>

OSCE (Organization for Security and Co-operation in Europe). 1993. *Principles Governing Conventional Arms Transfers*. <http://www.osce.org/documents/fsc/1993/11/4269_en.pdf>

—. 2000. *Document on Small Arms and Light Weapons*. FSC.DOC/1/00. Adopted 24 November. Vienna: Forum for Security Co-operation, OSCE. <http://www.osce.org/documents/fsc/2000/11/1873_en.pdf>

—. 2003. *Handbook of Best Practices on Small Arms and Light Weapons*. Vienna: OSCE. <http://www.osce.org/fsc/item_11_13550.html>

—. 2004. *Standard Elements of End-User Certificates and Verification Procedures for SALW Exports*. Decision No. 5/04. FSC.DEC/5/04 of 17 November. <http://www.osce.org/documents/fsc/2004/11/3809_en.pdf>

Parker, Sarah. 2008. *Implications of States' Views on an Arms Trade Treaty*. Geneva: UNIDIR, annexe A. <http://www.unidir.ch/pdf/ouvrages/pdf-1-92-9045-008-B-en.pdf>

—. 2009. 'Export Controls: Primary and Secondary Source Materials for Chapter Tables.' Unpublished background paper. Geneva: Small Arms Survey.

Portugal. 2008. *National Report on the Implementation of the UN Small Arms Programme of Action*. May. <http://www.un-casa.org/CASACountryProfile/PoANationalReports/2008@158@Portugal%202008.doc>

Pyadushkin, Maxim. 2008. *Firearms Legislation Project: Questionnaire (Russian Federation).* Unpublished background paper. Geneva: Small Arms Survey.

Republic of Korea. 2008. *National Report on the Implementation of the UN Small Arms Programme of Action.* <http://www.un-casa.org/CASACountryProfile/PoANationalReports/2008@104@Republic%20of%20Korea.doc>

Romania. 2005a. *Annual Report of the Romanian Arms Export Controls.* Bucharest: Ministry of Foreign Affairs/National Agency for Export Controls.

—. 2005b. *National Report on the Implementation of the UN Small Arms Programme of Action.* <http://www.un-casa.org/CASACountryProfile/PoANationalReports/2005@162@Romania.pdf>

—. 2008. *National Report on the Implementation of the UN Small Arms Programme of Action.* <http://disarmament.un.org/cab/bms3/1BMS3Pages/1NationalReports/Romania(E).PDF>

Russian Federation. 2007. *National Report on the Implementation of the UN Small Arms Programme of Action.* <http://www.un-casa.org/CASACountryProfile/PoANationalReports/2008@163@Russia%202008%20E.doc>

SEESAC (South Eastern and Eastern Europe Clearinghouse for the Control of Small Arms and Light Weapons). 2006. *Analysis of National Legislation on Arms Exports and Transfers in the Western Balkans.* 16 August.

Singapore. 2003. *Strategic Goods (Control) Act* (updated to 2007). <http://statutes.agc.gov.sg>

—. 2007. *Strategic Goods (Control) Order 2007.* <http://www.customs.gov.sg/NR/rdonlyres/6692B2E5-22C2-4BBD-B055-5F2426EC5890/0/SGCOrder2007.pdf>

—. 2008. *Handbook on the Strategic Trade Scheme (STS).* Singapore Customs. <http://www.customs.gov.sg/NR/rdonlyres/E5D64083-A9B0-424D-A585-87250213455A/21172/HandbookontheSTS23Jun08.pdf>

Small Arms Survey. 2007. *Small Arms Survey 2007: Guns and the City.* Cambridge: Cambridge University Press.

—. 2008. *Small Arms Survey: Risk and Resilience.* Cambridge: Cambridge University Press.

South Africa. 2002. *National Conventional Arms Control Act.* <http://us-cdn.creamermedia.co.za/assets/articles/attachments/00436_natconvarmscontact41.pdf>

—. 2003. *2003 and 2004 National Conventional Arms Control Committee's (NCACC) Annual Report(s).*

—. 2004. *National Conventional Arms Control Regulations.* <http://www.dti.gov.za/nonproliferation/ArmsControl.html> or <http://www.dod.mil.za/documents/documents.htm>

—. 2008. *National Conventional Arms Control Amendment Bill.* Government Gazette No. 31078. 23 May 2008. <http://www.parliament.gov.za/live/commonrepository/Processed/20081124/76319_1.pdf>

Spain. 2004a. *Royal Decree 1782/2004 of 30 July Approving the Control Regulation on the External Trade of Defence Material, Other Material and Dual-use Items and Technologies.* Unofficial translation.

—. 2004b. *National Report on the Implementation of the UN Small Arms Programme of Action.* <http://www.un-casa.org/CASACountryProfile/PoANationalReports/2008@178@Spain(E).doc>

—. 2007a. *Law 53/2007 of 28 December on Control of External Trade in Defence and Dual-use Material.* Unofficial translation.

—. 2007b. *Order ITC/713/2007, of 15 March 2007 with the Updating of Annex I of Royal Decree 1782/2004 of 30 July 2004 on the Control of External Trade in Defence Material, Other Material and Dual-use Goods and Technologies.* <http://www.boe.es/boe/dias/2007/03/26/pdfs/A12986-13043.pdf>

Sweden. 1992a. *The Military Equipment Act.* 1992:1300. Unofficial translation from the Ministry of Foreign Affairs.

—. 1992b. *The Military Equipment Ordinance* (1992:1303). Unofficial translation from the Ministry of Foreign Affairs.

—. 2000. *Act on Penalties for Smuggling.* 2000:1225, unofficial translation. <http://www.sweden.gov.se/content/1/c6/02/77/68/c656cb4d.pdf>

—. 2007. *Strategic Export Controls: Military Equipment and Dual-Use Products.* Government Communication 2007/08:114. Stockholm: Ministry of Foreign Affairs. 13 March.

—. 2008. *National Report on the Implementation of the UN Small Arms Programme of Action.* <http://www.un-casa.org/CASACountryProfile/PoANationalReports/2008@186@Sweden%202008.pdf>

—. n.d.a. Swedish Inspectorate of Strategic Products (ISP) Web site. <http://www.isp.se/sa/node.asp?node=410>

—. n.d.b. *Export Controls: Guidelines for Export Licence Decisions Related to War Materiel and Other War Materiel.* Unofficial translation. <http://www.sipri.org/contents/expcon/rikt.html>

Switzerland. 1996a. *Federal Act on the Control of Dual-Use Goods and of Specific Military Goods.* Unofficial translation provided by the State Secretariat for Economic Affairs. <http://www.seco.admin.ch/themen/00513/00600/00608/00613/index.html?lang=en>

—. 1996b. *Federal Act of 13 December 1996 on War Material* (War Material Act, WMA). Unofficial translation provided by the State Secretariat for Economic Affairs. <http://www.admin.ch/ch/e/rs/c514_51.html>

—. 1997. *Ordinance on the Export, Import and Transit of Dual Use Goods and Specific Military Goods.* Unofficial translation provided by the State Secretariat for Economic Affairs. <http://www.seco.admin.ch/themen/00513/00600/00608/00613/index.html?lang=en>

—. 1998. Ordinance of 25 February 1998 on War Material. Unofficial translation provided by the State Secretariat for Economic Affairs. <http://www.admin.ch/ch/e/rs/c514_511.html>

—. 2005. *National Report on the Implementation of the UN Small Arms Programme of Action.* <http://www.un-casa.org/CASACountryProfile/PoANationalReports/2005@187@Switzerland-e.pdf>

—. 2008. *National Report on the Implementation of the UN Small Arms Programme of Action.* <http://www.un-casa.org/CASACountryProfile/PoANationalReports/2008@187@Switzerland%202008.doc>

Teixeira, Vitor. 2007. *Firearms Legislation Project: Questionnaire (Portugal).* Unpublished background paper. Geneva: Small Arms Survey.

TrackerNet. n.d. Web site. <http://www.trackernet.org>

Turkey. 2008. *National Report on the Implementation of the UN Small Arms Programme of Action.* <http://www.un-casa.org/CASACountryProfile/PoANationalReports/2008@198@Turkey.pdf>

UK (United Kingdom). 1979. *Customs and Excise Management Act.*

—. 2000. *The Consolidated EU and National Arms Export Licensing Criteria.* 26 October. <http://www.fco.gov.uk/servlet/Front?pagename=OpenMarket/Xcelerate/ShowPage&c=Page&cid=1014918697565>

—. 2002. *Export Control Act 2002.* <http://www.opsi.gov.uk/acts/acts2002/20020028.htm>

—. 2008a. *National Report on the Implementation of the UN Small Arms Programme of Action.* <http://www.un-casa.org/CASACountryProfile/PoANationalReports/2008@205@UK%202008.doc>

—. 2008b. *Scrutiny of Arms Export Control (2008): UK Strategic Export Controls Annual Report 2006, Quarterly Reports for 2007, Licensing Policy and Review of Export Legislation.* London: House of Commons, Business and Enterprise, Defence, Foreign Affairs, and International Development Committees.

—. 2008c. *Review of Export Control Legislation (2007): Government's Further Response to the Public Consultation.* 21 July.

—. 2008d. *Guidance on the Export of Firearms.* January.

—. 2009. *UK Strategic Export Control Lists.* Accessed January 2009. <http://www.berr.gov.uk/files/file49410.pdf>

UKBERR (UK Department for Business Enterprise and Regulatory Reform). 2004. 'Export Licence: Open General Export Licence (Accompanied Personal Effects: Sporting Firearms).' 1 May. <http://www.berr.gov.uk/files/file7975.pdf>

—. 2007. *2007 Review of Export Control Legislation: A Consultative Document.* June.

—. 2008. 'Export Licence: Open General Export Licence (Exports or transfers in Support of UK Government Defence Contracts). 11 June. <http://www.berr.gov.uk/files/file45914.pdf>

—. n.d.a. Web site. <http://www.berr.gov.uk/whatwedo/europeandtrade/strategic-export-control/sanctions-embargoes/by-country/index.html>

—. n.d.b. 'Licences: Export, Trade Control and Transhipment.' <http://www.berr.gov.uk/whatwedo/europeandtrade/strategic-export-control/licences/index.html>

—. n.d.c. 'Goods Checker.' <http://www.ecochecker.co.uk/goodsChecker/>

Ukraine. 2003. *Law of Ukraine On State Control of International Transfers of Goods Designated for Military Purposes and Dual-Use Goods.* 20 February.

UN (United Nations). 1945. Charter of the United Nations. <http://www.un.org/aboutun/charter/>

—. n.d. Universal Human Rights Index. <http://www.universalhumanrightsindex.org/>

UNGA (United Nations General Assembly).1992. *Report of the Governmental Technical Experts on the Register of Conventional Arms.* A/47/342 of 14 August.

—. 2001. *Programme of Action to Prevent, Combat and Eradicate the Illicit Trade in Small Arms and Light Weapons in All Its Aspects ('UN Programme of Action').* A/CONF.192/15 of 20 July. <http://disarmament.un.org/cab/poa.html>

—. 2008. *Report of the Group of Governmental Experts to Examine the Feasibility, Scope and Draft Parameters for a Comprehensive, Legally Binding Instrument Establishing Common International Standards for the Import, Export and Transfer of Conventional Arms.* A/63/334 of 26 August.

Unisys. 2005. *Intra-Community Transfers of Defence Products.* Brussels: Uniysis. February.

UNSC (United Nations Security Council) Sanctions Committees. n.d. Web site. <http://www.un.org/sc/committees>

US (United States). 1997. Code of Federal Regulations. Title 15: Commerce and Foreign Trade, Part 748—Applications (Classification, Advisory, and License) and Documentation. As amended 9 May. <http://ecfr.gpoaccess.gov/cgi/t/text/text-idx?c=ecfr&sid=13301414b239804fce651268b1f4d133&rgn=div8&view=text&node=15:2.1.3.4.32.0.1.13&idno=15>

—. 2005a. Arms Export Control Act, ch. 39 of US Code Title 22: Foreign Relations and Intercourse, as amended in 2005. <http://www.access.gpo.gov/uscode/title22/chapter39_.html>

—. 2005b. *Foreign Assistance Act of 1961* (updated to 2005). <http://www.dsca.mil/programs/LPA/2006/faa_aeca.pdf>

—. 2006. *Defense Trade Controls Overview.* <http://www.pmddtc.state.gov/reports/documents/defense_trade_overview_2006.pdf>

—. 2007. International Traffic in Arms Regulations (ITAR): Consolidated Version 2007. <http://ecfr.gpoaccess.gov/cgi/t/text/text-idx?c=ecfr&sid=86c9428901a37ef1e99d6f446d59f3d6&rgn=div5&view=text&node=22:1.0.1.13.59&idno=22>

USDoD (United States Department of Defense). 2003. 'End-Use Monitoring (EUM).' In *Security Assistance Management Manual*, document DoD 5105.38-M, ch. 8. <http://www.dsca.osd.mil/samm/>

USDoS (United States Department of State). 2008. *National Report on the Implementation of the UN Small Arms Programme of Action.* <http://www.un-casa.org/CASACountryProfile/PoANationalReports/2008@207@US-Report.doc>

—. n.d. *Conventional Arms Transfer (CAT) Policy.* <http://www.state.gov/t/pm/rsat/c14023.htm#>

WA (Wassenaar Arrangement on Export Controls for Conventional Arms and Dual-Use Goods and Technologies). 1998. *Elements for Objective Analysis and Advice Concerning Potentially Destabilising Accumulations of Conventional Weapons.* 3 December. <http://www.wassenaar.org/guidelines/docs/Objective_analysis.pdf>

—. 2000. *Best Practices for Disposal of Surplus/Demilitarised Military Equipment.* 1 December. <http://www.wassenaar.org/publicdocuments/2000/2000_bestpracticesdisposal.html>

—. 2002. *Best Practice Guidelines for Exports of Small Arms and Light Weapons (SALW).* 12 December. <http://www.wassenaar.org/docs/best_practice_salw.htm>

—. 2008. *Munitions List.* Adopted and recorded in app. 5 to the Initial Elements, dated 19 December 1995; last updated 3 December 2008. WA-LIST (08). <http://www.wassenaar.org/controllists/>

Weidacher, Reinhilde. 2005. *Behind a Veil of Secrecy: Military Small Arms and Light Weapons Production in Western Europe.* Occasional Paper 16. Geneva: Small Arms Survey.

Wood, David. 2007. *Romania's Arms Transfer Control System at EU Accession: An Analysis.* London: Saferworld.

World Bank. n.d. Worldwide Governance Indicators. <http://web.worldbank.org/WBSITE/EXTERNAL/WBI/EXTWBIGOVANTCOR/0,,contentMDK:20771165~menuPK:1866365~pagePK:64168445~piPK:64168309~theSitePK:1740530,00.html>

ACKNOWLEDGEMENTS

Principal author

Sarah Parker

Contributors

Pablo Dreyfus, Aymeric Elluin, Fulvia Fallani, Sun Goo Lee, Bernhard Klob, Paavo Kotiaho, Elkana Laist, Erlend Leonhardsen, Mischa Liatowitsch, Virginie Moreau, Rebeca Perez, Maxim Pyadushkin, Vitor Teixeira

British military police examine an AKM-pattern rifle.
© Visar Kryeziu/AP Photo

Revealing Provenance

WEAPONS TRACING DURING AND AFTER CONFLICT

3

INTRODUCTION

Weapons are evidence. Most carry marks that, combined with their structural characteristics, identify them uniquely. If they can be identified uniquely, their ownership history may be traced and the point at which they were diverted into the illicit sphere revealed. Weapons tracing can help uncover illicit supply channels, providing a firm basis for disrupting such trade and prosecuting those involved in it.

In recent years, the international community has come to recognize that weapons tracing can be central to efforts designed to detect, and hence address, the illicit proliferation and misuse of small arms. For now, however, it remains primarily a law enforcement tool. Its potential application to conflict and post-conflict settings remains poorly understood.

This chapter explores the process and promise of weapons tracing in conflict and post-conflict situations. It is designed as a practical guide to the tracing of small arms, light weapons, and their ammunition in conflict and post-conflict settings. Its principal conclusions include the following:

- Between 1998 and 2008, the international community spent USD 2.3 billion on disarmament, demobilization, and reintegration (DDR) and other initiatives designed to address the problem of illicit small arms proliferation;
- There is no evidence to suggest that any of the 330,000 weapons registered during these initiatives have been comprehensively analysed to ascertain their types and origins;
- About 75 per cent of United Nations and associated weapons collection records reviewed for this chapter are too ambiguous to allow for weapons tracing;
- Few states import-mark military weapons in ways that would allow a non-expert to identify the manufacturer;
- Although they have a legal obligation to mark weapons, few of the 74 signatories to the *UN Firearms Protocol* do so.

The chapter's main conclusion is that, despite more than a decade of attention to small arms identification and tracing, the international community has yet to make significant use of these important tools in conflict and post-conflict contexts.

Organizations with post-conflict peacekeeping or disarmament mandates, such as the UN, devote very little attention to monitoring, recording, and tracing weapons. The international community, more generally, has given little thought to the value of weapons tracing or how to improve international cooperation with respect to tracing requests.

Efforts to control the illicit proliferation of small arms and light weapons need to be founded upon firm evidence of illicit trade and its specific dynamics. The weapons themselves can often provide such evidence—but only if organizations record weapons information comprehensively and states and commercial entities cooperate fully with tracing requests.

THE PROMISE OF TRACING

In 2003, the United Nations Panel of Experts on Liberia noted a significant number of Serbian manufactured Zastava M70 assault rifles in the hands of warring factions throughout Liberia, including government troops loyal to then President Charles Taylor and fighters belonging to the rebel group Liberians United for Reconciliation and Democracy, or LURD (UNSC, 2003a, paras. 71–73).[1]

The Panel recorded serial numbers from some of the weapons and provided them to the Serbian Ministry of Defence in Belgrade. The Serbian authorities confirmed that all of the serial numbers submitted by the Panel belonged to weapons that had been manufactured by the Serbian arms producer Zastava in 2001 and 2002. Their date of manufacture suggested that they had been manufactured (and hence transferred) either after or immediately prior to the March 2001 UN arms embargo on Liberia.[2]

The Serbian authorities reported that the serial numbers matched those of a shipment to Nigeria that had been brokered by the Belgrade-based company Temex. The Panel's earlier enquiries had revealed that the shipment to Nigeria declared by Temex had been arranged under a forged end-user certificate and that the arms had not been delivered to Nigeria, but had instead been supplied directly to forces under the control of Charles Taylor, in violation of the UN arms embargo (UNSC, 2002, paras. 64–82; 2003a, paras. 69–70).[3]

In response to the Panel's findings, in April 2003 the Government of Serbia reported that it had revoked all licences granted to Temex for the trade in arms and military equipment and had ordered all military manufacturers to cease cooperation with the company (UNSC, 2003b, para. 94).

The Panel's ability to identify the M70 assault rifles by their marks, and to trace their origins back to the manufacturer, yielded vital evidence in the investigation. The trace established a direct link between weapons in the hands of warring parties, the company that had manufactured them, and the illicit supply channels that had brought them to Liberia.

Weapons tracing is a powerful lever in efforts to control the illicit proliferation of small arms and light weapons because it can provide hard evidence of parties' involvement in illegal activities. The Liberia Panel's work is a textbook example of weapons tracing, but it remains a rare success. As the following sections note, weapons tracing is not always a difficult task, but it is one that requires much greater attention by the international community.

TRACING BASICS

Small arms tracing has been defined as the

> *systematic tracking of illicit small arms and light weapons found or seized on the territory of a State from the point of manufacture or the point of importation through the lines of supply to the point at which they became illicit.* (UNGA, 2005a, para. 5)

The first step in any tracing operation is to identify the weapon of interest uniquely on the basis of its physical characteristics and markings. Then, with the cooperation of the states that manufactured and imported the weapon, the second step is to track changes in ownership through available documentary records. The ultimate, but often elusive, goal of weapons tracing is to identify the point in the transfer chain at which the (typically) legal weapon entered the illicit market. The three pillars of marking, record-keeping, and cooperation are essential to successful tracing.

Marking: Unmarked weapons cannot be identified uniquely. While a weapon's design may enable interested parties to identify its manufacturer, marks indicating the manufacturer and country of manufacture are usually indispensable. In all cases, the presence of a unique serial number allows one weapon to be distinguished from hundreds or thousands of others that may have been produced at a particular factory. Moreover, if countries mark the weapons that they import, tracing efforts are far more likely to succeed.

Record-keeping: Key elements of a weapon's history—in particular, changes in ownership—must be recorded for tracing to be possible. Records must be accurate, comprehensive, and retrievable if investigators are to have any chance of piecing together the weapon's history. Essential information includes the weapon type and model, its serial number, and the party to which it was transferred.

Cooperation in tracing: Even if the necessary marking and record-keeping requirements have been met, tracing efforts will be brought to a swift halt if the countries of manufacture or import—or trading entities within those countries—do not cooperate with tracing requests. After having identified the weapon uniquely, an investigator seeking tracing assistance typically approaches the countries of manufacture and import for help. Sometimes investigators contact relevant trading companies directly. Thereafter they follow the record-keeping chain forward in time—if possible to the point at which the weapon was diverted to the illicit sphere.

Unmarked weapons cannot be identified uniquely.

Both the *International Tracing Instrument* (ITI)[4], adopted by the UN General Assembly on 8 December 2005 (UNGA, 2005a; 2005b), and the outcome of the first meeting to consider the implementation of the ITI underline the fundamental, mutually reinforcing nature of these three pillars of weapons tracing (UNGA, 2008, annex, para. 9(a)).[5] They also note that weapons tracing 'may be required in the context of all forms of crime and conflict situations' (UNGA, 2005a, preamb. para. 2).[6] Law enforcement officials often trace small arms when conducting criminal investigations. The tracing of weapons in conflict situations is rare, however, and usually restricted to the activities of some UN embargo-monitoring groups and a handful of research organizations.

CONFLICT TRACING: A USER'S GUIDE

Why attempt a weapons trace in a country experiencing ongoing armed conflict or having recently emerged from conflict? Illicit arms transfers fuel conflict and, in post-conflict situations, they allow protagonists to rearm for war or for crime. Whether at the height of warfare or in societies that have recently emerged from armed conflict, 'conflict tracing' may be used to monitor potentially escalatory influxes of weapons and to investigate particular cases of concern.

The application of conflict tracing is not limited to identifying direct transfers to warring parties. The process may also be applied in cases of weapons loss by armed forces. Whether through negligence or theft, loss is a type of diversion, and diverted weapons fuel crime and insurgency across the world (Bevan, 2008c, pp. 47–56). Conflict tracing can play a critical role in identifying which security forces leak weapons and, by extension, where the security of weapons needs to be improved.

Recent evidence indicates that in the post-conflict environment, peacekeepers are no less susceptible to diversion than state security forces. In 2006, for instance, the South African defence minister reported that 50,000 rounds of ammunition, 97 mortar bombs, 46 R-4 assault rifles, 3 light machine guns, 2 pistols, and 2 grenades had been lost or stolen in the course of peace support missions in Burundi (Glatz and Lumpe, 2007, p. 86). In such cases, tracing may also help identify weapons diverted from peacekeeping forces and highlight weaknesses in arms management.

Conflict tracing, regardless of the context in which it is applied, relies on observing the types of weapons in use (whether legally or illegally). This provides a baseline of weapons in a given region, one that can become the basis for detecting influxes of new or more numerous weapons—which might provide the 'seed' evidence for a subsequent, more detailed investigation. In the Liberia case described above, the large number of distinctive M70 assault rifles served as such evidence. These weapons stood out against the many older Kalashnikov-pattern weapons in the region and called for further investigation.

The following sections provide a detailed, operationally oriented description of conflict tracing procedures—from observing and monitoring the weapons in use, to uniquely identifying weapons of concern and tracing their transfer history through documentary evidence.

Weapons identification

Weapons identification is the process of observing and recording the physical characteristics of a weapon, including its type and design, along with any marks that have been applied to it (see Table 3.1). Three pieces of information are critical to weapons identification: the model of the weapon (including the calibre, which often differentiates one model from another), the manufacturer's marks, and the serial number. When available, import marks provide a crucial fourth piece of information.

Given the millions of weapons used in contemporary armed conflict, why choose to trace one weapon and not another? The decision often requires some basic knowledge of weapon types, manufacturers of these weapons, and where they are likely (or not likely) to be used.

Table 3.1 Information required to uniquely identify a weapon

Information	Comments
Critical information	
Model of weapon and calibre (often marked, otherwise necessitates visual examination of design features)	Identifies the specific type of weapon (potentially one among many types produced by a single manufacturer).
Manufacturer's marks	Identifies the manufacturer (factory or firm).
Serial number	Uniquely identifies the weapon in a production run. May be recorded in export, import, or within-country transfer documentation.
Import mark (when available)	Identifies a state that has, at one time, imported the weapon; that state may retain export or within-country transfer documentation.
Supplementary information	
Annotation (fire selector, sights, etc.)	May identify the manufacturer.
Weapon design	Certain features of the weapon that may help to identify the model and manufacturer (for example, the shape and composition of the stock or the design of the muzzle compensator).

Telling weapons apart requires great attention to detail. In attempting to distinguish between an AKM and an AK-105 (see Figure 3.1), for example, many people would (incorrectly) describe each as an AK-47. Yet the two weapons have differing calibres—7.62 x 39 mm and 5.45 x 39 mm, respectively—which indicates that each is part of a distinct market, whether legal or illicit. AKMs are standard in Darfur, for instance, but it would be unusual to encounter an AK-105 in the region. These kinds of observations prompt people to observe, record, and ultimately, to try and trace conflict weapons.

Figure 3.1 **AKM (top) and AK-105 (bottom)**

While expertise is not a prerequisite to tracing, it is essential to observe and take note of the types of weapons in circulation. It does not take an expert, for example, to note an influx of 'black AKs', such as the AK-105. The appearance of newly arrived weapons, particularly if their design is unusual or new, might be sufficient to prompt non-experts to examine their markings to determine their provenance.

In 2008, for example, researchers in Germany observed (from photographs) that Georgian security forces were using German-manufactured Heckler & Koch G36 assault rifles. The appearance of G36 weapons was unusual because Georgian forces had previously, and almost exclusively, used Kalashnikov-pattern weapons. Moreover, Germany had reportedly rejected Georgia's request to purchase weapons of this type on the grounds of 'unresolved conflicts within its territory' (Kucera, 2007; Deutsche Welle, 2008). The case is illustrative of the role that vigilance and monitoring can play in detecting cases worthy of further investigation.

Weapon model

Manufacturers often produce many different models of weapon (for example 'G3A3' or 'G3A4'), some of which differ only slightly from one another. In the context of weapons tracing, identifying the model of weapon precisely is important for two reasons. First, manufacturers tend to stamp production runs of one type of model with successive serial numbers; these records are subsequently stored together. Several decades can separate the production of two models of weapon by one manufacturer. Any records that might pertain to their transfer are likely to be stored separately. Knowing the model of weapon (and, by extension, the production period) can significantly reduce the volume of documentation that needs to be consulted when responding to a tracing request. Second, transfer documentation may likewise list weapons by their model designations. Any attempt to locate a weapon in manufacturing, export, or import records by serial number alone could be extremely time-consuming.[7]

Together with the serial number and manufacturer, the model is one of a weapon's three most important identifying features. In fact, the model of weapon may indicate the manufacturer, which means that identifying the model precisely can provide two of the three primary identifying features (model, manufacturer, and serial number).

Some manufacturers, however, do not mark their weapons with model designations. In other cases, it can be difficult to determine which marks indicate the model. For instance, the marks pictured in Figure 3.2 feature a model designator, which, to the non-expert (or non-Chinese literate), is undecipherable. From left to right, the marks read '5', '6', and 'Type'—a Type 56 assault rifle.

Figure 3.2 **Marks on the Type 56 assault rifle**

© James Bevan. Weapon courtesy of Royal Armouries, UK

Learning to identify specific models of weapon can take years of experience and there is no complete substitute for this level of knowledge. Nevertheless, it is important to note that most people—indeed most organizations—do not need to identify weapons on sight. This task can be performed by an expert later, as long as that person is given the right information (including photographs).

Table 3.2 reproduces part of a list of 4,868 weapons that were collected by the Kosovo Police Service during two years of weapons amnesties and seizures. The list has many errors (marked in red) and none of the model designations is accurate. Because the records are relatively expansive, however, an expert can still identify each of the weapons listed here.

In this case, the person recorded what was believed to be the serial number while inadvertently including the model designation as part of that number. This information reveals that the rifles are all Chinese (rather than another of the many Kalashnikov variants) and comprise two Type 56-1 and four Type 56-2 assault rifles, in addition to a Type 56S-1 rifle manufactured for the US sporting market.

Table 3.2 **Extract from a list of 4,868 weapons and associated items collected by the Kosovo Police Service, 2000-02 (errors marked in red)**

Manufacturer	Model	Firearm type	Calibre	Serial number
AK (Kalashnikov)	Unknown	Sub-machine gun	7.62	56-16140072
AK (Kalashnikov)	1969	Rifle	7.62	56-17097521
AK (Kalashnikov)	AK-47	Rifle	7.62	56-20024456
AK (Kalashnikov)	AK-47	Rifle	7.62	56-20103089
AK (Kalashnikov)	Unknown	Rifle	7.62	56-20103089
AK (Kalashnikov)	AK-47	Rifle	7.62	56-202261
AK (Kalashnikov)	AK-47	Rifle	7.62 mm	56S-1 900476

Note: Type 56 assault rifles are manufactured in both AK-47 and AKM patterns, so the designation AK-47 is deemed an error.
Source: KPIS (2002)

Box 3.1 **Weapons identification in practice**

The weapon model, the manufacturer's mark, the serial number, and, when available, import markings are the basic elements needed to trace a weapon in most transfer records. Very often, however, the model designation is not marked on a weapon. For instance, the only way to tell the difference between many varieties of Kalashnikov-pattern weapons is by their design features. Model recognition involves only basic weapons expertise, but most people (including some military personnel) lack such knowledge.

An example of a weapon that is difficult to identify is pictured in Figure 3.3. Due to years of use in a harsh environment, the model designation and manufacturer's marks on the weapon have become undecipherable to the naked eye. Although the Arabic serial number is still visible (lower right of the frame), identifying the weapon model and manufacturer requires observing some of the weapon's design features.

Figure 3.3 **Manufacturer's marks (centre) and serial number (lower right) on an Egyptian Misr assault rifle**

Egyptian Misr assault rifle on the Kenya-Sudan border, May 2008. © James Bevan

In this case, the relevant design features include the shape of the stock and the fire selector annotation (see Figure 3.4). Together with the Arabic serial number, this information identifies both the model and the manufacturer–a Misr assault rifle, manufactured by the Maadi factory of Cairo, Egypt. Despite its age and condition, this weapon thus provides sufficient information for a tracing process to begin.

There is, however, a deficit of interest in weapons identification among international organizations, few of which have staff with the skills required to identify weapons. The personnel who are best placed to observe illicit weapons are the peacekeepers and law enforcement staff deployed in conflict and post-conflict situations. Yet they often have neither the mandate nor the basic training to identify (or at least record) the weapons that often proliferate in large numbers in their theatre of operations. The United Nations, for example, does not instruct its personnel in basic weapons identification; nor do major international peacekeeping training programmes offer lessons in the subject.[8]

As a result, personnel overlook valuable conflict tracing information. Trends that should be of concern remain unnoticed. Even when evidence of illicit proliferation abounds, there are simply not enough experts on the ground to realize it and to begin tracing illicit weapons. The diagnostic value of weapons tracing is, therefore, absent from many conflicts of international concern.

These deficiencies would not arise if the necessary energy and resources were to be allocated to raising awareness among relevant personnel, particularly peacekeepers and other employees in affected areas. People do not need to be experts to contribute valuable information if they know where to look for it and how to record it.

There is also a largely untapped pool of weapons expertise that could be hired for specific missions or activities. While some groups, including a few UN embargo panels and development project personnel, have requested external assistance in tracing weapons, such contacts are informal and sporadic.[9] Putting expertise on the ground as a formal part of UN missions (possibly according to region or on a rotational basis) would have a positive impact on the international capacity to identify and trace illicit weapons.

Figure 3.4 **Identifying design features of the Egyptian Misr assault rifle**

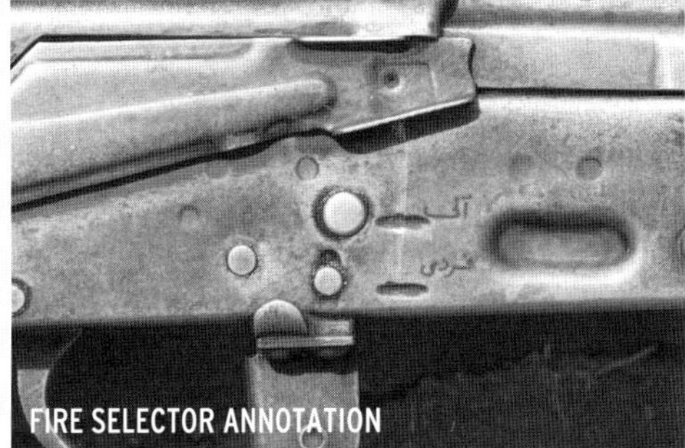

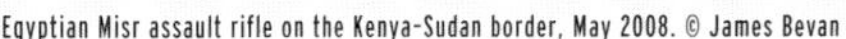
Egyptian Misr assault rifle on the Kenya-Sudan border, May 2008. © James Bevan

Two lessons may be drawn from the case presented in Box 3.1. First, the person recording the information does not have to be an expert to record information that can later be used to identify the weapon. Second, an expert may be able to make a positive identification by cross-referencing weapon characteristics and marks—particularly if the person recording the information records any mark, symbol, or letter in full, as it appears on the weapon.

Manufacturers' marks

Factories identify their products by marking them. Manufacturers' marks range from the name of the factory, written in plain text, to symbols and numerical codes. For example, the Serbian manufacturer Zastava uses both plain text and a symbol to brand its M70 assault rifles (see Figure 3.5). Other manufacturers use symbols and/or numerical combinations, as shown in Figure 3.6, which pictures a Chinese manufacturer's symbol featuring the number 66 inside a triangle.

Figure 3.5 Two varieties of the Zastava factory mark

Illustrations: © James Bevan

Most factories or manufacturing countries brand weapons with their own marks. The *International Tracing Instrument* notes that states are required to provide 'unique user-friendly marking with simple geometric symbols in combination with a numeric and/or alphanumeric code, permitting ready identification by all States of the country of manufacture' (UNGA, 2005a, para. 8(a)).

Table 3.3 Manufacturers' marks on various Kalashnikov-pattern assault rifles[10]

Proof mark	Country of origin
10	Bulgaria
66 五六式	China (Type 56 model)[a]
١٩٧٢ ١.١٢٣.٤	Egypt (date: 1972; factory mark; serial number)
تبوك عيار ٧,٦٢×٣٩ملم	Iraq (calibre; model: Tabuk; factory mark)[b]
68년 산	North Korea (Type 68 model)
	Romania (Cugir factory)[c]
	Russia (Izhevsk factory)

Notes:

[a] The mark translates literally as '5' '6' 'Type'.

[b] From right to left, the Arabic script in the proof mark reads: 'Tabuk' [proof mark] 'Calibre 7.62 x 39 mm'.

[c] The Cugir factory is now part of the ROMARM company.

Illustrations: © James Bevan

Figure 3.6 **Common marks on Kalashnikov-pattern weapon**

External marks:

Manufacturer Model Serial number

RECEIVER (LEFT SIDE)

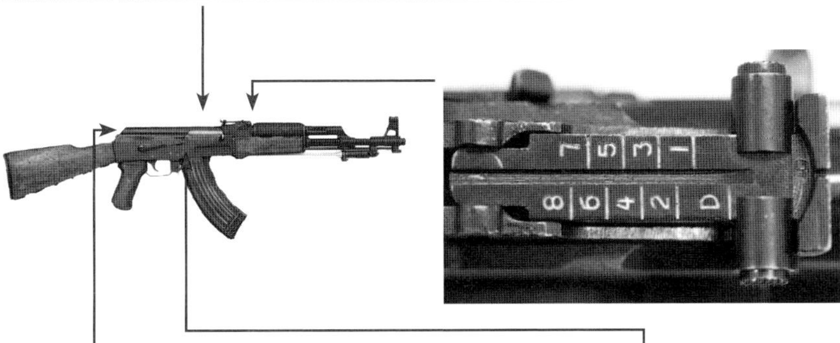

REAR SIGHT (TOP)

RECEIVER COVER (REAR)

FIRE SELECTOR, RECEIVER (RIGHT SIDE)

Internal marks:

BOLT CARRIER

RECOIL SPRING GUIDE

© James Bevan. Weapon courtesy of Royal Armouries, UK

Theoretically, these marks should make identifying a weapon's manufacturer a relatively easy task. However, many such marks cannot be described as either 'user-friendly' or easily identifiable 'by all States', as those reproduced in Table 3.3 illustrate. Many states do not, therefore, fulfill the marking requirements of the ITI.

At present, manufacturers employ such a wide range of diverse marks, including letters, numbers, symbols, and combinations thereof, that identifying them is similar to learning an extended alphabet.

If the manufacturer's mark is cryptic, the person recording the information should note any mark, symbol, or letter in full, as it appears on the weapon, as an expert will be able to identify it at a later time.

Serial number

Successful weapons tracing invariably depends on finding a serial number.[11] The serial number is the only way to identify a weapon uniquely with the naked eye and without extensive forensic research. Once recorded and submitted to a manufacturing, exporting, or importing country or company, the serial number can be used to identify an individual weapon in transfer records. Conflict weapons without serial numbers are relatively rare; in these cases, they have usually been worn away with time and rough handling. In contrast to serial numbers of weapons recovered from crime scenes, those of conflict weapons are seldom removed deliberately.[12]

Table 3.4 Serial number locations on various types of weapon

Weapon type (location)	Example
Pistol (slide)	Type 68, North Korea
Sub-machine gun (receiver)	MAC-10, USA
Rifle (receiver)	G3A3, Germany
Rocket launcher (pistol grip and sight mount)	Type 69, China

© James Bevan. Weapons courtesy of Royal Armouries, UK

Serial numbers appear in different places on weapons, although they are almost always stamped or engraved onto the main body of the weapon—the part of the weapon that is least likely to be removed or replaced (see Table 3.4). Manufacturers normally apply serial numbers to the slide, barrel, or frame of pistols and revolvers. They usually locate serial numbers on the receiver (main body) of sub-machine guns, rifles, assault rifles, and light and heavy machine guns.

For the non-expert the phrase serial number can be confusing because manufacturers use letters in addition to numbers. Establishing which marks (often among many) comprise a serial number is sometimes difficult. The upper image in Table 3.5, for instance, includes a date (1983) and a serial number (NH 6335). The date and serial number were applied at different times in the manufacturing process and the stamping font and positioning differs.

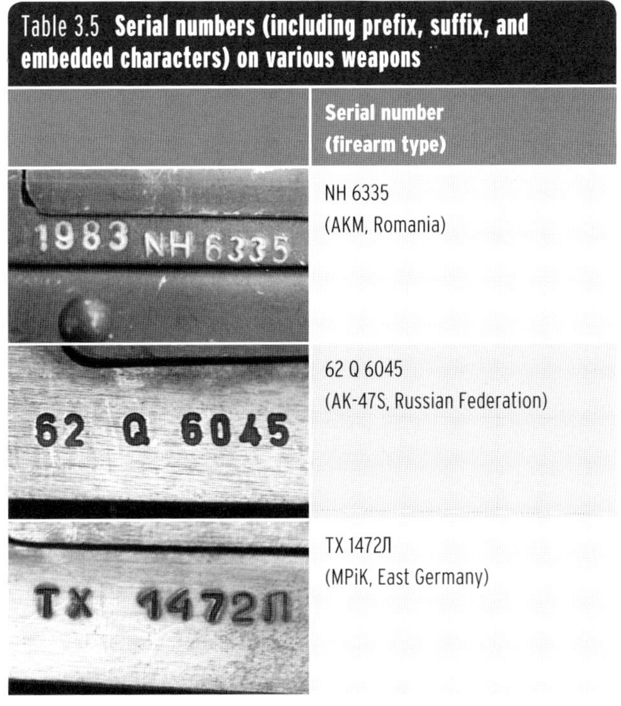

Table 3.5 **Serial numbers (including prefix, suffix, and embedded characters) on various weapons**

	Serial number (firearm type)
1983 NH 6335	NH 6335 (AKM, Romania)
62 Q 6045	62 Q 6045 (AK-47S, Russian Federation)
TX 1472Л	TX 1472Л (MPiK, East Germany)

© James Bevan. Weapons courtesy of Royal Armouries, UK

Furthermore, the serial numbers in Table 3.5 are alphanumeric: in each instance the serial number comprises both letters and numbers—prefix, body, and suffix. A failure to record the prefix and suffix letters ('NH' or 'Л') or embedded letters ('Q'), and the spaces between them, would render the serial number incomplete and make it impossible to find weapons among transfer records.

Box 3.2 **Identifying marks on ammunition**

Manufacturers rarely mark ammunition with a unique serial number, which makes it more difficult to trace than weapons. The most defining piece of information to be found on ammunition is usually a lot or batch number, which specifies the particular production run of the ammunition or of its component parts. In the case of light weapons ammunition, the lot or batch number is usually stencilled or stamped onto the body of the item (see Figure 3.7). Small arms cartridges are generally too small to accommodate such text and, instead, manufacturers apply lot or batch numbers to the packaging material rather than to the individual cartridges (Dreyfus, 2008).

Tracing ammunition by lot or batch number is not as precise as tracing a weapon using a serial number. Thousands of items may be part of the same lot and, therefore, feature identical markings. Moreover, ammunition from the same, identically marked lot might have been shipped to numerous recipients. If one party subsequently retransfers the ammunition illicitly, it is therefore extremely difficult to identify that party using lot markings. Furthermore, because most small arms cartridges are not lot-marked, removing them from their packaging separates them from their identifying lot or batch numbers.

Tracing ammunition usually necessitates finding relatively large numbers of one type of ammunition and then identifying, through a process of elimination, from where it is most likely to have been transferred (Bevan, 2008a). Most ammunition is marked with factory and year codes, which helps to narrow down the possible range of sources—even in the case of otherwise anonymous small arms cartridges (Bevan, 2008b). Complex, high-value ammunition, such as missiles for man-portable air defence systems (MANPADS), may feature unique serial numbers, which allow them to be traced in transfer records (Bevan, 2004).

Figure 3.7 **Marks on a PG-7 warhead and propelling charge (RPG-7 rocket launcher)**

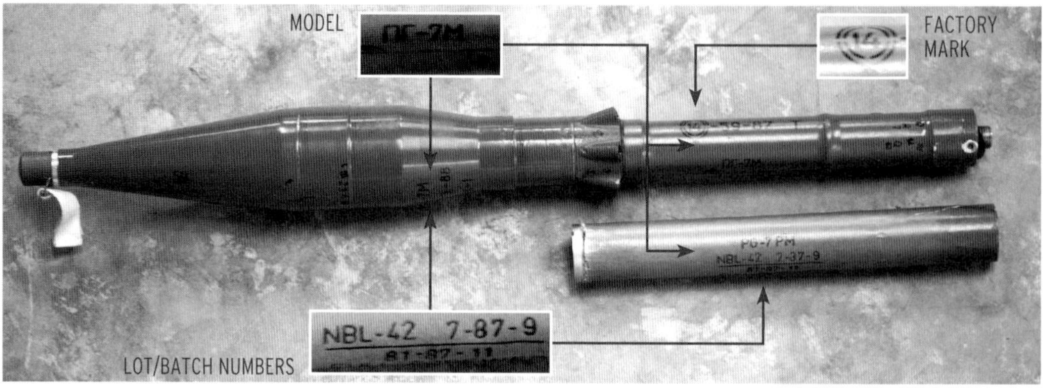

© James Bevan. Weapons courtesy of Royal Armouries, UK

The meaning behind the various configurations of prefix, suffix, and embedded letters is often known only to manufacturers and need not be familiar to people who identify and trace weapons. If the complete serial number, including all marks and symbols, is transmitted to the manufacturer and other record-holders, the weapon can be traced.

Import marks

Import markings are stamps or engravings applied to the weapon at the time of importation. These may be plain text, numbers, or symbols. Figure 3.8 displays the upper left receiver (body) of a Russian Izhevsk-manufactured AKM assault rifle. The marks include the Izhevsk 'arrow in a triangle', the year 1974, and the serial number. However, this weapon also features a triangular, pre-2003 Iraqi military mark between the two rivets. This is an import mark: it signifies that, at some point in the weapon's 34-year history, it was imported into Iraq.

Import marks have the potential to make weapons tracing much easier because they shorten the chain of possible transfers that need to be investigated when establishing how the weapon came to be on the illicit market.

When a weapon is marked only with a manufacturer's mark and serial number, the process of tracing the weapon needs to start with the manufacturer. The manufacturer may retain records that specify the country or entity to which the weapon was first delivered. However, even if these records are available, there is no guarantee that subsequent recipients will have kept similar, detailed export documentation. There is great potential for weapons to 'disappear' from the documentary record after the first transfer.

Figure 3.8 **Iraqi import mark on a Russian-manufactured AKM**

© James Bevan. Weapon courtesy of Royal Armouries, UK

Moreover, because weapons are durable and can remain operational for many decades, manufacturers may not retain records of a particular weapon's manufacture or sale. For instance, a manufacturer may have ceased business without transferring its records to relevant authorities. Paper records may have disintegrated, been lost, or been destroyed after the legal retention period—as little as ten years in some countries. Computerized records save space and lessen the risk that manufacturers will jettison records for space-saving reasons, but many of the world's conflict weapons pre-date the advent of computerized record-keeping systems.

If, however, the weapon has been import-marked, the process of tracing begins with the import-marking country. The chain of potential transfers is therefore significantly reduced and investigations need only focus on what happened to the weapon after it was re-exported from the import-marking country. If the import-marking country keeps records of export recipients, the trace can advance another step (i.e. with the identification of another entity in the transfer chain).

States party to the *UN Firearms Protocol* are required to mark all imported firearms 'permitting identification of the country of import and, where possible, the year of import' (UNGA, 2001, art. 8(1)(b)). The ITI reminds signatories of this obligation (UNGA, 2005a, annexe para. 8(b)). Import records are often retained long after the legal retention period as importers typically need to keep more information than manufacturers—for tax, customs, and consumer protection purposes. As a result, importer records are often maintained considerably longer than manufacturing records.

Tracing is enhanced if an import mark identifies not only the importing country, but also the year of import, as both the *UN Firearms Protocol* and ITI urge. Yet very few states mark weapons at import.

A few states, such as Brazil, Lebanon, and Venezuela, have requested that foreign manufacturers apply import marks to weapons prior to delivery. While these cases are not import marking in the strict sense since the mark is

Box 3.3 Import marking in the United States

The United States Gun Control Act of 1968 requires that licensed importers apply the following permanent marks on firearms: (a) if not already present, an individual serial number, not duplicating any other serial number used by that importer; (b) the model, calibre or gauge, the name of the manufacturer, and, when applicable, the name of the importer; and (c) the name of the country in which the firearm was manufactured and the city and state of the importer (US, 2008, sec. 478.92).

More specifically, the serial number must be marked on the frame or receiver of the firearm. The frame or receiver is the primary structural component of the firearm to which all the other components are attached. The remainder of the markings may be placed on the frame, receiver, or barrel of the weapon. All of the markings must be placed on the firearm permanently by engraving, casting, or stamping in a manner not susceptible to being readily obliterated, altered, or removed (US, 2004, sec. 923(i); US, 2008, sec. 478.92). Although there are many methods for marking firearms, some of them, such as stamping, are more resistant to obliteration or sanitization (OSCE, 2003, sec. II.3.3).

Recognizing that not all manufacturers will impress import markings at the time of manufacture just prior to shipment to the importing country, it is necessary to account for firearms that arrive at the importing state with no import markings at all, but merely manufacturing marks. In the United States, licensed importers are required to mark the firearms they import within 15 days of the date of release of the firearms from customs custody (US, 2008, sec. 478.112(d)). The failure to mark firearms as required by the law and the regulations is punishable by a fine of up to $250,000 and five years' imprisonment (US, 2004, sec. 924(a)(1)(D)).[13] The licence of a manufacturer or importer who willfully fails to mark firearms in accordance with the law and regulations may also be revoked (US, 2004, sec. 923(e)).

On 30 January 2002, the Bureau of Alcohol, Tobacco and Firearms[14] issued a final rule requiring a minimum height (1/16 inch / 1.587 mm) and depth (.003 inch / 0.076 mm) for all serial number markings placed on firearms by licensed importers and manufacturers, and standard depth (.003 inch / 0.076 mm) requirements for all other required markings (US, 2008, sec. 478.92(a)(1)(i); OFR, 2001, p. 40596). The change was designed to facilitate the tracing of firearms because lightly stamped markings wear more easily and become difficult to read. Uniform height and depth requirements help prevent recording and reporting errors and also make it more difficult to alter, remove, or obliterate firearms markings. Despite initial objections over the proposal, the agency and the industry determined that most industry members can and have satisfied the .003 inch depth requirement (OFR, 2001, p. 40598).

Source: Kullman (2008)

applied by the manufacturer-exporter (and not the importer), they serve the same purposes, provided that the mark clearly and correctly identifies the recipient country (and date of import). There is, of course, a small risk that weapons might be diverted while en route to the importing country, which would defeat the purpose of such marking. Yet since sellers are not normally paid until their products are received and approved by the buyer, they have a strong incentive to ensure the safe arrival of the weapons (Kullman, 2008).

The chief arguments against import markings are their cost, a lack of room on a weapon following repeated importations, and the 'defacement' of a rare or expensive firearm. In practice, countries that practice import marking have resolved each of these issues. For example, rare or expensive weapons may be marked in a different manner through a legislative fix known in the United States as a variance. This permits the US regulating agency, on a case-by-case basis, to allow an alternative method of marking a weapon and to require the retention of additional records. In the case of a rare or valuable weapon, markings may be permanently affixed on several parts of the weapon that are not as visible as ordinary marks (e.g. under the grip or under the stock). Certain other weapons may be encased in Lucite or permanently attached to frames that are also marked. Owners of such weapons may be legally required to keep proper records with the weapon at all times (Kullman, 2008).

Weapons tracing requires documentary evidence of transfers.

Weapons tracing

Weapons tracing entails using a weapon's identifying information—model, manufacturer, serial number, and (if available) import mark—to track changes in the weapon's ownership over time. As the following sections note, the tracing process is dependent, first, on the existence of documentary evidence of such changes—'the record-keeping chain'—and, second, on the willingness of parties that might hold such records to cooperate with tracing requests.

Following the record-keeping chain

The record-keeping chain is the entire documentary history of a weapon's transfer from one party to another. Although parts of the chain may be difficult to access, it can identify previous owners or users of a weapon, or reveal entities that were involved in its transfer. There may be many types of documentary evidence in the chain, including:

- **manufacturer's records** compiled by the factory, which document individual weapons, their dates of manufacture, and recipients;
- **quality control records** compiled by a (sometimes independent) organization responsible for ensuring that producers meet manufacturing standards;
- **export documentation** that specifies the recipient of the weapon, including export authorization and end-user certification;[15]
- **packing lists** that detail the weapons contained in boxes, crates, and other shipping containers;
- **shipping documents**, such as bills of lading, with which transport agents (air, land, and sea) acknowledge receipt of goods;
- **import documentation**, such as import licences and any registries of import-marked weapons;
- **transit documentation**, which details the origins and destinations of weapons shipped on or through the territory of a state;[16]
- **proof house records**, which certify a weapon as safe, reliable, or some other criteria (usually upon import, but also if a weapon has been deactivated); and
- **security force inventories**, which record weapons in stock, issued to particular units, or destroyed or demilitarized.

Once in possession of some or all of this documentary information, anyone who wishes to trace a weapon can begin to piece together its history. Manufacturer records may identify the entity to which the weapon was first sold (the first recipient). For example, in 2007, the UN Monitoring Group on Somalia requested that the Russian Federation trace two serial numbers found on MANPADS missiles.[17] The Russian Federation responded:

> *missile 9M39 from party 03-95 with number 03268 was produced in Russia in 1995 [. . .] This missile was shipped to Eritrea in the same year through the state company 'Rosvooruzhenie'.* (UNSC, 2008, para. 106)

Similarly, export records obtained from the first recipient may reveal a second recipient. Packing lists and shipping documentation may do likewise. In all cases, however, two factors condition the success of efforts to follow the record-keeping chain: (1) the accuracy and comprehensiveness of information specifying the model, manufacturer, serial number, and, where available, importer of the weapon, and (2) access to that documentation.

Cooperation in tracing

Cooperation is a prerequisite for successful conflict tracing. Following the record-keeping chain usually involves contacting manufacturers, exporting states, or any of a host of potential intermediaries that may have been responsible for a weapon's transfer. If the trace is to succeed in identifying the weapon's last legal owner or point of diversion, each of the parties needs to cooperate by releasing information that specifies the recipient of each transfer.

States responded to only 30 per cent of UN tracing requests.

Conflict tracing differs from traces conducted by domestic law enforcement authorities—so-called 'crime gun tracing'. In domestic traces, police departments may have to request information from another country, but, more often than not, their tracing activities begin and end at home. Weapons used in crime—particularly when civilian ownership in the country is widespread—frequently originate in the domestic civilian market (Bevan, 2008c, pp. 62–66). In these cases, law enforcement authorities consult firearm registration, sale, or resale records to determine the weapon's last legal owner.

Conflict tracing poses additional challenges. Countries in conflict or recovering from conflict often lack the records (import, sale, and licensing) necessary to conduct a domestic trace. Professional police forces, which might otherwise be instrumental in conducting a trace, are often in disarray. Under these circumstances, those maintaining order in conflict or post-conflict zones (e.g. international peacekeeping forces) or investigating the supply of arms to a country (e.g. UN sanctions panels) are best placed to trace conflict weapons. Their starting point is usually outside the country in question. In most cases, the only evidence presented to an investigator is the weapon itself, which means that the manufacturer (or, if known, most recent importer) is the first point of contact and the tracing process has to 'work forward' through the record-keeping chain.

There is, however, no comprehensive mechanism to facilitate conflict trace requests. When organizations or groups such as UN sanctions panels require information on weapon transfers to conflict zones, they tend to make ad hoc requests to national governments, export agencies, manufacturers, or other entities. The results are mixed. At present, a lack of cooperation by manufacturers and states is the norm rather than the exception. Between 2006 and 2007, for instance, states responded to only around 30 per cent of UN sanctions panels' tracing requests.[18]

Conflict tracing would prove more successful if major weapons-producing or exporting states cooperated more closely with local, regional, or UN-mandated investigators. Enhanced cooperation could be incorporated into existing law enforcement agreements at regional or international levels.[19] Among other things, such agreements would specify the modalities for accessing and using sensitive information.[20]

At the international level, INTERPOL facilitates cooperation between national police forces, including for weapons tracing, through its global communications system I-24/7. As of the end of 2008, a total of 514 agencies and organizations had access to the I-24/7 network.[21] These included the National Central Bureaus (NCBs) that serve as designated INTERPOL contact points within 186 member countries, as well as other law enforcement entities, customs offices, and international organizations specifically authorized to use the network. Law enforcement officials typically forward a tracing request to the country's INTERPOL NCB. The latter, using I-24/7, then dispatches the enquiry to the NCB in the country identified as the manufacturer or most recent importer of the weapon. That NCB then forwards the tracing request to the record-holders within the country, such as manufacturers or export authorities.

INTERPOL recently strengthened its weapons tracing infrastructure.

INTERPOL recently strengthened its weapons tracing infrastructure. In January 2009, INTERPOL's I-24/7 network introduced a new firearm trace form that standardizes the tracing process for member countries and enhances the organization's ability to analyse firearm trace data. The form also has a link to the INTERPOL Firearms Reference Table (IFRT), another component of the I-24/7 network. The IFRT was developed in cooperation with the Royal Canadian Mounted Police to address the widespread problem of improper firearm identification. It provides users with more than 250,000 firearm references and 57,000 high-quality digital images of firearms in order to assist them in properly identifying a firearm.

UN entities such as the civilian police components of peacekeeping operations and sanctions groups also access INTERPOL systems in the context of conflict tracing. A cooperation agreement concluded between the UN and INTERPOL in July 1997 provides the necessary legal framework for this cooperation (INTERPOL and UN, 1997). Both the UN Interim Administration Mission in Kosovo and the UN Mission in Liberia have been granted access to the INTERPOL communications network and databases, including to aspects that facilitate the exchange of information for weapons tracing (INTERPOL and UN, 2002; INTERPOL, 2005).[22]

WEAPONS COLLECTION: POST-CONFLICT RECORD-KEEPING

This chapter has noted that people decide to trace conflict weapons because they notice something that is worthy of further investigation. This entails vigilance, but there are other situations in which gathering tracing-relevant information is a much more passive process.

Weapons collection initiatives are one such activity. By recording details of all collected weapons, they provide a valuable pool of tracing information, even in the absence of weapons identification experts. If the weapons are recorded in sufficient detail, an expert will be able to identify any trends in the types and numbers of weapons listed. An expert review of many weapons (potentially tens of thousands) can reveal a preponderance of weapons that originate from a single factory or numerous weapons with consecutive serial numbers—strong indicators of single, possibly illicit, consignments of weapons.

Post-conflict weapons collection programmes are not designed with weapons tracing in mind, but they should record weapons in sufficient detail to trace them. The purpose of recording collected weapons is to verify that each weapon is disposed of properly, be they destroyed, demilitarized, or transferred to legitimate users, such as the security forces. Verification requires identifying each weapon uniquely, which means recording the same information that is required for weapons tracing: model, manufacturer, serial number, and (where applicable) import mark. Most

Box 3.4 Verification

Verification is the monitoring of weapons that have been stockpiled temporarily, pending disposal. It is designed to ensure that weapons are correctly disposed of and not stolen, misplaced, or diverted to illicit markets in the meantime. Verification is similar to the accounting processes that states with effective stockpile management systems use to monitor their stockpiles (Bevan, 2008a).

Verification necessitates compiling records that uniquely identify each weapon, which means that weapons must be registered by serial number. It is also preferable to record the specific type (model and manufacturer) of weapon for two practical reasons. First, weapons collection lists can become the basis of more permanent national stockpile inventories, particularly when post-conflict weapons are absorbed into a country's security force stockpiles (SEESAC, 2006). In these cases, recording types becomes important because security forces need to have qualitative information about the weapons at their disposal. Second, from the perspective of weapons collection initiatives, listing weapon types increases the chances of diagnosing security breaches.

Recording weapons in detail is not just preferable from the perspective of analysing trends in their distribution; it can also help secure those weapons against (re-)entering illicit markets.

weapons collection initiatives, therefore, attempt to record this information. If it is recorded accurately, the information can be used for a variety of purposes, including:

1. to identify any illicit weapons transfers that might have provided weapons to parties during a conflict (possibly in breach of UN arms embargoes);
2. to generate a baseline of the types of weapons present and thereby facilitate identification of future influxes of weapons that might allow spoilers to threaten peace, security, and peace-building;
3. to assess the age and quality of collected weapons in order to establish whether initiatives have successfully reduced the number of weapons in circulation—and not merely removed the old and less desirable models;
4. to monitor possible arms and ammunition losses from peacekeeping forces and to facilitate recovery of weapons that have been lost or stolen; and
5. to verify the destruction and disposal of weapons that have been collected during arms reduction initiatives, such as DDR programmes, arms seizures, and weapons amnesties (see Box 3.4).

Between 1998 and 2008, UN and associated initiatives collected around 330,000 weapons and made records of most of them.[23] These records are, potentially, of great value for efforts to understand the illicit trade in weapons and for monitoring the progress of countries recovering from conflict—including the efficacy of arms reduction initiatives.

Process

Compiling records of collected weapons is a simple process but requires the person conducting the registration to record all the information necessary to identify each weapon—model, manufacturer, and serial number. Many weapons registration initiatives fail to do this.

Table 3.6 Extract from a list of 348 weapons collected by the Burundian army, 2005-07

Série	Type	Numéro
#7	K.V. Ord	3809709
#8	K.V. Ord	6737
#9	K.V. Ord	17-0635

Source: Burundi (2007)

Table 3.7 Numbers of traceable weapons listed in records collated by UN agencies

Programme	Implementing agency	Number of weapons recorded*	Number of traceable weapons**	Percentage of traceable weapons
Republic of Congo (2006)	UN Development Programme	1,308	0	0.0
Liberia (2004)	UN Mission in Liberia	21,630	5,490	25.4
Kosovo (2000–02)	UN Development Programme, Kosovo Police Service	4,867	1,455	29.9
Total/average		**27,805**	**6,945**	**25.0**

* Figures exclude ammunition and ancillary items.

** The number of weapons that were recorded in sufficient detail to make a tracing request (without guarantee of success)—including model (and, or by extension, manufacturer) and serial number. The numbers are generous because they include some records that have multiple, successive serial numbers but no model designation—on the assumption that, with considerable research, the manufacturer of the weapons could probably be identified.

Sources: **Republic of Congo:** email correspondence with Hervé Gonsolin, CTP Armes Légères et Violence Armée, UNDP Burundi-BINUB, 2 September 2008; **Liberia:** UNMIL (2005); **Kosovo:** KPIS (2002)

A case in point is the Burundian army's collection of 348 weapons from former rebel groups in several locations in 2005–07. Of the 348 weapons recorded, only 40 could be identified by model, manufacturer, and serial number.[24] Most of the weapons were recorded simply as 'K.V. Ord', or ordinary Kalashnikov (see Table 3.6). The serial numbers were incompletely documented and, even when these were complete, it is impossible to establish where the weapons were manufactured because of the absence of accurate model designations and factory marks.

Burundi does not appear to be an exceptional case. Table 3.7 displays the results of an entry-by-entry review of around 28,000 weapons collated by UN agencies during three weapons collection initiatives. It shows that 75 per cent of the 28,000 weapons are recorded with insufficient accuracy to enable a trace. Most of the records (probably around 50 per cent) cannot be used to analyse the types and origins of weapons in circulation more broadly because they do not specify the model of weapon with sufficient accuracy.

These figures are compiled from a relatively small sample, but they suggest that there are serious flaws in current approaches to weapons registration. If they are representative of most weapons collection initiatives, then perhaps half of all weapons registered in post-conflict collection initiatives (more than 160,000 pieces of evidence) cannot be identified by model (let alone serial number) and their countries of origin cannot, therefore, be established.

Such inadequacies may help explain why the Small Arms Survey has found no evidence to suggest that any weapons registration lists compiled during 45 weapons collection and DDR programmes between 1998 and 2008 were analysed comprehensively. The most detailed analyses consisted of aggregating relative numbers of generic weapon types (i.e. pistols or machine guns) into brief reports. In many cases, however, these simple aggregations were inaccurate due to weapon misclassification during the registration process.

Improving the UN's approach to weapons registration

How might these issues be addressed? The three programmes listed in Table 3.7 managed only 25 per cent accuracy, but they achieved that accuracy rate without their personnel having been trained in weapons identification. Nor were the registration systems designed to generate information for tracing purposes. The more successful aspects of these programmes therefore provide some valuable insight into how the inaccuracy of weapons registration might be addressed in the future.

Republic of the Congo:[25] Led by the UN Development Programme (UNDP), the collection initiative recovered 1,308 weapons from November 2005 to March 2007.[26] The recording system was well-planned with predefined entry fields for generic weapon types, such as *fusil* (rifle) and *fusil mitrailleur* (assault rifle). The serial numbers were diligently recorded and reproduced with prefix, suffix, and embedded letters, including the faithful reproduction of Cyrillic characters. The database was designed to provide a breakdown of the relative quantities of weapon types (pistols, rifles, grenades, etc.) recovered for UNDP's reporting purposes, and it fulfilled that requirement. Unfortunately, however, the information is not sufficient for weapons tracing because the predefined entry system did not allow for entries of the specific model (and hence manufacturer) of each weapon collected.

Liberia: This list was compiled under the auspices of the UN Mission in Liberia between June and December 2004. Although the quality of data varies, some of the personnel responsible for identifying and recording weapons had significant expertise—often specifying the model of weapon with sufficient precision to identify the manufacturer. Other weapons registrars were apparently less able. For example, 6,839 weapons are entered simply as 'AK-47', followed by a serial number. One factor in the programme's favour was the prevalence of 2,664 Zastava-manufactured M70AB2 and 1,928 Chinese Type 56, 56-1, and 56-2 assault rifles, which, in each case, feature a stamped, plain text model designation. This made it easier for the personnel involved to identify and record the specific model of weapon.

An expert can identify weapons if marks are recorded comprehensively.

Kosovo: This list was compiled by the Kosovo Police Service, with the support of UNDP, between 2000 and 2002. It features a relatively large number of entry fields, but the individual entries differ in quality, which suggests that the personnel involved had varying degrees of expertise. Many of the records are misclassified (for example, assault rifles listed as pistols) and model designations are frequently recorded in place of serial numbers (often without the serial numbers present). In addition, the records include 810 'unknown' weapons, even though information that was incorrectly entered under the field 'serial number' identifies them as common types. As in Liberia, the weapons collectors were aided by the prevalence of weapons that were marked with model designations, such as Zastava-manufactured weapons (approximately 700) and numerous civilian-market models (usually clearly branded with model and manufacturer).

The most significant trend in the three programmes was that personnel were far more likely to compile accurate records when the weapons were clearly marked with a model designation, such as 'Serbian/Yugoslavian M70AB2' or 'Chinese Type 56' assault rifles. Conversely, weapons without model designations were least likely to be registered accurately. This means that most registration personnel did not identify the weapons, but rather reported what was written on them. Unfortunately, because they only recorded what they believed to be relevant, many important identifying marks were not recorded during the registration process. Very often this is fatal to weapons identification, but not always. Even though registration personnel recorded numerous weapons as unknown, additional information (even entered in the wrong places, such as in 'serial number' entry fields) can sometimes be used to identify them—as was the case during this review (see Table 3.2).

An expert can usually identify weapons if the relevant marks are recorded comprehensively, even if the person recording them does not make a positive identification. Unfortunately, many existing registration systems are limiting and discourage expansive recording of marks, as evidenced in the three weapons collection programmes reviewed above. A greater number of data entry fields (for example, seven in the case of Kosovo) made it more likely that personnel would record important information—even if that information was recorded under the wrong heading.

Taken as a whole, these observations suggest that registration problems occurred due to the convergence of two factors: poor training and the imperfect design of registration systems. Personnel had not been trained to record every

Box 3.5 UN weapons registration processes

The UN Integrated Disarmament, Demobilization and Reintegration Standards (IDDRS) require that all DDR programmes compile records that are 'accurate enough to ensure that every weapon registered as handed in must also be registered as destroyed' (UNDDR, 2006, sect. 4.10, p. 20). However, the IDDRS provides no guidance on how to record this information. Instead, it refers users to another UN document, entitled RMDS/G 04.20 (SEESAC, 2006, sect. 5.2, paras. b-c).

The RMDS notes that weapons data should include 'the quantities, types, serial numbers and sources of legal and surrendered weapons' (para. c). Unfortunately, the source does not explain how personnel should identify the 'types' of weapons, or how they should identify and record a serial number or other identifying features. The only expertise it calls for is for staff members to be 'trained in the use of computers' (para. b).

Neither the IDDRS nor RMDS, therefore, recognizes that personnel require training if they are to record weapons accurately. Each assumes that recording accurate information requires only technical infrastructure, such as accounting systems and computers; however, as anyone skilled in data management knows, no matter how good the system, its success rests on the quality of information entered.

A closer look at the systems on offer also reveals some fundamental failings. Both the IDDRS and RMDS refer practitioners to the UN DREAM database–an integrated system designed to support DDR processes and record weapons. This referral overlooks the need for the person using the system to have basic weapons expertise. Indeed, DREAM requires that the user enter various pieces of information including:

1. manufacturer
2. country
3. make
4. model
5. calibre
6. barrel length
7. action
8. magazine capacity

As noted above, many weapons do not have the information written on them to allow a non-specialist to complete fields 1-6 without inferring (or guessing) the correct information. Moreover, fields 7 and 8 are superfluous in a registration system and it is unclear why they appear in the database.

Because it is required by the IDDRS, weapons registration has become a formal part of UN DDR programmes, but without appropriate guidance UN personnel cannot fulfil its requirements. These observations suggest a need to revise existing UN approaches to weapons registration.

mark that was visible on weapons and were therefore unsure of what they should record. This was compounded by registration systems that did not accommodate comprehensive recording of marks and instead limited personnel, forcing them to make their own, often erroneous, judgements as to what constituted relevant information.

It is clear that registration systems need to be redesigned to accommodate more information that is of greater relevance. Personnel also need to receive guidance on the types of information that they need to record. The UN Integrated Disarmament, Demobilization and Reintegration Standards (IDDRS) do not currently specify adequate training requirements or provide sufficient basis for the development of registration systems (see Box 3.5).

Revising the system

No system is infallible. The people who collect weapons will never be able to make accurate records of every weapon they encounter. The challenge is to move the quality of weapons records beyond the 25 per cent accuracy range. This is desirable from the perspective of understanding illicit trade and necessary for verifying that weapons have been correctly disposed of.

To this end, the redesign of registration systems and the provision of adequate training are two fundamental improvements that need to be instituted. But it is also important to recognize that weapons collection records are valuable evidence and, if they are to be of utility, they need to be processed by an expert in order to assess their veracity and to identify significant trends in the distribution of weapons.

System redesign: Registration systems do not need to be complex, but they need to be redesigned to prioritize different types of information. Many entry fields—such as *calibre, manufacturer,* or *country of origin*—are unrealistic because they require information that is not written on the weapon. These could be replaced with fields that accept observable information—such as marks, symbols, or design features—that requires no background expertise to record. A photograph of each weapon's markings would help to verify whether the information has been entered accurately and confirm model identification. Many previous collection initiatives rely on spreadsheet systems such as Microsoft Excel, which are adequate for the task of recording all necessary information and are easy to amend. Dedicated databases, such as the UN DREAM system, could be adapted to include new fields with relative ease (including photographs). A model recording system, which has been designed to facilitate the recording of complex marks, is annexed to this chapter.

Basic training: The fact that some existing registries contain 25 per cent traceable records is evidence that, if personnel are able to recognize marks as meaningful, then they need little prompting to record them. However, personnel need to be trained to make records of all marks (regardless of whether they understand them) to help identify the precise model of weapon, in addition to recording serial numbers accurately (with prefix, suffix, and embedded letters). Weapons collection personnel need only know where to look for this information—something that can be accomplished in a matter of hours.

Expert analysis: Relatively few people have the expertise to analyse weapons collection lists. The task requires knowledge of weapons and the means of identifying them (marks and design), but also experience of broad trends in the global distribution of weapons. It is clear that demand for such expertise is intermittent because few weapons collection initiatives are in operation at any one time. Expertise is nevertheless necessary if the UN and other organizations involved in weapons collection are to maximize the value of weapons registration.

Table 3.8 Improving UN weapons records: projected costs (USD)

Weapons recorded	Weapons collection teams[a]	Expert analysis (500 weapons per day)		Support material[b]	Training		Total costs		Cost per weapon	
		Lower	Upper		Lower[c]	Upper[d]	Lower	Upper	Lower	Upper
1,000	1	1,200	1,600	120	1,320	3,360	2,640	5,080	2.64	5.08
10,000	2	12,000	16,000	200	2,200	5,600	14,400	21,800	1.44	2.18
100,000	20	120,000	160,000	2,000	22,000	56,000	144,000	218,000	1.44	2.18
Average cost per weapon									**1.84**	**3.15**

Note: The speed of expert analysis (weapons analysed per day) would be significantly enhanced by better quality records.

[a] Large collection programmes often have collection teams located in different areas. Training costs are assumed to be identical for each team (assumed here to number four persons). Each team is allocated an arbitrary weapons record of 5,000.

[b] Covers all publication costs (USD 50,000) for a peer-reviewed pocket guide to recording weapons, broken down into cost per guide (USD 25), with four copies issued to each team.

[c] Budget for one day (eight hours) of training, including the costs of short-distance air travel and accommodation for the trainer, plus remuneration at expert consultancy rates.

[d] Budget for one day (eight hours) of training, including the costs of long-distance travel and accommodation for the trainer, plus remuneration at expert consultancy rates.

Table 3.8 presents a cost estimate for the development of registration systems, training, and expert analysis to augment existing weapons collection processes. It suggests that improving weapons registration would range from USD 5 per weapon for the smallest programmes to USD 1.5 per weapon for larger initiatives—a range that reflects economies of scale.

System redesign, basic training, and expert analysis represent relatively minor investments when compared to overall international expenditure on weapons collection and DDR programmes. A review of four UN registration processes, presented in Table 3.9, suggests existing expenditures of between USD 2 and USD 6 per weapon. This expenditure (which is difficult to disaggregate from most programme expenditure) includes the cost of someone observing and recording the weapon's marks as well as the cost of maintaining a weapons registration database.

Although the additional costs of improving the system listed in Table 3.8 would, perhaps, double existing registration expenditure, it is important to recognize that these crucial improvements would comprise only a small fraction of disarmament budgeting. For example, an average increase of USD 3–4 per weapon, if applied to the 330,000 weapons collected between 1998 and 2008, would total USD 1.3 million[27]—a relatively small (0.06 per cent) addition to the USD 2.3 billion spent on weapons collection and DDR programmes in that period.

The case for recording and comprehensively analysing collected weapons can be stated quite simply:

> If weapons collection initiatives aim to reduce the impact of illicit weapons in circulation, would it not be valuable to know—by comprehensively analysing the age and types of weapons collected—whether new (or new types of) weapons are entering troubled regions and undermining those initiatives?

A slight increase in expenditure during weapons collection and destruction programmes would increase the international community's ability to monitor and trace weapons considerably. Such a measure could prove an important step in efforts to curb illicit proliferation.

Table 3.9 The costs of UN weapons records

Country programme	Lead agency	Number of collected weapons	Cost of compiling weapons records (USD)	Cost per weapon of compiling records (USD)
Bosnia and Herzegovina	UNDP	332	2,128	6
Republic of Congo	UNDP	1,308	7,137	5
Croatia*	UNDP	16,000	31,535	2
Nepal	UN Mission in Nepal (UNMIN)	3,475	8,303	2
Total/average		**21,115**	**49,103**	**4**

* Calculated for a seven-month period (December 2007–June 2008).

Note: Some of the costs of UN-organized weapons collection initiatives are borne by implementing partners. For example, local police or military forces often physically collect and record the weapons. Local partners may only receive limited per diems for volunteers and interns (MUP and UNDP, 2007, p. 7). These costs are included in the above table.

Sources: Bosnia and Hezegovina: UNDP (2007); correspondence with Amna Berbic, Chief Technical Advisor, Small Arms Control in BiH, EU Arms Control Programme, UNDP Bosnia and Herzegovina, 2 September 2008; Republic of Congo: correspondence with Hervé Gonsolin, CTP Armes Légères et Violence Armée, UNDP Burundi-BINUB, 2 September 2008; Croatia: UNDP (2008); correspondence with Leo Lisac, Project Assistant, Arms Control and Security, UNDP Bosnia and Herzegovina, 22 September 2008; Nepal: correspondence with Ingmar Hermansson, UNMIN, 3 September 2008

CONCLUSION

Conflict tracing is an emerging field of international interest. Yet despite spending more than USD 2 billion on initiatives to disarm post-conflict societies, the international community continues to devote too little attention to understanding how the weapons that are used in armed conflict arrive there in the first place and how they might continue to arrive in the future.

The monitoring, recording, and tracing of weapons offers the international community a vital opportunity to better understand the illicit trade in small arms and light weapons. Today, however, organizations such as the UN do not allocate sufficient resources to these activities.

Weapons can serve as evidence. In any conflict, the weapons that proliferate can provide the core physical information necessary to start a tracing process and, ultimately, to identify and apprehend the parties that trade illicit weapons. But to tap this potential, it is important that the relevant organizations identify and record weapons comprehensively and initiate weapons traces once they have done so. Two fundamental obstacles currently stand in the way of realizing this objective.

First, weapons identification skills remain restricted to a handful of individuals. The expertise of these individuals cannot easily be replicated, but it can be used to improve the ways in which international organizations—particularly those involved in weapons collection—record and identify weapons. This is not yet happening.

Second, the cooperation required to trace conflict weapons—among states, international organizations, and commercial entities—remains nascent and ad hoc. Requests for information inevitably involve a broad range of actors, but relevant organizations have given little thought as to how trace requests might be better coordinated.

Neither of these obstacles is insurmountable. This chapter provides firm indication that, given minimal resources and training, most people can record weapons in sufficient detail to allow an expert to identify them positively and uniquely. Once this process is complete, a trace request can proceed on firm evidence.

The current lack of cooperation in tracing requests is, arguably, a greater challenge. Existing mechanisms, such as those of INTERPOL, offer unrealized potential. Standing in the way of such potential advances, however, is the fact that international organizations—and ultimately states—need to recognize the value of conflict tracing and act on that knowledge. ■

ANNEXE 3.1: A MODEL RECORDING SYSTEM

This system is exclusively designed to record information that allows an expert to identify the weapon. The person recording the information can support the analysis by contributing an opinion (on type and model), but the identification is based primarily on the marks observed on the weapon and its physical properties. The entries are supported by a photograph. The system does not rely on the expertise of the person recording the information. In this case, the weapon is a 1974 Russian, Ishevsk-manufactured AKM assault rifle.

© James Bevan. Weapon courtesy of Royal Armouries, UK

Type of weapon (if known):	Kalashnikov		
Model of weapon (if known):	?		
Overall length of weapon:	88	**cm**	
Brief description (include fixed or folding stock, bayonets, sights, etc.):	Rifle with a fixed stock		
Colour of furniture/main body:	Wooden		
Marks/symbols (main group; as they appear, from left to right, or top to bottom, or around the headstamp of a cartridge):		859	
	Triangle with an arrow inside	1974	285859
Marks/symbols (other):	859	Russian characters on other side	

LIST OF ABBREVIATIONS

DDR	Disarmament, demobilization, and reintegration
IDDRS	UN Integrated Disarmament, Demobilization and Reintegration Standards
IFRT	INTERPOL Firearms Reference Table
INTERPOL	The International Criminal Police Organization
ITI	*International Tracing Instrument* (*International Instrument to Enable States to Identify and Trace, in a Timely and Reliable Manner, Illicit Small Arms and Light Weapons*)
MANPADS	Man-portable air defence system(s)
NCB	National Central Bureau (of INTERPOL)
UNDP	UN Development Programme

ENDNOTES

1 The Panel of Experts was appointed pursuant to para. 25 of Security Council resolution 1478 (2003) concerning Liberia.

2 Security Council resolution 1343 (UNSC, 2001, para. 5).

3 See McDonald (2008) for an overview of forged end-user certification.

4 For an analysis of the ITI's provisions, see McDonald (2006).

5 The ITI is structured on this premise. See UNGA (2005a, secs. III–V).

6 See UNGA (2008, annexe, para. 3(c)).

7 Furthermore, tracing that relies exclusively on records of serial numbers could potentially retrieve several weapons that share serial numbers although their models differ.

8 Organizations such as the Norwegian Defence International Centre, the Kofi Annan International Peacekeeping Training Centre in Ghana, and the Pearson Peacekeeping Centre in Canada have yet to introduce weapons identification training. See NODEFIC (n.d.), KAIPTC (n.d.), and PPC (n.d.).

9 The Small Arms Survey has received tracing-related requests from UN panels covering the Democratic Republic of the Congo (DRC), Liberia, and Sudan. It has also been asked to identify weapons and ammunition for UN Development Programme country offices, disarmament, demobilization, and reintegration programmes, and a number of civilian weapons collections.

10 An extensive list of Kalashnikov-pattern proof marks can be found in the Small Arms Survey's Weapons ID Sheet entitled 'Kalashnikov-pattern Weapons: Identifying Marks' at <http://weaponsid.smallarmssurvey.org/media/products/23/Kalashnikov_Marks.pdf?SASid=j2lfhiuu8frnbgrsg3une3f3m2>.

11 There are exceptions, but these are rare. For instance, the weapon could be so specialized (such as a made-to-order, customized sniper rifle) that the manufacturer could determine, without consulting serial number records, to which party it was transferred.

12 The author has viewed many thousands of military weapons, held by numerous parties to armed conflict, and has found few weapons that were not marked with a serial number (however faded or damaged). Reviews of thousands of weapons collection records (discussed later in this chapter) also suggest that the intentional removal of serial numbers is uncommon in the context of armed conflict. The probable reason is that, in contrast to crime situations in which criminals (notably illegal sellers) may fear discovery by law enforcement officials, most combatants have little reason to believe that their weapons will be subject to investigation.

13 As the firearms statute does not specify the amount of the fine, the default maximum for all US felony offences applies, namely USD 250,000 for individuals (US, 2007, sec. 3571(b)(3)).

14 The agency's name was changed to the Bureau of Alcohol, Tobacco, Firearms and Explosives in 2003.

15 See McDonald (2008).

16 See Wood and Peleman (1999, p. 119).

17 The Monitoring Group notes that it 'succeeded in obtaining the serial numbers of two SA-7/SA-18 surface-to-air missiles' (UNSC, 2008, para. 104).

18 The requests were not general enquiries about weapons submitted to manufacturers or national authorities. They included only specific weapon-tracing requests that were reported in UN panel reports on the following countries: Somalia (3 requests, 3 replies); DRC (18 requests, 2 replies); Côte d'Ivoire (1 request,1 reply); and Sudan (1 request,1 reply). See UNSC (2007c, para. 78; 2007d, paras. 20–22; 2007b, para. 27; 2008, paras. 104–05).

19 Bilateral agreement is another possibility, but the transnational nature of illicit arms trafficking makes multilateral frameworks for cooperation far more useful.

20 This issue is also regulated by para. 15 of the ITI (UNGA, 2005a; 2005b).

21 Correspondence with INTERPOL official, December 2008.

22 There have also been agreements for access with the international criminal courts for Rwanda and Yugoslavia, as well as the Special Court for Sierra Leone. Correspondence with INTERPOL official, January 2009.

23 Based on a review of 45 weapons collection initiatives (some multiple) in Afghanistan, Angola, Bosnia and Herzegovina, Burundi, Cambodia, Central African Republic, Chad, Colombia, Côte d'Ivoire, Croatia, Djibouti, DRC, Eritrea, Ethiopia, Ghana, Guatemala, Guinea–Bissau, Haiti, Indonesia (Aceh), Iraq, Kenya, Kosovo, Liberia, the former Yugoslav Republic of Macedonia, Montenegro, Nepal, Nicaragua–Honduras, Niger, Papua New Guinea, the Philippines, Republic of the Congo, Rwanda, Serbia and Montenegro, Sierra Leone, Solomon Islands, Somalia, Sudan, Timor–Leste, and Uganda.

24 These included 33 Chinese Type 56 and 56-1 assault rifles (indicated by the serial prefixes '56' and '56-1'); six G3 rifles manufactured by Fábrica Nacional de Munições de Armas Legeiras, Portugal (indicated by the prefix 'FMP'); and one Belgian MAG general-purpose machine gun, with the designation FN.

25 Complete list (with personal information omitted) supplied by UNDP Burundi. Email correspondence with Hervé Gonsolin, CTP Armes Légères et Violence Armée, UNDP Burundi–BINUB, 2 September 2008.

26 Ammunition (1,502 collective entries, totalling 628,937 items) was listed separately.

27 This figure is an extrapolation of the average cost per weapon (USD 4) presented in Table 3.9 to the 330,000 weapons collected and recorded in UN and other weapons collection programmes.

BIBLIOGRAPHY

Bevan, James. 2004. 'Big Issue, Big Problem? MANPADS.' In Small Arms Survey, ed. *Small Arms Survey 2004: Rights at Risk.* Oxford: Oxford University Press, pp. 77–97.

—. 2008a. 'Stockpile Management: Accounting.' In James Bevan, ed. *Conventional Ammunition in Surplus: A Reference Guide.* Geneva: Small Arms Survey, pp. 49–60.

—. 2008b. *Ammunition Tracing Kit: Protocols and Procedures for Recording Small-Calibre Ammunition.* Geneva: Small Arms Survey.

—. 2008c. 'Arsenals Adrift: Arms and Ammunition Diversion.' In Small Arms Survey, ed. *Small Arms Survey 2008: Risk and Resilience.* Cambridge: Cambridge University Press, pp. 42–75.

— and Pablo Dreyfus. 2008. 'Small Arms Ammunition Lot Marking.' In James Bevan, ed. *Conventional Ammunition in Surplus: A Reference Guide.* Geneva: Small Arms Survey. pp. 154-159.

Burundi. 2007. 'Comptage des armes.' Bujumbura: République du Burundi, Forces Armées, Etat-major général intègre.

Deutsche Welle. 2008. 'Georgians Illegally Armed with German Weapons, Report Says.' 17 August. <http://www.dw-world.de/dw/article/0,,3571263,00.html?maca=en-kalenderblatt_topthema_englisch-347-rdf>

Dreyfus, Pablo. 2008. 'Conventional Ammunition Marking.' In James Bevan, ed. *Conventional Ammunition in Surplus: A Reference Guide.* Geneva: Small Arms Survey, pp. 31–42.

Glatz, Anne-Kathrin and Lora Lumpe. 2007. 'Probing the Grey Area: Irresponsible Small Arms Transfers.' In Small Arms Survey, ed. *Small Arms Survey 2007: Guns and the City.* Cambridge: Cambridge University Press, pp. 73–115.

INTERPOL. 2005. Resolution AG-2005-RES-06. 19–22 September. <http://www.interpol.int/Public/ICPO/GeneralAssembly/AGN74/resolutions/AGN74RES06.asp>

— and UN. 1997. Co-operation Agreement between the United Nations and the International Criminal Police Organization—Interpol. 8 July. <http://www.interpol.int/Public/ICPO/LegalMaterials/cooperation/agreements/UN1997.asp>

—. 2002. *Memorandum of Understanding between the International Criminal Police Organization (Interpol) and the United Nations Interim Administration Mission in Kosovo on Co-operation in Crime Prevention and Criminal Justice.* 20 December. <http://www.interpol.int/Public/ICPO/LegalMaterials/cooperation/agreements/UNMIK.asp>

KAIPTC (Kofi Annan International Peacekeeping Training Centre). n.d. <http://www.kaiptc.org>

KPIS (Kosovo Police Information Service). 2002. 'Database on Reported and Committed Crimes.' Pristina: KPIS.

Kucera, Joshua. 2007. 'Georgia Meets Resistance in the West.' *Jane's Defence Weekly.* Coulsdon: Jane's Information Group. 13 June.

Kullman, William. 2008. *The Value of Marking at Import.* Unpublished background paper. Geneva: Small Arms Survey.

McDonald, Glenn. 2006. 'Connecting the Dots: The International Tracing Instrument.' In Small Arms Survey, ed. *Small Arms Survey 2006: Unfinished Business.* Oxford: Oxford University Press, pp. 95–117.

—. 2008. 'Who's Buying? End-User Certification.' In Small Arms Survey, ed. *Small Arms Survey 2008: Risk and Resilience.* Cambridge: Cambridge University Press, pp. 155–81.

MUP (Ministry of Internal Affairs, Croatia) and UNDP. 2007. 'Operation: SALW Civilian Collection (2007).' Protocol for Execution. Zagreb: MUP and UNDP.

NODEFIC (Norwegian Defence International Centre). n.d. <http://www.mil.no/felles/fokiv/>.

OFR (US Office of the Federal Register). 2001. *Federal Register.* Vol. 66, No. 150. Washington, D.C.: OFR, National Archives and Records Administration. 3 August. <http://frwebgate.access.gpo.gov/cgi-bin/getdoc.cgi?dbname=2001_register&docid=01-19418-filed.pdf>

OSCE (Organization for Security and Co-operation in Europe). 2003. *Handbook of Best Practices on Small Arms and Light Weapons.* Vienna: OSCE Forum for Security Co-operation. <http://www.osce.org/fsc/item_11_13550.html>

PPC (Pearson Peacekeeping Centre). n.d. <http://www.peaceoperations.org/>

SEESAC (South Eastern and Eastern Europe Clearinghouse for the Control of Small Arms and Light Weapons). 2006. 'RMDS/G 04.20: SALW Accounting.' 4th edition. Belgrade: SEESAC. <http://www.seesac.org/resources/RMDS%2004.20%20SALW%20Accounting%20(Edition%204).pdf>

UNDDR (UN Disarmament, Demobilization and Reintegration Resource Centre). 2006. *Integrated Disarmament, Demobilization and Reintegration Standards*. New York: UNDDR. <http://www.unddr.org/iddrs>

UNDP (UN Development Programme). 2007. 'UNDP Small Arms Control in BIH, SACBIH: Pilot Weapons Collection Project in the Municipalities of Novo Sarjevo and Istocna Ilidza.' Project Impact Report, PI/001. Sarajevo: UNDP. January.

—. 2008. 'Noteworthy Results from the Campaign "Less Weapons, Less Tragedies."' Zagreb: UNDP. 12 June. <http://www.undp.hr/show.jsp?shownewsrepcat=81912&page=81904&showsingle=95472>

UNGA (United Nations General Assembly). 2001. *Protocol against the Illicit Manufacturing of and Trafficking in Firearms, Their Parts and Components and Ammunition, Supplementing the United Nations Convention against Transnational Organized Crime ('UN Firearms Protocol')*. Adopted 31 May. Entered into force 3 July 2005. A/RES/55/255 of 8 June (annexe). <http://www.undcp.org/pdf/crime/a_res_55/255e.pdf>

—. 2005a. *International Instrument to Enable States to Identify and Trace, in a Timely and Reliable Manner, Illicit Small Arms and Light Weapons ('International Tracing Instrument')*. A/60/88 of 27 June (annexe). <http://www.un.org/events/smallarms2006/pdf/A.60.88%20(E).pdf>

—. 2005b. *International Instrument to Enable States to Identify and Trace, in a Timely and Reliable Manner, Illicit Small Arms and Light Weapons*. Decision no. 60/519 of 8 December. A/60/463, para. 95; A/60/PV.61, p. 41.

—. 2008. *Report of the Third Biennial Meeting of States to Consider the Implementation of the Programme of Action to Prevent, Combat and Eradicate the Illicit Trade in Small Arms and Light Weapons in All Its Aspects*. A/CONF.192/BMS/2008/3 of 20 August. <http://disarmament2.un.org/cab/bms3/1BMS3Pages/1thirdBMS.html>

UNMIL. 2005. 'Weapons Collection List (2004–05).' Monrovia: UNMIL, Joint Military Assessment Centre. May.

UNSC (United Nations Security Council). 2001. 'Resolution 1343 (2001).' S/RES/1343 (2001). 7 March. <http://daccessdds.un.org/doc/UNDOC/GEN/N01/276/08/PDF/N0127608.pdf?OpenElement>

—. 2002. 'Letter Dated 24 October 2002 from the Chairman of the Security Council Committee Established Pursuant to Resolution 1343 (2001) Concerning Liberia Addressed to the President of the Security Council.' S/2002/1115. 25 October. <http://daccessdds.un.org/doc/UNDOC/GEN/N02/626/79/IMG/N0262679.pdf?OpenElement>

—. 2003a. 'Letter Dated 24 April 2003 from the Chairman of the Security Council Committee Established Pursuant to Resolution 1343 (2001) Concerning Liberia Addressed to the President of the Security Council.' S/2003/498. 24 April. <http://www.un.org/Docs/sc/committees/Liberia2/LiberiaSelEng.htm>

—. 2003b. 'Letter Dated 28 October 2003 from the Chairman of the Security Council Committee Established Pursuant to Resolution 1343 (2001) Concerning Liberia Addressed to the President of the Security Council.' S/2003/937. 28 October. <http://daccessdds.un.org/doc/UNDOC/GEN/N03/543/25/IMG/N0354325.pdf?OpenElement>

—. 2007b. 'Letter Dated 16 July 2007 from the Chairman of the Security Council Committee Established Pursuant to Resolution 1533 (2004) Concerning the Democratic Republic of the Congo Addressed to the President of the Security Council.' S/2007/423. 18 July. <http://daccessdds.un.org/doc/UNDOC/GEN/N07/384/59/PDF/N0738459.pdf?OpenElement>

—. 2007c. 'Letter Dated 2 October 2007 from the Chairman of the Security Council Committee Established Pursuant to Resolution 1591 (2005) Concerning the Sudan Addressed to the President of the Security Council.' S/2007/584. 3 October. <http://daccessdds.un.org/doc/UNDOC/GEN/N07/491/00/PDF/N0749100.pdf?OpenElement>

—. 2007d. 'Letter Dated 17 October 2007 from the Chairman of the Security Council Committee Established Pursuant to Resolution 1572 (2004) Concerning Côte d'Ivoire addressed to the President of the Security Council.' S/2007/611. 18 October. <http://daccessdds.un.org/doc/UNDOC/GEN/N07/551/12/PDF/N0755112.pdf?OpenElement>

—. 2008. 'Letter Dated 24 April 2008 from the Chairman of the Security Council Committee Established Pursuant to Resolution 751 (1992) Concerning Somalia Addressed to the President of the Security Council.' S/2008/274. 24 April. <http://daccessdds.un.org/doc/UNDOC/GEN/N08/290/68/PDF/N0829068.pdf?OpenElement>

US (United States). 2004. *Firearms*, Chapter 44 of the United States Code Title 18 – Crimes and Criminal Procedure, as amended in 2004. <http://uscode.house.gov/download/pls/18C44.txt>

—. 2007. United States Code. Title 18: Crimes and Criminal Procedures; Ch. 227: Sentences. <http://uscode.house.gov/download/pls/18C227.txt>

—. 2008. United States Code of Federal Regulations. Title 27: Alcohol, Tobacco and Firearms, sec. 478: Commerce in Firearms and Ammunition. Accessed 1 April 2008. <http://ecfr.gpoaccess.gov/cgi/t/text/text-idx?c=ecfr&tpl=/ecfrbrowse/Title27/27cfr478_main_02.tpl>

Wood, Brian and Johan Peleman. 1999. 'The Arms Fixers: Controlling the Brokers and Shipping Agents.' PRIO Report 3/99. Oslo: International Peace Research Institute, Oslo.

ACKNOWLEDGEMENTS

Principal author

James Bevan

Contributors

William Kullman, Jasna Lazarevic, Glenn McDonald

Shoes of gunshot victims on display at a rally against arms trafficking near the United Nations in New York, July 2001.
© Peter Morgan/Reuters

Two Steps Forward

UN MEASURES UPDATE

4

INTRODUCTION

To vote or not to vote? That was the question confronting the Third Biennial Meeting of States (BMS3)[1] on its last day, as it pondered how to take implementation of the *UN Small Arms Programme of Action* a step forward. Governments, international organizations, and NGOs active on small arms issues were hoping the Meeting, the third in a series devoted to a 'consideration' of *Programme* implementation, would mark a clean break from the paralysis that had afflicted the earlier biennial meetings as well as the *Programme*'s 2006 Review Conference. Ideally, this meant consensus agreement on a relatively detailed, substantive outcome document. The substance was at hand, consensus not, in the last hours of BMS3.

In the event, the UN membership voted overwhelmingly, on 18 July 2008, to adopt the BMS3 report, including its outcome document. This capped a successful month at UN headquarters in New York. A week earlier, a Group of Governmental Experts (GGE) adopted, by consensus, its report on conventional ammunition stockpiles. That report, much like the BMS3 outcome document, contains text that can be used to translate relatively vague commitments contained in the *Programme*—in this case, for better stockpile management—into tangible improvements 'on the ground'.

In August 2008, UN headquarters in New York hosted the final meeting of the GEE on an Arms Trade Treaty (ATT). The results from this forum were less than sensational, however. The group could not reach any firm—or even tentative—conclusions on the scope, feasibility, and draft parameters of an ATT. Yet it did agree that the discussions should continue—success of a kind given the thorny nature of the subject matter, namely, possible restrictions on national arms transfer practices.

This chapter reviews these developments, including related follow-up at the autumn 2008 session of the UN General Assembly First Committee (Disarmament and International Security), and examines some of the implications for future work on small arms (and conventional arms) at the global level. Its principal conclusions include the following:

- The BMS3 outcome offers the promise, but not the certainty, of a reinvigorated UN small arms process, focused on 'implementation challenges and opportunities' in selected areas of the *Programme of Action*.
- There is also some indication that the UN small arms regime is inching towards the development of a more systematic and rigorous system for monitoring national implementation of *Programme* commitments; but again, this is more potential than reality.
- The decision of the Ammunition Expert Group to treat the issue of ammunition surplus within the broader framework of stockpile management ensures the report's practical relevance.
- The *Ammunition Report*, which has already prompted the UN to undertake the formulation of technical guidelines for ammunition management, could also be used to improve the management of weapons.

- The ATT Expert Group reached few, if any, firm conclusions; but it did pave the way for further, more inclusive consideration of the arms transfer issue among UN Member States.
- The future prospects for the ATT are unclear. For the moment, all options remain open, including those relating to the core goals and structure of a possible ATT.

The chapter begins its review of recent developments in the UN small arms process with an examination of BMS3 and the Ammunition GGE, before turning to the more difficult ATT meetings. It briefly recaps the history of these initiatives, analyses their outcomes, and considers the resulting implications for international small arms work. The chapter follows events up to the end of 2008, which includes follow-up measures decided at the 63rd session of the UN General Assembly.

THE THIRD BIENNIAL MEETING OF STATES

In July 2008, UN Member States met, for the third time, 'to consider the national, regional and global implementation of the Programme of Action' (UNGA, 2007, para. 4). The first two biennial meetings for the *Programme*, held in July 2003 and July 2005, had helped refocus global attention on the still nascent *Programme*, but had done little to catalyse implementation. Another opportunity to achieve this and more came and went in June–July 2006. The first Review Conference for the *Programme of Action,* characterized by much political wrangling, reached no substantive agreement of any kind (Small Arms Survey, 2007, ch. 4).

Meetings in 2003, 2005, and 2006 did little (or nothing) to advance *Programme* implementation.

The Review Conference had taken no decision on *Programme* follow-up meetings, but the UN General Assembly, in particular its First Committee (Disarmament and International Security), filled this gap later in 2006 by deciding that a third biennial meeting of states 'shall be held no later than in 2008, in New York' (UNGA, 2006b, para. 4). As with the first two biennial meetings, the third was to 'consider' *Programme* implementation, not reconsider the terms of the instrument; yet independent evaluations of progress made by states in fulfilling their commitments under the *Programme* had consistently shown that, while not entirely idle, they were by and large falling short (BtB with IANSA, 2006). The *Programme of Action* had been adopted in July 2001. The meetings in 2003, 2005, and 2006, cited above, had done relatively little to advance *Programme* implementation. A lot was therefore riding on BMS3.

There was, first, a need to restore overall confidence in the UN small arms process. As indicated elsewhere in this chapter, progress was being made on several related fronts, including illicit brokering, conventional ammunition stocks, and, to some extent, conventional arms transfers. But the future of the core UN framework for small arms, represented by the *Programme of Action,* was unclear following the Review Conference misfire. Many of the commitments in the *Programme* are open-ended in formulation. They articulate a range of important goals, often in unequivocal terms, but seldom enumerate the concrete steps that are needed to achieve them. There was a need, then, to 'unpack' some of these commitments—in essence to provide a more detailed guide to implementation.

BMS3 also offered states their first opportunity 'to consider the implementation' of the *International Tracing Instrument* (ITI)[2] (UNGA, 2006b, para. 5). One of the more tangible results of the UN small arms process, the ITI had been agreed in 2005 in an effort to enhance the traceability of small arms and light weapons through improved marking, record keeping, and international cooperation (Small Arms Survey, 2006, ch. 4; CONFLICT TRACING). Like the *Programme,* the ITI provides for biennial implementation meetings, to be held in conjunction with biennial meetings of states for the *Programme of Action* wherever possible (UNGA, 2005b, para. 37).[3]

Meeting preparations

Preparations for BMS3 got under way in earnest with the nomination of the Chair-designate, Ambassador Dalius Čekuolis of Lithuania, in December 2007. Given the scale of the challenge, this additional lead time—more than previous Chairs had enjoyed—proved instrumental to the success of the Meeting.

Beginning in January 2008, and continuing right up to and during the Meeting itself, the Chair-designate consulted extensively with individual countries, regional groups, the UN membership, and civil society (see Čekuolis, 2008, p. 23). This included meetings with the Geneva Process on small arms. The recommendation of a Geneva Process Working Group to focus BMS3 on a limited number of topics[4] had found imperfect expression in the general ('omnibus') resolution on small arms, adopted by the General Assembly in late 2007, which called upon states to use the Meeting to identify 'priority issues or topics of relevance'.[5] Ambassador Čekuolis took up the Working Group recommendation as originally formulated and instead sought to finalize the topics for priority discussion in advance of BMS3. This would enable the Meeting to get down to business from the first day, with a focused, in-depth discussion of *Programme* implementation in the selected areas.

National reporting was used to good effect for BMS3.

The Chair-designate's initial consultations confirmed that, in addition to the discussion of the ITI, there was strong support for a discussion of illicit brokering, along with stockpile management and surplus disposal. The subject of international cooperation, assistance, and national capacity-building was identified as a cross-cutting theme that would underpin all of the *Programme* discussions at BMS3 (Čekuolis, 2008, p. 20). In the same spirit, the General Assembly had already encouraged states to use the meeting 'to highlight . . . implementation challenges and opportunities' in the priority discussion areas (UNGA, 2007, para. 8). The choice of topics was not unanimous, necessitating lengthy negotiations over the Meeting agenda. At the end of the day, in order to satisfy countries that were pushing for a discussion of additional subjects at BMS3, Ambassador Čekuolis introduced an 'other issues' session.

Another innovation, at least for a UN small arms meeting, was the sustained use of facilitators, including during the preparatory phase.[6] Four facilitators were appointed in advance of the meeting: Colombia (international cooperation, assistance, and national capacity-building), Egypt (ITI), South Korea (illicit brokering), and Switzerland (stockpile management and surplus disposal). Canada (other issues) and Finland (illicit brokering) were added to the list at BMS3. Of the initial group of four, the appointment of two facilitators from the Geneva diplomatic missions (as well as two from New York) reflected the Chair-designate's desire to make optimal use of the small arms expertise found in Geneva (Čekuolis, 2008, pp. 22–23).

In contrast to the Conference that resulted in adoption of the *Programme of Action* in 2001 and the Review Conference in 2006, there was no formal preparatory process for BMS3. The facilitators provided an (informal) structure for the preparatory process and, crucially, allowed consultations to be conducted simultaneously on each of the focus discussion topics in advance of BMS3 and at the Meeting itself. In June 2008 the facilitators produced discussion papers that were based on their consultations, as well as their analysis of national reporting in their subject area. These papers were among the primary inputs for the eventual BMS3 outcome document.

Unlike many other UN policy initiatives, the *UN Programme of Action* has no formal monitoring process. No mechanisms or bodies have been established for purposes of assessing states' compliance with their commitments under the *Programme*. Aside from the biennial implementation meetings—and so far a single, unsuccessful Review Conference—the *Programme of Action* merely mentions the possibility of 'voluntary' reporting on national implementation (UNGA, 2001, para. II.33).[7] Reporting, however, was used to good effect for BMS3 (see Box 4.1). Echoing the General

Box 4.1 National reporting on the UN Programme of Action

The *UN Programme of Action* encourages states to share information on their implementation efforts (UNGA, 2001, para. II.33). The voluntary nature of this mechanism, coupled with the absence of basic parameters for reporting, has affected both the frequency and quality of national reports.

There has been a high level of participation in *UN Programme* reporting. Between 2002 and 2008, 148 UN Member States (77 per cent) submitted at least one report, while 44 others (23 per cent) have never reported. Of the total 466 national reports submitted since 2001, the majority have coincided with years in which a biennial meeting of states or review conference has been held, as indicated in Figure 4.1. Reporting rates have also varied greatly between regions. For example, 95 per cent of European states have reported at least once since 2001, while the figure for Oceania is 43 per cent.

The absence of a prescribed format for reporting has contributed to a divergence in reporting practices. States have submitted reports varying from one-page general descriptions of small arms activities to long, highly structured, and detailed accounts of national policies in *Programme*–and even non-*Programme*–related areas. In presenting this information, they have also used different formats, sometimes changing formats over time. This variation has affected the nature of the information exchanged, its level of detail, and, perhaps most importantly, its comparability.

A lack of comparability obviously hampers an overall assessment of progress in *Programme of Action* implementation. A reporting template, developed by UNDP, UNIDIR, UNODA, and the Small Arms Survey,[10] has been used at least once by about half of all states that reported during the 2003–08 period (Cattaneo and Parker, 2008). There has, however, been considerable variation in the use states make of the template, with some answering, or attempting to answer, all of its questions and others employing it much more selectively. Where states have used the reporting template comprehensively, reporting tends to be more complete; states report on all issues addressed in the *Programme*, even where this entails a 'non-applicable' reply.

The consistent use of a single template would clearly enhance the comparability of national reports. So too the development of detailed standards or benchmarks for *Programme* implementation. Comparability is in fact limited, not only by divergent reporting practices, but also by a lack of specificity in many provisions of the *Programme*. Under the vague heading 'measures to address illegal stockpiling',[11] for example, states have provided information on the regulation of civilian firearms ownership, standards for storage, and the collection of illicit weapons from civilians.

Problems stemming from the lack of a standard reporting format and the open-ended nature of many *Programme* provisions are compounded by weaknesses in national reporting practices. Much of the information states provide is not sufficiently detailed to assess *Programme* implementation, or is unrelated to the relevant provision. For instance, many states simply report that they have adequate stockpile management procedures in place (UNGA, 2001, para. II.17); yet general affirmations of compliance give little sense of *actual* controls. Unless states provide further details–such as the type and extent of the physical security measures they employ–it is impossible to determine whether they have met their *Programme* commitments or not.

Another weakness in national reporting is that states give little or no information on the impact of measures taken under the *Programme of Action*. Many include specifics of the number of seized weapons or surplus arms that have been destroyed. One state has indicated, for example, that the number of thefts from state stockpiles has declined as evidence of the effectiveness of new stockpile management procedures. But overall such data is lacking. For example, no state has provided information on the number of arrests made for illicit manufacturing or trading, despite the *Programme* stipulation that states 'take action' under national laws against groups and individuals involved in such practices (UNGA, 2001, para. II.6).

As recognized at BMS3, the effective implementation of the *Programme of Action* depends, in many cases, on the development of adequate capacity. Some states are using their national reports to communicate their assistance needs, but it is unclear whether donors are taking advantage of this information. The BMS3 outcome document calls upon states to make increasing use of their national reports for this purpose (UNGA, 2008b, para. 7i).

Seven years of reporting on *Programme of Action* implementation yield a mixed picture. A lack of comparability, coupled with inadequate or incomplete information and the vagueness of certain *Programme* commitments, make reporting, overall, only moderately useful. Participation rates suggest that, notwithstanding its voluntary nature, states consider reporting to be important. These reports undoubtedly constitute a central–sometimes the only–source of information on states' efforts to tackle the small arms problem. They help to sustain broad momentum on the small arms issue and, crucially, provide some information on progress made in fulfilling *Programme* commitments. But they do not yet provide a comprehensive or detailed account of the state of *Programme* implementation.

Source: Cattaneo and Parker (2009)

Figure 4.1 **Number of reports submitted annually, 2002-08**

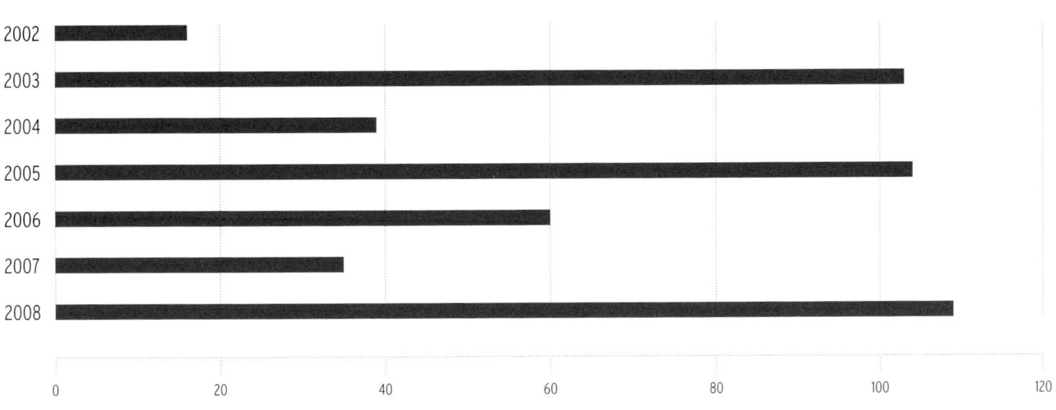

Note: Biennial meetings of states for the UN Programme of Action were held in 2003, 2005, and 2008, with one Review Conference convened in 2006.

Source: Cattaneo and Parker (2008, p. 4)

Assembly's general resolution on small arms (UNGA, 2007, para. 6), Amb. Čekuolis urged states to submit their reports 'well in advance' of BMS3 so that the Meeting discussions and outcome document could take account of them.[8] The Small Arms Survey and United Nations Institute for Disarmament Research (UNIDIR) also prepared a draft analysis of reporting on the BMS3 focus topics.[9]

The national reports and the analysis of reporting constituted, along with the facilitator papers, the main inputs for the draft outcome document that Amb. Čekuolis circulated to states the week before the start of BMS3. The latter included initial draft text for each of the Meeting themes, including the ITI, but excluding 'other issues'. There were no conclusions, however. What came to be called 'The way forward' sections were developed during BMS3.

The Third Biennial Meeting

BMS3 was held at UN headquarters in New York during 14–18 July 2008. The United States did not attend the sessions devoted to the implementation of the *Programme of Action,* though it did attend, and participate in, the two meetings held on 17 July on the ITI.[12] The Meeting completed its consideration of procedural matters on the morning of Monday 14 July, immediately launching into the first item of substance, namely, international cooperation, assistance, and national capacity-building. BMS3 then proceeded, more or less on schedule, to consider the other substantive areas, including 'other issues'. Draft conclusions ('The way forward' sections) were prepared by the Chair following each day's discussion, with the UN translating these overnight and immediately issuing them to the UN membership in the organization's six official languages (including online posting).

Throughout the Meeting, states generally followed the Chair's request to focus their interventions on the items under discussion. The 'general exchange of views' that had stolen much time from previous UN small arms meetings was omitted from the BMS3 Programme of Work. During the thematic discussions, states mostly read selectively from longer statements and *Programme* implementation reports, in many cases posting full versions of these documents on the website of UNODA (United Nations Office for Disarmament Affairs). Facilitators or civil society experts gave presentations at the beginning of each thematic discussion that focused on the technical aspects of the relevant subject.

Amb. Čekuolis also kept control of the outcome document, issuing successive drafts or parts of drafts under his own authority despite pressure from Iran, in particular, to initiate 'line-by-line negotiations' on the text. The latter approach had resulted in the loss of valuable time at the Review Conference as states piled amendment upon amendment to the draft under discussion. In an article published after BMS3, the Chair has argued that neither the time available at the Meeting (five working days) nor the nature of the discussions (focused on the *implementation* of an *existing* instrument) justified formal, treaty-like negotiations (Čekuolis, 2008, p. 22). Instead, the facilitators worked in parallel with the Meeting discussions to solicit inputs from states and to facilitate compromises on matters of dispute. Late in the evening of Wednesday 16 July, Amb. Čekuolis issued an initial draft of the outcome document, incorporating all sections (except for the ITI) and their recommendations. Following the ITI discussions and further consultations, a revised version of the document was distributed to states late on Thursday night. As far as one can tell, this document, reviewed by states on the Meeting's last day, Friday 18 July, enjoyed consensus support—with the exception of Iran, which again objected to the working method.

Box 4.2 Civil society at BMS3

The BMS3 Chair made extensive use of civil society expertise prior to and during BMS3 (see Čekuolis, 2008, p. 23). Although other fields of UN activity, such as the environment, have included civil society experts in discussions among governments, rules of procedure adopted for the 2001 UN Small Arms Conference and used in subsequent *Programme* meetings have limited civil society participation to a set-piece intervention occupying part of a single day. Civil society has also been excluded from UN experts' meetings on small arms and from formal negotiating sessions, such as those relating to the ITI and Review Conference outcome. While there was no consensus on allowing civil society, generally, a more interactive role at BMS3, representatives of Amnesty International and the Small Arms Survey were able to give presentations at the beginning of the (governmental) sessions devoted to illicit brokering and the ITI. Continuing a practice begun by earlier BMS Chairs, Amb. Čekuolis also encouraged governments to include members of civil society in their BMS3 delegations.

Many states and others active on small arms issues had hoped that BMS3 would result in a restoration of the consensus decision-making that had marked the initial phases of the UN small arms process but, as of 2005, had increasingly yielded to formal voting. Iran, however, indicated it would not join the consensus. As a result, the draft Meeting Report, including the outcome document, was put to a vote. It was adopted by a vote of 134 states in favour, with two abstaining (Iran, Zimbabwe) and none opposed.[13]

Half full: the BMS3 outcome

Of course, any agreed result was better than the non-results that the first two biennial meetings, and also the Review Conference, had produced. But in fact, while not perfect, the BMS3 outcome document has much to recommend it. It does not augment or extend states' existing commitments in the three thematic areas. But it does give these commitments somewhat more detailed—and practical—expression. As recommended by the UN General Assembly, it points to 'implementation challenges and opportunities' in the three areas, providing, above all, a set of benchmarks against which future implementation efforts can be assessed—whether by the state concerned or by independent monitors.

The best example of this is the stockpiles section. The *Programme of Action* articulates the key principles that underpin good stockpile management, but, in so doing, leaves many questions unanswered. When are stockpile management standards and procedures 'adequate' (UNGA, 2001, para. II.17)? How do states go about clearly identifying stocks that are surplus to national requirements (para. II.18)? What do they need to consider when responsibly disposing, preferably through destruction, of their surpluses (para. II.18)? What are the resource implications of such measures? The BMS3 outcome document provides useful answers to each of these questions,[14] while highlighting the close relationship between the different sectors, especially surplus identification and effective stockpile management.[15]

The section of the outcome document devoted to 'International cooperation, assistance and national capacity-building' similarly unpacks various parts of the *Programme of Action* in useful ways. After years of talk at the UN about improving the matching of needs and resources, the BMS3 outcome spotlights several practical means of achieving this. It cites UNODA's Programme of Action Implementation Support System and a relevant database prepared by the United Nations Institute for Disarmament Research (UNGA, 2008b, paras. 2, 3, 7k).[16] It also underlines the utility of national reporting on the *Programme of Action,* both for purposes of bringing donors and recipients together (UNGA, 2008b, paras. 3, 7d, 7i),[17] and for exchanging information on the broader range of areas covered by the BMS3 document (*Programme* and ITI outcomes).[18] As one might expect, the BMS3 cooperation text borrows liberally from the *Programme of Action,* yet pure repetition is rare. Even those paragraphs that are clearly based on the *Programme* tend to incorporate new elements.[19] And in several areas the BMS3 outcome breaks new ground, for example in emphasizing the responsibility of states seeking assistance to assess their own needs and to convey these with some specificity (UNGA, 2008b, paras. 7g–h), and in highlighting the importance of inter-regional cooperation (para. 7l).

The section on illicit brokering is shorter than the other two, but covers several key points. States acknowledge the 'global' nature of the problem (para. 10) and the need to adopt 'a comprehensive approach' to it, citing, in this regard, the potential relevance of 'associated activities', such as financing and transportation, in developing relevant regulations (para. 11). End-user certification, including verification measures, and international cooperation are also emphasized (paras. 12, 16c). Last but not least, the BMS3 outcome gives the report of the GGE on illicit brokering a boost, underlining its utility to national efforts to tackle the problem. The brokering section does not develop corre-

Box 4.3 First steps on the ITI

The first meeting on ITI implementation provided evidence that the Instrument has the firm support of many UN Member States, yet also raised questions about the extent to which it has been embraced in national legislation and practice. The day-long discussion devoted to the ITI was practical and focused, with states enumerating various measures they were taking in the areas of weapons marking, record keeping, and tracing. The ITI outcome document[20] lays down certain markers for Instrument implementation. Initial steps, such as bringing national systems into line with the ITI (UNGA, 2008b, Annex, para. 9b) and designating national points of contact (para. 9c), are emphasized. The ITI outcome also underscores the 'mutually reinforcing' nature of weapons marking, record keeping, and tracing (para. 9a), along with the need to build national capacity for effective implementation.[21]

On the basis of meeting discussions and resulting outcome, one could conclude that the ITI is a huge success. Yet an analysis of the national reports on ITI implementation tells a different story. While reporting under the *Programme of Action* has been voluntary from the beginning, states decided to write a *requirement* for biennial reporting into the text of the Instrument (UNGA, 2005b, para. 36). Nevertheless, less than one-third of the UN membership (62 of 192 states) submitted information on their implementation of the ITI in 2008 (Cattaneo and Parker, 2008, p. 97).[22] Response rates were considerably lower in many areas of importance. For example, as of 13 December 2007, two years after the ITI's adoption by the General Assembly (and simultaneous application to all UN Member States), only 27 countries had provided UNODA with name and contact information for their national point of contact (Cattaneo and Parker, 2008, p. 113).[23] Only 24 states reported having established legal requirements or practices for the marking of small arms held by government defence and security forces (p. 116).[24] Only 20 states provided information relating to the tracing cooperation sections of the Instrument (p. 120),[25] raising doubts as to whether it is being used to conduct tracing operations in crime and conflict situations as it was designed to do.

States have provided relatively more information on their implementation of the marking and tracing provisions of the *Programme of Action*;[26] yet, as the authors of the UNIDIR study note, the ITI covers these areas in far more detail (p. 124). The current silence maintained by most states on their use of the ITI could reflect a lack of familiarity with the new instrument's reporting requirements, but could also reflect a failure to follow through on their commitments.

sponding *Programme* commitments to the extent that the stockpile and cooperation sections do. Yet, given the existence of the GGE report, this isn't necessary. It is, in fact, the latter that provides the benchmarks for implementation in this area.

In relation to brokering, then, as in relation to stockpile management and international cooperation and assistance, the BMS3 outcome provides states with concrete, practical guidance for enhanced *Programme* implementation. Yet the utility of the document will depend on tangible improvements in such implementation. While, as already noted, much of the text offers a useful elaboration of *Programme* commitments, weak language tends to dominate. Most often, states are 'encouraged' to take certain action. In a way, this is logical. No new commitments were agreed at the Third Biennial Meeting. It makes sense to leave the means of implementation to the discretion of states. Nevertheless, the question is left open.

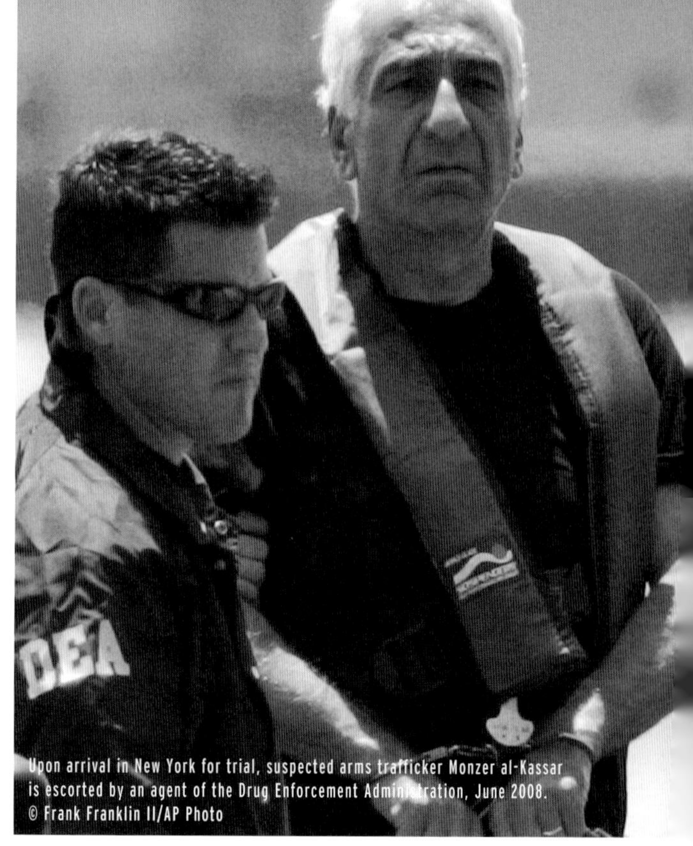

Upon arrival in New York for trial, suspected arms trafficker Monzer al-Kassar is escorted by an agent of the Drug Enforcement Administration, June 2008. © Frank Franklin II/AP Photo

A forward-looking implementation agenda

Although no firm decisions were taken, the BMS3 outcome document provides a tentative road map for the next phase(s) of the UN small arms process. Among the 'ideas and proposals for a forward-looking implementation agenda for the Programme of Action', it mentions:

> *a) Reporting on a biennial basis, reporting templates and the analysis of reports;*
> *b) Follow-up meetings on the Programme of Action, including periodic meetings of governmental experts;*
> *c) Regional meetings that could be used to support subsequent United Nations meetings on the Programme of Action.* (UNGA, 2008b, para. 29)

The notion of 'reporting templates' is echoed elsewhere in the document (paras. 3, 7i), as is the idea of convening regional meetings in non-BMS years in order to advance *Programme* implementation (paras. 6, 7n) and 'periodic meetings of governmental experts' (para. 7o). The BMS3 outcome document also lists 24 'other issues' that 'some States indicated . . . were important to the implementation of the Programme of Action' (para. 28).

The core elements of the BMS3 outcome's 'forward-looking implementation agenda' were taken up by the UN General Assembly's First Committee when it met in October 2008. The General Assembly's principal resolution on small arms, Resolution 63/72, provides for a fourth biennial meeting of states (and second ITI implementation meeting) in 2010, with an 'open-ended meeting of governmental experts' and second review conference following in 2011 and 2012 respectively (UNGA, 2008e, paras. 6–7, 13–14). The resolution also follows up the BMS3 recommendation that regional meetings be used to support the *Programme of Action* process (para. 15).[27] As of the end of 2008, it was expected that one or more such meetings would be convened during 2009 in order to help pave the way for the fourth BMS.

Both the ITI[28] and the brokering process[29] receive their due in Resolution 63/72, but it is its emphasis on national reporting that is most striking.[30] Paragraph 8 provides a link between BMS3 and future *UN Programme* meetings, encouraging states to include in their national reports 'information on progress made in the implementation of the measures highlighted in the report of the third biennial meeting of States'.[31] The proposal for biennial reporting (less frequent but more effective) contained in the BMS3 outcome finds implicit support in that Resolution 63/72 sets the end of 2009 as the next deadline for reporting (para. 8). In essence, these reports will feed into deliberations at BMS4. The same paragraph also encourages states to use the existing reporting template (in order to improve comparability between countries and over time). The analysis of reports is also backed, to some extent, with the mention of the UNIDIR–Small Arms Survey study that provided key inputs for BMS3 and its outcome (pream. para. 8). As reflected in the resolution, all these aspects of reporting remain underdeveloped—especially the importance of assessing implementation through some sort of analysis—but the basic elements are present. BMS3 and Resolution 63/72 offer the potential—but only the potential—of a more systematic, rigorous use of national reporting for purposes of assessing overall progress made in *Programme of Action* (and ITI) implementation.

The key to the success or failure of the *Programme* and ITI remains implementation.

Among the issues the BMS3 outcome lists as potential themes for future UN small arms meetings, Resolution 63/72 picks no favourites; but in sketching out the path towards BMS4 it backs the BMS3 method of focusing on a limited number of 'priority issues or topics of relevance' and, importantly, specifies that these be identified 'well in advance' of the meeting (UNGA, 2008e, para. 12). Applying another lesson from BMS3, the resolution also '[s]tresses the importance of the early designation of the Chair', proposing a date of October 2009 for that nomination (para. 11).

It is no exaggeration to say that BMS3 and the follow-up General Assembly Resolution have breathed new life into the *UN Programme of Action*. Resolution 63/72 outlines a more sophisticated and—at least potentially—dynamic process comprising regional meetings, a fourth biennial meeting, a meeting of governmental experts, and a second review conference. The challenge for 2009 and 2010 will be to ensure that these meetings complement and reinforce one another, and that the links between the regional and the global levels are strengthened. It is equally important that the outlines of an implementation monitoring mechanism, as tentatively drawn in both the BMS3 outcome document and Resolution 63/72, take somewhat firmer shape. The new meetings may prove to be useful, but the key to the success or failure of the *Programme of Action* (and the ITI) remains implementation.

THE AMMUNITION GGE

In 2008 a UN Group of Governmental Experts (GGE) convened to consider means of enhancing cooperation in addressing the problem of surplus conventional ammunition (UNGA, 2006c, para. 7). Conventional ammunition includes a wide range of munitions, ranging from the largest-calibre artillery shells and free-flight rockets to the cartridges, grenades, rockets, and guided missiles that are used in small arms and light weapons. It is a category that encompasses both small arms and major conventional weapons.

The problems posed by conventional ammunition are threefold. First, a growing death toll from explosions at ammunition stockpile facilities vividly illustrates the safety risks posed by poorly managed, decaying stockpiles of

A Bosnian soldier walks past destroyed ammunition and mortar rounds at the Bosnian Government Ordinance Facility in Doboj, November 2006. © Amel Emric/AP Photo

ammunition (Wilkinson, 2008, p. 134). Second, loss and theft from national stockpiles diverts ammunition to fuel armed violence and insurgency (Small Arms Survey, 2008, pp. 47–62). Third, and specific to surplus, states are often tempted to transfer excess ammunition stocks to parts of the world where they are used indiscriminately and/or proliferate without control (Bevan, 2008, pp. 3–4).

Despite these problems, however, states have traditionally marginalized conventional ammunition within the broader arms control debate. Nowhere is this more evident than in international efforts to regulate the trade in small arms and light weapons. Although states continue to transfer surplus small-arms cartridges abroad, sometimes in dubious circumstances,[32] the *UN Programme of Action* does not address ammunition clearly and specifically. Moreover, states have recently excluded ammunition from associated instruments, such as the ITI.

The 2008 GGE *Surplus Ammunition Report* partially redresses the balance. It provides a framework for action to address excessive ammunition surpluses and suggests ways in which improved national policies, coupled with enhanced international cooperation, can encourage the safe and secure management of ammunition stockpiles. Although the scope of the *Surplus Ammunition Report* is limited to national stockpiles (ammunition held by state security forces), it adds an important dimension to international efforts to address the illicit proliferation of small arms and light weapons ammunition.

In from the cold

In 1997, the *Report of the Panel of Governmental Experts on Small Arms (UN Panel Report)* listed ammunition alongside the small arms and light weapons of 'main concern' to the United Nations (UNGA, 1997, paras. 24, 26c). This appraisal was supported by the 1999 *Report of the Group of Experts on the Problem of Ammunition and Explosives (Ammunition Report)*. States, however, quickly realized that ammunition could not be treated in exactly the same way as small arms and light weapons. Many types of ammunition contain explosives and states were wary of broadening the scope of debate to include issues as diverse as commercial explosives, military demolition stores, and the component parts of major conventional weapons.

The subsequent 1999 *Report of the Group of Governmental Experts on Small Arms (Small Arms Report)* reflected these emerging tensions. While noting the need to control ammunition, it was careful to put the issue behind that of small arms proliferation in the list of priorities (UNGA, 1999b, paras. 118, 129–30). As Greene (2006, p. 7) notes, some states feared that any reference to ammunition in the 1999 *Small Arms Report* would encourage other states to request the addition of the phrase 'and explosives' in the text. As a result, the report avoided focusing on ammunition by referring to small arms and light weapons as a generic category, one in which the role of ammunition was implied rather than explicitly defined. The group's recommendations were limited to encouraging states (UNGA, 1999b, para. 118) to review the 1999 *Ammunition Report* (UNGA, 1999a).

The recommendations of the *Ammunition Report,* however, went unheeded during preparations for the 2001 UN Small Arms Conference and in the *Programme of Action* that emerged from the Conference. Since 2001, the *Programme* has been the touchstone of most international efforts to address illicit small arms proliferation, but the document does not use the word 'ammunition'. While certain provisions of the *Programme,* such as those pertaining to stockpile management and surplus destruction, could arguably apply to ammunition—as well as weapons—this is left to the discretion of UN Member States.

The marginalization of ammunition arguably reached its height in the *International Tracing Instrument,* agreed in 2005. It recommended that 'small arms and light weapons ammunition be addressed in a comprehensive manner as part of a separate process conducted within the framework of the United Nations' (UNGA, 2005a, para. 27). This translated the desire of a few states to push any discussion of small arms ammunition firmly away from the consideration of small arms control within the UN framework.

With explicit reference to the ITI recommendation,[33] in 2005 France and Germany presented a draft document that was to become UN General Assembly Resolution 61/72. The resolution appealed to all states to assess the size and security of national stockpiles and to evaluate whether they might require external assistance to reduce any risks that their assessments might reveal (UNGA, 2006c, para. 2). It also encouraged states to assist other national governments in their efforts to improve stockpile management, whether bilaterally or through international or regional organizations (para. 3). Last but not least, states requested that, no later than 2008, the Secretary General establish a group of governmental experts to consider 'further steps to enhance cooperation with regard to the issue of conventional ammunition stockpiles in surplus' (para. 7). The group, consisting of experts from 17 states,[34] met three times: in Geneva in January 2008, and in New York in March–April and July 2008.

Usefully, the Ammunition Group addressed the issue of surplus as part of stockpile management.

A pragmatic approach

The most important decision taken by the Ammunition GGE was to address the issue of surplus within the wider context of stockpile management. Surpluses arise, the group noted, primarily because states do not have the stockpile management systems in place to detect and curb their growth. Moreover, ineffective stockpile management also encourages unsafe storage and handling practices and facilitates the diversion (loss or theft) of ammunition to illicit markets. By framing the issue as a stockpile management problem, the group addressed not only the issue of surplus but also the wider safety and security issues inherent in national management of ammunition stockpiles.

The group's decision to focus on stockpile management rather than surplus alone allowed it to skirt some potentially divisive issues, such as surplus 'thresholds' or an 'acceptable level' of surplus. The problem thus became, not the size or level of surpluses, but the ways in which states managed the safety and security of such stocks. States often accrue excessive surpluses because they do not have the necessary monitoring systems with which to assess the quality and quantity of stockpiled ammunition. They may assume that 'more ammunition is better' and therefore retain large stocks of aging, unserviceable, and often dangerous ammunition. Moreover, even where surplus stocks are stored safely and securely, countries incur corresponding storage, maintenance, and security costs.

The group, therefore, recognized that the decision to retain surpluses was a national prerogative, but that, if it is to serve national interests, ammunition should be safely stored and monitored to ensure that it is serviceable and secured against loss or theft (UNGA, 2008a, paras. 8–10). Specific solutions included the installation of accounting systems to allow states to gauge what was in their national stockpiles and the deployment of associated technical means that would enable them to determine its condition (para. 19). With these systems in place, countries can make a more informed decision as to what constitutes an 'acceptable level' of surplus, taking account of cost, security, and safety implications.

The group undertook a systematic review of the major components of effective ammunition management. These include: planning the location and management of national stockpiles; procedures for ammunition storage and handling; monitoring, surveillance, and testing of ammunition; accounting, stocktaking, and forecasting of ammunition requirements; ensuring the physical security of stockpiled and deployed ammunition; and a range of disposal and destruction methods (paras. 21–45). All of these elements, the group noted, were interconnected. Together they constituted an integrated system spanning the ammunition life cycle (paras. 19–20).

The GGE Report recognizes the need to improve the coordination of assistance programmes and to raise awareness among potential recipient countries of the range of programmes on offer. It emphasizes the need to enhance and sustain stockpile management capacity— through both national efforts and bilateral and multilateral assistance (para. 60). It also underlines the need for peacekeeping forces to maintain effective stockpile management systems (paras. 12, 60, 74), an implicit admission that such forces have, in the past, been prone to engage in diversion.

While the report lays out a full range of stockpile management improvements, it does not explain how states might begin this process. It does not, for example, encourage states to review their existing stockpile arrangements, undoubtedly a prerequisite to the identification of existing problems and available resources. Resolution 61/72 (UNGA, 2006c, para. 2) and the BMS3 outcome document (UNGA, 2008b, para. 24), by contrast, do call for such a review. Nor does the *Surplus Ammunition Report* broach the question of international transfer criteria. Although addressing this topic would undoubtedly have tested the limits of the group's mandate, it merits consideration. Many states with problematic surpluses continue to import ammunition. Exporting states have obvious leverage in such cases. The Wassenaar Arrangement's *Elements for Export Controls of MANPADS*, for example, stipulates that exporters should consider stockpile security arrangements in the recipient state before transferring man-portable air defence systems (WA, 2003, paras. 3.7, 3.9). Export criteria that made all ammunition transfers contingent on the safety and security of national stockpiles might encourage recipient countries to remedy ineffective stockpile management practices.

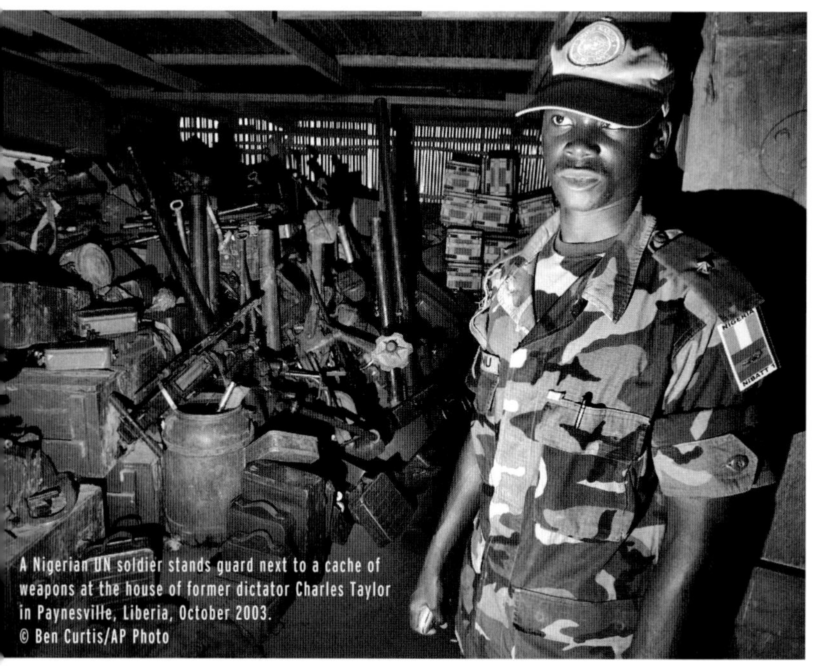
A Nigerian UN soldier stands guard next to a cache of weapons at the house of former dictator Charles Taylor in Paynesville, Liberia, October 2003.
© Ben Curtis/AP Photo

The *Ammunition Report* offers detailed, practical guidance for the improvement of stockpile management. Recognizing that international best practice is a distant goal for many countries, it does not seek to develop a new normative framework. The group noted, however, that relatively minor improvements to national stockpile management—such as fitting locks to storage facilities or observing safety distances—could dramatically reduce states' exposure to security and safety risks.

Given the gulf between international best practice and the often haphazard systems in many states, the group recommended the development of technical guidelines that would be 'sequenced to allow states gradually to attain a series of progressively more comprehensive stockpile management systems'. These would be designed to enable states 'to prioritize and address the most serious safety and security risks first'. The group envisaged a 'realistic process' aimed at improving ammunition management to the greatest extent possible (UNGA, 2008a, para. 61). In late 2008, the German government agreed to co-fund the development of these guidelines within the UN system.

Although this is never stated explicitly, many of the *Ammunition Report* recommendations apply as much to the management of arms as they do to ammunition. If implemented, they would do much to reduce the proliferation of weapons (as well as of ammunition) already circulating on illicit markets. The report, then, which has already prompted the UN to undertake the formulation of technical guidelines, has the potential to spark wider change. That said, it is no substitute for more comprehensive international efforts to regulate the ammunition trade. The GGE Report does not address broader issues related to illicit proliferation, such as the need for more effective export controls—particularly governing shipments to recipient states with a history of poor stockpile security. Curbing the proliferation of illicit ammunition, like the weapons themselves, requires a series of mutually reinforcing measures, of which stockpile management is only one.

Many Ammunition Group recommendations also apply to the management of weapons.

THE ATT GGE

By and large, the international arms trade has dodged international control efforts notwithstanding some tentative steps in this regard, notably in the *UN Programme of Action*.[35] Such regulation has traditionally been resisted on the grounds that arms transfers are a matter of state sovereignty and national security, and that the right to self-defence under Article 51 of the UN Charter carries with it a right to buy and sell arms. Indeed, arms, ammunition, and other military equipment are excluded from World Trade Organization rules pursuant to a national security exemption (GATT, 1948, art. XXI). Since the end of the cold war, however, the imposition of an increasing number of UN arms embargoes and a surge in the number of regional arrangements affecting arms transfers have, in theory, imposed greater discipline on international arms transfers. More recently, arms control advocates and sympathetic states have set their sights on a goal of global regulation.

History of the ATT

The current initiative for an Arms Trade Treaty (ATT) can be traced back to 1995, when a group of Nobel Peace Prize Laureates, led by Oscar Arias, began campaigning for an international agreement to prevent irresponsible arms transfers. The concept found traction among various civil society groups, with Amnesty International, the International Action Network on Small Arms, and Oxfam launching, in 2003, the Control Arms campaign for purposes of promoting agreement on a global, legally binding ATT. Since 2003, many states have lent their support to the initiative, including the United Kingdom, which began urging the development of global guidelines on the transfer of small arms and light weapons earlier that year.

In October 2006, a large majority of UN Member States voted to adopt the first ATT Resolution during the meeting of the General Assembly's First Committee (UNGA, 2006a), with an even larger majority supporting it in the General Assembly plenary session two months later (UNGA, 2006d) (see Table 4.1). In the first instance, the resolution called on the Secretary General to:

> *seek the views of Member States on the feasibility, scope and draft parameters for a comprehensive, legally binding instrument establishing common international standards for the import, export and transfer of conventional arms* (para. 1).

Activists campaigning for a global arms trade treaty hold placards during a protest in New Delhi, September 2006. © Adnan Abidi/Reuters

The resolution also instructed the Secretary General to establish a group of governmental experts (GGE) to examine the feasibility, scope, and draft parameters of such an instrument. A total of 99 states and two regional organizations submitted their views on an ATT to the Secretary General in 2007.[36] The GGE, comprising experts from 28 countries,[37] conducted its work over three one-week sessions in 2008,[38] and delivered its report to the Secretary General in August 2008. A further ATT resolution was adopted by the First Committee at its October 2008 meeting (UNGA, 2008d) and by the General Assembly in December 2008 (UNGA, 2008f) (second ATT Resolution). This resolution established an open-ended working group (OEWG), commencing in 2009, that will serve to open up the ATT for discussion among the broader UN membership.

The political landscape

While, as reflected in General Assembly voting patterns, the ATT process has attracted considerable support among states, it has also, not surprisingly, encountered a certain amount of resistance. The level and nature of states' support for (and opposition to) an ATT can be gleaned from two major sources: the patterns of voting on the ATT resolutions and the national submissions to the Secretary General.

General Assembly resolutions

A clear majority of states appear to favour the adoption of a legally binding ATT. The United States, the world's largest exporter of conventional arms,[39] is the only country that has consistently voted against the ATT resolutions (see Table 4.1).[40] A comparison of 'yes' votes and abstentions reveals further divergences among the major arms exporters. The United Kingdom, the fifth-largest exporter of conventional weapons (and eighth-largest exporter of small arms),[41] has been instrumental in driving the ATT process forward. Five of the other ten largest exporters of conventional arms co-sponsored the second ATT Resolution,[42] as did three of the largest importers of conventional arms.[43] Furthermore, 23 of the 30 largest exporters of conventional arms[44] and 19 of the 30 largest importers of conventional arms[45] voted

Table 4.1 Voting on the ATT resolutions

Resolution	Voting forum	Yes	Abstained	No	Not voting
First ATT Resolution	First Committee 2006	139	24	1	28
	General Assembly 2006*	153	24	1	14
Second ATT Resolution	First Committee 2008	145	18	2	27
	General Assembly 2008	133	19	1	39

* There were slight variations between the states that voted in favour of the ATT Resolution at the First Committee and those that voted in favour at the General Assembly (plenary meeting). Most importantly, Cuba and Djibouti abstained from the First Committee vote, but voted in favour of the resolution at the General Assembly. See WILPF (2008).

in favour of the first ATT Resolution at the General Assembly.[46] Five of the 30 largest exporters[47] of conventional arms and nine of the 30 largest importers[48] abstained from the vote, however.

States' views

The vast majority of the 99 states that submitted views (91) indicated that they believed an ATT was feasible and desirable. Eight, however, asserted that they did not think an ATT was feasible. Not surprisingly, all but one of these countries (Cuba) abstained from voting on the first ATT Resolution. Significantly, some of the states that asserted that an ATT was feasible, including several of the largest arms exporters, pointed out that there might be practical obstacles to agreeing an ATT. These included a lack of political will to negotiate an instrument and the possibility that some of the major exporting states would not participate constructively. The declared ATT sceptics expressed a range of other concerns. They asserted that an ATT process was premature; that universal agreement on a set of standards would be difficult to achieve; that compliance with regional-level commitments should instead be prioritized; and finally that the instrument should be politically, not legally, binding, like the *Programme of Action*. Although the United States did not submit its views on an ATT to the UN Secretary General, US government officials have been quoted as saying that an ATT would weaken existing transfer controls by setting a low universal threshold (see Box 4.4).[49]

Based on both General Assembly voting and the views submitted to the UN Secretary General, it seems clear that, while a large number of states support the idea of an ATT, several major arms exporters and importers have yet to be convinced. This was reflected in the outcome of ATT GGE discussions.

Box 4.4 The US position: not at all or wait and see?

The United States' declared opposition to the ATT resolutions appears to be at odds with domestic legislation adopted in 1999. The *International Arms Sales Code of Conduct Act of 1999* directed the President, within 120 days of enactment, to begin negotiations 'within appropriate international fora . . . to establish an international regime to promote global transparency with respect to arms transfers' (US, 1999, sec. 1262(a)). It provides a list of criteria that should be included in such an international arms sales code of conduct, including respect for human rights. Although the United States took some initial steps towards a multilateral arms transfer code of conduct,[50] it appears to have abandoned these efforts.[51]

The GGE report

Given the disparity of views within the GGE, its adoption of a consensus report represented something of an accomplishment. Had it failed to agree on an outcome, the Chairperson would have been forced to submit what is known as a 'procedural report', which simply states that the experts met at certain times and discussed certain issues, but is devoid of substantive outcomes. Nevertheless, the group's substantive report does not—in its content—extend much beyond a procedural report.

From the text of the GGE report, one could conclude that the group did fulfil its mandate 'to *examine* . . . the feasibility, scope and draft parameters for a comprehensive, legally binding instrument establishing common international standards for the import, export and transfer of conventional arms' (UNGA 2006d, para. 2; emphasis added). Indeed, the report is riddled with references to the fact that the group 'discussed', 'observed', 'recognized', 'noted', 'considered', and 'examined' various aspects of ATT feasibility, scope, and draft parameters. It appears, however, that the group did little more than 'examine' these issues, and was unable to arrive at substantive findings or agreement. There is only one instance in the report where the group appeared to 'agree' on something, namely, 'that principles enshrined in the Charter of the United Nations would be central to any potential arms trade treaty' (UNGA, 2008c, para. 24).

Feasibility

The group did not conclude that an ATT was feasible. Rather, it identified various factors on which, it claimed, feasibility depended (UNGA, 2008c, part IV). These were:

- collectively agreed objectives;
- resistance to political abuse;
- potential for universality;
- respect for the sovereignty of every state;
- respect for the territorial integrity of every state;
- practical applicability;
- clear definitions;
- scope; and
- parameters.

Two aspects of feasibility received some emphasis in the GGE Report: universality and agreed objectives. The need for an ATT to be universal (all states participating) was repeated several times in the report. One of the concerns or criticisms of the current system of regional transfer control arrangements is that not all states are party to them. Nor are they identical—which creates potential gaps and loopholes. Universality is in fact viewed by many ATT proponents as the initiative's very raison d'être—all states would be governed by the same principles and restrictions.

Scope

Under scope, the group discussed the types of weapons, activities, or transactions that might be included in an ATT. Although the GGE considered using the seven weapons categories contained in the United Nations Register of Conventional Arms,[52] plus small arms and light weapons, as a starting point for follow-up discussions on the

Blood stains the ground near shadows of Afghan police officers following an attack on foreigners in Kabul, Afghanistan, October 2008. © Ahmad Masood/Reuters

scope of an ATT, its members were unable to agree on this (UNGA, 2008c, para. 21). They also considered whether categories such as ammunition, explosives, components, defence services, and manufacturing technology should be included in an ATT, but, again, no agreement was possible. In addition, the group discussed the possible inclusion in an ATT of the following types of activities or transactions: exports, imports, re-exports, transit, trans-shipment, licensing, transportation, technology transfer, manufacturing and foreign licensed production, illicit arms brokering, and arms transfers to non-state actors (UNGA, 2008c, para. 22).

Draft parameters

Discussions of possible draft parameters for an ATT centred on the criteria that should be applied by states when considering whether to authorize an arms transfer. The group mentioned the following factors as potentially relevant to such a determination: preventing terrorism, organized crime, and other criminal activities; maintaining regional stability; promoting socio-economic development; preventing unlawful transfers to non-state actors, unauthorized re-export, unlicensed production, and illicit brokering; respecting the right to manufacture and import; utilizing end use/end-user assurances; combating diversion; and ensuring compliance with Security Council arms embargoes and other existing international obligations (UNGA, 2008c, para. 25). The group also discussed possible mechanisms, such as information sharing, reporting, and international cooperation and assistance, that could underpin the implementation of an ATT. Yet no firm conclusions were reached in this area either (para. 26).

Agreeing to disagree

It seems clear that the GGE did little to pave the way for concrete discussions, let alone negotiations, on an Arms Trade Treaty. It did not agree on a list of weapons or transactions that should be included in an ATT; it did not agree on draft parameters; most importantly, it did not even agree that there is a need for an ATT, or that such an instrument is 'feasible'. Nevertheless, the group did open the door to a continuation of the process, specifically by concluding that 'further consideration of efforts within the United Nations to address the international trade in conventional arms is required on a step-by-step basis in an open and transparent manner' (UNGA, 2008c, para. 27). The second ATT Resolution took full advantage of this possibility.

All options open

The General Assembly took up the GGE report in the autumn of 2008. Its second ATT Resolution 'endorses' the report and '[e]ncourages all states to implement and address' its recommendations to prevent the diversion of conventional arms and ensure that national transfer control systems are 'at the highest possible standards' (UNGA, 2008f, paras. 1–2 ; 2008c, paras. 28–29). Most importantly, the resolution establishes an open-ended working group (OEWG) to continue the consideration of international arms transfer issues begun by the GGE, this time with the participation of all UN Member States (UNGA, 2008f, paras. 3, 5; 2008c, para. 27). The OEWG will 'meet for up to six one-week sessions starting in 2009'. In its first year, the OEWG is to 'further consider those elements' of the GGE report 'where consensus could be developed for their inclusion in an eventual legally binding treaty' on conventional arms transfers (UNGA, 2008f, paras. 3, 5).

As of the end of 2008, the future prospects for the ATT were unclear. Given the reservations some states expressed about the initiative, it did well to survive the GGE process. One might think that agreement in the OEWG, among all UN Member States, will prove at least as elusive as in the GGE; yet states intent on blocking particular outcomes may find this more difficult in the more inclusive working group setting. Nevertheless, given the GGE's failure to agree on basic transfer control issues, the ATT OEWG is more or less obliged to start from scratch. The OEWG is, in essence, free to explore all the options. This includes the core goals and structure of a possible ATT. Nothing can be ruled out at this stage, but neither can anything be ruled in.

CONCLUSION

On paper, at least, the UN small arms process took two steps forward in 2008. BMS3 and the follow-up General Assembly Resolution breathed new life into the *UN Programme of Action,* while the Ammunition GGE produced a useful report that brings ammunition (as well as weapons) firmly into the global arms control picture. As of the end of 2008, it was unclear whether the decision to establish an open-ended working group for purposes of continuing discussions on a possible arms trade treaty would, eventually, yield similar dividends. The documents produced by BMS3 and the Ammunition GGE are important since, coupled with those produced earlier on weapons tracing and brokering, they help establish a set of benchmarks for implementation in the areas they cover. In essence, they provide detailed guidance for the implementation of frequently vague *Programme of Action* norms.

The year 2008 was also important in that fundamental questions regarding the implementation of these instruments gained new force. While the first meeting on ITI implementation saw states engaging with the details of weapons marking, record keeping, and tracing, their national reports (or lack thereof) suggested otherwise. In particular, it appears that the primary function of the ITI, namely, to facilitate small arms tracing in both crime and conflict situations, is so far unfulfilled. Similarly, there are questions about the implementation of the *Programme of Action*. National reporting appears to have the broad support of UN Member States; yet, while undoubtedly useful, it does not yet allow us to evaluate overall progress in *Programme* implementation.

The development of specific benchmarks for implementation will, to the extent these are integrated into national reporting practices, assist in this task. So too will the emergence, at least in broad outline, of a more systematic and rigorous monitoring system. It appears that national reporting for the *Programme of Action,* as well as the ITI, is shifting to a biennial schedule. This will obviously ease the often disparaged 'reporting burden', while encouraging states to provide more detailed and comprehensive information. The increased use of reporting templates will help improve comparability among reports (between states and over time), while the analysis of such information, barely begun in 2008, can be expected, if strengthened, to spur implementation efforts across the board.

The new developments at the UN offer a wealth of possibilities for international small arms work in the coming months and years. But, for now, these are possibilities, not realities. The production of new documents, important as they might be, is only progress on paper. Eight years after the adoption of the *UN Programme of Action,* the priority remains implementation.

LIST OF ABBREVIATIONS

ATT	Arms Trade Treaty
BMS3	Third Biennial Meeting of States to Consider the Implementation of the Programme of Action to Prevent, Combat and Eradicate the Illicit Trade in Small Arms and Light Weapons in All Its Aspects
GGE	Group of Governmental Experts (United Nations)
ITI	*International Tracing Instrument*
OEWG	Open-ended working group (United Nations)
UNDP	United Nations Development Programme
UNIDIR	United Nations Institute for Disarmament Research
UNODA	United Nations Office for Disarmament Affairs

ENDNOTES

1 Full title: Third Biennial Meeting of States to Consider the Implementation of the Programme of Action to Prevent, Combat and Eradicate the Illicit Trade in Small Arms and Light Weapons in All Its Aspects.

2 *International Instrument to Enable States to Identify and Trace, in a Timely and Reliable Manner, Illicit Small Arms and Light Weapons* (UNGA, 2005b).

3 ITI implementation meetings are to be combined with *Programme* implementation meetings 'where such meetings are in fact convened'. In essence, states have committed themselves to meeting biennially on ITI implementation, whatever the fortunes of the broader UN small arms process. But, wherever possible (where *Programme* implementation meetings 'are in fact convened.') the two meetings are to be combined (UNGA, 2005b, para. 37).

4 See Geneva Process on Small Arms, Working Group on BMS (2007).

5 Paragraph 8 of the resolution '*Calls upon* States, in considering the implementation of the Programme of Action, to take full advantage of the biennial meetings of States to identify priority issues or topics of relevance in the illicit trade in small arms and light weapons in all its aspects' (UNGA, 2007). To some extent, this is what happened at the 2006 Review Conference with various states and groups of states competing to ensure the issues they considered most important received their due in the outcome document under negotiation.

6 Facilitators were also used during the negotiations on the ITI, but only towards the end of the process, in an effort to break deadlock in four key areas. See Small Arms Survey (2006, p. 99).

7 See also Small Arms Survey (2004, ch. 8).

8 He asked states to submit their reports by the end of March 2008. A large number of reports were, in fact, received by that date or shortly thereafter. By the end of BMS3, a record 109 states had submitted a national report on their implementation of the *Programme of Action*.

9 The final report, prepared some months after BMS3, has been published as Cattaneo and Parker (2008).

10 The Assistance Package was first developed in 2003 and revised in 2005; it can be downloaded at <http://www.poa-iss.org/PoA/PoA.aspx>.

11 See UNGA (2001, paras. II.3, II.6).

12 In both 2006 and 2007, the United States voted against the UN General Assembly's general ('omnibus') resolution on small arms as it opposed a continuation of biennial meetings—in fact, any formal UN follow-up—for the *Programme of Action,* a position it also defended at the 2006 Review Conference. See, for example, Small Arms Survey (2007, p. 125).

13 Ten countries that did not participate in the vote subsequently informed the UN Secretariat of their support for the BMS3 Report (UNGA, 2008b, p. 7 (note 1)).

14 Standards and procedures for stockpile management are addressed in UNGA (2008b, paras. 20, 22, 24, 27b–c, e); the identification of surplus in UNGA (2008b, paras. 20, 23, 25–26, 27a); surplus disposal/destruction in UNGA (2008b, paras. 22–23, 27e); and resources in UNGA (2008b, paras. 21–23, 27d).

15 See UNGA (2008b, paras. 20, 25).

16 See also UNGA (2008b, Annex, para. 9f).

17 See also UNGA (2008b, para. 27f and Annex, para. 9d).

18 See UNGA (2008b, paras. 9, 14, 27h, Annex, paras. 2 and 9d).

19 Compare, for example: UNGA (2008b, para. 7c) with UNGA (2001, paras. II.4, III.18); and UNGA (2008b, para. 7f) with UNGA (2001, paras. III.3, III.10).

20 Formally, the ITI outcome was separate from that devoted to the *Programme of Action*. For this reason, it appears in an annex to the BMS3 report, rather than forming an integral part of the same.

21 See in particular UNGA (2008b, Annex, paras. 7, 9a, 9e).

22 Up to 17 September. During the same period, 109 national reports were received on the implementation of the *Programme of Action* (Cattaneo and Parker, 2008, chart 1 (p. 4)).

23 See UNGA (2005b, para. 31a).

24 See UNGA (2005b, para. 8d).

25 See UNGA (2005b, sec. V).

26 See Cattaneo and Parker (2008, pp. 97–112).

27 See also pream. paras. 9–10.

28 See UNGA (2008e, pream. paras. 3, 5, paras. 7, 9, 15).

29 See UNGA (2008e, pream. para. 11, para. 3).

30 See UNGA (2008e, pream. paras. 6–8, paras. 8–10).

31 See also paras. 4–5. Other themes of the Meeting are reflected in paras. 18 (matching needs with resources) and 19 ('coherent identification of needs') of the resolution.

32 See, for example, Chivers (2008).

33 Discussions over surplus conventional ammunition precede the 2005 ITI, but were nevertheless catalysed by it. See UNGA (2004; 2005c).

34 Bangladesh, Bolivia, Cameroon, Chile, China, the Czech Republic, France, Germany, Morocco, Norway, Peru, the Republic of Korea, the Russian Federation, Serbia, South Africa, the United Kingdom, and the United States. See UNGA (2008a, Annex 2).

35 Attempts to regulate the international arms trade include efforts by the League of Nations dating back to 1920. See Parker (2008, pp. 2–5).

36 The two regional organizations that submitted their views were the Caribbean Community (CARICOM) and the European Union. For a full list of the states that submitted their views, see UNODA (2007).

37 Not coincidentally, one assumes, the experts came from most of the world's top arms suppliers and many of the top arms recipients. For the names of the experts and their countries, see UNGA (2008c, pp. 5–10).

38 Exact dates were: first session, 11–15 February 2008; second session, 12–16 May 2008; and third session, 28 July–8 August 2008.

39 The United States is also the world's largest exporter and importer of small arms and light weapons (TRANSFERS).

40 Zimbabwe voted against the ATT resolution at the First Committee meeting in October 2008. Yet it voted in favour of the resolution when the General Assembly met in plenary in December 2008.

41 This is the ranking for 2005. See the Small Arms Survey website for the latest information.

42 Rankings for conventional arms transfers are taken from SIPRI (2008). The five largest exporters that co-sponsored the resolution are France, Germany, Italy, the Netherlands, and Sweden.

43 Australia, Greece and Turkey.

44 Austria, Belgium, Brazil, Bulgaria, Canada, Czech Republic, Denmark, Finland, France, Germany, Italy, Montenegro, the Netherlands, Norway, Poland, Republic of Korea, South Africa, Spain, Sweden, Switzerland, Turkey, Ukraine, and the United Kingdom.

45 Algeria, Australia, Canada, Chile, Germany, Greece, Indonesia, Italy, Japan, Malaysia, Norway, Poland, Republic of Korea, Romania, Singapore, South Africa, Spain, Turkey, and the United Kingdom.

46 Note that there is some double counting as certain major exporters of conventional arms are also major importers.

47 Belarus, China, Israel, Libya, and the Russian Federation.

48 China, Egypt, India, Iran, Israel, Pakistan, Saudi Arabia, United Arab Emirates, and Venezuela.

49 'The only way to convince all major exporters to sign on to the ATT would be to weaken its provisions. Concluding a weak ATT would legitimize an international standard based on a lowest common denominator that would not address the problem of illicit and irresponsible transfers' (Explanation of vote on Draft Resolution L.39 (Arms Trade Treaty) by Ambassador Christina Rocca, permanent representative of the United States delegation to the Conference on Disarmament, 31 October 2008, para. 2; <http://www.reachingcriticalwill.org/political/1com/1com08/EOV/USL39.pdf>). See also Norton-Taylor (2006).

50 See, for example, EU and US (2000).

51 In the years following the Act's 1999 adoption, the US State Department included a multilateral Arms Transfer Code of Conduct in a list of performance indicators for 'Regional Stability' that figured in its annual *Performance and Accountability* reports. The code indicator was, however, 'discontinued' in the 2002 report. The State Department indicated that 'because arms sales reflect national foreign policies, we do not foresee significant non-European adherence to the code in the near- to long-term'. It concluded that, as several 'influential countries' were 'preparing their own versions' of a code of conduct 'and developing strategies for widespread adoption', '[i]t is to our advantage to let other countries develop their own text for a code before continuing further' (US DoS, 2003, p. 272). There has been no further mention of the code of conduct goal in the State Department reports.

52 The seven major categories of weapons under the UN Register of Conventional Arms are: battle tanks, armoured combat vehicles, large-calibre artillery systems, combat aircraft, attack helicopters, warships (including submarines), and missiles and missile-launchers.

53 The author was Special Advisor to Ammunition GGE Chairperson, Michael Hasenau. The views expressed in this chapter are the author's alone and should not be attributed to Mr Hasenau or the Government of Germany.

54 The author was Special Advisor to BMS3 Chairperson, Ambassador Dalius Čekuolis. The views expressed in this chapter are the author's alone and should not be attributed to Ambassador Čekuolis or the Government of Lithuania.

BIBLIOGRAPHY

Bevan, James, ed. 2008. *Conventional Ammunition in Surplus: A Reference Guide*. Geneva: Small Arms Survey. January.

BtB (Biting the Bullet Project: International Alert, Saferworld, University of Bradford) with IANSA (International Action Network on Small Arms). 2006. *Reviewing Action on Small Arms 2006: Assessing the First Five Years of the UN Programme of Action*. London: Biting the Bullet. <http://www.iansa.org/un/review2006/redbook2006/>

Cattaneo, Silvia and Sarah Parker. 2008. *Implementing the United Nations Programme of Action on Small Arms and Light Weapons: Analysis of the National Reports Submitted by States from 2002 to 2008*. Geneva: United Nations Institute for Disarmament Research (UNIDIR). December. <http://www.unidir.ch/bdd/fiche-ouvrage.php?ref_ouvrage=92-9045-008-H-en>

—. 2009. *Analysis of National Reporting on PoA Implementation*. Unpublished background paper. Geneva: Small Arms Survey.

Čekuolis, Dalius. 2008. 'Tackling the Illicit Small Arms Trade: The Chairman Speaks.' *Arms Control Today*, Vol. 38, No. 8. October, pp. 19–24. <http://www.armscontrol.org/act/2008_10/Cekuolis>

Chivers, Chris. 2008. 'Supplier Under Scrutiny on Arms for Afghans.' *New York Times*. 27 March. <http://www.nytimes.com/2008/03/27/world/asia/27ammo.html?_r=2&pagewanted=print>

EU (European Union) and US (United States). 2000. *Declaration by the European Union and the United States on the Responsibilities of States and on Transparency Regarding Arms Exports*. Conclusions of the EU–US Summit, Washington, DC. 18 December. <http://www.eurunion.org/partner/summit/Summit0012/ArmsExpts.htm>

GATT (*General Agreement on Tariffs and Trade*). 1948. Entered into force 1 January. Geneva: World Trade Organization, July 1986 (consolidated version). <http://www.wto.org/english/docs_e/legal_e/gatt47_e.pdf>

Geneva Process on Small Arms. Working Group on BMS. 2007. *Options and Proposals for Making Biennial Meetings of States as Effective as Possible in Advancing Implementation of the UN Programme of Action on Small Arms*. Unpublished paper. 1 June.

Greene, Owen. 2006. 'Ammunition for Small Arms and Light Weapons: Understanding the Issues and Addressing the Challenges.' In Stéphanie Pézard and Holger Anders, eds. *Targeting Ammunition: A Primer*. Geneva: Small Arms Survey. June, pp. 1–13.

Norton–Taylor, Richard. 2006. 'UN Vote Paves Way for Arms Treaty.' *Guardian* (London). 28 October. <http://www.guardian.co.uk/world/2006/oct/28/armstrade.richardnortontaylor>

Parker, Sarah. 2008. *Implications of States Views on an Arms Trade Treaty*. Geneva: United Nations Institute for Disarmament Research (UNIDIR). January. <http://www.unidir.ch/bdd/fiche-ouvrage.php?ref_ouvrage=92-9045-008-B-en>

SIPRI (Stockholm International Peace Research Institute). 2008. *SIPRI Yearbook 2008: Armaments, Disarmament and International Security*. Oxford: Oxford University Press. <http://yearbook2008.sipri.org/>

Small Arms Survey. 2004. *Small Arms Survey 2004: Rights at Risk*. Oxford: Oxford University Press.

—. 2006. *Small Arms Survey 2006: Unfinished Business*. Oxford: Oxford University Press.

—. 2007. *Small Arms Survey 2007: Guns and the City*. Cambridge: Cambridge University Press.

—. 2008. *Small Arms Survey 2008: Risk and Resilience*. Cambridge: Cambridge University Press.

UNGA (United Nations General Assembly). 1997. *Report of the Panel of Governmental Experts on Small Arms (UN Panel Report)*. A/52/298 of 27 August (annexe). <http://disarmament.un.org/cab/smallarms/docs/rep52298.pdf>

—. 1999a. *Report of the Group of Experts on the Problem of Ammunition and Explosives (Ammunition Report)*. A/54/155 of 29 June. <http://disarmament.un.org/cab/smallarms/docs/rep54155.pdf>

—. 1999b. *Report of the Group of Governmental Experts on Small Arms (Small Arms Report)*. A/54/258 of 19 August. <http://disarmament.un.org/cab/smallarms/docs/rep54258e.pdf>

—. 2001. *Programme of Action to Prevent, Combat and Eradicate the Illicit Trade in Small Arms and Light Weapons in All Its Aspects ('UN Programme of Action')*. 20 July. A/CONF.192/15. <http://disarmament.un.org/cab/smallarms/files/aconf192_15.pdf>

—. 2004. *Problems Arising from the Accumulation of Conventional Ammunition Stockpiles in Surplus*. Decision 59/515 of 3 December.

—. 2005a. *Report of the Open-ended Working Group to Negotiate an International Instrument to Enable States to Identify and Trace, in a Timely and Reliable Manner, Illicit Small Arms and Light Weapons*. A/60/88 of 27 June. <http://www.un.org/events/smallarms2006/pdf/A.60.88%20(E).pdf>

—. 2005b. *International Instrument to Enable States to Identify and Trace, in a Timely and Reliable Manner, Illicit Small Arms and Light Weapons ('International Tracing Instrument')*. A/60/88 of 27 June (annexe). <http://www.un.org/events/smallarms2006/pdf/A.60.88%20(E).pdf>

—. 2005c. *Problems Arising from the Accumulation of Conventional Ammunition Stockpiles in Surplus*. Resolution 60/74 of 8 December. Reproduced in A/RES/60/74 of 11 January 2006.

—. 2006a. *Towards an Arms Trade Treaty: Establishing Common International Standards for the Import, Export and Transfer of Conventional Arms*. Draft Resolution A/C.1/61/L.55 of 12 October.

—. 2006b. *The Illicit Trade in Small Arms and Light Weapons in All Its Aspects*. Resolution 61/66 of 6 December. Reproduced in A/RES/61/66 of 3 January 2007.

—. 2006c. *Problems Arising from the Accumulation of Conventional Ammunition Stockpiles in Surplus*. Resolution 61/72 of 6 December. Reproduced in A/RES/61/72 of 3 January 2007.

—. 2006d. *Towards an Arms Trade Treaty: Establishing Common International Standards for the Import, Export and Transfer of Conventional Arms*. Resolution 61/89 of 6 December. Reproduced in A/RES/61/89 of 18 December.

—. 2007. *The Illicit Trade in Small Arms and Light Weapons in All Its Aspects*. Resolution 62/47 of 5 December. Reproduced in A/RES/62/47 of 10 January 2008.

—. 2008a. *Report of the Group of Governmental Experts Established Pursuant to General Assembly Resolution 61/72 to Consider Further Steps to Enhance Cooperation with Regard to the Issue of Conventional Ammunition Stockpiles In Surplus (Surplus Ammunition Report)*. A/63/182 of 28 July. <http://www.poa-iss.org/DocsUpcomingEvents/a-63-182-e.pdf>

—. 2008b. *Report of the Third Biennial Meeting of States to Consider the Implementation of the Programme of Action to Prevent, Combat and Eradicate the Illicit Trade in Small Arms and Light Weapons in All Its Aspects*. A/CONF.192/BMS/2008/3 of 20 August. <http://disarmament2.un.org/cab/bms3/1BMS3Pages/1thirdBMS.html>

—. 2008c. *Report of the Group of Governmental Experts to Examine the Feasibility, Scope and Draft Parameters for a Comprehensive, Legally Binding Instrument Establishing Common International Standards for the Import, Export and Transfer of Conventional Arms*. A/63/334 of 26 August. <http://www.poa-iss.org/DocsUpcomingEvents/a-63-334-e.pdf>

—. 2008d. *Towards an Arms Trade Treaty: Establishing Common International Standards for the Import, Export and Transfer of Conventional Arms*. Draft Resolution. A/C.1/63/L.39 of 17 October.

—. 2008e. *The Illicit Trade in Small Arms and Light Weapons in All Its Aspects*. Resolution 63/72 of 2 December. Reproduced in A/RES/63/72 of 12 January 2009.

—. 2008f. *Towards an Arms Trade Treaty: Establishing Common International Standards for the Import, Export and Transfer of Conventional Arms*. Resolution 63/240 of 24 December. Reproduced in A/RES/63/240 of 8 January 2009.

UNODA (United Nations Office for Disarmament Affairs). 2007. Towards an Arms Trade Treaty. <http://disarmament.un.org/cab/ATT/index.html>

US (United States). 1999. *International Arms Sales Code of Conduct Act of 1999*. 22 U.S.C. 2551. <http://uscode.house.gov/uscode-cgi/fastweb.exe?getdoc+uscview+t21t25+2469+1++%28%29%20%20A>

—. DoS (Department of State). 2003. *Fiscal Year 2002 Performance and Accountability Report*. February.
<http://www.state.gov/documents/organization/18552.pdf>

WA (Wassenaar Arrangement). 2003. *Elements for Export Controls of Man-Portable Air Defence Systems*. 12 December.
<http://www.wassenaar.org/publicdocuments/2007/docs/Elements_for_Export_Controls_of_Manpads.pdf>

Wilkinson, Adrian. 2008. 'Ammunition Depot Explosions.' In James Bevan, ed. *Conventional Ammunition in Surplus: A Reference Guide*. Geneva: Small Arms Survey. January, pp. 129–35.

WILPF (Women's International League for Peace and Freedom). 2008. 'Draft Resolutions from the First Committee on Disarmament and International Security 2006, October 2–October 31, 2006.' Reaching Critical Will.
<http://www.reachingcriticalwill.org/political/1com/1com06/res/resindex.html>

ACKNOWLEDGEMENTS

Principal authors

James Bevan,[53] Glenn McDonald,[54] Sarah Parker

An ex-combatant brings weapons to a disarmament point set up by the United Nations Mission in Liberia, April 2004.
© Tim A. Hetherington/Panos Pictures

Man, the State, and War

THE THREE FACES OF SMALL ARMS DISARMAMENT

5

INTRODUCTION

Small arms and light weapons disarmament measures are becoming routine and widespread. When the United Nations Development Programme announced an initiative in late 2008 to disarm and demobilize 182,900 former combatants in Sudan, the news was neither surprising nor unprecedented (IRIN, 2008). Perhaps the most striking aspect was its very normalcy. Several comparable initiatives were unveiled elsewhere in 2008, as were other new small arms collection and disarmament projects.

Small arms control stresses core goals and common procedures, with results that fall far short of international uniformity, but at least seem generally consistent. Small arms disarmament, by comparison, has been continuously reinvented, leading to an ever-growing canon of projects, many of which seem tailored to unique circumstances, without broader relevance. This chapter seeks to clarify the accomplishments and limitations of small arms collection and disarmament as it affects civilians, the state, and non-state actors. It challenges writers like Colin Gray, who argue that disarmament eliminates weapons best when it is needed least (Gray, 1992). The chapter shows that, whether it is a cause of change or a correlate, collection and disarmament measures usually are associated with a reduction of armed violence and promotion of political stability. Among its key findings:

- Destruction of state-owned small arms has been roughly comparable in scale to that of civilian firearms.
- Disarmament of non-state forces is by far the smallest quantitatively, but it may be most important for international and domestic security.
- The best prospects for further large-scale disarmament involve destruction of state surpluses.
- Disarmament has destroyed 40 per cent of some military arsenals and as much as 20 per cent of civilian weapons.
- Extrapolated globally, the findings suggest that at least 76 million military small arms and 120 million civilian firearms could be eliminated.
- Whether voluntary or compulsory, civilian weapons collection and destruction is most effective when accepted as legitimate. Coercive disarmament efforts often fail.
- While the impact of civilian weapons collection and destruction is difficult to separate from other reforms, it is associated with reduction or control of homicide and suicide rates.

Disarmament is an enormous subject, relevant to the full spectrum of 'deadly quarrels', from disputes between individuals to the 'clash of civilizations' (Richardson, 1960; Huntington, 1996). Small arms, light weapons, and their ammunition are part of this spectrum of human conflict, ranging from domestic violence to world war, with a role for disarmament in all. Disarmament measures, moreover, can take many forms, from reducing a particular type of weapon to complete elimination of a whole category (see Box 5.1). An overarching theory of small arms disarmament—

explaining when it is possible, how it is implemented, and what it achieves—remains a distant goal. Although a thorough understanding of disarmament progress requires such insight, this chapter does not explicitly consider such fundamental issues.

Box 5.1 Arms control vs. disarmament

Small arms control refers to regulations establishing conditions on ownership, limiting acquisition of certain quantities or types of weapons or ammunition, or restricting storage, transfer, and resale. Control does not aim to reduce weapons numbers, but rather to ensure greater safety of existing and future inventories.

Small arms disarmament is a process involving collection and destruction of weapons, sometimes combined with erecting barriers against acquisition of new weapons. It can be incremental, partial, or comprehensive.

This chapter instead provides an empirical review of the contributions disarmament processes have made to conflict and violence abatement. It focuses not on enhanced control over arms inventories or tighter regulation of firearms ownership, but on systematic weapons collection, followed by outright destruction. Similarly, it explores the role of collection and disarmament among all three major actors affected by the use of small arms and light weapons: society, state agencies, and non-state combatants.

Disarmament can mean the absolute elimination of an entire category of weapon, as called for by the 1993 Chemical Weapons Convention or the 1997 Anti-Personnel Landmines Treaty, but in practice it is usually a process of incremental steps and partially attained accomplishments. Small arms disarmament has more in common with agreements that reduced armaments without eliminating them, such as the 1990 Treaty on Conventional Armed Forces in Europe or the 1991 Strategic Arms Reduction Treaty. All too often, disarmament occurs in a conflicted political atmosphere, where destruction of old weapons is accompanied by acquisition of new models. Other forces are also shaping events. Part of an environment full of conflicting impulses and parallel efforts, small arms disarmament rarely yields to easy assessment. Small arms collection and disarmament, rather, is a realm of weak generalizations.

The chapter introduces three major categories of small arms and light weapons disarmament, each stressing particular actors, methods, and trends. Examining in turn the disarmament experience among civilians, states, and non-state actors, each section assesses overall data and illustrative case studies. The chapter reaffirms the diverse forms of small arms collection and disarmament, each of which relies on separate methods, produces data that is difficult to compare, and achieves distinct goals. Civilian arms collection and destruction, for example, is all about reducing violence. State disarmament reduces stockpiles to diminish costs and illicit diversion. Disarmament of non-state actors is largely about symbolic dividends, including confidence building and restoration of state authority. Consequently, there is no single way to compare disarmament performance; each subfield, sometimes each experience, must be evaluated separately.

THREE FACES OF DISARMAMENT

All small arms, light weapons, and ammunition disarmament undertakings share a desire to transcend the limits of arms control, to minimize the dangers of armed violence through outright destruction of weapons and ammunition. In application, though, disarmament programmes differ depending on the nature of the parties involved. Reducing the small arms holdings of individual owners involves very different goals and mechanisms from the trimming of state arsenals or the disarmament of insurgent forces. These three categories are summarized here as *man*, the *state*, and *war* (Waltz, 1959). They differ in terms of rationales, symbolism, and measures of success to such a degree that they share little more than the definitive act of weapons destruction.

Civilian weapons collection and destruction addresses the safety and social environment of individuals. Participants are usually otherwise ordinary men and women. They may be former combatants but are no longer organized or responsive to military command. The state usually is the crucial actor organizing civilian collection and disarmament processes, although inter-governmental and even non-governmental organizations can play important roles. But, in this case, the state is not giving up its own weapons. Civilian weapons collection and destruction can be principally symbolic. As weapons become part of a dialogue about social goals, their number or quality may be less important than the ceremonies designed to transform their meaning, potentially making guns and gun use less heroic and more repugnant. In many cases, success is measured not so much in absolute numbers of weapons as in social outcomes, such as the reduction of domestic or criminal violence or, more modestly, changed attitudes towards weapons possession and use.

State disarmament is usually undertaken by governments to reduce their own arsenals. Except for enforced disarmament of defeated states after wars, state disarmament is usually essentially home-grown, driven by the priorities and capabilities of the state. Foreign governments and multilateral organizations can play facilitating roles, but the crucial decisions belong to the state that controls the weapons. State disarmament can have symbolic elements, but it is intended primarily to improve the security of the state and its citizens by reducing dangers of weapons diversion and, in the case of ammunition, depot explosions. It also promises economic savings. The success of state disarmament is readily measured in terms of the absolute number or proportion of total weapons eliminated, especially in relation to identified surplus.[1]

Gun destruction is a symbol of commitment more than an impediment to renewed fighting.

Disarmament of non-state actors is about reducing the risks of (renewed) warfare and (continuing) armed violence. With the decline of state-to-state war, conflict disarmament today typically applies to non-state combatants (Mack, 2005). Former government soldiers or militiamen may be included, but the emphasis of formal disarmament, demobilization, and reintegration (DDR) is on building domestic and regional security by facilitating reintegration of former combatants into civilian life. With the quantity and quality of weapons secondary to the goal of social and political reintegration (ACEH), the numbers or types of weapons eliminated is often less important. Former insurgents are seldom willing to surrender all their weapons, least of all when embarking upon a peace process of uncertain resilience. With only a limited share of weaponry involved, destruction is valued as a symbol of commitment more than a physical impediment to the resumption of fighting. Quantity and quality are still relevant, but even modest disarmament may be enough to advance a political process.

Through much of the 20th century, disarmament advocates pressed their preferred instrument as a transformative tool, one that would make many other security policies unnecessary. Elimination of weapons of mass destruction or major conventional weapons systems was expected to change the nature of international relations (Myrdal, 1976; Noel-Baker, 1926). Small arms disarmament, by contrast, is rarely promoted today as an end in and of itself. Only in very specific circumstances is disarmament the dominant goal; destruction of excess man-portable air defence systems (MANPADS) may be the best example of this.

As the dominant actor in international small arms processes, states are vital to the business of disarmament, largely determining where it is emphasized and what it can achieve. The way states view disarmament is revealed

Table 5.1 **Government seizure and destruction information for 49 countries**

Country	Year(s)	Description	Military	Civilian	Police	Combatant
Angola	2006	small arms and light weapons		75,323		
Argentina	2002-03	firearms		7,396		
Austria	2006	surplus	82,252			
Bosnia and Herzegovina	2007	small arms and light weapons	95,000			
Botswana	2006	firearms		1,159		
Brazil	2004-05	small arms		253,321		
Bulgaria	2002	surplus	75,612			
Cambodia	1999-2007	small arms and light weapons		242,000		
Canada	2003	surplus revolvers			20,000	
China	1996-2004	illegal		4,000,000		
Croatia	2008	small arms and light weapons	27,741			
Czech Republic	2006	seized		4,500		
Ecuador	2003-07	firearms		15,519		
El Salvador	1996-2004	small arms		24,566		
Estonia	2006	pistols	6,000			
Finland	2007		12,368	3,283		
France	1998-2000	small arms	140,000			
Germany	1990-2007	surplus	2,155,892			
Ghana	2001-07			2,500		
Greece	2001-02		570	1,190		
Haiti	2002*			249		
India	1990-2007	terrorist				49,953
Italy	2007	small arms and light weapons	169,925			
Kazakhstan	2004	firearms		875		

Kenya	2003-08	small arms and light weapons		20,136		
Lesotho	2001-04	firearms		3,800		
Lithuania	2001			1,004		
Macedonia, former Yugoslav Republic of	2003-07	weapons		17,000		
Mexico	2007			28,302		
Namibia	2007			1,426		
New Zealand	2007	police rifles			750	
Nicaragua	2004	MANPADS	333			
Niger	2000-04	confiscated		1,746		
Nigeria	2004	assorted				1,466
Norway	2004	firearms		29,308		
Paraguay	2003	firearms		2,615		
Peru	2002-05	firearms		3,736		
Philippines	2007-08	captured				57,200
Portugal	2006	apprehended		1,215		
Romania	2002-03	small arms and light weapons	195,510			
Serbia	2001-04	small arms		108,789		
Solomon Islands	2003-04	former military				2,542
South Africa	1999-04	small arms	271,867	42,642	162,000	
Sri Lanka	2005	captured		35,000		
Tanzania	2001-05	illicit		8,540		
Togo	2006	firearms		8,062		
Turkey	1984-2007	terrorist				89,381
Uganda	2005-06	seized		53,000		
Uruguay	2008	civilian		8,000		
Total			**3,233,070**	**5,006,202**	**182,750**	**200,452**

* The year for Haiti is approximate.

Sources: Parker and Cattaneo (2008) for all countries except Angola (2006, p. 10); Finland (2008, pp. 6, 10); India (2008, p. 5); Mexico (2008, p. 3); Norway (2005, p. 9); and Turkey (2008, p. 1)

in their statements about the issue. Table 5.1 collects official disarmament information from annual reports on implementation of the 2001 UN *Programme of Action*.[2] These reports do not provide a complete picture of global disarmament. Many countries have not reported at all while others do not offer much information about their disarmament activities. They may, for example, only report on their assistance for disarmament in other countries. Despite their great variation, these reports constitute the single most comprehensive repository of information about national disarmament practices available today (Parker and Cattaneo, 2008).

Equally important, the disarmament activities that governments emphasize in their reporting reveal much about their policies and priorities. While the civilian, state, and ex-combatant categories feature regularly in the reports, individual submissions usually focus on a particular aspect of small arms disarmament. Of the 49 governments providing disarmament data in Table 5.1, only South Africa reports on all actors of state and society (military, police, and civilians, but not non-state combatants). Most countries focus on either state or civilian disarmament. Regardless of emphasis, though, the total quantities of weapons involved in each of the two categories are roughly comparable. Removing the biggest statistical outliers (China and Germany) makes the overall categories of state and civilian disarmament even more similar.

Purely voluntary gun turn-ins can be surprisingly effective.

As shown in Table 5.1, few governments reporting on their implementation of the *Programme of Action* say much about the disarmament of non-state armed groups. The quantities of weapons involved in such cases can be much smaller than disarmament of state agencies or collection of weapons from civilians, a reflection of the relatively smaller size of most insurgencies, as well as their ambivalence about participating. No less revealing, governments that stress armed groups in their reporting do not describe any disarmament of national military or law enforcement agencies.

MAN: COLLECTING CIVILIAN GUNS

Although civilian weapons collection is principally governed by domestic small arms policy, the pool of shared experience is expanding as a result of the efforts of particular countries. The need to reduce arms supply often continues well after armed conflict has ended and former combatants have been disarmed and demobilized. Armed civilians—rather than insurgents or the state—are often at the centre of the worst cycles of today's violence in countries such as Brazil, Guatemala, Haiti, Jamaica, Mexico, South Africa, and Venezuela. State forces are hardly blameless; often they are heavily implicated in social chaos. In most of these countries, though, civilian inventories—sometimes augmented by warfare and terrorism—are most likely to be used in acts of violence.

Civilian weapons collection in post-conflict countries ideally includes three parallel processes: weapon turn-ins (voluntary, with some form of individual compensation, or weapons-for-development exchanges), combined with regulatory reform to inhibit sudden or sustained rearming or acquisition of more powerful firearms, and institutional reform to enhance local security and weaken demand for new weapons. Such projects, like any others, require meticulous management. Success is most likely when all three aspects are pursued simultaneously, minimizing uncertainty and discouraging rearming (Buchanan and Widmer, 2006, pp. 11–18).

When it comes to civilian weapons, most of the states listed in Table 5.1 seem happiest to emphasize the collection and destruction of crime guns. This section, however, pays greater attention to systematic efforts to eliminate whole categories of civilian weapons, as illustrated by five major examples in Australia, Brazil, Britain, the Solomon Islands, and South Africa. Although such initiatives are few in number, the resulting reduction in civilian ownership tends to be much greater, making their lessons especially important.

Preconditions of civilian weapons collection

To its most vociferous critics, civilian disarmament is eternally associated with the crimes of Nazi Germany, when Jews and Communists were denied weapons permits and required to turn in their firearms. The effort to stain civilian weapons collection with the blood of the Holocaust is a common trope of gun rights advocacy (Halbrook, 2000). This obscures basic realities: except for police seizure of crime guns, the most successful undertakings are highly consensual. Just as careful assessment questions whether Nazi gun policy actually achieved much at all (Harcourt, 2004), it appears that other civilian collection programmes have been quite effective fulfilling limited aims. That said, the preconditions for success can seem just as demanding as those for disarmament between rival states counting nuclear warheads.

Civilian weapons collection and destruction varies greatly, from the complete cessation of legal civilian gun ownership, as in the Solomon Islands since 2002 and proposed under the 2005 Brazilian referendum, to ending legal ownership of particular categories of firearms, such as handguns in Britain and automatic weapons in Australia, to simply banning carrying firearms in public, as in parts of Yemen since 2005. Uniting these measures are restrictions on previously permissible ownership, usually involving a reduction in the number or types of guns civilians are permitted to own.

One of the most difficult issues for civilian weapons collection is whether a programme should be voluntary or compulsory. In practice, a mixture of both may be necessary. Purely voluntary turn-ins can be surprisingly effective. The most successful experiences banning particular types of firearms—in Australia and Britain—involved stronger measures (see below). While civilian collection and destruction cannot be effective without widespread support, it may not be taken seriously without threat of sanctions. In lieu of some compulsion, moreover, free-rider problems can undermine cooperation (everyone gains security regardless of whether each individual participates). But sanctions without support are not politically sustainable either. In the short run, the fastest implementation appears to come through the combination of strong public support with a legal requirement for mandatory compliance. Whether voluntary or compulsory, civilian weapons collection and destruction is most effective when its legitimacy is accepted (see Box 5.2). Experiences with *coercive* disarmament, involving the threat or use of state force, may not be universally disastrous, but they tend to fail (see Box 5.3).

To be effective over the longer term, civilian weapons collection must be combined with arms trade control to minimize rapid replacement. The Burundi example shows that this is not easily done by weak states with porous borders (Pézard and Florquin, 2007). Geography undoubtedly plays a major role in the effectiveness of such efforts, yet, in the long run, reducing *demand* may be even more critical.

A major source of doubt in any evaluation is the inability to isolate the effect of civilian weapons collection from other measures implemented simultaneously to reduce crime

Box 5.2 Preferred circumstances for effective civilian collection

- High *public support* for collection measures;
- Widespread acceptance of *government authority*;
- Public belief in *state institutions* to assure personal security;
- Carefully calibrated *compensation*;
- Corresponding *restrictions* on replacement purchases; and
- Readily *controlled international borders*.

and illegal gun use. The issue is part of the enigma surrounding crime decline anywhere (Zimring, 2006). The causes of crime increases can often be isolated, with a small number of key factors at work. The same cannot usually be said of crime declines, typically the result of a combination of social forces and policy choices. In every case examined here, civilian weapons collection was part of a larger reform package, typically including gun control (such as purchasing restrictions, changes in the right to carry arms, and gun registration) and better law enforcement. Community activism and demographic change (an ageing population) often were at work as well. Further clouding our understanding of the specific role of civilian collection and destruction, all the cases examined here involved only partial measures. Most eliminated only a small proportion of the country's total civilian arsenal.

For want of systematic data on any but the most ephemeral aspects of crime gun seizures, this section relies instead on careful examination of five prominent experiences: Australia, Britain, Brazil, the Solomon Islands, and South Africa (see Table 5.2). Although the sample is small, these cases suggest that elimination of roughly 20 per cent of a country's civilian inventory may be entirely feasible financially and politically. Of a global civilian inventory of some 650 million guns, this amounts to at least 120 million readily suitable for collection and destruction.[3] Whether such actions are thought worthwhile, however, is typically determined by local circumstances. The distinctiveness of each case is striking, none more so than that of China. Chinese economic and social statistics are often received sceptically, complicating interpretation (Small Arms Survey, 2002, pp. 94–96). The Chinese example noted in Tables 5.1 and 5.2 is huge and has been emphasized by officials, but it is not examined further here. While none of these cases proves that weapons collection was instrumental in reducing armed violence, most were followed by such a reduction. More broadly, even if it is not possible to confirm exactly what disarmament measures have accomplished, it is clear that in no case reviewed here was disarmament progress associated with an increase in firearms homicide. Only in Britain was weapons collection followed by deteriorating social stability ('anti-social behaviour'), and this remains small by international standards (ASB, 2003). Although methodological barriers make it difficult to prove exactly how much disarmament helped in these cases, none suggest it led to an increase in the number of deaths.

Table 5.2 Examples of major civilian collection programmes

Country	Registered civilian guns	Est. total civilian guns[a]	Destroyed	Years	Proportion destroyed
Australia	3,200,000	3,900,000	713,000	1997-2003	18%
Brazil	3,688,506	15,000,000	748,177	1998-2005	5%
China	680,000	40,000,000	4,000,000	1996-2006	10%
Solomon Islands	n/a	3,520	3,714	2003-04	106%[c]
South Africa	3,737,676	5,950,000	442,337[d]	2001-05	7%
United Kingdom[b]	1,934,633	3,700,000	162,198	1997-98	4%

Notes:

[a] Estimated total civilian guns before destruction.

[b] United Kingdom data here refers only to England, Scotland, and Wales.

[c] The number of weapons in the Solomon Islands was underestimated; more were destroyed than previously thought to exist.

[d] The South African disarmament total subtracts 88,640 decommissioned police weapons (Gould et al., 2004, p. 243).

Sources: **Australia:** Chapman et al. (2006, p. 365); Lee and Suardi (2008, p. 23). **Brazil:** Dreyfus and Nascimento (forthcoming). **China:** Parker and Cattaneo (2008). **Solomon Islands:** AP (2004); Muggah and Alpers (2003). **South Africa:** Lamb (2008, p. 20); Gould et al. (2004, p. 243). **United Kingdom:** UK Parliament (1999). **Other data:** Small Arms Survey (2007a, ch. 2, app. 3).

Box 5.3 **Coercive disarmament and the mistakes of others**

Governments struggling to impose control over parts of their territory may see forced disarmament as the best solution to their problems. Actual experience, however, suggests otherwise. *Compulsory disarmament*–legally mandated and regulated–can be highly effective when the preconditions discussed earlier are met. This approach is different from coercive disarmament, which relies on the threat or use of state force. The risks of *coercive disarmament* have been shown repeatedly in north-east Africa, where heavily armed tribesmen and former militiamen are a powerful force.

The trans-border region of Ethiopia-Kenya-Sudan-Uganda has long been unstable due to migratory lifestyles of major cattle herding tribes (the Karimojong, Pokot, Toposa, and Turkana) and their tendency for 'predatory expansion' (Mburu, 2007, p. 71). Persistent drought and acquisition of automatic rifles, both intensifying in the mid-1990s, aggravated traditional instability. Guns increased the risks of raiding and cattle theft but also the potential rewards for such crime (Leff, 2007). The result is a classic arms spiral; gun ownership no longer assured individual security, but disarmament was too risky in the absence of sufficient state power. Instead, disarmament was imposed in all these countries to restore state authority and regional stability.

In southern Sudan, disarmament of civilians has been used repeatedly in an effort to consolidate the authority of the Sudan People's Liberation Army-led government and to promote stability, but the results vary. The most controversial events occurred in 2006, though accounts are complex and confusing. Local observers regarded some aspects of the disarmament of rival militias in Jonglei state as relatively successful. Although described as 'voluntary', the most successful were organized on a command basis through local chiefs. This yielded roughly 3,300 weapons, many of good quality. Other elements of the programme were disastrous, provoking military resistance from the White Army and the Lou Nuer tribe. Although roughly 1,400 small arms and light weapons were seized in this part of the process, it led to widespread fighting, with hundreds of deaths and serious dislocation (Small Arms Survey, 2007b, pp. 4-5). Research in Jonglei by the Small Arms Survey shows a substantial decline in criminal victimization since the peace process and disarmament. In various Jonglei regions, 76.4 to 84.0 per cent of survey respondents report feeling more secure or about the same, while 12.4 to 18.1 per cent report feeling less secure (Garfield, 2007, pp. 28-29).

There is nothing new about disarmament in the Ugandan region of Karamoja: James Bevan records nine campaigns from 1945 to 2007. As a response to chronic Karimojong attacks on neighbouring tribes, the highly publicized 2001-02 campaign was intended to restrain Karimojong power. More than 10,000 firearms were seized, roughly one-quarter of the estimated Karimojong arsenal. But the heavy-handed campaign turned the Karimojong from government supporters into enemies, a situation that further deteriorated when the Ugandan Army withdrew from the region in 2002. Another campaign by the Ugandan Army to restore order and take Karimojong weapons in 2005-06 achieved few positive results (Bevan, 2008a, pp. 54-60).

In all these cases, coercive disarmament initially was seen as an instrument for restoring the authority of the state and rule of law. Yet experience reveals that there are no shortcuts to nation-building. While collecting unwanted guns such as those found in unguarded village caches in north-east Africa contributed to security, taking weapons from groups still convinced of their vulnerability had the opposite effect. Studies by the Small Arms Survey conclude that disarmament works best when preceded by restoration of state authority, not the other way around (Bevan, 2008a, p. 18; Leff, 2007, p. 5; Garfield, 2007, p. 38).

A radically different critique comes from US gun advocates who embrace the Karimojong as fellow victims, wrongfully stigmatized because 'for countless generations, cattle rustling has been a traditional . . . pursuit' (Kopel, Gallant, and Eisen, 2008, p. 38). Even this perspective does not dispute that proliferation of automatic rifles dramatically worsened tribal violence in north-east Africa. Nor do its advocates offer evidence that additional guns will have a positive effect. The only promising solution appears to be state-building and restoration of the rule of law to suppress cattle theft, prior to consensual disarmament.

Australia

Not only did Australia enact one of the proportionately largest civilian firearms collection and destruction schemes ever attempted, but it also has become the centre of an important debate on its effectiveness.

Firearms licensing and registration was established in the 1970s, but laws were permissive and had little effect on the country's gun culture, which permitted ownership of military-style weapons, although handguns were more regulated. Change came after a series of mass killings that began in the 1980s and culminated in the Port Arthur

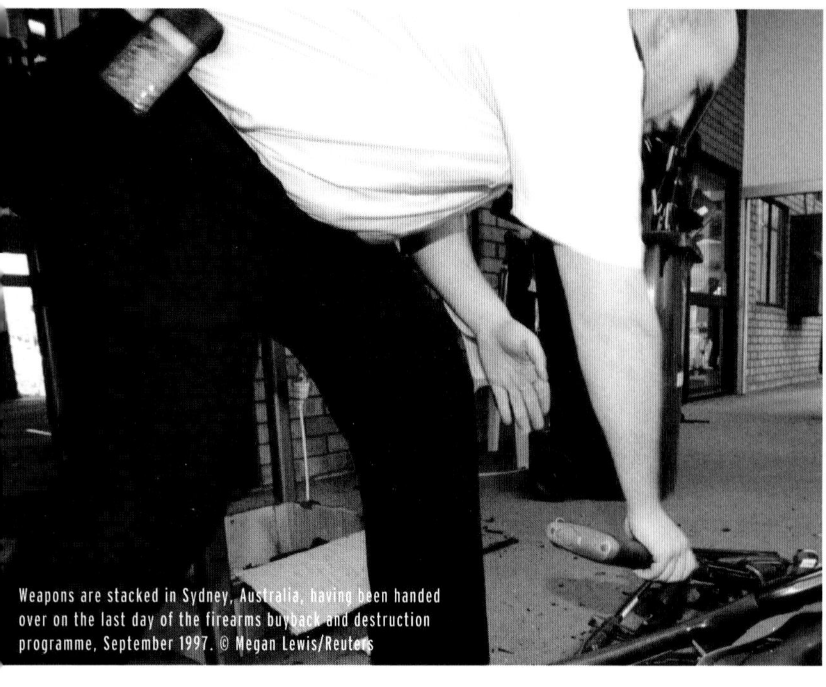
Weapons are stacked in Sydney, Australia, having been handed over on the last day of the firearms buyback and destruction programme, September 1997. © Megan Lewis/Reuters

massacre of 28 April 1996, when a lone gunman murdered 35 people and wounded 18 more (Chapman and Alpers, 2006). The major legislative response was Australia's 1996–97 National Firearms Agreement, which bans civilian ownership of automatic and semi-automatic rifles and shotguns. The subsequent buyback and destruction programme eliminated 643,726 semi-automatic rifles, pump-action shotguns, and other unwanted firearms, bought back from their owners at market value (Reuter and Mouzos, 2003). A second campaign was launched after an incident on 21 October 2002 at Monash University of Melbourne, in which a gunman killed two people and wounded five. The National Handgun Buyback, which ran from July to December 2003, collected and destroyed 70,000 handguns, for a total of more than 713,000 firearms surrendered in all (Lee and Suardi, 2008).

Figure 5.1 **Homicide in Australia, 1995-2007**

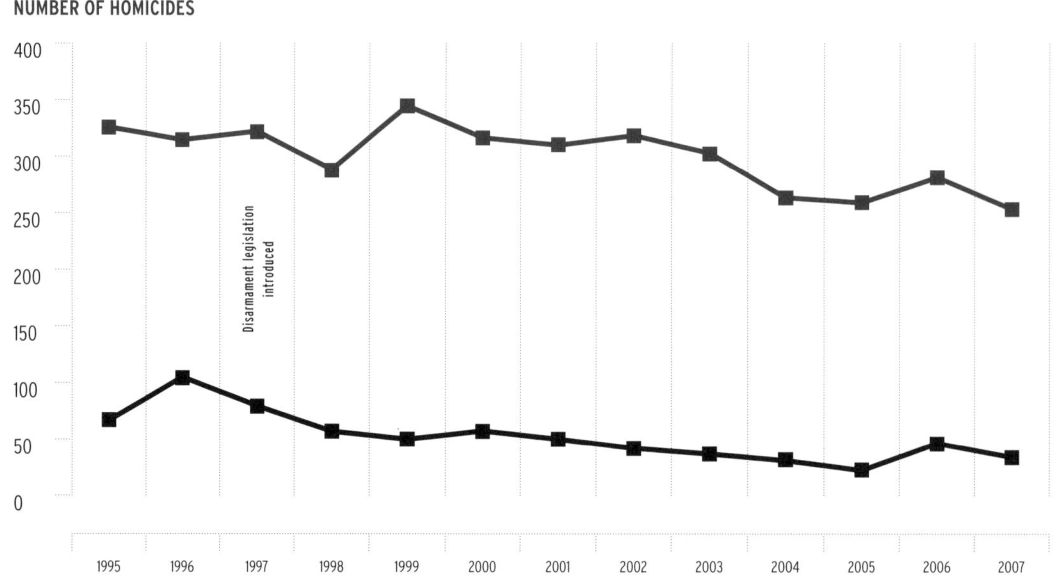

Sources: 1995-97: Chapman et al. (2006, p. 369); other data: ABS (2008, p. 9)

The impact of these measures has been the subject of extensive research and intense debate. Death from homicide and suicide had already been declining in Australia and continued after weapons destruction was done, sparking a major dispute over the effect of the initiative (see Figure 5.1). Did partial disarmament actually reduce gun crime or suicide? The total scale of the reforms was not small, eliminating roughly 20 per cent of the firearms held by the country's civilians, if one accepts the estimate of a total of 3,900,000 civilian guns before disarmament (Chapman et al., 2006; Small Arms Survey, 2007a, app. 3). Australian gun ownership advocates prefer an estimate of four to six million, which would dilute the relative size of the collection programme (Christie, 1999).

The debate has continued for more than a decade, making this the most sustained and focused gun policy dialogue outside the United States. The clearest effect is the total elimination of *mass* murders. Between 1979 and 1996, Australia endured 13 mass shootings, each causing at least five deaths. In these events, 112 people were shot dead and at least another 52 were wounded. There have been no comparable incidents since 1996 (Chapman et al., 2006). The rate of firearms homicide and suicide has also continued to decline. Some observers argue that by removing one-fifth of the country's firearms, including much of the public inventory of its most destructive types, these measures accelerated an existing trend. The same analysis stresses the impact on suicide, especially the 70 per cent drop in the rate of male firearm suicide between 1997 and 2003. In absolute terms, it fell from 3.1 to 1.8 per 100,000 (Chapman et al., 2006).

Other researchers have challenged these findings, noting the lack of strong causal models or correlation. Any effect, they maintain, is largely coincidental, the apparent result of more fundamental changes in Australian society, or dumb luck (Baker and McPhedran, 2007; 2008). Others note more charitably that any statistical impact of partial disarmament may well be masked by continuing trends of declining murder and suicide rates (Lee and Suardi, 2008). Australian and British statistical analyses are complicated by the low level of homicide, which magnifies otherwise inconsequential annual variations (Neill and Leigh, 2007). Even after allowing for such uncertainty, though, this review supports the conclusion that the effects of partial disarmament in societies such as Australia and Britain are real but small. Others note the rising use of handguns in homicides and suicide, a new development that might undo some of the gains of the previous decade (Davies and Mouzos, 2007, p. 2). A middle perspective concludes that the debate probably cannot be resolved, but 'to the extent that this evidence points anywhere, it is towards the firearms buyback reducing gun deaths' (Neill and Leigh, 2007, p. ii).

Brazil

The specific role of civilian weapons collection is difficult to isolate from the broad constellation of factors commonly associated with the decline of social violence in Brazil. It was one dimension in a renaissance of community-based social activism, more systematic

Rifles and assault guns are burnt in Rio de Janeiro, 6 July 2003, as part of an event involving the destruction of 4,000 firearms. © Antonio Scorza/AFP

integration of official policy and community needs, and improved law enforcement. Buttressing this was the introduction of civilian arms control in 2003 and disarmament measures in 2004. These changes coincide with a marked decline in homicide, and particularly gun homicide. Although civil violence remains high by any standard and the decline should not be exaggerated, Brazil has lost its rank among the world's most deadly societies.

A virtually unrestricted gun culture—along with organized crime and police corruption—was a major force behind the steady deterioration of public security in the 1980s and 1990s. Brazilian cities became some of the most violent places on earth. Between 1979 and 2003, some 550,000 Brazilians were killed by firearms (Waiselfisz, 2005). Firearms were the overwhelming weapons of choice, figuring in 68.8 per cent of murders. Homicide peaked in 2003, the same year the long-debated firearms Disarmament Law came into effect. The law ended the right to carry weapons, restricted sales, and required registration (Gawryszewski and Mercy, 2004). Although a referendum to ban public gun ownership was decisively defeated, a voluntary turn-in campaign reduced ownership by 460,000 guns (Dreyfus and Nascimento, forthcoming).

In 2004, firearms homicide rates began to decline (see Figure 5.2). In the state of São Paulo, the murder rate plummeted from 36 per 100,000 in 1999 to 11.6 per 100,000 in 2007. In Rio de Janeiro state, the murder rate dropped from a high of 46.1 per 100,000 in 2002 to 39.5 per 100,000 in 2006, according to police figures (Downie, 2008).[4] Compared to extrapolations from previous trends, the total number of lives saved by declining homicide rates was estimated at approximately 5,563 people in 2004 and roughly 23,961 people between 2004 and late 2007 (De Souza et al., 2007; CS, 2007).

Figure 5.2 **Homicide in Brazil, 1994-2006**

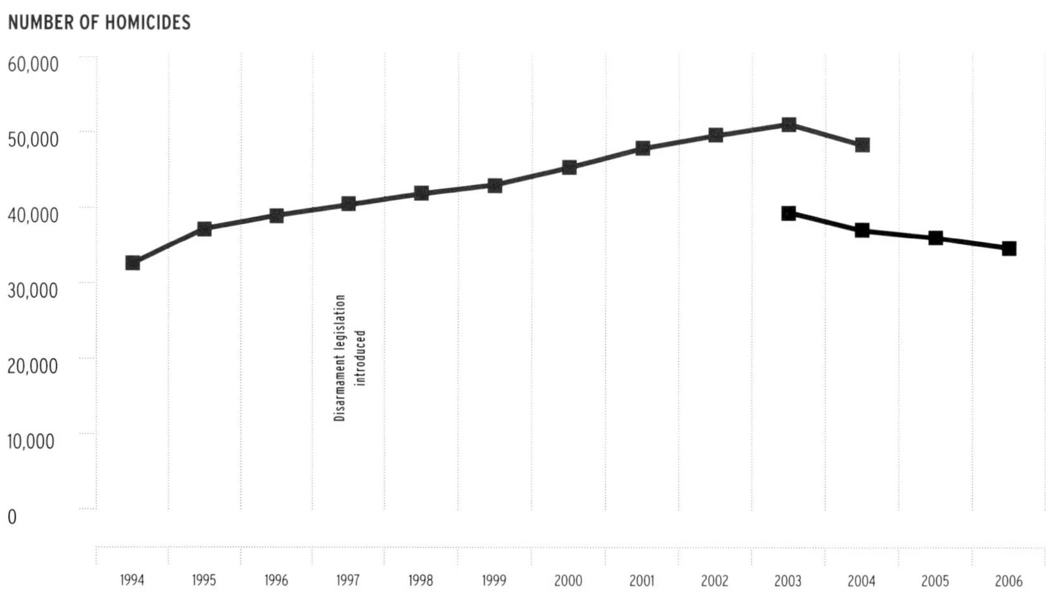

Note: Not all firearms deaths are homicides. According to Waiselfisz (2007, p. 136): 'In 2004 Brazil registered 37,113 deaths under this chapter: 92.1% being homicides; 3.3% suicides; 0.5% accidents involving firearms; and 4% of undetermined intent.'

Sources: CS (2007); Waiselfisz (2007, p. 124)

The exact contribution of weapons collection to these trends is elusive. Most of the weapons destroyed by the Brazilian Army—the agency responsible for small arms destruction—were seized by law enforcement officials during criminal investigations and arrests. According to the officer responsible, the Brazilian Army destroyed 748,177 civilian small arms between 1998 and 2005. These included 253,321 of the 460,000 weapons received through voluntary disarmament from August 2004 to July 2005 (Dreyfus and Nascimento, forthcoming). Reduction of civilian inventories by 460,000 firearms also had the effect of reducing the pool of weapons available for theft. Although causality is difficult to pin down, cautious researchers agree that the decline in gun killing is 'a fact directly attributable to the disarmament policies implemented that year' (Waiselfisz, 2007). Other studies stress the importance of improved law enforcement and community initiatives but also conclude that 'gun control was another important factor in the crime drop' (Kahn and Goertzel, 2007).

The Brazilian case prompts further qualifications, however. Unlike Australia and Britain, for example, Brazil's extremely high homicide rates eliminate most problems of trend detection, but not the problem of statistical masking. Moreover, even after a cumulative drop in firearms deaths of 18 per cent, gun crime remains very high by global standards. Improvements are slight for specific groups—above all, poor young men—and particular regions (Ruediger, Riccio, and Britto, 2007). For example, in Recife, Brazil's most violent big city, the homicide rate declined, but less dramatically, from a high of 58.9 per 100,000 in 2001 to 53.9 per 100,000 in 2007 (Downie, 2008). For Brazil as a nation, losing the status of *most murderous* is an important accomplishment. It is easy to sense the euphoria implicit in the observation of Julio Jacobo Waiselfisz that, 'for the first time in Brazilian history, we have had three years in which the measures of fatal violence have fallen' (Downie, 2008). Instead, it is the Venezuelan capital of Caracas that has emerged as the most dangerous city on the continent, with an annual murder rate of 130 per 100,000 residents (Llana, 2008; Romero, 2006).

Great Britain

British gun policy was transformed by mass killings with legally owned firearms.[5] After the killing of 16 people and wounding of 15 in Hungerford in 1987 by a lone gunman with semi-automatic weapons, legislation banned semi-automatic rifles, pump shotguns, and several other categories of firearm. The killing of 16 primary-school students and their teacher and the wounding of 17 more in Dunblane, Scotland, again by a single gunman with legally owned handguns, in 1996, led to further amendments to the Firearms Acts, prohibiting private ownership of virtually all handguns (Cullen, 1996). The result was some of the strictest gun legislation anywhere and a series of campaigns to collect the banned weapons.

Firearms collection is a regular feature of British gun policy. During the 1988 general amnesty that followed the Hungerford massacre, 48,000 firearms were surrendered (Cusick, 1996). The collection programme mandated under the 1997 Firearms (Amendment) Act only applied to one part of the civilian arsenal: banned handguns. Between 1 July 1997 and 28 February 1998, a total of 162,198 handguns were received by police in England, Scotland, and Wales (UK Parliament, 1999). A general amnesty in 2003 received nearly 44,000

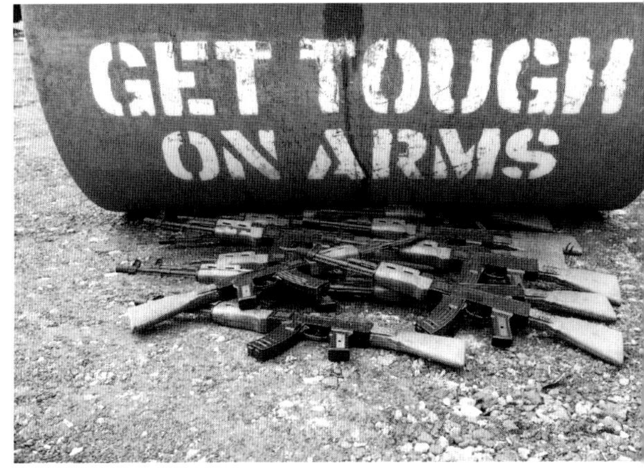

The symbolic destruction of firearms in London, 9 July 2004.
© Alessandro Abbonizio/AFP

Table 5.3 **Weapons collection in Britain**

Year	Firearms type	Legal status	Quantity collected
1966	Various	Voluntary amnesty	25,000
1988	Various	Voluntary amnesty	48,000
1996	Various	Voluntary amnesty	20,000
1997-98	Handguns	Mandatory	162,198
2003	Various	Voluntary amnesty	43,908

Sources: Cusick (1996); Hales, Lewis, and Silverstone (2006, p. 7); Hales (2009); UK Parliament (1999)

guns (Hales, Lewis, and Silverstone, 2006, p. 7). Many thousands more have been collected through criminal seizures and have often been destroyed. Since 1996, a combined total of approximately 226,000 firearms have been eliminated through such measures (see Table 5.3). The net result is the elimination of virtually all previously legal handguns but a smaller proportion of rifles and shotguns. Of about four million publicly owned firearms held in England, Scotland, and Wales (registered and estimated unregistered) in 1997, about six per cent were removed (Small Arms Survey, 2007a, app. 3).[6] This was a relatively comprehensive but narrowly targeted campaign, stressing specific types of firearms, mostly registered handguns. Britain destroyed proportionately fewer weapons than most of the countries examined here, but they were the type most suited for crime and domestic violence (Small Arms Survey, 2007a, app. 3).[7]

Figure 5.3 **Intentional firearms death in England and Wales, 1994-2006**

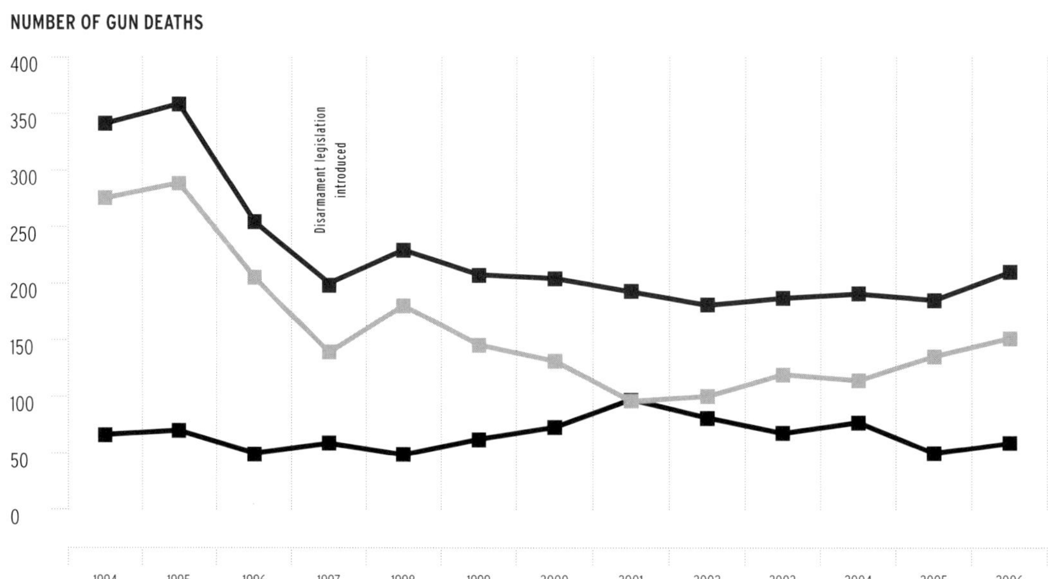

Sources: Kaiza (2008); Povey (2004, p. 49)

Figure 5.4 **Firearms offences in England and Wales, 1990-2006/07**

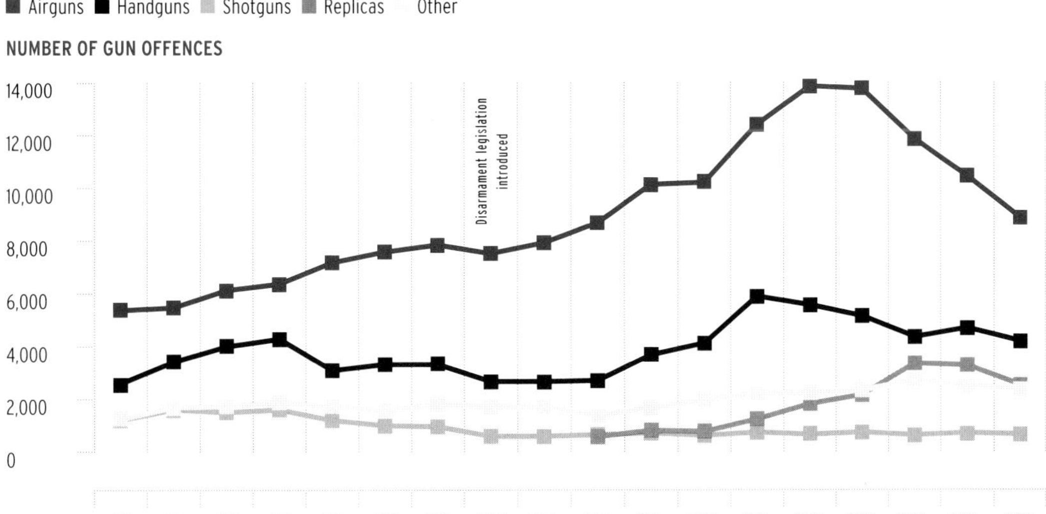

Notes:

Airguns use compressed gas to propel a non-explosive cartridge.

Replicas include 'softair'guns, such as BB guns.

Other guns include paintball guns, rifles, stun guns, incapacitating gas devices, machine guns, and unidentified guns, among others.

Source: GCN (2007); Kaiza (2008, p. 48)

Gun killings in Britain remain relatively rare. In 2007–08, there were 59 firearms homicides in England and Wales, perpetuating one of the lowest rates in the world (see Figure 5.3). Intentional firearm deaths declined significantly just before Dunblane and have since stabilized, although firearms suicides appear to be increasing (see Figure 5.3). Firearms homicides stand at 0.15 per 100,000, less than half the rate in Finland, one-third that in Switzerland, and one-fifth that in Italy (Squires, Grimshaw, and Solomon, 2008, p. 16). In recent years, guns were used in eight per cent of all homicides (Povey, 2004, p. 1). Yet, since the Dunblane massacre and the 1997 Firearms Act, overall gun crime has increased by one-third, hitting its peak in 2003–04 (see Figure 5.4). This has included a significant increase in the criminal use of imitation firearms and compressed airguns.

Not surprisingly, then, much of the British discussion stresses not murder or violence, but the much broader category of 'gun crime'. The British definition of 'firearm' covers weapons such as air guns, imitations, and replicas that are excluded in most societies. Indicative of the great sensitivity of British society, official statistics also track crimes with imitation and replica guns that might be overlooked elsewhere (Hales, 2006). In a country that bans handguns outright, any possession is criminal (Squires, Grimshaw, and Solomon, 2008). Headlines such as 'Gun Crime Soars by 35%' are often driven by events involving imitations. Crime data may also be inflated by changes in reporting practices and police priorities (BBC, 2003; Hales, 2006, pp. 6, 10; Hales, Lewis, and Silverstone, 2006, p. 115).

A major problem in understanding the connections between British firearms policy and gun crime—even the most serious, such as attempted murder—is imperfect reporting. 'Previous qualitative research on gun crime highlights the fact that even very serious firearms offences, such as attempted murder, may go unreported, particularly if the victim is himself involved in criminal activity'—a problem hardly unique to the United Kingdom (Hales, 2006). Limits in official reporting mechanisms also preclude clear determinations of the proportion of crimes committed with legally owned or illicit, unregistered guns (Coaker, 2007).[8] A further irony of the Dunblane legislative reforms is that they coincided with an apparent smuggling boom, partially fuelled by the end of war in Bosnia and Herzegovina (Bryan, 2004; Gallagher, 2004). In general, however, little is known about the numbers and sources of British crime guns.

The effects of the legislative changes on murder, armed violence, and broader gun crime remain unclear. It is certainly possible that the post-Dunblane reforms have suppressed gun theft and criminal use, sparing the United Kingdom even worse problems of gun proliferation, but this remains unproven. Foreign smuggling, use of air guns and replicas, and unreported theft all appear to be important elements of the 'gun crime problem', but no firm evidence reveals how much any one element contributes (Summers, 2007). Despite the seriousness of such questions, there is no discussion in the United Kingdom comparable to Australian debates on the effects of its 1997 Firearms Act. There is less statistically based research as well. This is probably a measure of a stronger national consensus on current policy and commitment to tight controls on ownership. More attention is devoted to the question of how to deal with gun violence among the worst-affected social groups, especially gangs and ethnic minorities.

Jimmy Rasta, commander of Solomon Islands militia, turns in weapons and ammunition on 15 August 2003. © Reuters

Solomon Islands

While the other cases considered here focus on criminal violence and suicide, the Solomon Islands endured outright warfare. Although isolated and small (with a population of 581,318), this situation points to basic problems of managing civilian armaments in post-conflict environments. The example is especially relevant to other countries afflicted with high levels of post-conflict violence.

The problems of post-conflict environments are well known: a potentially poisonous mix of weak institutions, insecure and vulnerable populations, and plentiful reserves of weapons and ammunition. As instruments acquired for military dominance are turned to factional, sectarian, and criminal purposes, the level of armed violence previously associated with warfare can be sustained for years or can even increase (POST-CONFLICT SECURITY). The most common mechanism for dealing with post-conflict situations is DDR. But, as shown below, this is best for symbolic disarmament designed to reassure former enemies of peaceful intentions, not for the sustainable removal of large quantities or proportions of lethal equipment (Geneva Declaration Secretariat, 2008). By the time conditions were ripe for disarmament in the Solomon Islands, warring groups had largely evaporated, and the issue had become post-conflict crime suppression and civilian weapons collection.

The conflict that broke out in December 1998 had its roots in tensions between the native Gwale of Guadalcanal and Malaitan migrants. The Guadalcanal Revolutionary Army (also know as the Isatabu Freedom Movement) began attacking Malaitans, provoking large-scale displacement and the emergence of the Malaita Eagle Force (Fraenkel, 2004; Moore, 2004). The conflict continued until July 2003, when Parliament welcomed intervention by a Commonwealth force of 300 police and 1,800 soldiers from 15 countries led by Australia. The Regional Assistance Mission to Solomon Islands is a long-term, well-funded intervention that has been cited as a model for other stability-building initiatives (Dobbins et al., 2008).

The Solomon Islands did not endure the rise in post-conflict violence common elsewhere.

Assuring security was the most immediate goal. There was no formal DDR element, although in July 2002 and July 2004 the UN Development Programme helped retrain more than 1,000 police special constables, most of whom were recruited from former armed groups (Dobbins et al., 2008, p. 188). Disarmament of civilians—mostly former militiamen—was a prominent element of the intervention. The option had been considered before, leading some critics to inveigh against 'the madness of civilian disarmament in the South Pacific', which they predicted would lead to Rwanda-like genocide (Kopel, Gallant, and Eisen, 2000). The actual results were very different. With security assured, disarmament was widely accepted and reinforced the end of armed violence.

A total of 3,714 firearms were received in response to a series of appeals from 2003 to 2004 (Llewellyn, 2004). This was more than the total number of weapons previously estimated in the country, as shown in Table 5.2 (Muggah and Alpers, 2003). This example demonstrates both the conservatism of conventional estimating procedures and the problems they can cause by underestimating the weapons to be collected. Even with participation levels that were higher than expected, the programme left an unknown number of weapons available, including hundreds of military rifles.[9]

The Solomon Islands did not endure the precipitous rise in post-conflict violence all too common elsewhere. Studies stress the importance of disarmament, among other factors, in the virtual cessation of armed violence. In that regard, the islands compare favorably to cases such as those of the Democratic Republic of the Congo, East Timor, or Haiti, where removal of weapons has proven very difficult, making any outburst of tensions potentially dire (Muggah, 2009). Yet the Solomons have reportedly seen new security problems, such as an increase in crocodile attacks, which now requires action from officials instead of armed civilians (ABC, 2003; AP, 2004; Dunnigan, 2004). The greatest test of disarmament and security building was the civil unrest of April 2006, following highly contested elections. The resulting political instability and rioting showed the Solomon Islands remain far from fully peaceful. Nevertheless, the situation has been managed without a resumption of deadly violence, evidence that disarmament may have inhibited escalation to fatal violence.

While the Solomon Islands are the primary example of civilian post-conflict disarmament examined here, it is in many respects too distinct for easy comparison. The Solomons are, above all, small and insular; import of large quantities of arms and ammunition is more difficult than for many other places. They also had the advantage of a large and sustained intervention by an international peacekeeping force, undoubtedly instrumental in ensuring security and political stability.

South Africa

After the Solomon Islands, South Africa has enacted the most ambitious disarmament measures of the countries examined here, eliminating surplus military, law enforcement, and civilian weapons in roughly equal quantities. All potentially contribute to the decline of violence, but the impact of such programmes in South Africa seems weaker than in other cases considered here.

The role of poorly controlled state arsenals is especially relevant in South Africa. In some cases, the connection between state arsenals and civilian effects can be overwhelming, as illustrated by the experiences of Afghanistan, Albania, Iraq, Somalia, and Uganda (Bhatia and Sedra, 2008; Bevan, 2008a). In South Africa, the flow is less extreme but nonetheless consequential. Leakage from the armed forces and law enforcement appears to be an important source of crime guns. Theft or loss of well over 2,000 law enforcement and military firearms is reported annually, including many of the most powerful small arms released into South African society (see Figure 5.5). In 1994–2003, a total of 208,090 firearms were reported lost or stolen from civilian owners (Gould et al., 2004, p. 201). Actual theft is undoubtedly greater, since owners of unregistered weapons must be cautious about reporting.

South African civilian gun policy reform began in the early 1990s, responding to rising concern over easier access to guns and apparent changes in society, most visibly higher crime, including homicide. Between 1995 and 1998, the proportion of all murders committed with firearms increased from 41.5 to 49.3 per cent (Hennop, Potgieter, and Jefferson, 2001). This percentage appears to have increased since, but a lack of disaggregated crime data since 2000 makes it impossible to categorize murders by the immediate cause of death. The causal impact of better gun control and partial disarmament is difficult to evaluate, although it is associated with declining violence (Lamb, 2008, p. 2).

Figure 5.5 **Reported firearms theft and loss in South Africa, 1994-2007**

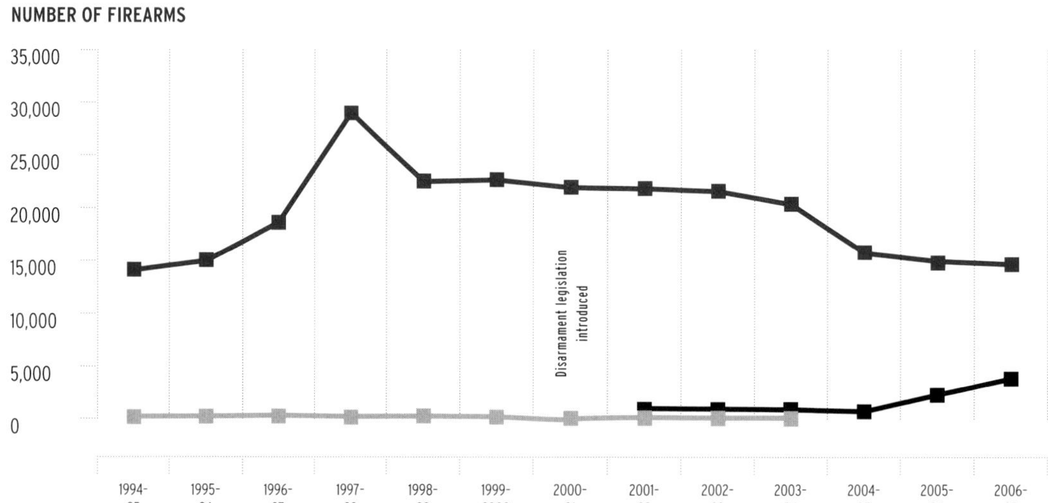

Sources: **Civilian losses:** Lamb (2008, p. 8). Police losses: Lamb (2008, pp. 12-13). **Military losses:** Gould et al. (2004, p. 158)

Continuous gun amnesties, turn-ins, recoveries, and seizures became prominent, framing attitudes and expectations. Some of the most publicized focused on suppression of gun trafficking from neighboring Mozambique—reportedly the origins of many illegal guns—but, in recent years, attention shifted to the illegal and unwanted guns of South Africa itself. The most important reform was the 2000 Firearms Control Act. It introduced new requirements for firearms licensing, ended automatic licence renewal, and required secure storage. After four years of negotiations to complete regulatory aspects, the Act came into effect in July 2004. Implementation has been controversial, especially among gun owners who complain of inadequate support for licensing and registration. Weapons collection has been among the most visible aspects of implementation, with major turn-in campaigns accelerating the collection of unwanted guns. An amnesty in 2005 elicited more than 100,000 firearms, handed in without financial compensation (Kirsten, 2006).

The South African Police Service reports that it has destroyed a total of 530,977 guns since 2000. This is in addition to 271,867 small arms destroyed by the armed forces and far in excess of the 42,642 civilian guns reported as destroyed in the country's reports to the UN (Lamb, 2008, p. 20; see Table 5.1). There is some confusion about exactly whose guns these were, though. Police destruction seems to include 88,640 decommissioned police firearms (Gould et al., 2004, p. 243). The weapons destroyed more recently in routine disarmament ceremonies appear overwhelmingly civilian. These include military or police weapons that were apparently received or seized from civilian owners (van Lill, 2006). In all, weapons collection has probably reduced South Africa's total civilian arsenal by some 440,000 guns (Lamb, 2008, p. 20).[10] Better law enforcement reinforces further disarmament, shown by declining gun theft, with the curious exception of theft and loss from police (see Figure 5.5). Sustained disarmament by all sectors of South African society—civilian and state—has corresponded with a decline in homicide. Lack of comprehensive data on gun homicide and other crime leaves considerable uncertainty, but trends appear to indicate declining firearm homicide rates (see Figure 5.6).

Figure 5.6 **Homicide and seizures of illegal guns in South Africa, 1994-2007**

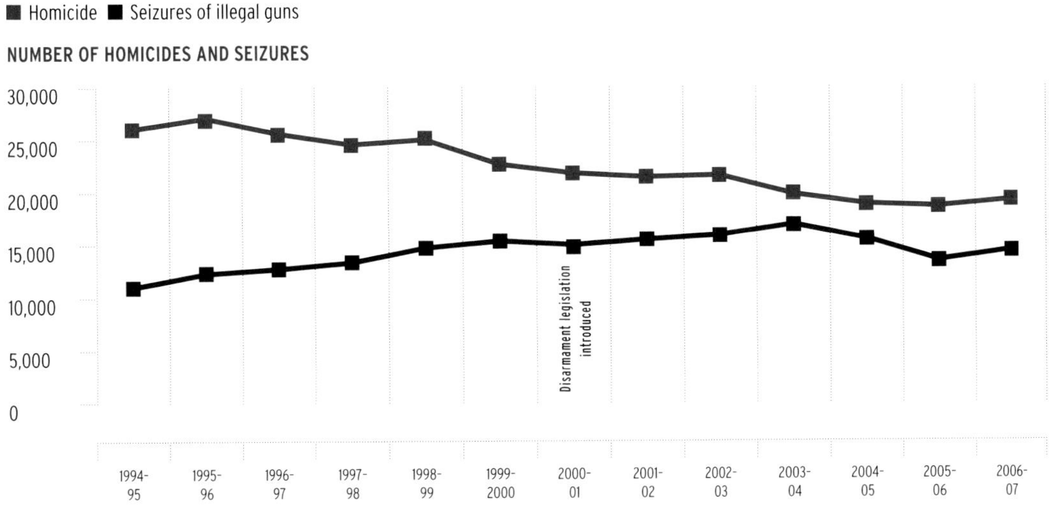

Source: Lamb (2008, p. 2)

THE STATE: CUTTING NATIONAL ARSENALS

Disarmament policy of donor governments and international institutions stresses destruction of surplus small arms, light weapons, and ammunition held by state militaries (Courtney-Green, 2008; Kryvonos and Kytömäki, 2008).[11] This tendency might seem surprising, since civilians have most of the world's firearms. As noted in previous editions of the *Small Arms Survey,* there are at least 875 million firearms in the world today, with roughly three-quarters of these in civilian hands. This translates as 650 million civilian, 200 million military, 26 million law enforcement, and fewer than 1 million insurgent firearms distributed around the world (see Figure 5.7; Small Arms Survey, 2007a, p. 43). State surplus destruction, rather, is most valuable for reducing costs and the risk of depot explosions, illicit diversion, or irresponsible transfers to regions in conflict.

The quantitative dominance of civilian firearms inventories, while real, is exaggerated by the unique contribution of the United States, where private owners control roughly 270 million firearms (Small Arms Survey, 2007a, p. 39). When the United States is dropped from the totals, a more balanced view emerges of typical distributions across the rest of the world (see Figures 5.7 and 5.8). From this perspective, civilians still have the most firearms, but military inventories rise from one-quarter to one-third of the global total. Private and state inventories are evenly matched in many countries, and the armed forces almost always control more powerful small arms, as well as light weapons rarely seen anywhere in civilian hands. Of the 200 million modern military firearms worldwide, at least 76 million are surplus, priority candidates for destruction (Small Arms Survey, 2008, p. 77). By this standard, then, official arsenals are neither puny nor inconsequential, with a rightful place on the international disarmament agenda.

Although their firepower is often greater, military weapons are, in a sense, less destructive than their civilian counterparts. Of the estimated 300,000 gun deaths every year, at least 60 per cent are homicides and suicides unrelated to armed conflict or crime (Wille and Krause, 2005). While almost two-thirds of all homicides are committed with firearms, most are the result of crime—including domestic violence—and not warfare (Geneva Declaration Secretariat, 2008, pp. 9, 67, 69). Of course, military small arms are exceptionally dangerous in other ways. Not only are they generally more powerful than civilian or law enforcement weapons, but they also tend to be the only small arms that are routinely stockpiled. Militaries are ideally positioned to collect and ship tens of thousands of rifles overnight. History has repeatedly shown how military surpluses, delivered to sensitive locations, can instantly bring down a government, plunge a country into civil war, or otherwise transform conflict. Other people's surpluses were crucial in recent wars in Liberia and Sierra Leone and help perpetuate armed conflict in the Democratic Republic of the Congo and Somalia today (HRW, 2003;

A Kalashnikov rifle is destroyed in Ukraine as part of a NATO-sponsored project to eliminate 1.5 million excess Ukrainian military firearms and 133,000 tons of ammunition, January 2007. © Sergei Supinsky/AFP

Figure 5.7 **Global small arms distribution, with the United States, 2007**

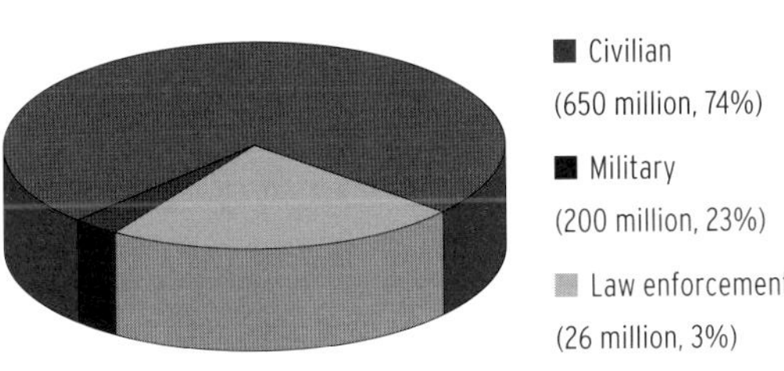

Figure 5.8 **Global small arms distribution, without the United States, 2007**

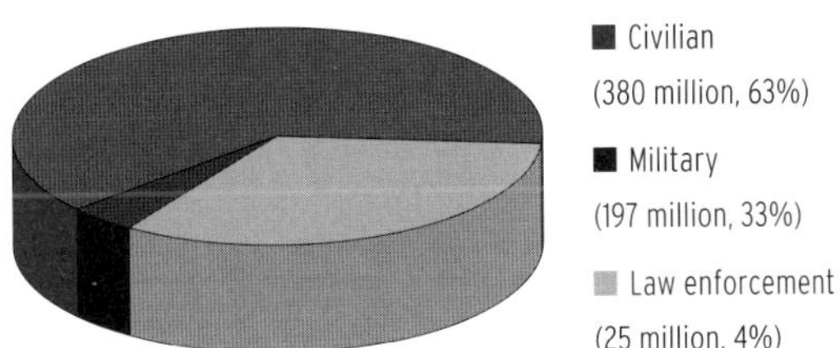

Sources: Small Arms Survey (2006, ch. 2; 2007a, ch. 2)

UNSC, 2008, pp. 33–36). State disarmament is the sensible alternative to long-term storage, uncontrolled diversion, and irresponsible transfer abroad.

Military small arms, light weapons, and ammunition are handled very differently from other disarmament candidates. A distinctive characteristic of small arms disarmament is the lack of treaty obligations. Unlike other forms of state disarmament, small arms destruction is neither reciprocal nor managed through bilateral or multilateral arrangements. None of the examples of state disarmament shown in Figure 5.9 involved one country destroying part of its small arms inventory on the condition that another do the same. These were all unilateral, national decisions. Some states received foreign support—such as Bulgaria, Romania, and Ukraine—but pressure from donors appears to have

Figure 5.9 **Selected state military small arms disarmament, by proportion destroyed**

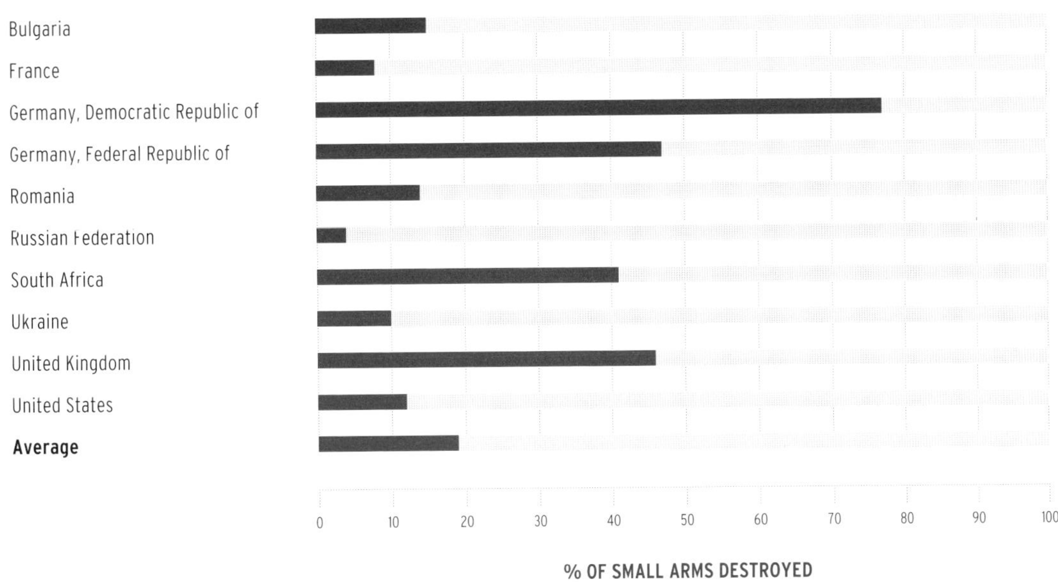

Notes: This graph is based on figures for completed destruction only, not planned. Destruction in the German Democratic Republic does not include about 304,000 former small arms that were transferred abroad (Beeck, 2008, p. 60). Destruction in the Federal Republic of Germany includes a total of 2,155,892 destroyed, minus 1 million counted as destruction in the GDR (Germany, 2008, p. 21; Beeck, 2008). US totals include 3,054,553 in 2005 inventories plus the destruction of 830,000 firearms and the known foreign transfer of 1.2 million weapons since 1990. Additional US weapons were estimated statistically. The average is calculated by dropping statistical outliers.

Sources: **Germany:** Germany (2008, p. 21); Beeck (2008). **Romania:** Faltas (2008, p. 95). **Estimates:** Small Arms Survey (2006, ch. 2, pp. 44, 46).

been minimal. The UN *Programme of Action* and several regional instruments commit states to dispose of and (preferably) destroy surplus, but the practical role of donor governments and multilateral institutions is encouragement and help. These processes lack the classic signifiers of disarmament progress: there are no international summits, treaty-signing ceremonies, or generous media attention. DDR programmes aimed primarily at non-state actors, examined below, are much closer to those traditional models.

Although state disarmament tends to be domestically driven, it produces significant results. The destruction projects shown in Figure 5.9 are among the best-publicized cases. They demonstrate the freedom of states to destroy very large proportions and absolute quantities of weapons. Based on such experiences, the destruction of roughly 20 per cent of any country's small arms and light weapons arsenal is typically possible, and 40 per cent or more in many cases, a finding that confirms similar conclusions achieved through analysis of military doctrine (Small Arms Survey, 2008, p. 77).

Disarmament alone minimizes the cost and dangers of weapons and ammunition storage.

Surpluses arise when military requirements change, eliminating any clear need for the equipment. While surpluses can be stored, this is problematic over the longer term. The dangers of ammunition storage are made clear enough by the reality of catastrophic depot explosions. Surplus weapons do not explode but may be lost or stolen—especially if stockpile security is weak, as it often is for surplus equipment. Disarmament alone minimizes financial cost and the dangers of poorly supervised weapons and ammunition, especially depot catastrophes, pilferage, and illegal diversion (Bevan, 2008b).

WAR: DISARMING NON-STATE ARMED GROUPS

Disarmament, demobilization, and reintegration may be the most rigorously studied aspect of small arms disarmament. It is far and away the most visible and best funded. More than 60 programmes have been launched since the late 1980s (Muggah, 2009, p. 6). As of 2008, at least 19 internationally sponsored DDR projects were in progress, involving some 1.1 million participants, with combined budgets of $1.6 billion (Caramés and Sanz, 2008, pp. 1–2). This is roughly 25 times the total amount allocated in any one year for destruction of state small arms, light weapons, and ammunition surpluses (Karp, 2008).

While most research on conflict termination and post-conflict reconstruction stresses problems of successful reintegration of former fighters, this section focuses on the narrow issue of disarmament in DDR. Why is there a *disarmament* element in DDR? To be sure, DDR is always a broad programme and should not be judged by one component. Nor should any component be unevaluated. As shown here, the cumulative effect of disarmament on the arsenals of insurgent groups is often dubious. Yet disarmament remains a foundational element of international efforts to bring fighting to a close and restrain resumption of armed conflict. Disarmament of non-state combatants may not collect most insurgent weapons, nor their best weapons, but it is associated with many of the most successful examples of conflict resolution. Why is disarmament so important in this context?

Conceptual approaches

The greatest barrier to evaluating the role of disarmament in DDR is the sheer diversity of such projects. Unlike other forms of international disarmament, regulated through a single treaty such as the 1993 Chemical Weapons Convention or the 1997 Ottawa Convention banning anti-personnel landmines, DDR is a set of practices adapted to the unique characteristics of each situation. Its harshest critics focus exclusively on DDR failures—of which there are many—and ignore its numerous successes (Kopel, Gallant, and Eisen, 2008; Malcolm, 2005). Such criticism overlooks the typical complexity of human conflict. Just as disarmament cannot ensure sustainable peace by itself, so it almost always is too limited to cause the worst ills attributed to it, such as vulnerability to genocide. The lessons from actual disarmament experience tend instead to be ambiguous, reflecting the messy reality of post-conflict situations.

Disarmament is regarded as the easiest phase of DDR to implement, more mechanical and self-contained than the more context-dependent demobilization and reintegration. Given the limited quantities and quality of weapons that may be collected in such interventions, it is frequently argued that disarmament is mostly symbolic. This is the core of Colin Gray's biting critique that disarmament works only when it is not needed (Gray, 1992). But symbolic does not mean unimportant. As culturally sensitive writers note, some of the most vicious conflicts have been fought for purely symbolic goals (Diamond, 2005; Keegan, 1994). Some research finds more measurable results, especially reduction in killing; one such study concludes that DDR in Colombia reduced homicides by 13 per cent in areas of operation of demobilized groups, averting between 650 and 2,300 homicides in its first year (Restrepo and Muggah, 2009, p. 43). Others question any effect, arguing that, 'combatants not exposed to the DDR programme appear to reintegrate just as successfully as those that participated' (Humphreys and Weinstein, 2009, p. 49).

Confusion over effectiveness is exacerbated by the multiple goals of many disarmament programmes, in which the specific contribution of disarmament often is poorly articulated or unrelated to other steps in demobilization. According to Béatrice Pouligny, this obscurity is not accidental. Rather,

> *disarmament is an integral symbolic and practical element of the demobilization process, of which it is often an essential part. Yet it should be noted that disarmament can also take place before, during and after demobilization, and that it can be separate from the latter process.* (Pouligny, 2004, p. 5)

The reason lies in the fundamental goal of DDR, which 'is more than just about putting weapons beyond use, but is rather about changing attitudes' (Pouligny, 2004, p. 5). From this perspective, the disarmament element of DDR serves no inherent purpose; the real function of the overall programme essentially is veterans support for rebels (Peake, 2009). Others stress the empirical benefits of post-conflict disarmament. In Pouligny's words, 'when disarmament is not undertaken . . . small arms frequently reappear in acts of organized and spontaneous violence. They constitute genuine threats to international, regional and domestic security' (Pouligny, 2004, p. 14). Others, like Robert Muggah, maintain that disarmament is most useful as a measurable index of performance in otherwise nebulous environments where outcomes are poorly documented; the number of guns is easier to measure than ethnic or sectarian tension (Muggah, 2006, p. 197).

The lessons from disarmament experience tend to be ambiguous, reflecting a messy post-conflict reality.

Disarmament's role in DDR may be largely symbolic. But even limited arms collection and destruction can help promote conflict resolution. Strategic theory stresses the importance of reciprocal arms limitations for confidence building, persuading participants of the safety of further détente and cooperation, vital in all armed conflicts (Spear, 2006, p. 173). The symbolic power of disarmament also contributes to the transformation of social priorities and expectations, suppressing the visibility and importance of weapons in post-conflict affairs. Although they often are hard to measure, the practical effects should not be discounted. Experience with disarmament of combatants within ongoing armed conflicts shows that all sides often can agree on the mutual benefits of specific forms of disarmament activity (see Box 5.4).

Box 5.4 Disarming before peace?

The greatest disadvantage of the DDR paradigm is that it postpones disarmament until the end of an armed conflict. The parties to a conflict agree to DDR, in other words, because they are done fighting. While this is the best-funded and most prominent approach for dealing with insurgent armament, there are alternatives.

An important option is going directly to the armed groups, before or independently of any peace settlement. This is often controversial; it can mean abandoning rhetorical commitments not to bargain with terrorists. And it can be sensitive; groups confronted with requests to disarm too early may abandon negotiations altogether (Hottinger, 2008). But there are important precedents to build upon. As in many other aspects of small arms policy, an illustrative path was staked out by work on landmines. The most active NGO in this field, Geneva Call, reports agreements to ban anti-personnel mines with 35 non-state actors (NSAs) (Geneva Call, 2008, p. 4). Other organizations, most prominently the Danish Demining Group and Landmine Action, have led actual destruction of NSA landmine stockpiles. In Iraqi Kurdistan, Mine Advisory Group and Norwegian People's Aid are assisting 'the world's largest indigenous mine action (destruction) programme' (Geneva Call, 2008, p. 28).

Landmines are covered by a global ban. The prospects for small arms are different since they are not the subject of an international prohibition. They also constitute the military mainstay of virtually all insurgent forces. Even advocates are cautious:

> engaging armed groups on a total ban on small arms would be asking them to come to the negotiation table and eventually to renounce the armed struggle. . . . NSAs will not surrender small arms before peace has been achieved. (Sjöberg, 2007, p. 35)

This may exaggerate the barriers; for non-state actors, disarmament does not mean giving up completely, but it probably requires them to accept that they cannot win through force of arms alone. The most promising approach appears to be banning particular categories of small arms, light weapons, and ammunition, those already renounced by most states. Another promising path is opening dialogue on weapons storage, security, and re-transfers (Florquin and Warner, 2008, pp. 21–22).

Even within the counter-terrorist paradigm, there are important disarmament options. The best way to keep a weapon out of terrorist hands, as is often noted in other contexts, is to ban it outright. Although states may not be ready to renounce their own right to such weapons, outright banning may be the best way to achieve counter-terror goals. Usually, this logic is expressed in the context of nuclear weapons and other forms of weapons of mass destruction. But it can also be applied to specific forms of light weapons. Banning highly accurate munitions such as GPS-guided mortar shells may be politically feasible (Bonomo et al., 2007, p. xix). Other candidates are high-power sniper weapons and MANPADS.

Colombian soldiers watch the destruction of landmines and explosives in Valle del Cauca province, 31 August 2004. © Eduardo Munoz/Reuters

Empirical insight

Many of these issues can also be illuminated by a look at the evidence. The 45 DDR programmes identified in Table 5.4 have spent almost USD 2.7 billion overall, with the disarmament components yielding more than 430,000 small arms and light weapons. Among the 20 programmes with complete performance data, the cost of removing a weapon, measured against total programme cost, was approximately USD 18,750 each (after dropping outliers). But since it is virtually impossible to separate the disarmament element from demobilization and reintegration, these figures include the complete cost of DDR. Albert Caramés and Eneko Sanz find that disarmament and demobilization are the quickest and cheapest part of a typical programme, estimated to consume 6 to 10 per cent of a total DDR budget (Caramés and Sanz, 2008, p. 2). This suggests disarmament alone costs about USD 1,900 per weapon or less.

In practice, the *most costly* programmes are often *least successful* in disarmament terms. Prominent examples are the Democratic Republic of the Congo, Haiti, and Côte d'Ivoire. The cheapest tend to be those that achieved the most disarmament. There is a logic here: disarmament presumes political accommodation, which reduces costs and greatly facilitates the likelihood of overall success. Large outlays per weapon tend to reveal a programme in trouble.

Much more difficult to evaluate is the *effectiveness* of DDR as a disarmament tool. What proportion of insurgent small arms and light weapons are actually recovered? A straightforward assessment of the data in Table 5.4 suggests the total proportion is relatively low—an average of roughly 14 per cent for factions reporting sufficient data. Although limited, this is not dramatically different from the average for state disarmament of 19 per cent (see Figure 5.9). There are obvious incentives for former combatants to hedge by withholding weapons. This accounts for the well-known tendency for DDR to recover few weapons or rusted metal. In reality, disarmament performance often is much better, although this must be set against the common (but not universal) tendency for non-state factions to inflate their personnel numbers to improve bargaining strength.

With this problem in mind, thresholds of success become somewhat clearer. A review of the examples in Table 5.4 reveals the weakness of current evidence. Despite the breadth of DDR experience, there is a dearth of systematic evidence for comparison or establishing a clear threshold for disarmament success. Several well-

Table 5.4 Summary of disarmament outcomes in 45 DDR programmes

Country	Year(s)	Number of weapons collected	Total programme cost* (USD)	Cost per weapon (USD)	Combatants demobilized	Weapons collected/ combatant	Est. total arsenal**	Proportion collected
Afghanistan	2003-	131,811	141,200,000	1,326	63,380	1.7	101,408	130%
Angola	1991-92	32,731	132,000,000	3,089	134,289	0.3	214,862	15%
	1994-98				115,980		185,568	
	2002-	33,000	184,000,000	5,576	97,390		155,824	15%
Bosnia and Herzegovina	1995-99		8,500,000		400,000		640,000	
	2000-04		17,510,000		22,666		36,266	
	2002-		11,000,000		13,500		21,600	
Burundi	2004-	5,404	87,900,000	16,266	22,688	0.2	36,301	15%
Central African Republic	2004-07		13,100,000		7,565		12,104	
Chad	2005-				9,000		14,400	
Colombia	2003-06	18,051	302,600,000	16,763	31,761		50,818	36%
Congo, Democratic Republic of the	2004-	2,332	208,000,000	3,355	124,059	0.1	198,494	1%
Congo, Republic of the	2000-03	1,776	17,000,000	1,443	10,100	1.2	16,160	11%
Côte d'Ivoire	2006-	110	150,000,000	1,363,636	981	0.1	1,570	7%
Djibouti	1993-2002		29,900,000		15,000		24,000	
East Timor	1999-2003		12,000,000		1,308		2,093	
El Salvador	1991-96	10,200			38,000	0.3	60,800	17%
Eritrea	1993-97		68,800,000		54,000		86,400	
	2001-06		197,000,000		200,000		320,000	
Ethiopia	1991-96				350,000		560,000	
	2001-05		174,100,000		148,000		236,800	
Guatemala	1996-98	1,818			3,000	0.6	4,800	38%
Guinea-Bissau	2000-05		26,000,000		11,445		18,312	
Haiti	1993-96		8,600,000		5,482		8,771	
	2006-	200	15,700,000	78,500	500	0.4	800	25%

Indonesia	2005-	840	35,000,000	41,667	6,145	0.1	9,832	9%
Liberia	1994-97	10,036	99,300,000	9,894	41,647	0.2	66,635	15%
	2003-06	28,314	91,000,000	3,214	103,019	0.3	164,830	17%
Mali	1995	2,700	2,000,000	741	12,000	0.2	19,200	14%
Mozambique	1992-97	200,000	112,900,000	2,444	92,881	0.5	148,610	135%
Namibia	1989-96		41,200,000		57,000		91,200	
Nepal	2007-	3,475	18,400,000	5,295	19,602	0.2	31,363	11%
Nicaragua-Honduras	1989-2002	17,883	92,000,000	5,145	22,383	0.8	35,813	50%
Niger	1995-06	166	2,400,000	14,458	3,160	0.1	5,056	3%
Philippines	1996-2004		16,100,000		7,500		12,000	
	2006-				0		0	
Rwanda	1997-2001		19,400,000		18,692		29,907	
	2002-		65,500,000		35,367		56,587	
Sierra Leone	1996-2004	56,163	100,000,000		71,043	0.4	113,669	49%
Solomon Islands	2002-04	3,730	1,200,000	322	1,424	2.6	2,278	164%
Somalia	1992-95		1,600,000				0	
	2000-		32,800,000		1,266		2,026	
Sudan	2005-		69,440,000		91,000		145,600	
Uganda	1992-97		43,200,000		36,358		58,173	
	2002-		7,400,000		16,245		25,992	
Totals		**560,740**	**2,655,750,000**	**18,750**	**2,516,826**		**4,026,922**	**14%**

Notes: Blank cells reflect a lack of data.

* Since published budgets rarely disaggregate components, these figures include demobilization and reintegration expenses, usually the most expensive elements of DDR programmes. Blank cells indicate a lack of data, not a lack of activity.

** Estimated at 1.6 firearms per combatant for all countries.

Source: based on compilations by Robert Muggah and Katherine Aguirre for the Small Arms Survey

regarded programmes involved collection and destruction of as little as 15 per cent of estimated insurgent weapons. Other projects were less successful establishing an enduring peace, despite collection of 50 per cent or more. Most striking are programmes collecting more than 100 per cent of the estimated number of combatant weapons—Afghanistan, Mozambique, and the Solomon Islands—a curiosity that underlines the dangers of relying on any estimate of guerrilla forces. In the absence of reliable baseline estimates of total insurgent weapons, it is virtually impossible to analyse disarmament accomplishments. Thus, the preference among many observers is to stress not the number of weapons but security outcomes.

This tendency also reflects the important symbolic role of disarmament in DDR. Traditional security-based approaches view disarmament as an end in and of itself, proof of completion of a process of political reconciliation.

DDR partially reverses this ordering. It uses disarmament less as a goal and more as an incentive for further rewards (Hartzell and Hoddie, 2006, p. 161). Without the transparency or enforcement needed to reassure concerns about cheating (withholding weapons), small arms disarmament cannot assure security by itself. It functions not as an impediment to resumption of fighting, but—like civilian weapons collection—as a confidence-building measure (Spear, 2006, p. 173). Former combatants present their weapons both as an index of individual commitment and as a token of the greater goal of secure demobilization and social reintegration.

DDR planners have been accused of contributing to this haziness by avoiding concrete goals. There is no commonly accepted definition of successful disarmament in the DDR context (Muggah, 2006, p. 198). The DDR community generally does not define success in terms of raw numbers or proportions of weapons recovered. Indeed, criteria for success, much less definitions of success itself, are seldom articulated. Instead, there is a tendency to justify DDR as a process rather than an end-state, with success described alternately as 'the reduced risk of recurrent armed conflict, the neutralization of potential spoilers, the building of confidence between stakeholders or the promotion of long-term development' (Muggah, 2006, p. 195). Even when weapons are collected, they may not actually be destroyed. Surrendered weapons and ammunition are typically turned over to the peacekeepers, national armed forces, or police for safe storage or destruction. 'However, in most countries, there is reck-

Box 5.5 **The US Army embraces DDR**

If further evidence were needed of the near-universal acceptance of post-conflict disarmament and the increasingly synergistic appreciation of its relationship with security reform, nation-building, and peace-building, it could be found with the United States Army. As recently as 2003, US Army doctrine barely concealed prejudices against counter-insurgency and peace-building, prejudices inherited from the Vietnam War. The legacy of the Weinberger-Powell Doctrine left little sympathy for long engagements and tactical restraint (Bacevich, 2005, pp. 47–52; Nagl, 2005). These attitudes began to change in response to pressure to support state-building and conflict resolution in the 1990s (Dobbins et al., 2005). The challenges of war in Afghanistan and Iraq accelerated this trend. By 2008, disarmament had become a major element of US Army policy for conflict resolution.

In 2003, just weeks before the invasion of Iraq, the US Army published a new field manual for Stability Operations, its principle guidance on what to do after territory is taken. This showed all the disdain for disarmament that might be expected during the Rumsfeld era, when US strategy focused on rapid conquest, not long occupation. The document recognized disarmament only as a 'typical flash point' (US Army, 2003, p. 01-14). Its only other words on the subject were to warn commanders that, 'the mandate may require the (Peace Enforcement) force to disarm or demobilize the belligerent parties. These tasks are complex, difficult, and often dangerous' (US Army, 2003, p. 03-07). The tone was clear: avoid when possible.

The 2008 version of the guidance, by comparison, is highly sensitive to the imperatives and problems of military occupation and security assistance. Obviously influenced by the experiences of Afghanistan, Iraq, and many less conspicuous missions, it explicitly embraces DDR as an important element of nation-building and devotes considerable space to these issues (US Army, 2008, ch. 6). In a dramatic shift from its predecessor, the document states:

> Often the situation requires disarming, demobilizing, and reintegrating personnel associated with armed forces or belligerent groups before and as part of SSR [security sector reform]. Military forces can expect to assume a primary role in disarmament . . . The DDR program is a critical component of peace and restoration processes and is accounted for in initial planning . . . The DDR program is a central contributor to long-term peace, security, and development. (US Army, 2008, pp. 6-5, 6-21)

The US Army approach is distinctive. Its doctrine also implies military ownership or control over programmes more typically associated with UN civilian mandates. But this does not reduce the scale of the change in US thinking. To eliminate any remaining doubt, 'disarmament' is also included in a list of 'New Army Terms' (US Army, 2008, p. G-3).

lessness and scarce monitoring of the final destinations of surrendered arms. These arms risk diversion in the very region in which they are collected' (Caramés and Sanz, 2008, p. 25).

Even successful DDR programmes often generate limited or disappointing disarmament accomplishments. These include relatively successful cases, such as Colombia, Liberia, and Sierra Leone, where weapons received varied between 15 and 49 per cent (see Table 5.4). Yet, all these countries saw a marked improvement in political stability and greatly reduced armed violence. The limits of DDR disarmament have been exposed more notably in cases such as the Democratic Republic of the Congo, Haiti, and Côte d'Ivoire, where participation was not forthcoming and conflict could not be brought under control. But criteria for success need to be adapted to the situation (Hänggi and Scherrer, 2008). Programmes that are considered weapons collection failures by some, such as that in Kosovo, are successful in the sense that the parties involved have not returned to fighting. This may help explain the unprecedented embrace of DDR by previously disapproving institutions such as the US Army (see Box 5.5).

Even incomplete disarmament can contribute to political stability and reductions in armed violence.

CONCLUSION

For centuries, the vision of disarmament has tantalized and teased with revolutionary possibilities to transform relations between peoples and governments. The data and examples in this chapter support a more modest understanding of the prospects for small arms collection and disarmament. It should arouse neither 'irrational exuberance', nor dismissiveness or anxiety (FRB, 1996). The experiences recounted here show it is neither a universal antidote for armed violence and political instability, nor, when undertaken with public consent, a threat to liberty and security. Polemics conceal a nuanced reality. Disarmament's contribution may be largely positive—it may even be essential in some situations—but it is rarely sufficient to achieve major improvements in human security by itself.

Recent small arms collection and destruction successes—such as civilian programmes in Brazil and the Solomon Islands; state disarmament in Germany and South Africa; or the disarming of non-state actors in Colombia, Liberia, and Mozambique—were not stand-alone events. Each was a complex, integrated effort. In every case, success truly had many fathers. Similarly, more controversial examples—such as partial civilian disarmament in the United Kingdom, state destruction in the Russian Federation or Ukraine, and many DDR experiences show few, if any, negative effects. Even with obvious failures—such as DDR in Haiti—it is extremely difficult to show that voluntary collection and disarmament efforts are detrimental. Measured against trends in homicide and suicide, surplus stockpile disasters, or the maintenance of political stability, even highly incomplete disarmament typically helps. The only evidence of systematic harm is associated exclusively with coercive disarmament. Except when used to disarm defeated states, it has rarely been tried and almost always appears to be a mistake.

The prospects for further small arms collection and disarmament are considerable. Roughly 40 per cent of state arsenals—some 76 million small arms—appear to be surplus to requirements and highly suitable for destruction. State disarmament appears to be the easiest to negotiate and simplest to implement, although, even here, frustrations are common. Collection and destruction seems readily feasible for perhaps 20 per cent of all civilian firearms—at least 120 million altogether. Disarmament of former non-state combatants will never elicit comparable numbers of weapons, but, as these are some of the most destabilizing and symbolically important weapons, they warrant disproportionate attention. As shown here, though, even relatively small and incomplete undertakings can have invaluable symbolic effects, influencing possibilities and expectations.

Collection and disarmament therefore appears to be an extremely important instrument of small arms policy, but it is only one among many. It has a well-established role in managing small arms proliferation, but there is no evidence that it works in isolation from other tools of social reform. With effects difficult to isolate from simultaneous social policies, it appears to rely on interaction with other measures, although further research is needed to better understand how all these elements fit together. Small arms collection and disarmament, in other words, is not an alternative to social policy, but a potentially important element in any comprehensive programme for reducing the dangers of armed violence and instability. Given the possibilities, there is a tremendous need for rigorous dialogue on how to make better use of its potential.

LIST OF ABBREVIATIONS

DDR	Disarmament, demobilization, and reintegration
MANPADS	Man-portable air defence system(s)
NSA	Non-state actors

ENDNOTES

1 For a discussion of such processes, see Bevan (2008a).

2 In 2001, the United Nations General Assembly adopted the *Programme of Action to Prevent, Combat and Eradicate the Illicit Trade in Small Arms and Light Weapons in All Its Aspects* ('*Programme of Action*'); see UNGA (2001). For details on the implementation of the *Programme of Action* regarding export controls, see EXPORT CONTROLS.

3 Total civilian firearms are estimated in Small Arms Survey (2007a, ch. 2).

4 Sources disagree on the extent of the decline. More impressive figures are cited in the *Economist*, which reports that the homicide rate in Rio de Janeiro fell from 64 per 100,000 people in the mid-1990s to 39 per 100,000 in 2007. In São Paulo, the murder rate reportedly fell from 112 per 100,000 people in 1995 to 33 in 2006 (*Economist*, 2008).

5 Britain is used here to mean England, Scotland, and Wales. Data in this section does not include Northern Ireland.

6 If airguns are included, the total number of guns probably exceeds one million. Unlike softair guns, airguns are potentially lethal, yet neither requires a licence. The author thanks Gavin Hales for clarifying this point.

7 Gun ownership in the United Kingdom may be much more common than is often assumed. For England and Wales, estimates of registered and unregistered firearms range from 2.0 to 4.7 million, for an average of 3.4 million (Small Arms Survey, 2007a, app. 3; Squires, Grimshaw, and Solomon, 2008, p. 19). For the United Kingdom as a whole (including Northern Ireland and Scotland) combined totals vary from 2.5 to 5.5 million, for an average of 4 million estimated civilian guns. While the actual total cannot be declared with certainty, the United Kingdom appears to be armed at an average level for Europe (Small Arms Survey, 2004, ch. 2; 2007a, ch. 2).

8 Better information may emerge through the newly established National Ballistics Intelligence Service, a data sharing and tracing system for all police constabularies of England and Wales, designed to facilitate the tracing of illicit and suspect firearms (Terry, 2008).

9 Robert Muggah and Philip Alpers estimate that the Solomon Islands had a pre-conflict total of 1,010 to 1,270 military and commercially manufactured rifles. Only 300 of these appear to have been recovered (Dunnigan, 2004; Muggah and Alpers, 2003).

10 The South African disarmament total subtracts 88,640 decommissioned police weapons (Gould et al., 2004, p. 243).

11 This section on state armed forces and law enforcement agencies is designed as a brief overview, partially recapitulating themes covered in the *Small Arms Survey 2008* (Small Arms Survey, 2008).

BIBLIOGRAPHY

ABC (Australian Broadcasting Corporation). 2003. 'Law and Order Improve Dramatically in the Solomons.' 1 October.

ABS (Australian Bureau of Statistics). 2008. *Recorded Crime: Victims, Australia, 2007*. Canberra: ABS. 26 June.

Angola. 2006. *National Report of the Republic of Angola on the Implementation of the United Nations Programme of Action to Prevent, Combat and Eradicate the Illicit Trade in Small Arms and Light Weapons in All Its Aspects*. June, p. 10.

AP (Associated Press). 2004. 'Crocodiles Thrive on Disarmament.' 8 June.

ASB (Anti-social Behaviour Act). 2003. Anti-social Behaviour Act 2003 (c. 38). London: Office of Public Sector Information.

Bacevich, Andrew J. 2005. *The New American Militarism*. Oxford: Oxford University Press.

Baker, Jeanine and Samara McPhedran. 2007. 'Gun Laws and Sudden Death: Did the Australian Firearms Legislation of 1996 Make a Difference?' *British Journal of Criminology*, Vol. 47, No. 3, pp. 455–69.

—. 2008. 'Australian Firearms Legislation and Unintentional Firearm Deaths: A Theoretical Explanation for the Absence of Decline following the 1996 Gun Laws.' *Public Health*, Vol. 122, No. 3. March, pp. 297–99.

BBC (British Broadcasting Corporation). 2003. 'Gun Crime Soars by 35%.' 12 January. <http://news.bbc.co.uk/1/hi/uk_politics/2640817.stm>

Beeck, Christina. 2008. 'Germany: From Surplus Exports to Destruction.' *Contemporary Security Policy*, Vol. 29, No. 1. April.

Bevan, James. 2008a. *Crisis in Karamoja: Armed Violence and the Failure of Disarmament in Uganda's Most Deprived Region*. Occasional Paper No. 21. Geneva: Small Arms Survey. June.

—, ed. 2008b. *Conventional Ammunition in Surplus*. Geneva: Small Arms Survey.

Bhatia, Michael and Mark Sedra. 2008. *Afghanistan, Arms and Conflict: Armed Groups, Disarmament and Security in a Post-War Society*. London: Routledge, ch. 4.

Bonomo, Giacomo Bergamo et al. 2007. *Stealing the Sword: Limiting Terrorist Use of Advanced Conventional Weapons*. Santa Monica: Rand Corporation, ch. 3.

Bryan, John. 2004. *Illegal Firearms in the United Kingdom*. Working Paper No. 3. London: Centre for Defence Studies, pp. 31–34.

Buchanan, Cate and Mireille Widmer. 2006. *Civilians, Guns and Peace Processes: Approaches and Possibilities*. Geneva: Centre for Humanitarian Dialogue. October.

Caramés, Albert and Eneko Sanz, 2008. *DDR 2008: Analysis of Disarmament, Demobilisation and Reintegration (DDR) programmes in the World during 2007*. School for a Culture of Peace, Autonomous University of Barcelona, n.d.

Chapman, Simon and Philip Alpers. 2006. 'Tight Gun Controls the Most Powerful Weapon.' *Sydney Morning Herald*. 27 April.

— et al. 2006. 'Australia's 1996 Gun Law Reforms: Faster Falls in Firearm Deaths, Firearm Suicides, and a Decade without Mass Shootings.' *Injury Prevention*, No. 12. December, pp. 365–72.

Christie, Louis. 1999. *Australian Gun Controls: Should More Be Done?* Coalition of Law Abiding Sporting Shooters.

Coaker, Vernon. 2007. 'Minister's Answers on Gun Crime.' BBC News. 15 November.

Courtney-Green, Peter. 2008. 'NATO and Demilitarization of Surplus Weapons and Ammunition.' *Contemporary Security Policy*, Vol. 29, No. 1. April.

CS (Comunidade Segura). 2007. 'Gun-related Deaths Fall 12% in Brazil.' 15 November. <http://www.comunidadesegura.org/?q=en/node/37237>

Cullen, W. Douglas. 1996. *The Public Inquiry into the Shootings at Dunblane Primary School on 13 March 1996: List of Victims*. London: The Stationery Office.

Cusick, James. 1996. 'Nationwide gun amnesty is ordered.' *Independent*. 22 March.

Davies, Megan and Jenny Mouzos. 2007. *Homicide in Australia: 2005–06 National Homicide Monitoring Program Annual Report*. Canberra: Australian Institute of Criminology, p. 3.

Diamond, Jared. 2005. *Collapse: How Societies Choose to Fail or Succeed*. New York: Viking, ch. 2.

Dobbins, James et al. 2005. *America's Role in Nation-Building: From Germany to Iraq*. Santa Monica: Rand Corporation.

—. 2008. *Europe's Role in Nation-Building from the Balkans to the Congo*. Rand Corporation, pp. 173–206.

Downie, Andrew. 2008. 'Crime: Effort to Mend a Violent Reputation.' *Financial Times*. 7 July.

Dreyfus, Pablo and Marcelo de Sousa Nascimento. Forthcoming. 'Brazil.' In Aaron Karp and Jorge Restrepo, eds. *Small Arms of South America*. Geneva: Small Arms Survey.

Dunnigan, James. 2004. 'Disarmament, Peacekeeping and Giant Crocodiles.' 24 June. <http://www.strategypage.com/dls/articles2004/2004624.asp>

Economist. 2008. 'Not as Violent as You Thought.' 21 August.

Faltas, Sami. 2008. 'Bulgaria and Romania: Quick Start, Ambiguous Progress.' *Contemporary Security Policy*, Vol. 29, No. 1. April.

Finland. 2008. *National Report of Finland on the Implementation of the United Nations Programme of Action to Prevent, Combat and Eradicate the Illicit Trade in Small Arms and Light Weapons in All Its Aspects*. Helsinki: Ministry of Foreign Affairs.

Florquin, Nicolas and Elizabeth Decrey Warner. 2008. 'Engaging Non-State Armed Groups or Listing Terrorists? Implications for the Arms Control Community.' *Disarmament Forum*, No. 1. April, pp. 17–25.

Fraenkel, Jon. 2004. *The Manipulation of Custom: From Uprising to Intervention in the Solomon Islands*. Wellington and Canberra: Victoria University Press and Pandanus Books.

FRB (Federal Reserve Board). 1996. 'The Challenge of Central Banking in a Democratic Society.' Remarks by Chairman Alan Greenspan at the Annual Dinner and Francis Boyer Lecture of The American Enterprise Institute for Public Policy Research, Washington, DC. 5 December. <http://www.federalreserve.gov/boarddocs/speeches/1996/19961205.htm>

Gallagher, Thomas. 2004. 'Criminal Law: Are Gun-Related Offences on the Increase in the UK?' <http://www.lawyerintl.com/law-articles/>

Garfield, Richard. 2007. *Violence and Victimization after Civilian Disarmament: The Case of Jonglei*. Sudan Working Paper No. 11. Geneva: Small Arms Survey. December.

Gawryszewski, Vilma Pinheiro and James A. Mercy. 2004. 'Homicide Trends and Characteristics: Brazil, 1980–2002.' *Morbidity and Mortality Weekly Report*, Vol. 53, No. 8. 5 March, pp. 169–171.

GCN (Gun Control Network). 2007. 'Firearms Offences: England and Wales, 1989–2005.' <http://www.gun-control-network.org/A018.htm>

Geneva Call. 2008. *Annual Report 2007*. Geneva: Geneva Call.

Geneva Declaration Secretariat. 2008. *Global Burden of Armed Violence*. Geneva: Geneva Declaration Secreatriat, ch. 3.

Germany. 2008. *National Report on the Implementation of the United Nations Programme of Action to Prevent, Combat and Eradicate the Illicit Trade in Small Arms and Light Weapons in All Its Aspects, Federal Republic of Germany*. Berlin: Federal Foreign Office. 21 March.

Gould, Chandré et al. 2004. 'South Africa.' In Chandré Gould and Guy Lamb, eds. *Hide and Seek: Taking Account of Small Arms in Southern Africa*. Pretoria: Institute for Security Studies.

Gray, Colin. 1992. *House of Cards: Why Arms Control Must Fail*. Ithaca, NY: Cornell University Press.

Halbrook, Stephen. 2000. 'Nazi firearms law and disarming of the German Jews.' *Arizona Journal of International and Comparative Law*, No. 3, pp. 483–535.

Hales, Gavin. 2006. *A Guide to and Review of Home Office Gun Crime Statistics*. Portsmouth: Institute of Criminal Justice Studies, University of Portsmouth. November.

—. 2009. Letter to author. 16 January.

—, Chris Lewis, and Daniel Silverstone. 2006. *Gun Crime: The Market in and Use of Illegal Firearms*. Home Office Research Study 298. London: Home Office. December.

Hänggi, Heiner and Vincenza Scherrer. 2008. 'Recent Experience of UN Integrated Missions in Security Sector Reform.' In Heiner Hänggi and Vincenza Scherrer, eds. *Security Sector Reform and UN Integrated Missions: Experience from Burundi, the Democratic Republic of Congo, Haiti and Kosovo*. Münster and Geneva: Lit Verlag and Geneva Centre for the Democratic Control of Armed Forces, ch. 1.

Harcourt, Bernard. 2004. 'On the NRA, Adolph Hitler, Gun Registration, and the Nazi Gun Laws: Exploding the Culture Wars.' *Public Law Working Paper*, No. 67. Chicago: University of Chicago. June.

Hartzell, Caroline and Matthew Hoddie. 2006. 'From Anarchy to Security: Comparing Theoretical Approaches to the Process of Disarmament following Civil War.' *Contemporary Security Policy*, Vol. 27, No. 1. April, pp. 155–67.

Hennop, Ettienne, Jakkie Potgieter, and Clare Jefferson. 2001. *The Role of Firearms in Crime in South Africa: A Detailed Analysis of Police Dockets*. Monograph No. 55. May, ch. 2.

Hottinger, Julian Thomas. 2008. 'Engaging Non-state Armed Groups in Disarmament.' *Disarmament Forum*, No. 1. April, pp. 27–35.

HRW (Human Rights Watch). 2003. *Weapons Sanctions, Military Supplies, and Human Suffering: Illegal Arms Flows to Liberia and the June–July 2003 Shelling of Monrovia*. New York: HRW, 3 November.

Humphreys, Macartan and Jeremy Weinstein. 2009. 'Assessing Progress toward Demobilization and Reintegration in Sierra Leone.' In Robert Muggah, ed. *Security and Post-Conflict Reconstruction*. London: Routledge, ch. 2.

Huntington, Samuel. 1996. *The Clash of Civilizations and the Remaking of World Order*. New York: Simon and Schuster.

India. 2008. *India: Integrated National Report on the Implementation of the United Nations Programme of Action to Prevent, Combat and Eradicate the Illicit Trade in Small Arms and Light Weapons in All Its Aspects*. New Delhi: Ministry of External Affairs. 31 March.

IRIN. 2008. 'Sudan: Preparing for Massive Demobilization.' 21 October.

Kahn, Túlio and Ted Goertzel. 2007. 'The Great São Paulo Homicide Drop.' *Fórum Brasileiro de Segurança Pública*. 28 May.

Kaiza, Peter. 2008. 'Homicides, Recorded Crimes Involving Firearms.' In David Povey et al., eds. *Homicides, Firearm Offences and Intimate Violence 2006/07: Supplementary Vol. 2 to Crime in England and Wales 2006/07*. London: Home Office. 31 January.

Karp, Aaron. 2008. 'Introduction: Inconspicuous Disarmament.' *Contemporary Security Policy*, Vol. 29, No. 1. April.

Keegan, John. 1994. *A History of Warfare*. New York: Knopf, chs. 1, 2.

Kirsten, Adèle. 2006. *Assessing the Impact of Firearm Amnesties for South Africa*. Pretoria: Institute for Security Studies. November.

Kopel, David, Paul Gallant, and Joanne Eisen. 2000. 'Solomon Says: The Madness of Civilian Disarmament in the South Pacific.' *National Review*. 27 November.

—. 2008. 'Uganda: We're from the Government and We're Here to Help You.' *America's 1st Freedom*. January, pp. 38–39, 60.

Kryvonos, Yurii and Elli Kytömäki. 2008. 'The OSCE Experience with Surplus Small Arms and Ammunition.' *Contemporary Security Policy*, Vol. 29, No. 1. April.

Lamb, Guy. 2008. *Under the Gun: An Assessment of Firearm Crime and Violence in South Africa*. Pretoria: Institute for Security Studies. March.

Lee, Wang-Sheng and Sandy Suardi. 2008. *The Australian Firearms Buyback and Its Effect on Gun Deaths*. Melbourne Institute Working Paper No. 17/08. Melbourne: Melbourne Institute of Applied Economic and Social Research. August.

Leff, Jonah. 2007. *Responses to Pastoral Wars: A Review of Violence Reduction Efforts in Sudan, Uganda, and Kenya*. Geneva: Small Arms Survey. September.

Llana, Sara Miller. 2008. 'Will Venezuela's Murder Rate Hurt Chávez?' *Christian Science Monitor*. 3 December.

Llewellyn, Ian. 2004. 'Crocs Breach Peace in Solomons Disarmament.' *The Age* (Melbourne). 8 June.

Mack, Andrew. 2005. 'Why the Dramatic Decline in Armed Conflict?' In Human Security Report Project. *Human Security Report 2005*. Oxford: Oxford University Press, ch. 5.

Malcolm, Joyce Lee. 2005. 'The UN's Global Effort to Disarm Civilians: Wisdom or Folly?' *Breakthroughs*, Vol. XIV, No. 1. Spring.

Mburu, Nene. 2007. 'Warriors and Guns: The Anthropology of Cattle Rustling in Northeastern Africa.' In Charles Fruehling Springwood, ed. *Open Fire: Understanding Global Gun Cultures*. Oxford: Berg, ch. 6.

Mexico. 2008. *Report of the Government of Mexico on the Implementation of the United Nations Programme of Action to Prevent, Combat and Eradicate the Illicit Trade in Small Arms and Light Weapons in All Its Aspects*. 31 March.

Moore, Clive. 2004. *Happy Isles in Crisis: The Historical Causes for a Failing State in Solomon Islands, 1998–2004*. Canberra: Asia Pacific Press.

Muggah, Robert. 2006. 'Emerging from the Shadow of War: A Critical Perspective on DDR and Weapons Reduction in the Post-conflict Period.' *Contemporary Security Policy*, Vol. 27, No. 1. April, pp. 190–205.

—. 2009. 'The Emperor's Clothes?' In Muggah, ed. *Security and Post-Conflict Reconstruction*. London: Routledge.

— and Philip Alpers. 2003. *Reconsidering Small Arms in the Solomon Islands: Findings*. Unpublished background paper. Geneva: Small Arms Survey. 1 August.

Myrdal, Alva. 1976. *The Game of Disarmament: How the United States and Russia Run the Arms Race*. New York: Pantheon.

Nagl, John A. 2005. *Counterinsurgency Lessons from Malaya and Vietnam: Learning to Eat Soup with a Knife*, revised edn. Chicago: University of Chicago Press.

Neill, Christine and Andrew Leigh. 2007. 'Weak Tests and Strong Conclusions: A Re-Analysis of Gun Deaths and the Australian Firearms Buyback.' Australian National University Discussion Paper No. 555.

Noel-Baker, Philip. 1926. *Disarmament*. London: Hogarth Press, p. 2.

Norway. 2005. Norway: *National Report on the Implementation of the United Nations Programme of Action to Prevent, Combat and Eradicate the Illicit Trade in Small Arms and Light Weapons in All Its Aspects*. Oslo: Ministry of Foreign Affairs. 30 April.

Parker, Sarah and Silvia Cattaneo. 2008. *Implementing the UN Programme of Action on Small Arms and Light Weapons: Analysis of the National Reports Submitted by States from 2002 to 2008*. Draft report. Geneva: United Nations Institute for Disarmament Research. July.

Peake, Gordon. 2009. 'What the Veterans Say: Unpacking DDR Programmes in Timor–Leste.' In Robert Muggah, ed. *Security and Post-Conflict Reconstruction*. London: Routledge, ch. 6.

Pézard, Stéphanie and Nicolas Florquin. 2007. *Small Arms in Burundi: Disarming the Civilian Population in Peacetime*. Geneva: Small Arms Survey, pp. 2, 5, 21–23, 76.

Pouligny, Béatrice. 2004. *The Politics and Anti-Politics of Contemporary Disarmament, Demobilization and Reintegration Programs*. Paris: Centre d'Etudes et de Recherches Internationales, Sciences Po, Secrétariat Général de la Défense Nationale. September.

Povey, David. 2004. *Crime in England and Wales 2002/2003—Supplementary Vol. 1: Homicide and Gun Crime 01/04*. London: Home Office. January, p. 49.

Restrepo, Jorge A. and Robert Muggah. 2009. 'Colombia's Quiet Demobilization: A Security Dividend? Reviewing the Evidence.' In Robert Muggah, ed. *Security and Post-Conflict Reconstruction*. London: Routledge, ch. 1.

Reuter, Peter and Jenny Mouzos. 2003. 'Australia: A Massive Buyback of Low-Risk Guns.' In Jens Ludwig and Philip J. Cook, eds. *Evaluating Gun Policy: Effects on Crime and Violence*. Washington, DC: Brookings Institution Press.

Richardson, Lewis Fry. 1960. *Statistics of Deadly Quarrels*. Pacific Grove: Boxwood Press.

Romero, Simon. 2006. 'As Crime Soars for Venezuela, Chávez Coasts.' *New York Times*. 2 December.

Ruediger, Marco Aurelio, Vicente Riccio, and Angela Britto. 2007. 'Homicides in Rio de Janeiro State, Brazil: A Geographical Distribution and Its Impacts for Public Policies Concerning Crime Reduction.' Paper presented at the annual meeting of The Law and Society Association, Berlin, Germany. 25 July.

Sjöberg, Anki. 2007. *Armed Non-State Actors and Landmines Volume III: Towards a Holistic Approach to Armed Non-State Actors?* Geneva: Geneva Call. November.

Small Arms Survey. 2002. *Small Arms Survey 2002: Counting the Human Cost*. Oxford: Oxford University Press.

—. 2004. *Small Arms Survey 2004: Rights at Risk*. Oxford: Oxford University Press, ch. 2.

—. 2006. *Small Arms Survey 2006: Unfinished Business*. Cambridge: Cambridge University Press, ch. 2.

—. 2007a. *Small Arms Survey 2007: Guns and the City*. Cambridge: Cambridge University Press.

—. 2007b. *Anatomy of Civilian Disarmament in Jonglei State*. Sudan Issue Brief No. 3, 2nd edn. Geneva: Small Arms Survey.

—. 2008. 'A Semi-automatic Process? Identifying and Destroying Military Surplus.' In Small Arms Survey. *Small Arms Survey 2008: Risks and Resilience*. Cambridge: Cambridge University Press, ch. 3.

de Souza, Maria de Fátima Marinho et al. 2007. 'Reductions in Firearm-Related Mortality and Hospitalizations in Brazil after Gun Control.' *Health Affairs*, Vol. 26, No. 2, pp. 575–84.

Spear, Joanna. 2006. 'From Political Economies of War to Political Economies of Peace: Contributions of DDR after Wars of Predation.' *Contemporary Security Policy*, Vol. 27, No. 1. April, pp. 168–89.

Squires, Peter, Roger Grimshaw, and Enver Solomon. 2008. *'Gun Crime': A Review of Evidence and Policy*. London: Centre for Crime and Justice Studies, King's College London. June.

Summers, Chris. 2007. 'Who Supplies the Guns on Our Streets?' BBC News. 12 November.

Terry, Nick. 2008. 'Database to Boost Gun Crime Fight.' BBC News. 10 March.

Turkey. 2008. *Turkey: National Report on the Implementation of the United Nations Programme of Action to Prevent, Combat and Eradicate the Illicit Trade in Small Arms and Light Weapons in All Its Aspects*. Ankara: Ministry of Foreign Affairs, April.

UK Parliament. 1999. 'Handgun Surrender Figures.' Hansard. 27 May. <http://hansard.millbanksystems.com/written_answers/1999/may/27/handgun-surrender-figures>

UNGA (United Nations General Assembly). 2001. *Programme of Action to Prevent, Combat and Eradicate the Illicit Trade in Small Arms and Light Weapons in All Its Aspects ('UN Programme of Action')*. 20 July. A/CONF.192/15 of 20 July. <http://disarmament.un.org/cab/poa.html>

UNSC (United Nations Security Council). 2008. *Final Report of the Group of Experts on the Democratic Republic of the Congo*. S/2008/773 of 12 December.

US Army. 2003. *Stability Operations and Support Operations*, FM 3-07 (FM 100-20). Washington, DC: Department of the Army. February.

—. 2008. *Stability Operations*, FM 3-07. Washington, DC: Department of the Army. October.

van Lill, André. 2006. 'Western Cape: Firearms destruction.' *SAPS Journal*. Pretoria: South African Police Service. July, p. 33.

Waiselfisz, Julio Jacobo. 2005. *Mortes matadas por armas de fogo no Brasil, 1979/2003*. Brasília: Unesco.

—. 2007. 'Map of Violent deaths.' *Estudos Avançados* (São Paulo), Vol. 21, No. 61. September/December.

Waltz, Kenneth. 1959. *Man, the State and War: A Theoretical Analysis*. New York: Columbia University Press.

Wille, Christina and Keith Krause, 2005. 'Behind the Numbers: Small Arms Conflict Deaths.' In Small Arms Survey. *Small Arms Survey 2005: Weapons at War*. Oxford: Oxford University Press, ch. 9.

Zimring, Franklin. 2006. *The Great American Crime Decline*. Oxford: Oxford University Press. November.

ACKNOWLEDGEMENTS

Principal author

Aaron Karp

Students walk past the destroyed Sakheen elementary school, where they used to study, Gaza, January 2009.
© Jenny Matthews/Panos Pictures

Large and Small

IMPACTS OF ARMED VIOLENCE ON CHILDREN AND YOUTH

6

INTRODUCTION

Over the last decade, children and youth have been recognized as being specifically and disproportionately affected by consequences of armed violence. Along with a growing appreciation of children's rights—enshrined in the 1989 Convention on the Rights of the Child—this recognition has led researchers and implementing agencies to begin treating children and youth as special stakeholders in their assessments of and programming for situations of armed violence.

Most of the related research has been conducted in conflict settings. The landmark 1996 report by Graça Machel entitled *Impact of Armed Conflict on Children* documents how death and injury, malnutrition, loss of education, and conscription by government forces, paramilitaries, and non-state armed groups affect the youngest segment of the population (UN, 1996). Published ten years later, a strategic review of the Machel study emphasizes the indirect consequences of war, including the loss of basic services and rise of poverty (UN, 2007). This review also notes how the changing nature of conflicts—now mainly conducted by small, ill-trained, and lightly armed groups—affects civilians, who are increasingly targeted and bear the brunt of the consequences of hostilities (UN, 2007; UNCAAC and UNICEF, 2007).

Several multi-country studies attempt to capture the effects of armed violence on children.[1] The UN's recent *World Report on Violence against Children* has helped bring the hidden problem of violence against children into the international spotlight (Pinheiro, 2006). Today it is understood that although male adolescents and young men generally form the majority of the direct victims of armed violence through death, injury, and psychosocial trauma, children are also victims through targeted attacks on civilians or recruitment into armed groups. Blurring the line between victimization and perpetration, recruited children also play the role of combatant, wielding weapons with startling ease (Wiseman, 2006; Sommers, 2006; Stohl et al., 2001).

The chapter's main findings are as follows:

- Children and youth are directly and indirectly impacted by armed violence in ways that are different and, at times, more severe than adults. They are victims, witnesses, and perpetrators of armed violence.
- Estimates of direct conflict deaths have ranged from as low as 52,000 per year (Geneva Declaration Secretariat, 2008, p. 9) to as high as 184,000 (WHO, 2008, p. 58). The World Health Organization estimates that almost half of these deaths occur in persons 0 to 29 years of age (47 per cent), of whom the vast majority are young males 15 to 29 years old (73 per cent) (WHO, 2008).
- In addition to death, many children and youths suffer injuries and psychological trauma. For every youth homicide, there are an estimated 20 to 40 non-fatal firearm injuries (WHO, 2002).

- Children and youth are indirectly affected by armed violence through displacement, the death or injury of a family member, and reduced access to social services.
- Schools and hospitals may close or be difficult to access during hostilities. Some may be deliberately targeted in conflict. Reduced access to education disproportionately affects school-aged children, while the deterioration in health care provision has implications for children's physical development. A deterioration in reproductive health services affects girls and young women, especially those who are pregnant or have been raped.
- Half the world's out-of-school population—39 million children—live in conflict-affected fragile states, even though these countries account for just 13 per cent of the world's population (International Save the Children Alliance, 2007, p. 4).
- Despite their vulnerabilities, children and youth demonstrate enormous resilience and an ability to cope in the face of adversity.

Box 6.1 Definitions

Children
Persons aged 0-18 years (UN, 1989, art. 1)

Youth
Persons aged 15-24 years (UN definition)[2]

The chapter provides a comprehensive overview of direct and indirect impacts of armed violence on children and youth. It argues that they are affected by armed violence—physiologically, psychologically, and socially—but that they also demonstrate enormous resilience. The chapter ends by outlining steps for a way forward, which emphasize the importance of child protection initiatives and the need for further research and consolidation of best practices that identify and strengthen resilience and coping strategies.

IMPACTS OF ARMED VIOLENCE ON CHILDREN AND YOUTH

Children and youth are exposed to armed violence in a number of different ways—as witnesses, victims, and perpetrators—during and after conflict, as well as in times of peace. This section reviews the direct consequences of armed violence for children and youth, including death, injury, and psychosocial trauma. While many lose their lives in battle or other forms of armed conflict, the number of wounded, disabled, and traumatized is far greater. Capturing the scope of these impacts—some of which may be long-lasting or permanent—raises a number of conceptual, methodological, and practical challenges.

This chapter distinguishes between the 'direct' and 'indirect' impacts of armed violence on children and youth based on the proximity between cause and effect. Direct impacts, such as death, injury, and psychosocial trauma,

Table 6.1 Armed violence impacts: examples relating to children and youth

Direct impacts	• Death and injury • Psychosocial trauma
Indirect impacts	• Changes resulting from the death and injury of family and peers • Displacement • Reduced access to or quality of education • Reduced access to or quality of health care

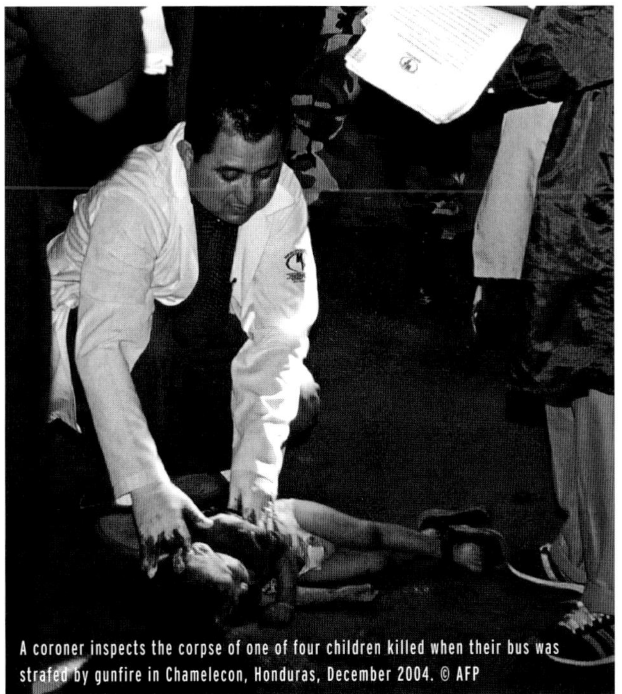
A coroner inspects the corpse of one of four children killed when their bus was strafed by gunfire in Chamelecon, Honduras, December 2004. © AFP

stem from an individual's first-hand encounter with armed violence. By contrast, indirect impacts arise when armed violence affects someone removed from the violent event. These impacts include displacement and impaired education (see Table 6.1).

DIRECT IMPACTS

Death and injury

There is insufficient data to capture the global impact of armed violence on children and youth, including the numbers killed and injured. Estimates of direct conflict deaths have ranged from as low as 52,000 per year to as high as 184,000 (Geneva Declaration Secretariat, 2008, p. 9; WHO, 2008, p. 58).[3] The World Health Organization estimates that almost half of these deaths occur in persons 0 to 29 years of age (47 per cent), of whom the vast majority are young males 15 to 29 years old (73 per cent, see Figure 6.1) (WHO, 2008). The number of direct conflict deaths for the 0–29 age group may thus be as low as 24,000 or as high as 86,000.[4]

Figure 6.1 **Distribution of deaths by sex and age group (years) in 'war and civil conflict' for 2004 (WHO, 2008)**[5]

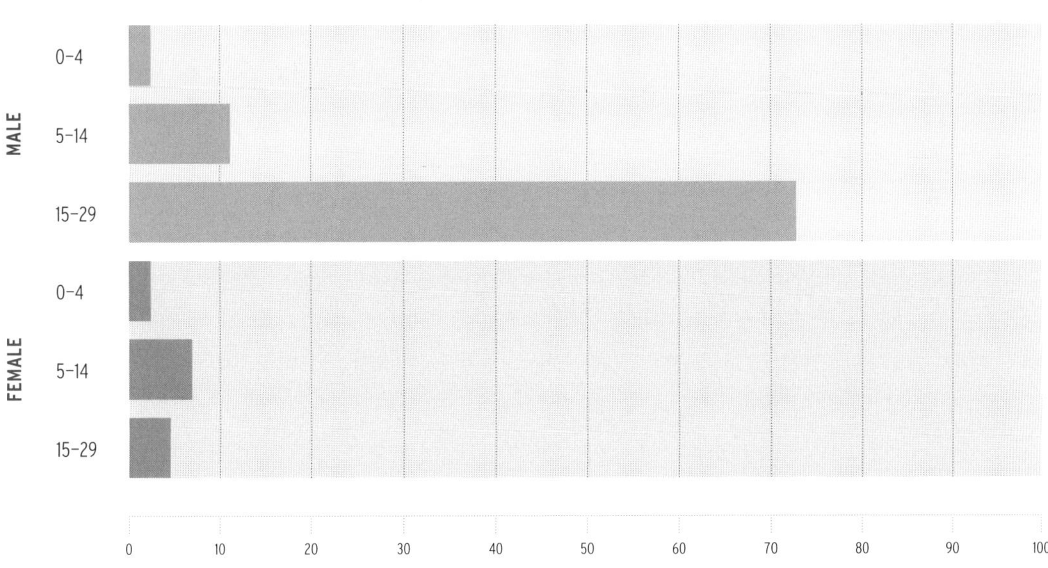

In addition to causing countless fatalities, armed violence brings about untold physical suffering for children and youth in both conflict and non-conflict settings. Studies of non-fatal violence reveal that, for every youth homicide, there are around 20–40 victims of non-fatal youth violence receiving hospital treatment (WHO, 2002, p. 27). The total number of children injured or permanently disabled as a result of armed violence is not known (Geneva Declaration Secretariat, 2008, pp. 13, 34).

In conflict settings, children and youth can be recruited into armed groups and thereby encounter the extreme violence of modern war and the risk of death, injury, malnourishment, and exposure to drugs or alcohol. Many are forced to become perpetrators of violence, sometimes inflicted on their own communities and families. The most frequent injuries for child soldiers include loss of hearing, eyesight, and limbs (UN, 1996). Impacts on child soldiers are compounded by the separation from their families and the breakdown of social structures, which, in turn, have implications for their long-term physical and psychological health (see Box 6.2). Other young victims of conflict may suffer similar consequences, with trauma being manifested in a number of different ways, both 'visibly' through physical injury or disability and 'invisibly' through psychological disturbances.

Girls and young women are at risk of sexual violence and exploitation.

Small arms are used to commit or facilitate human rights abuses against children and youth, including extra-judicial executions, forced disappearances, and torture (Stohl, 2001, p. 5). Girls are particularly vulnerable to sexual exploitation, including rape and sexual slavery. Beyond the associated physical and emotional trauma, rape may lead to infection with HIV/AIDS and unwanted pregnancies. Women and girls in West Africa, specifically Côte d'Ivoire, the Democratic Republic of the Congo (DRC), Liberia, and Sierra Leone, are extremely vulnerable to gender-based violence and in need of special protection measures (UNICEF, 2005). In the DRC, for example, research has shown severe sexual violence involving arms, with accounts of men being forced at gunpoint to rape their mothers, sisters, or daughters (Wakabi, 2008).

Homicide and violence-related injury of children occur in communities all around the world but are more frequent in poor urban areas where there is corruption, lawlessness, and a lack of social services and employment opportunities. Children and youth—especially boys and young men—may express frustration and anger through fights and anti-social behaviour (Pinheiro, 2006). The World Health Organization estimates that boys are two to three times more likely than girls to get involved in fighting (WHO, 2002, p. 29). They may also participate in organized armed violence, such as gangs, drug factions, cartels, death squads, paramilitaries, and revolutionary groups. Research on urban armed violence in ten different countries reveals striking similarities in the risk factors and motives of children and youth using firearms and violence against others (Dowdney, 2005). Meanwhile, the diversity in youth gangs—in terms of their structure, motivation, dynamics, and activities—has also been emphasized (Strocka, 2006). Where firearms and other weapons are widely available and affordable, fights are more likely to lead to severe injuries and death. The situation is worsened where boys are encouraged to exhibit aggressive masculinity, weapons skills, private codes of loyalty and revenge, and general risk-taking (Pinheiro, 2006, p. 287; Luz, 2007).

Easy access to firearms and other weapons increases the risk of interpersonal violence, including domestic violence against women and children. A 2003 study from the United States shows that having a gun in the home increased the overall risk of someone in the household being murdered by 42 per cent, and, for women in particular, the risk was nearly tripled (Wiebe, 2003). Access to firearms has also been shown to be a risk factor for suicide (Hemenway and Miller, 2002). A study of the global burden of disease by the World Health Organization reveals that suicides are the largest source of 'intentional injury burden' in developed countries, while in developing countries

Box 6.2 **Child soldiers**

Child soldiers are most generally defined as any person under the age of 18 years who is a member of or attached to government armed forces or any other regular or irregular armed force or armed group, regardless of whether an armed conflict exists (Coalition to Stop the Use of Child Soldiers, 2008a, p. 411). Not all child soldiers are direct combatants. While some children serve on the front lines, others are used in combat support roles as messengers, spies, porters, or cooks. Both young girls and boys serve in these roles (Denov and Maclure, 2005; McKay and Mazurana, 2004).

Children become involved with armed groups for a variety of reasons. Some children take up arms to respond to a perceived need to ensure their own defence; others are abducted by forces that attack villages and massacre families. Some children join government military or rebel forces 'voluntarily' because they have lost their families and are seeking protection. Others perceive military service as a substitute for the support structure that disappears when conflict erodes families and communities. They may also believe that joining an armed group is the only way to be assured of food, clothing, and shelter. Or they may 'volunteer' because they feel compelled to protect their hometowns, are encouraged by their parents to enlist, or are persuaded to fight for social causes, religious expression, or national liberation.

The use of child soldiers often changes the dynamics of conflict. In some cases, conflicts could not continue without the extra strength provided by child soldiers. Examples include Sierra Leone and Liberia in the 1990s and early years of the following decade, when numerous child-led groups waged war against the government and themselves. In Uganda today, the Lord's Resistance Army relies almost solely on child soldiers to wage war against the Government of Uganda; the group is believed to be made up of 80 per cent child soldiers (Coalition to Stop the Use of Child Soldiers, 2009).

Child soldiers are subjected to life-threatening risks–even beyond the normal dangers of war. Child soldiers are given dangerous tasks, such as landmine clearance, because they are seen as easily replaceable and therefore expendable. Girl soldiers face additional hardships. Some are assigned as 'wives' of their commanders and may become pregnant. Child soldiers are often tortured and endure psychological and sexual abuse. Sexually transmitted diseases are not uncommon. Child soldiers are often plied with drugs and alcohol to make it 'easier' for them to undertake combat activities.

A child soldier belonging to the Lord's Resistance Army stands guard, Uganda, August 2006. © Adam Pletts/WPN

A large body of international law is intended to protect children from being used as soldiers. The most significant is the Optional Protocol to the Convention on the Rights of the Child on the Involvement of Children in Armed Conflict. This widely accepted international standard on the use of children in armed conflict was ratified by more than 120 countries (see Box 6.9). Yet the Coalition to Stop the Use of Child Soldiers emphasizes the lack of best practices for addressing the special needs of child soldiers in disarmament, demobilization, and reintegration (DDR) programmes. Indeed, long-term support and funding for former child soldiers are often altogether absent from DDR activities. Lessons learned from past efforts continue to be overlooked in the implementation of official DDR and rehabilitation programmes. For example, the unique injuries and trauma faced by girls are often ignored (Stohl, 2009).

The challenge is how to ensure rehabilitation and justice for the victims of a conflict, both the population and the former child soldiers (Coalition to Stop the Use of Child Soldiers, 2008a, p. 16). Although protection for children after conflict may vary from country to country, rebuilding processes generally attempt to hold adult parties responsible for the use of child soldiers and therefore accountable for the children's actions. An example is the trial at the International Criminal Court–the first of its kind–of a former Congolese warlord charged with recruiting and using hundreds of children under 15 years of age to fight (BBC, 2009a).

Source: Stohl (2009)

violence and war are the largest source (WHO, 2008, p. 49). Youth suicide in developing countries has nevertheless been identified as an important and potentially growing issue, especially among subgroups (Aaron et al., 2004; Kim and Singh, 2004). Research in the Caribbean, for example, has found that suicide is a serious concern among school-going adolescents (UNICEF, 2006a, p. 22). There is, however, insufficient literature to draw conclusions on the role of armed violence and the availability of arms in causing or contributing to self-directed violence among young people globally.

Psychosocial trauma[6]

In addition to causing death and physical injury, armed violence can affect children's psychological and social behaviour and development, thereby temporarily or permanently altering their lives. They may show symptoms indicative of depression, anxiety, and post-traumatic stress disorder (PTSD; see Box 6.3), which, in turn, may lead to aggression, fear, bedwetting, nightmares, and social isolation (Heptinstall, Sethna, and Taylor, 2004; Polusny and Follette, 1995; Ackerman et al., 1998). This behaviour can affect children's school work or relationships with friends and family (Paolucci et al., 2001; Ackerman et al., 1998). Both victims and perpetrators of armed violence may experience psychosocial trauma (Hauff, 2007).

Individual characteristics, such as age, sex, and culture, play an important role in determining how, and to what extent, psychosocial trauma manifests itself. For example, in order to express their opinions, children under three years of age tend to resort to play, whereas a preschool-age child may rely more on words (Dinicola, 1996). Equally, preschool children may be less equipped to hide their emotions than school-age children (Sayfan et al., 2008). Signs of psychological trauma, therefore, may be more subtle and nuanced and difficult to detect in older, as opposed to younger, children. Moreover, an aggregation of US data on trauma for the past 25 years shows that girls are significantly more susceptible than boys to long-term psychosocial effects as a result of a non-sexual assault (Tolin and Foa, 2006, p. 972). Finally, important ethnic and cultural differences pose challenges to the conceptualization and measurement of psychosocial trauma, including PTSD (see Box 6.3).

Research conducted in the Gaza Strip has shown that childhood traumatization as a result of armed violence can lead to symptoms of depression, persistent post-traumatic stress behaviour, and a decreased satisfaction with one's quality of life (Qouta et al., 2008). The long-term nature of armed violence traumatization was also reported in Croatia, where the experiencing or witnessing

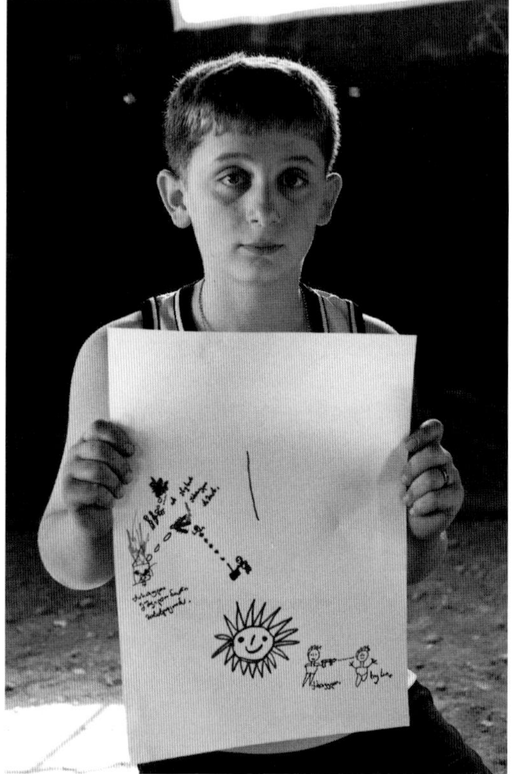

A child in a camp for displaced families in Gori, Georgia, shows his drawing depicting scenes of violence, August 2008. © Cliff Volpe/Getty Images

Box 6.3 Post-traumatic stress disorder: practical challenges to measurement

Post-traumatic stress disorder (PTSD) has been defined as a series of maladaptive emotional or behavioural reactions in response to the experience of a stressful event, or repeated stressful events, such as armed violence, natural disasters, injury, and loss (APA, 1995; WHO, 1992). Manifestations vary according to age, sex, and culture. Young children, for example, typically exhibit PTSD in response to violent events through repetitive play, re-enactment behaviour, reduced interest in usual activities, memory and sleep disturbances, irritability and anger, difficulty concentrating, and an exaggerated startle response (Dinicola, 1996; APA, 1995).

Diagnosing and treating post-traumatic stress in children from culturally diverse regions presents a host of practical challenges to clinicians (Sayfan, 2008; Nader, 2007; Dinicola, 1996). Ethnic and cultural norms determine which types of childhood behaviour and emotions are 'acceptable' within a specific community and thereby define limits on how children may express themselves (Nader, 2007; Dyregrov et al., 2000; Dinicola, 1996). For instance, in certain Bosnian cultures, until the age of 18 years, children are considered to be under the authority of the parent or caretaker. Without permission from a parent or caretaker, these children may be less able or less willing to express themselves (Dyregrov et al., 2000).

Many factors specific to the individual affect the expression and nature of PTSD, including age, sex, ethnocultural norms, and the type and severity of the traumatic incident experienced. Together, these factors pose challenges to defining, evaluating, and diagnosing psychosocial trauma in children and youth. Further qualitative research is needed to explore the role of ethnicity and culture in determining how psychosocial trauma is manifested and to explore whether Western models of mental illness are universally appropriate.

Source: Murray (2009)

of war and various atrocities during childhood predicted aggressive behaviour in adolescence (Qouta, Punamäki, and El Sarraj, 2008). Finally, a US study shows that women who were sexually abused during childhood are twice as likely to attempt suicide than those who had no such history (Dominguez, Nelke, and Perry, 2002).

Fortunately, there is not only bad news. Research shows that, in spite of persistent fear and anxiety, children who experience war or chronic violence may be endowed with internal resilience mechanisms that help them cope (Sagi-Schwartz, 2008; Ehntholt and Yule, 2006; Baker, 1990). It has been shown that children who have a mild temperament and positive self-esteem adapt better in the face of adverse circumstances (Ehnthold and Yule, 2006). National identity, religion, and political ideology may also help maintain the child's self-identity and pride, thereby protecting her or him from developing psychosocial problems (Laor et al., 2006; Servan-Schreiber et al., 1998; Punamäki, 1988).

In addition to internal resilience factors, external resilience factors may also play a role in helping children cope. A supportive home, school, and community environment can promote and strengthen coping strategies (Jackson, 2006; Laor et al., 2006). Important elements of supportive environments include: community support, family cohesion, a healthy attachment to caregivers, the mother's psychological health and her capacity to cope, adequate health systems, and social infrastructure. Such environments may reinforce personal resilience, while reducing the severity and duration of psychosocial impacts that may result from armed violence.[7]

INDIRECT IMPACTS OF ARMED VIOLENCE ON CHILDREN AND YOUTH

While direct impacts of armed violence are often visible and more easily measurable, the indirect impacts, including disrupted education, disease, and malnutrition, affect a greater number of people worldwide (UN, 1996, p. 32; Geneva Declaration Secretariat, 2008, p. 31). These impacts can be difficult to capture in statistics, especially in times of war, when reliable data is scarce. It can also be conceptually and methodologically difficult to disentangle the impacts attributable to armed violence from other causes—such as natural disasters or economic or political turmoil—as they often come hand in hand. Despite these challenges, there is substantial evidence that armed violence may exacerbate an already poor situation by contributing to the rise of poverty, malnutrition, and disease, which have serious impacts on children and youth (UNCAAC and UNICEF, 2007; UNDP, 2008).

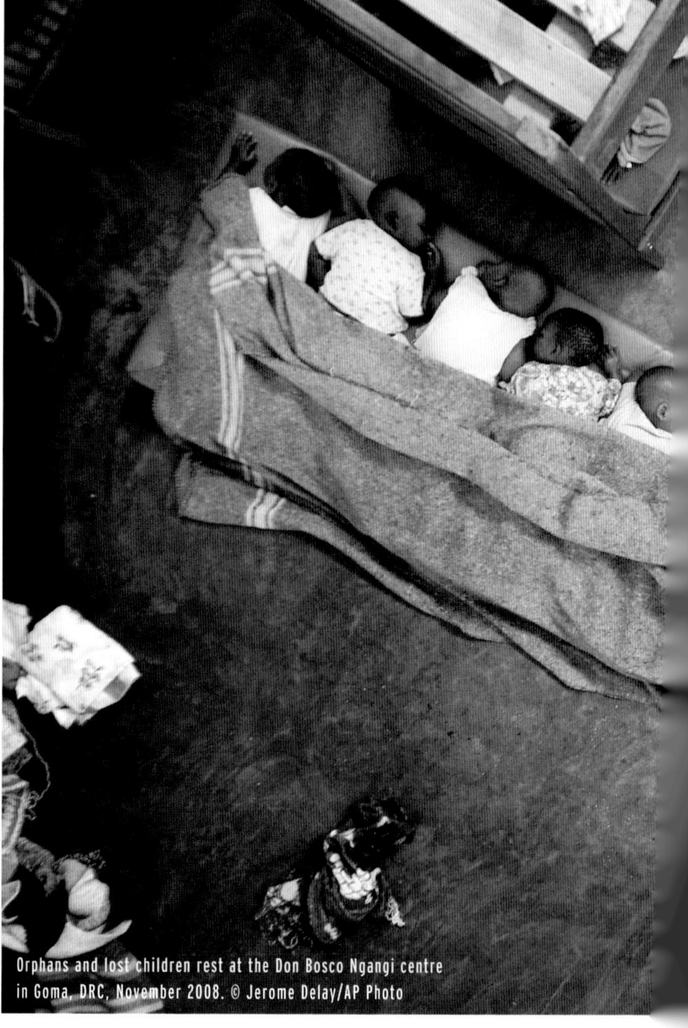
Orphans and lost children rest at the Don Bosco Ngangi centre in Goma, DRC, November 2008. © Jerome Delay/AP Photo

Changes resulting from the death and injury of family and peers

Sudden changes in family circumstances, such as the death or disappearance of parents or family members, can affect children and youth in different ways. On top of the psychological distress associated with losing a loved one, children and youth may be left without guidance, role models, and sustenance. The death or serious injury of a parent or caretaker may force children to take on new responsibilities, including working to earn money, caring for younger siblings, and managing their own and their family's health (WCRWC, 2000, pp. 8, 26; Boyden and Mann, 2005). Children whose parents have been killed may also join armed groups or gangs to seek the perceived protection that these groups offer (UN, 1996, p. 12).

A survey of 266 students in Nepal's Terai region finds that 15 per cent reported having had a parent or caretaker who was shot by a firearm. Of those, more than half said that it had altered their role in the family in some capacity.[8] The majority of children indicated that they had to take on jobs to supplement their family's income. In some countries, including Afghanistan, India, Pakistan, and Yemen, the death of a father or husband can have especially severe consequences for a surviving mother and her children (Boyden et al., 2002, p. 34) (see Box 6.4).

In the chaos of conflict, many children become separated from their parents or relatives. For a variety of reasons, separation from parents and family is usually detrimental for the overall well-being and development of the child (UNICEF, 2006b). For example, in Rwanda, more than 119,000 children were registered as unaccompanied by the end of 1997 (Merkelbach, 2000). Unaccompanied children and child-headed households face special risks during

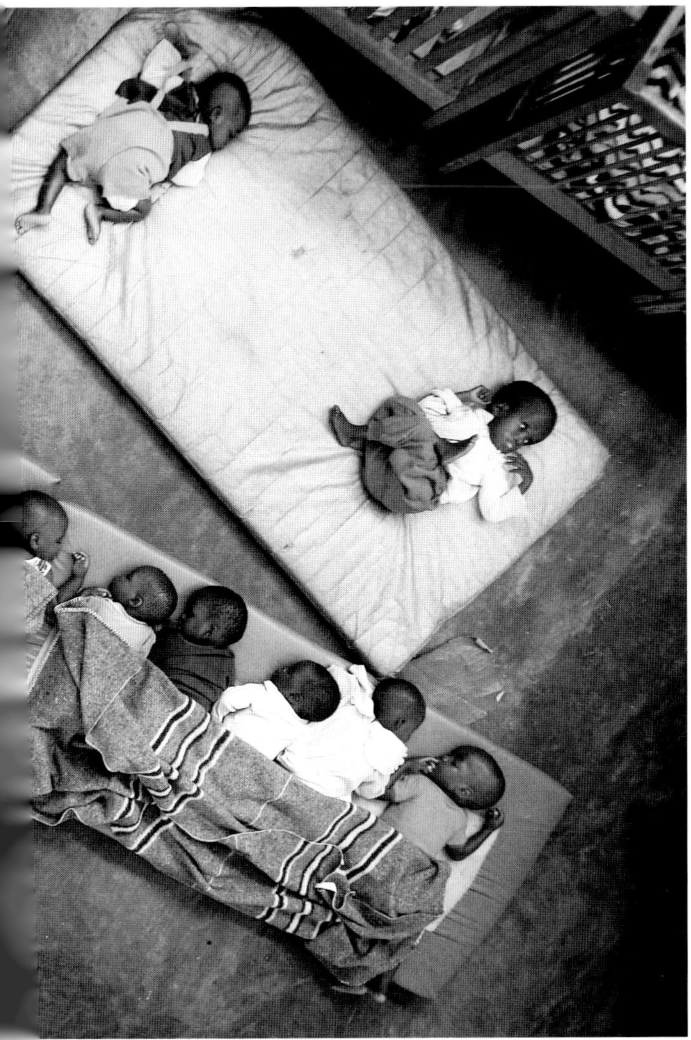

Box 6.4 Indirect impacts of Yemeni revenge killing

Revenge killing is the most common form of non-conflict armed violence in Yemen. It is customary for families to settle disputes outside the rule of law. Usually men (fathers or brothers) are responsible for seeking revenge by taking the life of a male member of another family.

In addition to the death of the victim, there are grave indirect impacts of revenge killing for the widow and her children. The loss of a father, the main source of income, creates extreme hardship for the rest of the family.

In cases in which a mother has only given birth to daughters, the husband's family is permitted under customary law to expel the widow and her daughters from their home, leaving them destitute. This scenario does not apply when the couple has boys, who have the right to remain in the husband's family's home. If a widow and her daughters are expelled from their home, they can go to the widow's parental home or face destitution and homelessness. The husband's family may also decide to take care of all the children, but not the widow, resulting in the splitting up of the family. If the widow remarries, new husbands sometimes mistreat or reject the daughters of the first marriage.

Source: Research conducted by the Small Arms Survey for UNICEF, Yemen, March 2008[9]

and even after conflicts, as they lack adult protection and care. They often struggle to earn a living and are forced to drop out of school, causing them to forgo potential opportunities and face social marginalization (Mirza, 2006). Children without parental care, including street children, are also at risk of becoming victims of further violence (Thomas de Benítez, 2007).

Displacement

The threat of harm and destabilization in areas affected by conflict and high levels of criminal violence often forces families to flee their homes in search of more secure environments, such as to camps for refugees or internally displaced persons (IDPs). Children and youth also flee areas of armed conflict to avoid recruitment into armed groups (see Box 6.5). According to the 2007 Report of the Special Representative of the Secretary-General for Children and Armed Conflict, an estimated 5.8 million children had become refugees as a result of armed conflict, and 8.8 million

Family members from Timor-Leste look out from their shelter as UN staff arrive at their refugee camp in Atenbua, West Timor, November 1999. © Darren Whiteside/Reuters

were internally displaced in 2006 (UN, 2007, p. 19). The UN estimates that children constitute half of the total number of refugees worldwide (UNCAAC, 2008a).

Although well-run refugee camps can be safe havens for their inhabitants, physical insecurity can pose a serious concern, especially in terms of gender-based violence (Pinheiro, 2006, p. 299). A 13-country study by the United Nations High Commissioner for Refugees highlights the extent of the problem. It shows that a high proportion of crimes and disputes in all the surveyed refugee camps fall under the broad category of sexual and gender-based violence. In Sierra Leone, domestic violence was second only to theft as the most pervasive justice issue arising in the camps (da Costa, 2006, p. 10).

Box 6.5 The 'night commuters' of northern Uganda

Known as 'night commuters', rural children in northern Uganda traveled to towns each night in 2003-04. They sought to escape attacks and the risk of abduction by the Lord's Resistance Army and a general climate of insecurity (AI, 2005a). At night, children and youths would leave their villages or IDP camps in search of safe haven in nearby urban centres, where they would sleep in shelters, displacement camps, churches, hospitals, or even on the street. Aid agencies had set up the shelters in view of the Ugandan government's inability to end the brutal war and protect its citizens from rebel attacks. However, without proper security and supervision, the children were victims of physical and sexual violence along transit routes and in the sleeping spaces in town centres. Girls were exposed to the risks of pregnancy and of contracting HIV and other sexually transmitted diseases, with many turning to 'survival sex' in exchange for food or money (UNICEF, 2005, pp. 49-50).

In addition to increasing the risk of gender-based abuse, displacement impacts children's access to education, nutrition, and health care, potentially severing the networks of community, family, and friends who normally provide emotional and financial support. Mortality and malnutrition, including deficiencies in micronutrients such as iron and vitamin A, are often extremely high among refugee and displaced children (Moss et al., 2006; Mason, 2002).

Many refugee camps have become militarized. Studies show that armed groups target refugee communities, where, in addition to recruiting young men and women, they carry out such abuses as rape, forced prostitution, and slavery (Boyden et al., 2002, p. 32; Muggah, 2006; UNHCR, 2006, p. 65). Without official registration or proper identity documents, IDPs face additional difficulties in accessing government assistance, employment, health care, and education. Even after a conflict has subsided, many families still fear a return to their homes because of persistent insecurity (Stohl, 2002).

Children and youth risk being drawn into gang warfare in areas affected by violence. This risk can result in displacement from cities to suburban and rural areas and vice versa (UNHCR, 2006, p. 170). For instance, during Haiti's most violent years of confrontation—a combination of political conflict and armed criminality—many families transferred their children from urban areas, the site of the worst fighting, to the homes of relatives in the countryside. Between 2004 and 2005, some 13,600 children and adolescents were moved to rural areas from Bel Air, a Port-au-Prince neighbourhood with a population of roughly 80,000 inhabitants (Botton, 2008).[10]

Education: reduction in access and quality

Education is a fundamental human right: every child is entitled to it (UNGA, 1948, art. 26). Unfortunately, rather than being safe havens for children, schools can be dangerous places for many. Schools may not function due to rampant instability or due to the fear that students will be abducted or attacked on the way to school. The restriction of access to and quality of education represents one of the main indirect impacts of armed violence on children and youth.

Schools are deliberately targeted, for political and practical reasons.

Education is disrupted when fighting forces specifically target schools and teachers themselves. Schools may be deliberately attacked for political reasons—for example, because schools are government assets and hence perceived as 'soft targets'—or for practical reasons. School buildings may be occupied and used as bases for fighting forces because they have decent facilities, including toilets and kitchens. A UNESCO report finds that some of the highest numbers of attacks on schools and teachers in recent years took place in Afghanistan, Colombia, Iraq, Nepal, the Occupied Palestinian Territory, Thailand, and Zimbabwe (O'Malley, 2007, p. 6). Incidents include the bombing, assassination, abduction, illegal detention, and torture of staff, students, education officials, and trade unionists; the risk of such incidents occurring—and of children being forcibly recruited by armed groups—increases with the bombing and burning of educational buildings and the closure of institutions.

According to a 2007 report by Save the Children, half the world's out-of-school population—39 million children—live in conflict-affected fragile states, even though these countries make up just 13 per cent of the world's population (International Save the Children Alliance, 2007, p. 4). In such environments, a child's ability to travel safely between home and school is often limited. Additionally, risk of abduction, rape, landmines, or being shot may make travel to school perilous, and, in extreme cases, may cause schools to shut down completely (see Box 6.6). In Afghanistan and northern Pakistan, the number of attacks on schools, particularly girls' schools, limits access to education. Many of the attacks on girls' schools are carried out by extremist Islamic groups (BBC, 2009b; O'Malley, 2007). In Afghanistan, the Ministry of Education has reported that militants attacked 250 schools between 2005 and 2008 (IRIN,

2008). In January 2008, 400 schools remained closed, mostly in the southern provinces of Afghanistan, due to attacks or the fear of attacks (IRIN, 2008).

In some countries, teachers are deliberately targeted because they are seen as 'thought leaders' with influence in the local community or because they are seen as representatives of the government or an opposing group. In Colombia, for example, 310 teachers were murdered between 2000 and 2006 because they took political positions on human rights or social justice on behalf of their community (FECODE, 2007; O'Malley, 2007). As the most educated members of the local population, many of them were spokespeople on local issues (O'Malley, 2007, pp. 16–17). Similarly in Iraq, militants have recently targeted teachers as part of their efforts to drive out Baghdad's remaining intellectuals and middle class. Up to 40 per cent of Iraqi professionals had fled the country since 2003 according to the Iraq Index, compiled by the Brookings Institution in Washington and released in December 2006 (O'Malley, 2007, pp. 18–19).

Box 6.6 Kidnapping of school children in Haiti

Haiti is a fragile state afflicted by intermittent surges in armed violence. In addition to the weak capacity of public security institutions, the root causes of armed violence are also related to underdevelopment, lack of opportunities, and limited access to basic resources, such as water and food. Not only are children being deprived of their most basic needs, but in recent years they have also become targets of organized crime through acts such as kidnapping.

Research has revealed that children are one of the main targets of Haiti's criminal gangs. In many cases, kidnappers demand large sums of money from the families of the kidnapped child. Children are also used in the perpetration of kidnapping, either as informants or for logistical tasks. Due to a surge in kidnappings between October and December 2006, the Ministry of National Education decided to close schools throughout the country for the month of December 2006.

Source: Research conducted by Viva Rio for UNICEF, Haiti, January 2008[11]

In Nepal, even before the armed conflict broke out in 1996, access to education was already extremely limited. Conflict caused additional disruptions. Maoists and the Royal Nepalese Army targeted schools to further their offensives during the civil war. Some schools closed—both temporarily and permanently—due to damage to facilities, lack of staff, and military operations by both the Maoists and the Nepalese government (AI, 2005b). The Watchlist on Children and Armed Conflict reports that several hundred schools were shut down due to the armed conflict, affecting at least 100,000 students (WCAC, 2005, p. 21).

Armed violence prevents both students and teachers from moving freely to and from school without the risk of being shot, sexually violated, or abducted. Schools located in areas subsumed by armed violence may therefore find it difficult to recruit well-qualified staff. In the Occupied Palestinian Territory, for example, movement restrictions, bombardment of schools, and closures have all limited children's and teachers' access to schools. Restrictions on movement in the West Bank include roadblocks and checkpoints, often accompanied by body searches and reported harassment by Israeli security (DCI/PS, 2006, pp. 55–62).

In many developed countries, weapons are being carried and used in fights between peers within and around schools. A study of 35 developed countries finds that anywhere from 10 to 21 per cent of boys and 2 to 5 per cent of girls carry a weapon. Among weapon carriers, 7 to 22 per cent of boys and 3 to 11 per cent of girls opt for a firearm. In nearly all countries included in the study, both physical fighting and weapon carrying associated with an increased risk of injury (Picket et al., 2005).

The nature of violence within schools often reflects the levels and patterns of violence in the communities that surround them, and prevailing political and socioeconomic conditions, attitudes, traditions, values, laws, and law enforcement (Pinheiro, 2006, p. 111). A 2002 UNESCO study assesses the security level of 340 schools throughout

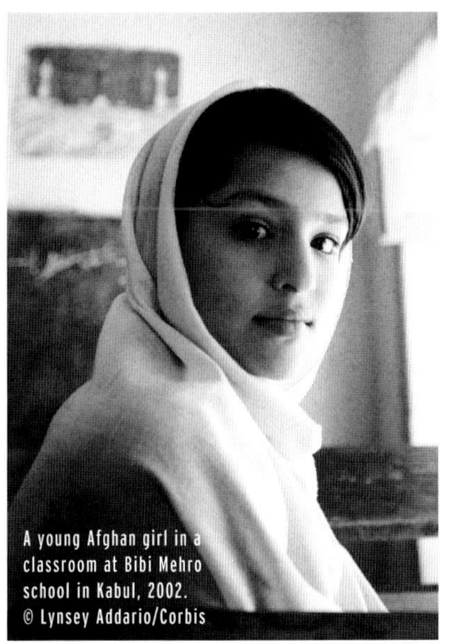
A young Afghan girl in a classroom at Bibi Mehro school in Kabul, 2002. © Lynsey Addario/Corbis

Brazil (Abramovay, 2002).[12] More than half the schools investigated are considered 'insecure environments' (53 per cent of private schools and 65 per cent of public schools).[13] In South Africa, there are reports of widespread gang-related armed violence in or around school premises. Turf wars between gangs take place not only on the street but also on school grounds, where gangs seek to establish a base for selling drugs and recruiting new members (Legget, 2005).

Health impacts: reduction in access and quality

Mortality rates are one of the key indicators of the impact of armed violence. Although a significant number of children and youths are killed and injured every year as a result of armed conflict, many more who are exposed to armed conflict die from malnutrition and disease (UN, 1996, p. 32). In the DRC, for example, fewer than ten per cent of deaths due to conflict have been found to be 'direct' or 'violent', while 90 per cent were 'indirect' conflict deaths (see Box 6.7).

While young men are at the highest risk of direct conflict death, indirect deaths affect all age groups, including children under five years of age. Children die as a result of the rise in diarrheal diseases, severe malnutrition, respiratory infections, and measles (UN, 1996; Salignon et al., 2000; O'Hare and Southall, 2007). Many of today's armed conflicts take place in some of the world's poorest countries. High levels of malnutrition and disease are exacerbated

Box 6.7 **Excess deaths of children and youth due to conflict**

The under-five, or child, mortality rate is often used as an indicator of the human cost of armed conflict. The Machel study estimates that 2 million children died due to conflict between 1986 and 1996 (UN, 1996, p. 2). Although frequently quoted, this statistic is out of date and potentially misleading. The more recent Machel Strategic Review finds that 'an attempt to aggregate numbers would give inaccurate results, and instead describes specific issues and contexts illustrating the impact of conflict on children' (UN, 2007, para. 16).

One reason why it is impossible to provide an accurate aggregate figure is that mortality data in conflict zones is not always disaggregated by age. In addition, the calculation of excess child deaths requires a baseline, or a pre-conflict, mortality rate, which is often difficult to obtain. Finally, the calculation of excess deaths is also heavily dependent on the estimated population size (Checchi and Roberts, 2005; Geneva Declaration Secretariat, 2008).

Despite the challenges, efforts are being made to quantify the impact of conflict on mortality, disease, and disease transmission at the country level. In Sudan, for example, the use of survey data and contextual information leads to an estimate of 135,000 deaths of adults and children for the period September 2003-January 2005, about 112,000 of which are in excess of the expected number of deaths and are thus attributed to the conflict (Guha-Sapir and Degomme, 2006, p. 11). A recent survey that documents the humanitarian impact of war in the DRC since 1998 reveals that 5.4 million excess deaths occurred between 1998 and 2007 and concludes that the vast majority of deaths (90 per cent) were due to preventable infectious diseases, malnutrition, and neo-natal and pregnancy-related conditions (Coghlan et al., 2008). The study estimates that although children under five make up only one-fifth of the overall population, they account for nearly half of the deaths—approximately 343,000 excess deaths over the 15-month period from January 2006 to April 2007[14] (Coghlan et al., 2008, pp. 7-8).

While perhaps not representative of all recent conflicts, the results from the DRC emphasize the high vulnerability of children in conflict situations.

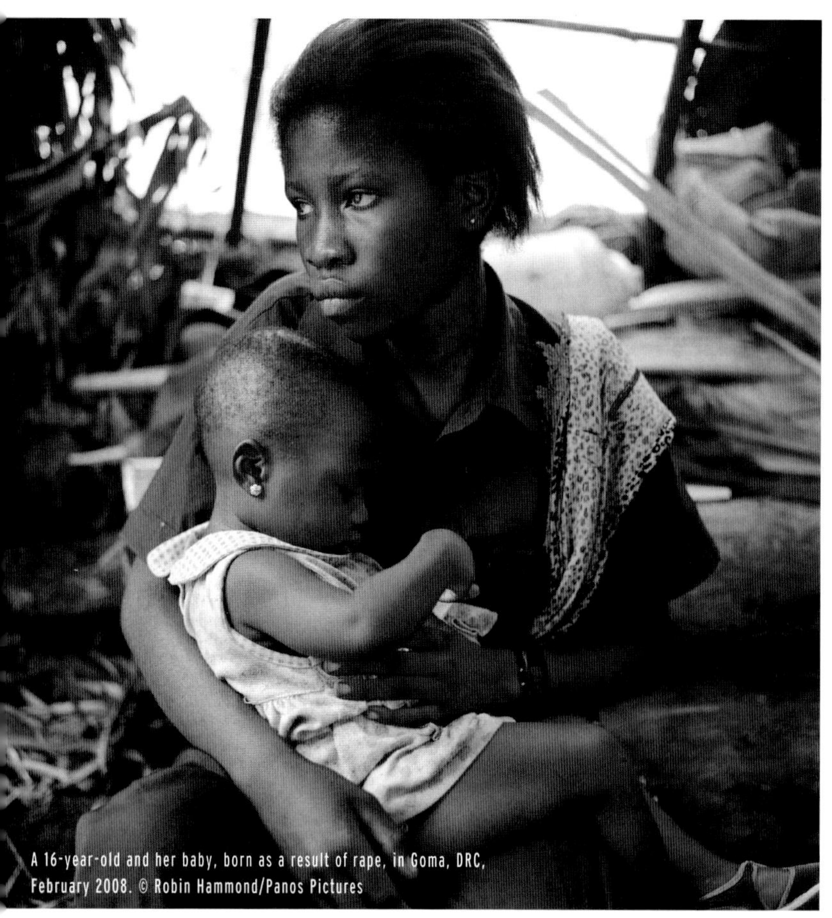
A 16-year-old and her baby, born as a result of rape, in Goma, DRC, February 2008. © Robin Hammond/Panos Pictures

by disruption of food production and supplies, disruption in the delivery of humanitarian aid, disintegration of families and communities, displacement of populations, and destruction of educational and health services as well as water and sanitation systems. Children under five years of age are known to be vulnerable to malnutrition and infection, though their relative risk of dying during conflict compared with older age groups needs further investigation (Guha-Sapir and van Panhuis, 2004).

Conflict limits access to health care. In most wars, health facilities come under direct attack. Those that remain open are often looted, lose their staff, or are forced to close down. The remaining facilities are sometimes difficult to reach because of restrictions on movement (see Box 6.8). As a result of the breakdown of health systems, children die from preventable diseases, including malnutrition, malaria, diarrhoea, acute respiratory infections, measles, and tuberculosis (Oxfam, 2001, p. 29; WCAC, 2006, p. 6). Infants and children are particularly prone to malnutrition because of their proportionally high nutritional requirements (WHO, 2000, p. 4). In Uganda, during the offensive of the Lord's Resistance Army in Kitgum, hospitals and health clinics were targeted, with drugs and medical personnel seized. This seriously impeded access to health care facilities and the ability of health workers to monitor the spread of disease. As a result, children were dying of curable and preventable diseases, in particular malaria, diarrhoea, pneumonia, and acute respiratory tract infection (Oxfam, 2001, p. 29). In Afghanistan, health centres were used for voter registration sites in preparation for the 2009 presidential elections, leading to targeted attacks by Taliban insurgents. Eventually, the Afghanistan government was forced to stop using health centres in the election process (IRIN, 2009).

In areas prone to armed violence, children and their families may bear the burden when governments divert resources from social services, such as education and health care, towards conflict-related expenditures. Health facilities often become under-funded and under-staffed, as health workers decide to relocate to more secure environments. The problem of 'brain drain' in places experiencing conflict, such as Sri Lanka, has greatly reduced the number of qualified health specialists practising in affected countries. Inexperienced volunteers and health workers tend to fill the gap (Boyden et al., 2002, p. 37). In Iraq, the emigration of doctors fleeing violence—including threats, kidnappings, and killing of medical staff—is further weakening the country's strained health infrastructure (Zarocostas, 2007).

Box 6.8 **Roadblocks to health care in the Occupied Palestinian Territory**

Restrictions on movement through the West Bank and from the Gaza Strip to Israel limit the movement of people and the transport of goods and services. Crucially, the separation wall, roadblocks, and numerous checkpoints throughout the West Bank limit access to health care. From 2000 to 2006, 2,029 ambulances were prevented from reaching hospitals, 403 ambulances were attacked, and 140 patients died at Israeli checkpoints, according to the Palestinian Ministry of Health.[15]

Those seeking medical attention in the Gaza Strip have faced different challenges. Because Gaza lacks sophisticated medical care, patients requiring advanced medical procedures have had to apply for a referral to receive more advanced care in Israeli health centres or in the West Bank.[16] Israel decides whether to grant or refuse these permits.

The recent conflict in Gaza (December 2008-January 2009) has severely affected civilians, including children. According to the Gaza health ministry, as of 17 January 2009, 1,193 people had been killed, including 410 children and 108 women (BBC, 2009c). Movement of civilian and aid workers has been severely restricted, with parents unable to bring ill children to the hospital. The World Health Organization has reported difficulties in getting medical supplies to the places where they are needed. As a result, life-saving medical supplies cannot reach those in need, and access to care is compromised (Reuters AlertNet, 2009).

Source: Humanitarian Monitor (2007)

Reproductive health is crucial for the health of pregnant adolescents and women, as well as their children. Girls who give birth before the age of 15 are five times more likely to die in childbirth than women in their twenties (UNICEF , 2009, p. 32). If medical services decline during armed conflict, the situation for young expecting mothers deteriorates. Health education, care, and counselling are especially important for women and girls who have been raped. Access to quality reproductive health has implications not only for the health and survival of the mother but also for her child. A study of 3,000 pregnancies among women besieged in Sarajevo found that the number of live births decreased from 10,000 per year before the war to 2,000 per year during the war. Contraceptive use during the siege decreased to about 5 per cent, while the number of abortions increased until there were more than two abortions for every live birth. The data reveals increases in perinatal mortality (from 15.3 to 38.6 per 1,000 live births), low birth weight (from 5.3 to 12.8 per 1,000), and congenital abnormalities (from 0.37 per cent to 3.00 per cent) (Carballo, Simic, and Zeric, 1996).

THE WAY FORWARD

This section begins with a presentation of key child protection initiatives that build upon existing international standards in seeking to prevent and respond to the problem of armed violence for children and youth. It subsequently examines the research agenda as well as the ongoing need to consolidate best practices. The section highlights, in particular, the utility of policies and programmes that explicitly recognize the mixture of vulnerability and resilience of young people affected by armed violence.

International measures and initiatives

Existing standards in international law relevant to armed violence against children are comprehensive and detailed. Children and youth, as human beings, are entitled to enjoy all the rights guaranteed by the various international human rights treaties that have developed from the Universal Declaration of Human Rights. Children and youth are also entitled to the protection laid down in international legal instruments relating to international criminal, humanitarian, and labour law (Pinheiro, 2006, p. 31).

The key international agreements safeguarding the protection of children and youth are: the Geneva Conventions, the Convention on the Rights of the Child (CRC), and the Optional Protocol to the CRC on the involvement of children in armed conflict (see Box 6.9). A number of other international initiatives also aim to increase the protection of children and youth, especially in armed conflict settings, such as the appointment of a UN Special Representative of the Secretary-General for Children and Armed Conflict, who, in close collaboration with the United Nations Children's Fund (UNICEF), has sought to raise global awareness on the issue of children and armed conflict (UN, 1997). Another important step forward has been the adoption of UN Security Council resolution 1612, which represents the first systematic attempt to collect and disseminate information on grave violations of international norms regarding children and armed conflict, including attacks against hospitals and schools (UNSC, 2005). The 2006 Integrated Disarmament, Demobilization and Reintegration Standards and the 2007 Paris Principles and Guidelines on Children Associated with Armed Forces or Armed Groups represent two normative frameworks for mainstreaming child-sensitive reintegration into post-conflict recovery programmes (UNDDR, 2006; Paris Principles, 2007).

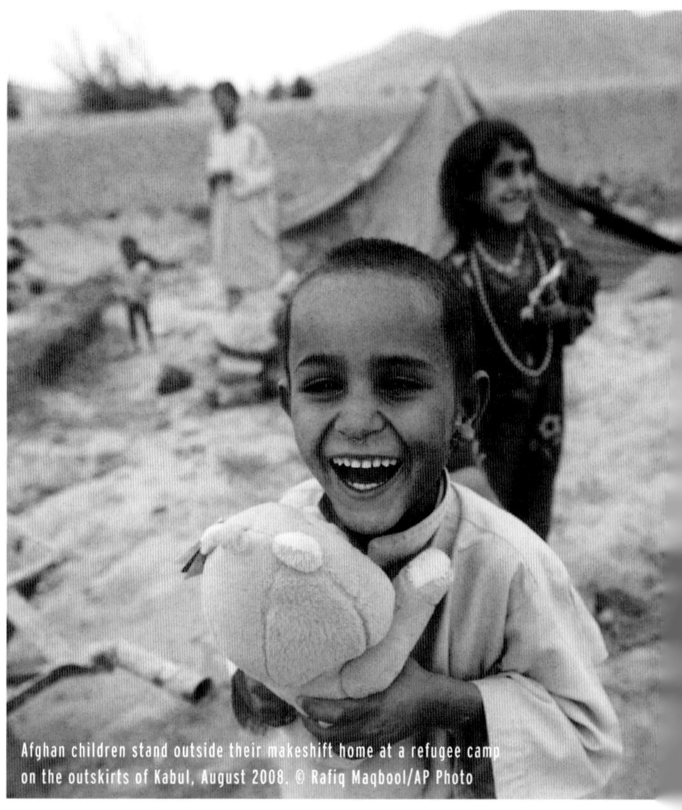
Afghan children stand outside their makeshift home at a refugee camp on the outskirts of Kabul, August 2008. © Rafiq Maqbool/AP Photo

Most governments have ratified the international instruments. However, there remains little oversight and few mechanisms of enforcement. A 2006 report on children and small arms argues that, although most states are bound to the various international instruments that address children and armed violence, they have been slow to incorporate them into national legislation and operational practice (World Vision, 2006, p. 6).

A focus on children and youth is provided by UNICEF, the lead UN agency for child protection. Working with governments and partners at local, national, and regional levels, UNICEF takes a preventive and rights-based approach to the problem of violence against children in all settings. UNICEF has put forward its 'Protective Environment Framework' to ensure that governments fulfil their obligations by addressing the underlying systems that fail to protect children, such as social sector policies and capacities (Landgren, 2005). UNICEF promotes the separation of DDR processes for children from formal DDR procedures and advocates that children who have participated in hostilities should be seen primarily as 'victims'. Programmes should promote the best interest of children, aim to enhance self-esteem, and prevent the use of children in conflict.[17] UNICEF also promotes the participation of children and youth in research and programming in line with the Convention on the Rights of the Child (Landsdown, 2001).

Box 6.9 **Key international agreements**

The growth of children's rights as reflected in international and transnational law has transformed the post-war legal landscape.[18] The most important international agreements to protect children and youth from armed violence are listed below. Nations that ratify these conventions are bound to them by international law.

The 1949 Geneva Conventions and the Additional Protocols I and II (1977) are part of international humanitarian law, a whole system of legal safeguards that cover the way wars may be fought and the protection of individuals. The Geneva Conventions specifically protect people who do not take part in the fighting (civilians, medics, chaplains, aid workers) and those who can no longer fight (wounded, sick and shipwrecked troops, prisoners of war). The Geneva Conventions have been acceded to by 194 states and enjoy universal acceptance.

The 1989 UN Convention of the Rights of the Child (CRC) sets out the civil, political, economic, social, and cultural rights of children (0–18 years). It sets up a framework of legal principles and detailed standards that should govern law, policy, and practice affecting children, including the promotion of prevention of violence and responses to protect all children from all forms of violence. The CRC was adopted by the UN General Assembly in 1989 and came into force in 1990. It is the most widely accepted human rights treaty (UNOHCHR, 1998). As of December 2008, 193 countries had ratified it, including every member of the UN except the United States and Somalia.

The 2000 Optional Protocol to the Convention of the Rights of the Child on the Involvement of Children in Armed Conflict was adopted on 25 May 2000 by the UN General Assembly. This agreement represents a milestone in protecting children from participation in armed conflicts, requiring ratifying governments to ensure that children under 18 years of age are not recruited compulsorily into their armed forces. The protocol came into force in 2002. As of January 2009, 126 nations were party to the Protocol, including the United States, which has not ratified the Convention (UNOHCHR, 2000). Other provisions of the Optional Protocol commit states to supporting processes of rehabilitation and reintegration (UNGA, 2000; UNICEF, 2003). The Optional Protocol:

- requires that states 'take all feasible measures' to ensure that members of their armed forces under the age of 18 years do not participate in hostilities;
- prohibits the conscription of anyone under the age of 18 into the armed forces;
- requires states to raise the age of voluntary recruitment from 15 and to deposit a binding declaration of the minimum age for recruitment into its armed forces;
- and prohibits the recruitment or use in hostilities of children under the age of 18 by rebel or other non-governmental armed groups and requires states to criminalize such practices (UNOHCHR, 2000).

A number of other international[19] and regional[20] instruments reaffirm the provisions on children outlined in the CRC and its Optional Protocol.

Addressing knowledge gaps

While children and youth are sometimes passive victims of violence, very often their relationship to armed violence is more dynamic. Many perpetrate such violence, either voluntarily or under duress. At the same time, children and youths who are exposed to armed violence frequently demonstrate immense bravery and persistence in the face of hardship (Boyden and Mann, 2005; Boyden, 2003; Wiseman, 2006). Many survivors are forced to discover and develop survival strategies that are tested under extreme conditions and many carry heavy responsibilities, such as earning a living and caring for family members.

A recent review of the literature on youth in conflict and post-conflict settings has provided useful insight into the resilience and capabilities of youth and the consequent implications for rehabilitation and reintegration programming (Sommers, 2006). Nevertheless, more research is needed on the concept of resilience and for improving understanding of the factors that help individuals cope in the face of adversity (Dowdney, 2007). Considerable research has been done in the field of domestic child abuse, showing that children exposed to violence at home are more likely to experience or perpetrate violence as adults.[21] However, relatively few studies have examined the influence of culture and trauma in perpetuating violence from one generation to the next (Weingarten, 2007).

Indirect impacts of armed violence on children and youth also warrant further attention. Until recently, most research focused on the immediate and direct impacts of armed violence on children and youth (such as death, injury, and psychosocial trauma), with fewer studies aiming to capture and quantify the broader and indirect impacts of armed violence caused, for example, by the breakdown of social services.

There are several reasons why researching indirect impacts is not an easy task. First, it is inherently difficult to disentangle the indirect effects of armed violence from other factors, such as poverty and natural disasters. Second, violence itself is under-reported (e.g. domestic armed violence remains hidden and under-recognized). And, third, the manifestation of some impacts (especially psychosocial trauma) varies by age, sex, and culture; socially constructed notions of childhood and health may determine how impacts are expressed, experienced, and perceived (Clark-Kazak, forthcoming; Dowdney, 2007).

Despite the methodological challenges involved, it is important that researchers continue to treat children and youth as a distinctive stakeholder group, while simultaneously examining the interactions between individuals, families, communities, and societies. Additional multi-country and longitudinal data is needed to build the evidence base for policy and programming. This information could be complemented by smaller-scale qualitative studies that explore perceptions of armed violence and security and generate local knowledge.

Consolidating lessons learned

A scarcity of impact evaluations has meant that there is a lack of proven techniques that generate lasting, positive results for children and youth (Sommers, 2006). As a result, there is much debate among experts about 'what works'. For example, in the area of child reintegration—where the major challenge is to provide immediate assistance to ex-combatants before they are enticed into another conflict or a livelihood in crime—some potential good practices have been identified from specific settings, although systematic evaluations are lacking (Dowdney, 2007; Luthar and Cicchetti, 2000).

A young gang member holds a gun in the hallway of a housing project in the Brooklyn neighbourhood of Bedford-Stuyvesant, USA, 2006. © Boogie/WPN

In conflict settings, an example of potential good practice comes from Côte d'Ivoire, where UNICEF has used an integrated approach to provide psychosocial, socio-professional, and educational assistance to 3,000 children formerly associated with armed forces or at risk of recruitment. It has been argued that the project was effective because it addressed other protection issues caused or aggravated by the conflict and therefore benefited other children made vulnerable by the crisis. The project dealt with issues such as education, access to health care, and the fight against HIV/AIDS (UNICEF, 2006c). Evidence from Uganda similarly points to the need to include a greater number of vulnerable children and

Box 6.10 Reintegration of child soldiers in Uganda

Research was conducted with children who had been abducted by the Lord's Resistance Army (LRA) in 2003. Focus group discussions were held with 116 children and youths to document their experience of abduction and return to their communities.

The research shows that abduction affected children in a number of ways, leading to pain, disability, and frequent ill health as a result of abuse or wounds. Girls suffered the pain and distress resulting from sexual violence and the fear of being HIV-positive or having other sexually transmitted diseases. The physical symptoms made it difficult for some to work or attend school. The majority of returnees suffered anxiety, visual and auditory hallucinations, and suicidal thinking.

Children reported that their families usually welcomed them home after abduction but that problems were reported with regards to siblings, who initially both feared and rejected them. They said they felt stigmatized and rejected by their communities and were bullied at school. The most rejected sub-group of returnees was girls who had suffered sexual violence. Infants born as a result of that violence were also vulnerable to rejection and stigmatization. Children's age, sex, and stage of physical and psychological development affected community perceptions of their responsibility for actions committed by the LRA.

At the same time, children displayed many signs of resilience, demonstrating persistence and courage in the face of rejection. Coping strategies included seeking strength and comfort in religion, social interaction with others, and recreational activities. Developing skills for self-control and distancing themselves from their siblings were reported to be effective in fostering better relationships over the longer term. While the children showed resilience, they also showed vulnerabilities, highlighting the absence of an opportunity to talk with others or to receive advice and guidance that could foster their coping skills.

Source: Coalition to Stop the Use of Child Soldiers (2008b)

scale up education programmes (see Box 6.10). Complementing these findings, the survey of war-affected youth in Uganda finds that the targeting of former abductees has been less successful in reducing vulnerability and improving long-term reintegration, mainly because abduction status is a crude and unreliable predictor of need (Annan, Blattman, and Horton, 2006). In addition to broad-based programmes aimed at all vulnerable children, it is still strongly argued that special programmes are needed that target ex-combatants, children, women, and the disabled because these groups have specific needs and face particular challenges (Hazen, 2007; Willibald, 2006).

In non-conflict settings, gang violence is an area where consolidation of best practices is needed. Key knowledge gaps include: the acquisition of weapons (demand), the misuse of the same (armed violence), and the joining or leaving of gangs. Gang violence research has traditionally focused on 'youth delinquency' and the linkages between violence, crime, and drug abuse. More recently, however, studies have begun to touch on a number of related issues, such as children's rights, child labour, urban renewal, and justice. For example, a study from Sao Paulo in Brazil revealed systemic causes of armed violence, such as a lack of investment in law enforcement and social services (Cardia, 2000). Other studies have examined the significance of inequality, social exclusion, and 'social identities' or the specific roles and motivations of children and adolescents in gangs (Strocka, 2006; Dowdney, 2003). The structure and impact of organized armed violence vary from place to place and over time. In Nicaragua, a longitudinal ethnographic study highlighted the dynamic nature of youth violence, which, from 1996 to 2002, 'evolved from a form of collective social violence to a more individually and economically motivated type of brutality' (Rodgers, 2006). Further research is needed to shed light on factors of resilience and vulnerability, which—as for the reintegration of former child soldiers—may inform community-based interventions that build upon and boost resilience (Dowdney, 2007).

CONCLUSION

Children and youth are specifically and disproportionately affected by many consequences of armed violence, whether physiological, psychological, or social. Although male adolescents and young men generally form the majority of the direct victims of armed violence (through death, injury, and psychosocial trauma), younger children may also suffer through targeted attacks on civilians or recruitment into armed groups.

In addition to death, injury, and psychosocial trauma, children and youth are vulnerable to indirect impacts of armed violence when a family member dies or is injured, when the family has to move, or when basic social services break down. For example, a disruption of education systems disproportionately affects school-aged children, while a lack of access to health care has implications for children's physical development. Armed violence can contribute to the rise of poverty, malnutrition, and disease, which have serious long-term consequences for the lives of children and youth.

Impacts vary by age, sex, culture, and the specific circumstance of the individual. It is therefore important that researchers consider socially constructed notions of childhood and health, including mental health, because these will determine how impacts are expressed, experienced, and perceived.

Despite their vulnerabilities, children and youth demonstrate enormous resilience and an ability to cope. More research is needed to improve the general understanding of resilience, as well as the individual and contextual factors involved, and to identify interventions that promote and strengthen coping strategies. Effective interventions would also reduce the risk of future perpetration of violence, thereby limiting the potential for its intergenerational transmission.

While there have been many programmes aimed at reducing the impacts of armed violence on children and youth, lessons learned have not been systematically documented and built upon. Robust multi-country and longitudinal data needs to be complemented with qualitative studies that, together, form the basis for policy that explicitly recognizes the needs, rights, and resilience of children and youth. ■

ABBREVIATIONS

CRC	Convention on the Rights of the Child	LRA	Lord's Resistance Army
DRC	Democratic Republic of the Congo	PTSD	Post-traumatic stress disorder
DDR	Disarmament, demobilization, and reintegration	UNICEF	UN Children's Fund
IDP	Internally displaced person	WHO	World Health Organization

ENDNOTES

1 See, for example, Coalition to Stop the Use of Child Soldiers (2001; 2004; 2008a); Luz (2007); Small Arms Survey and Viva Rio (forthcoming); Pinheiro (2006); Geneva Declaration Secretariat (2008).

2 An explanation of the definition of 'youth' can be found at UN (n.d.). Several studies have generated statistics that identify adolescents and youth as important groups; see Giacaman (2007); Luz (2007); and WCRWC (2000; 2004).

3 The *Global Burden of Armed Violence* report finds that between 2004 and 2007 at least 208,300 violent deaths were recorded in armed conflicts, an average of 52,000 people killed per year (Geneva Declaration Secretariat, p. 2). This estimate was calculated by pooling a variety of incident-based data-sets (p. 46). It is considered a conservative estimate because it includes only recorded deaths; the real total may be much higher

(p. 2). This conflict deaths estimate thus represents the lower end of the range while the World Health Organization (WHO) estimate lies at the upper end.

4 The upper estimate of the number of direct conflict deaths of persons aged 0–29 years (86,000) is provided by the WHO directly; see WHO (n.d.). The lower estimate (24,000) was calculated here by applying the WHO age ratio to the total estimate (52,000) provided in the *Global Burden of Armed Violence* report (Geneva Declaration Secretariat, p. 2). This approach assumes that, despite the different methods of data collection and analysis, there is no systematic bias in the reporting of age–sex disaggregated data.

5 See WHO (n.d.) for age-disaggregated estimates for 2004. Note that WHO estimates by age group are not in line with the UN definition of 'youth' (15–24 years of age).

6 This section is based on Murray (2009).

7 Sagi-Schwartz (2008); Jackson (2006); Laor et al. (2006); Zahr (1996); Baker (1990).

8 Research conducted by the Small Arms Survey for UNICEF, Nepal, May 2008. The findings are not representative of Nepal as a whole or of the Terai region. See also Small Arms Survey and Viva Rio (forthcoming).

9 See also Small Arms Survey and Viva Rio (forthcoming).

10 This estimate is based on the work of more than 40 Viva Rio researchers who visited some 32,000 people living in nearly 10,000 homes in Bel Air in 2008.

11 See also Small Arms Survey and Viva Rio (forthcoming).

12 This research was conducted in 340 public and private schools of 14 municipalities in Brazil between 2000 and 2002, covering a sample of 55,000 persons—parents, students, and teachers.

13 'Insecure environments' are defined by criteria such as presence of conflicts at school, presence of armed students, robbery, drug dealing, and sexual violence.

14 The study estimates the total death toll from the conflict (between January 2006 and April 2007) at 727,000, of which 47.2 per cent were under-fives (Coghlan et al., 2008, pp. 7–8). Children under five thus account for 343,000 deaths.

15 Data provided by the Palestinian Ministry of Health, 7 February 2008.

16 It is uncertain to what extent children have been affected by ambulatory and medical referral restrictions.

17 For more details on UNICEF's role, see UNDDR (n.d.).

18 See Zeldin (2007) for a full account.

19 See, for example, the Geneva Declaration on Armed Violence and Development (Geneva Declaration, 2006); the Rome Statute of the International Criminal Court (ICC, 1998); the United Nations Programme of Action to Prevent, Combat and Eradicate the Illicit Trade in Small Arms and Light Weapons in All Its Aspects (UN, 2001); and the International Labour Organization's Convention Concerning the Prohibition and Immediate Action for the Elimination of the Worst Forms of Child Labour (ILO, 1999).

20 See, for example, the European Union Guidelines on Children and Armed Conflict (EU, 2003) and the African Charter on the Rights and Welfare of the Child (OAU, 1999).

21 Neugebauer (2000); Ertem, Leventhal, and Dobbs (2000); Bouvier (2003); Ehrensaft (2003).

BIBLIOGRAPHY

Aaron, Rita et al. 2004. 'Suicides in Young People in Rural Southern India.' *The Lancet*, Vol. 363, Iss. 9415, pp. 1117–18.

Abramovay, Miriam and Maria das Graças Rua. 2002. *Violências nas escolas*. Brasília: UNESCO. <http://unesdoc.unesco.org/images/0012/001257/125791porb.pdf>

Ackerman, Peggy T. et al. 1998. 'Prevalence of Post Traumatic Stress Disorder and Other Psychiatric Diagnoses in Three Groups of Abused Children (Sexual, Physical, and Both).' *Child Abuse & Neglect*, Vol. 22, Iss. 8, pp. 759–74.

AI (Amnesty International). 2005a. 'Uganda: Child Night Commuters.' London: AI. <http://www.amnesty.org/en/library/info/AFR59/013/2005>

—. 2005b. 'Nepal: Children Caught in the Conflict.' 26 July. <http://www.amnesty.org/en/library/asset/ASA31/054/2005/en/dom-ASA310542005en.html>

Annan, Jeannie, Christopher Blattman, and Roger Horton. 2006. *The State of Youth and Youth Protection in Northern Uganda: Findings from the Survey for War-Affected Youth*. A Report for UNICEF Uganda. September.

APA (American Psychiatric Association). 1995. *Diagnostic and Statistical Manual of Mental Disorders: International Version*. Washington, DC: APA.

Baker, Ahmad M. 1990. 'The Psychological Impact of the Intifada on Palestinian Children in the Occupied West Bank and Gaza: An Exploratory Study.' *American Journal of Orthopsychiatry*, Vol. 60, Iss. 4, pp. 496–505.

BBC (British Broadcasting Service). 2009a. 'Congo Warlord Denies War Crime.' 26 January. <http://news.bbc.co.uk/2/hi/africa/7850397.stm>

—. 2009b. 'Fresh Attacks on Pakistan Schools.' 19 January. <http://news.bbc.co.uk/2/hi/south_asia/7836875.stm>

—. 2009c. 'Thousands Protest in UK over Gaza.' 17 January. <http://news.bbc.co.uk/2/hi/south_asia/7836875.stm>

Botton, Shelley de. 2008. *Haiti: Armed Conflict Displaces Thousands of Children*. 4 March. Rio de Janeiro: Comunidad segura portal, Viva Rio. <http://www.comunidadesegura.org/?q=en/node/38451>

Bouvier, Paul. 2003. 'Child Sexual Abuse: Vicious Circles of Fate or Paths to Resilience?' *The Lancet*, Vol. 361, Iss. 9356. 8 February, pp. 446–47.

Boyden, Jo. 2003. 'Children under Fire: Challenging Assumptions about Children's Resilience.' *Children, Youth and Environments*, Vol. 13, No. 1. <http://www.colorado.edu/journals/cye/13_1/Vol13_1Articles/CYE_CurrentIssue_Article_ChildrenUnderFire_Boyden.htm>

— and Gillian Mann. 2005. 'Children's Risk, Resilience, and Coping in Extreme Situations.' In Michael Ungar, ed. *Handbook for Working with Children and Youth: Pathways to Resilience Across Cultures and Contexts*. Thousand Oaks: Sage Publications, pp. 3–25. <http://www.sagepub.com/Ungar%20I%20Proof%20Chapter%201_5336.pdf>

— et al. 2002. *Children Affected by Armed Conflict in South Asia: A Review of Trends and Issues Identified through Secondary Research*. Refugee Studies Centre Working Paper No. 7. Oxford: International Development Centre, University of Oxford.

Carballo, M., S. Simic, and D. Zeric. 1996. 'Health in Countries Torn by Conflict: Lessons from Sarajevo.' *The Lancet*, Vol. 348, Iss. 9031, pp. 872–74.

Cardia, Nancy. 2000. *Urban Violence in São Paulo*. Washington, DC: Woodrow Wilson International Center for Scholars.

Checchi, Francesco and Les Roberts. 2005. 'Interpreting and Using Mortality Data in Humanitarian Emergencies: A Primer for Non-epidemiologists.' *HPN Network Paper*, Iss. 52. London: Overseas Development Institute.

Clark-Kazak, Christina. Forthcoming. 'Towards a Working Definition and Application of Social Age in International Development Studies'. *Journal of Development Studies*.

Coalition to Stop the Use of Child Soldiers. 2001. *Global Report*. London: Coalition to Stop the Use of Child Soldiers.

—. 2004. *Global Report*. London: Coalition to Stop the Use of Child Soldiers.

—. 2008a. *Global Report*. London: Coalition to Stop the Use of Child Soldiers.

—. 2008b. *Returning Home—Children's Perspectives on Reintegration: A Case Study of Children Abducted by the Lord's Resistance Army in Teso, Eastern Uganda*. London: Coalition to Stop the Use of Child Soldiers.

—. 2009. 'Questions and Answers.' <http://www.child-soldiers.org/childsoldiers/questions-and-answers>

Coghlan, Benjamin et al. 2008. 'Mortality in the Democratic Republic of Congo: An Ongoing Crisis.' New York: International Rescue Committee. <http://www.theirc.org/resources/2007/2006-7_congomortalitysurvey.pdf>

da Costa, Rosa. 2006. *The Administration of Justice in Refugee Camps: A Study of Practice*. Legal and Protection Policy Research Series. Geneva: Department of International Protection, United Nations High Commissioner for Refugees.

DCI/PS (Defence for Children International Palestine Section). 2006. 'Sustained Occupation, Suspended Dreams.' Jerusalem: DCI/PS. <http://www.dci-pal.org/english/publ/research/2006/sustained.pdf>

Denov, Myriam and Richard Maclure. 2005. 'Girls and Small Arms in Sierra Leone: Victimization, Participation and Resistance.' Paper presented for the International Studies Association Conference, Honolulu, Hawaii. March. <http://www.allacademic.com//meta/p_mla_apa_research_citation/0/7/0/0/2/pages70020/p70020-1.php>

Dinicola, Vincenzo F. 1996. 'Ethnocultural Aspects of PTSD and Related Disorders among Children and Adolescents.' In Anthony Marsella et al. *Ethnocultural Aspects of Posttraumatic Stress Disorder: Issues, Research, and Clinical Applications*. Washington, DC: American Psychological Association, pp. 389–414.

Dominguez, Renee, Connie Nelke, and Bruce Perry. 2002. 'Child Sexual Abuse.' In David Levinson, ed. *Encyclopedia of Crime and Punishment*, Vol. 1. Thousand Oaks: Sage Publications, pp. 202–07.

Dowdney, Luke. 2003. *Children of the Drug Trade: A Case Study of Children in Organized Armed Violence in Rio de Janeiro*. Rio de Janeiro: 7letras.

—. 2005. *Neither War Nor Peace: International Comparisons of Children and Youth in Organised Armed Violence*. Rio de Janeiro: Children in Organised Armed Violence.

—. 2007. *Trauma, Resilience and Cultural Healing: How Do We Move Forward?* London: Coalition to Stop the Use of Child Soldiers. <http://www.child-soldiers.org/psycho-social/Trauma_Resilience_and_Cultural_Healing_2007.pdf>

Dyregrov, Kari et al. 2000. 'Refugee families' experience of research participation.' *Journal of Traumatic Stress*, Vol. 13, Iss. 3, pp. 413–26.

Ehntholt, Kimberly A. and William Yule. 2006. 'Practitioner Review: Assessment and Treatment of Refugee Children and Adolescents Who Have Experienced War-related Trauma.' *Journal of Child Psychology and Psychiatry*, Vol. 47, Iss. 12, pp. 1197–1210.

Ehrensaft, Miriam K. 2003. 'Intergenerational Transmission of Partner Violence: A 20-Year Prospective Study.' *Journal of Consulting and Clinical Psychology*, Vol. 71, No. 4, pp. 741–753. <http://www.apa.org/journals/releases/ccp714741.pdf>

Ertem, Ilgi Ozturk, John M. Leventhal, and Sara Dobbs. 2000. 'Intergenerational Continuity of Child Physical Abuse: How Good Is the Evidence?' *The Lancet*, Vol. 356, Iss. 9232. 2 September, pp. 814–19.

EU (European Union). 2003. European Union Guidelines on Children and Armed Conflict. <http://www.consilium.europa.eu/uedocs/cmsUpload/GuidelinesChildren.pdf>

FECODE (Federación Colombiana de Educadores). 2007. 'La lucha integral por los derechos humanos y Fecode.' <http://fecode.edu.co/descargas/dh/informe%20_comision_dh.pdf>

Geneva Declaration. 2006. Geneva Declaration on Armed Violence and Development. <http://genevadeclaration.org/geneva-declaration.html>

Geneva Declaration Secretariat. 2008. *Global Burden of Armed Violence*. Geneva: Geneva Declaration Secretariat. <http://www.genevadeclaration.org/pdfs/Global-Burden-of-Armed-Violence.pdf>

Giacaman, Rita et al. 2007. 'Individual and Collective Exposure to Political Violence: Palestinian Adolescents Coping with Conflict.' *European Journal of Public Health*, Vol. 17, No. 4, pp. 361–68.

Guha-Sapir, Debarati and Olivier Degomme. 2006. 'Counting the Deaths in Darfur: Estimating Mortality from Multiple Survey Data.' HiCN Working Paper 15. Brighton: Institute of Development Studies, University of Sussex. <http://www.hicn.org/papers/wp15.pdf>

Guha-Sapir, Debarati and Willem Gijsbert van Panhuis. 2004. 'Conflict-related Mortality: An Analysis of 37 Datasets.' *Disasters*, Vol. 28, Iss. 4, pp. 418–28.

Hauff, Edvard. 2007. 'Loss, Reconnection and Reconstruction: A Former Child Soldier's Return to Cambodia.' In Boris Drozdek and John P. Wilson, eds. *Voices of Trauma: Treating Survivors Across Cultures*. Washington, DC: Springer, pp. 175–89.

Hazen, Jennifer. 2007. 'Social Integration of Ex-Combatants after Civil War.' <http://www.un.org/esa/socdev/sib/egm/paper/Jennifer%20Hazen.pdf>

Hemenway, David and Matthew Miller. 2002. 'Association of Rates of Household Handgun Ownership, Lifetime Major Depression, and Serious Suicidal Thoughts with Rates of Suicide across US Census Regions.' *Injury Prevention*, Vol. 8, pp. 313–16.

Heptinstall, Ellen, Vaheshta Sethna, and Eric Taylor. 2004. 'PTSD and Depression in Refugee Children: Associations with Pre-migration Trauma and Post-migration Stress.' *European Child and Adolescent Psychiatry*, Vol. 13, No. 6, pp. 373–80.

Humanitarian Monitor. 2007. 'Occupied Palestinian Territory.' No. 20. December, pp. 1–25. <http://www.ochaopt.org/documents/Humanitarian_Monitor_Dec_07.pdf>

ICC (International Criminal Court). 1998. Rome Statute of the International Criminal Court. <http://untreaty.un.org/cod/icc/statute/romefra.htm>

ILO (International Labour Organization). 1999. Convention Concerning the Prohibition and Immediate Action for the Elimination of the Worst Forms of Child Labour. <http://www.ilo.org/public/english/standards/relm/ilc/ilc87/com-chic.htm>

International Save the Children Alliance. 2007. 'Last in Line, Last in School: How Donors are Failing Children in Conflict-affected Fragile States.' <http://www.savethechildren.org/publications/rewrite-the-future/RTF_Last_in_Line_Last_in_School_report_FINAL.pdf>

IRIN. 2008. 'Afghanistan: Some Schools More Vulnerable to Attack Than Others?' 2 January. <http://www.irinnews.org/PrintReport.aspx?ReportId=76067#>

—. 2009. 'Afghanistan: Government Abandons Voter Registration at Health Centres.' 14 January. <http://www.irinnews.org/report.aspx?ReportID=82352>

Jackson, Diana. 2006. 'Playgroups as Protective Environments for Refugee People at Risk of Trauma.' *Australian Journal of Early Childhood*, Vol. 31, No. 5, pp. 1–5.

Kim, Wun Jung and Tanvir Singh. 2004. 'Trends and Dynamics of Youth Suicides in Developing Countries.' *The Lancet*, Vol. 363, Iss. 9415, p. 1090–91.

Landgren, Karen. 2005. 'The Protective Environment: Development Support for Child Protection.' *Human Rights Quarterly*, Vol. 27, No. 1, pp. 214–48.

Landsdown, Gerison. 2001. *Promoting Children's Participation in Democratic Decision-making*. Florence: UNICEF Innocenti Research Centre.

Laor, Nathaniel et al. 2006. 'Risk and Protective Factors Mediating Psychological Symptoms and Ideological Commitment of Adolescents Facing Continuous Terrorism.' *Journal of Nervous and Mental Disease*, Vol. 194, Iss. 4, pp. 279–86.

Legget, Ted. 2005. *Terugskiet (Returning Fire): Growing up on the Street Corners of Manenberg, South Africa*. Rio de Janeiro: Children in Organised Armed Violence. <http://www.coav.org.br/publique/media/Report%20%C3%81frica%20do%20Sul.pdf>

Luthar, Suniya and Dante Cicchetti. 2000. 'The Construct of Resilience: Implications for Interventions and Social Policies.' *Development and Psychopathology*, Vol. 12, Iss. 4, pp. 857–85.

Luz, Daniel. 2007. 'The Impact of Small Arms on Children and Adolescents in Central America and the Caribbean: A Case Study of El Salvador, Guatemala, Jamaica and Trinidad and Tobago.' Panama City: UNICEF.

McKay, Susan and Dyan Mazurana. 2004. 'Where Are the Girls? Girls in Fighting Forces in Northern Uganda, Sierra Leone and Mozambique: Their Lives during and after War.' *Rights & Democracy*. March. <http://www.dd-rd.ca/site/publications/index.php?subsection=catalogue&lang=en&id=1401>

Mason, John B. 2002. 'Lessons on Nutrition of Displaced People.' *Journal of Nutrition*, Vol. 132, Iss. 7, pp. 2096S–2103S.

Merkelbach, Maarten. 2000. 'Reuniting Children Separated from Their Families after the Rwandan Crisis of 1994: The Relative Value of a Centralized Database.' *International Review of the Red Cross*, No. 838, pp. 351–67. <http://www.icrc.org/Web/Eng/siteeng0.nsf/html/57JQHH>

Mirza, Sadaf. 2006. 'Childhood Bypassed: Rwanda's Youth-Headed Households.' *SAIS Review*, Vol. 26, No. 2. Summer–Fall, pp. 179–80.

Moss, William J. et al. 2006. 'Child Health in Complex Emergencies.' *Bulletin of the World Health Organization*, Vol. 84, No. 1, pp. 58–64. <http://www.who.int/entity/bulletin/volumes/84/1/58.pdf>

Muggah, Robert, ed. 2006. *No Refuge: The Crisis of Refugee Militarization in Africa*. London: Zed Books.

Murray, Ryan. 2009. 'Psychosocial Trauma from Armed Violence in Youths and Adolescents.' Unpublished background paper. Geneva: Small Arms Survey.

Nader, Kathleen. 2007. 'Culture and the Assessment of Trauma in Youths.' In John P. Wilson and Catherine So-kum Tang, eds. *Cross-Cultural Assessment of Psychological Trauma and PTSD*. Washington, DC: Springer, pp. 169–96.

Neugebauer, Richard. 2000. 'Research on Intergenerational Transmission of Violence: The Next Generation.' *The Lancet*, Vol. 355, Iss. 9210. 1 April, pp. 1116–17.

O'Hare, Bernadette and David Southall. 2007. 'First Do No Harm: The Impact of Recent Armed Conflict on Maternal and Child Health in Sub-Saharan Africa.' *Journal of the Royal Society of Medicine*, Vol. 100, No. 12, pp. 564–70.

O'Malley, Brendan. 2007. *Education under Attack: A Global Study on Targeted Political and Military Violence against Education Staff, Students, Teachers, Union and Government Officials, and Institutions*. Paris: UNESCO. <http://www.unesco.org/education/attack/>

OAU (Organization of African Unity). 1999. African Charter on the Rights and Welfare of the Child. <http://www.africa-union.org/Official_documents/Treaties_%20Conventions_%20Protocols/A.%20C.%20ON%20THE%20RIGHT%20AND%20WELF%20OF%20CHILD.pdf>

Oxfam. 2001. 'Conflict's Children: The Human Cost of Small Arms in Kitgum and Kotido, Uganda.' Oxford: Oxfam. <http://www.oxfam.org.uk/resources/policy/conflict_disasters/downloads/conflict_uganda.pdf>

Paolucci, Elisabeth O. et al. 2001. 'A Meta-analysis of the Published Research on the Effects of Child Sexual Abuse.' *Journal of Psychology*, Vol. 135, Iss. 1, pp. 17–36.

Paris Principles. 2007. 'The Principles and Guidelines on Children Associated with Armed Forces or Armed Groups.' <http://www.un.org/children/conflict/_documents/parisprinciples/ParisPrinciples_EN.pdf>

Picket, William et al. 2005. 'Cross-national Study of Fighting and Weapon Carrying as Determinants of Adolescent Injury.' *Pediatrics*, Vol. 116, No. 6, pp. e855–63.

Pinheiro, Paulo Sérgio. 2006. 'World Report on Violence against Children.' Geneva: United Nations Secretary-General's Study on Violence against Children. <http://www.violencestudy.org/r242>

Polusny, Melissa and Victoria Follette. 1995. 'Long-term Correlates of Child Sexual Abuse: Theory and Review of the Empirical Literature.' *Applied & Preventive Psychology*, Vol. 4, pp.143–66.

Punamäki, Rajaa-Leena. 1988. 'Historical-political and Individualistic Determinants of Coping Modes and Fears among Palestinian Children.' *International Journal of Psychology*, Vol. 23, pp. 721–39.

Qouta, Samir, Rajaa-Leena Punamäki, and Eyad El Sarraj. 2008. 'Child Development and Family Mental Health in War and Military Violence: The Palestinian Experience.' *International Journal of Behavioral Development*, Vol. 32, No. 4, pp. 310–21.

Reuters AlertNet. 2009. 'Newborns and Babies in Gaza Face Increasing Health Threats.' 11 January. <http://www.alertnet.org/thenews/fromthefield/SaveChAlli/635d765dcb1da8850c426dc9e9db7584.htm>

Rodgers, Dennis. 2006. 'Living in the Shadow of Death: Gangs, Violence and Social Order in Urban Nicaragua, 1996–2002.' *Journal of Latin American Studies*, Vol. 38, Iss. 2, pp. 267–92.

Sagi-Schwartz, Abraham. 2008. 'The Well Being of Children Living in Chronic War Zones: The Palestinian–Israeli Case.' *International Journal of Behavioral Development*, Vol. 32, No. 4, pp. 322–36.

Salignon, Pierre et al. 2000. 'Health and War in Congo-Brazzaville.' *The Lancet*, Vol. 356, No. 9243, p. 1762.

Sayfan, Liat et al. 2008. 'Children's Expressed Emotions When Disclosing Maltreatment.' *Child Abuse & Neglect*, Vol. 32, Iss. 11, pp. 1026–36.

Servan-Schreiber, David et al. 1998. 'Prevalence of Posttraumatic Stress Disorder and Major Depressive Disorder in Tibetan Refugee Children.' *American Academy of Child and Adolescent Psychiatry*, Vol. 37, Iss. 8, pp. 874–79.

Small Arms Survey and Viva Rio. Forthcoming. *The Impacts of Small Arms and Light Weapons on Children*. New York: UNICEF.

Sommers, Marc. 2006. *Youth and Conflict: A Brief Review of Available Literature*. Washington, DC: Equip 3/Youth Trust. May.

Stohl, Rachel. 2002. 'Under the Gun: Children and Small Arms.' *Africa Security Review*, Vol. 11, No. 3. <http://www.iss.co.za/ASR/11No3/Stohl.html>

—. 2009. *Child Soldiers*. Unpublished background paper. Geneva: Small Arms Survey.

— et al. 2001.'Putting Children First: Background Report.' London: Biting the Bullet Project, December.

Strocka, Cordula. 2006. 'Youth Gangs in Latin America.' *SAIS Review*, Vol. 26, No. 2, pp. 133–46.

Thomas de Benítez, Sarah. 2007. *State of the World's Street Children: Violence*. London: Consortium for Street Children. <http://www.streetchildren.org.uk/reports/State of the World's Street Children-Violence.pdf>

Tolin, David F. and Edna Foa. 2006. 'Sex Differences in Trauma and Posttraumatic Stress Disorder: A Quantitative Review of 25 Years of Research.' *Psychological Bulletin*, Vol. 132, Iss. 6, pp. 959–92.

UN (United Nations). 1989. *Convention on the Rights of the Child*. A/RES/44/25 of 20 November 1989. <http://www.un-documents.net/a44r25.htm>

—. 1996. *Impact of Armed Conflict on Children*. A/51/306 of 26 August. <http://www.un.org/documents/ga/docs/51/plenary/a51-306.htm>

—. 1997. *Resolution Adopted by the General Assembly: Rights of the Child*. A/RES/51/77 of 20 February. <http://www.un.org/documents/ga/res/51/ares51-77.htm>

—. 2001. Programme of Action to Prevent, Combat and Eradicate the Illicit Trade in Small Arms and Light Weapons in All Its Aspects. A/CONF.192/15. <http://disarmament.un.org/cab/poa.html>

—. 2007. *Report of the Special Representative of the Secretary-General for Children and Armed Conflict*. A/62/228 of 13 August. <http://daccess-ods.un.org/TMP/5614680.html>

—. n.d. 'Youth and the United Nations: Frequently Asked Questions.' <http://www.un.org/esa/socdev/unyin/qanda.htm>

UNCAAC (United Nations Office of the Special Representative of the Secretary-General for Children and Armed Conflict). 2008a. 'Office of the Special Representative of the Secretary-General for Children and Armed Conflict.' <http://www.un.org/children/conflict/english/theoffice.html>

— and UNICEF (United Nations Children's Fund). 2007. *Report of the Special Representative of the Secretary-General for Children and Armed Conflict*. Part Two (Strategic Review). A/62/228 of 13 August. <http://www.un.org/children/conflict/english/machelreports.html>

UNDDR (United Nations Disarmament, Demobilization and Reintegration Resource Centre). 2006. 'Integrated Disarmament, Demobilization and Reintegration Standards.' <http://www.unddr.org/iddrs/download/full_iddrs.pdf>

—. n.d. 'UN Partners.' <http://www.unddr.org/partners.php?id=3>

UNDP (United Nations Development Programme). 2008. *Post-Conflict Economic Recovery: Enabling Local Ingenuity*. Crisis Prevention and Recovery Report. New York: UNDP.

UNGA (United Nations General Assembly). 1948. Universal Declaration of Human Rights. UNGA resolution 217 A (III) of 10 December. <http://www.un.org/Overview/rights.html>

—. 2000. Optional Protocol to the Convention on the Rights of the Child on the Involvement of Children in Armed Conflicts. A/RES/54/263 of 25 May. <http://www.un-documents.net/a54r263.htm>

UNHCR (United Nations High Commissioner for Refugees). 2006. *The State of the World's Refugees 2006: Human Displacement in the New Millennium*. Geneva: UNHCR.

UNICEF (United Nations Children's Fund). 2003. *Guide to the Optional Protocol on the Involvement of Children in Armed Conflict.* <http://www.unicef.org/publications/files/option_protocol_conflict.pdf>

—. 2005a. 'The Impact of Conflict on Women and Girls in West and Central Africa and the UNICEF Response.' New York: UNICEF. <http://www.unicef.org/publications/index_25262.html>

—. 2006a. 'UN Secretary General's Study on Violence against Children: Violence against Children in the Caribbean Regional Assessment.' Panama City: UNICEF Regional Office for Latin America and the Caribbean. <http://www.uwi.edu/ccdc/downloads/Violence_against_children.pdf>

—. 2006b. 'Children without Parental Care.' Child Protection Information Sheet. <http://www.unicef.org/protection/files/Parental_Care.pdf>

—. 2006c. 'Côte d'Ivoire: Prevention, Demobilization and Reintegration—Children Associated with Armed Groups.' <http://www.unicef.org/evaluation/files/cote_divoire_2006(3).doc>

—. 2009. *State of the World's Children: Maternal and Child Health*. New York: UNICEF

UNOHCHR (United Nations Office of the High Commissioner for Human Rights). 1989. Convention on the Rights of the Child: Status of Ratification. General Assembly resolution 44/25 of 20 November. <http://www.unhchr.ch/html/menu3/b/k2crc.htm>

—. 2000. Optional Protocol to the Convention on the Rights of the Child on the Involvement of Children in Armed Conflict: Status of Ratifications. General Assembly resolution A/RES/54/263 of 25 May. <http://www.unhchr.ch/html/menu2/6/protocolchild.htm>

UNSC (United Nations Security Council). 2005. Security Council resolution 1612. S/RES/1612 of 26 July. <http://daccess-ods.un.org/access.nsf/Get?Open&DS=S/RES/1612%20(2005)&Lang=E&Area=UNDOC>

Wakabi, Wairagala. 2008. 'Sexual Violence Increasing in Democratic Republic of Congo.' *The Lancet,* Vol. 371, Iss. 9605. January, pp. 15–16.

WCAC (Watchlist on Children and Armed Conflict). 2005. 'Caught in the Middle: Mounting Violations against Children in Nepal's Armed Conflict.' New York: WCAC. <http://www.watchlist.org/reports/pdf/nepal.report.20050120.pdf>

—. 2006. 'Struggling to Survive: Children in Armed Conflict in the Democratic Republic of the Congo.' New York: WCAC. <http://www.watchlist.org/reports/files/dr_congo.report.20060426.php>

WCRWC (Women's Commission for Refugee Women and Children). 2000. 'Untapped Potential: Adolescents Affected by Armed Conflict.' New York: WCRWC. <http://www.unicef.org/emerg/files/adolescents_armed_conflict.pdf>

—. 2004. 'Global Survey on Education in Emergencies.' New York: WCRWC. <http://www.womenscommission.org/pdf/Ed_Emerg.pdf>

Weingarten, Kaethe. 2007. 'Witnessing the Effects of Political Violence in Families: Mechanisms of Intergenerational Transmission and Clinical Intervention.' *Journal of Marital and Family Therapy,* Vol. 30, Iss. 1, pp. 45–59.

WHO (World Health Organization). 1992. 'The ICD-10 Classification of Mental and Behavioural Disorders.' Geneva: WHO.

—. 2000. 'The Management of Nutrition in Major Emergencies.' Geneva: WHO.

—. 2002. *First World Report on Violence and Health*. Geneva: WHO.

—. 2008. *Global Burden of Disease: 2004 Update*. Geneva: WHO. <http://www.who.int/healthinfo/global_burden_disease/GBD_report_2004update_full.pdf>

—. n.d. 'Deaths by Cause in WHO Regions: Estimates for 2004.' <http://www.who.int/entity/healthinfo/global_burden_disease/DTH6%202004.xls>

Wiebe, D.J. 2003. 'Homicide and Suicide Risks Associated with Firearms in the Home: A National Case-Control Study.' *Annals of Emergency Medicine,* Vol. 41, No. 6, pp. 771–82. <http://download.journals.elsevierhealth.com/pdfs/journals/0196-0644/PIIS0196064403002567.pdf>

Willibald, Sigrid. 2006. 'Does Money Work? Cash Transfers to Ex-combatants in Disarmament, Demobilisation and Reintegration Processes.' *Disasters,* Vol. 30, No. 3, pp. 316–39.

Wiseman, Marianne. 2006. *A Review of Literature on Safety Education: Implications for Education on Small Arms*. Belgrade: South Eastern and Eastern Europe Clearinghouse for the Control of Small Arms and Light Weapons. <http://www.seesac.org/reports/safety%20educ1.pdf>

World Vision. 2006. 'Small Arms and Children: Progress since 2001 and Recommendations for Further Action.' Ontario: World Vision.

Zahr, Lina Kurdahi. 1996. 'Effects of War on the Behavior of Lebanese Preschool Children: The Influence of Home Environment and Family Functioning.' *American Journal of Orthopsychiatry,* Vol. 66, Iss. 3, pp. 401–08.

Zarocostas, John. 2007. 'Exodus of Medical Staff Strains Iraq's Health Facilities.' *BMJ,* Vol. 334, p. 865.

Zeldin, Wendy. 2007. *Children's Rights: International Laws*. Law Library of Congress. LL File No. 2007-04112. <http://www.loc.gov/law/help/child-rights/international-law.php>

ACKNOWLEDGEMENTS

Principal authors

Jonah Leff and Helen Moestue

Contributors

Ryan Murray and Rachel Stohl

A UN peacekeeper stands near the Mugunga camp for internally displaced persons in Goma, Democratic Republic of the Congo, November 2008. © Les Neuhaus

Securing the Peace

POST-CONFLICT SECURITY PROMOTION

7

INTRODUCTION

Acute armed violence can persist long after formal war comes to an end, with some so-called 'post-conflict' environments presenting as many, or more, direct and indirect threats to civilians than the armed conflicts that preceded them.[1] Anticipating the many expressions of armed violence during the post-conflict period is key to achieving human security and, eventually, national stability.

Yet few programmes that seek to promote post-war security are designed to deal with the many facets of such violence. Ceasefires, peace agreements, and even popular elections—important as they may be—do not necessarily deliver tangible improvements in the safety of individuals and communities.

Some of the reasons why armed violence continues to simmer or mutates in the aftermath of war are well known. Many armed conflicts end without a strong commitment to a ceasefire or peace agreement, resulting in a precarious transitional period. Moreover, efforts to impose victors' justice can unintentionally worsen the situation (Kreutz, Marsh, and Torre, 2007; Licklider, 1995). Some armed groups—and particularly senior officers and commanders from the 'losing side'—may be dissatisfied with the new political dispensation and therefore fuel future instability (Weinstein, 2007; Darby, 2001; Stedman, 1997). Scholars and practitioners have observed how predatory networks and patronage structures associated with the war economy may remain intact and even emerge strengthened after protracted warfare.[2]

The intensity and distribution of post-conflict armed violence—and the victimization it inflicts—tend to change over time. Societies emerging from war can experience a surge in predatory and organized criminal violence due to risk factors and vulnerability associated with the war and post-conflict period. A fluid constellation of state agents and armed groups use various forms of coercion in pursuit of competing (and often overlapping) motivations and interests. The causes of armed violence—whether political, economic, or communal—may shift in complex ways. Likewise, armed violence once concentrated in specific locales, such as the rural hinterland or international frontiers, may diffuse into urban slums or seep into wealthier neighbourhoods (Rodgers, 2004; 2007).

Quelling post-war armed violence is a major preoccupation for multilateral and bilateral agencies promoting peace- and state-building. Given the way violence can undermine day-to-day security and social order, it is an even more urgent priority for affected states and civil societies. This chapter considers some of the challenges inherent in defining a society as 'post-conflict'. It first examines how, far from heralding a return to normalcy, such contexts are frequently as unsafe as war-affected environments. The chapter then highlights an array of newer security promotion measures that, when combined with conventional interventions such as disarmament, demobilization, and reintegration (DDR) programmes, can reduce the risks of armed violence and promote personal safety and long-term stabilization of war-ravaged communities. Its findings include the following:

- Certain post-conflict societies and population groups suffer rates of direct armed violence comparable to (or even higher than) the armed conflicts that preceded them.
- Excess (non-violent) mortality can also remain high in post-conflict societies—often much higher than violent death rates—long after the shooting stops.
- The risk of armed conflict recurring in post-war societies appears to be greater than the risk of war erupting in societies that have not experienced armed conflict.
- Proximate and structural risks in post-conflict environments—from alcohol, narcotics, and arms availability to high rates of unemployment among men and concentrations of displaced populations—can influence the onset, intensity, and duration of armed violence.
- Conventional security promotion activities such as DDR have a mixed record and, on their own, may not be suited to deal with many of the dynamic forms of post-conflict armed violence.
- Interim stabilization measures, tightly connected to the overarching peace- and state-building framework, serve as 'holding strategies' in the immediate post-conflict period.
- Second-generation security promotion interventions—routinely undertaken in combination with or following DDR and security sector reform (SSR)—are evidence-led and community-focused.

Interim stabilization and second-generation promotion can complement and reinforce conventional security promotion.

The chapter documents an abundance of strategies that are designed to prevent and reduce armed violence around the world. While many of these unfold in post-conflict (as well as ostensibly non-conflict) contexts, solid evidence of what works and what does not is still lacking. Beyond expectations of security, order, and reductions in armed violence, clear benchmarks of 'success' are seldom established. There are comparatively few credible impact or cost–benefit evaluations of such activities.[3] Nevertheless, a modest but convincing evidence base suggests that 'interim stabilization' and 'second-generation security promotion' interventions offer promising means of diminishing the risks and effects of post-conflict violence (Colletta, Berts, and Samuelsson Schjörlien et al., 2008; WOLA, 2008; Muggah, 2008b). Taken together with more conventional approaches such as DDR and arms control, these measures comprise a broader, more sophisticated set of tools for enhancing security in the aftermath of war.

Interim stabilization initiatives are undertaken during the sensitive period coinciding with or immediately following the end of armed conflict. Designed to create space before more formal and large-scale security promotion activities take place, they can include activities such as the promotion of civilian service corps, military integration arrangements, transitional security forces, dialogue and sensitization programmes, and differentiated forms of transitional autonomy. *Second-generation* measures are usually deployed later, overlapping with or following DDR and SSR. They include community security and safer-city interventions, weapons for development programmes, and more targeted evidence-based activities focusing on at-risk youth and hot spots. Key factors distinguishing such initiatives from conventional security promotion include their data-driven approach, a municipal or community focus, and emphasis on risk and symptom mitigation.

Conventional security promotion frequently lacks clear standards of effectiveness.[4] Since it aims to establish political stability, this type of intervention is often unable to contend with the criminal and quasi-political violence that frequently overtakes politically oriented violence in the post-conflict period (Muggah and Krause, 2009). Interim stabilization and second-generation security promotion—by focusing on key risks, enhancing resilience in affected communities, and concentrating on reducing indicators of armed violence—can complement and reinforce conventional security promotion. While no panacea, these measures may be especially useful if targeted at specific groups at risk for, or vulnerable to, armed violence, and at potential 'spoilers' of war-to-peace transitions.

DISAGGREGATING POST-CONFLICT ARMED VIOLENCE

A widespread assumption held by diplomats and donors is that when wars come to an end, safety and security will improve and normality will resume. A period of relative stability—or peace consolidation—is expected to follow the conclusion of a peace agreement and the deployment of peacekeepers.[5]

But these expectations are routinely confounded by experience on the ground. While direct violent deaths can and often do rapidly decline when wars end, particularly in the wake of UN-supported peace-support operations, it is important to recognize that new forms of armed violence also routinely emerge (Fortna, 2008). As discussed below, violent killings may start to rise once more, particularly among youthful segments of the population. What is more, the incidence of excess mortality can remain comparatively high until access to basic services is re-established and armed violence diminished.[6]

Map 7.1 **Violence and instability by district in the DRC, 2006-08**

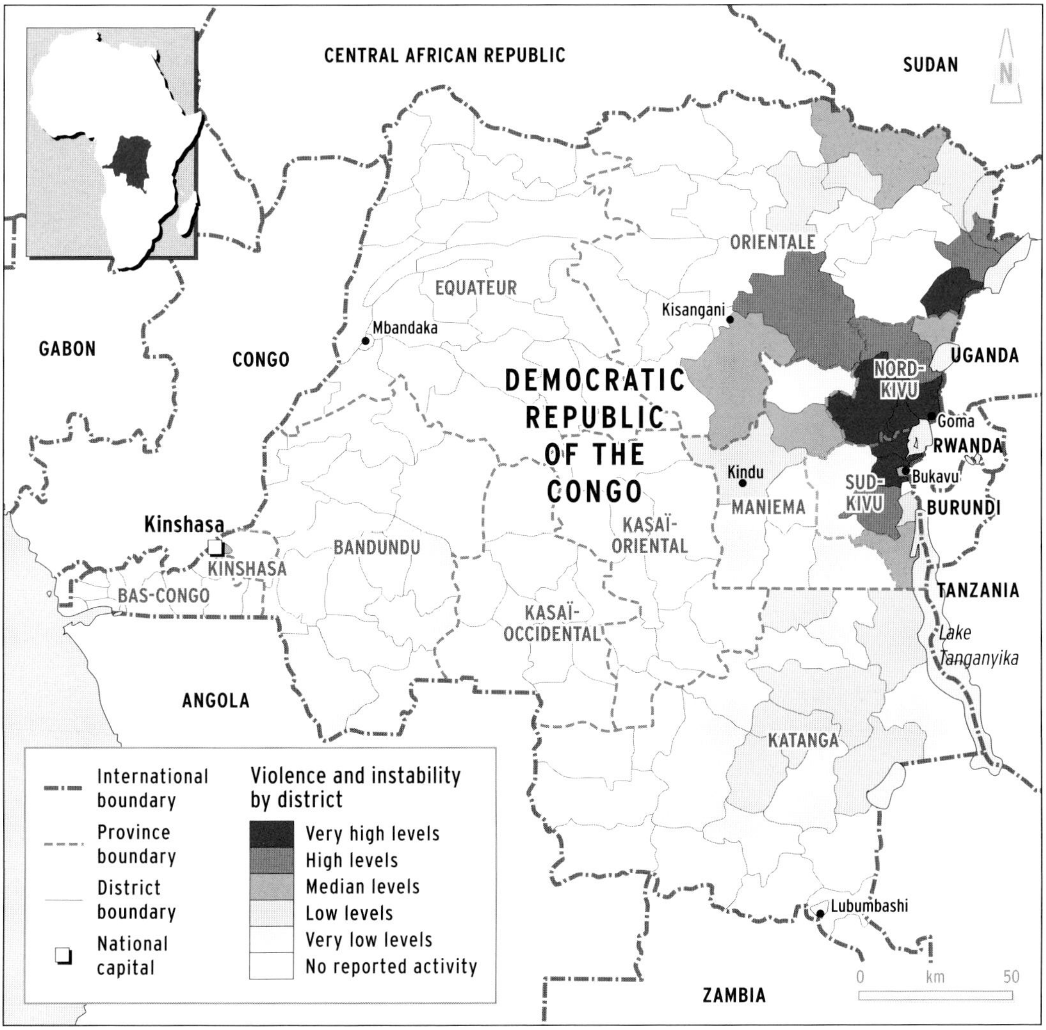

Source: ACLED (2008)

Armed violence may assume qualitatively different characteristics during the post-war period than during the preceding armed conflict. For one, post-conflict armed violence transforms and can become entrenched in new geographic areas and among specific demographic and socio-economic population clusters. In some cases, as in Afghanistan, Iraq, and Sri Lanka, post-conflict armed violence can escalate and exceed wartime rates (Small Arms Survey, 2005). These escalations may be at odds with regional tendencies. At the same time, post-conflict armed violence can substantially increase the exposure of civilians, especially women and children, the elderly, and the displaced, to excessive rates of non-violent mortality and morbidity (see Box 7.1).[7] In the wake of the 1990–91 Gulf War, for example, one expert observed how 'far more persons died from post-conflict health effects than from direct war effects' (Daponte, 1993). Where wars are especially severe and protracted, abnormally high levels of mortality and morbidity can persist after the formal end of armed conflict.

Targeted efforts to prevent and reduce armed violence in the post-conflict period may not only reduce intentional killings, but also diminish excess mortality and morbidity. Even so, it should be noted that focused interventions to minimize instability such as peacekeeping and DDR—while important—achieve only so much (see Box 7.2). Other factors shaping excess post-conflict non-violent mortality and morbidity are not tied only to rising crime or communal violence, but also to real and relative investments in human and public infrastructure, including health care. Following a war, the professional health workforce may be seriously

Box 7.1 Excess mortality in 'post-war' Congo

In countries such as Angola, the Democratic Republic of the Congo (DRC), Liberia, Sierra Leone, and Sudan, post-conflict excess mortality rates declined but remained elevated for an unspecified period.[8] These high rates are a major challenge for humanitarian and recovery operations. Indeed, far more resources are devoted to reconstructing basic health infrastructure than to negotiating ceasefires or disarming and demobilizing former soldiers.

The relative vulnerability of a population combined with the inability of public authorities to rehabilitate and resume basic service delivery can contribute to an increase in mortality. The DRC was affected by systemic conflict for more than a decade, with devastating implications for societal vulnerability and ultimately health. The acute period of armed conflict (1998–2002) contributed to a dramatic escalation in violent death, together with displacement and excess mortality.

After the signing of a formal peace accord in 2002 and a sharp reduction in armed violence, persistent tensions in several eastern provinces continued to exact a monumental human toll. A robust UN peacekeeping effort supported by the United Nations Mission in the DRC (MONUC) has shored up the security situation since 2004. Following sustained onslaughts by rebel leader Laurent Nkunda's forces in North Kivu, the situation remained precarious, particularly in eastern areas of the country (see Map 7.1). Nkunda's arrest in Rwanda in early 2009 could contribute to important changes in the region.

On the basis of five surveys conducted between 2000 and 2007, the International Rescue Committee (IRC) estimates that more than 5.4 million excess deaths occurred after 1998. An estimated 2.1 million of these occurred since the formal 'end' of war in 2002. More than six years after the signing of the formal peace agreement, the country's national crude mortality rate (CMR) is roughly 2.0 deaths per 1,000 per month—more than 50 per cent higher than the sub-Saharan African average (IRC, 2008, p. ii). As Table 7.1 shows, these rates are even higher in eastern areas of the country. Crucially, fewer than one per cent of these deaths were attributed to armed violence. The vast majority died as a result of easily preventable diseases such as malaria, diarrhoea, pneumonia, and malnutrition (IRC, 2008, p.iii).

A Rwandan ex-rebel looks away during a UN film presentation in Kimuwa, DRC, May 2008. © Lionel Healing/AFP

Table 7.1 Approximate crude mortality rates (CMR) in east and west DRC: 1999–2007*

Year	Percentage CMR due to violence**	CMR in east DRC (per 1,000)	CMR in west DRC (per 1,000)
1999	11.1	5.4	n/a
2000	n/a	5.4	n/a
2001	9.4	5.4	n/a
2002	n/a	3.5	2.0
2003	1.6	2.9	1.8
2004	n/a	2.9	1.8
2006	n/a	2.6	2.0
2007	0.6	2.6	2.0

* Surveys were not undertaken in 2005.

** Figures refer to 'proportion of violent deaths in conflict east' and therefore are not representative of the whole country. See IRC (2007, p. 13).

Source: IRC (2008, pp. 9–13)

depleted, often taking generations to recover.[9] Rapid reductions in excess post-conflict mortality also depend on the length and intensity of an armed conflict, the extent of dispersion of populations, and the level of aid provided during various stages of the war and post-war period. Because surveillance and monitoring systems may also collapse, there are serious challenges to defining and tracking the global burden of post-conflict armed violence.[10]

Another impediment to better diagnosing and therefore responding to the dynamics of post-conflict armed violence is semantic. There are routine disagreements over basic definitions of 'conflict' and 'war' on the one hand,[11] and 'post-conflict' and 'post-war' on the other. For the purposes of this chapter, 'armed conflict' and 'war' are treated as synonymous. And while a debate persists among conflict specialists over the characteristics of different types of 'war', it is useful to recall that 'conflict' is a socially embedded and arguably necessary feature of all societies. In other words, notwithstanding the popularity of the term in policy-making and practitioner circles, there is in fact no such thing as a 'post-conflict' society if one understands that term to include non-violent forms of conflict.

There are also a series of practical challenges in determining whether and when a country is classified as 'post-conflict'. This is

The shadow of a peacekeeper is projected onto a metal gate riddled with bullet holes in South Ossetia, Georgia, August 2004. © Dmitry Chebotayev/WPN

Box 7.2 Does peacekeeping work?

International peacekeeping was only seldom used to maintain peace and quell violence in civil wars during the cold war. The number, scope, and size of peacekeeping missions have exploded since 1989. Yet early optimism about their potential diminished soon after initial failures in Bosnia and Herzegovina, Rwanda, and Somalia in 1993–94. Nevertheless, the breadth and reach of 21st-century peace-support operations is unprecedented: nearly twice as many blue helmets are deployed in post-conflict theatres today as at the peak of UN missions in the 1990s.

Debates over whether peacekeeping increases the chances of durable peace have been hampered by the absence of reliable data and systematic comparisons. On the one hand, the most well-known missions tend to be those that failed spectacularly, while quieter success stories are less likely to make the news. On the other hand, most studies of peacekeeping examine only cases where peacekeepers were deployed, and therefore cannot assess what difference peacekeeping makes. In the absence of research on whether peace is more likely to endure when peacekeepers are present than when they are absent, opponents of peacekeeping have argued that it is irrelevant and even counterproductive while supporters have not been able to back up their more positive accounts with solid evidence.

Drawing on new data, researcher Virginia Fortna finds that peacekeeping greatly improves the chances that peace will last, reducing the risk of another civil war by 50–80 per cent (Fortna, 2008). She argues that the positive effect of peacekeeping is probabilistic rather than deterministic. In other words, peacekeepers will not ensure lasting peace in every case, but they significantly improve the chances that peace will endure relative to cases where belligerents are left to their own devices after civil war. Drawing on quantitative analysis of a dataset encompassing all ceasefires in civil wars form 1989 to 2000 and in-depth case studies, she controls for variables to handle the fact that peacekeepers are not deployed at random.[12] Peacekeeping is an effective tool: it can help change the incentives of warring parties, provide credible information about negotiating parties' intentions, manage ceasefire violations, and prevent opposing sides from hijacking the political process.

Peacekeeping missions are not all alike and can be divided into smaller 'observation missions', 'inter-positional missions', 'multidimensional missions', and more militarily robust 'peace-enforcement missions'. Intriguingly, Fortna finds relatively little difference in the effectiveness of non-coercive and coercive missions, because most of the ways peacekeeping makes a difference are political and economic rather than military in nature.

Source: Fortna (2009)

not altogether surprising. Just as there is frequently disagreement among international humanitarian lawyers about when countries are considered to be 'at war', decision-makers, mediators, and relief workers actively grapple with the question of when a war has ended (see Box 7.3). This is not a simple semantic challenge. In fact, the label or categorization shapes concrete decisions relating to the design of peace agreements, humanitarian intervention, withdrawal of peacekeeping forces and relief personnel, and budgeting and funding cycles.

Multilateral and bilateral aid agencies often struggle to distinguish between their conflict and post-conflict portfolios. The World Bank, for example, seldom provides lending or grant support to countries 'at war'. Between the early 1980s and late 1990s, however, the agency increased lending to post-conflict countries by more than 800 per cent with reconstruction operations reaching across multiple sectors (World Bank, 1998b). In 1998, the World Bank identified a range of possible indicators for determining whether a country could be considered 'post-conflict'.[13] The World Bank noted at the time that it should 'examine this issue and explore the development of indicators to determine when the "post-conflict" period ends and "normalcy" begins' (World Bank, 1998b, p. 44). Surprisingly, the agency's *Fragile and Conflict-affected Countries Group* recently abandoned defining 'post-war' scenarios after many years of trying. Operational protocol 8.5 featured indicators, but the latest version quietly dropped them.[14]

Just as it is difficult to determine when a 'post-conflict' situation begins, it is equally hard to know when it can be said to have ended.[15] When can a society be considered to be experiencing a durable or sustainable 'peace'? There

Box 7.3 Does a peace agreement signal a war's end?

Since 1990, more than half of all civil wars have ended in a peace agreement. This translates into more than 600 separate peace agreements (often occurring in the same country) in more than 80 separate contexts. The rising number of peace settlements in the past two decades has been attributed to heightened international attention to armed conflict in the post-cold war period, the emergence of a common approach to conflict resolution that treats governments and warring parties as (near) equals, and the importance attached to ceasefires followed by politico-legal agreements for maintaining stability.

There is widespread acceptance of the importance of peace agreements in resolving war. But is this causal assumption borne out by the evidence? Indeed, what exactly is a peace agreement? The concept is in fact more poorly understood than commonly believed. At the beginning of the 1990s, a peace agreement laying out provisions for a ceasefire along with other internal constitutional changes represented the end point of a mediation process. Increasingly, peace agreements are viewed as the starting point of an ongoing complex phase of recovery and reconstruction in which mediators may remain involved. Christine Bell distinguishes between pre-negotiation agreements (e.g. 'talks about talks'), framework and substantive agreements (e.g. 'aimed at linking ceasefires to blueprints for constitutional settlements'), and implementation agreements (e.g. which seek to 'deepen key aspects of peace frameworks') (Bell, 2006; 2008).

The normative structure of peace agreements appears to be an important determinant in shaping post-conflict violence. For example, precise and coherent commitments, it is argued, can facilitate what Bell refers to as 'compliance pull' or the willingness of parties to commit to the terms of a given settlement (Bell, 2006). Precision is especially important with respect to laying down the terms of a ceasefire and separating and demobilizing troops. Although constructive ambiguity may be politically expedient, it can also enable agreement on certain texts, by offering baseline principles. The content of such peace agreements–the extent to which they feature rights protections, constitutional provisions, or third-party delegation–can also play a key role in shaping their effectiveness in relation to armed violence reduction.

Source: Bell (2009)

is in fact no consensus as to whether a post-conflict situation ends after a comprehensive ceasefire is put in place, within a certain number of months or years after a peace agreement is signed, following the withdrawal of a peace support operation, or even in the wake of a sharp reduction in the incidence of collective armed violence. A number of multilateral and bilateral agencies introduced temporal thresholds—five to ten years after a war is officially declared 'over'—but diplomats and aid officials frequently acknowledge that these markers are arbitrary.[16]

Post-conflict environments are more easily described than defined. As noted above, the challenges of defining which countries are post-conflict are often as intractable as those of determining what is (or is not) 'war' (HSRP, 2005; Small Arms Survey, 2005; Stedman, Rothchild, and Cousens, 2002). It may well be easier to define the broad parameters of a 'post-conflict' situation than to determine precisely when it begins or ends. For the purposes of this chapter, a post-conflict situation can be described as:

> *a period following an armed conflict, characterized by a clear victory of one party, a declared cessation of war (i.e. ceasefire and/or peace agreement), and/or a dramatic de-escalation in armed violence in comparison to the 'wartime' period.*

The above description coincides with recent efforts by the United Nations Development Programme to establish 'peace milestones' or benchmarks of transition (UNDP, 2008).[17]

Reflecting concurrence among key armed conflict datasets and a variety of other reports, Table 7.2 lists a selection of areas where wars officially ended as of 1990. The generation of such a list reveals practical difficulties inherent in designating when a war ends. For many countries, comparatively high rates of political violence, criminal violence, and counter-insurgency persist or increase after the war has officially been declared 'over'. Such cases—including Afghanistan and Iraq—are not included in the table.

Table 7.2 **Selected post-conflict countries: 1990-2008**

	Post-conflict start date	Outcome
Angola	2002	Peace agreement
Bosnia and Herzegovina	1995	Peace agreement
Burundi	2003	Peace agreement
Cambodia	1991	Peace agreement
Cameroon	1996	Reduced conflict
Central African Republic	2007	Reduced conflict
Comoros	1999	Ceasefire
Congo, Democratic Republic	1999, 2002	Ceasefire
Congo, Republic of the	2000	Peace agreement
Côte d'Ivoire	2003	Peace agreement
Croatia	1995	Peace agreement
Ecuador	1991	Peace agreement
El Salvador	1992	Peace agreement
Federal Republic of Yugoslavia[a]	1999	Ceasefire
Guatemala	1996	Peace agreement
Haiti[b]	1994, 2004	Reduced conflict
Indonesia (Aceh)	2005	Peace agreement
Indonesia (Timor-Leste)	1999	Peace agreement
Kosovo[c]	1999	Ceasefire
Lesotho	1998	Victory
Liberia	2003	Peace agreement
Macedonia, former Yugoslav Republic of	2001	Peace agreement
Mexico	1996	Reduced conflict
Mozambique	1992	Peace agreement
Nepal	2006	Peace agreement
Papua New Guinea (Bougainville)	2001	Peace agreement
Peru	1992	Reduced conflict
Rwanda	2002	Peace agreement[e]
Senegal (Casamance)	2004	Peace agreement
Sierra Leone	1999	Peace agreement
Slovenia	1991	Peace agreement

Solomon Islands	2003	Intervention
South Africa	1994	Peace agreement
Sudan (South)	2005	Peace agreement
Togo	2006	Victory
Tajikistan	1997	Peace agreement
United Kingdom (Northern Ireland)	1998	Peace agreement

Notes: An explanation of the methodology employed for this table is available at http://www.smallarmssurvey.org/files/sas/publications/yearb2009.html

[a] In 2003 the name Federal Republic of Yugoslavia was dropped by Serbia and Montenegro. In 2006 Montenegro declared independence and subsequently Serbia declared itself the lawful successor to Serbia and Montenegro.

[b] While it was subjected to repeated coups and more than seven peacekeeping missions since 1991, Haiti was never theoretically 'at war'. As such, it offers a challenge to conventional definitions of 'conflict', which require two or more organized fighting forces.

[c] Kosovo unilaterally declared independence from Serbia in February of 2008.

Sources: Data compiled by CERAC and the Small Arms Survey using UCDP (2008); Geneva Declaration Secretariat (2008); UNDP (2008); IISS (various dates); academic and media reports

Disagreements over semantics can generate contradictions that inhibit a clear understanding of post-conflict environments. For example, owing in part to the terminological disagreement signalled above, there are routine disputes among political scientists, forensics specialists, and epidemiologists over how to 'count' violent deaths, human rights violations, and criminal violence during and after wars (Small Arms Survey, 2005, pp. 229–57). Likewise, certain governments may feel they have legitimate reasons to shield the true magnitude of armed violence from public scrutiny.[18] As a result, comparatively limited analysis has been carried out on post-conflict armed violence, and only a few comprehensive datasets explain patterns and trends both during and after war.[19]

Although quantitative data on post-conflict armed violence is limited and of mixed quality, certain broad qualitative generalizations can be rendered about different post-war contexts. For example, Chaudhary and Suhrke (2008) contend that post-conflict societies can be distinguished according to the specific character and form of armed violence they experience. One group of countries that emerged from war, such as El Salvador, Guatemala, and Nicaragua, continue to exhibit stable or rising rates of homicidal violence—sometimes equivalent to peak periods of armed conflict (see Table 7.3).[20] These effects are especially pronounced among youthful segments of the population, in particular young males. Other countries, such as Mozambique, Peru, Sierra Leone, and the Solomon Islands, appear to have more successfully transitioned into periods marked by greater personal security for the civilian population.

Members of the United Self-Defence Forces of Colombia (AUC) are demobilized at a ceremony in Tibu, Colombia, December 2004. © Luis Acosta/AFP

Table 7.3 **National and youth homicide rates in selected Latin American countries (homicide rates per 100,000 population)**

	1995	1996	1997	1998	1999	2000	2001	2002	2003	2004	2005
El Salvador youth	74.7	73.7	59.5	71.8	64.1	58.3	60.2	52.1	57.1	74.4	92.3
El Salvador national	45.5	44.7	38.0	44.2	38.3	35.8	35.1	30.8	32.3	39.6	48.8
Guatemala youth	28.0	29.7	44.0	41.0	27.8	31.8	34.9	45.5	55.1	55.4	n/a
Guatemala national	19.6	21.1	28.6	26.2	18.1	19.4	20.3	24.2	28.5	28.5	n/a
Nicaragua youth	n/a	10.6	9.0	9.5	9.3	12.4	12.0	11.3	16.1	15.5	16.6
Nicaragua national	n/a	6.3	6.2	5.5	6.5	6.8	7.3	6.8	9.4	10.0	10.4
Colombia national	64.4	67.0	60.1	64.2	66.0	72.2	74.3	77.3	61.3	52.6	43.8
Mexico national	16.8	15.4	14.1	14.0	12.4	10.7	10.0	9.7	9.6	8.8	9.3

Source: Waiselfisz (2008)

It is possible to identify a range of different, potentially overlapping post-conflict scenarios (see Table 7.4). These include societies affected by *political violence, routine state-led violence, economic and crime-related violence, community and informal justice, and post-war property-related disputes*.[21] These are not necessarily mutually exclusive; they can be overlapping as the case of Aceh readily shows (ACEH). It is important to recall that post-conflict environments do not emerge in a vacuum—they imperfectly reflect the armed conflicts that precede them. They may continue to feature government-supported militia, quasi-insurgent groups, and organized crime. On the other hand, these groups may rely on new forms of capital and encourage the progressive militarization of society, including in the service of economic and political elites.

Table 7.4 **Types of post-conflict armed violence**

Type of violence	Indicators	Examples
Political violence	Extra-judicial killings, explosives attacks, kidnappings, routine torture, population displacement, organized riots	Cambodia, Guatemala, South Sudan
Routine state-led violence	Excessively violent law enforcement activities, encounter killings, social cleansing operations, routine torture	Angola, Mozambique
Economic and crime-related violence	Armed robbery, extortions, kidnappings for ransom, control of markets through violence	Afghanistan, El Salvador, Guatemala, Liberia
Community and informal justice	Lynchings, vigilante action, mob justice	Liberia, Mozambique, Northern Ireland
Post-conflict property-related disputes	Clashes over land, revenge killings, small-scale 'ethnic cleansing'	Afghanistan, Guatemala, Kosovo, Liberia

Source: Chaudhary and Suhrke (2008)

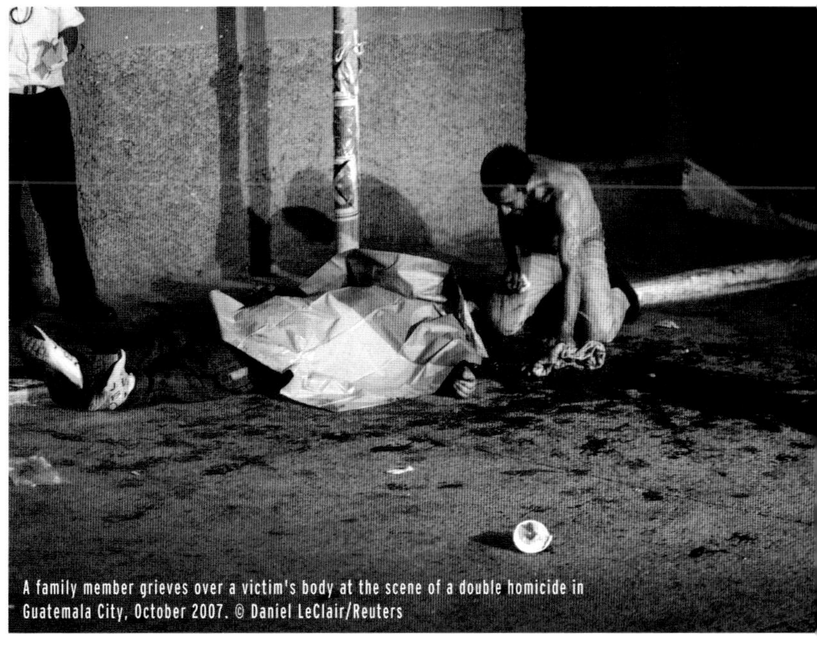
A family member grieves over a victim's body at the scene of a double homicide in Guatemala City, October 2007. © Daniel LeClair/Reuters

What are the factors that keep the incidence of post-war armed violence unexpectedly high, and why does its form change over time? One reason is that the domestic balance of power is usually fundamentally realigned after an armed conflict. Whether as a result of concessions made during peace negotiations, the disarmament and demobilization of commanders and rank and file, or efforts to install or institutionalize democratic reforms, different winners and losers emerge during the post-conflict period. Political elites operating in the public and private spheres may rely on political violence to shore up their negotiating positions and advance their personal agendas. The shape and direction of such armed violence will be informed by, among other factors, the dynamics of a given peace settlement or internationally supported recovery strategy.

Escalating *political violence* is common in the aftermath of war. If one party 'wins' the war and controls a strong security apparatus, violent purges and retributive acts to eliminate remnants of the enemy may ensue, as was the case in Rwanda following the 1994 genocide.[22] Alternatively, if a war ends with an inclusive or widely accepted settlement overseen by peacekeeping forces, there may be fewer instances of flagrant violations. In the latter case, erstwhile and newly posted political authorities, military personnel, and private elites may resort to violent intimidation against possible foes. Such actions may be reported erroneously as common or petty crime. Even more problematic, in some post-conflict settings experiencing fragmentation and division, political violence can appear to take on more anarchic characteristics. Following the US-led armed invasion of Afghanistan in 2001, for example, the factionalization of the security sector contributed to an escalation in warlord-inspired violence and the emergence of under-governed spaces (AFGHANISTAN).[23]

Many post-conflict environments are characterized by routine *state-led armed violence* perpetrated by the security apparatus. In certain countries, such as Angola, Guatemala, or Mozambique, the military, police, and paramilitary forces may be more inclined to pursue violent strategies than to deliver public security (Chaudhary and Suhrke, 2008). These actions may be implicitly sanctioned, even if not explicitly authorized, by politicians and public authorities who may not be susceptible to the same intensity of (pre-war) oversight and scrutiny. Such violence often features extra-judicial killing of suspected criminals rather than arrest or prosecution. It also includes the systematic use of torture. Security agencies may also condone social cleansing operations in slums and shantytowns as part of law and order—or *mano dura* (heavy hand)—operations (Jütersonke, Muggah, and Rodgers, 2009).

Another common feature of post-conflict societies is *economically motivated armed violence*. Countries such as Liberia, South Africa, and others in Central America experienced violent crime waves in the aftermath of war

(Chaudhary and Suhrke, 2008). Policy-makers and social science researchers have focused on the way illegal war economies, including their complex (and frequently transnational) networks of patronage, contribute to persistent armed violence after war in states such as Afghanistan, Bosnia and Herzegovina, Haiti, and elsewhere.[24] Armed groups that were not effectively disarmed and demobilized may morph into private security entities and organized criminal networks, as in the case of the Balkans and Timor-Leste.[25] Such violence becomes increasingly normalized and entrenched due to the continued presence of armed ex-combatants lacking credible opportunities for employment and income generation. Government and state security forces may also seek to continue to profit from illegal rents. Indeed, organized crime of a certain scale cannot continue without some degree of official complicity (Muggah and Krause, 2009).

An under-reported but nevertheless important category of post-conflict armed violence relates to *community and informal justice*. The sudden imposition of 'modern' forms of law enforcement can be heavily contested in post-conflict societies. Moreover, owing to the failure of transitional governments to provide adequate security, informal, if often locally legitimate, forms of community justice delivery, vigilantism, and militia 'policing' can come to the fore. The lines between these various 'justice' mechanisms are fluid and shifting. For example, vigilante groups are often formally structured and draw on popular support (Höglund and Zartman, 2006). Related armed violence may derive legitimacy from the real and perceived protection offered civilians, often with complicity from public authorities. In Liberia, for instance, the Ministry of Justice (controversially) called for the formation of vigilante groups to counter increasing violent crime in the capital, Monrovia (Chaudhary and Suhrke, 2008). Lynching and mob justice also appear to enforce certain forms of order and moral codes.[26] Neighbourhood gangs established along ethnic or community lines may also establish elements of local control through the provision of 'protection services', as has occurred in post-conflict Timor-Leste and Nicaragua.[27]

Post-conflict societies are subject to proximate and structural risks that can shape patterns of armed violence onset and intensity.

A final category of post-conflict armed violence is prompted by *property disputes* arising from competing claims registered by displaced or recently resettled populations. Large-scale dislocation can generate renewed armed violence if repatriated or returning families find that others have seized their houses, lands, or assets. In certain cases, entire villages and population groups may have been coercively evicted, as was the case with certain Tamil and Sinhalese populations in Sri Lanka from 1983 to 2001 and since 2005 (Muggah, 2008a). Mandingo Liberians who fled during the war found their land occupied by other ethnic groups when they returned, and attempts to reclaim it led to rioting and new forms of communal violence (Chaudhary and Suhrke, 2008). Likewise, in post-war Kosovo, the Serb minority was particularly exposed to Kosovar Albanians seeking to establish an ethnically homogeneous territory. Revenge or retribution killings over the death or maiming of family and community members are also common in many post-conflict societies.[28] In certain instances, such killings can escalate and intensify smouldering tensions (Mac Ginty, 2006).

RISK FACTORS FACING POST-CONFLICT SOCIETIES

International concern with post-war armed violence is motivated by a number of factors. A major preoccupation relates to the susceptibility of such countries and municipalities to renewed full-scale armed conflict. Relatedly, policy-makers are worried that if armed violence is left unchecked, it can contribute to continued fatal injuries and indirect mortality, unnecessary suffering, and escalating human rights violations, while also undermining investments in state-building. Post-conflict states are, in the vernacular, 'fragile states'.[29] In order to stay their collapse, considerable attention has been devoted to promoting armed conflict prevention, humanitarian intervention, and peace-building initiatives, including transitional justice and security sector reform.[30]

Box 7.4 When do post-conflict societies return to war?

The claim that post-conflict countries had a 40-50 per cent risk of going back to war within a decade of war was established as part of an enquiry led by the World Bank into the economic aspects of armed conflict. The assessment was overseen by the World Bank's then Development Research Group director Paul Collier and associates (Collier et al., 2003). The figure rapidly circulated in the academic world, the UN system, and the international donor community and was subsequently used as a justification for the establishment of the Peacebuilding Commission.

Numerous social scientists contend that the figure is misleading and probably too high. Revised figures suggest a lower magnitude of risk of armed conflict recurrence–approximately 20-25 per cent within the first five years. This revision is based on the use of alternative datasets and independent retesting of the original data (Walter, 2004; Suhrke and Samset, 2007). The authors of the World Bank study revised their earlier figure downwards to 40 per cent (Collier, Hoeffler, and Söderboom, 2006, p. 14).

Macro-level research suggests that many post-conflict societies are vulnerable to a disproportionately high risk of war recurrence, in addition to rates of armed violence that are higher than expected. But the extent to which societies emerging from armed conflict are at risk is a subject of much controversy (see Box 7.4). Indeed, the oft-cited statistic that post-conflict countries have a 40–50 per cent risk of sliding back to open warfare within ten years is probably overly pessimistic, but the risk is still likely to be in the order of 20–25 per cent. The reasons why certain countries do not succumb to renewed armed conflict has also eluded close examination.[31] According to Charles Tilly, however, knowledge of discrete 'causes' of war and war recurrence may be less important than a more sophisticated understanding of the nature of the resulting armed conflicts and post-conflict environments (Tilly, 1995).

Nevertheless, better evidence is needed on these macro-level risks, since these differences matter for policy and programming. Some researchers fear that if the estimated risk of war recurrence is exaggerated, it could encourage decision-makers to resort more easily to (military) interventions, including peacekeepers (Easterly, 2008). Yet if the risks are downplayed, they contend that outsiders may be more inclined to adopt 'softer' tactics and a more cautious approach that emphasizes diplomacy and targeted sanctions. These concerns do not appear to be borne out by reality: even where there is solid evidence of post-conflict countries sliding back into war—as in the DRC, Somalia, and Sri Lanka—UN member states have rarely pursued assertive military interventions.[32] On the contrary: even in those countries where international engagement is comparatively strong—as in Afghanistan, Iraq, and Sudan—outsiders are hardly rushing in to assist, much less with well-resourced military operations.

Meanwhile, post-conflict societies are subject to proximate and structural risks that can shape patterns of armed violence onset and intensity (Geneva Declaration Secretariat, 2008; OECD, 2008b; Small Arms Survey, 2008).[33] Many of these same factors are relevant in ostensibly 'peaceful' environments as well. Understanding why armed violence occurs in either context, who commits violent acts, and who is at risk of victimization is at the core of effective strategies for armed violence prevention and reduction. Successful security promotion interventions typically focus not only on minimizing the symptoms of armed violence, but also on targeting the proximate risk factors associated with perpetration, enhancing resilience and better understanding the historical, political, economic, and socio-cultural 'embeddedness' of violence in a given society.

Proximate risk factors for heightened armed violence include unregulated small arms and light weapons availability, substance abuse, a history of victimization, abuse in the home, and prevailing attitudes that support the use of coercion.[34] While the presence of these risk factors is routinely correlated with the increased likelihood of armed violence, different forms of violence appear to be shaped by distinct combinations of risk factors. For example, in the case of youth violence, predictors include exposure to warfare, the presence of gangs in the neighbourhood, having an older sibling who is in a gang, perceptions of insecurity at school or in the neighbourhood, and lack of economic opportunities. Likewise, substance abuse, association with delinquent peers, and school bullying also appear to be associated with the onset of certain forms of youth violence, especially in post-conflict societies where support services are comparatively limited (WHO, 2008b).

War-torn cities serve as magnets for the young, and youths are the most likely to perpetrate and be victimized by armed violence.

Structural factors such as social and economic exclusion, rapid and unregulated urbanization and social dislocation, unequal access to basic public services, systemic unemployment, and living in poorer and socially marginalized areas can also be correlated with a higher risk of armed violence (Small Arms Survey, 2007; 2008; UNODC, 2005). But these factors on their own offer only limited insight. Understanding how they are connected in specific contexts is potentially even more important. In some cases, as in post-conflict societies throughout West and Central Africa, youths are rapidly recruited (voluntarily and forcibly) from urban slums into more organized institutions such as militia or even rebel groups (Small Arms Survey, 2006, pp. 295–322). Similar phenomena have been observed in Central America among gang members, many of whom were formerly combatants (or sons of combatants) during local civil wars (Muggah and Stevenson, forthcoming). Given that many of these factors are associated with rapid urbanization, greater attention to the dynamics of post-conflict urban armed violence is warranted. War-torn cities serve as magnets for the young, and youths are the most likely to perpetrate and be victimized by armed violence (WHO, 2008b; Graham, 2004).

Meanwhile, other structural risk factors are being linked to the recurrence of war. Sharp macro-economic shocks (Collier et al., 2003), rising levels of horizontal inequality (Diprose and Stewart, 2008; Diprose and Ukiwo, 2008), the expansion of unemployed youth populations (Collier et al., 2003), the persistence of 'bad neighbourhoods', and simmering identity-related grievances have all been offered as explanations for the onset of armed conflict as well as its contagion across borders. Although debates continue over the influence of these risks, the fact that a high number of countries afflicted by war slip back into armed conflict would imply that security promotion, peace-building, and development interventions should place a priority on minimizing proximate and structural risks (OECD, 2008a; 2008c; 2008d).

Although knowledge about proximate and structural risk factors for the onset and duration of war appears to be growing, a number of important issues remain unresolved. For example, the abovementioned distinction between proximate and structural risk factors does not adequately capture the instrumental mobilization of violence, including by so-called 'violence entrepreneurs', as is often the case in 'ethnicized armed conflicts'.[35] More attention also needs to be paid to the factors that contribute to the resilience of individuals and societies in the face of the extreme adversity that often characterizes post-conflict settings. Given the potential (and contested) role of 'youth bulges' and 'horizontal inequality' as factors explaining armed conflict and violence, a better understanding of these specific risk factors—whether for political, economic, state-led, communal, or property-related armed violence—is warranted.[36]

PROMOTING SECURITY AFTER WAR

Although the number and intensity of armed conflicts appear to be in decline since the early 1990s,[37] armed violence simmers on in many post-conflict countries. Encouragingly, certain lessons associated with preventing and reducing armed violence in such environments are being learned. Some of these are emerging from unexpected sources, including the crime and justice sectors. For example, in addition to the importance attached by military and development actors to peace-support interventions and conventional security promotion such as DDR, there is growing awareness of the critical role to be played by functioning and punitive security sectors.[38]

Over the past decade, it appears that some security promotion activities have begun adjusting to the dynamic landscapes of post-conflict armed violence. Many have focused deliberately on manipulating and mitigating proximate risk factors for post-conflict violence.[39] In some cases, these newer interventions have consciously sought to alter the incentives of violence entrepreneurs, disrupt enabling factors for armed violence onset, and change the built environment in which armed violence occurs. Adapted from or reinforcing conventional approaches, these newer activities have borrowed liberally from criminology, urban geography, and epidemiological disciplines.

Table 7.5 A selection of security promotion activities

	Type	Examples
Interim stabilization	Civilian service corps	South African Service Corps and the Kosovo Protection Corps
	Military integration arrangements	*Brassage* of the DRC, UNITA in Angola
	Transitional security forces	Afghan Military Forces, Sunni Awakening Councils in Iraq
	Dialogue and sensitization programmes	Rwandan *Ingando* process, Labora farm experiment in Uganda
	Differentiated forms of transitional autonomy	Khmer Rouge in Cambodia and Mindanao Autonomy Zone in the Philippines
Second-generation	Community security mechanisms	Community security fund in Sudan, community violence reduction in Haiti, Safer Cities in the former Yugoslav Republic of Macedonia
	At-risk youth and gang programmes	Gang violence reduction programmes in El Salvador, education and recreation programmes in Brazilian *favelas* (slums)
	Weapons for development and weapons lotteries	Weapons in exchange for development in Albania, Bosnia and Herzegovina, Mali, and Niger and weapons lotteries in Haiti, Mozambique, and the Republic of the Congo
	Urban renewal and population health programmes	Targeted slum development in Caracas (Venezuela), health-based interventions in Medellín and Cali (Colombia) and Kingston (Jamaica)

Source: Muggah and Colletta (2009)

Creative approaches to security promotion are fast emerging in post-conflict theatres as a result of experimentation on the ground. Conventional interventions such as DDR and SSR are routinely being transformed and adapted as practitioners seek to reorient activities towards (proximate) risk reduction and enhancing resilience. Likewise, designers of security promotion activities are increasingly reducing incoherence and competitive friction among relevant agencies by developing collaborative and inter-sector interventions (ACEH, AFGHANISTAN, LEBANON). Conventional interventions focused more broadly on promoting national stability and civilian accountability over the agents and means of violence are in some cases giving way to (or being complemented by) interim stabilization interventions and second-generation security promotion on the ground.

The incremental evolution of post-conflict security promotion reveals a degree of pragmatism among security and development practitioners. It is suggestive of the way in which military, policing, and development actors are registering and responding to known risks on the ground and seeking to promote 'whole-of-government' approaches (OECD, 2008a; Easterly, 2008). Alongside mainstream peace-building activities including mine clearance, transitional justice, and international criminal courts, newer interventions designed to promote safety and security are flourishing. And while the extent of their effectiveness remains subject to debate, they appear to complement and reinforce conventional security promotion strategies, expanding the menu of options available to prevent and reduce armed violence (see Table 7.5).

Interim stabilization

As noted above, there are a variety of reasons why many negotiated peace accords collapse within five years. More often than not reversions occur because the conditions are not ripe in the fragile post-conflict environment for the implementation of key security sector reforms or the social and economic reintegration of former combatants.[40] In the rush to declare peace and finalize an exit strategy, and faced with looming security vacuums, negotiating parties may forgo the detailed planning and programming required of carefully timed and phased interim stabilization measures that accompany conventional security promotion.[41] Alternatively, such interventions may not be pursued by peace mediators and negotiating parties if they run up against the vested interests of powerful elites and armed groups.[42]

Interim stabilization measures are part of a broader transitional integration process that seeks to balance adequate security with necessary development. While no guarantee of stability, such interventions can create and sustain a 'holding pattern', keeping former combatant cohesiveness intact within a military or civilian structure, and also buying time and creating space for political dialogue and the formation of an enabling environment for legitimate social and economic reintegration (Colletta, Berts, and Samuelsson Schjörlein, 2008).[43]

Interim stabilization measures aim to set clear, immediate, and limited objectives. These are to: dramatically reduce armed violence; improve real and perceived security; build confidence and trust; and buy time and space for longer-term conventional security promotion activities, including second-generation initiatives. Buying time and space is more important than it may at first appear. After all, peace agreements are often only the beginning rather than the end of the peace process. It is crucial to continue constructive dialogue among warring parties in order to develop a conventional DDR or SSR framework that outlines parameters for specific interventions if these are not part of the peace agreement.

Time is required in order to constitute administrative structures and legal instruments essential to DDR, including related reintegration commissions, veterans' bureaus, amnesties, and peace and justice laws. There is a need to create space for participants to understand and ultimately play a part in conventional security promotion. As expectations of a peace dividend begin to rise, time may also be required to allow the state to reinforce its capacity and reach, to promote community involvement in local security provision, and to facilitate opportunities for markets to regenerate and allow for rapid labour absorption.

The various types of emerging interim stabilization measures include: (i) the establishment of civilian service corps; (ii) military or security sector integration arrangements; (iii) the creation of transitional security forces; (iv) dialogue and sensitization programmes and related halfway-house arrangements; and (v) differentiated forms of transitional autonomy. These categories are not necessarily mutually exclusive. In most cases, interim stabilization measures integrate elements of two or more of these categories. These activities aim to convert potential spoilers into stakeholders during the transition period (particularly with regard to the security sector) and allow for the eventual management of small arms and armies.

Civilian service corps arrangements are usefully illustrated with the cases of the South African Service Corps and the Kosovo Protection Corps. These transitional organizations transform former military groups into transitional civilian organizations (e.g. reconstruction brigades, environmental protection–civilian conservation corps, and natural disaster prevention and response corps) through the maintenance of social

A former child soldier hands ammunition over to the UN, Monrovia, Liberia, December 2003.
© Sven Torfinn/Panos Pictures

structures and cohesion but with changed functions. They address the need to (at least temporarily) employ and occupy former combatants in some form of controlled, meaningful civilian activity. In addition to providing clear incentives to participate in the post-conflict recovery process, this type of arrangement may allow the time and space required for demobilization and reintegration to be pursued, while also permitting individuals to strengthen their life and vocational skills as they ease into civilian life.

Military or security sector integration is another common strategy employed in societies emerging from war (Hoddie and Hartzell, 2003). It is a key interim stabilization mechanism for 'right-sizing' military and policing structures by bringing erstwhile warring parties together in a single entity and ensuring that potential spoilers and legitimate servicemen and -women are provided with ample livelihood. Military integration is exemplified by the *brassage* process in the DRC, the parallel integration and reintegration programme in Burundi, and the demobilization of the UNITA rebel group in Angola (Colletta, Berts, and Samuelsson Schjörlein, 2008). Variations of the strategy have been employed in many other post-conflict zones (e.g. Afghanistan, the Philippines, Rwanda, and Uganda) where military integration and the consolidation of security within a single unified national security apparatus preceded a more structured demobilization of rebel groups (Colletta and Muggah, 2009).

Interim stabilization may allow the time and space required for demobilization and reintegration to be pursued.

The creation of more temporary *transitional security forces* is another clear interim stabilization measure. The formation of the Afghan Military Forces bringing together various militia under a single decentralized force and uniform payroll in Afghanistan following the US-led invasion is one clear example of a transitional security force. Many of these combatants were later demobilized or integrated into the new national Afghan security system (AFGHANISTAN). The more recent experience with the Sunni Awakening Councils in Iraq is an example whereby local militia with strong ethnic, religious, or tribal 'identity' roots were incorporated into local community security forces. In this way they were provided with recognition and paid a salary. Local tribal or culturally based leadership was situated within a loose national command structure. It was intended that these groups eventually integrate into formal security forces or be demobilized when local security, governance, and economic conditions permitted (Colletta, Berts, and Samuelsson Schjörlein, 2008).

Other interim arrangements include *dialogue, sensitization programmes, and halfway-house arrangements*. This category is illustrated by the Rwandan *Ingando* process. Former combatants were gathered into camps for problem-solving dialogue sessions in order to review the causes of violence and to take ownership of the tragedy. The process also served as a forum for the exposure of myths and stereotypes, and afforded an opportunity to rekindle trust following the deep trauma of the 1994 genocide (Colletta, Berts, and Samuelsson Schjörlein, 2008). Many of the characteristics of this category can also be seen in the Labora farm experiment, an agricultural collective in Uganda,[44] and in the creation of a non-governmental organization for former paramilitaries in Colombia (Muggah, 2008b; Colletta and Muggah, 2009). The effects of long-term economic and social marginalization and stigmatization are addressed in halfway-house arrangements, be they urban cooperatives, agricultural farms, or new NGOs created to enable a resocialization process and adjustment of mindsets and behaviour.

Another type of interim stabilization mechanism is enhanced *autonomy during a transitional period*. The primary example of such schemes is the agreement between the Government of Cambodia and the Khmer Rouge, with Hun Sen's Win–Win Policy (Colleta, Berts, and Samuelsson Schjörlein, 2008). In this case, social cohesion, local control over governance (including security) and natural resources, and livelihood were exchanged in a clearly defined time period (e.g. three years) for a public affirmation of loyalty to the state.

The above examples of interim stabilization are particularly successful when control and cohesiveness of rank-and-file combatants are maintained until such time as existing command structures are reshaped, emphasizing civilian authority, and conditions are ripe for social and economic reintegration or military integration. This approach typically plays out at three tiers: at the *state* level as it establishes power sharing and attendant institutional, legal, and administrative frameworks for transitional governance; at the *community* level, where sensitization, transitional justice, and reconciliation mechanisms are established; and at the *individual* level by way of improved security, transitional employment, the re-establishment of property rights (asset base), or the provision of life skills training and psychosocial support.

The effectiveness of interim stabilization arrangements depends on a careful appreciation of the key proximate and structural risks and other contextual factors. Ensuring that ground level realities are acknowledged is central to shaping the dynamics of intervention strategies, highlighting again the importance of effective and ongoing diagnosis and analysis. There is no 'one size fits all' approach. A range of incentives and organizational or institutional arrangements are possible—from non-governmental agencies, political parties, rural agri-business, urban public and private service delivery to military, police customs, and intelligence service integration. Moreover, there is a recognition that interim stabilization arrangements should be tightly connected to the over-arching peace- and state-building framework, and that they require adequate provisions for financing, coordination, and monitoring.

Second-generation security promotion

Second-generation security promotion approaches are fast emerging as alternatives and add-ons to DDR and SSR, particularly in Latin America and the Caribbean.[45] They clearly overlap with conventional security promotion, but also represent the expanding toolkit of post-conflict interventions available to planners and practitioners. In contrast to conventional measures—particularly DDR—they tend to be evidence-led, focusing at the outset on identifying and mitigating demonstrated risk factors, enhancing resilience and protective factors at the municipal and community levels, and constructing interventions on the basis of identified needs. The World Bank and the Inter-American Development Bank, for example, have been supporting second-generation security promotion for more than a decade (see Box 7.5).

Second-generation security promotion approaches are fast emerging as alternatives and add-ons to DDR and SSR.

The emergence of second-generation security promotion is linked to a growing awareness of the limitations of conventional approaches such as DDR. In complex environments such as Southern Sudan and Haiti, for example, more 'classic' DDR programmes, focused on collecting weapons, cantonment, and reintegration of individual ex-combatants, swiftly gave way to a series of alternative interventions (Muggah, 2007). These activities sought to draw explicitly on local cultural norms rather than rigid externally provided incentives, put weapons beyond use rather than taking them (temporarily) out of circulation, target civilians and gang members rather than former soldiers, and draw on community-based leaders and associations rather than national public institutions.

Second-generation security promotion activities shift the emphasis away from top–down interventions designed by outsiders to more community-designed and -executed approaches. In certain cases, they include activities that carefully map out and respond to known proximate risk factors and that focus on the motivations and behavioural factors associated with actual and would-be perpetrators. From Timor–Leste to El Salvador, examples of second-generation approaches include (i) *community security mechanisms,* (ii) *schemes focusing on at-risk youth and gangs, (iii) weapons for development activities and weapons lotteries,* and (iv) *urban renewal and population health programming.*

Box 7.5 The World Bank and second-generation programmes

The World Bank's Small Grants Programme for Violence Prevention supports municipal-level initiatives that advance community-based approaches to reducing criminal armed violence and assisting victims. Initiatives focus on reducing the number of arms in circulation, altering the attitudes and behaviour of the agents who might potentially use them, and strengthening public and private institutions for enhanced security and good governance.

Lessons emerging from the agency's experience emphasize the importance of:

- *Multi-sector strategies:* these are grounded in a common vision of the risks affecting citizen security among a wide range of public and private entities.
- *Diagnostics and data-cost sharing:* evidence-based diagnostics are critical for a common vision and the development of local and national strategies.
- *Long-term implementation plans with inter-agency coordination:* matching public sector budgetary allocations for security with commensurate allocations for preventive action.
- *Focusing on those at risk of involvement in crime and reinforcing existing security mechanisms:* promoting local customs and social rules to generate a sense of belonging, facilitate peaceful coexistence, and encourage respect for common heritage, civic rights, and duties.
- *Seeking local solutions and targeting 'hot spots':* this should be done together with initiatives that bring the police and community closer together in designing participatory security promotion.
- *Balancing sticks and carrots:* upholding law and order through the accountable punishment of those who harm public well-being, while supporting those who foster peace, solidarity, respect, and community cohesion.

Source: OECD (2008a)

Community security mechanisms tend to emerge in response to, or independently of, DDR activities grafted into UN-mandated peace-support operations. By virtue of their proximity to affected communities, field-based practitioners and local organizations are frequently more attuned to local contextual factors than decision-makers and peace negotiators charged with formulating conventional security packages. Community security mechanisms tend to adopt area-based approaches to security promotion, endorse collective incentives to enhance compliance and community participation, and harness the influence of indigenous power brokers and agents of change. 'Community security funds' and 'violence reduction committees' such as those introduced in South Sudan and Haiti are prominent examples (Muggah, 2007). Community security initiatives tend to feature integrated and multi-sector strategies. They foster confidence and legitimacy through the routine involvement of formal and informal security agents and affected communities. Crucially, their durability and scalability may depend on strong and decentralized local authorities and civil society actors—institutions that are often severely compromised or weakened by protracted armed conflict.

Gang members of the Mara 18 are held in El Hoyón prison in Escuintla, Guatemala, August 2005. © Victor James Blue/WPN

Activities related to *youth and gang-related violence* in post-conflict countries throughout Central America can also be categorized as second-generation security promotion. Violence prevention and reduction interventions focused on so-called 'clikas' and subgroups connected to the *Mara Salvatrucha* or *Barrio Dieciocho* have been pursued from San Salvador (El Salvador) to forced migrant communities in the United States. Community-led initiatives—such as Homeboy Industries in the United States or the Centro de Formación y Orientación in El Salvador—appear to demonstrably enhance the resilience of at-risk youth, former gang members, and post-conflict communities. Specifically, they aim to reinforce coordinated public and private sector responses to post-conflict economic violence and to provide mentorship, risk education, and alternative livelihoods for would-be perpetrators and victims, especially boys and young men in poor and marginal communities (WOLA, 2008).[46] They offer important alternatives to enforcement-based *mano dura* approaches that are popular in the region (Muggah and Stevenson, forthcoming).

Box 7.6 Community-based disarmament in Somaliland

When the Somali National Movement (SNM) came to power in the early 1990s, large quantities of weapons remained in the hands of the civilian population. Young men quickly established new clan-based militias and armed bandit *deydey* gangs. While the former had some legitimacy in the eyes of the people, being seen as clan defence organizations, the latter preyed on the civilian population and were viewed as criminals. Both types of groups extorted 'taxes' from the civilian population and were often indistinguishable in practice.

The SNM's nascent police and army were incapable of dealing with either the clan militias or the *deydey* bandits, and unable to establish law and order. Crime, shoot-outs, and an atmosphere of armed terror and impunity pervaded Somaliland. Although the new government formally announced a disarmament and integration process, it lacked the capacity and authority to implement it. The international community was not prepared to help secure the post-war peace.

Instead, a popular community-based effort involving traders, civil society groups, traditional and religious leaders, women's groups, and female kiosk traders successfully built a 'NO GUN' campaign, in which men with guns were shunned, heckled on the streets, and refused services. In one decisive instance, women in the city of Berbera disarmed a militia checkpoint, capturing weapons and an armed vehicle, hurling both the vehicle and the weapons into the sea. Poets and musicians joined the campaign with public anti-gun performances while sheikhs preached against the carrying of weapons at Friday mosque.

In a matter of weeks this campaign cleared the streets of weapons and created sufficient popular pressure to persuade clan militias to disarm and join the national security forces. To this day, although Somaliland's sub-national groups have not formally disarmed and few personal weapons have actually been collected, guns are seldom if ever seen in public. The new national police and army remain, in the public eye, the only legitimate persons entitled to carry weapons.

Source: OECD (2008a)

Second-generation interventions aim to promote ownership and locally legitimate activities by focusing on existing social institutions rather than forming or relying solely on (new) national entities and associated structures (see Box 7.6). They also advance a demand-side approach to arms control, emphasizing the importance of influencing the means and motivations rather than strictly reducing access to hardware. The introduction of *weapons for development* projects in Liberia, Mali, and the Republic of the Congo, *weapons lotteries* in Mozambique and Haiti's slums, and gun-free zones in Brazil and South Africa are examples of innovative and context-specific approaches to reducing gun violence.[47] Rather than focusing narrowly on removing the tools of violence, the emphasis is instead on reshaping the conditions that foster their misuse (Brauer and Muggah, 2006). Such activities often complement more traditional approaches to post-conflict arms control, including the strengthening of national regulatory frameworks associated with civilian arms ownership, weapons stockpile management, and civilian oversight over the security sector.

Meanwhile, urban renewal—including *Safer Community and Safer City design strategies*—are other examples of second-generation approaches. There is growing evidence that innovative environmental design and effective use of the built environment by city planners, architects, social scientists, and community leaders can contribute to a reduction in opportunities for predatory violence and related fear of victimization in post-conflict settings (Moser, 2004; 2006). Interventions that support 'positive territoriality' by fostering neighbourhood interaction and vigilance, enhance 'public-led surveillance' through the identification of 'hot spots', establish 'hierarchy of space' through the encouragement of use and ownership of public spaces, emphasize 'target hardening' through the strategic use of physical barriers and security devices, contribute to 'environment harmonizing' by reducing space for armed violence and victimization to occur, and strengthen 'image maintenance' by creating well-maintained and lit public and private spaces all appear to enhance local resilience against violence.[48] Safer Community activities that consciously integrate at-risk youth also reportedly improve routine safety and security in post-conflict societies.[49]

A number of critical lessons are emerging from second-generation security promotion activities. An underlying principle appears to be a more scaled-back and facilitative role for international agencies. Rather than recreating new national-level institutions such as commissions or focal points or relying on blunt instruments, second-generation security promotion activities are forged on the basis of formal and informal cooperation with existing (including customary) local institutions. Where possible, the initiative, control, and responsibility of overseeing interventions resides in the hands of local partners; community ownership is therefore a hallmark of such initiatives. Although many second-generation initiatives are nascent and empirically demonstrated evidence of their effectiveness is only gradually being assembled, they potentially offer an important contribution to redressing post-conflict insecurity.[50]

CONCLUSION

Any serious investment in post-conflict security promotion needs to take account of the many dimensions of armed violence. This means investing in diagnosing and ultimately reducing known risk factors and promoting armed violence-sensitive interventions. A failure to address effectively and comprehensively the immediate and underlying correlates of post-conflict armed violence means that the embers can smoulder, waiting for the next spark to reignite into war.

Conventional forms of post-conflict security promotion are often narrowly conceived and constructed as part of a general peace-support operation. They typically apply a limited range of measures to armed violence reduction and focus on specific categories of armed actors. Predictably, they also struggle to contend with the geographical and demographic complexities of armed violence before, during, and after war's 'end'.

Part of the reason for this is political and administrative. Programmes such as DDR, international policing, and small arms control are routinely introduced as part of a UN Security Council resolution or pursuant to a peace agreement with clear prescriptions on how such interventions should be executed. As such, they assume that war has passed its 'peak' and that some form of normalization (or stability) will ensue in the post-conflict period. Interventions are seldom developed on the basis of solid baseline evidence on the ground, or adequately equipped to handle the diverse types of armed violence and their interconnections.

A number of newer approaches appear to be more successful at containing arms and spoilers in post-conflict contexts. These draw upon emerging experiences of armed violence prevention and reduction in chronically violence-affected societies. In addition to creating space for conventional security promotion to take hold, they tend to focus on identifying and responding to risk factors, enhancing resilience at the municipal or community level, and constructing interventions based on identified needs. Interim stabilization measures and second-generation security promotion activities launched from Afghanistan and Cambodia to Colombia and Haiti have explicitly targeted the diverse dimensions of arms availability. More importantly, on the basis of sound information and analysis, they have also homed in on the preferences of actors using weapons and the real and perceived factors contributing to armed violence.

Mirroring the logic of mainstream community development, the design, control, and supervision of such armed violence reduction activities rests at least as much with local partners as with external actors. Although such interventions are nascent, and evidence of their effectiveness is still accumulating, they offer a promising means of keeping some of the more pernicious aspects of post-conflict violence in check.

LIST OF ABBREVIATIONS

CMR	Crude mortality rate
DRC	Democratic Republic of the Congo
SNM	Somali National Movement
DDR	Disarmament, demobilization, and reintegration
SSR	Security sector reform

ENDNOTES

1 See, for example, Geneva Declaration Secretariat (2008) and Small Arms Survey (2005) for a review of direct and indirect conflict deaths during and after war.

2 See, for example, Spear (2006) and Pugh (2005).

3 Notable exceptions include Dobbins et al. (2005), Doyle and Sambanis (2006), Zuercher (2006), and Fortna (2008).

4 The recent launch of standards and guidelines to assist DDR and SSR—including the *Integrated DDR Standards* (UN DDR, 2006) and the SSR *Handbook* of the Organisation for Economic Co-operation and Development (OECD–DAC, 2007)—should change this situation.

5 Violence does sometimes decline dramatically in the immediate aftermath of armed conflict and, in certain cases, during wartime itself. Indeed, noted 19th-century sociologist Emile Durkheim argues that suicide rates can fall during war and post-conflict periods. This conclusion is backed by empirical evidence involving an analysis of suicide rates in France from 1826 to 1913, which indicates that suicide rates were lower during years of war than during years of peace (Lester, 1993). Similar trends were observed more recently in other war-affected areas such as Sri Lanka (Somasundaram and Rajadurai, 1995). Likewise, there are examples of the general health actually improving for populations during and following wars, as was the case of World War II Great Britain and, to a lesser extent, certain affected population groups in war-affected countries of Africa. Correspondence with Alex de Waal, November 2008.

6 For a review of the epidemiological literature on post-conflict armed violence, consult Small Arms Survey (2005). See also Columbia University (2008) for a review of incident reporting on collective violence in a selection of countries.

7 See, for example, WHO (2008a; 2008b) and Ghobarah, Huth, and Russett (2003).

8 See, for example, the Complex Emergency Database (CE-DAT) of the Centre for the Research of Epidemiology of Disasters (CRED, n.d.).

9 See, for example, Geneva Declaration Secretariat (2008) and Hoeffler and Reynal-Querol (2003).

10 As discussed in the *Global Burden of Armed Violence*, reporting biases are common in post-conflict environments (Geneva Declaration Secretariat, 2008). In some cases, post-conflict killing may be classified as common crime rather than banditry. In other cases, the sudden and rapid expansion of reporting may give a false impression that criminal violence is on the increase. See, for example, Collier et al. (2003).

11 Small and Singer (1982) first defined civil war as armed conflicts involving active participation of the national government, military action internal to a country's sovereign borders, and effective resistance by both sides. The principle difference between civil (internal or intra-state) war and colonial or imperial war was the internality of war to the territory of a sovereign state and the participation of the government as a combatant. Tilly (2003) describes war more broadly as a form of 'coordinated destruction'—a typology that includes various forms of political violence that in turn generate 'short-run damage' and are perpetrated by coordinated, organized actors. Sambanis (2004) argues that classifying war is more problematic than presented by Small and Singer or Tilly, owing to: (i) challenges of distinguishing extra- from inter-state armed conflicts; (ii) the difficulties of determining what degree of organization is needed to separate war from other forms of one-sided state-sponsored violence; (iii) the obstacles associated with establishing a numerical threshold to identify wars (e.g. more than 1,000 or more than 25); and (iv) the challenges associated with deciding when an old war stops and a new one begins (as distinct from terrorism or other forms of armed violence).

12 Fortna correctly observes that since peacekeeping is not instated randomly, measuring whether it 'works' is not straightforward. Peacekeeping is most likely to be used where the chances that peace will last are otherwise comparatively low, that is, in the most difficult cases. A comparison of whether (and how long) peace endures with and without peacekeeping would therefore yield misleading results unless these underlying prospects for peace were controlled for. See Fortna (2008).

13 These indicators include: '(1) macroeconomic stability and its probable sustainability; (2) recovery of private sector confidence, as measured by the investment ratio; and (3) the effectiveness with which institutional arrangements and the political system are coping with the tensions, schisms and behaviors that lay behind the conflicts' (World Bank, 1998b, p. 44).

14 Operation protocol 8.5 was originally designed for reconstruction after natural disasters. It mentions a 'Stage Five: Return to Normal Operations' defined as 'when the emergency phase is over and operations are once more carried out under normal lending procedures, and the consciousness of conflict begins to wane' (World Bank, 1998a, p. 9). Indicators are left vague and under-developed. Guidance is also provided by the *Framework for World Bank Involvement in Post-Conflict Countries* (World Bank, 1997).

15 Alex de Waal notes that the 'post-conflict' concept is founded on normative assumptions about the direction of causality: 'A checklist approach might find that a post-conflict country also fits the criteria for a pre-conflict one.' Correspondence with Alex de Waal, November 2008.

16 For a review of these concerns, consult Muggah (2008b) and Muggah and Krause (2009).

17 These peace milestones include 'a cessation of hostilities and violence; signing of peace agreements; inception of demobilization, disarmament and reintegration; return of refugees and [internally displaced persons]; establishment of the foundations of a functioning state; initiation of reconciliation and societal integration; and the start of economic recovery' (UNDP, 2008, p. 5).

18 Journalists and human rights agencies may also under-report the incidence and scale of violence due to state repression and self-censorship. In an era heavily influenced by the so-called 'war on terror', governments may also describe simmering violence as 'terrorism', concealing ongoing domestic struggles and legitimate grievances.

19 For casualty information, consult, for example, UCDP (2008), COW (n.d.), IISS (n.d.), and ACLED (2008).

20 Since the end of civil war in all three countries criminal violence has exploded—especially in urban areas. Although under-reporting and under-recording is significant, in Nicaragua, for example, the absolute number of crimes tripled between 1990 and 2003. Crime perception surveys confirm rising fear among the population at large. See Rodgers (2004).

21 This framework draws explicitly from Chaudhary and Suhrke (2008) and the Geneva Declaration Secretariat (2008). It should be noted that there are also instances of societies emerging from war that do not experience egregious rates of violence, though this category is not included.

22 The Rwandan Patriotic Front, which took control of the state after the 1994 genocide, used military means to pursue the *genocidaires* and the ethnic group associated with them as they fled into neighbouring DRC, reportedly killing tens if not hundreds of thousands of people (Chaudhary and Suhrke, 2008).

23 For instance, militia leaders and rivals Abdul Rashid Dostum and Atta Mohammed have repeatedly clashed in their attempts to control the country's northern provinces. See Chaudhary and Suhrke (2008).

24 See, for example, Cooper (2006), Spear (2006), Goodhand (2005), and Pugh (2005).

25 For details, see *Issue Briefs* on armed violence, private security, and gangs in Timor-Leste (TLAVA, n.d.).

26 This is not new. Lynchings of African-Americans in the post-Civil War United States were sometimes announced in newspapers beforehand. See, for example, Moses (1997).

27 For more information on Timor–Leste, see TLAVA (n.d.). In post-conflict Nicaragua, urban youth gangs evolved from 'providing micro-regimes of order as well as communal forms of belonging' in the mid-1990s, to forming predatory organizations 'concerned with regulating an emergent drug economy in the exclusive interest of the individual gang members instead of protecting their local neighbourhood' (Rodgers, 2006, p. 321).

28 Such killings tend to reflect the interests of narrow groups, which distinguish them from the community and informal justice described above.

29 See, for example, OECD (2008c, 2008d).

30 See, for example, OECD (2008b). The *Human Security Report* has made the claim that robust peace-support operations and peace-building activities are correlated with reductions in armed conflict, though the authors do not examine the micro-level determinants of how such activities prevent war renewal (HSRP, 2005).

31 Apprehending the factors that enhance resilience in post-conflict societies is the subject of www.urban-resilience.org and will also be explored in future editions of the *Small Arms Survey*.

32 See, for example, Regan (2009) and Doyle and Sambanis (2006) for a review of what makes peacekeepers more likely to intervene.

33 These risks have been divided into discrete descriptive categories by Roy Licklider: (i) external (e.g. neighbouring countries, behaviour of peacekeepers, support or lack of it from the international community), (ii) societal (e.g. unemployment, weak respect for the law, limited experience with democracy, arms availability), (iii) the nature of the settlement (e.g. imposed from above, exclusion of key groups, inadequate provisions for enforcement), (iv) governmental (e.g. lack of legitimacy, inability to generate revenues or respond to social demands, limited tradition of legitimate opposition), and (v) important groups within the country (e.g. spoilers, victims and key leaders). Correspondence with Licklider, November 2008.

34 See, for example, Geneva Declaration Secretariat (2008) and WHO (2008b).

35 See, for example, Keen (1998).

36 The *Global Burden of Armed Violence* is an important step towards expanding the evidence base. See, for example, Geneva Declaration Secretariat (2008) and Cincotta (2008).

37 See, for example, HSRP (2005).

38 See, for example, OECD (2007) and the burgeoning work on security sector reform and international policekeeping including Cockayne and Malone (2004).

39 At the same time, multilateral and bilateral development donors have sought to alter structural risk factors through targeted assistance and investment. See Easterly (2008).

40 Fortna (2009) also points to other factors that shape the likelihood of war onset, such as the decisiveness of military victory, history of conflict between belligerents before the war, balance of power between actors, costs of wars, and issues at stake.

41 A recent three-country (Cambodia, Colombia, and Uganda) exploratory study financed by the Swedish government as a follow up to the Stockholm Initiative on Disarmament Demobilisation Reintegration accents the importance of assessing contextual factors, unbundling reintegration processes, and identifying interim stabilization measures that support sufficient security in the short term in order to create the enabling conditions for sustainable development in the long term (Colletta, Berts, and Samuelsson Schjörlein, 2008).

42 See, for example, the work of the Centre for Humanitarian Dialogue for a review of mediator approaches to DDR and other forms of security promotion during peace negotiations (CHD, n.d.).

43 Social and economic reintegration are not to be confused with reinsertion or sustainable reintegration.

44 See, for example, Colletta, Berts, and Samuelsson Schjörlein (2008).

45 See, for example, Colletta and Muggah (2009) and Muggah (2008b; 2005) for a review of second-generation security promotion.

46 Other gang-violence reduction programmes that appear to have contributed to sharp reductions in armed violence in the United States include Identity (Montgomery County, Maryland), Community Mobilization Initiative (Herndon, Virginia), and Gang Intervention Partnership (Columbia Heights, Washington, DC). Examples of Central American activities include Grupo Ceiba (Guatemala), Paz y Justicia (Honduras), and Equipo Nahual (El Salvador). See, for example, WOLA (2008).

47 See, for example, Colletta and Muggah (2009), Small Arms Survey (2005), and Atwood, Glatz, and Muggah (2006) for reviews of these second-generation approaches.

48 Prominent examples of this in post-conflict contexts include work undertaken by Saferworld, the Balkan Youth Union, the Centre for Security Studies in Bosnia and Herzegovina, and CIVIL and the Forum for Civic Initiatives (FIQ) in South-eastern Europe. See, for example, Saferworld et al. (2006).

49 Examples of how youth can be engaged range from participating in bicycle and foot patrols, neighbourhood watches, and early warning systems to advancing crime reduction education, prevention strategies, and escort services. See CSIC (2006).

50 In Colombia, for example, a rash of targeted second-generation security promotion programmes focusing on temporary alcohol and weapons-carrying restrictions, and related activities focused on prospective gang members and urban renewal, contributed to the fastest decline in homicidal violence yet recorded in the Western hemisphere. See, for example, Muggah (2008b) and Small Arms Survey (2006, pp. 295–322).

BIBLIOGRAPHY

ACLED (Armed Conflict Location and Event Dataset). 2008. *ACLED Report: Democratic Republic of Congo*. Mimeo. 1 August–3 September.

Atwood, David, Anne-Kathrin Glatz, and Robert Muggah. 2006. *Demanding Attention: Addressing the Dynamics of Small Arms Demand*. Occasional Paper 18. Geneva: Small Arms Survey.

Bastick, Megan, Karin Grimm, and Rahel Kunz. 2007. *Sexual Violence in Armed Conflict: Global Overview and Implications for the Security Sector*. Geneva: Democratic Control of Armed Forces.

Bell, Christine. 2006. 'Peace Agreements: Their Nature and Legal Status.' *American Journal of International Law*, Vol. 100, No. 373, pp. 373–412.

—. 2008. *On the Law of Peace: The New Law of the Peacemaker*. Oxford: Oxford University Press.

—. 2009. 'Deconstructing Peace Agreements.' Unpublished background paper. Geneva: Small Arms Survey.

Brauer, Jurgen and Robert Muggah. 2006. 'Completing the Circle: Building a Theory of Small Arms Demand.' *Journal of Contemporary Security Policy*, Vol. 27, No. 1, pp. 138–54.

Caumartin, Corinne. 2005. *Racism, Violence, and Inequality: An Overview of the Guatemalan Case*. Working Paper No. 11. Oxford: Centre for Research on Inequality, Human Security and Ethnicity, University of Oxford.

CERAC (Conflict Analysis Resource Center). n.d. <http://www.cerac.org.co>

Chaudhary, Torunn and Astri Suhrke. 2008. *Post-war Violence*. Unpublished background paper. Geneva: Small Arms Survey.

CHD (Center for Humanitarian Dialogue). n.d. 'Negotiating Disarmament.' <http://www.hdcentre.org/projects/negotiating-disarmament>

Cincotta, Richard. 2008. *Young Guns: The Demographics of Discord*. Unpublished background paper. Geneva: Small Arms Survey.

Cockayne, James and David Malone. 2004. 'United Nations Peace Operations Then and Now.' *International Peacekeeping*, Vol. 9, pp. 1–26.

Cohen, Lawrence E. and Kenneth C. Land. 1987. 'Age Structure and Crime: Symmetry Versus Asymmetry and the Projection of Crime Rates through the 1990s.' *American Sociological Review*, Vol. 52, No. 2. April, pp. 170–83.

Colletta, Nat, Hannes Berts, and Jens Samuelsson Schjörlien. 2008. *Balancing Security and Development: An Exploratory Study of Interim Stabilization Measures in Colombia, Cambodia and Uganda*. Stockholm: Folke Bernadotte Academy.

— and Robert Muggah. Forthcoming. 'Rethinking Post-Conflict Security Promotion: Interim Stabilization and Second-Generation Approaches to DDR and SSR.' *Journal of Conflict, Security and Development*, special edn., spring/summer.

Collier, Paul and Anke Hoeffler. 2004. *Murder by Numbers: Socio-economic Determinants of Homicide and Civil War*. Working Paper No. 2004–10. Oxford: Centre for the Study of African Economies, University of Oxford.

—, and Måns Söderboom. 2006. *Post-Conflict Risks*. Working Paper No. 256. Oxford: Centre for the Study of African Economies, University of Oxford. <http://www.bepress.com/csae/paper256>

— et al. 2003. *Breaking the Conflict Trap: Civil War and Development Policy*. Washington, DC: World Bank.

Columbia University. 2008. *Monthly Deaths by Collective Violence from News Reports*. <http://www.columbia.edu/~cds81/docs/violence_graphs.pdf>

Cooper, Neil. 2006. 'Peaceful Warriors and Warring Peacemakers.' *Economics of Peace and Security Journal*, Vol. 1, No. 1. January, pp. 20–24.

COW (Correlates of War). n.d. Datasets. <http://www.correlatesofwar.org/>

Cramer, Christopher. 2002. 'Homo Economicus Goes to War: Methodological Individualism, Rational Choice and the Political Economy of War.' *World Development*, Vol. 30, No. 11. November, pp. 1845–64.

— and Jonathan Goodhand. 2003. 'Try Again, Fail Again, Fail Better? War, the State and the "Post-Conflict" Challenge in Afghanistan.' In Jennifer Milliken, ed. *State Failure, Collapse and Reconstruction*. London: Blackwell Publishers, pp. 131–55.

CRED (Centre for the Research of Epidemiology of Disasters). n.d. Complex Emergency Database (CE-DAT). <http://www.cedat.be/database>

CSIC (Centre for Strategic and International Studies). 2006. *Engaging Youth to Build Safer Communities*. New York: CSIC.

Daponte, Beth. 1993. 'A Case Study in Estimating Casualties from War and Its Aftermath: The 1991 Persian Gulf War.' *PSR Quarterly*, Vol. 3, No. 2, pp. 57–66.

Darby, John. 2001. *The Effects of Violence on Peace Processes*. Washington, DC: United States Institute of Peace.

Diprose, Rachael and Frances Stewart. 2008. *Horizontal Inequalities and Violent Conflict*. Unpublished background paper. Geneva: Small Arms Survey.

— and Ukiha Ukiwo. 2008. *Decentralization and Conflict Management in Indonesia and Nigeria*. Working Paper No. 49. Oxford: Centre for Research on Inequality, Human Security and Ethnicity, University of Oxford.

Dobbins, James et al. 2005. *The UN's Role in Nation-Building. From the Congo to Iraq*. Santa Monica: RAND Corporation.

Doyle, Michael W. and Nicholas Sambanis. 2006. *Making War and Building Peace: United Nations Peace Operations*. Princeton: Princeton University Press.

Easterly, William. 2008. 'The Bottom Billion: Why the Poorest Countries Are Failing and What Can Be Done About It.' *New York Review of Books*. 4 December.

Fearon, James and David Laitin. 1996. 'Explaining Interethnic Cooperation.' *American Political Science Review*, Vol. 90, No. 4, pp. 715–35.

Ford Institute for Human Security. 2008. *What Makes a Camp Safe? The Protection of Children from Abduction in Internally Displaced Persons and Refugee Camps*. Pittsburgh: University of Pittsburgh. <http://www.fordinstitute.pitt.edu/docs/23182ReportPR11.pdf>

Fortna, Virginia. 2008. *Does Peacekeeping Work? Shaping Belligerents' Choices after Civil War*. Princeton: Princeton University Press.

—. 2009. 'What Is the Impact of Peacekeeping?' Unpublished background paper. Geneva: Small Arms Survey.

Geneva Declaration Secretariat. 2008. *The Global Burden of Armed Violence*. Geneva: Geneva Declaration Secretariat. <http://www.genevadeclaration.org/pdfs/Global-Burden-of-Armed-Violence.pdf>

Ghobarah, Hazem, Paul Huth, and Bruce Russett. 2003. 'Civil Wars Kill and Maim People—Long after the Shooting Stops.' *American Political Science Review*, Vol. 97, No. 2. May, pp. 189–202.

Goodhand, Jonathan. 2005. 'Frontiers and Wars: The Opium Economy in Afghanistan.' *Journal of Agrarian Change*, Vol. 5, No. 2, pp. 191–216.

Graham, Stephen. 2004. *Cities, War and Terrorism: Towards an Urban Geopolitics*. London: Blackwell Publishing.

Hoddie, Matthew and Caroline Hartzell. 2003. 'Civil War Settlements and the Implementation of Military Power-Sharing Arrangements.' *Journal of Peace Research*, Vol. 40, No. 3, pp 303–20.

Hoeffler, Anke and Marta Reynal-Querol. 2003. *Measuring the Costs of Conflict*. Oxford: Centre for the Studies of African Economies, University of Oxford.

Höglund, Kristine and I. William Zartman. 2006. 'Violence by the State: Official Spoilers and Their Allies.' In John Darby, ed. *Violence and Reconstruction*. South Bend, Indiana: University of Notre Dame Press, pp. 11–31.

HSRP (Human Security Report Project). 2005. *Human Security Report 2005: War and Peace in the 21st Century*. Oxford: Oxford University Press.

ICG (International Crisis Group). 2008. *Burundi: Restarting Political Dialogue*. New York: ICG. <http://www.crisisgroup.org/home/index.cfm?id=5632&l=1>

IDMC (Internal Displacement Monitoring Center). 2008. *Internal Displacement: Global Overview of Trends and Developments in 2007*. Geneva: IDMC and Norwegian Refugee Council. <http://www.unhcr.org/refworld/docid/48074b842.html>

IISS (International Institute for Strategic Studies). n.d. Armed Conflict Database. <http://www.iiss.org/publications/armed-conflict-database/>

IRC (International Rescue Committee). 2007. *Mortality in the Democratic Republic of Congo: An Ongoing Crisis*. Atlanta: IRC and Burnet Institute. <http://www.theirc.org/resources/2007/2006-7_congomortalitysurvey.pdf>

IRIN (Integrated Regional Information Network). 2008. 'Sierra Leone: Sex Crimes Continue in Peacetime.' Freetown: IRIN. 20 June. <http://www.irinnews.org/report.aspx?ReportID=78853>

Jütersonke, Oliver, Robert Muggah, and Dennis Rodgers. 2009. 'Urban Violence and Security Promotion in Central America.' *Security Dialogue*, Vol. 50, Nos. 4–5, special edn.

Keen, David. 1998. 'The Economic Functions of Violence in Civil Wars.' *Adelphi Paper 320*. London: International Institute for Strategic Studies.

Kellah, Amie-Tejan. 2007. 'Establishing Services in Post-conflict Sierra Leone.' *Forced Migration Review*, No. 27. January.

Kreutz, Joakim, Nicholas Marsh, and Manuela Torre. 2007. *Regaining State Control: Arms and Violence in Post-Conflict Countries*. Unpublished background paper. Oslo: International Peace Research Institute.

Langer, A. 2008. 'When Do Horizontal Inequalities Lead to Conflict? Lessons from a Comparative Study of Ghana and Côte d'Ivoire.' In Frances Stewart, ed. *Horizontal Inequalities and Conflict: Understanding Group Violence in Multiethnic Societies*. London: Palgrave Macmillan, pp. 163–89.

Lester, David. 1993. 'The Effect of War on Suicide Rates: A Study of France from 1826 to 1913.' *European Archives of Psychiatry and Clinical Neuroscience*, Vol. 242, No. 4, pp. 248–49.

Licklider, Roy. 1995. 'The Consequences of Negotiated Settlements in Civil Wars, 1945–1993.' *American Political Science Review*, Vol. 89, No. 3, pp. 681–90.

Mac Ginty, Roger. 2006. 'Post-Accord Crime.' In John Darby, ed. *Violence and Reconstruction.* Notre Dame, IN: University of Notre Dame, pp. 101–19.

Mancini, Luca. 2008. 'Horizontal Inequality and Communal Violence: Evidence from Indonesian Districts.' In Frances Stewart, ed. *Horizontal Inequalities and Conflict: Understanding Group Violence in Multiethnic Societies.* London: Palgrave Macmillan, pp. 106–135.

Moser, Caroline. 2004. 'Urban Violence and Insecurity: An Introductory Roadmap.' *Environment and Urbanization,* Vol. 16, No. 2. October, pp. 3–16.

—. 2006. 'Reducing Urban Violence in Developing Countries.' *Global Views,* No 1. Washington, DC: Brookings Institution.

Moses, Norton. 1997. *Lynching and Vigilantism in the United States: An Annotated Bibliography.* Westport, CT: Greenwood Press.

Muggah, Robert. 2005. 'No Magic Bullet: A Critical Perspective on Disarmament, Demobilization and Reintegration (DDR) and Weapons Reduction in Post-Conflict Contexts.' *The Commonwealth Journal of International Affairs,* Vol. 94, No. 379, pp. 239–52.

—. 2007. 'Great Expectations: (Dis)Integrated DDR in Haiti and Sudan.' *Humanitarian Exchange Magazine,* Iss. 37. March. <http://www.odihpn.org/report.asp?id=2878>

—. 2008a. *Relocation Failures in Sri Lanka: A Short History of Internal Displacement and Resettlement.* London: Zed Books.

—, ed. 2008b. *Security and Post-Conflict Reconstruction: Dealing with Fighters in the Aftermath of War.* New York: Routledge.

— and Stevenson, Chris. Forthcoming. 'On the Edge: Armed Violence in Central America.' *World Bank Regional Report: Central America.* Washington, DC: World Bank.

— and Nat Colletta. 2009. 'Promoting Post-Conflict Security from the Bottom Up.' *Journal of Security Sector Management,* March.

— and Keith Krause. 2009. 'Closing the Gap between Peace Operations and Post-Conflict Insecurity: Towards a Violence Reduction Agenda.' *International Peacekeeping,* Vol. 16 No. 1, pp. 136–50.

Nathan, Laurie. 2005. 'The Frightful Inadequacy of Most of the Statistics: A Critique of Collier and Hoeffler on Causes of Civil War.' *Discussion Paper No. 11.* London: Crisis States Research Centre, London School of Economics and Political Science.

OECD–DAC (Organisation for Economic Co-operation and Development–Development Assistance Committee). 2007. *Handbook on Security Sector Reform: Supporting Security and Justice.* Paris: OECD.

—. 2008a. *Armed Violence Reduction Policy Paper.* Paris: Small Arms Survey/The SecDev Group.

—. 2008b. *Guidance on Evaluating Conflict Prevention and Peacebuilding Activities.* Paris: OECD.

—. 2008c. *Concepts and Dilemmas of State Building in Fragile Situations: From Fragility to Resilience.* Paris: OECD.

—. 2008d. *State Building in Situations of Fragility: Initial Findings.* Paris: OECD. <http://www.oecd.org/dataoecd/62/9/41212290.pdf>

Østby, Gudrun. 2008. 'Polarization, Horizontal Inequalities and Violent Civil Conflict.' *Journal of Peace Research,* Vol. 45, No. 2, pp. 143–62.

Pugh, Michael. 2005. 'The Political Economy of Peacebuilding: A Critical Theory Perspective.' *International Journal of Peace Studies,* Vol. 10, No. 2, pp. 23–42.

Regan, Patrick. 2009. *Sixteen Million and One.* New York: Paradigm Press.

Reynal-Querol, Marta. 2002. 'Ethnicity, Political Systems, and Civil Wars'. *Journal of Conflict Resolution,* Vol. 46, No. 1, pp. 29–54.

Rodgers, Dennis. 2004. '"Disembedding" the City: Crime, Insecurity and Spatial Organization in Managua, Nicaragua'. *Environment and Urbanization,* Vol. 16, No. 2, pp. 113–24.

—. 2006. 'The State as a Gang: Conceptualizing the Governmentality of Violence in Contemporary Nicaragua.' *Critique of Anthropology,* Vol. 26, No. 3, pp. 315–30.

—. 2007. 'Slum Wars of the 21st Century: The New Geography of Conflict in Central America.' Working Paper No. 10. London: Crisis States Research Centre, London School of Economics and Political Science.

Roggio, Bill. 2007. *The Long War Journal: The Sunni Awakening.* 3 May. <http://www.longwarjournal.org/archives/2007/05/the_sunni_awakening.php>

Rusagara, Frank. 2004. 'Military Integration as an Integral Part of the Peacebuilding Process in Transition to Democratic Governance.' Unpublished mimeo. Kigali, Rwanda.

Saferworld et al. 2006. *Creating Safer Communities: Lessons from South Eastern Europe.* London: Balkan Youth Union, Centre for Security Studies, CIVIL, Forum for Civic Initiatives, and Saferworld. <http://www.saferworld.org.uk/publications.php?id=236>

Sambanis, Nicholas. 2004. 'What Is Civil War? Conceptual and Empirical Complexities of an Operational Definition.' *Journal of Conflict Resolution,* Vol 48, No. 6, pp. 814–58.

Sisk, Timothy. 2001. 'Peacemaking in Civil Wars: Obstacles, Options and Opportunities.' Occasional Paper 20. Notre Dame, IL: Kroc Institute of International Peace Studies, University of Notre Dame.

Small, Melvin and David Singer. 1982. *Resort to Arms: International and Civil Wars, 1816–1980.* Beverly Hills, CA: Sage.

Small Arms Survey. 2005. *Small Arms Survey 2005: Weapons at War.* Oxford: Oxford University Press, pp. 229–89.

—. 2006. *Small Arms Survey 2006: Unfinished Business.* Oxford: Oxford University Press.

—. 2007. *Small Arms Survey 2007: Guns and the City.* Cambridge: Cambridge University Press, pp. 161–88.

—. 2008. *Small Arms Survey 2008: Risk and Resilience.* Cambridge: Cambridge University Press, pp. 211–98.

Somasundaram, D. J. and S. Rajadurai. 1995. 'War and Suicide in Northern Sri Lanka.' *Acta Psychiatrica Scandinavica,* Vol. 91, No. 1, pp. 1–4.

Spear, Joanna. 2006. 'From Political Economies of War to Political Economies of Peace: The Contribution of DDR after Wars of Predation.' *Contemporary Security Policy,* Vol. 27, No. 1, pp. 168–89.

Staveteig, Sarah. 2005. 'The Young and the Restless: Population Age Structure and Civil War.' *Environmental Change and Security Project Report,* Iss. 11, pp. 12–19.

Stedman, Stephen. 1997. 'Spoiler Problems in Peace Processes.' *International Security*, Vol. 22, No. 2, pp. 5–53.

—, Donald Rothchild, and Elizabeth Cousens. 2002. *Ending Civil Wars: The Implementation of Peace Agreements*. Boulder: Lynne Rienner Publishers.

Stewart, Frances. 2008. 'Horizontal Inequalities and Conflict: An Introduction and Some Hypotheses.' In Frances Stewart, ed. *Horizontal Inequalities and Conflict: Understanding Group Violence in Multiethnic Societies*. London: Palgrave Macmillan, pp. 3–24.

—, Graham Brown, and Arnim Langer. 2008. 'Policies towards Horizontal Inequalities.' In Frances Stewart, ed. *Horizontal Inequalities and Conflict: Understanding Group Violence in Multiethnic Societies*. London: Palgrave Macmillan, pp. 301–25.

Suhrke, Astri and Ingrid Samset. 2007. 'What's in a Figure? Estimating Recurrence of Civil War.' *International Peacekeeping*, Vol. 14, No. 2, pp. 195–203.

Tilly, Charles. 1995. 'Democracy is a Lake.' In George Reid Andrews and Herrick Chapman, eds. *The Social Construction of Democracy, 1870–1990*. New York: New York University Press, pp. 365–87.

—. 2003. *The Politics of Collective Violence*. Cambridge: Cambridge University Press.

TLAVA (Timor–Leste Armed Violence Assessment). n.d. <http://www.timor-leste-violence.org/>

UCDP (Uppsala Conflict Data Program). 2008. Conflict Termination Dataset, v. 2.0, 1946–2006. Data retrieved 18 June 2008. Uppsala: Department of Peace and Conflict Research.

UNDDR (United Nations Disarmament, Demobilization and Reintegration Resource Centre). 2006. *Integrated Disarmament, Demobilization and Reintegration Standards*. New York: UNDDR. <http://www.unddr.org/iddrs>

UNDP (United Nations Development Programme). 2008. *Post-Conflict Economic Recovery: Enabling Local Ingenuity*. New York: UNDP. <http://www.undp.org/cpr/content/economic_recovery/PCER_rev.pdf>

UNFPA (United Nations Population Division). 2007. *Population Prospects, the 2006 Revision*. New York: United Nations. <http://www.un.org/esa/population/publications/wpp2006/wpp2006.htm>

UNGA (United Nations General Assembly). 2008. 'The Situation in Afghanistan and Its Implications for International Peace and Security.' A/62/722–S/2008/159. 6 March.

UNHCR (United Nations High Commissioner for Refugees). 2008. *2007 Global Trends: Refugees, Asylum-seekers, Returnees, Internally Displaced and Stateless Persons*. Geneva: UNHCR.

UNICEF (United Nations Children's Fund). 2005. *The Impact of Conflict on Women and Girls in West and Central Africa and the UNICEF Response*. UNICEF. February.

UNODC (United Nations Office on Drugs and Crime). 2005. *Crime and Development in Africa*. Vienna: UNODC.

UNOWA (United Nations Office for West Africa). 2007. *Urbanization and Insecurity in West Africa: Populations Movements, Mega Cities and Regional Stability*. Dakar: UNOWA.

Urdal, Henrik. 2006. 'A Clash of Generations? Youth Bulges and Political Violence.' *International Studies Quarterly*, Vol. 50, No. 3, pp. 607–30.

USDOJ (United States Department of Justice). *Bureau of Justice Statistics: Data Online*. Accessed 1 May 2008. <http://www.ojp.usdoj.gov/bjs>

Waiselfisz, Julio Jacobo. 2008. *Mapa da Violência: Os Jovens da América Latina: 2008*. Brasilia: Instituto Sangari. <http://www.ritla.net/index.php?option=com_content&task=view&id=4759&Itemid=284>

Walter, Barbara F. 2004. 'Does Conflict Beget Conflict? Explaining Recurring Civil War.' *Journal of Peace Research*, Vol. 41, No. 3, pp. 371–88.

Weinstein, Jeremy. 2007. *Inside Rebellion: The Politics of Insurgent Violence*. Cambridge: Cambridge University Press.

White, Richard. 1981. 'Outlaw Gangs of the Middle Border: American Social Bandits.' *Western Historical Quarterly*, Vol. 12, No. 4, pp. 387–408.

WHO (World Health Organization). 2008a. *A Hard Pill to Swallow: Collective Violence in Africa*. WHO Report on Violence in Africa. Oxford: Oxford University Press.

—. 2008b. *Preventing Violence and Reducing Its Impact: How Development Agencies and Governments Can Help*. Geneva: WHO.

WOLA (Washington Office for Latin America). 2008. *Daring to Care: Community-Based Responses to Youth Gang Violence in Central America and Central American Immigrant Communities in the United States*. WOLA Special Report. Washington, DC: WOLA.

World Bank. 1997. *Framework for World Bank Involvement in Post-Conflict Countries*. Washington, DC: World Bank.

—. 1998a. *Post-Conflict Reconstruction: The Role of the World Bank*. Washington, DC: World Bank.

—. 1998b. *The World Bank's Experience with Post-Conflict Reconstruction*. Washington, DC: World Bank.

Zuercher, Christoph. 2006. 'Is More Better? Evaluating External-Led State-Building after 1989.' CDDRL Working Papers, No. 54. April.

ACKNOWLEDGEMENTS

Principal author

Robert Muggah

Contributors

Katherine Aguirre Tobón, Christine Bell, and Virginia Fortna

Former members of the Free Aceh Movement hold up their weapons before handing them over to the Aceh Monitoring Mission in Banda Aceh, December 2005. © Tarmizy Harva/Reuters

The Limits of DDR

REINTEGRATION LESSONS FROM ACEH

8

INTRODUCTION

The signing of the Helsinki peace agreement in August 2005 sought to bring an end to nearly 30 years of secessionist conflict in Aceh. The province, at Indonesia's western-most tip, provided a setting for reintegration programming aimed at consolidating a nascent peace. Under the Helsinki Memorandum of Understanding (MoU), the rebel Free Aceh Movement (Gerakan Aceh Merdeka or GAM) was to hand in 840 weapons and its members were to be demobilized (GoI and GAM, 2005, paras. 4.3, 4.2). Section three of the agreement focused on reintegration with clauses stipulating assistance for former combatants, pardoned political prisoners, and victims of war. The Indonesian government established a reintegration agency (Badan Reintegrasi-Damai Aceh, the BRA) and international agencies lined up to support reintegration programmes and processes.

Three-and-a-half years on, Aceh is a much more peaceful place. GAM handed in its firearms, which were subsequently destroyed, Indonesian troops moved out of Aceh, and elections for a provincial governor and district heads passed off smoothly. A former rebel leader won the governorship, many former GAM rebels were installed as district heads, and GAM transformed itself into a political party (Partai Aceh) ready to contest local legislative elections in April 2009. Security has improved markedly and support for peace in Aceh is almost universal. Unsurprisingly, Aceh has been presented as a model with potential application for other troubled spots (Morfit, 2007; Husain, 2007).[1] The award of the Nobel Peace Prize to former Finnish President Martti Ahtisaari, who chaired the Helsinki talks, was but confirmation of the massive turn-around in Aceh.

Yet while the Aceh post-war story is a broadly positive one, the experience of delivering reintegration support to former combatants and others is not. There has been widespread disillusionment with the ways in which reintegration assistance has been provided and the impacts it has had. The year 2008 saw a rise in localized violent conflict, often involving former combatants. Many of the people who were affected by the conflict remain much worse off than others in the province. Ineffective reintegration assistance is viewed by many in Aceh and Jakarta as a cause of these problems and a potential 'time bomb' for the peace process (Hariyanto, 2008). There are concerns that the peace is more fragile than some suspect (ICG, 2007a; 2008). As Aceh enters its fourth year of peace, the finding that only around half of countries coming out of armed conflict make it through ten years without relapse is frequently cited in Aceh (Collier et al., 2003; POST-CONFLICT SECURITY).

In exploring the reasons why peace has held thus far in Aceh and the role reintegration programmes have played, this chapter seeks to draw out lessons for international disarmament, demobilization, and reintegration (DDR) programming. It features new and original data on reintegration in Aceh, drawing upon a number of World Bank studies conducted in the province over the past four years. These include two representative surveys of former combatants carried out in 2006 and 2008 (the latter also including interviews with more than 3,000 civilian households), ongoing conflict monitoring, an Aceh-wide survey of infrastructure damage and social relations, and a provincial poverty

Map 8.1 **Aceh**

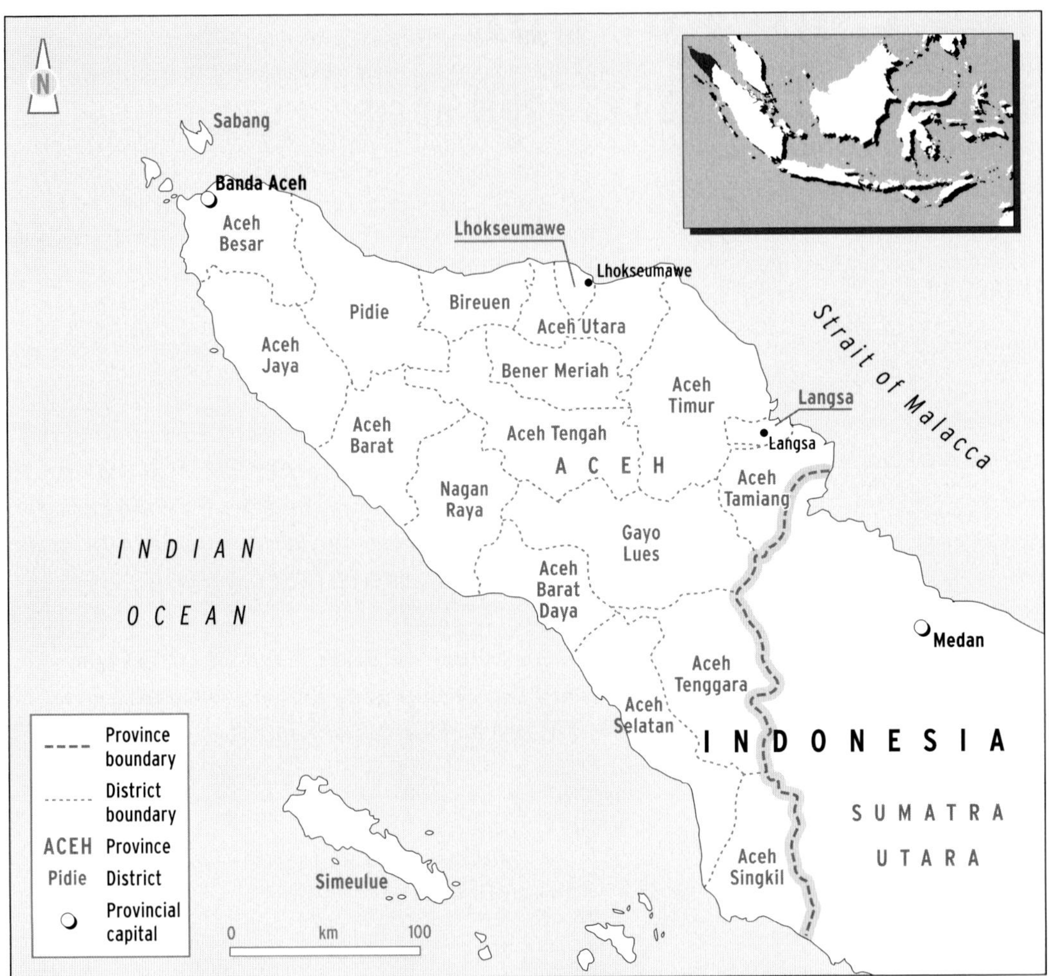

assessment (see Box 8.1). The chapter, and the data it uses, builds upon a growing body of micro-studies and surveys of ex-combatants that have been conducted in post-war countries such as Colombia, Ethiopia, Liberia, Sierra Leone, Timor–Leste, and Uganda.[2] Such data allows for a rigorous evaluation of how reintegration efforts have proceeded and how these programmes have succeeded (or failed) and why.

Among the main findings of the chapter are the following:

- The main reasons for the success of the peace process in Aceh to date are the high-level commitment from the leadership of both sides and widespread support for peace among the people of Aceh.
- Reintegration programmes for former combatants have not played a key role in supporting peace. At times, the way assistance has been provided has increased tensions.
- The approach to reintegration implemented in Aceh stems in part from a set of assumptions about the situation of former combatants and their relationship with non-combatants. Derived from other post-war settings, many of these do not fit well with the Aceh experience.

- Social cohesion between combatants and non-combatants is strong in Aceh. Former combatants are more likely to be employed than non-combatants, rendering targeted assistance unnecessary in many cases.
- The provision of cash to individuals has had little impact on their welfare and has instead fuelled disillusionment among many former combatants and non-combatants.
- The failure to link—even partially—the reintegration programme to tsunami reconstruction and broader development efforts left key post-war issues unresolved and, moreover, exacerbated inequality in Aceh.

The chapter proceeds by summarizing the genesis, evolution, and settlement of the Aceh conflict and highlights some of the emerging problems in the post-war period. It then looks at how reintegration programmes have been implemented in Aceh, including the extent of their reliance on principles derived from international experience. The chapter then focuses on three weaknesses of the reintegration and broader post-war programme in Aceh using data from the World Bank studies. It concludes with a short summary of potential ways forward in the province, drawing attention to the implications of the Aceh experience for reintegration programming elsewhere.

Box 8.1 Data sources used in this chapter

The **GAM Reintegration Needs Assessment** was conducted by the World Bank between October 2005 and March 2006. Qualitative fieldwork in half of Aceh's districts explored progress on reintegration, emerging post-conflict issues, and how people had benefited from aid. A statistically representative survey of 642 former GAM combatants and prisoners was implemented with members of the European Union-led Aceh Monitoring Mission (AMM) acting as enumerators. The World Bank has outlined the results (World Bank, 2006a).

The **Aceh Reintegration and Livelihoods Surveys (ARLS)** comprise original data on more than 3,000 civilians, a statistically representative sample of more than 1,000 ex-combatants, and more than 800 village heads. The surveys were conducted in all 248 of Aceh's urban and rural sub-districts. They collect information on numerous factors that affect the reintegration of civilians and ex-combatants, including social cohesion, economic livelihoods, attitudes towards government, and conflict-affectedness. The ARLS was designed by researchers from Columbia and Stanford universities together with the World Bank and was implemented in July-September 2008.[4]

Data on conflict trends in Aceh is from the World Bank's **Aceh Conflict Monitoring Updates**, which are published monthly. Local media are monitored, with all incidents of reported conflict clipped, coded, and entered into a master database. The monitoring also involves regular field trips around the province to investigate particular incidents and emerging trends.

The 2008 **Aceh Poverty Assessment** looks at the impact of the conflict, the tsunami, and reconstruction on poverty (World Bank, 2008e). It draws on data from government surveys such as SUSENAS,[5] which it combines with secondary data collected on the ground in Aceh.

The **Aceh Village Survey** was administered through the World Bank/Government of Indonesia's Kecamatan Development Program (World Bank/KDP, 2007). Local facilitators in almost all rural villages in Aceh collected data on the degree of infrastructure damage from the conflict and tsunami, and on various dimensions of local social life including flows of internally displaced persons (IDPs), social cohesion, and access to information.

CONFLICT AND PEACE IN ACEH

Armed conflict in Aceh has ebbed and flowed since 1976, resulting in somewhere between 12,000 and 20,000 violent deaths (Aspinall, forthcoming). As with most wars, a number of plausible explanations can be given for why it occurred and persisted. The most common relate to the capture of rents from natural resource extraction, state-perpetuated violence and repression, and the mobilization of a distinct Acehnese identity for violent purposes (Barron and Clark, 2006). Grievances among the Acehnese over the capture of oil and gas revenues by the central government added to prior resentment of a perceived domination of national Indonesian culture by the island of Java (Sulaiman, 2006; Ross, 2005). Promises that Aceh would receive political and cultural autonomy were broken, compounding dissatisfaction (Miller, 2006). The horrific counter-insurgency tactics of the Indonesian military served to increase perceived alienation and GAM was able to recruit widely across the province (Schulze, 2004). Lack of economic development despite Aceh's abundant resources, and the perceived ineptitude and corruption of the state, led many in Aceh to feel that separation from Indonesia was necessary (Barron and Clark, 2006).

The establishment of a military operations zone, with tens of thousands of Indonesian troops pouring into Aceh, led to an escalation of conflict in 1989. A series of failed attempts at negotiating peace from 2000 resulted in the implementation of martial law in Aceh in May 2003 (Sukma, 2004). Aceh was largely closed off to the outside world as all-out war led to serious human rights abuses (HRW, 2003; AI, 2004).

Three factors coalesced in late 2004 and early 2005 to make Aceh ripe for peace. First, the election of President Susilo Bambang Yudhoyono and his deputy, Jusuf Kalla, resulted in a new impetus from Jakarta to find a peaceful solution. Kalla had been involved in past attempts to bring peace to other troubled parts of Indonesia and had used intermediaries to probe the GAM leadership's desire for a settlement (Husain, 2007). Yudhoyono, a former military leader, commanded respect from the army's top brass. He quickly replaced some senior military leaders with reformists, thereby securing a new ability to guarantee peace once an agreement was found (Morfit, 2007).

Second, there was a change in calculus from GAM. The movement had been decimated by martial law, with many combatants killed or imprisoned and many others leaving Aceh. GAM leaders also realized that support for independence from the international community was increasingly unlikely, given the lack of international support for the independence of a small Muslim state astride the shipping lanes of the Strait of Malacca in the post-9/11 environment; GAM turned to a strategy of demanding increased political and economic autonomy (Barron and Burke, 2008, pp. 10–11).

A worker builds a house for a tsunami victim near Banda
December 2007. © Tarmizy Harva/Reuters

Third, the Indian Ocean tsunami of December 2004, which killed at least 167,000 people in Aceh alone, played a part. Thousands of aid agencies poured into the troubled province. In this environment, all-out offences from either side could not take place (Awaluddin, 2008). The tsunami created a face-saving opportunity for both sides to acknowledge that different approaches were needed. The preamble to the Helsinki MoU noted the moral imperative of both parties to work towards peace. The windfall of post-tsunami aid also strengthened the incentives of GAM to support peace, with former combatants having opportunities as direct beneficiaries and with jobs and contracts for reconstruction work.[6] International demands that reconstruction funds be used effectively made a continuation of war unthinkable for a government keen on boosting its image as a rising democratic power (Barron and Burke, 2008).

Five rounds of negotiations resulted in the Helsinki MoU, which the Government of Indonesia and GAM signed on 15 August 2005. An unarmed Aceh Monitoring Mission (AMM), staffed and funded by the European Union (EU) and the Association of Southeast Asian Nations (ASEAN), arrived to oversee the implementation of the deal. Relatively problem-free early implementation of the agreement was accompanied by a remarkable improvement in security. Predictions of a spate of revenge attacks issued at the time the MoU was signed proved incorrect (Barron, Clark, and Daud, 2005; ICG, 2005a); throughout 2006, only three serious incidents involving GAM and the military were reported by the local media. Where incidents occurred, both sides worked together to resolve them and local tensions did not escalate (World Bank, 2006b).

Yet while high-level commitment to the peace agreement from both sides has remained intact, cases of violence in Aceh were on the rise in 2008 (see Figure 8.1). As in other post-war contexts, these acts of violence differed in nature from those of the war era (POST-CONFLICT SECURITY). Whereas past clashes tended to be between GAM combatants and government troops, new incidents involved a wider range of actors. On 1 March 2008, five former combatants were brutally murdered in the central highlands by a gang affiliated with pro-Indonesia militias (World Bank, 2008a). In May and June, a series of incidents along the central highlands and North Aceh border conflated community-level problems with broader political tensions (World Bank, 2008b). In July, a shoot-out between police and a group of renegade former GAM fighters resulted in four deaths

Figure 8.1 **Violent conflicts in Aceh, January 2005–December 2008**

■ Local-level violent incidents ■ GAM-GoI incidents

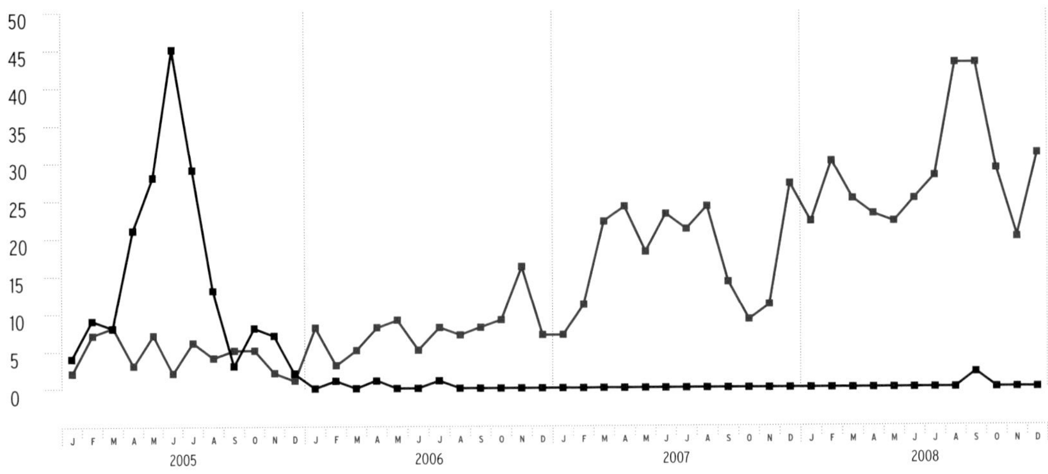

Source: Correspondence with Adrian Morel, head of World Bank conflict monitoring work, February 2009

(ICG, 2008). In July and August 2008, 19 people died from conflicts in Aceh, with 23 injured in August alone. Forty-three cases of violent conflict were reported in August 2008, 70 per cent higher than the average monthly total from January to July 2008 (World Bank, 2008c); the number of new violent conflict incidents remained the same in September 2008 (World Bank, 2008d).[7] The number of cases of violence subsequently fell, only to rise sharply in December 2008. From October 2006 to the end of 2008, World Bank monitoring shows 39 violent conflict incidents involving the use of firearms and 20 violent conflict incidents involving the use of explosives.[8]

The police have claimed that the number of armed crimes is 22 times higher than before the Helsinki MoU was signed (Jones, 2008), although no doubt crime was to some extent hidden during the conflict era, with criminal incidents reported and recorded as conflict incidents.[9] Influential think tanks such as the International Crisis Group, aid agencies, government officials, and GAM itself have frequently attributed these problems to the ineffective implementation of reintegration programmes in Aceh (ICG, 2007a; World Bank/DSF, 2007, p. 5; Bean and Knezevic, 2008).

INTERNATIONAL MODELS FOR REINTEGRATION

There is global consensus on the importance of programmes to support the reintegration of former combatants into civilian life following peace settlements. Since 1989, when the United Nations Security Council sanctioned an operation in Namibia, more than 60 DDR programmes have been launched (Muggah, 2009). As development agencies have increasingly invested in DDR as a 'central pillar of military–civilian transition operations', such programmes have proliferated (Muggah, 2005). As Kees Kingma notes, reintegration, along with disarmament and demobilization, 'are now compulsory elements of new peacekeeping and peace enforcement operations' (Kingma, 2001, p. 1).[10]

The rapid rise of DDR as a tool for post-war support—by 2007, the annual budget for DDR exceeded USD 630 million (Muggah, 2009)—has not been accompanied by an extensive discussion on its suitability to all post-war contexts.

This is particularly worrying given the broad lack of empirical evidence allowing for an assessment of impacts as well as comparative analyses of where different approaches work (or not) and why (Humphreys and Weinstein, 2007).

A set of orthodoxies informing the design and implementation of reintegration programmes in a vast array of post-war environments has emerged nevertheless. A number of frameworks for DDR, most notably the UN Integrated DDR Standards (IDDRS) and the Stockholm Initiative on DDR, have been developed (UNDDR, 2006; Swedish MFA, 2006). These reflect decades of policy and practice and consolidate 'best practice' and 'lessons learned'; as such, they are the repository of a kind of conventional wisdom. The principles embodied in such frameworks provided a rationale for reintegration programming in Aceh and helped shape the design of such programmes.[11] The reintegration model is based on the following five tenets.

A set of orthodoxies informing reintegration programmes has emerged.

Unique challenges for former combatants. The fundamental basis for reintegration programming is the recognition that there are immediate and unique challenges associated with consolidating peace at both the individual and the community level. Individuals who fought during the war era face incentive structures that may discourage them from pursuing peaceful lives. Former combatants may not have the skills to undertake new non-violent, income-generating activities. These difficulties may be compounded by the lack of working opportunities in post-conflict economies (Collier, 1994). Unemployed combatants can place strains on the social fabric of communities, dependent on support networks that were weakened by war. Experience of conflict, and resultant trauma, can lead to behaviour that increases tensions and the risk of local conflict (Husain et al., 1998).

Targeted reintegration programmes preferred. The natural extension of this logic is that there is a need for reintegration programmes focusing specifically on the economic, social, and political needs of former combatants. The market and regular development expenditures are unlikely to provide for former combatants for a number of reasons, including: relative lack of education of former combatants compared to the general population; discrimination in hiring them; risk avoidance from those implementing development programmes; and anti-social or uncooperative attitudes acquired by combatants during wartime. Reintegration programmes tend to assume that they can identify a cadre of former combatants who should be targeted for reintegration assistance. The IDDRS, the key reference for reintegration programmers, sets out procedures for data collection to determine the size of the caseload (UNDDR, 2006, module 4.30, pp. 8–9, 20). It then calls for provision of assistance to individual combatants (UNDDR, 2006, pp. 17–18, 25–26).

Prioritizing security over development. The primary aim of assisting combatants and affected communities is to stabilize peace. Complex political and economic interests shape the extent to which different individuals and groups are motivated to invest in peace; spoilers may aim to wreck peace efforts through conflictual behaviour (Stedman, 1997). In the short run, buying off these groups or individuals is viewed as being more important than pursuing development impacts. Programmes focusing on development and broader recovery, and benefiting broader populations, can come later. As the IDDRS observes, 'DDR is a *precondition,* and not a substitute, for recovery interventions aimed specifically at vulnerable groups' (UNDDR, 2006, module 4.30, p. 6, emphasis added). This overriding security focus can justify a certain lack of transparency and inequitable targeting of reintegration assistance in the short run (UNDDR, 2006, module 2.10, pp. 8–11).[12]

Building state capacity not the immediate priority. The reintegration model emphasizes the importance of support being delivered quickly on the ground at the expense of a longer-term emphasis on enhancing the ability of the state to assume this role. This guideline largely reflects the fact that almost two-thirds of reintegration initiatives have been implemented in African countries (Muggah, 2009, p. 6). While it is recognized that conflict is often a result of weak or illegitimate state structures and practices, and that conflict in turn weakens these further, the primary focus of reintegration is not on building state capacity or citizen–state relations. According to the prevailing doctrine, such considerations can be addressed later, once immediate security challenges are dealt with.[13]

Separate implementation structures. The importance of ensuring that programmes are delivered quickly, combined with the weakness of state bodies in most post-conflict contexts, may necessitate the development of implementation structures outside of regular government systems. The IDDRS assumes that the UN will play a coordinating role and that international funds will be the primary resources for reintegration.[14]

DDR IN ACEH

The Helsinki MoU contains a set of provisions that form the basis of Aceh's DDR programme. GAM was to demobilize all of its 3,000 military troops while decommissioning all 'arms, ammunition and explosives' held by its members (GoI and GAM, 2006, paras. 4.2, 4.3). As discussed in Box 8.2, 840 weapons were to be handed to the Aceh Monitoring Mission.

Box 8.2 Disposing of the guns

The Helsinki agreement committed GAM to handing 840 arms to AMM in four stages by 31 December 2005, just four-and-a-half months after the MoU was signed. Table 8.1 lists the number of weapons collected during the process.

In addition, 4,849 rounds of assorted ammunition were handed over and destroyed, as well as many explosives, largely home-made 40 mm grenades (exact numbers are not available).

Firearms were of varying quality. The MoU did not stipulate what an eligible firearm was but GAM and the Government of Indonesia subsequently agreed on a basic set of standards: the gun had to have a steel chamber and barrel and had to be capable of firing munitions. Firearms, munitions, and explosives were submitted in bulk by GAM representatives at public ceremonies across the province. AMM monitors publicly cut each weapon into three parts using 1.7-kw rotary cutting machines powered by mobile generators after AMM had 'verified' each weapon to ensure it met with the required standards. The last weapon-cutting ceremony took place in Banda Aceh on 21 December 2005. The decommissioning was declared a success by GAM, the military, and AMM.

It is widely felt that more weapons exist in Aceh, and that former rebels (and others) can access these. However, the weapons destruction helped build confidence between the two sides and no one from either side has publicly discussed the issue of remaining arms. Where former combatants have been involved in armed crime, GAM spokespersons have said that they are acting alone, as GAM has already surrendered its guns.

Sources: AMM internal reports; Frodin (2008)

Table 8.1 Firearms collected by AMM during four-phase decommissioning, 2005

Phase	Date	No. of firearms handed in	Number of firearms accepted by AMM*
1	15-18 September	279	243
2	mid-October	291	233
3	mid-November	286	222
4	December	162	142
Total		**1,018**	**840**

* The AMM only accepted fully functional firearms.

The MoU also contains provisions for a reintegration programme. 'Economic assistance' of undefined levels and forms was to be given to former combatants, amnestied prisoners, and civilian victims. Infrastructure damaged by the conflict was also to be repaired (see Box 8.3).

The impetus for including the reintegration provisions came from the international officials who were brokering the Helsinki talks (Kingsbury, 2006, p. 41). Reintegration was not a priority for either GAM or the Indonesian government negotiators. GAM disliked the use of the term reintegration from the start as they felt it implied a division between combatant and community members that did not exist. On several occasions during early post-Helsinki sittings of the Committee on Security Arrangements (the meetings between GAM and the Indonesian government chaired by the Aceh Monitoring Mission), GAM asked that the word not be used in discussions (Barron and Burke, 2008, p. 35). From the government's perspective, reintegration was a side issue, of much less importance than other issues such as security and the legal status of Aceh. While neither side objected to the reintegration provisions being included, it was a low-priority part of the deal. This meant there was little if any haggling over the MoU's reintegration clauses.

Box 8.3 The Helsinki MoU and reintegration

The Helsinki MoU provides the basis for reintegration programming in Aceh in the following stipulations:

- Measures should be taken to 'assist persons who have participated in GAM activities to facilitate their reintegration into civil society'. This involves the provision of 'economic assistance to former combatants, political prisoners and affected civilians' (para. 3.2.3).
- Public and private property destroyed or damaged in the conflict should be rehabilitated (para 3.2.4).
- 'Farming land, employment or, in the case of incapacity to work, adequate social security' should be given to the same population groups (para. 3.2.5).
- A Reintegration Fund to pay for these programmes should be established by the authorities of Aceh (para. 3.2.3).

Aceh's reintegration programme

Soon after the agreement was signed, the government started the process of working out what would be provided and to whom. The MoU stipulated that reintegration programmes were to be funded and administered by the Government of Indonesia and the Aceh authorities; the government in Jakarta consequently allocated a considerable sum of money, almost USD 190 million, to fund reintegration efforts. Donors sought to support the reintegration programme, too, contributing around USD 160 million (MSR, forthcoming).

A new reintegration agency under the control of the local Acehnese authorities, the Aceh Reintegration Agency, or BRA, was established in early 2006 to manage reintegration funds from Jakarta and local government and to coordinate assistance from the international donors. Together with Bappenas, Indonesia's powerful national planning agency in Jakarta, a programme was developed to provide assistance to former combatants and conflict-affected persons (see Table 8.2).

There were thus a number of BRA programmes:

- Programmes targeted former combatants on both sides of the conflict. Military troops leaving Aceh also received bonuses, although this came from a separate government allocation outside of the reintegration budget (Mietzner, 2006, p. 51).
- Programmes provided cash payments to others affected by the conflict. This includes cash payments to 1,059 victims, yearly compensation paid to people who lost family members, and assistance for physically disabled persons. While conflict victims' assistance was originally given to affected communities, with communities decid-

Table 8.2 **BRA reintegration programmes, 2005–07**[15]

No.	Category	Planned no. of beneficiaries	Form of assistance	Amount (USD)
Assistance to former conflict actors				
1	GAM combatants	3,000	Cash	2,500/person
2	GAM 'non-combatants'	6,200	Cash	1,000/person
3	Political prisoners	2,035	Cash	1,000/person
4	Pro-Indonesia militia group	5,000	Cash	1,000/person
5	GAM who surrendered before MoU (and who usually joined the militia groups)	3,204	Cash	500/person
6	Medical assistance	3 packets[16]	In-kind assistance	500,000/year
Assistance to conflict-affected persons				
7	Village-based assistance (2006–mid-2007)	1,724 villages	Village grants	6,000–17,000/village
8	Individual conflict victim assistance (mid- to late 2007)	1,059 persons	Cash	1,000/person
9	Compensation for loss of family member (*diyat*)	33,424 persons	Cash	300/person per year
10	Housing assistance	31,187 units	Cash allocation	3,000/house
11	Assistance for the physically disabled	14,932 persons	Cash	1,000/person

Note: This table uses the exchange rate USD 1 = IDR 10,000.

Sources: Forbes Damai Aceh (2007a; 2007b); BRA (2008); communication with BRA members

ing how to allocate funds, the approach was changed after one round to individually targeted cash payments (Aspinall, 2008; Barron and Burke, 2008, pp. 50–51; ICG, 2007a).

- Money was provided for houses for conflict victims and medical services for those in need.

Donor reintegration support

Donors funded three streams of programmes.[17] The first was technical assistance and advisory support provided to the BRA and Bappenas. UNDP and the US Agency for International Development (USAID) funded a cadre of national and international advisers who worked closely with both agencies to help shape the emerging reintegration programme. The United States established a Forum Bersama (Joint Forum) and Aceh Peace Resource Center, both of which aimed to create spaces and mechanisms for international actors to provide advice to the local and national bodies. Other aid agencies, including the World Bank, the International Organization for Migration (IOM), and the European Commission, also worked closely with the BRA and Bappenas, providing consultants, ad-hoc advice, and funding workshops and overseas trips to conferences and training on DDR and peace-building.

The second stream involved IOM's reintegration programme. IOM was the biggest international actor directly implementing reintegration programmes and has provided almost USD 20 million to former combatants and amnestied prisoners. In-kind assistance was issued to beneficiaries through Information Counselling and Referral Service centers, a standard model used by IOM in other post-war locations. In addition, IOM has been involved in providing cash grants to affected communities (approximately USD 6 million), in giving medicines and counselling to traumatized victims (approximately USD 2 million), and in providing training for the police (around USD 10 million).[18] A wide range of donors has supported these programmes, including the European Commission, Japan, USAID, UNDP, the World Bank, the Netherlands, Canada, and Norway. By and large, these projects have been implemented in parallel with BRA programmes. Despite efforts to share data on beneficiaries and divide up the caseload, few mechanisms were in place to ensure the same people did not get targeted by more than one programme (and, indeed, many did) (Barron and Burke, 2008).

Donors also funded local and international NGOs working in a range of reintegration-related areas. These have included support to IDPs, local capacity building, public information programmes, and conflict resolution training. The scale of such programmes, which collectively totalled around USD 70 million, was small compared with the amount of aid for post-tsunami reconstruction (see below). Around USD 5 million of analytical work on conflict issues was also conducted, primarily by the World Bank.

Internationally, many DDR programmes are financed through pooled funding mechanisms. In Aceh, this approach never materialized. A Multi-Donor Fund existed for tsunami reconstruction but reintegration and post-war reconstruction were not part of its mandate. The government sought to avoid the creation of a second fund, fearing that international stakeholders might attempt to take the lead in reintegration programming, thereby displacing the government. As a result, donors and aid agencies implemented their programmes in parallel, with relatively little coordination, and a common strategy was not developed (Barron and Burke, 2008).

While the post-war challenges in Aceh are not unique, they differ from those the reintegration model aims to address.

MISDIAGNOSING THE PROBLEM: REINTEGRATION NEEDS IN ACEH

The reintegration paradigm is built upon a number of assumptions about the social, political, and economic challenges former combatants face and this, in turn, has shaped the goals of reintegration programmes (Humphreys and Weinstein, 2007). These reflect the fact that most reintegration programmes have been implemented in sub-Saharan Africa, where civil wars have been largely of a 'symmetric, non-conventional' nature, with the loyalties of the population split between different factions and the state (Kalyvas, 2008). The civil war in Aceh was of a different nature: it was a popular movement for increased autonomy for Aceh rather than a (relatively) balanced struggle between competing groups for control of state resources. While the types of post-war challenges in Aceh are by no means unique, many of them differ from those that the reintegration model aims to address.

Social reintegration

In many civil wars, there are multiple conflicting parties, each of which command loyalty from sections of the local population. Reintegration programmes are designed to help heal the divides between former rivals, both combatants and their supporters. Tensions can also exist between former combatants and civilians if atrocities have been committed. The Aceh reintegration programme aimed to provide support to a wide range of groups in parallel in order to ensure that any latent tensions were not accentuated, and both donors and the government funded a number of local peace-building initiatives aimed at healing divides (Barron and Burke 2008).

Yet, in Aceh, intra- and inter-community relationships did not pose a major threat to peace. Relationships between GAM fighters and the civilian population remained strong throughout the conflict (ICG, 2007b).[19] Indeed, the boundaries between who was a combatant (in the jungle) and who was a sympathizer (in the village) were often blurred (Frodin, 2008). During the war, combatants returned to their villages for periods of rest or for special occasions; even during the height of the armed conflict, GAM members would go back to their villages at least once every few months to visit their families (Barron, Clark, and Daud, 2005, p. 29). Combatants also rotated, serving for limited periods of time before others took over their role. Many non-combatants played important supporting roles, sheltering those who were armed, providing them with food, reporting on military movements, and raising funds for the struggle. There was strong support for GAM's goals, if not always its means, among the civilian population in most areas of Aceh (Barron, Clark, and Daud, 2005, p. 28).

In Aceh, intra- and inter-community relationships did not pose a major threat to peace.

As a result, there was acceptance, indeed often celebrations, when combatants returned home after the peace deal, a situation that has been observed in other post-war cases such as Timor–Leste (Peake, 2009). Six months after the Helsinki MoU, a survey of 642 former combatants found that 90 per cent had experienced no problems on their return. In more than three-quarters of villages surveyed, traditional *peusijuk* (welcoming) ceremonies were held to celebrate the return of the combatants (World Bank, 2006a, p. 25). Even where active anti-GAM groups existed, such as in the central highlands, returnees experienced few problems of acceptance.

Many returning combatants felt such acceptance and celebrations were natural. As one former combatant explained:

> *We are the same as the villagers. We are their fathers, sons and grandsons; it's impossible for them not to accept us back into the village. Which parent would not accept the return of their son? It's like a happy reunion now.* (World Bank, 2006a, p. 23)

Indeed, the return of combatants has in most cases helped improve social cohesion. A World Bank survey in every village in Aceh in 2007 found almost two-thirds to have reported improvements in village solidarity since the MoU (World Bank/KDP, 2007, p. 78). Only 7.4 per cent of villagers interviewed said that there were low levels of trust between 'those who just returned from the mountain' and some other community members (p. 77).

As time has gone on, trust between former combatants and non-combatant villagers has not diminished. Of the more than 1,000 former GAM members surveyed in mid-2008, only seven have reported some difficulties in being accepted since they returned to their villages. In some areas of the central highlands, where pro-government militia were strong due to the presence of non-Acehnese ethnic groups such as the Gayo and Javanese, tensions are greater. Yet even here trust has been gradually growing, although there have been isolated cases of unrest, as discussed above. Across all of the areas surveyed, 97 per cent of female community members and 96 per cent of civilian men reported that the presence of former combatants was not a source of division within their village. Class differentials and, particularly, unequal access to aid were more likely to cause problems, as discussed below.

Survey evidence also shows remarkably high levels of trust between former combatants and non-combatant community members three years after the MoU (see Table 8.3). Ninety-five per cent of civilian men and 97 per cent of civilian women said that former combatants should be fully welcome in their village; 94 per cent and 95 per cent, respectively, said that they should be allowed membership of community associations. Around 90 per cent of informants said they would be happy to welcome former combatants into their family through marriage and that former combatants could be among their close friends.

Table 8.3 Dimensions of trust in former combatants: civilian respondents, by sex, mid-2008

Survey questions about ex-combatants	Percentage of positive responses	
	Men (n=1,794)	Women (n=1,237)
Should they be fully welcomed in this village?	95%	97%
Should they be allowed membership in community associations?	94%	95%
Could they be among your close friends?	92%	89%
Would you welcome them into your family through marriage?	89%	88%

Source: ARLS (2008)

Strong social relations between former combatants and the civilian population is reflected in the role that former combatants have been playing in community activities. Overall, this role is as large as that played by civilians. Former combatants are not facing major barriers to participating in village associations and community activities. As Table 8.4 shows, former combatants are actually more active in certain areas than non-combatant civilians. Larger proportions are active in religious groups, cultural and ethnic associations, and youth or sports groups. Ex-combatants are less likely to be involved in development and finance groups. However, they are more likely to be involved in other groups that involve a wide range of community members such as youth and sports groups or religious bodies (for men only).[20] The higher figures for membership in political groups for former combatants is likely to reflect their membership in the Komite Peralihan Aceh (Aceh Transition Committee, or KPA), the civilian body set up to represent the interests of former GAM. In the 2008 survey, all of the 1,086 ex-combatants interviewed reported never having been prevented from using social services, such as accessing health or educational services or participating in associations, by other villagers.

Table 8.4 Participation in community activities: GAM vs. civilians, by sex, mid-2008

Community group	Men		Women	
	Ex-combatant (n=1,024)	Civilian (n=1,794)	Ex-combatant (n=29)	Civilian (n=1,237)
Farmers or trader group, or professional association	37%	44%	31%	23%
Credit/finance group	15%	22%	0%	18%
Community development/self-help group	6%	37%	0%	26%
Religious group	80%	77%	54%	74%
Cultural/ethnic association	41%	28%	0%	9%
Political group	74%	14%	100%	2%
Youth or sports group	70%	44%	27%	6%
Women's group	3%	4%	38%	51%

Source: ARLS (2008)

These findings differ from those in some other post-war contexts. For example, a recent study in Liberia found evidence of friction between ex-combatants and their communities: 35 per cent of former combatants interviewed felt they were not viewed positively by their communities. These findings are also likely to be representative of the ex-combatant situation in neighbouring countries such as Sierra Leone and Côte d'Ivoire (Hill, Taylor, and Temin, 2008).[21]

Whether such acceptance will remain intact over a longer period of time is still an open question. Yet the findings thus far suggest that the focus of the reintegration model, and of some programmes in Aceh, on peace-building within and between communities may have relatively little relevance in Aceh.

Political reintegration

Successful post-war transitions inherently involve a move from the use of violent means to competition mediated through political processes (Paris, 2004). Ultimately, former combatants need to accept the legitimacy of state institutions. In many post-war contexts, this can be difficult, in particular where, as in Aceh, war has been ended through a negotiated settlement rather than an outright victory for the rebel group. It might have been expected that senior GAM commanders and representatives would be frustrated at their lack of immediate influence over policy-making. For lower-level combatants, accepting that power is mediated through formal political processes can also be difficult.

Yet survey evidence shows high levels of political participation by former combatants in Aceh. Former combatants were more likely to vote than the civilian population in the gubernatorial elections of late 2006 (see Table 8.5). In mid-2008, combatants and civilians were almost equally likely to say that they would vote in the elections for the next governor of Aceh. Only one-third of former combatants voted in the last presidential elections, compared with more than four-fifths of civilians. Yet by the middle of 2008, almost all former combatants said they would vote in the presidential elections taking place in 2009.

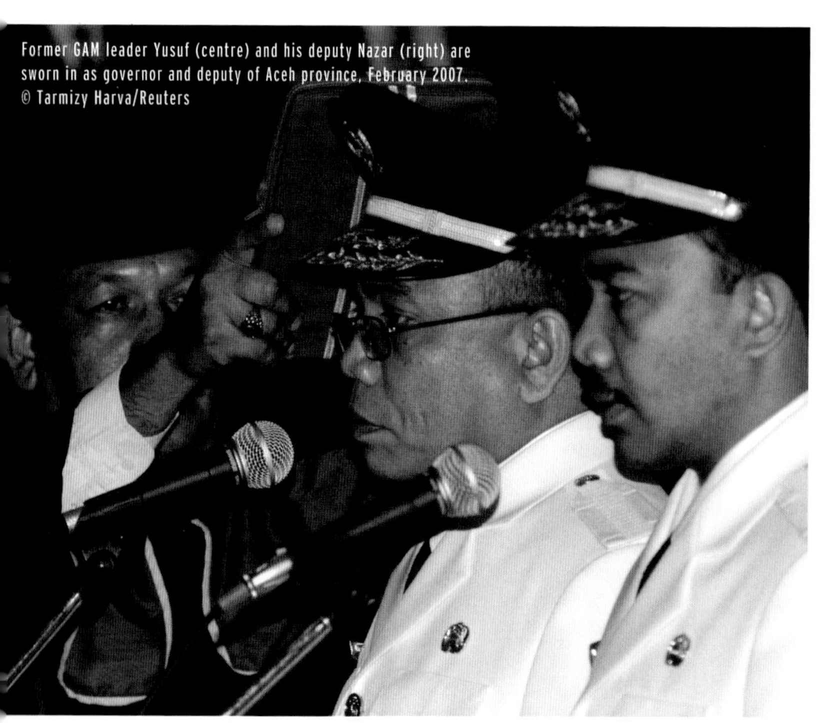
Former GAM leader Yusuf (centre) and his deputy Nazar (right) are sworn in as governor and deputy of Aceh province, February 2007. © Tarmizy Harva/Reuters

These findings reflect broad acceptance of political institutions and processes by former combatants. Political participation is not merely motivated by tactical or strategic considerations but by a desire to take advantage of the new opportunities afforded by the peace deal. For former GAM members, the Helsinki MoU provided rapid access to positions of power in the province. The gubernatorial and district head elections in December 2006 resulted in a landslide for the ex-rebel group. Irwandi Yusuf, the former GAM representative to the Aceh Monitoring Mission, and his running partner, Nazar, a former leader of the pro-independence referendum SIRA movement, beat the establishment candidates in one round for the governorship. GAM won in almost half of Aceh's districts. Elsewhere, candidates sought

Table 8.5 **Political activities: GAM vs. civilians, by sex, mid-2008**

Survey question	Men		Women	
	Ex-combatant (n=1,024)	Civilian (n=1,794)	Ex-combatant (n=29)	Civilian (n=1,237)
Did you vote in the last election for the governor of Aceh?	92%	88%	90%	88%
Do you plan to vote in the next election for the governor of Aceh? *(almost certainly or very likely)*	98%	97%	100%	97%
Did you vote in the last election for the Indonesian president?	39%	89%	45%	86%
Do you plan to vote in the next presidential election? *(almost certainly or very likely)*	91%	97%	100%	98%

Source: ARLS (2008)

deals with GAM commanders to ensure success (Clark and Palmer, 2008). Unsurprisingly, former combatants were more likely than the general population to support the winning gubernatorial pairing.[22] Communities also revealed that they were open to former combatants assuming local leadership positions: 83 per cent of civilian men and 87 per cent of civilian women said they would be happy for ex-combatants to take formal leadership roles in their villages (ARLS, 2008).[23]

This is not to say that all former combatants properly understand the mechanics and norms of democracy. On several occasions during the start of the campaign for the 2009 legislative elections, for example, GAM's political party, Partai Aceh, pursued thuggish tactics to intimidate the electorate into voting for them (World Bank, 2008g). Rather than stemming from an aversion to democracy among the former rebel group, this conduct is associated with the broader challenges of consolidating democracy in a transitioning state. Democracy is still relatively new to Aceh and to Indonesia, and candidates of all parties and stripes tend to try to utilize muscle to gain votes (Barron, Nathan, and Welsh, 2005). Dealing with such issues requires the strengthening of electoral institutions and broader political education for candidates and voters, activities not normally associated with reintegration programming.

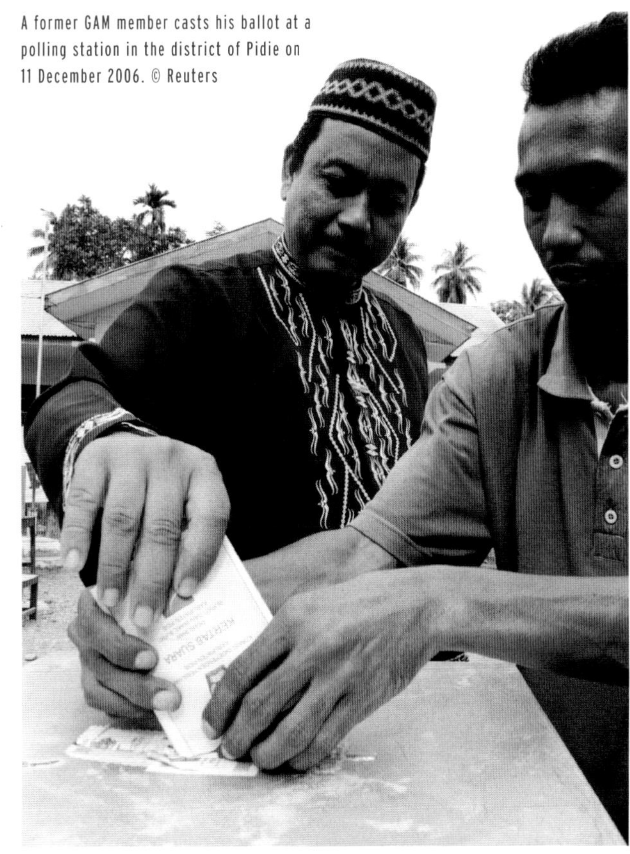
A former GAM member casts his ballot at a polling station in the district of Pidie on 11 December 2006. © Reuters

Economic reintegration

A basic assumption of the reintegration model is that former combatants are likely to face significant barriers to returning to work or pursuing their livelihoods. Providing assistance to former combatants that enables them to get jobs, start their own businesses, or productively work the land is viewed as being necessary to help them make the transition to civilian life. Once they are working, they are less likely to partake in violence.

The GAM Needs Assessment, conducted in the first year after the signing of the Helsinki MoU, showed that unemployment for former combatants was a major issue. Seventy-five per cent of the 642 ex-combatants interviewed said they were lacking regular work (World Bank, 2006a, p. 16).

Yet the situation two years later is very different. Table 8.6 shows that very few former combatants are un- or underemployed. Indeed, former combatants are *more* likely to have full-time employment than are civilians. Access to reintegration support does not appear to be key in determining employment status. Former combatants who received assistance from the BRA or IOM are no less likely to be unemployed than those who did not receive any support.[24]

The Aceh Poverty Assessment shows the extent to which the end of the armed conflict itself created an important peace dividend (World Bank, 2008e). Improvements in security—in part a function of the disarmament of GAM and the withdrawal of Indonesian troops, but largely not related to reintegration efforts—led to increased mobility of labour and reduced transaction costs and risk for investment. One result is that poverty levels dropped substantially in areas that were greatly affected by the armed conflict. While in 2005 people in high-conflict areas were 43 per cent more likely to live below the poverty line, by 2006 they were 4 per cent less likely than the average person in Aceh (World Bank, 2008e, p. 15). The massive tsunami reconstruction effort also had an impact, although this was lower in conflict-affected areas, which received significantly less help. Agriculture, a sector in which almost half of Acehnese are employed, grew by 4.5 per cent in the first half of 2008 (World Bank, 2008f).

The growth in farming has created working opportunities for many former combatants. The GAM Needs Assessment found that prior to joining the movement, 94.6 per cent of former combatants and prisoners were employed, with most working as farmers or small traders (World Bank, 2006a, p. 16). These figures are similar to those of the wider Aceh population. Land scarcity and access to farming land are not a problem in Aceh—one reason why there have been few complaints from former combatants that the land promised to them in the MoU has not yet been

Table 8.6 Work situation: GAM vs. civilians, mid-2008

Which option best describes your employment situation?	Men		Women	
	Ex-combatant (n=1,024)	Civilian (n=1,794)	Ex-combatant (n=29)	Civilian (n=1,237)
Full-time employment	85%	78%	45%	29%
Consistent part-time/contract work	6%	6%	7%	5%
Some part-time/contract work	6%	4%	14%	6%
Unemployed	1%	3%	0%	1%
Student	0%	5%	0%	4%

Source: ARLS (2008)

Figure 8.2 **Education levels: GAM vs. civilians**

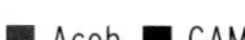

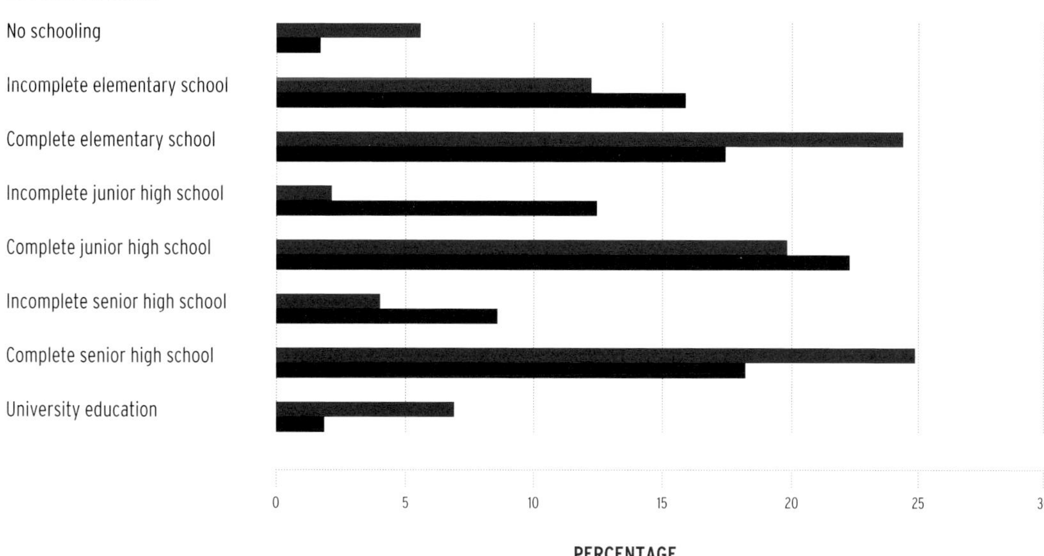

Source: World Bank (2006a)

provided (see Box 8.3). Few if any barriers prevent former combatants and others from working the land. Lower employment rates for younger combatants might be a result of fewer familial responsibilities for members of this group. As a result, they may choose not to work, or to take part-time jobs with less frequent income, relying on their parents or other family members for support.[25]

For other jobs, GAM members are also competitive. The GAM needs assessment conducted in 2006 clearly shows how similar former combatants are to the civilian population in terms of education levels (World Bank, 2006a). Compared to the rest of the population, GAM members are more likely to have completed some schooling, although they are less likely to have a high level of education (see Figure 8.2).

In post-war Aceh, educated former combatants, who are most likely to live in urban areas and have commanding roles, have an additional advantage when seeking out work. Edward Aspinall shows how recent political developments have increased economic opportunities for some former combatants (Aspinall, 2009). He estimates, for example, that 500 former combatants received jobs at the tsunami reconstruction agency BRR. Senior GAM figures, such as Teuku Kamaruzzaman, have been appointed to high-level positions, which have allowed them to influence other appointments. Others have received positions as security guards or in monitoring teams.

New opportunities in contracting and other important sectors of Aceh's economy have been even more important. Aspinall outlines how former combatants have become key players in the construction industry, which is booming due to tsunami reconstruction. At higher levels, this provides a source of revenues, a portion of which flows down through the GAM/KPA hierarchy. Most notably, former GAM leader Muzakkir Manaf now runs a large contractor firm, PT Pulau Gading. In Aceh Barat Daya, it is alleged that the *bupati* (district head) has allocated IDR 12 billion (USD 1.3 million) in contracts to companies owned by KPA members, all of whom are former GAM (World Bank/

DSF, 2007). George Aditijondro cites projects that Muzakkir's company has won, including a IDR 2.4 billion (more than USD 200,000) project to construct a bridge in the city of Lhoksuemawe (Aditijondro, 2008). At lower levels, construction contracts provide opportunities for manual work for less educated former combatants. One GAM figure estimates that 25–30 per cent of the 3,000 former combatants in Aceh Besar were employed in some capacity in construction projects (Aspinall, 2009).[26]

Stabilizing security in Aceh

Many of the social, political, and economic challenges that reintegration programmes are traditionally designed to address were not present in post-war Aceh. By and large, there are no great divides between former combatants and the communities to which they have returned. Strong relationships existed between combatants and civilians in the conflict period and these have endured in the post-war era. Former combatants are participating in the political processes that provide means to mediate differences now that the war has ended. The local elections of 2006–07 saw the accession of many former GAM figures to power; the positions and the interests of the former rebel movement are strongly represented in provincial and district decision-making bodies (Clark and Palmer, 2008). The large majority of former combatants are not facing barriers to income-generating activities and, indeed, are less likely to be unemployed than the population at large.

Former combatants are less likely to be unemployed than the population at large.

This is not to say that there are not important social, economic, and political dimensions to Aceh's transition from war to peace. Helping those affected by war—combatants and non-combatants alike—to overcome experiences of violence is vital (IOM et al., 2007). While former GAM members have access to political power, this does not mean that they are fully versed in the norms of how democratic decision-making should work. Among the few former combatants who have only part-time work, some may be involved in violent criminal acts. Increasing intra-GAM squabbles related to competition over economic resources such as construction contracts is also leading to violence.[27]

Dealing with these issues will be vital if peace is to be consolidated. But, by and large, these are not the types of problems that reintegration programmes can conceivably impact in a large way.

PROBLEMS WITH INDIVIDUAL TARGETING

Programmes focusing on former combatants in Aceh have had two main characteristics. First, assistance has been targeted largely at individuals through specially created reintegration programmes aimed at all who were members of the former rebel group. This has been true for both BRA and donor programmes. Second, for BRA programmes the predominant modality has been the provision of cash aimed primarily at compensating former combatants rather than improving their welfare (see below). The characteristics of Aceh mean that these approaches have had minimal impact in improving the prospects of former combatants or in satisfying them. This has fuelled disillusionment and has at times led to low-level tensions on the ground.

Assisting which former combatants?

From the beginning, a real difficulty for reintegration programmers in Aceh was working out to whom assistance should be provided. Reintegration programmes tend to assume that there is a cadre of former combatants who can be identified for reinsertion and reintegration assistance. Normally former combatants are registered when they hand in their guns. Assessments of the needs of each individual are then conducted and ID cards are provided entitling recipients to reintegration support (Colletta, Kostner, and Wiederhofer, 2003). Such methods, when implemented well, allow for the identification of a clear caseload to whom assistance can be provided and who can be monitored over time (UNDDR, 2006, module 4.10). In Aceh, attempts to follow such an approach proved ineffective. This was not because of poor programme design—international expertise was on hand to support combatant registration—but because these methods could not be applied given the local politics and the nature of the GAM movement. Reintegration support continued to be provided to individual combatants. Due to unclear selection criteria and verification mechanisms, however, much of it did not reach intended beneficiaries and others needing help.

The distinction between GAM combatants and sympathizers is a finely grained one in Aceh. Membership of GAM was extremely fuzzy. The movement had general support from much of Aceh's population. This created immense challenges for targeting. The MoU called for the demobilization of 3,000 GAM members who were to receive assistance and provided the basis for the number of ex-combatant benefit packages to be financed. Yet, as in many post-war situations, there were far more people who felt they were eligible for support, rendering extremely difficult the identification of those who were entitled to assistance.

There were significantly more ex-combatants than the 3,000 noted in the MoU.

The extent of this problem became clear early on. IOM, at the request of the Indonesian government, had run an extremely effective reinsertion programme for amnestied prisoners. They had provided cash assistance, health checks, and transport home. The programme adopted the approach used by IOM elsewhere and was widely viewed as a success (World Bank, 2006a). However, attempts to extend the programme to the former combatants who had not been imprisoned met with difficulties. IOM envisioned that, in conformity with international practice and norms, they would provide reinsertion assistance and enrol former combatants in reintegration programmes as they handed in their guns. Yet while guns were handed in on time, ex-combatants did not emerge from hiding, so there was no one to enrol (Barron and Burke, 2008, p. 37).

Without clear beneficiaries to target, IOM sought a list of the 3,000 combatants from GAM's leadership. However, GAM refused to provide the list, partly because of security concerns. Yet the larger problem was that there were significantly more ex-combatants out there than the 3,000 noted in the MoU.[28] GAM's leadership, eager to maintain control and influence over members, did not want to decide who would receive benefits and who would not (ICG, 2005b; Barron and Burke, 2008, p. 38). Without a list, IOM's programme stalled. Politically, there was little space to acknowledge that more than 3,000 former combatants existed as this number had been cast in stone in the MoU, or that it might be more effective if reintegration benefits for former combatants were spread more widely.[29] Yet little effort was made by IOM, or indeed other aid agencies, to make the case for wider targeting.

Subsequent efforts to work out the size of the former combatant caseload were not fruitful. GAM eventually provided a list of 3,000 but it was clear that this did not represent all their members. Negotiations between the government and GAM led to the inclusion of another 6,200 'non-combatants' in the reintegration programme (Aspinall 2008, p. 23). Those who made the list(s) were those likely to be connected to high-level leaders in the movement.

To get around the numbers problem, the government tried several approaches. First, money was given to former GAM commanders who redistributed the resources across the former combatant base as well as to some supporters. Three rounds of assistance of IDR 1 million (around USD 100) per head were provided by local government for 3,000 combatants in late 2005 and early 2006. Subsequent monitoring found that funds had been spread widely, with GAM supporters and some civilians receiving money. Forty per cent of former combatants received less than IDR 200,000 over the three rounds, with some receiving as little as IDR 30,000, or just over USD 3 (World Bank, 2006a).

Many who did not receive money felt they should have. In early 2006, a new scheme involved GAM leaders setting up micro-projects involving their former cadres. Names were listed. Yet funds were again transferred to GAM leaders, and in the majority of cases were then shared widely across the combatant population and sometimes with other GAM supporters (Zurstrassen, 2006).

IOM continued to provide reintegration packets to former combatants, although they were not worried about whether recipients were part of the official 3,000. Programmes targeted female combatants and vulnerable youth. The result was some overlap between government and IOM programmes, different levels of assistance, and varying quality of assistance. Some former combatants missed out all together.[30]

Providing targeted assistance to individuals assumes that a clear caseload can be identified. In Aceh, as in many other post-war places (Jensen and Stepputat, 2001), the development of a clear list of combatants was neither politically possible (given concerns within the GAM leadership about revealing the names of former combatants) nor technically feasible (given the fuzzy dividing line between combatants and civilians). This led to serious limitations as to what could be achieved through individual targeting. Assistance was spread widely within GAM as a means of minimizing jealousies, but consequently levels of support were so low that impacts were limited. Further, the low amount of assistance only served to increase dissatisfaction among many former combatants who had been expecting more support (ICG, 2005b, pp. 5–6).

The reintegration programme was largely ineffective but not initially harmful.

Limited welfare impacts

There is a debate in DDR literature over whether the provision of cash is more effective than in-kind assistance for reintegrating former combatants (Knight and Özerdem, 2004; Willibald, 2006). The decision to provide cash in Aceh was not one based on an assessment of whether it would have greater impacts than in-kind aid. Rather, the primary purpose of BRA assistance for former combatants was viewed—by GAM and the BRA alike—as compensation for former fighters.[31] As Bill Rolston notes, the provision of compensation may be necessary after wars end to avoid potentially destabilizing political disaffection (Rolston, 2007, pp. 262–63). There is a strong case to be made that providing compensation is just as vital an element of transitional justice as prosecuting human rights offenders (Aspinall, 2008). Yet this approach was always unlikely to exert much influence on the key drivers of conflict in Aceh.

In general, money from the BRA was given in lump sums with no requirements on how it should be spent and with no technical assistance provided to help recipients use it effectively (Zurstrassen, 2006). In essence the money was an attempted pay-off to potential spoilers. Flowing from the logic of the reintegration model, in the early days the primary focus of assistance was to ensure security. This, in the eyes of the programme's supporters, justified a lack of transparency and unequal targeting of reintegration assistance. Yet the focus on solely getting cash to former combatants, without concern for the effective use of funds, has been counter-productive. Funds have been spread widely (and thus funding per capita has been reduced) and a large proportion of assistance has been used for unproductive consumption with few longer-term impacts (Zurstrassen, 2006). Former combatants, too, asked why they were only being given *uang rokok* (money for cigarettes) when they deserved more and when the MoU mandated that assistance should economically empower them (World Bank, 2006a, p. 31).

The resulting programme was largely ineffective but not harmful, at least initially. Funds generally did not enhance former combatants' ability to enter the labour market, but they did satisfy political pressures for the government to be seen to be implementing the reintegration provisions of the MoU. With the passing of time, however, the approach does appear to have had some negative consequences. One has been the creation of new demands for assistance from former combatants and rising disillusionment when this was not forthcoming. A second has been increasing suspicions—from ex-combatants and non-combatants alike—that Jakarta and the Acehnese authorities do not care about their needs and that they are reneging on the promises of the peace deal.

The missing dimension: building state legitimacy

Scepticism about the motives of the government, and particularly the BRA, has grown among both former combatants and civilians in Aceh. Unequal access to benefits, lack of transparency in delivery mechanisms, and perceptions of corruption have tainted the image of local government.[32] Tarmizi, the director of a local NGO, notes the potential for conflict:

> *The reintegration programme only benefits the elite in GAM. This will have a big impact on horizontal conflict at the village level. . . . I think they have to change the programmes—do regional development in areas affected by the conflict, make infrastructure, make small-scale economic activity, but now they only make a priority of some [people].* (Aguswandi and Large, 2008, p. 51)

Discontent with how reintegration assistance is being provided is not unusual in post-war settings. In Aceh, however, the approach risked accentuating many of the underlying causes of the conflict. A lack of state legitimacy was one of the factors that drove the conflict initially and that could provide a basis for future unrest (Barron and Clark, 2006). This related to both the Jakarta government and the Acehnese authorities, with the latter often seen as puppets of Jakarta (McGibbon, 2006). Historically, conflict in Aceh has been driven by the perceived unresponsiveness of elites to the needs of the Acehnese people (Aspinall, forthcoming). Anthony Reid identifies cycles of violence being triggered whenever such dissatisfaction reaches a tipping point (Reid, 2006; 2009). The activities and programmes of the BRA were closely monitored among the Acehnese population, former combatants and non-combatants alike, in part because the agency's functioning served as a bellwether for the extent to which the local government could provide for the Acehnese people in the autonomy era. With the BRA failing, murmurs of dissatisfaction about what the local government could achieve in the post-war period increased to the point that one local analyst predicted that the agency could lead to the downfall of Governor Irwandi (Hariyanto, 2008).

The reintegration approach risked accentuating the underlying causes of the conflict.

Clearly a well-functioning BRA and effective reintegration programme alone would not build the legitimacy of the state that had eroded in the conflict era. Yet reintegration assistance as it was implemented does risk contributing to the very processes that triggered armed violence in Aceh in the first place. International approaches tend to prioritize the disbursement of funds to potential problem groups over transparency concerns. Yet in the Aceh case, this was problematic because the major conflict cleavage had always been between society and the state. Reintegration funds could have been used to help build state legitimacy, although this is a long-term endeavour. That these funds were not used in this way was not only a missed opportunity; it could also contribute to an undermining of peace in the longer run.[33]

A 'MAXIMALIST' APPROACH TO REINTEGRATION

'Maximalist' conceptions of reintegration emphasize the need to connect initial combatant-focused assistance to a broader set of activities aimed at supporting the war-to-peace transition. Early DDR programmes tended to focus primarily on a narrow set of goals around establishing security. Over time, the goals have expanded with a focus on linking to other efforts aimed at promoting development and broader forms of security promotion (Jennings, 2008; Muggah, 2006; POST-CONFLICT SECURITY).

Objectives of DDR programmes around the world now also include provisions for dependants of former combatants, strengthening state institutions, promoting property rights, and addressing distortions in state spending (Muggah, 2009). This expansion of focus has been the result of lessons learned about how security-promoting activities can have little impact if they are not joined to broader strategies that aim to address the short-, medium-, and longer-term causes of conflict. In most post-war countries, funding for the reintegration of former combatants is just one element of broader approaches that also seek to repair the economy of conflict-devastated areas (Colletta, Kostner, and Wiederhofer, 2003). A number of experienced practitioners have argued for a relatively quick integration of traditionally conceived reintegration activities into mainstream development efforts (Ball, 1997).

In Aceh, there was clearly a need for this wider approach given the nature and extent of the post-war challenges. Foremost among these are ensuring that the economy grows and produces sustainable, well-paying jobs (World Bank, 2008e). Former combatants may be more likely to be employed than others, but the quality of such jobs is often poor and many are still living at or below the poverty line.[34] Growth rates in Aceh for the first half of 2008 were less than half of those across Indonesia as a whole, with Aceh's economy actually contracting by 5.8 per cent over the first six months of 2008 (World Bank, 2008f). As Rolston points out, it does not make sense merely to 'reintegrate ex-combatants into poverty' (Rolston, 2007, p. 265); such a move can lead to fresh conflict or a rise in violent crime (Babiker and Özerdem, 2003; Baare, 2001). Improving the lot of the Acehnese (including former combatants) requires structural changes to the economy that in turn will create jobs and improve returns to work.

As with most areas affected by war, there are also vast reconstruction needs in Aceh. Tens of thousands of houses were damaged or destroyed by the conflict. From 1989 to 1998, when Aceh was declared an 'area of military operations' in an attempt to root out the rebels, 527 schools were burned; another 880 schools closed due to damage in the second half of 2003, when martial law was re-established following the collapse of the Cessation of Hostilities Agreement (Barron, 2008). Twenty-two per cent of village health clinics and 11–20 per cent of transport infrastructure were directly damaged by the conflict; 28 per cent of rice fields and 45 per cent of other crop land were damaged or destroyed. Lack of maintenance, closely related to the presence of conflict, resulted in even more damage (MSR, forthcoming). A preliminary estimate places the costs of post-war reconstruction and recovering losses from the conflict era at more than USD 1.4 billion, a figure that only includes the 2003–06 period (MSR, forthcoming).

An Acehnese woman runs as a primary school burns in front of her house, May 2003. © Choo Youn-Kong/AFP Photo

Aceh provided a potential arena for the implementation of a 'maximalist' approach to reintegration and recovery. Unlike many post-war settings, resources were not scarce in Aceh. In their review of six peace processes, Shepard Forman and Stewart Patrick cite a lack of money and failure to follow up on pledges as major problems (Forman and Patrick, 2000). Yet in Aceh resources abounded: the tsunami resulted in the arrival of around USD 8 billion of reconstruction and development resources (Barron, 2008); 3,645 international NGOs were registered in Aceh by January 2006 (Schulze, 2006).

These funds offered a potential means to promote growth and the development of conflict-affected areas in ways that would help consolidate peace. However, reintegration programmes, and post-war strategies, were separated from those aimed at tsunami reconstruction or broader development. As a result, relatively few of these resources have made it into war-affected areas. This has created inequalities that are driving new tensions.

Limitations on the use of tsunami aid

The vast majority of donor aid that arrived in Aceh was tied. Limitations were placed on where it could be spent (the tsunami-affected coastal areas) and who could receive assistance (those directly affected by the tsunami) (Schiller, 2008). The Multi-Donor Fund, a USD 600 million plus pot of money for tsunami reconstruction assistance, for example, could not get permission from its donors to expand into conflict programming. In particular, the United States argued that changing the mandate of the fund to include broader development and post-war reconstruction

A couple views the destruction caused by the tsunami to their former residential area in Banda Aceh, January 2005. © Dimas Ardian/Getty Images

Figure 8.3 **Conflict damage, tsunami damage, and tsunami funding, per district**

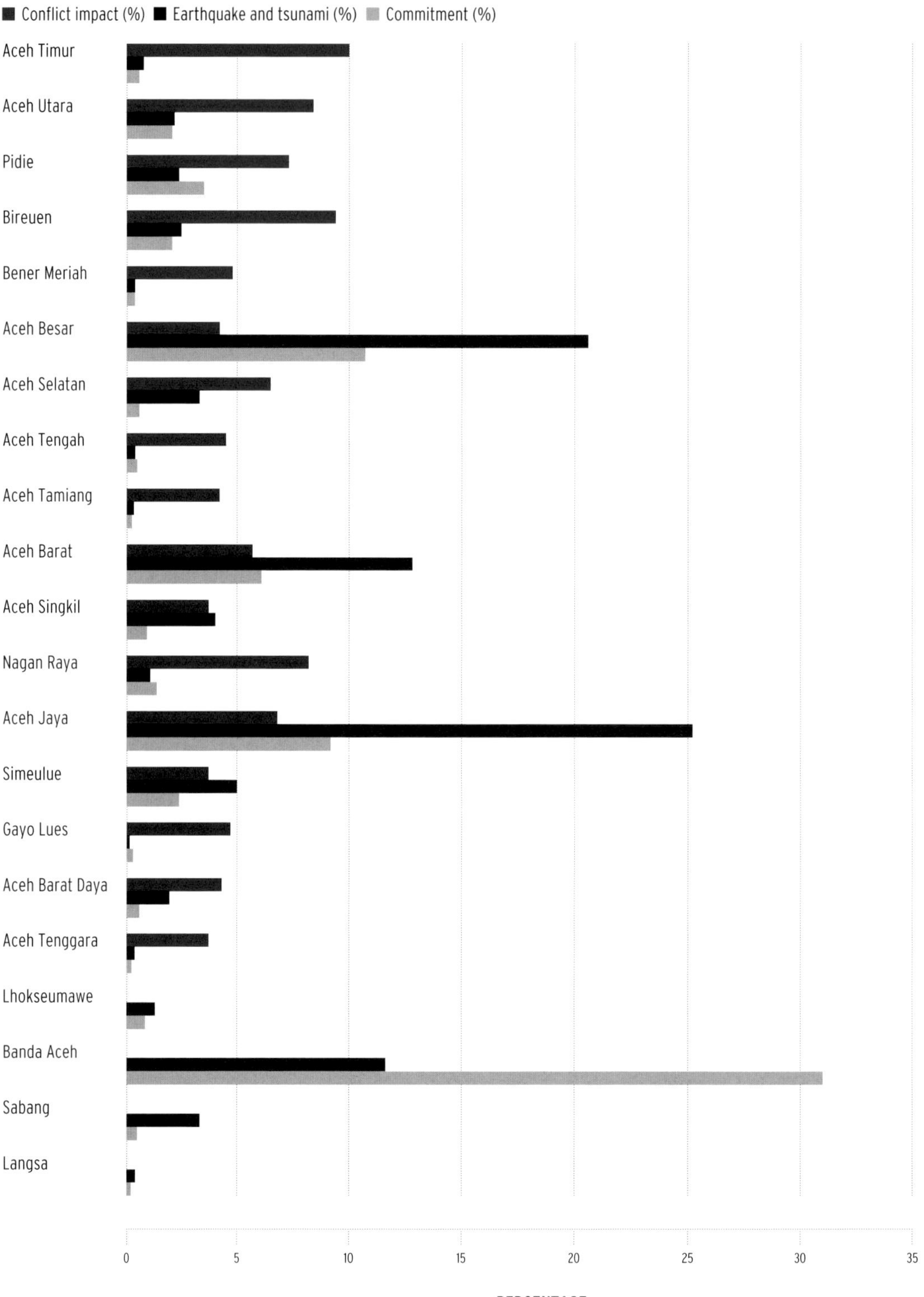

Source: World Bank estimates, November 2008

programming would require approval from Congress. Given this, they, along with other donors such as the European Union, strongly resisted pressures to move into conflict-affected areas situated away from the tsunami-hit coasts (Barron and Burke, 2008). While more and more agencies became interested in peace-building issues over time, most found that they could not use their resources in some of the regions that were hardest hit by the conflict in Aceh (Burke and Afnan, 2005).

These restrictions were understandable given the immensity of the tsunami's impacts and the enormous post-tsunami needs. Yet while tsunami funds could not be used for key post-war needs, few additional sources arrived to support many of the province's most conflict-torn areas. There was a perception among donor nations that it was difficult to make a case for significant funding for post-war reconstruction when Aceh was already receiving such high levels of tsunami aid. As mentioned, only certain parts of Aceh were receiving such aid. Government tsunami reconstruction money, much of it from Jakarta, avoided many conflict-affected areas and explicit funding for peace support programmes was relatively limited.

As a result, there was a massive discrepancy between the amount of resources available for tsunami and conflict programming, with resources for the former over 20 times larger than those for reintegration.[35] Around seven per cent of the 'tsunami funds' reached areas affected by conflict that were not hit by the tsunami.[36] This did help. But, overall, there were large funding gaps for post-war reconstruction and development in many of the areas hit hardest by the conflict. As Figure 8.3 shows, the districts in Aceh with the highest levels of conflict damage (Aceh Timur, Bireuen, Aceh Utara, Pidie, and Nagan Raya) all received very little tsunami money.[37]

The resources available for tsunami programming were over 20 times larger than those for reintegration.

Post-conflict donor money that did arrive tended to be focused on reintegration issues (such as livelihoods for former combatants and conflict victims or psychosocial support) and a narrow range of peace-building efforts (such as conflict mediation training, public information, gender awareness). There was little money to work on other vital areas such as infrastructure reconstruction and broader economic development. (Post-)conflict programming and reintegration assistance became synonymous in Aceh. As a result there was a key gap with respect to the provision of post-war development aid aimed at rebuilding conflict-affected infrastructure, creating sustainable livelihoods, and strengthening local institutions.

Lack of synergy between tsunami and conflict programming

A second issue relates to the lack of synergy between strategies and programmes providing tsunami and conflict assistance. On the Jakarta and Aceh government side, there were few incentives for the agencies responsible for reintegration (BRA) and tsunami reconstruction (BRR) to work together. From the outset, BRR viewed their mandate as only relating to tsunami reconstruction. In the days leading up to the signing of the Helsinki MoU, discussions were held about what role BRR would play with reintegration and post-war reconstruction programmes. The agency had sufficient capacity and expanding its mandate to cover these areas would ensure that the vast pool of tsunami funds could be tapped for peace-building purposes. However, BRR representatives were understandably reluctant to take part in the formation and implementation of the reintegration programme or for broader post-conflict work. They were already struggling to deal with the immense challenges of tsunami reconstruction and wanted to avoid what was seen as bumpy political terrain (Barron and Burke, 2008).

There was also little interest from the BRA to work with BRR. This was partly due to jealousy: BRR not only had far more resources to spend, but also far more capacity, and the agency received much greater attention from both the Jakarta government and donors. Most importantly, BRR had a far greater level of authority, and a wider mandate, than did the BRA. At no point was there significant collaboration between the BRA and BRR in strategy development or programme implementation.

Rising inequality and tension

The separation of tsunami and post-conflict programming had a number of consequences. First, there was a lack of conflict sensitivity in the use of tsunami funding. With a separate government agency deemed responsible for 'conflict issues', BRR deliberately remained 'conflict blind'. Yet many areas where tsunami programmes were operating had been affected to some extent by the conflict. Former combatants and conflict victims lived across the province. Lack of conflict sensitivity in tsunami programming, reflected in the failure to tap the expertise and networks of those working on the reintegration agenda, was pervasive (Burke and Afnan, 2005).

Second, one result of the vastly different funding levels for post-war and tsunami support has been rising inequality between tsunami- and conflict-affected areas (Barron, 2008). At one level, the larger support for tsunami victims is understandable given the immense impacts of that disaster. Yet the armed conflict caused about half as much infrastructure damage as did the tsunami (World Bank/KDP, 2007, p. 4).

Table 8.7 Sources of division and violence within communities: non-combatant community members, by sex, mid-2008

Difference between [. . .] is a source of division	Men	Women	Of the men and women who reported divisions		
	Source of division	Source of division	n=	Escalated into violence in last 6 months	Prevented you from carrying out economic activities
Rich and poor	22%	21%	435	11%	12%
Men and women	6%	7%	110	13%	8%
Younger and older generations	5%	5%	99	10%	4%
Returnees/IDPs and other community members	2%	2%	31	4%	4%
New migrants and other community members	3%	2%	59	5%	2%
Ex-combatants and village members	3%	4%	72	9%	2%
Different ethnic groups	3%	4%	61	11%	4%
People who have received special assistance from government and those who have not	44%	43%	970	9%	7%
People in this village and people from neighbouring villages	5%	7%	106	3%	2%

Source: ARLS (2008)

Those affected by the conflict have been far less likely to receive help than those hit by the tsunami. By mid-2008, 47 per cent of those whose houses were damaged or destroyed by the tsunami had received compensation compared with 16 per cent of those whose houses or workplaces were damaged or destroyed by the conflict.[38] In areas affected by the tsunami and the armed conflict, victims of the former were often prioritized when receiving assistance such as a new house. Conflict-affected infrastructure is only being built back at half the speed of that affected by the tsunami (World Bank/KDP, 2007, p. 38). Levels of post-war assistance also tended to be significantly lower than tsunami support. On average EUR 7,000 (USD 11,000) was allocated for each new tsunami house compared with EUR 3,500 (USD 5,500) if the same house was destroyed by the conflict (Frodin, 2008).

This discrepancy has fuelled resentment. The 2008 survey asked community members what sources of division existed in their village. As Table 8.7 shows, differences between men and women, young and old, ethnic groups, and returning IDPs and community members were not viewed as a great source of disputes. Fewer than four per cent said divisions between former combatants and village members were a source of friction. On occasion, conflicts related to these divisions escalated into violence or prevented economic activities from being conducted, but the number of cases is very low. Far more problematic was unequal access to government assistance, which 44 per cent of men and 43 per cent of women cited as a source of tension. Eighty-seven informants reported that these divisions had escalated into violence.[39] From March 2007, disputes over the delivery of aid recorded in the World Bank's conflict monitoring averaged almost 30 per month (Barron, 2008).

Conflict-affected infrastructure is being built back at half the speed of that affected by the tsunami.

Local government funds: opportunities and risks

These problems were not the fault of the reintegration programme alone. Rather, they were a result of a poorly conceived and executed conflict recovery and peace-building strategy that failed to synchronize short-term reintegration assistance with other ongoing programmes and funds in the province. The arrival of fresh government resources from 2008 has offered an opportunity to redress some of the mistakes already made. But it also accentuates risks if funding is not spent equitably and transparently.

From 2008 onwards, tsunami and reintegration funds will be supplemented by substantial extra resources for regular development spending. The Law on Governing Aceh (national law 11/2006), which implements many of the provisions of the MoU, stipulates that 70 per cent of the revenues from current and future hydrocarbon deposits are to remain in Aceh. Of more significance, given declining gas deposits, an additional two per cent of the Indonesia-wide DAU (the discretionary block grant from the centre to the regions aimed at equalizing the fiscal capacity of regional governments) will be given to Aceh for 15 years, and one per cent for the following five years (Barron and Clark, 2007). With this extra *dana otsus,* the budget of the Acehnese authorities in 2008 was USD 1.4 billion, six times as much as in 1999 (World Bank, 2006c, p. 39) (see Figure 8.4). Even as tsunami assistance leaves Aceh, the money available to develop the province will remain fairly constant.

This creates big opportunities in Aceh but also risks. The ways in which these resources are spent and the extent to which they can successfully spur equitable economic growth and improve the delivery of services will in part determine the likelihood of large-scale violence re-emerging. Armed conflict in the past was driven by a perceived gap between the wealth of Aceh and the ways in which local people benefit from the province's development (Ross, 2005). If the vast resources that Aceh will control do not translate into economic growth and improvements in living standards for ordinary villagers, violent conflict may arise again.

Figure 8.4 **Resources available for development in Aceh**

TRILLION IDR (CONSTANT 2005 PRICES)

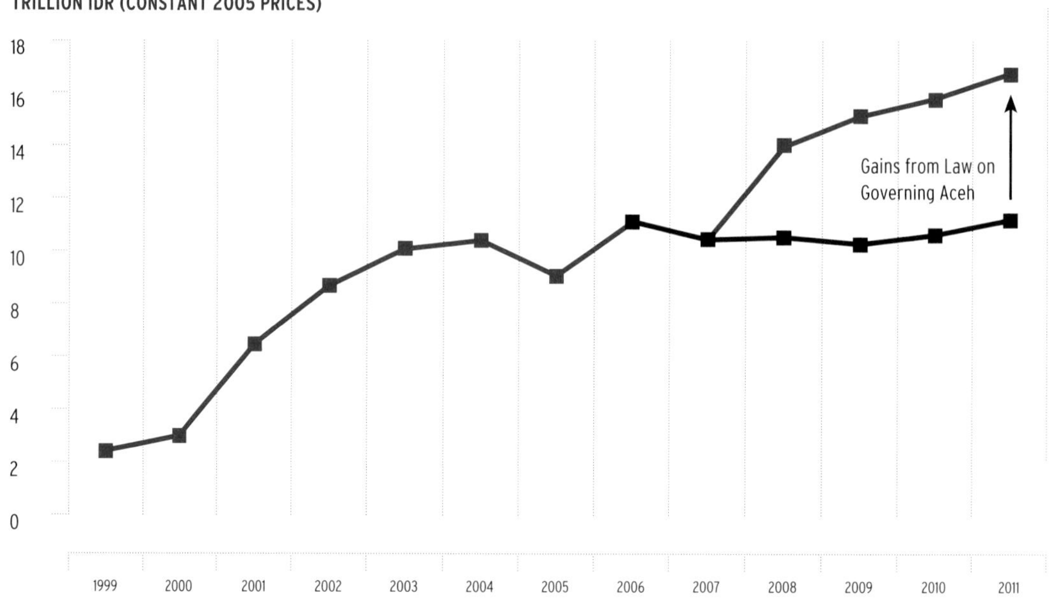

Note: In view of the strong fluctuations in the exchange rate between the USD and IDR, this graph presents only IDR figures.

Source: World Bank estimates, January 2009 (based on oil at USD 60/barrel)

It is unlikely that such a conflict would pit GAM against the Jakarta government, at least in the short term. GAM's leaders, and many former GAM members, are fully committed to the peace deal; Aceh's special autonomy provisions give them unprecedented power over the province's vast resources. Yet rebellion may come from other sources. Those excluded from power (including elites who have lost their positions of prominence since the war has ended) may seek to mobilize Acehnese villagers, disappointed at not seeing a greater peace dividend. If Aceh does not grow, and this growth does not move people out of poverty, there is a real risk that people will feel that the special autonomy provisions are not enough and that outright independence is necessary. Aceh's history shows that times of peace are less common than periods of war.[40]

Despite this, donors have paid relatively little attention to building local capacity in ways that strengthen the performance and legitimacy of the state and which build links between those in power and the governed. Relatively little assistance has been provided to the governor, district heads, and parliament members to help them manage their budgets in ways that ensure effective and equitable use of funds. Where such support has been provided, limited attention has been paid to how fund distribution may affect (post-)conflict dynamics.

In the longer term, wider geographically targeted programmes aimed at promoting economic growth, creating jobs, delivering services, reforming the security sector, and strengthening state institutions are more likely to contribute to reintegration and conflict prevention than more finely targeted programmes. Strategies for spurring reintegration and post-war development in Aceh need to take account of the wide range of funding sources (including for non-conflict-focused programmes) and the diverse types of programmes needed (not all of which are directly conflict-related).

CONCLUSION

This chapter has argued that reintegration programmes in Aceh have been largely ineffective. In part, this is because many of their key design characteristics have flowed from a set of assumptions derived from post-war settings that are very different from the one encountered in Aceh.

First, the orthodoxies of reintegration, as encapsulated in documents such as the IDDRS, reflect a set of post-war challenges that were of minimal importance in Aceh. Social relations and trust between combatants and the non-combatant population were, and are, strong. The Helsinki process created close-to-immediate opportunities for former rebels to assume political positions and former combatants largely accepted that power should be achieved through political processes rather than by force. Most importantly, former combatants have not faced major barriers to work; any barriers also affect Aceh's non-combatant population. Aceh's reintegration needs thus differ from those of many places emerging from war.

Second, the mechanisms by which reintegration assistance was provided in Aceh were also ill-conceived. Reintegration programmes followed the international model in that they attempted to target individual ex-combatants in ways that prioritized security over broader development or welfare impacts. Government funds were distributed in cash without the provision of technical assistance or monitoring to ensure they were productively used, and without mechanisms to identify those most in need. At the same time, however, it is hard to envision how cash assistance to individual ex-combatants could have been successfully provided.

International practice has increasingly emphasized 'maximalist' conceptions of reintegration, where short-term support to former combatants is linked to broader strategies aimed at restarting economic growth, improving institutions, and dealing with other peace-building issues. Such approaches were needed in Aceh, where many of the post-war challenges related to larger, structural economic and political issues. Yet a wider programme was only partially—and very selectively—implemented in Aceh. International and domestic funding for tsunami reconstruction, for example, was massive. But funds generally could not be spent in the most conflict-affected areas; the reintegration programme became divorced from other development work going on in the province. The separation of reintegration efforts (which became synonymous with *all* post-conflict support) and broader reconstruction and development work has contributed to rising inequality across the province. This is fuelling resentment and tensions, although it is still too early to see whether there will be serious long-term consequences.

To date, these failings have not had a disastrous impact for a number of reasons. First, former elites within the rebel group were successfully (re-)integrated into political institutions, a development that was not a result of any post-conflict programming but of the structure of the peace deal. This helped bind leaders and their followers into continuing to support peace. Second, the end of the armed conflict created a peace dividend in and of itself that helped reduce poverty and led to new opportunities for work. In this environment, GAM's swift accession to power allowed for a channelling of resources to (some) former combatants. Unequal and non-transparent distribution of reintegration resources has caused tensions. But in an environment where opportunities exist to access far larger sums of money (for example, through construction contracts), getting effective reintegration help was never going to be of utmost importance to most combatants.

Serious post-war challenges exist in Aceh. However, the mechanisms to deal with them relate far more to issues of state-building and ensuring longer-term economic growth and development, than to helping a small subset of the population (that is difficult to define). In Aceh, the challenge now is how to make the transition effectively from targeted assistance to efforts aimed at supporting long-term conflict-sensitive development. The reintegration tool kit says little about how to engineer that shift.

The weaknesses of reintegration programmes in Aceh raise broader questions about the efficacy of the reintegration model for some post-war places. Reintegration frameworks such as the IDDRS arguably have far more utility for many of the states of sub-Saharan Africa, where conflicts have destroyed economies and devastated the social fabric, where democracy needs to be built from scratch, and where limited domestic resources or capacity exists (Peake, 2009). Yet these are not the only places where wars occur and where peace agreements are reached. Aceh is part of a strong, rapidly democratizing Indonesian state. Finding models to support peace processes in middle-income countries where markets still function is vitally important. ■

LIST OF ABBREVIATIONS

AMM	Aceh Monitoring Mission
ARLS	Aceh Reintegration and Livelihoods Surveys
ASEAN	Association of Southeast Asian Nations
BRA	Badan Reintegrasi-Damai Aceh (Aceh Reintegration Agency)
BRR	Badan Rekonstruksi dan Rehabilitasi (Tsunami Reconstruction and Rehabilitation Agency)
GAM	Gerakan Aceh Merdeka (Free Aceh Movement)
IDDRS	Integrated Disarmament, Demobilization and Reintegration Standards (United Nations)
IDP	Internally displaced person
IDR	Indonesian rupiah
IOM	International Organization for Migration
KDP	Kecamatan (Sub-district) Development Program
KPA	Komite Peralihan Aceh (Aceh Transition Committee)
MoU	Memorandum of Understanding (signed by GAM and the Government of Indonesia)
USAID	United States Agency for International Development

ENDNOTES

1 At this writing, Indonesians involved in the Helsinki peace process (including Vice President Jusuf Kalla and his senior adviser, Farid Husain) are attempting to broker peace talks aimed at ending the conflict in southern Thailand (Khalik, 2008).

2 See, for example, Muggah (2009); Muggah and Baare (2009); and Muggah and Bennett (2009).

3 For reports related to these data sources, see Conflict and Development Program (n.d.).

4 Data from the ARLS used in this chapter is weighted. For male civilian respondents, weighting allows for projections to be made for the full provincial population, rather than just for the population sampled. For female civilian respondents, the data is not representative of all of Aceh but only the areas where the survey was conducted. The data for ex-combatants is representative of the full former combatant population.

5 SUSENAS is the National Socio-Economic Household Survey administered by the Indonesian Bureau of Statistics.

6 The Helsinki MoU calls on GAM to nominate representatives to the tsunami reconstruction agency, known as the Badan Rekonstruksi dan Rehabilitasi or BRR (GoI and GAM, 2005, para. 1.3.9). Senior GAM leader Teuku Kamaruzzaman was subsequently appointed as secretary of the BRR. Employment opportunities for former GAM members in BRR are discussed in more detail below.

7 The following definition of 'violent conflict' is used: any physical action between individuals or groups that results in deaths, injuries, or property destruction, and that is not an act of violent crime. 'Violent crime' is defined as incidents of violence where there is no issue over which the actors are disputing, and where an ideology or identity is not explicitly mobilized in the incident. Figure 8.1 shows only violent conflict, not violent crime.

8 These figures do not include incidents of violent crime, for which use of firearms was higher. Correspondence with Adrian Morel, head of World Bank conflict monitoring work, February 2009.

9 World Bank conflict monitoring shows that levels of violent crime climbed sharply through 2007 but started to fall from the end of the first quarter of 2008. The monitoring does not record incidents before October 2006, so it is not possible to confirm or dismiss the police assertion. It is also too early to see whether the fall in violent crime is a temporary or longer-term phenomenon.

10 The United Nations *Integrated Disarmament, Demobilization and Reintegration Standards* specify that 'The UN should, wherever it is possible, and when in keeping with the mandate of the peacekeeping mission, establish an integrated DDR unit in the mission' (UNDDR, 2006, module 2.10, p. 13).

11 Reintegration advisers in Aceh rarely made explicit reference to the IDDRS or SDDRS. However, many of them had been involved in the process of developing the frameworks and, as such, their advice reflected the contents of the documents.

12 Over time, DDR objectives have expanded from a narrow security focus to include broader forms of security promotion as well as development goals. See the section on 'A 'maximalist' approach to reintegration', below.

13 Explicit statements about prioritizing security over development are rare. Yet the basic premise of DDR, as outlined in the IDDRS, is that it will be an internationally led endeavour with the UN establishing an integrated DDR unit (UNDDR, 2006, module 2.10, p. 13). That DDR Unit reports to the Deputy Special Representative of the Secretary-General (module 2.30, p. 9). Planning for DDR is to be situated within the UN mission's broader strategic plan (module 3.10). DDR should support national institutions through capacity building, legal framework development, policy planning and implementation, financial management, logistics assistance, and community development work (module 3.30). However, implementation of projects is not envisioned through regular government mechanisms, but through either ad-hoc institutions or directly by international agencies or NGOs (module 3.30).

14 See previous endnote.

15 A final year (2008) of assistance from national government is planned. Funds for 2008 still have to arrive in Aceh and it is unclear how they will be used. Some of the programmes listed here are still being implemented.

16 Grants of USD 500,000 per year were provided to cover the health expenses of former combatants. It is unclear which mechanisms were used for distributing these sums. It appears that some system is in place for clinics and hospitals to receive reimbursements for expenses they incur when treating former combatants for free. Interviews with Asmawati, head of BRA social section, and Fuady, BRA secretary of the social department, Banda Aceh, November 2008.

17 See Barron and Burke (2008) for a broader summary and discussion.

18 Interview with IOM Banda Aceh team, Banda Aceh, November 2008.

19 This is by no means unique to Aceh. In Ethiopia, for example, many returning combatants from the front with Eritrea had close links with the communities to which they were returning (Muggah and Bennett, 2009).

20 Aceh is largely religiously homogenous: Muslim. Prayer and Koran recital groups are an important part of the social fabric of each village. It appears that former combatants are participating extensively in such groups.

21 It should be noted that Aceh is by no means unique. Evidence from a diverse range of cases, such as Ethiopia (Muggah and Bennett, 2009), Timor-Leste (Peake, 2009), and even Uganda (Muggah and Baare, 2009), points to strong relations between combatants and civilians.

22 Among former combatants under 30, 93.5 per cent said they voted for Irwandi–Nazar, compared with 73.6 per cent of civilians under 30. For those who are 30 or older, the difference was even greater: 87.5 per cent of former combatants said they voted for Irwandi–Nazar compared with 43.1 per cent of civilians in the same age bracket (ARLS, 2008).

23 N = 3,046.

24 This does not mean that the BRA or IOM programmes have not had positive impacts. If former combatants who were less likely to get a job by themselves were disproportionately likely to receive assistance, then the programmes may have had a positive effect. Unfortunately, it is difficult to assess rigorously the impacts of these programmes, largely because neither has a monitoring and evaluation system that allows for comparisons to be made between those who received assistance and those who did not. Indeed, there is a lack of such evaluations in almost all post-war environments (Humphreys and Weinstein, 2007).

25 Email correspondence with Yuhki Tajima, Harvard University, December 2008.

26 This raises questions about what happens when the tsunami reconstruction boom ends. However, as discussed below, provincial and district government budgets are high (and rising) and it is likely that construction will continue to be a major sector of Aceh's economy.

27 See World Bank (2008a–d; 2008g).

28 A number of theories have been propagated as to why the MoU contains such a low figure. One version is that GAM deliberately gave a low number in order to minimize the number of guns they had to hand in. Military intelligence estimated there was one gun for every 3.5 combatants. Another version is that GAM were asked how many people they had *active* at the time of negotiations. GAM had 3,000 combatants active at that time (interview with Irwandi Yusuf, Banda Aceh, May 2006); however the movement's numbers were larger because combatants tended to work in shifts, fighting for three or four months before being replaced by other fighters. In any case, it appears the implications of the 3,000 number for the number of reintegration packages was not clear to GAM at the time of the Helsinki negotiations (interview with Nur Djuli, head of BRA, Banda Aceh, June 2007).

29 These sensitivities became particularly clear when an early draft of a needs assessment conducted by the World Bank noted that there were considerably more than 3,000 former combatants in Aceh. The country director of the World Bank was told forcefully by the Coordinating Minister for the Economy to stay out of what was a political matter (Barron and Burke, 2008, p. 39).

30 Forty-one per cent of male former combatants have not received any assistance; 23 per cent have received two or more forms of assistance (ARLS, 2008, n=1,024).

31 This view was less true for the IOM combatant programmes. The Information Counselling and Referral Service offices provided advice and technical assistance as well as funds to former combatants (Bean and Knezevic, 2008). However, it is impossible to assess whether this approach was more or less effective than BRA's because data was not collected on combatants who did not receive help to allow for an evaluation of programme impacts.

32 In particular, there have been allegations and protests against money being skimmed by local government officials from BRA housing programmes. In the central highlands, it is alleged that around 40 per cent of funds were not delivered to communities, with BRA housing being of a sub-standard nature as a result. Large protests in Banda Aceh led to BRA compensating affected housing recipients to the tune of IDR 10 million (around USD 1,000) per household. Interviews with villagers and NGO workers in the central highlands, September 2008.

33 Only time will tell how this will play out. In his analysis of GAM's role in the construction sector, Aspinall correctly identifies access to resources through non-transparent means as being important for 'buying in' GAM to peace in the short term (Aspinall, 2009). However, his historical analysis of the roots of and motivations for conflict in Aceh highlights a consistent pattern. When Acehnese have felt that governing powers are not representing their interests, resentment has risen, often taking violent form. See Aspinall (forthcoming) and Reid (2009).

34 More than 26 per cent of Acehnese households lived below the poverty line in 2006, significantly higher than for Indonesia as a whole. In rural areas, poverty levels are over 30 per cent (World Bank, 2008e, p. 8).

35 From ongoing World Bank monitoring.

36 From ongoing World Bank monitoring.

37 For each district, the percentage given is the amount of damage in that district as a proportion of the overall damage total across the province.

38 Tsunami figures include only those affected by the tsunami and not by the conflict; conflict figures include only those affected by the conflict and not by the tsunami. Sample size for the former is 708, for the latter it is 777 (ARLS, 2008).

39 The problem of unequal access to aid is also confirmed by other case study and key informant data collected as part of the MSR (forthcoming).

40 Substantial numbers of Acehnese have been in armed resistance against Jakarta's authority for 86 of the past 132 years, making times of peace the more unusual since 1873 (Reid, 2009).

BIBLIOGRAPHY

Aditijondro, George Junus. 2008. 'Profiting from Peace: The Political Economy of Aceh's Post-Helsinki Reconstruction.' INFID Working Paper No. 3. Jakarta: International NGO Forum on Indonesian Development.

Aguswandi and Judith Large, eds. 2008. *Reconfiguring Politics: The Indonesia–Aceh Peace Process*. London: Conciliation Resources.

AI (Amnesty International). 2004. 'New Military Operations, Old Patterns of Human Rights Abuses in Aceh (Nanggroe Aceh Darussalam, NAD).' 7 October. <http://web.amnesty.org/library/pdf/ASA210332004ENGLISH/$File/ASA2103304.pdf>

ARLS (Aceh Reintegration and Livelihoods Surveys). 2008. Columbia University, Stanford University, and the World Bank.

Aspinall, Edward. 2008. 'Peace without Justice? The Helsinki Peace Process in Aceh.' Geneva: Centre for Humanitarian Dialogue.

—. 2009. 'Combatants to Contractors: The Political Economy of Peace in Aceh.' *Indonesia*, Vol. 87. April.

—. Forthcoming. *Islam and Nation: Separatist Rebellion in Aceh, Indonesia*. Stanford: Stanford University Press.

Awaluddin, Hamid. 2008. 'Why Is Peace in Aceh Successful?' In Aguswandi and Judith Large, eds., pp. 25–27.

Baare, Anton. 2001. 'Demobilization and Reintegration: Revisiting the Uganda Experience.' Paper presented at the USAID Workshop on Demobilization and Reintegration Programs, Nairobi. 20–21 March.

Babiker, Mohammed Hassan and Alpaslan Özerdem. 2003. 'A Future Disarmament, Demobilisation, and Reintegration Process in Sudan: Lessons Learned from Ethiopia, Mozambique and Uganda.' *Conflict, Security and Development,* Vol. 3, No. 2, pp. 211–32.

Ball, Nicole. 1997. 'Demobilizing and Reintegration Soldiers: Lessons from Africa.' In Krishna Kumar, ed. *Rebuilding Societies after Civil War.* Boulder, CO: Lynne Rienner.

Barron, Patrick. 2008. 'Managing the Resources for Peace: Reconstruction and Peacebuilding in Aceh.' In Aguswandi and Judith Large, eds., pp. 58–61.

— and Adam Burke. 2008. 'Supporting Peace in Aceh: Development Agencies and International Involvement.' *Policy Studies,* No. 47. Washington, DC: East–West Center.

— and Samuel Clark. 2006. 'Decentralizing Inequality? Center–Periphery Relations, Local Governance, and Conflict in Aceh.' *Conflict Prevention and Reconstruction Paper,* No. 39. Washington, DC: World Bank.

—, Samuel Clark, and Muslahuddin Daud. 2005. *Conflict and Recovery in Aceh: An Assessment of Conflict Dynamics and Options for Supporting the Peace Process.* Jakarta/Banda Aceh: World Bank.

—, Melina Nathan, and Bridget Welsh. 2005. 'Consolidating Indonesia's Democracy: Conflict, Institutions and the "Local" in the 2004 Legislative Elections.' Conflict Prevention and Reconstruction Paper No. 31. Washington, DC: World Bank.

Bean, James and Neven Knezevic . 2008. *Meta Analysis: Vulnerability, Stability, Displacement and Reintegration—Issues Facing the Peace Process in Aceh, Indonesia.* Geneva: International Organization for Migration.

BRA (Aceh Reintegration Agency). 2008. Economic Section Update. Unpublished document. November.

Burke, Adam and Afnan. 2005. 'Aceh: Reconstruction in a Conflict Environment.' *Indonesian Social Development Paper,* No. 8. Jakarta: World Bank.

Clark, Samuel and Blair Palmer. 2008. 'Peaceful Pilkada, Dubious Democracy: Aceh's Post-Conflict Elections and Their Implications.' *Indonesian Social Development Paper,* No. 11. Jakarta: World Bank.

Colletta, Nat, Markus Kostner, and Ingo Wiederhofer. 2003. 'Disarmament, Demobilization, and Reintegration: Lessons and Liabilities in Reconstruction.' In Robert I. Rotberg, ed. *When States Fail: Causes and Consequences.* Princeton, NJ: Princeton University Press.

Collier, Paul. 1994. 'Demobilization and Insecurity: A Study in the Economics of the Transition from War to Peace.' *Journal of International Development,* Vol. 6, No. 3, pp. 343–51.

— et al. 2003. *Breaking the Conflict Trap: Civil War and Development Policy.* Washington, DC: World Bank and Oxford University Press.

Conflict and Development Program. n.d. Web site. Jakarta: Conflict and Development Program. <http://www.conflictanddevelopment.org>

Forbes Damai Aceh. 2007a. Update. 5 June.

—. 2007b. Update. October.

Forman, Shepard and Stewart Patrick, eds. 2000. *Good Intentions: Pledges of Aid for Postconflict Recovery.* Boulder, CO: Lynne Rienner.

Frodin, Lina. 2008. 'The Challenges of Reintegration in Aceh.' In Aguswandi and Judith Large, eds., pp. 54–57.

GoI and GAM (Government of Indonesia and the Free Aceh Movement). 2005. *Memorandum of Understanding between the Government of the Republic of Indonesia and the Free Aceh Movement.* Helsinki. 15 August. <http://www.aceh-mm.org/download/english/Helsinki%20MoU.pdf>

Hariyanto, Dadang. 2008. 'BRA: BOM Waktu Bagi Irwandi?' *Modus,* February (week 2).

Hill, Richard, Gwendolyn Taylor, and Jonathan Temin. 2008. *Would You Fight Again? Understanding Liberian Ex-Combatant Reintegration.* United States Institute of Peace Special Report. Washington, DC: United States Institute of Peace.

HRW (Human Rights Watch). 2003. 'Aceh under Martial Law: Inside the Secret War.' Vol. 15, No. 10. December. <http://hrw.org/reports/2003/indonesia1203/indonesia1203.pdf>

Humphreys, Macartan and Jeremy Weinstein. 2007. 'Demobilization and Reintegration.' *Journal of Conflict Resolution,* Vol. 51, No. 4, pp. 531–67.

Husain, Farid. 2007. *To See the Unseen: Scenes Behind the Aceh Peace Treaty.* Jakarta: Health & Hospital Indonesia.

Husain, Syed Arshad et al. 1998. 'Stress Reactions of Children and Adolescents in War and Siege Conditions.' *American Journal of Psychiatry,* Vol. 155, No. 12, pp. 1718–19.

ICG (International Crisis Group). 2005a. *Aceh: A New Chance for Peace.* Asia Briefing No. 40. Jakarta/Brussels: ICG. 15 August.

—. 2005b. *Aceh: So Far, So Good.* Asia Briefing No. 44. Jakarta/Brussels: ICG. 13 December.

—. 2007a. *Aceh: Post-conflict Complications.* Asia Report No. 139. Jakarta/Brussels: ICG.

—. 2007b. *Indonesia: How GAM Won in Aceh.* Asia Briefing No. 61. Jakarta/Brussels: ICG. 22 March.

—. 2008. *Indonesia: Pre-Election Anxieties in Aceh.* Asia Briefing No. 81. Jakarta/Brussels: ICG. 9 September.

IOM (International Organization for Migration) et al. 2007. *A Psychological Needs Assessment of Communities in 14 Conflict-Affected Districts in Aceh.* Jakarta: IOM.

Jennings, Kathleen. 2008. 'Seeing DDR from Below: Challenges and Dilemmas Raised by the Experiences of Ex-Combatants in Liberia.' *FAFO Report*, No. 3. Oslo: FAFO.

Jensen, Steffen and Finn Stepputat. 2001. 'Demobilizing Armed Civilians.' *CDR Policy Paper.* Copenhagen: Centre for Development Research.

Jones, Sidney. 2008. 'Keeping the Peace: Security in Aceh.' In Aguswandi and Judith Large, eds., pp. 72–75.

Kalyvas, Stathis N. 2008. 'Ethnicity and the Dynamics of Civil War.' Paper presented at the Rethinking Ethnicity and Ethnic Strife Conference, Budapest.

Khalik, Abdul. 2008. 'VP Shuns Foreign Ministry in Thai Talks.' *Jakarta Post*. 23 September. <http://old.thejakartapost.com/detailheadlines.asp?fileid=20080923.@03&irec=4>

Kingma, Kees. 2001. *Demobilisation and Reintegration of Ex-combatants in Post-war and Transition Countries*. Eschborn: Deutsche Gesellschaft für Technische Zusammernarbeit.

Kingsbury, Damian. 2006. *Peace in Aceh: A Personal Account of the Helsinki Peace Process.* Jakarta: Equinox.

Knight, Mark and Alpaslan Özerdem. 2004. 'Guns, Camps and Cash: Disarmament, Demobilization and Reinsertion of Former Combatants in Transitions from War to Peace.' *Journal of Peace Research,* Vol. 41, 4, pp. 499–516.

McGibbon, Rodd. 2006. 'Local Leadership and the Aceh Conflict.' In Anthony Reid, pp. 315–59.

Mietzner, Marcus. 2006. 'The Politics of Military Reform in Post-Suharto Indonesia: Elite Conflict, Nationalism, and International Resistance.' *Policy Studies,* No. 23. Washington, DC: East–West Center.

Miller, Michelle Ann. 2006. 'What's Special about Special Autonomy in Aceh?' In Anthony Reid, pp. 292–314.

Morfit, Michael. 2007. 'The Road to Helsinki: The Aceh Agreement and Indonesia's Democratic Development.' *International Negotiation,* Vol. 12, pp. 111–43.

MSR (Multi-Stakeholder Review of Post-Conflict Programming in Aceh). Forthcoming. <http://www.conflictanddevelopment.org/msr>

Muggah, Robert. 2005. 'No Magic Bullet: A Critical Perspective on Disarmament, Demobilization and Reintegration (DDR) and Weapons Reduction in Post-conflict Contexts.' *Round Table,* Vol. 94, No. 379, pp. 239–52.

—. 2006. 'Emerging from the Shadow of War: A Critical Perspective on DDR and Weapons Reduction in the Post-Conflict Period.' *Journal of Contemporary Security,* Vol. 27, No. 1, pp. 190–205.

—. 2009. 'Introduction: The Emporer's Clothes.' In Robert Muggah, ed. *Security and Post-Conflict Reconstruction: Dealing with Fighters in the Aftermath of War.* London and New York: Routledge.

— and Anton Baare. 2009. 'Negotiating Reintegration in Uganda: Dealing with Combatants during Peace Processes.' In Robert Muggah, ed. *Security and Post-Conflict Reconstruction: Dealing with Fighters in the Aftermath of War.* London and New York: Routledge.

— and Jon Bennett. 2009. 'Context Matters in Ethiopia: Reflections on a Demobilization and Reintegration Programme.' In Robert Muggah, ed. *Security and Post-Conflict Reconstruction: Dealing with Fighters in the Aftermath of War.* London and New York: Routledge.

Paris, Roland. 2004. *At War's End: Building Peace After Civil Conflict*. Cambridge: Cambridge University Press.

Peake, Gordon. 2009. 'What the Timorese Veterans Say: Unpacking Security Promotion in Timor–Leste.' In Robert Muggah, ed. *Security and Post-Conflict Reconstruction: Dealing with Fighters in the Aftermath of War.* London and New York: Routledge, pp. 165–89.

Reid, Anthony. 2009. 'The Aceh Conflict: A Long-term View for Long-Term Solutions.' Mimeo. Multi-stakeholder Review of Post-Conflict Programming.

— ed. 2006. *Verandah of Violence: The Background to the Aceh Problem*. Singapore: Singapore University Press and University of Washington Press.

Rolston, Bill. 2007. 'Demobilization and Reintegration of Ex-Combatants: The Irish Case in International Perspective.' *Social & Legal Studies,* Vol. 16, No. 2, pp. 259–80.

Ross, Michael L. 2005. 'Resources and Rebellion in Indonesia.' In Paul Collier and Nicholas Sambanis, eds. *Understanding Civil War: Europe, Central Asia, and Other Regions*. Washington, DC: World Bank and Oxford University Press.

Schiller, Rachel. 2008. 'The Impacts of Peacebuilding Work on the Aceh Conflict: Reflecting on Peace Practice—Cumulative Impacts Case Study.' Cambridge, MA: Collaborative Learning Projects.

Schulze, Kirsten. 2004. 'The Free Aceh Movement (GAM): Anatomy of a Separatist Organization.' *Policy Studies,* No. 2. Washington, DC: East–West Center.

—. 2006. 'Dealing with Destruction: Aceh—A Year after the Tsunami.' *World Today,* Vol. 62, No. 1, pp. 12–13.

Stedman, Stephen. 1997. 'Spoiler Problems in Peace Processes.' *International Security,* Vol. 22, No. 2, pp. 5–53.

Sukma, Rizal. 2004. 'Security Operations in Aceh: Goals, Consequences, and Lessons.' *Policy Studies,* No. 3. Washington, DC: East–West Center.

Sulaiman, M. Isa. 2006. 'From Autonomy to Periphery: A Critical Evaluation of the Acehnese Nationalist Movement.' In Anthony Reid, pp. 121–48.

Swedish MFA (Ministry for Foreign Affairs). 2006. *Stockholm Initiative on Disarmament Demobilisation Reintegration: Final Report*. Stockholm: MFA. <http://www.regeringen.se/sb/d/4890>

UNDDR (United Nations Disarmament, Demobilization and Reintegration Resource Centre). 2006. *Integrated Disarmament, Demobilization and Reintegration Standards*. New York: UNDDR. <http://www.unddr.org/iddrs>

Willibald, Sigrid. 2006. 'Does Money Work? Cash Transfers to Ex-combatants in Disarmament, Demobilization and Reintegration Processes.' *Disasters*, Vol. 30, Iss. 3, pp. 316–39.

World Bank. 2006a. *GAM Reintegration Needs Assessment: Enhancing Peace through Community-level Development Programming*. Banda Aceh: World Bank.

—. 2006b. *The Aceh Peace Agreement: How Far Have We Come?* Briefing Note. December. <http://www.conflictanddevelopment.org/data/brief/Conflict%20briefing%20note-eng.pdf>

—. 2006c. *Aceh Public Expenditure Analysis: Spending for Reconstruction and Poverty Reduction*. Jakarta: World Bank.

—. 2008a. *Aceh Conflict Monitoring Update: January 1st–February 29th*. Banda Aceh: World Bank.

—. 2008b. *Aceh Conflict Monitoring Update: May 1st–June 30th*. Banda Aceh: World Bank.

—. 2008c. *Aceh Conflict Monitoring Update: July 1st–August 31st*. Banda Aceh: World Bank.

—. 2008d. *Aceh Conflict Monitoring Update: September 1st–30th*. Banda Aceh: World Bank.

—. 2008e. *Aceh Poverty Assessment 2008: The Impact of the Conflict, the Tsunami, and Reconstruction on Poverty in Aceh*. Jakarta: World Bank.

—. 2008f. *Aceh Economic Update: October 2008*. Jakarta/Banda Aceh: World Bank/Bank Indonesia/Multi-Donor Fund.

—. 2008g. *Aceh Conflict Monitoring Update: October 1st–November 30th*. Banda Aceh: World Bank.

—/DSF (Decentralization Support Facility). 2007. *Aceh Conflict Monitoring Update: September 2007*. Banda Aceh: World Bank/DSF.

—/KDP (Kecamatan Development Program). 2007. *2006 Village Survey in Aceh: An Assessment of Village Infrastructure and Social Conditions*. Banda Aceh/Jakarta: World Bank/Government of Indonesia.

Zurstrassen, Matthew. 2006. 'An Evaluation of BRA Support to Former Combatants.' Unpublished World Bank evaluation report for BRA. 10 September.

ACKNOWLEDGEMENTS

Principal author

Patrick Barron

Contributors

Wasi Abbas, Macartan Humphreys, Adrian Morel, Laura Paler, Yuhki Tajima, Jeremy Weinstein, Rob Wrobel

Afghan militiamen hand over weapons during a disarmament ceremony in Herat, July 2004. © Marcelo Salinas/WPN

DDR in Afghanistan

WHEN STATE-BUILDING AND INSECURITY COLLIDE

9

INTRODUCTION

By December 2001, after less than three months' fighting, Coalition and allied Afghan forces had driven the five-year-old Taliban government from power, taken the capital Kabul, and overpowered further armed resistance in the strategic cities of Mazar-e-Sharif, Kunduz, Kandahar, and elsewhere.[1] In the wake of these successes, Western donors moved quickly to establish a transitional government and begin planning security promotion efforts. These would eventually include disarmament, demobilization, and reintegration (DDR), an illegal armed group disbandment programme, and a host of associated weapons control and security measures. Donor governments mobilized to support these programmes with contributions of more than USD 180 million (Sedra, 2008a, pp. 124, 138).

By 2006, however, the security situation had deteriorated significantly. Taliban, al-Qaeda, and other insurgent forces had grown in strength along Afghanistan's mountainous southern border.[2] Supported by the Pakistani intelligence service and poppy cultivation proceeds, these fighters developed into an intensive and effective insurgency, modifying their tactics and launching increasingly deadly attacks on Afghan security forces, civilians, aid workers, and foreign troops. In response, the US-led Operation Enduring Freedom (OEF) force, together with the NATO-led International Security Assistance Force (ISAF), stepped up counter-insurgency operations. Whereas violence was previously confined to the provinces, from 2007 onwards the Taliban increasingly carried out attacks on government targets in the heart of Kabul.[3] The spreading insecurity has led some Afghans to voice nostalgia for the stability and relative safety of the Taliban era.

Insecurity has other faces in post-2001 Afghanistan. The loyalty ties, power structures, and influence of armed groups of former anti-Taliban forces, as well as criminal groups, have persisted inside and outside the new government. Warlords influence swathes of territory in some regions; if they have not been absorbed into the national or regional security apparatus, they may continue operations under the banner of private security firms for hire by domestic and foreign actors. Criminality, the drug trade, and inter-group conflict—in a society where small arms are virtually ubiquitous—are defining features of the landscape. For all of these reasons, security remains a major concern for many Afghans.[4]

As the other case studies in the *Small Arms Survey 2009* demonstrate, no two post-conflict contexts are identical (ACEH, LEBANON). But the complexity and ongoing violence in Afghanistan challenge the label 'post-conflict'. Armed violence and insecurity have shadowed the experience of state-building in Afghanistan since 2002 and have led at least one analyst to conclude that 'the post-9/11 era in Afghanistan . . . should still be viewed as a renewed period of conflict and mobilization' (Bhatia, 2008a, p. 14). In this context, Afghanistan, perhaps to a larger extent than other societies plagued by armed violence, has also demonstrated the intrinsically political nature of DDR and the inextricable linkages between DDR and security sector reform (SSR).

This chapter reviews the development and implementation of the primary DDR and demilitarization measures in Afghanistan. Among its findings:

- The Afghanistan DDR programme disarmed and demobilized some 63,000 members of the Afghan Military Forces (AMF) from October 2003 to July 2005. Much of the country reaped security benefits—whose impact remains difficult to quantify—after the removal of AMF commanders from the government payroll and the release of AMF soldiers from service.
- Through December 2008, DDR interventions and the follow-on Disbandment of Illegal Armed Groups (DIAG) programme removed about 100,000 small arms, light weapons, and other weapons, about half of which were destroyed. Based on previous estimates, however, arms possession remains widespread among militia, state, and insurgent forces and the civilian population.
- Tasked with simultaneously breaking apart and reintegrating AMF militias, recruiting and training a new national police and army, and establishing a representative government practically from scratch, DDR planners were forced to make difficult decisions about the pacing, terms, and extent of disarmament and demobilization efforts.

Map 9.1 **Afghanistan**

The inability of the state to provide security during DDR and DIAG, in particular, circumscribed the possibilities for successful armed group disarmament and demobilization in the country.

- DDR suffered early on from a highly factionalized government that saw AMF commanders, warlords, and drug lords manipulating the programme to their benefit, targeting their enemies, and maintaining their power bases. However, the DIAG programme has reduced the influence of these figures to some degree in national and provincial governments.
- Generations of armed violence and the dynamics of mobilization, legitimacy, and patronage in Afghanistan have combined to create commander–militiamen links that are difficult to break, and DDR and DIAG have proven unable to do so. In recent years, under pressure from the rising insurgency and inadequate state security forces, the government has increasingly turned back to militia and other auxiliary forces for support.

This chapter sketches out the complex history of armed conflict in Afghanistan since the Soviet period through to Taliban rule, including relevant social, historical, and geopolitical perspectives. It then describes the main events of the 'war on terrorism' as it played out in Afghanistan, and the international community's subsequent development of programming designed to stabilize and bring security to the country.

While a range of security programmes has been instituted in Afghanistan since 2002, this chapter focuses specifically on the DDR and illegal armed group disbandment projects of the Afghan New Beginnings Programme (ANBP). After examining how these programmes were designed and executed, the chapter offers reflections on their outcomes, both in terms of their stated goals and objectives, and measured against other qualitative and quantitative security indicators.

CONTEXT: ARMED GROUPS AND CONFLICT IN AFGHANISTAN

In 2001 Barakat and Wardell distilled and categorized the phases of 23 years of Afghan conflict as follows (Barakat and Wardell, 2001[5]):

1979–88	jihad in a cold-war context, various Mujaheddin factions fight against the Soviet military forces
1989–1992	armed conflict between the Soviet-backed government in Kabul and Mujaheddin factions
1992–96	factional war among Mujaheddin groups
1996–2001	regional proxy war between the Taliban and the Northern Alliance
late 2001	US-led international 'war on terrorism'

Some further detail on these phases is important. In 1978, community and military rebellions evolved into a decade-long sustained insurgency against the Soviet-backed Karmal and Najibullah governments. The Soviet withdrawal in 1989 was accompanied by an acceleration of armed conflict between the state and competing political–military parties. When the Najibullah regime collapsed in 1992, inter-factional conflict erupted, dividing the country into fiefdoms of varying sizes. One of the many groups to emerge was the Taliban, formed in 1994 largely of youths from Pakistani refugee camps with little connection to local community structures (*Talib* means 'student' or 'cadet' in Arabic, and many members of the Taliban emerged from radicalized *madrasas* in the border areas). While the Taliban enjoyed some local legitimacy in Kandahar, where they were welcomed because of the security they provided, the faction grew into a more powerful player primarily due to financial and military support from Pakistan's Inter-Services Intelligence. The Taliban's popularity among Afghans would wane as they applied their conservative brand of Islam.

Through negotiation and open fighting, the Taliban were able to conquer and administer up to 90 per cent of the country by 1996. Remaining armed groups, many of which competed with one another in a bewildering array of alliances, joined to oppose the Taliban under the banner of the Northern Alliance (known within the country as the United Islamic Front for the Salvation of Afghanistan). Many of the groups within the alliance remained dormant or suffered significant losses until the United States offered military and financial backing in 2000–01 (Bhatia, 2008a, p. 14).

Following the terrorist attacks on the United States and the subsequent identification of al-Qaeda and Osama bin Laden as the primary perpetrators, the United States government issued an ultimatum to the Taliban government demanding the extradition of all al-Qaeda leaders in the country. When this demand was not met, the United States planned, sponsored, and led an invasion to uproot the Taliban and al-Qaeda from the country and capture bin Laden. In partnership with the United Kingdom, the United States initiated OEF-Afghanistan on 7 October 2001 with an aerial bombardment campaign in and around the cities of Kabul, Jalalabad, and Kandahar.

The subsequent ground war was fought by the Northern Alliance, assisted primarily by soldiers from the United States, Britain, and Canada. In fact, financial assistance was offered to almost anyone willing to pick up arms against the Taliban forces. This had the effect of not only remobilizing previously active fighters but also drawing in new (violence) entrepreneurs.

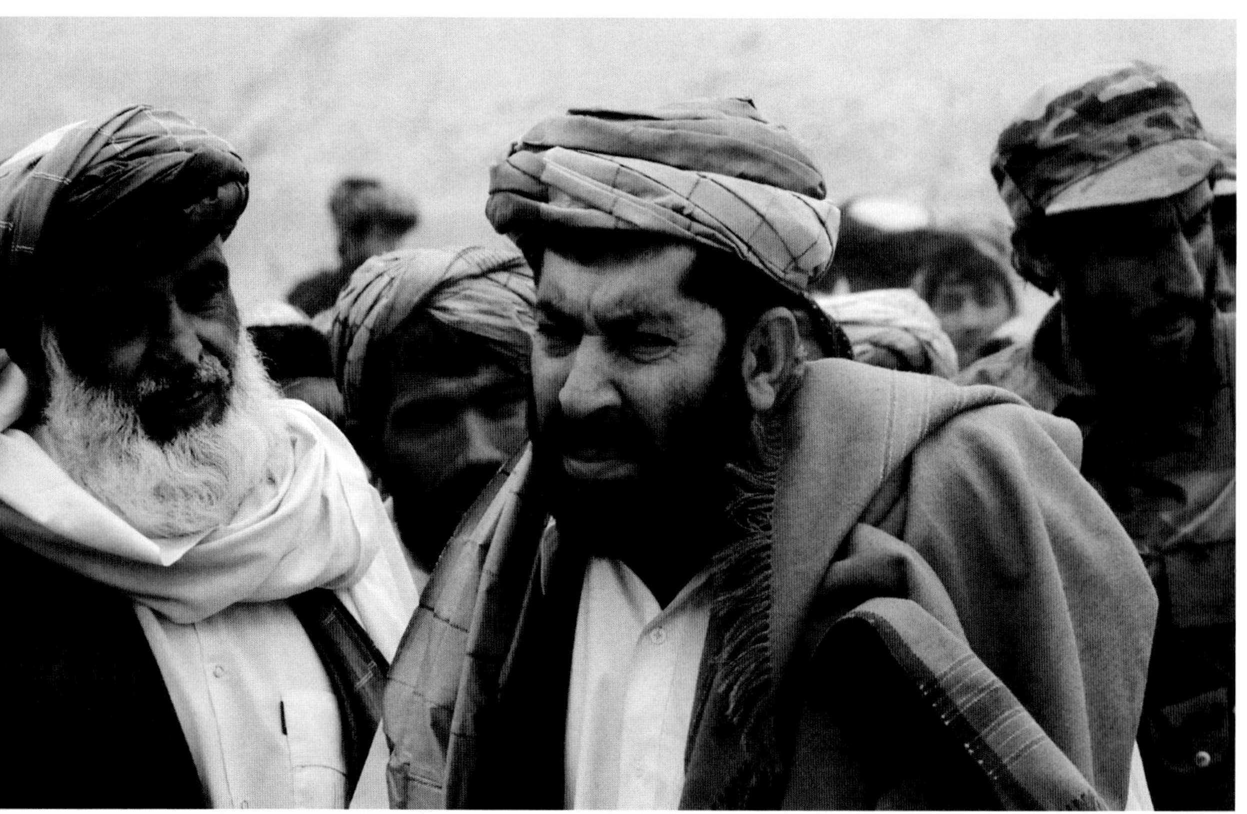

Former warlord Gul Agha Sherzai, centre, became governor of Kandahar in 2001 and of Nangarhar Province in 2004, despite accusations of ongoing criminal activity. © John Moore/AP Photo

At the outset, OEF's primary objective was to overthrow the Taliban and clear the country of al-Qaeda. Kabul was recaptured on 13 November 2001 and the rest of the Taliban strongholds around the country fell shortly thereafter. After another month of fighting with al-Qaeda loyalists in the cave complex of Tora Bora near the Pakistan border, it was widely believed that remaining combatant forces were limited and contained in a fixed area. Following these actions, OEF deployed mainly to the south and east of the country and engaged in offensive combat operations under the direct command of a US-led coalition. Until 2006, a separate NATO-led ISAF force was involved mostly in central, northern, and western areas and engaged in stability and support operations. Since 2006, both have mandates to operate over the entire country, and both are engaged in offensive military operations, but they remain separate.

At the local and regional levels, in the months following the collapse of the Taliban regime, militias that had collaborated with the Coalition or taken advantage of a security vacuum assumed power. Most were led by commanders who had exercised power in the pre-Taliban era. The landscape had become a patchwork of militia fiefdoms with varying levels of internal organization (ICG, 2003, p. 2). These groupings were eventually the basis of the transitional Afghan Military Forces. Crucially, as particular militia found favour or successfully exerted themselves with Kabul, the composition of key government agencies soon reflected this influence, contributing to the factionalization and even ethnicization of the main security institutions (Bhatia, 2008a, p. 18).

Box 9.1 **Estimating armed violence-related mortality in Afghanistan, 2004-08**

Estimating the number of deaths in Afghanistan's 'post-conflict' phase is challenging. In the absence of victimization surveys–such as have been conducted in Iraq–analysts must rely on incident reporting, which compiles conflict-related events from news reports, state and NGO data, and whatever can be obtained from hospitals and morgue reporting. While this technique has improved in recent years due to the advent of Internet search engines and parsing programmes that automatically identify appropriate data, the method suffers from the intrinsic limitations of its information sources. Whereas direct conflict deaths may be estimated using incident reporting, indirect deaths remain largely out of reach of this method.

The *Global Burden of Armed Violence* report analyses direct conflict deaths from a range of cross-country and individual country datasets. It finds that 12,417 direct conflict deaths occurred in Afghanistan from 2004 through 2007 (see Table 9.1). These include both civilian and combatant deaths caused by war-related attacks and injuries (as caused by bullets, bombs, mines, and other war weapons).

Complete data is not yet available for 2008. However, the UN Assistance Mission in Afghanistan reported in September 2008 that 1,445 civilians had been killed from January to August, a 39 per cent increase over the previous year (UNOHCHR, 2008). These included deaths from insurgent attacks, deaths caused by government and allied military operations, suicide bombings, and summary executions.

To these figures must be added indirect conflict deaths (also known as excess mortality). These arise from the worsening of social, economic, and health conditions and include deaths from reduced access to health services, destruction of health infrastructure, malnutrition and disease due to displacement and agricultural destruction, and food insecurity. Public health research indicates that indirect deaths can be three to 15 times greater than the number of direct deaths, depending on the nature of the conflict, the parties involved, and other factors. Applying a conservative average multiplier of four indirect deaths for every direct death yields 50,000 excess deaths in Afghanistan since 2004. Even if the ratio were reduced to three to one, as studies have suggested was the ratio in Iraq, the combined direct and indirect deaths for Afghanistan for these four years alone would exceed 50,000.

Source: Geneva Declaration Secretariat (2008, pp. 18, 27, 32, 40)

Table 9.1 **Direct conflict deaths in Afghanistan, 2004-07**

Year	Number of direct deaths	Mortality rate per 100,000
2004	917	3.21
2005	1,000	3.35
2006	4,000	12.87
2007	6,500	20.15
	Total: 12,417	**Average: 9.89**

Box 9.2 The dynamics of mobilization in Afghanistan

In Afghanistan there is no generic armed group 'type' or one fixed or static motive guiding combatant behaviour; presumptions of homogeneity can thus be counterproductive for DDR and demilitarization initiatives. A narrow focus on presumed 'greed'–whereby combatants are treated as undifferentiated rational utility-maximizers–neglects crucial issues such as the role of the state and local legitimacy, the malleable *perception* of legitimacy, and community reliance on commanders for protection.[7]

Not all Afghan armed groups are ideologically driven Islamists, warlords, or tribal militias. Michael Bhatia identifies three 'ideal types' of Afghan armed groups: *political-military parties* (also known as *tanzims*), *warlords and strongmen*, and *community militia*, each with distinctive dynamics of authority, activities, and weapons acquisition and distribution patterns (see Table 9.2).

Importantly for DDR and demilitarization, armed groups are linked to and guided by different sources of authority depending on their type. For example, a community militia is tied to the *qawm-e-mesharan* (local elders), is based on community consent, and is generally limited to local protection. Local strongmen can acquire enough power either to rise autonomously or to dominate the *qawm-e-mesharan* and hold a direct relationship with combatants. In contrast, contemporary militarized *tanzims* are primarily administrative organizations propagating a specific ideology.

Most armed groups in Afghanistan are fluid and dynamic, combining features of each type. Moreover, an armed group can evolve from one type to another over time. Thus, various types of armed groups dominate in different regions, with distinct constellations of community militias, strongmen, government-armed groups (official and informal militias), foreign forces, and political-military parties operating in each region.

Just as there is no generic armed group, there is no prototypical combatant in Afghanistan. Interviews reveal a diverse array of life narratives and histories of involvement in the conflict, whether as temporary combatants, community militia members, local strongmen, or in service with political-military parties. There is no one dominating motive for mobilization, though interviewed demobilizing combatants point to the significance of family, tribal, and customary institutions; the protection of families; coercive mobilization (in the north-east of the country especially); and multiple and often interlocking forms of authority. These motives are not necessarily equally distributed by region or tribal grouping. Thus, viewing mobilization through the narrow lenses of economic livelihoods, ideology, or grievance alone would be a great mistake.

Source: Bhatia and Muggah (2008, pp. 140–43)

Information on the number of combatants, violent victimization patterns, and presence of small arms and light weapons is difficult to obtain. A 2003 Small Arms Survey estimate places the number of small arms and light weapons in Afghanistan somewhere between 500,000 to 1.5 million (Small Arms Survey, 2003, p. 74). The International Institute for Strategic Studies reports that at most 533,000 individuals were mobilized after the Soviet withdrawal in 1989; it counts at least 102,400 fatalities from 1992 to 2008, of which 26,440 occurred from 2001 onwards (IISS, 2008). The Human Security Report Project suggests that the country experienced 480,000 direct conflict deaths in 1978–2005 (HSRP, 2008, p. 31). The *Global Burden of Armed Violence* report estimates that 12,417 violent deaths took place from 2004 to 2007 (see Box 9.1). These figures should be treated with caution since they are based on media reports and government sources that are almost impossible to verify.[6]

For Afghanistan, the post-9/11 period is but one phase of a 30-year cycle of violent conflict under the influence of foreign nations, proxy forces, tribalism, and criminality. The country may be considered 'post-war' in the sense that the war to overthrow the Taliban regime led to the establishment of a new government, but that war spawned an insurgency and counter-insurgency that increasingly threaten the viability of the state.

Central to the dynamics of conflict in Afghanistan is the role of local commanders and armed groups. These individuals and groups were empowered by literally billions of dollars in financial, material, and military assistance. Pakistan, the Soviet Union, the United States, and Saudi Arabia have all at one time or another provided infusions of start-up or venture capital in armed groups, allowing them to enhance their influence over the economy, village,

Table 9.2 **'Ideal types' of Afghan armed groups**

Type of armed group	Source of authority	Composition	Activities	Weapons ownership	Internal weapons distribution	Examples
Political-military party	Organization and indoctrination, charisma	Detribalized, delocalized, and ideologically oriented	Contest for national power or regional autonomy	Party stockpiles with central distribution	Tactical units oriented towards external enemy, mix of heavy weapons, infantry, specialized units	Hezb-e-Islam Gulbuddin Hekmatyar
Warlords and strongmen	Charisma, force, and patronage	Both community members and other delocalized elites	Contest for regional, provincial, or local power and autonomy	Individually owned weapons and commander stockpiles	Relatives, close affiliates, and *nazm-e-khas* (special force) given special weapons for predation and internal enforcement	Regional: Ismail Khan; local: Abdul Salaam Reza (Ghor)
Community militia	Tradition and charisma	Local community members	Local protection and predation; autonomy	Individually owned weapons	All combatants possess similar weapons	Paktya *arbakian* (tribal police)

Source: Bhatia (2008b, p. 77)

and provincial politics and *shuras* (local consultative bodies). Once armed and funded, commanders became largely self-sufficient, gaining control of customs posts, opium trafficking routes, and other economic activities (Rubin, 2003). Standard DDR and demilitarization theory would call for the disbandment and disarmament of these various groups. In the Afghan context, however, this approach has not been straightforward, as discussed below.

Afghan groups display an extraordinary level of heterogeneity and include multiple Mujaheddin parties, tribal militias, warlords, paramilitary organizations, a trained state officer corps, armed intelligence services, and both mono-ethnic and multi-ethnic armed groups and alliances (Bhatia and Muggah, 2008, p. 129). As the Coalition, its allies, and the transitional government authorities recognized early on, commanders, warlords, and armed groups would continue to play a decisive role in post-Taliban Afghanistan. The complexities of armed group mobilization are key to understanding the shifting power dynamics and their relationship to efforts to disarm and demobilize Afghan fighters (see Box 9.2).

THE PROGRESSION OF DDR PROGRAMMING IN AFGHANISTAN

The Afghanistan demilitarization effort has four 'pillars': the DDR of the formal militias associated with the government, which proceeded from October 2003 to June 2006; the disbandment of illegal armed groups (DIAG) programme, which began in September 2005 and is ongoing; the cantonment of heavy weapons; and the collection and destruction of anti-personnel mines and ammunition stocks. This chapter focuses primarily on DDR and DIAG.[8]

These efforts proceeded in parallel with not only security sector reform but also security sector *creation*, in particular the formation of a national army and a national police force. Thus, while the government was engaged in disarmament, it was simultaneously working to extend and enforce its monopoly over the legitimate use of force. These parallel moves were fraught with difficult choices and compromises that affected the design, implementation, and outcomes of the DDR and DIAG programmes.

A false start: the National Disarmament Commission

By the end of the Coalition-led military intervention, peace-building and state-building efforts were intimately connected. The first steps were taken even before fighting in the southern border areas was declared over. On 5 December 2001, under the auspices of the United Nations, prominent Afghanis signed the Bonn Agreement, establishing an Afghan Interim Authority (AIA) with a six-month mandate; the AIA was superseded by a Transitional Authority following a nationwide emergency *loya jirga,* a traditional convocation of Afghan leaders to address pressing challenges (see Figure 9.1). The Bonn Agreement also established a commission charged with developing a new constitution and a judicial commission to guide the rehabilitation of the justice system in accord with Islamic law and international standards.

The AIA was not a unitary actor but a patchwork of victorious commanders.

The agreement was not a peace agreement in the classic sense, as the Taliban and allied groups were completely ignored; rather, it was a power-sharing arrangement. Many of the top posts in the AIA were distributed primarily among four Afghan factions. It was especially relevant for future disarmament and demobilization programmes that the Northern Alliance held the key ministries of defence, foreign affairs, and the interior. Thus the AIA was not a unitary actor but a patchwork of victorious commanders, regardless of their earlier orientation to the state (Özerdem, 2002, p. 965).

Under these circumstances it is not surprising that the Bonn Agreement treaded softly on the question of the disarmament of the armed groups that contributed to the Coalition victory. The one limited stipulation was that 'upon the official transfer of power, all Mujaheddin, Afghan armed forces and armed groups in the country shall come under the command and control of the new Interim Authority, and be reorganized according to the requirements of the new Afghan security and armed forces' (Bonn Agreement, para. V, art. 1). In the view of the government, requiring the Northern Alliance to disarm was potentially risky, not to mention against the personal interests of some new leaders. Disarmament of armed groups would thus have been likely to 'remain unresolved in the near future' (Özerdem, 2002, p. 973).

In January 2003 President Karzai appointed four Defence Commissions: (1) the National Disarmament Commission (NDC), established to oversee the collection and destruction of weapons; (2) the Demobilization and Reintegration (D&R) Commission; (3) the Officer Recruiting and Training Commission; and (4) the Soldier Recruiting and Training Commission. These commissions were created for the dual purpose of asserting Afghan ownership over the DDR process and coordinating the multiplicity of actors involved in its implementation.

The primary purpose of the NDC was to approve the final version of the disarmament plan developed through discussions with the Afghan Ministry of Defence (MoD) and the ANBP and to provide some oversight of its implementation. From its inception, however, the commission sought to expand its mandate, positioning itself as the main implementing actor for the process and launching its own disarmament initiative before the ANBP could assert itself as

Figure 9.1 **Timeline of key events in Afghanistan, 2001-06**

October 2001
Military campaign against Taliban begins

November 2001
Taliban regime overthrown

December 2001
Bonn Agreement establishes Afghan Interim Authority (AIA)

March 2002
UN Assistance Mission in Afghanistan (UNAMA) established

June 2002
Loya jirga elects Hamid Karzai interim head of state

December 2002
Afghanistan Transitional Authority (ATA) establishes Afghan National Army

January 2003
ATA establishes National Disarmament Commission, Demobilization and Reintegration Commission

March 2003
Afghan New Beginnings Programme (ANBP) established

August 2003
NATO takes command of International Security Assistance Force (ISAF)

January 2004
Loya jirga adopts new constitution

August 2004
EUROCORPS takes command of ISAF

October 2004
Presidential elections held, Hamid Karzai elected

June 2005
Afghan Military Forces (AMF) declared disbanded

July 2005
Disbandment of Illegal Armed Groups (DIAG) project initiated

September 2005
Lower house of parliament and provincial council elections

December 2005
New parliament inaugurated

May-June 2006
Rapid escalation in insurgent violence

the focal point of the process. In this manner, it attempted to pre-empt the nascent ANBP and impose an 'Afghan solution' to the security crisis (Sedra, 2008a, p. 120).

The stated goal of the programme was to collect one million weapons and pieces of military equipment (Wali, 2002). Collection efforts took place in five northern provinces, targeting Afghan Military Forces personnel—the various militias, most under the umbrella of the Northern Alliance, that came to power in the wake of the Taliban's collapse. Weapons collected were to be stored in local facilities until they could be moved to the national MoD depot in Kabul (Wali, 2002).

The NDC programme suffered from a lack of clarity of process and reported outcomes. It appears that fighters were promised compensation for their weapons, but that funds were sometimes not delivered. There were also allegations that weapons collected were transferred to other militias instead of being stockpiled—a problem that would soon recur. By mid-2002, however, the government claimed that 50,000 pieces of military equipment had been collected, including both small arms and light weapons, and heavy military equipment such as tanks and armoured vehicles. This news of success was used to justify the extension of the programme throughout the rest of the country, but final figures for weapons collected in the expanded programme have yet to be made available. In the end, questions about the programme's impact, transparency, and neutrality remained. According to some analysts, the NDC programme was less an effort by an accountable and neutral government body to bring security than an attempt by factional actors within the MoD, aligned primarily with the Northern Alliance's Shura-e-Nezar (supervisory council) militia,[9] to consolidate their control over the country's military assets (Sedra, 2008a, p. 121).

The Afghan New Beginnings Programme[10]

Widespread recognition of the NDC's shortcomings fed eagerness to move to a formal and internationally driven DDR effort. In February 2003, President Karzai outlined the Afghan New Beginnings Programme at a donor conference in Tokyo (see Box 9.3). The ANBP was designed for implementation by the United Nations Development Programme (UNDP) on behalf of the government. The Transitional Authority and UNDP signed the agreement on 6 April, and the final approval to proceed was given on 8 October. With the establishment of the ANBP, the NDC was dissolved and its mandates integrated into the MoD. Of the four original commissions, only the D&R Commission remained active after 2005; disarmament was added to its duties, though it did not develop the capacity to assume this role.

The DDR programme was to be voluntary in nature and focus solely on militias associated with the AMF. The stated objectives were 'to decommission formations and units up to a total of 100,000 officers and solders and in the process collect, store and deactivate weapons currently in their possession in order to be able to reconstruct the Afghan National Army and return those not required to civilian life' (Sedra, 2004, p. 3).

In fact, though disarmament appears to occupy a central function here, the real goal was 'to break the historic patriarchal chain of command existing between the former combatants and their men; and to provide the demobilized personnel with the ability to become economically independent' (ANBP, 2006, p. 3). Unlike DDR programmes in many other contexts, this programme 'was never mandated to disarm the population per se or provide direct employment but to assist AMF military personnel to transition from military into civilian life' (ANBP, 2006, p. 3). The disarmament aspect of the ANBP was designed to be largely symbolic, indicating individual soldiers' commitment to peace (Sedra, 2008a, p. 124). Neither commanders nor soldiers were obliged to submit all of their weapons.

At the outset of the programme there was no clear picture of the number of AMF personnel who would qualify: estimates ranged from 50,000 to 250,000. A compromise figure of 100,000 participants was soon agreed, though it was a not based on a needs assessment. While the AMF had an interest in inflating its ranks to increase benefits, some of the uncertainty grew out of the part-time nature of militia activities and the spontaneous demobilization of many militia members—partly due to low or irregular pay—after the defeat of the Taliban (ICG, 2003, p. i). After 13 months of operations the ANBP quietly dropped its target to 60,000. The number and quality of weapons in militia hands was virtually unknown, relying on 'crude and outdated' estimates (Sedra, 2008a, p. 124).

At this point in the process, DDR best practices would typically call for skills and needs assessments and other preparatory measures such as militia mapping, surveying of groups' composition and structure, and soldier and commander profiling to inform programme design. None of these steps were taken prior to the launch of the ANBP. Nor did the programme seek to engage commanders in the process, whether with carrots or sticks, despite the focus on breaking militia chains of command.

Box 9.3 **Time and money**

Eight donor governments contributed to the ANBP for a total of USD 142.2 million. These were: Japan (USD 91 million); the United Kingdom (USD 19 million); Canada (USD 16 million); the United States (USD 9 million); the Netherlands (USD 4 million); the European Commission (USD 1.9 million); Norway (USD 0.8 million); and Switzerland (USD 0.5 million).

Donor conditions and deadlines shaped the programming from the start. The Japanese government, responsible for almost two-thirds of the ANBP budget, called for reforms to the MoD prior to the commencement of DDR operations, which resulted in a delay of four months. In fact, the MoD never did meet all of the requirements for personnel changes; donors decided to forgo the outstanding reforms as they would have caused additional, serious delays.

Time limits also controlled what could be offered. According to donor guidelines, the programme had to be completed in three years. By one analyst's estimate, it took 18 months to establish the ANBP, recruit staff, purchase vehicles, visit AMF units, and plan and negotiate the DDR process, leaving only 18 months to implement a highly complex and logistically challenging programme.

Partly for these reasons, some potential options were not proposed, including literacy training, despite the fact that more than 80 per cent of all demobilized ex-combatants were unable to read or write as of September 2004 (SRSG, 2004).

Sources: Sedra (2008a, p. 124); Poulton (2008, p. 14)

Table 9.3 The AMF disarmament process

	List of candidates →	Verifications of MoD list →	Disarmament →	Weapons collection
Actors	Ministry of Defence	ANBP's regional verification committee	Soldiers and officers, international observers	ANBP's mobile disarmament units
Tasks	Provides comprehensive list of AMF personnel	Verifies MoD list and modifies as appropriate; flags special cases (e.g. drug users, child soldiers); ensures special conditions are in place	Combatants hand in weapons to commanding officers; ceremony at garrison: medals, certificates of honour, honour parade	Collect and register weapons

Source: Sedra (2008a, p. 125)

The ANBP would grow to a staff of 700—mostly Afghans—with up to 70 international actors. The central office was located in Kabul and eight regional offices in Kunduz, Kabul/Parwan, Gardez, Mazar-e-Sharif, Kandahar, Bamyan, Jalalabad, and Herat. The programme proceeded as follows: AMF units would submit a list of their personnel to the regional office. After verification by the MoD, these lists would be vetted by prominent and trusted leaders from the region (see Table 9.3). Entry into the programme was limited to those who had at least eight months of military service and who could turn in a serviceable weapon to a mobile disarmament unit. No attempt was made to collect or even identify all the weapons held by the militia.[11]

Nevertheless, the trigger that guided an individual's movement through the programme was the surrendering of a weapon. Collected firearms were engraved with an alphanumeric code and registered into a database in the central ANBP office along with information on the owner. Eventually they were moved to the national arms depot and were held under a dual key system, with one key held by the MoD and the other by the International Observer Group, a body of international monitors. Upon completion of the programme the weapons were to be turned over to the Afghan National Army (ANA).

Once this step was taken, each individual was directed to a case worker for demobilization at an ANBP regional office. This consisted of an interview to determine the skills, experiences, education levels, and desires of ex-combatants. After taking an oath not to engage in further fighting, the former militiamen were given a medal for distinguished service and a certificate for honourable discharge. A cash payment of USD 200 was discontinued after a pilot project revealed that commanders were forcing ex-soldiers to turn over part or all of this money (Sedra, 2004, pp. 3–7).

The ex-combatant then passed into reintegration, which consisted of a choice of several packages or entry into the ANA following qualification. While the latter option may have been attractive to many militia members, stringent age requirements (18–28) excluded the vast majority: only 2.42 per cent of ex-combatants receiving reintegration assistance joined the ANA (Sedra, 2008a, p. 127). Ex-combatants often ended up with a reintegration package based on considerations of programme availability and administrative expediency rather than needs, skills, and market gaps (Dennys, 2005, p. 4).

Complications arose almost immediately. First, AMF commanders wilfully and systematically manipulated the process. They submitted the least loyal soldiers and least functional weapons, retaining control of the vast majority

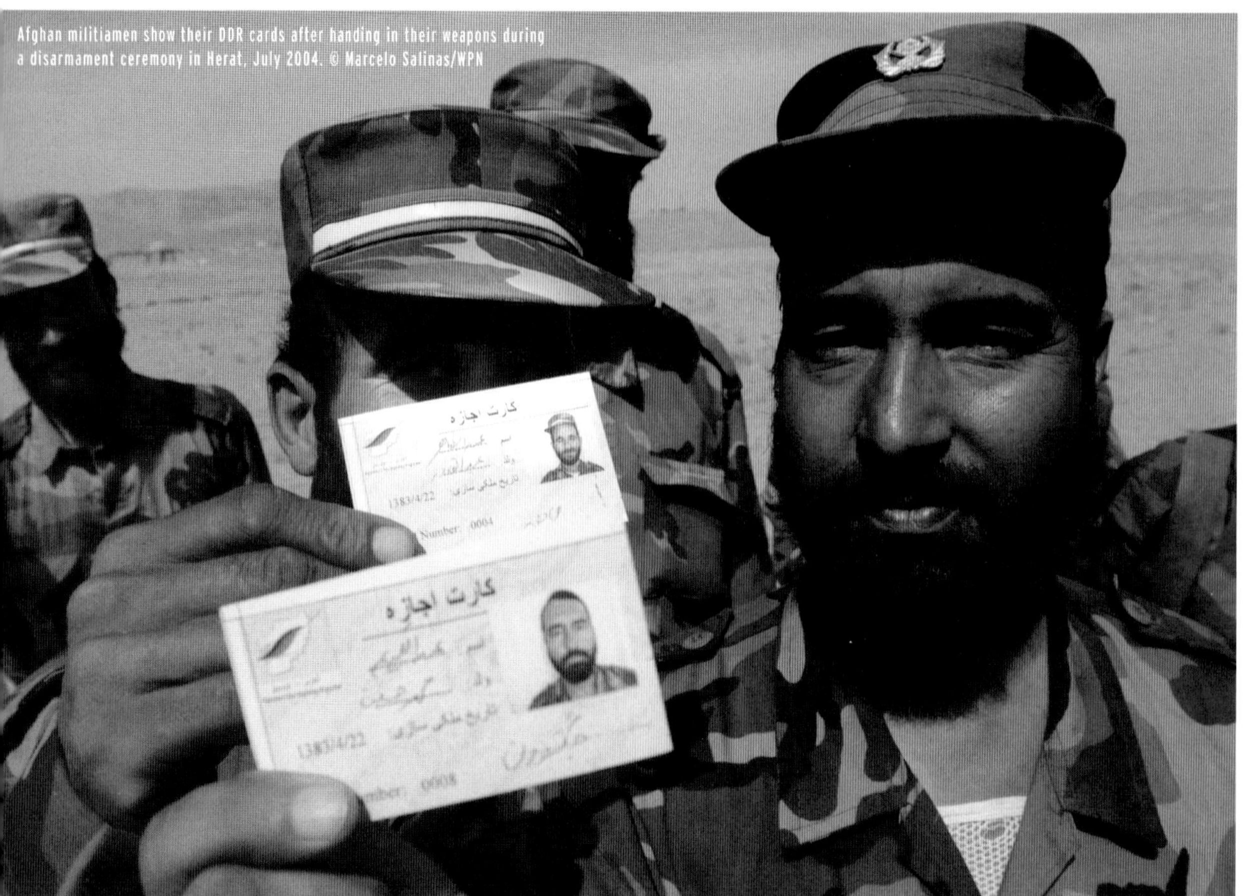

Afghan militiamen show their DDR cards after handing in their weapons during a disarmament ceremony in Herat, July 2004. © Marcelo Salinas/WPN

of their working armaments (Sedra, 2008a, p. 128). As noted, they pilfered reintegration assistance until it was discontinued. Commanders who had been appointed to official civilian roles were also able to use their positions to shuffle militia members into police units under their authority. In short, the programme was not successful in dismantling many commander–soldier linkages or in breaking the integrity of patronage networks. This behaviour was perhaps to be expected, since commanders were not the intended beneficiaries of DDR and naturally looked for ways to secure material gains when few other options presented themselves.

Secondly, the programme was beset by fraud. Many ex-combatants who did not qualify for the programme were admitted with falsified identification. The regional distribution of the benefits of DDR was also suspicious: the two regions under direct control of the Shura-e-Nezar faction accounted for at least 56 per cent of all militiamen who entered the process nationwide (Rossi and Giustozzi, 2006, p. 5).

In late 2004, the ANBP responded to these problems by launching the Commander Incentive Programme, which provided a monthly stipend, the offer of training abroad (in Japan), and possibly a government post in exchange for compliance with the DDR effort. This two-year, USD 5 million programme, funded by Japan, ended in September 2007. Of the 550 commanders who were identified, 460 had participated in the programme by June 2006 (Sedra, 2008a, p. 129). For a number of warlords, however, the training component could not be carried out because they were denied travel visas.[12]

A former Afghan militia soldier undergoes carpentry training as part of his reintegration after disarmament and demobilization, November 2004. © Gurinder Osan/AP Photo

Two other steps were taken that helped limit the obstruction of commanders. First, a law promulgated in October 2003 prohibits political parties from having a militia wing or even associating with armed groups, thereby restricting the activities of militia commanders with political ambitions and promoting their compliance with DDR. Many commanders rapidly entered their men into the programme in anticipation of the October 2004 presidential elections. Second, the United States changed its policy of ambivalence to the DDR of AMF groups, which it relied on to support Coalition forces against the Taliban in many areas, and instead applied pressure on those forces to comply with the programme. This may have been linked to the strategic shift by the United States towards the reduction of opium farming, which sustained some commanders.

The disarmament and demobilization process ended in July 2005. By that time, 63,380 ex-combatants had been demobilized through the ANBP (see Table 9.4), 259 AMF units formally decommissioned, some 57,629 light and medium weapons collected, and 100,000 soldiers 'de-financed' (i.e. formally removed from payrolls), freeing up some USD 120 million annually from state budgets. By the end of the reintegration phase in June 2006, benefits were delivered to some 55,804 ex-combatants, or 88 per cent of all who had demobilized. Agricultural training, vocational training, and small business operations together accounted for 93.3 per cent of the skills transferred (see Figure 9.2). An ANBP Client Evaluation Survey of 5,000 beneficiaries who had received six to nine months of reintegration assistance found that 93 per cent of respondents were satisfied with the assistance and 90 per cent were still employed.

Table 9.4 DDR phases in Afghanistan and selected outcomes

Phase	Start date	End date	Total disarmed	Total demobilized
Pilot phase	1 October 2003	31 May 2004	6,271	7,550
Main phase 1	1 June 2004	30 August 2004	8,551	7,257
Main phase 2	1 September 2004	30 October 2004	7,169	3,733
Main phase 3	1 November 2004	31 March 2005	22,440	20,375
Main phase 4	1 April 2005	31 July 2005	18,949	23,461
Totals			**63,380**	**62,376**

Source: UNDDR (2008)

Disbanding the AMF units had undeniably positive outcomes of the daily lives of community members and the security sector. Security checkpoints and AMF units belonging to rival ethnic or militia groups stationed in communities were closed, removing a security threat. Many AMF soldiers, bonded to their commanders but receiving little or no pay, were freed from service and no longer had to report to their commanders. AMF commanders lost the privilege of driving around in official vehicles with numerous bodyguards, which they also lost. The government was able to stop paying the force, freeing millions of dollars desperately needed elsewhere.[13]

In view of the severely inhospitable conditions on the ground, these achievements are significant. The number of AMF militiamen targeted for demobilization was met and valued training and assistance provided to ex-combatants. Complete disarmament was not a goal of the programme, but a significant number of weapons were removed from militias and transferred to the army.

Figure 9.2 Reintegration training benefits, 2003-06

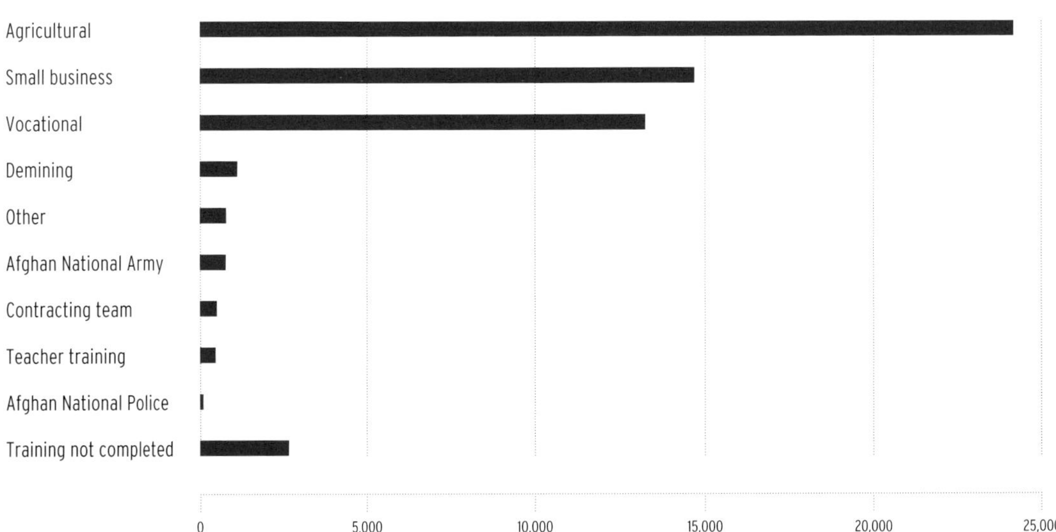

Source: UNDDR (2008)

In terms of its primary objective, however, it is unclear to what extent DDR interrupted commander–militiamen lines of influence. The reality is most likely that even the AMF units that were formally decommissioned could be reconstituted by commanders with access to guns, money, and unemployed militiamen. Most of these conditions remain in place today.

Disbanding illegal armed groups

The ANBP DDR programme targeted AMF militia only, but a large variety of armed groups, strongmen, warlords, and others with the power to mobilize followers remain outside the AMF (Sedra, 2008a, p. 134). These groups, which present further threats to the legitimacy of the government and act as potential spoilers, also seriously threaten security and functional governance. They collect illegal taxes, obstructing government revenue collection; they are involved in the illegal exploitation of natural resources; and, in some cases, they have assumed control over state-owned industries. As such, they subvert reform processes, intimidate local government officials and security forces, and drive the illegal economy, most notably the narcotics trade (Islamic Republic of Afghanistan, 2006, annexe A, p. 4). The power that these groups wield stems from their monopolization of the means of violence in their regional strongholds. Their access to guns has enabled them to insulate their interests, carve out mini-fiefdoms, and curtail the expansion of government authority into the periphery.

In July 2004, Presidential Decree 50 defined all groups falling outside the AMF as illegal (President of the Islamic Government of Afghanistan, 2004). In February 2005, as formal DDR of AMF groups was about to enter its final phase, the Canadian government provided a grant to develop and implement a programme to address illegal groups, to be called Disbandment of Illegal Armed Groups. Early feasibility studies identified some 1,870 illegal militias, including roughly 129,000 men. The government estimated that these groups possessed about 336,000 small arms and light weapons, 56,000 of which were concealed by AMF groups during DDR. But the actual number is probably much higher given arms flows into the country and the size of some caches uncovered by Coalition forces (Sedra, 2008a, p.135).

In July 2004, non-AMF armed groups were declared illegal.

In 2006, the government defined illegal armed groups as: 'a group of five or more armed individuals operating outside the law, drawing its cohesion from (a) loyalty to a commander, (b) material benefits, (c) impunity enjoyed by members, [and] (d) shared ethnic or social background' (Islamic Republic of Afghanistan, 2006, p. 2). AMF remnant groups were subsequently declared illegal, including units that had gone through DDR merely to receive the benefits, without any intention of disbanding.

DIAG has two stated objectives: '(1) to improve security through the disarmament and disbandment of illegal armed groups; and (2) to provide basic development support to communities freed from threats posed by illegal armed groups' (GoA, UNAMA, and UNDP, 2006, p. 2). The latter objective was deemed important in promoting the 'full integration' of groups back into their communities, providing an incentive for communities to remain arms-free, and preventing the resurgence of criminal and predatory groups. It was therefore considered an 'essential and integral part of the security sector reform process' (GoA, UNAMA, and UNDP, 2006, p. 1).

The government presented DIAG as a way of curtailing actors involved in 'drug smuggling, human trafficking, and human rights violations' and threatening communities in the absence of a robust rule of law; indeed, the government recognized that these groups undermined the peace process, hindered democratic development, and forced the withdrawal of international aid organizations. DIAG offered illegal armed group members the opportunity to 'honourably' conform to state authority requiring them to disarm and disband. The government also promulgated national gun laws criminalizing arms carrying and establishing an owner licensing and registration system (President of the Islamic Republic of Afghanistan, 2005). The project was pushed forward on an emergency basis to address armed groups in the period leading up to the Afghan National Assembly elections of September 2005.

DIAG incentives are provided to communities, not to individual militiamen.

DIAG aims to disrupt the relationship between commanders and their militiamen through disarmament. But whereas DDR was designed on the basis of a monetized incentive system, DIAG approaches illegal armed groups from a law enforcement perspective (Sedra, 2008a, p. 136). Moreover, incentives are provided collectively to communities, and not on an individual basis to militiamen. Likewise, coercive tactics are authorized for groups that fail to cooperate.

Another important distinction between the two programmes is that DDR was internationally driven while DIAG is overseen by the D&R Commission, reporting to a national coordinating body chaired by the president, the Security Coordination Forum (Sedra, 2008a, p. 136). DIAG is centrally planned, implemented by local actors in the provinces, and flexible, allowing for individual regional strategies and responses to specific local circumstances.

DIAG has applied a three-stage process. The first stage sought to force the demilitarization of illegal armed groups associated with commanders who wished to pursue legislative careers. Officially designated the National Assembly and Provincial Council Elections (NAPCE) phase, the programme employed a strategy similar to the one previously used in the DDR campaign to sever ties by AMF commanders who wanted to enter politics. In advance of the September 2005 legislative elections, 1,108 of around 6,000 lower parliament and provincial council candidates were identified as having possible links to armed groups. From this list, the Electoral Complaints Commission provisionally disqualified 207 candidates, pending their compliance with the terms of disarmament (ANBP, 2006, p. 12). While 124 candidates did turn in 4,857 weapons, the rest on the list chose not to comply, to say nothing of commanders who were never listed in the first place.[14] Pressure from the government and the international community led to the exclusion of only 34 candidates from the ballot. As a result, it was estimated that more than 80 per cent of the winning candidates in the provinces and 60 per cent in Kabul maintained ties to armed groups. Candidates' ties to armed groups were also a factor in the relatively low voter turnout (6.8 million votes cast out of 12.4 million registered voters), according to human rights groups (IRIN, 2005).[15]

The second stage focused on elected government officials who maintained ties to illegal armed groups—the so-called Government Officials with Links to Illegal Armed Groups phase. As of September 2005, it was suspected that at least 450 officials were thus connected (UNDP, 2008b). But a consensus could only be reached with 13 of them. A second round forced another eight groups to comply, and they submitted more than 1,000 weapons (Islamic Government of Afghanistan, 2006, p. 10). But those who have not complied—mostly employed by the Ministry of the Interior, a key stakeholder in the DIAG process—have yet to be forced out. The Ministry has shifted, rather than fired, many of the others, demonstrating how deeply entrenched patronage networks are in the government and society. The linkages between commanders and militiamen and their government sponsors remained largely intact after this stage (Sedra, 2008a, p.140).

The third—and main—stage of DIAG began in May 2006 after a pilot had been used to develop a three-phase strategy of voluntary, negotiated, and enforced compliance (see Table 9.5). Compliance is considered obtained if 70 per cent of all weapons in possession of the armed group are turned in within 30 days. Like the DDR exercise, DIAG initially required only that turned-in weapons were functional; later the threshold of acceptability was raised to weapons that could be utilized by security institutions.[16] Since under this scheme development incentives are provided to the community, religious and local leaders are encouraged to pressure groups to comply with the law.

Table 9.5 **Three phases of the DIAG (main stage)**

	Phase 1: voluntary compliance	Phase 2: negotiated compliance	Phase 3: enforced compliance
Political levers	Public information campaign; presidential decree; law on weapons	Public information reinforcement; negotiation at national level; use of political parties; negotiation at provincial or local level; legal deadline	Public information residual; law enforcement; shame list; forcible compliance or removal
Cultural levers	Influence via *shuras* or elders	Negotiation by *shuras* or elders; influence through *jirga*	–
Religious levers	Influence via *fatwa* or mosque	Negotiation by *fatwa*; influence through mosques	–
Economic levers	Influence via access to incentive programmes	Influence via access to incentive programmes; programme deadline	Denied access to all development programmes

Source: Islamic Republic of Afghanistan (2005)[17]

If an armed group refuses to comply within the voluntary compliance period, a negotiation phase commences, using national and local actors, including village *mullahs* and *shuras,* as needed. If this, too, should fail, the process can assume a more coercive tenor: the Ministry of Interior and Afghan National Police are invested with enforcement powers and, in theory, the ANA could be used to assist. However, it appears that forcible disarmament has rarely, if ever, been conducted.[18] At this stage, community development assistance is (temporarily) suspended.

As of December 2008, the programme had reportedly disbanded 382 illegally armed groups and collected 42,369 weapons. A further 14,805 weapons have been registered and 14,000 destroyed or retained by ISAF (Islamic Republic of Afghanistan, 2008). But, as in the DDR exercise, militias are reportedly surrendering their least serviceable weapons (ammunition was not a focus but fell under another programme; see Box 9.4). DIAG also lacked a plan to engage commanders directly (Sedra, 2008a, p.144). Whereas the Commander Incentive Programme was eventually created to generate incentives for AMF commanders, incentives were deemed inappropriate in the case of outright illegal groups.

Theoretically, DIAG was supposed to target illegal armed groups that were not covered by DDR. In reality, the majority of the listed groups were ex-AMF commanders who were retargeted. Three-quarters of the weapons recovered through DIAG came from Northern Alliance areas, leaving other heavily armed areas as yet unaddressed. It is also worth mentioning that most of the 1,870 listed militias were inactive—meaning that they did not seem to be involved in any illegal activities, particularly in those regions where the security situation was reasonably good.[19]

It is possible that intelligence problems played a role in this regional imbalance. In many cases it was extremely difficult to obtain reliable information about illegal armed groups to inform targeting. The illegal armed group (IAG) lists, normally emanating from the National Security Department, were often out of date and sometimes targeted the wrong people. There are several cases of former commanders appearing on IAG lists with an unrealistically low number of weapons next to their names.[20]

In this way, some militia leaders have persisted in their roles, protected by someone inside the government. They, in turn, have protected affiliated groups from government pressure to disarm. This applies not only to ethnic and

Box 9.4 Mine and ammunition stockpile destruction

With more than 30 years of proxy arming and a robust regional arms and ammunition trade, Afghanistan reportedly has one of the largest ammunition stockpiles in the world. Neither the NDC disarmament exercise nor the DIAG project focused on ammunition collection and destruction. In November 2004 the government of Canada funded an assessment that estimated the national ammunition stockpile at 100,000 metric tons, much of which was abandoned or unguarded (Sedra, 2008a, p. 146; ANBP, 2006, p. 7). A significant proportion had been exposed to the elements and had become volatile. In May 2005 at least 28 people were killed and 70 wounded when an illegal ammunition cache–including artillery, tank shells, and rocket-propelled grenades–accidentally exploded in Baghlan Province (Sedra, 2008a, p. 146).

To address the vast scale of ammunition proliferation in the country, the Ministry of Defence and UNDP established the Anti-Personnel Mines and Ammunition Stockpile Destruction project in December 2004, which got under way in July 2005. The project was funded by Canada, the United Kingdom, the European Union, UNDP, and other donors at USD 16 million for two years. It is primarily a detect-and-destroy programme, carried out by ammunition survey teams (ASTs).

Using all available intelligence resources to locate caches, ASTs move ammunition to a safe location and separate usable from unusable materiel. The usable ammunition is packaged and shipped to one of 12 MoD consolidation points and the rest is destroyed. To date, about one-third of the initial estimated ammunition stockpile has been surveyed (see Table 9.6). An interim Coalition-supported security force, the Afghan Guard Force, is charged with protecting new, official ammunition depots. There has also been a contemporaneous refurbishment of two national ammunition depots around Kabul, the rearrangement of 54 existing ammunition bunkers around the country, the creation of 22 new bunkers, and a comprehensive inventory process (Sedra, 2008a, p. 149).

Sources: ANBP (2008)

Table 9.6 Ammunition and landmines surveyed and destroyed as of 27 November 2008

AMF ammunition surveyed	33,878 tons
DIAG ammunition surveyed	2,961 tons
Total ammunition surveyed	**36,839 tons**
Ammunition consolidated	9,699 tons
Ammunition destroyed	20,943 tons
Anti-personnel mines destroyed	503,174 pieces
Anti-tank mines destroyed	22,503 pieces
Total mines destroyed	**525,677 pieces**

An explosive ordnance disposal team stacks weapons in Zabul Province, August 2004. © Teun Voeten/Panos Pictures

tribal militia but also to entities involved in the drug trade, whose spoils represent significant incentives to corrupt government officials. The upper house of parliament voted in May 2006 to halt DIAG due to the alleged need for Afghans to keep their guns for self-defence—possibly more a reflection of illegal armed group influence in the parliament than evidence of sound security planning (Sedra, 2008a, p. 144).

Yet in terms of key positions in the national government, at least, IAG influence has waned from its peak four to six years ago. While they continue to pose a threat to security and the rule of law, IAG commander capabilities were reduced in recent years, both militarily and politically. In 2002 and 2003, the majority of cabinet ministers had links to ex-AMF, illegal armed groups, or jihadi groups or were backed by them. Today no more than three cabinet members have such ties. Reductions have also been recognized in the lower government, though they still hold a significant number of positions there. Ex-armed group figures now represent a political opposition force rather than part of the government.[21]

DISCUSSION: PRESSURES AND REALITIES

More than three years have passed since DDR ended in Afghanistan, though the attempt to disband armed groups continues. But in the sometimes precarious security environment local commanders are increasingly resistant to turning over weapons and in some cases are reportedly rearming (Semple, Robbins, and Harris, 2007). It is tempting to focus on missed opportunities based on ideal conditions, but doing so underestimates the incredible complexity of the Afghan context and the immense domestic, regional, and international pressures bearing down on the government.

The following section discusses some of the dilemmas affecting the design, implementation, and outcomes of DDR and illegal armed group disbandment in the country. In particular, it focuses on the disarmament–security dilemma; the efficacy of using disarmament to break commander–militiamen links; the development challenges facing reintegrating soldiers; the role of the opium economy; and the revitalized insurgency. There are no easy answers to these questions, even in retrospect.

The disarmament–security dilemma

The government presented DIAG as a 'crucial element' of SSR.

Since 2002, the new government has fallen prey to a classic security dilemma. In order to secure its monopoly on the use of force, large numbers of armed groups need to be neutralized through DDR or through direct co-option. But disarmament is difficult to achieve without a robust and accountable security sector to back up disarmament actions with the threat of coercive force. The government presented DIAG as a 'crucial element' of SSR (Islamic Republic of Afghanistan, 2005). Yet the main organs of the security sector—the Afghan National Army and Afghan National Police—were in the process of being created from scratch almost simultaneously with DDR.[22] In many areas, neither was operational; the police, in particular, remain qualitatively weak and subject to corruption. Coalition forces were unwilling to serve as the enforcement mechanism. In a security vacuum such as this, demand for arms naturally tends to increase, and commanders acquire added legitimacy as arbiters of local disputes and as security providers (Bhatia, 2008a, p. 11). Indeed, the open operation of criminals, warlords, and insurgents leads private citizens to arm themselves for protection, thus perpetuating the militarization cycle (Sedra and Muggah, 2007).

Two other interrelated factors increase the complexity of this dilemma. The first is the factional nature of the government. The dominance of Shura-e-Nezar militia members in the Ministry of Defence and other ministries casts

Afghan National Army soldiers march in a graduation ceremony, Kabul, September 2003. © Richard Vogel/AP Photo

suspicion on the DDR programme, which came to be seen as a means by which certain warlords and commanders sought to consolidate power and suppress competitors. While strides have been made in this regard, efforts to disempower high-profile warlords continue. Success will require the full support of the international community, which has itself supported leaders with ties to illegal armed groups.

The historically decentralized nature of Afghan society makes this project all the more difficult. Afghanistan has never been a Western-style, centralized democratic state with national political leaders who respond to citizens' needs and provide services. Instead, it is predominantly a land of local autonomy, where tribal authority has provided identity, community, and patronage. While there is hope for improvement of central government services and a reduction in corruption, loyalties to local structures and organizations persist. Despite these realities, the international community is making development assistance contingent on the government's capacity to create provincial institutions and administration (London Conference on Afghanistan, 2006, p. 3). For these reasons some analysts have come to believe that achieving legitimacy requires accepting and working within local power structures, including armed strongmen and other opportunistic commanders, whether formerly affiliated with the AMF or fundamentally 'illegal' (Poulton, 2008).

DDR without disarmament

DDR is typically conceived of as a continuum, sometimes occurring in parallel or in overlapping phases, but usually with disarmament taking place early and reintegration falling last. This logic may not have been applicable or even possible in Afghanistan. In fact, the assumption that universal disarmament should be the first step in post-war securitization was quickly rejected in view of the realities on the ground, which suggested an emphasis on demobilization of both legal and illegal armed groups—with disarmament a concern for a much later phase (Özerdem, 2002, p. 965). Was this the right approach?

Some analysts have seen crucial missed opportunities to institutionalize and implement widespread disarmament in the early stages of the post-Taliban period, and to tie the main power brokers to demilitarization. The first failure, according to this analysis, was the vague language of the Bonn Agreement, which did not call for 'universal' DDR. This omission allowed the Mujaheddin to continue to enforce a populist narrative of participation in jihad and against the Taliban; they then used this position to justify their presence in parliament and government ministries—as well as to legitimize their use of armed violence (Sedra, 2008b, p. 113). Was the international community's failure to address the so-called ownership gap in the NDC disarmament initiative another missed entry point for robust and comprehensive disarmament?

While the classic post-war reconstruction model would call for local commanders to be disarmed, in the absence of a functioning security sector, and given the dynamics of traditional mobilization, the strategy of adopting and absorbing local commanders in state and provincial government appears to have been one of the few realistic strategies available. It must be recalled that in the early post-Taliban phase, strongmen and commanders' militias had benefited from new infusions of assistance from the United States. Many members of the fledgling government felt that earnest disarmament would risk turning those allies into enemies. The government possibly reasoned that strongmen were a potential asset to be retained for the future because they were sources of local authority who could direct men in combat.

In fact, in early 2009 Afghan authorities were seeking to once again deputize villagers in Wardak Province, south of Kabul, in an effort to increase local counter-insurgency capacities.[23] The US-backed Afghan Public Protection Force is intended to fill the shortage of police capacity, especially in distant areas (Moncrieff, 2009). According to the vice-chair of the D&R Commission, villagers would be asked to supply their own weapons, but conflicting reports suggest the United States will provide additional weapons (Boone, 2008; Faiez, 2009).[24] The forces would supposedly be subject to clear command and control mechanisms and tied directly to village *shuras*.[25]

DDR and DIAG were never intended to entirely disarm the country's militias.

Collecting weapons was always a side product of DDR and DIAG, which were never intended to entirely disarm the country's militias. This misperception that universal disarmament had been planned remains widespread among Afghans, however, contributing to their low opinion of the programmes. In general, weapons possession, particularly in the rural areas, continues to be viewed as a means of defence; this opinion is not likely to change until confidence in the newly established security institutions rises to an acceptable level, among both former armed group members as well as many civilians.[26]

For these reasons, the strategy of using disarmament to break the relationship between commanders and their soldiers is probably not sufficient. Though they have been significantly weakened by DDR and DIAG, these bonds remain and will continue to exist until effective, non-factionalized security institutions fill this security gap.[27] The UN Secretary-General's Deputy Special Representative to Afghanistan probably spoke for many analysts when he suggested in June 2008 that illegal armed groups would never completely disappear from the Afghan landscape. The challenge, he said, was reducing them from a national security threat to a problem that can be managed by law enforcement (UNAMA, 2008).

Reintegration without development

Afghanistan is found near the bottom of UNDP's Human Development Index in life expectancy (42.9 years), literacy (28 per cent), primary, secondary, and tertiary education enrolment (42.8 per cent), and mortality for under-five-year-olds (257 per 1,000), ranking 174 out of 178 countries measured. Recent years have seen some 'tremendous' improvements: per capita GDP has increased from USD 683 in 2002 to USD 964 in 2005; the number of telephone users rose to 2.5 million, or 10 per cent of the population; school enrolment has grown from 900,000 to nearly 5.4 million; and the rate of malaria and tuberculosis has dropped dramatically (UNDP, 2007, p. 3). But it is unquestionable that citizens remain in dire need of large-scale development assistance.

Box 9.5 Current challenges to suppressing the drug economy

Besides subsistence and small-scale farming, poppy cultivation remains among the most lucrative occupations in Afghanistan. The international community has taken a zero-tolerance approach, primarily focused on crop eradication, as reflected in the Afghanistan Compact:

> Meeting the threat that the narcotics industry poses to national, regional and international security as well as the development and governance of the country and the well-being of Afghans will be a priority for the Government and the international community. The aim will be to achieve a sustained and significant reduction in the production and trafficking of narcotics with a view to complete elimination. (London Conference on Afghanistan, 2006, p. 4)

Crop destruction can be effective in curtailing production, but without micro-credit programmes or incentives to switch to other crops (such as wheat), farmers become destitute and turn to insurgents for assistance. In exchange for security and start-up capital, poppy farmers turn over a portion of the proceeds to the insurgents, thus supporting their operations, funding their weapons purchases, and contributing to further instability. Insurgents, together with warlords and drug lords, are thought to have extracted almost half a billion dollars of tax revenue from drug farming, production, and trafficking in 2008 (UNODC, 2008, p. 2).

In fact, the distinction between opium GDP and non-opium GDP is somewhat artificial, since the multiplier effect from growth in the illicit economy has a direct impact on the growth of legal economy (Sedra and Middlebrook, 2005). Thus crop eradication alone tends to bring down the regional economy as a whole. In Nangarhar Province, for example, a 70 per cent reduction in opium production in 2004–05 triggered a general decline in household incomes, slowing down local economic growth overall, as well as employment. Invariably, then, poppy eradication will precipitate a decline in total per capita income (Sedra and Middlebrook, 2005).

In 2006 the Ministry of Counter-Narcotics released its five-year strategy to reduce the 'opium economy', which President Karzai called 'the single greatest challenge to the long-term security, development, and effective governance of Afghanistan' and to the stability of the region (MoCN, 2006, p. 4). The strategy has eight pillars, of which Alternative Livelihoods is the most costly, calling for crop substitution and other rural development initiatives to wean farmers and others off poppy production and sales (MoCN, 2006, p. 29). To date, however, alternative livelihood assistance has not been provided effectively.

Some recent news is encouraging. Opium production reportedly declined by almost 19 per cent in 2008, to pre-2006 levels, though the greatest declines occurred outside the southern region, where the vast majority of cultivation occurs (UNODC, 2008, pp. 7, 11). The export value of opium-based drugs decreased from about USD 4 billion in 2007 to about USD 3.4 billion in 2008 (UNODC, 2008, p. 29). This drop is due not to eradication, but to a combination of factors including decreased planting after pressure from governors, *shuras*, and village elders; decreased demand for opium due to market saturation; and increasing demand for wheat, primarily due to drought (UNODC, 2008, p. 2). For the moment, the dynamics in opium and wheat markets have made wheat a more attractive option than it used to be.[28] The trend is also having some development impacts. Nangarhar received USD 10 million from the Good Performers Initiative, a programme funded by the United States and Britain that provides development assistance to communities leading the fight against the poppy in Afghanistan (VOA, 2009).

DDR provided demobilizing AMF members with skills training, and satisfaction with the training was high. Yet many militiamen expected not just training but long-term employment. In the period under review, however, the international community, recognizing the lack of rule of law and the ongoing problems associated with illegal armed groups, did not invest in large-scale development projects.

Conversely, one of DIAG's primary goals was to support the economic development of communities once they complied with the programme. The development rewards were slow in coming, however. Mahmoud Raqi district in Kapisa Province was the first community to be declared in compliance with DIAG, earning a canal rehabilitation and cleaning project launched in April 2007—almost two years after DIAG began. The project expects to rehabilitate 95 km of waterways in the district serving 240,000 inhabitants (ANBP, 2007). To date, only five DIAG development projects have been completed (UNDP, 2008a).

To date, only five DIAG development projects have been completed.

A larger development strategy for Afghanistan, which aims to rehabilitate dormant industrial facilities and agricultural projects, has been even slower to materialize. In 2006 the Government of Afghanistan and the international community agreed to a set of conditions on which development assistance would be provided. Improvements would need to be made in three broad categories: security; governance, rule of law, and human rights; and economic and social development (London Conference on Afghanistan, 2006, p. 2). The Afghanistan National Development Strategy was the follow-up to these steps.

While efforts to control the opium trade have not met projected goals (see Box 9.5), the reconstruction of roads, bridges, buildings, schools, and other investments in the 'peace economy' also lags behind. Reconstruction assistance accounts for a fraction of military spending, per capita aid to the country is far below that received in places such as Bosnia and Herzegovina and Timor-Leste, and leading donors are failing to meet their aid commitments. The result is an aid shortfall of USD 10 billion. Furthermore, a significant portion of development assistance coming into the country ends up leaving it quickly: up to 40 per cent finds its way into corporate profits and consultant fees (Waldman, 2008, p.1).

Reconciliation and insurgency

Despite its claims to recognize 'the right of the people of Afghanistan to freely determine their own political future in accordance with the principles of Islam, democracy, pluralism and social justice' (Bonn Agreement, 2001, preamb.), the Taliban have generally been marginalized from the political process since October 2001. The military victory was not followed by a peace agreement; the power-sharing arrangement did not include Taliban leaders. What reconciliation was on offer was ad hoc, top-down, and predicated on the willingness of former Taliban commanders to work within a new government system that they had no hand in helping create.

The central government made piecemeal attempts to reach out to insurgents old and new. As early as 2003 President Karzai gave almost all insurgents operating under the name of the Taliban the opportunity to become full citizens by denouncing violence, disarming, and recognizing the authority of the government. This offer was generally not taken up. In 2007, two years after some ex-Taliban commanders were elected to the lower parliament (Gall, 2005), a more emphatic invitation to ongoing insurgents to lay down arms and enter talks was issued. Karzai suggested that he would even consider giving Taliban leaders deputy minister positions or entire departments in key ministries (Chu, 2007).

Now that the insurgency has grown to include a range of domestic and foreign-sourced groups with differing goals and capacities, the question of reconciliation is even more complex. The United States, the most important con-

A young boy cries while being taken out of the Ministry of Justice building during an attack by Taliban suicide bombers in Kabul, February 2009. © Lynsey Addario/Corbis

tributor of military and financial assistance to the government, has given mixed signals about the possibility of talks with the Taliban (VOA, 2008; CNN, 2008). As the counter-insurgency has become increasingly bogged down, however, NATO and US forces commander General David McKiernan appeared to acknowledge that reconciliation at the local levels, through *shuras,* should include commanders aligned with the insurgency (Radio Free Europe, 2008).

Among the many impacts of the insurgency is a counter-productive effect on DIAG programming. As the southern insurgency gains momentum, commanders in the other areas of the country fear that the Taliban and associated groups are growing in influence and that they may soon reach well beyond the southern territories. These commanders are increasingly reluctant to turn in weapons. Indeed, the director of DIAG in the northern state of Mazar-e-Sharif indicated that northern commanders who had complied with weapons turn-in were rearming and stashing weapons in late 2007; such arming is probably occurring elsewhere as well (Semple, Robbins, and Harris, 2007). The government's focus on supplying the predominantly Pashtun southern provinces with development assistance and weapons has also made the northern, largely Tajik and Uzbek commanders put pressure on Kabul for increased power and resources.

CONCLUSION

The Afghan experience of DDR was more atypical than most, starting with the fact that it did not arise from a peace agreement between two parties but from an internationally driven military victory (that was presumed complete). It was of necessity launched in conjunction with the wholesale creation of a new national government and security apparatus in one of the most underdeveloped regions of the world, in a country of multiple armed groups and widespread arms availability, and amidst the lucrative and corrupting influence of the world's largest opium-producing centre.

With the close involvement of the international community, DDR itself was designed and executed by a government that was initially non-representative and factionalized. Cleansing the Ministry of Defence of partisan actors has already taken years and is not yet complete. Power alliances and government–commander relations did not only affect the design of these programmes (who was targeted, when, and how), but also the terms (qualifications for entry, arms surrender) and the actors (implementation agencies).

It is difficult to imagine a more challenging environment for DDR programming, and under these circumstances its achievements should not be undervalued. In additional to some 63,000 AMF disarmed and demobilized and the removal of some 100,000 weapons and 30,000 tons of ammunition from the population, the programme led to palpable security gains in many areas. As the DIAG programme progressed, many warlords, drug lords, and other IAG commanders were removed from the government. Corruption and factionalization have clearly obstructed progress on disarming groups, but much has been accomplished.

Afghanistan has not returned to full-scale warfare, but it is difficult to label the country 'post-conflict' so long as an armed insurgency rages and spreads. The experience of the ANBP and DIAG emphasize the limits of what can be achieved in a context where state-building, peace-building, counter-insurgency, and counter-narcotics operations converge. Preventing future mobilization depends in part on the state's ability to define, regulate, and contain legitimate and illegitimate force—by establishing and enforcing the rule of law and providing security for the population. In many cases the government has chosen to try to work with local command structures—and this move is probably unavoidable under the current circumstances. Nevertheless, it underlines the Afghan state's inability to establish a monopoly on the legitimate use of force throughout the country. Despite the many important accomplishments of the past few years, state-building and security promotion in Afghanistan remain, for the moment, works in progress. ■

LIST OF ABBREVIATIONS

AIA	Afghan Interim Authority
AMF	Afghan Military Forces
ANA	Afghan National Army
ANBP	Afghanistan New Beginnings Programme
AST	Ammunition survey team
ATA	Afghanistan Transitional Authority
DDR	Disarmament, demobilization, and reintegration
DIAG	Disbandment of Illegal Armed Groups
D&R Commission	Demobilization and Reintegration Commission
IAG	Illegal armed group
ISAF	International Security Assistance Force
MoD	Ministry of Defence
NAPCE	National Assembly and Provincial Council Elections

NDC	National Disarmament Commission	UNAMA	United Nations Assistance Mission in Afghanistan
OEF	Operation Enduring Freedom	UNDP	United Nations Development Programme
SSR	Security sector reform		

ENDNOTES

1 The initial phase (October–December 2001) of Operation Enduring Freedom was led by the United States and the United Kingdom with contributions and pledges of military or intelligence support from 75 states and bilateral and multilateral organizations (CRS, 2001).

2 The Coalition collectively labels these insurgents Anti-Government Forces or Anti-Coalition Forces. The insurgency is highly heterogeneous and includes separate Pakistani and home-grown Taliban groups, Glubuddin Hekmatyer's Hezb-i-Islami, the Haqqani network, al-Qaeda, and other smaller forces. For a discussion of the various factions that made up the insurgency in Afghanistan in 2008, see Gopal (2008).

3 Most dramatic among these strikes was the coordinated attack by eight Taliban militants on three separate government buildings on the morning of 11 February 2009, in which 20 people were killed (AP, 2009).

4 In 2007, the percentage of Afghans polled who cited security as their main concern rose from 22 to 32 per cent, with regional variations. In regions where citizens felt the country was headed in the right direction, this response was partly attributed to good security (Asia Foundation, 2007, p. 5).

5 See also Özerdem (2002, p. 963).

6 For a discussion of incidence monitoring and its limitations, see Small Arms Survey (2005, pp. 240–41) and Geneva Declaration Secretariat (2008, pp. 10–11).

7 There is an established literature on greed and grievance as motivations in mobilization. See, for example, Berdal and Malone (2000) and Collier and Hoeffler (2004).

8 Much of the material that follows relies on Bhatia and Muggah (2008) and Sedra (2008a).

9 The militia is a regional military and political structure founded by Ahmed Shah Massoud and hailing largely from the Panjshir Valley.

10 This and the following section draw primarily on Sedra (2008a).

11 Sedra reports that the Japanese government considered dropping the disarmament requirement altogether on the premise that, under the security conditions existing at the time, militiamen would be more willing to take part in demobilization and reintegration if they were allowed to retain their weapons for self-defence (Sedra, 2008a, p. 131).

12 Communication with Mark Sedra, 22 January 2009.

13 Communication with Hameed Quraishi, former ANBP official, 29 December 2008.

14 Sedra reports that even the commanders who did engage with the NAPCE process may not have fully complied and probably only submitted samples of their weapons stocks (Sedra, 2008a, p. 139).

15 The enshrining of warlord power notwithstanding, the fact that in less than four years the country was able to promulgate a progressive constitution and peacefully elect a president and a parliament—the first parliament in more than three decades—is a remarkable feat.

16 Communication with Hameed Quraishi, former ANBP official, 28 December 2008.

17 Reproduced from Bhatia and Sedra (2008, p. 141).

18 Communication with Mark Sedra, 3 January 2009.

19 Communication with Hameed Quaraishi, former ANBP official, 29 December 2008.

20 Communication with Hameed Quaraishi, former ANBP official, 29 December 2008.

21 Communication with Hameed Quaraishi, former ANBP official, 29 December 2008.

22 Rather than re-establishing a police force upon taking control of Kabul in 1996, the Taliban created a 'Vice and Virtue Police' in support of the Department for the Promotion of Virtue and the Prevention of Vice. Consequently, no civilian police force existed after the fall of the Taliban (UNDP, 2007, p. 82).

23 This strategy is under way on the other side of the Pakistan border, where *lashkar* (militia) fighters are being armed with Chinese AK-47s and other small arms to combat Taliban and al-Qaeda in the Federally Administered Tribal Areas. At least three *lashkars*, totaling 14,000 men, have reportedly been established in Bajaur (DeYoung, 2008).

24 The plans to arm and train a new civilian militia were announced shortly before evidence emerged that the United States had failed to follow basic record-keeping measures in its arming of the Afghan security forces in December 2004–June 2008. Some 87,000 rifles, pistols, mortars, and other weapons supplied by the United States could not be properly tracked (Schmidt, 2009).

25 The memory of a failed Canadian-financed 2006 effort to recruit auxiliary police lingers over this new US-backed effort. The previous campaign, hastily conceived and executed, drew only poorly trained men, many of whom were drug addicts. It was quietly ended in mid-2008 (Brewster, 2008).

26 Communication with Hameed Quaraishi, former ANBP official, 29 December 2008.

27 Communication with Hameed Quaraishi, former ANBP official, 29 December 2008.

28 One dark cloud sits on the horizon of this scenario. Given that Afghan opium production has exceeded global demand for many years, analysts suggest that prices should be far lower than they are. One explanation is that insurgents are hoarding opium and even supporting further decreases in production, which will revalue their stocks and increase their war finances. Worse still, such market manipulation combined with fluctuations in wheat prices could prove damaging to the provinces that have voluntarily given up poppy production (UNODC, 2008, p. 3).

BIBLIOGRAPHY

ANBP (Afghanistan New Beginnings Programme). 2006. *Brochure for the Second Tokyo Conference on Consolidation of Peace in Afghanistan*. Kabul: ANBP. 15 June.

—. 2007. 'Inauguration of DIAG First Development Project: Mahmoud Raqi-Kapisa Province.' Press release. 5 April.

—. 2008. Web site. Accessed 15 December 2008. <http://www.undpanbp.org>

AP (Associated Press). 2009. 'Suicide Bombing at Ministry in Kabul.' 11 February.

Asia Foundation. *Afghanistan in 2007: A Survey of the Afghan People*. Kabul: Asia Foundation.

Barakat, Sultan and Gareth Wardell. 2001. *Capitalizing on Capacities of Afghan Women: Women's Role in Afghanistan's Reconstruction and Development*. InFocus Programme on Crisis Response and Reconstruction, Working Paper 4. Geneva: International Labour Organization.

Berdal, Mats and David Malone. 2000. *Greed and Grievance: Economic Agendas in Civil Wars*. Boulder and London: Lynne Rienner.

Bhatia, Michael. 2008a. 'Violence in Afghanistan: An Overview.' In Michael Bhatia and Mark Sedra, pp. 11–37.

—. 2008b. 'Armed Groups in Afghanistan.' In Michael Bhatia and Mark Sedra, pp. 72–110.

— and Robert Muggah. 2008. 'The Politics of Demobilization in Afghanistan.' In Robert Muggah, ed. *Security and Post-Conflict Reconstruction: Dealing with Fighters in the Aftermath of War*. London: Routledge, pp. 126–64.

— and Mark Sedra. 2008. *Afghanistan, Arms and Conflict: Armed Groups, Disarmament and Security in a Post-war Society*. London: Routledge.

Bonn Agreement (Agreement on Provisional Arrangements in Afghanistan Pending the Re-Establishment of Permanent Government Institutions). 2001. 5 December.

Boone, Jon. 2008. 'Afghans Fear US Plan to Rearm Villagers.' *Financial Times*. 13 January.

Brewster, Murray. 2008. 'NATO Disbands Afghan Auxiliary Police.' *Edmonton Sun* (Canada). 15 May.

Chu, Henry. 2007. 'In Peace Bid, Karzai Opens Up to Taliban.' *Los Angeles Times*. 9 November.

CNN (Cable News Network). 2008. 'Gates: U.S. Would Support Afghan Peace Talks with Taliban.' 10 October.

Collier, Paul and Anke Hoeffler. 2004. 'Greed and Grievance in Civil War.' *Oxford Economic Papers*, Vol. 56, No. 4, pp. 563–95.

CRS (Congressional Research Service). 2001. 'Operation Enduring Freedom: Foreign Pledges of Military and Intelligence Support.' CRS Report for Congress. Code RL31152. 17 October. <http://fpc.state.gov/documents/organization/6207.pdf>

Dennys, Christian. 2005. 'Disarmament, Demobilization and Rearmament? The Effects of Disarmament in Afghanistan.' Japan Afghan NGO Network. June.

DeYoung, Karen. 2008. 'Pakistan Will Give Arms to Tribal Militias.' *Washington Post*. 23 October.

Faiez, Rahim. 2009. 'US-funded Program to Arm Afghan Groups Begins.' Associated Press. 31 January.

Gall, Carlotta. 2005. 'Islamists and Mujahideen Score Victory in Afghan Vote.' *New York Times*. 23 October.

Geneva Declaration Secretariat. 2008. *Global Burden of Armed Violence*. Geneva: Geneva Declaration Secretariat. September. <http://www.genevadeclaration.org>

Gopal, Anand. 2008. 'Who Are the Taliban? The Afghan War Deciphered.' TomDispatch.com. 4 December. <http://www.tomdispatch.com/post/175010>

GoA, UNAMA, and UNDP (Government of Afghanistan, United Nations Assitance Mission in Afghanistan, and United Nations Development Programme). 2006. 'Disbandment of Illegal Armed Groups (DIAG).' June. <http://www.undp.org/cpr/documents/ddr/pro_docs/Project_Doc_PRODOC_DIAG_Jan._2005_-_June_2006.pdf>

HSRP (Human Security Report Project). 2008. *miniAtlas of Human Security*. Vancouver: Simon Frasier University. <http://www.miniatlasofhumansecurity.info>

ICG (International Crisis Group). 2003. 'Disarmament and Reintegration in Afghanistan.' ICG Asia Report No. 65. Kabul/Brussels: International Crisis Group. 30 September.

IISS (International Institute for Strategic Studies). 2008. Armed Conflict Database: Afghanistan. Accessed 7 November 2008. <http://acd.iiss.org/armedconflict/MainPages/dsp_ConflictSummary.asp?ConflictID=181>

IRIN (Integrated Regional Information Network). 2005. 'Rights Body Warns of Warlords' Success in Elections.' 18 October.

Islamic Republic of Afghanistan. 2005. DIAG JPCC Planning Documents. Draft 5, unpublished. 12 May.

—. 2006. 'Strategy for Disbandment of Illegal Armed Groups in Afghanistan.' Kabul: Islamic Republic of Afghanistan. January.

—. 2008. *DIAG Implementation Report*. 1 December. Accessed 15 December 2008. <http://www.diag.gov.af/fastfact>

London Conference on Afghanistan. 2006. *Afghanistan Compact*. <http://www.nato.int/isaf/docu/epub/pdf/afghanistan_compact.pdf>

MoCN (Ministry of Counter-Narcotics). 2006. National Drug Control Strategy. Kabul: Islamic Republic of Afghanistan. January. <http://www.fco.gov.uk/resources/en/pdf/pdf18/fco_nationaldrugcontrolstrategy>

Moncrieff, Virginia. 2009. 'US, NATO Forces in Advanced Plans to Create Citizen Militias in Afghanistan: Reveals Leaked Email.' Huffingtonpost.com. 11 February. <http://www.huffingtonpost.com/virginia-moncrieff/us-nato-forces-in-advance_b_165998.html>

Özerdem, Alpaslan. 2002. 'Disarmament, Demobilisation and Reintegration of Former Combatants in Afghanistan: Lessons Learned from a Cross-cultural Perspective.' *Third World Quarterly*, Vol. 23, No. 5, pp. 961–75.

Poulton, Robin. 2008. *Afghanistan and the Experience of DDR in a Time of War*. Unpublished background paper. Geneva: Small Arms Survey.

President of the Islamic Government of Afghanistan. 2004. Presidential Decree No. 50. 14 July.

—. 2005. Presidential Decree No. 20. 24 June.

Radio Free Europe. 2008. 'U.S. Commander in Afghanistan Puts Forward Reconciliation Plan.' 19 November.

Rossi, Simonetta and Antonio Giustozzi. 2006. 'Disarmament, Demobilization and Reintegration of Ex-Combatants in Afghanistan: Constraints and Limited Capabilities.' Working Paper No. 2, series No. 2. London: Crisis States Research Centre, London School of Economics and Political Science.

Rubin, Barnett. 2003. 'Identifying Options and Entry Points for Disarmament, Demobilization, and Reintegration in Afghanistan.' New York: Center on International Cooperation, New York University.

Schmidt, Eric. 2009. 'Afghan Arms Are at Risk, Report Says.' *New York Times*. 12 February.

Sedra, Mark. 2004. *Securing Afghanistan's Future: Accomplishments and Strategic Pathway Forward—Disarmament, Demobilization and Reintegration of Ex-Combatants Technical Annex*. Kabul: Islamic Transitional State of Afghanistan.

—. 2008a. 'The Four Pillars of Demilitarization in Afghanistan.' In Michael Bhatia and Mark Sedra. *Afghanistan, Arms and Conflict: Armed Groups, Disarmament and Security in a Post-war Society*. London: Routledge, pp. 119–57.

—. 2008b. 'Addressing the Small Arms in Afghanistan: Introduction.' In Michael Bhatia and Mark Sedra, pp. 113–18.

— and Peter Middlebrook. 2005. 'Revisioning the International Compact for Afghanistan.' Foreign Policy Focus. 2 November. <http://www.fpif.org/fpiftxt/2912#_edn13>

— and Robert Muggah. 2007. 'Afghanistan's Fearful Culture.' *Ottawa Citizen*. 6 September. <http://www.canada.com/ottawacitizen/news/opinion/story.html?id=fefcd650-a201-4c0c-bdd6-8cc40ba91891>

Semple, Kirk, Ed Robbins, and Shayla Harris. 2007. 'Disarming Northern Afghanistan.' *New York Times* (video news report). October. <http://video.nytimes.com/video/2007/10/23/world/1194817109420/disarming-northern-afghanistan.html?scp=1&sq=Disarming%20Northern%20Afghanistan&st=cse>

Small Arms Survey. 2003. *Small Arms Survey 2003: Development Denied*. Oxford: Oxford University Press.

—. 2005. *Small Arms Survey 2005: Weapons at War*. Oxford: Oxford University Press.

UNAMA (United Nations Assistance Mission in Afghanistan). 2008. Press conference transcript. 2 June. <http://www.unama-afg.org/news/_pc/_english/2008/08june02.html#>

UNDDR (United Nations Disarmament, Demobilization and Reintegration Unit). 2008. 'Country Programme: Afghanistan.' Accessed 15 December 2008. <http://www.unddr.org/countryprogrammes.php?c121#approach>

UNDP (United Nations Development Programme). 2007. *Afghanistan Human Development Report 2007: Bridging Modernity and Tradition—the Rule of Law and the Search for Justice*. Kabul: UNDP. <http://hdr.undp.org/en/reports/nationalreports/asiathepacific/afghanistan/nhdr2007.pdf>

—. 2008a. 'DIAG Development Update.' Accessed 15 December 2008. <http://www.undpanbp.org/daig-update/diagupdate.html>

—. 2008b. 'DIAG Update.' Accessed 15 December 2008. <http://www.undpanbp.org/diag-strategy>

UNODC (United Nations Office on Drugs and Crime). 2008. *Afghanistan: Opium Survey 2008*. Vienna: UNODC. November.

UNOHCHR (United Nations Office of the High Commissioner for Human Rights). 2008. 'New UN Figures Show Sharp Rise in Afghan Civilian Casualties.' Press release. 16 September. <http://www.reliefweb.int/rw/rwb.nsf/db900SID/EGUA-7JJM7B?OpenDocument&RSS20=18>

VOA (Voice of America). 2008. 'US Rules Out Reconciliation with Taliban Leader Mullah Omar.' 29 October.

—. 2009. 'Progress against Poppy Production.' 17 January. <http://www.voanews.com/uspolicy/2009-01-17-voa2.cfm>

Waldman, Matt. 2008. 'Falling Short: Aid Effectiveness in Afghanistan.' Agency Coordinating Body for Afghan Relief (ACBAR). Kabul: ACBAR.

Wali, Abdel. 2002. 'Disarmament Drive.' *Afghanistan Recovery Report*, No. 20. Institute for War & Peace Reporting, 25 July. <http://www.iwpr.net/?p=arr&s=f&o=153669&apc_state=heniarr2002>

ACKNOWLEDGEMENTS

Principal authors

Michael Bhatia, Emile LeBrun, Robert Muggah, and Mark Sedra

Contributors

Bradford Adams and Robin Poulton

IN MEMORIAM

Michael Vinay Bhatia
23 August 1976–7 May 2008

The Small Arms Survey staff is deeply saddened by the premature death of Michael Bhatia. Michael was widely recognized for his compassion and ability to lend people a voice in war-torn parts of the world. In addition to the research he undertook for the Small Arms Survey, he carried out studies in Afghanistan for the Overseas Development Institute, the Afghanistan Research and Evaluation Unit, the UK Department for International Development, and the Organization for Security and Co-operation in Europe. At Oxford University's St. Antony's College, he was completing research for his doctoral dissertation, *The Mujahideen: A Study of Combatant Motives in Afghanistan,* 1978–2004.

During the last seven months of his life, Michael served as a social scientist embedded with the US Army in Afghanistan. He was a highly regarded member of the Human Terrain programme. 'There's a big academic controversy involved,' he wrote of his work there, 'but in my mind we're actually serving to better attune the military to Afghan concerns and views.' In the course of his efforts to enhance understanding between Afghans and fighting forces, Michael was killed in Khost Province.

Michael will be remembered fondly by his academic peers–as a talented and committed researcher and an enthusiastic colleague. His confidence and exuberance were infectious. His insight will be sorely missed but his intellectual legacy will inspire young scholars for years to come.

© Aleksandr Pakhay/iStockphoto

Two Hizbollah fighters walk through the destroyed town of Aitta Shaab, 16 August 2006. © Jason Howe/WPN

Testing Received Wisdom

PERCEPTIONS OF SECURITY IN SOUTHERN LEBANON

10

INTRODUCTION

The Israeli–Lebanese border has been the site of numerous armed attacks since 2000, when Israel withdrew from Southern Lebanon. The 2006 war between Israel and Hizbollah killed approximately 1,000 people in Southern Lebanon, decimated its infrastructure, and led to the displacement of an estimated one million people in both countries. It also illustrated the region's continuing volatility.

Although many have written about the situation in Southern Lebanon, a number of questions remain unanswered. Namely, in the wake of a devastating war, how do the people of Southern Lebanon feel about their security? Whom do they look to for protection against local and external threats? Which political parties do they support? How many households own weapons, and what are their views on arms control, including the regulation of non-state armed groups?

This chapter presents the results of a household survey conducted in Southern Lebanon in March–May 2008 to explore these and other questions. Its key findings include the following:

- Some 1,000 people were killed and 5,800 injured in Southern Lebanon as a direct result of the 2006 war, while combat activity resulted in the damaging or destruction of approximately 69,000 homes in this area.
- The people of the south, whatever their political affiliations, express strong support for state security institutions, with the Lebanese army and police consistently cited as preferred security providers.
- Less than a quarter of the population believes that expanding the presence of the United Nations Interim Force in Lebanon (UNIFIL) on the border with Israel would enhance community safety.
- Although it is often assumed that Hizbollah is broadly popular among southerners, it appears that support for non-state armed groups in general—and Hizbollah in particular—is at least partially overestimated.
- The extent of civilian firearm ownership in Southern Lebanon is unknown but is probably much higher than that captured in survey responses. There is also evidence that arms flows to non-state groups such as Hizbollah continue despite a 2006 UN Security Council arms embargo.
- There is significant support among the people of Southern Lebanon for government control of civilian weapons ownership, as well as the outlawing of armed militias; those who back opposition parties, such as Hizbollah, are much less likely to favour such initiatives.

The chapter begins by outlining the turbulent history of Southern Lebanon and Lebanon as a whole. It provides historical background to the 2006 war and describes the key players and principal dynamics of that conflict. The chapter then presents the findings of the Southern Lebanon Armed Violence Assessment, devoting particular attention to those relating to insecurity during and after the 2006 war, attitudes towards security provision, party affiliation, and gun ownership and control.

SOUTHERN LEBANON: A HISTORY OF CONFLICT

The conflict with Israel has been central to recent Lebanese history, but in no part of the country has this been truer than in the south. Some commentators blame the Lebanese civil war on outside actors—Israel, Syria, Iran, France, the United States, and others—but other factors were also at work. The civil war was not exclusively a symptom of the Israeli–Palestinian conflict, but in the south that conflict does seem to overshadow all else. A capsule summary of Lebanon's modern history cannot do justice to the complex dynamics and range of actors influencing it. In this section, emphasis is given to the major events and trends that have shaped the experience of Southern Lebanon from 1975 onwards.

Map 10.1 **Southern Lebanon**

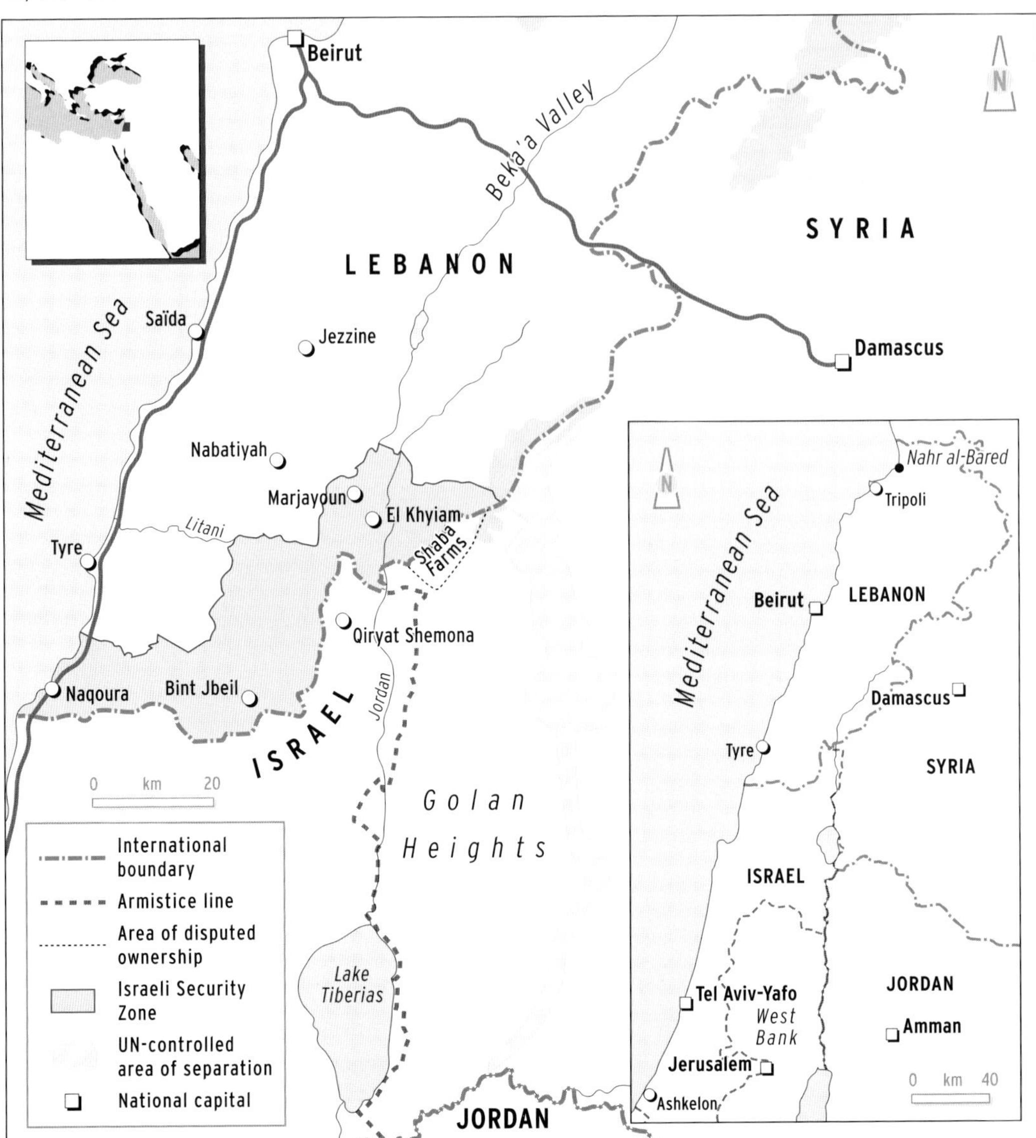

Lebanon did not truly gain independence from France until 1943, when the fledgling state established a confessional government that was dominated by Christians, though the population was and remains a diverse mix of Shi'ite and Sunni Muslim, Druze, Maronite Christian, and Greek Orthodox, among many other groups. With the rise of pan-Arab nationalism in the Middle East in the 1950s, however, Lebanese Muslims became increasingly dissatisfied with the sectarian political system. Ideologically driven groups also opposed the elitist, status quo character of the government that was partly a hold-over from the pre-independence period. A brief civil war in 1958 manifested as essentially a Christian–Muslim conflict over the nature of the Lebanese state. US military intervention was instrumental in ending militia fighting but did little to address the underlying antagonisms (Rabinovich, 1985, pp. 25–28).

By the late 1960s the Lebanese political system struggled to manage the domestic effects of rivalries between competing Arab states and especially the Arab–Israeli conflict. Most importantly, Lebanon was by then home to some 300,000 Palestinian refugees, mostly unwanted by the Lebanese and increasingly militarized following the establishment of the Palestine Liberation Organization (PLO) in 1964. The Cairo Agreement of 1969 granted the PLO a semi-autonomous base of operations in Southern Lebanon from which to organize their armed struggle with growing military and financial support from Arab governments (Cobban, 1984, p. 47). Itamar Rabinovich calls this the era of 'controlled tension' prior to the collapse of the state (Rabinovich, 1985, p. 32).

By the late 1960s Lebanon was home to some 300,000 Palestinian refugees.

Sectarian tensions ignited once more in 1975, precipitating a bloody multi-phase, multi-party civil war that would last until 1990, claim around 150,000 lives, and decimate representational government. The inter-sectarian militia violence soon drew in foreign actors. Syrian troops intervened in 1976 in an attempt to quell the fighting. Threatened by the proximity of Syrian forces and responding to PLO attacks, the Israel Defense Forces (IDF) invaded the country in 1978, progressing as far as the Litani River, the traditional dividing line between Northern and Southern Lebanon. Though the IDF withdrew in response to UN Security Council resolutions (UNSC, 1978a; 1978c), Israel maintained influence through allied Christian Lebanese militias, leading to ongoing violence in the south. The Security Council-mandated UN Interim Force in Lebanon was largely unable to provide security (ICG, 2006).

Following an assassination attempt on the Israeli ambassador to the United Kingdom and a bus bombing in Israel, the IDF bombed and then invaded the country once again in June 1982 in an attempt to expel the PLO from Southern Lebanon. The fighting also brought Israel into direct battle with Syrian, leftist, and Lebanese Muslim forces. In August, a multinational force composed of Italian, French, and US troops arrived to oversee the withdrawal of PLO fighters from Lebanon (ICG, 2006). By 1985 Israel had withdrawn most of its troops but established a Security Zone within Southern Lebanon, which it deemed crucial for its security and in which IDF troops patrolled. But much of Southern Lebanon remained in the hands of an Israeli-allied militia (the South Lebanon Army), which faced growing opposition from the emerging Shi'ite Islamist militia, Hizbollah.

Hizbollah came to dominate the Shi'ite landscape in Lebanon, supplanting the Amal Movement as the principal militia force in the south (see Box 10.1). It also waged low-intensity warfare against IDF forces in the Security Zone, prompting Israel to launch two short, but intensive, military campaigns in Southern Lebanon in July 1993 and April 1996.

Following failed US mediation between Israel and Syria over Lebanon, Israel unilaterally abandoned the Security Zone in 2000 in the face of protracted guerrilla engagement from Hizbollah. The Lebanese government left a power vacuum in the border area that was soon filled by Hizbollah and Amal fighters with the government's blessing. But the south remained unstable and poorly serviced by the government (Norton, 2000, pp. 35, 39, 40).

Hizbollah and Amal meanwhile pursued new grievances with Israel over the Shaba Farms, an Israeli-occupied area in the disputed Golan Heights zone. Only months after the IDF withdrawal in 2000, escalating Israeli–Palestinian violence sparked an engagement between the IDF and Palestinians on the Israel–Lebanon border, prompting

Box 10.1 Key players

Amal Movement

Harakat AMAL or the Amal Movement was founded in 1975 as the military wing of the Movement of the Disinherited, a political reform group established by Iranian-born Imam Sayyed Mousa al-Sadr, Lebanese parliamentarian Hussein al-Husseini, and other young Shi'ites. At its outset the movement was distinctively Shi'ite but communal in orientation, seeking to improve living conditions for all Lebanese (Collelo, 1989). Historically it has been aligned with Syrian interests, but not exclusively.

After the disappearance of al-Sadr in Libya in 1978, the movement went through a series of leadership changes. By 1980, Nabih Berri was in control, and with Syrian assistance the group entered the Lebanese civil war against anti-Syrian Palestinian and left-wing groups such as the Druze-led Progressive Socialist Party (PSP). In 1982 Husayn al-Musawi, deputy head of Amal, broke away to form Islamist-oriented Islamic Amal, supported by Iran. Islamic Amal quickly drew away much of the movement's support base. By 1984, Islamic Amal was absorbed into Hizbollah, which was to clash with Amal within the context of the broader, ongoing Lebanese civil war.

In 1985–89 Amal engaged in the 'War of the Camps', a series of battles with Hizbollah- and PSP-supported Palestinian groups prompted by years of mistreatment by Palestinians (Collelo, 2003, p. 142). These battles formed an important component of the civil war's latter phase. Following the 1989 Ta'if Agreement that ended the civil war and cemented Lebanese-Syrian relations, Amal became a mainstream political party in the national government. Nabih Berri was appointed a cabinet minister and elected speaker of the National Assembly (head of Parliament) in 1992, a position he still holds at this writing. Since 2005 Amal has allied itself with Hizbollah in elections. Following Syria's withdrawal in 2005 and Hizbollah's 2006 war with Israel, Amal entered into the Shi'ite-opposition March 8 Alliance with its former enemy. It also participated in the Hizbollah-led May 2008 military occupation of the predominantly pro-government Sunni areas of West Beirut (described below).

Hizbollah

Hizbollah was formed by defectors from Amal who were radicalized in response to the 1979 Iranian Islamic Revolution and the 1982 Israeli invasion of Lebanon, during which nationalist Palestinian and left-wing Lebanese groups failed to defend mainly Shi'ite communities located in the south, the southern suburbs of Beirut, and the Beka'a Valley. Iran provided early financial and military support to the group and sent 1,500 members of the Iranian Revolutionary Guard to provide training in 1982, though a small number had already been there since 1979 (Butler, 2006, p. 60).

Early activities included suicide bombings against the US Marines and French forces in Beirut in 1983, the assassination of left-wing intellectuals and leaders in 1984–85, and the hijacking of a US passenger jet in 1985. Hizbollah was formally founded in February 1985. In its manifesto it undertook to expel colonial forces from Lebanon, avenge civil war killings committed by right-wing Lebanese Christian militias, and establish a consensual (rather than coercive) Islamic state in Lebanon (Hizbollah, 1985). The party was led by secretary-general Sayyed Abbas Al-Moussawi.

Soon after its inception, and following successful anti-Israeli guerrilla warfare in the south, Hizbollah challenged Amal in an intra-Shi'ite war from which it emerged victorious in 1989. While the Ta'if Agreement, adopted the same year, called for the disbandment of all non-state armed groups, the Lebanese government considered Hizbollah exempt as a 'national resistance group' (Ta'if Agreement, 1989; UNSC, 2004b, para. 19). In 1992 Al-Moussawi was assassinated by Israel and succeeded by Sayyed Hassan Nasrallah.

In the absence of strong Lebanese state authority in most Shi'ite areas, and with the financial backing of Iran, the party was able to develop an elaborate social welfare network in poverty-stricken neighbourhoods and assist in the rebuilding of communities destroyed or damaged by Israeli bombardments (Salamey and Pearson, 2007). Later it branched into road repair and other infrastructure projects. It appears unique in Lebanon for its resistance to corruption (Butler, 2006, p. 59).

Following the Israeli withdrawal in 2000 and Syrian pullout in 2005, the party captured 14 out of 128 parliamentary seats in the 2005 elections and held two out of 24 cabinet ministries in the largely non-Shi'ite, anti-Syrian coalition government. While its perceived victory in the 2006 war with Israel further consolidated its influence and importance in Southern Lebanon and regionally, concern over Hizbollah's armed presence was growing in the Beirut government.

In May 2008 a long-standing political crisis exploded when the ruling coalition sought to shut down Hizbollah's military telecommunications network and remove an airport security chief allegedly close to the party. Hizbollah and its opposition partners responded by seizing control of most of pro-government West Beirut. The conflict, which threatened to return the country to civil war, ended only when the ruling majority agreed to key political demands of the Hizbollah-led opposition (BBC,

2008). During the Israeli occupation, Hizbollah is thought to have had only 450-500 active fighters. In 2006, its strength was estimated to be 1,000-1,200 active members and 6,000-10,000 volunteers operating on reserve (Butler, 2006, p. 62; Rao, 2006).

Lebanese Armed Forces

The Lebanese Armed Forces (LAF) has historically been regarded as a weak, poorly resourced, and ineffective fighting force. This weakness is a reflection of long-standing sectarian tension. From independence onwards, ruling elites had an interest in suppressing the army's power and authority, though Islamic groups in particular hoped the LAF would be competent enough to defend the country from Israeli attack (Collelo, 2003, p. 157).

During the civil war, the LAF was divided along sectarian lines, with some soldiers siding with the government and others defecting to the militias. In 1987 the entire military consisted of an estimated 15,000-18,000 men, supplied with minimal US, British, and French weapons (Collelo, 1989). The army has rarely undertaken offensive engagements; it has traditionally deployed to supervise elections (Collelo, 2003, p. 157).

Prior to the 2006 Hizbollah-Israel war, there was no Lebanese army presence in the former Israeli Security Zone; the LAF was largely a bystander to the 2006 conflict (Nerguizian, 2009, p. 12). For purposes of extending the government's control over the region, UN Security Council Resolution 1701 called for the deployment of Lebanese troops throughout Southern Lebanon with UNIFIL support (UNSC, 2006b, para. 2). About 15,000 troops had been deployed south of the Litani River as of late 2007, with a further 8,000 in the Lebanese-Syrian border area (Nerguizian, 2009, p. 33).

In May 2007, 2,000 LAF soldiers took part in suppressing a violent attack by Fatah al-Islam, an Islamist group of uncertain origin, in the Nahr al-Bared refugee camp in Northern Lebanon. This episode, in which 169 LAF, 222 militants, and 42 civilians were killed, is the most significant military engagement the LAF has carried out in the post-civil war period. While the casualties were high, it demonstrated that the army could be effective, despite being ill-equipped and suffering from coordination difficulties (Nerguizian, 2009, pp. 17-18).

In fact, the LAF has shown that it is one of the few Lebanese institutions in the post-Syrian era that most citizens trust. One recent analysis finds that it has become more representative, balanced, and capable, though it is still far from being able to secure the state's monopoly on the use of force (Nerguizian, 2009, p. 31). In 2008 the LAF had a combined strength of about 54,000 men (Nerguizian, 2009, p. 33). The government ended mandatory conscription in 2007 and so the LAF is now composed entirely of voluntary recruits.

UNIFIL

UNIFIL was created by UN Security Council Resolutions 425 and 426 of 1978 to confirm the withdrawal of Israeli armed forces following their invasion of Southern Lebanon and to assist the government in asserting control over the region (UNSC, 1978a; 1978b). Since its inception it has been accused of bias by both parties to the conflict and has been unable to provide tangible security in the south (ICG, 2006). During the 1982 invasion and subsequent occupation, UNIFIL remained behind Israeli lines and was largely prevented from fulfilling its mandate. In the wake of Israel's rapid, unilateral withdrawal in 2000, the UN force confirmed the withdrawal and monitored violations. Lebanese security forces also deployed to the south but left control of the border area to Hizbollah (UNDPKO, 2006). Following the 2006 Hizbollah-Israel war, the Security Council increased UNIFIL's maximum troop strength to 15,000. It was again mandated to support the deployment of Lebanese armed forces throughout the south, and to help ensure humanitarian access to civilians and the return of displaced persons (UNSC, 2006b, para. 11).

Hizbollah to launch its first operation in Shaba, killing three Israeli soldiers (Norton, 2000, p. 41). In response, Israel resumed violations of Lebanese airspace and waters. While tensions remained acute for the next six years, casualties on both sides were low. This was a period of 'harassing fire, aggressive patrolling, and heated rhetoric' from both parties within informally agreed boundaries (Butler, 2006, pp. 57–58).

The 2006 War

In July 2006, Hizbollah initiated a series of attacks and cross-border incursions that killed a number of Israeli military personnel and civilians. Two IDF personnel were kidnapped and taken back to Lebanon for the purposes of prisoner exchange (Butler, 2006, p. 64). An unsuccessful Israeli rescue operation led to the deaths of five more IDF

Box 10.2 The arming of Hizbollah

By the time of the 2006 war, the UN Security Council had repeatedly called for the withdrawal of foreign forces and influence from Lebanon and the disbandment and disarmament of all militias.[1] While Syria, a primary target of the UN resolutions, withdrew after international pressure and Lebanese protests prompted by the assassination of former prime minister Rafik Hariri in February 2005, the Lebanese government took no steps to disarm Hizbollah.

UN Security Council Resolution 1701 of August 2006 again emphasized 'the importance of the extension of the control of the Government of Lebanon over all Lebanese territory' and underlined the need for it 'to exercise its full sovereignty, so that there will be no weapons without the consent of the Government of Lebanon and no authority other than that of the Government of Lebanon' (UNSC, 2006b, para. 3). It also prohibited the supply of arms, related material, technical training, and assistance to any entity or individual in Lebanon not authorized by the Lebanese government or UNIFIL (para. 15).

The primary source of Hizbollah's weapons has always been thought to be Iran, operating with the cooperation of Syria and elements of the Lebanese government. Following Resolution 1701, Syrian President Bashar al-Assad pledged to honour the embargo (Hoge, 2006). Only a week after the end of the war, however, Turkish authorities reportedly intercepted five Iranian cargo planes and a Syrian aircraft carrying rocket launchers and crates of C-802 anti-ship missiles, the same weapon that disabled an Israeli boat on the third day of the war. According to Nicholas Blanford, a long-time observer of Hizbollah, the group's traditional conduit for arms is Lebanon's eastern border with Syria, but 'the party has devised alternative means of procuring weapons in the event of a closed land route' (Blanford, 2008).

During the 2006 war, Hizbollah fired approximately 3,970 surface-to-surface rockets (Rubin, 2007, p. 10). The origin of smaller, 107 mm and 122 mm rockets is difficult to determine conclusively; the 70-year-old designs are widely manufactured. More distinctive are the larger rockets–some weighing several tons–of which at least 457 were fired into Israel in 2006. Based mostly on Chinese designs, these are produced in Iran and Syria (Rubin, 2007, p. 11). Uzi Rubin reports that Hizbollah initially received Syrian-made 220 mm and 302 mm rockets, with ranges of 70–100 km. Later, Iranian-made 240 mm Fadjr-3 and 320 mm Fadjr-5 rockets were transferred through Syria. Larger versions with ranges of more than 200 km are suspected (Rubin, 2007, pp. 4–5).

Other reports have indicated that Hizbollah possesses Russian-designed or -manufactured anti-tank systems (RPG-29 and Metis-M) and French-made Milan missiles, in addition to less reliable Russian Katyushas and Iranian-made Fajr-3 and Fajr-5 missiles (Bazzi, 2006). It should be noted that Russian-labelled equipment may originate in any of several sympathetic Russian client states.

The clearest evidence of supply relationships comes from weapons uniquely produced in a single country. Hizbollah is reportedly in possession of several dozen Iranian Zelzal rockets, with a range of 120 miles and capable of carrying 1,300 lbs of explosives (Bazzi, 2006; Prier, 2008). Thus Iranian surface-to-surface rockets are important as evidence of an arms relationship otherwise largely kept covert.

Hizbollah leader Sayyed Hassan Nasrallah routinely emphasizes the scale of the group's arsenal, which appears to have grown considerably in recent years. In 2005 Nasrallah claimed Hizbollah possessed 12,000 rockets; in 2006, he claimed 20,000; in 2007 the number had grown to 33,000 rockets that could 'reach deep into Israel' (Rubin, 2007, p. 5; AP, 2007). He is more discrete about suppliers.

Israeli spokesmen have reported that Hizbollah is retransferring Iranian-made 122 mm, 20 km-range rockets to Hamas in Gaza (Fishman, 2008). These presumably are the rockets that began to hit Israeli cities further from the border–notably Ashkelon–in late 2008.

soldiers. Israel then initiated a 34-day systematic bombing and ground campaign designed to completely destroy Hizbollah's fighting capacity. The campaign failed to achieve its objective, however.

Israel reported 12 IDF and 43 Israeli civilian deaths as a result of the 2006 conflict. Fatalities in all of Lebanon were estimated at between 1,000 and 1,200, the 'vast majority' of which were probably civilians, and between 4,000–4,400 non-fatal injuries (HRW, 2007, p. 4; LHRC, 2009). Southern Lebanon's infrastructure had also been decimated, and an estimated one million civilians were displaced (AI, 2006, p. 2). It was the deadliest engagement between Israel and Lebanon-based forces since the Israeli invasion of 1982.

UN Security Council Resolution 1701 marked the official end of the war. It called for a 'full cessation of hostilities' between Hizbollah and Israel, the withdrawal of Israeli forces, the withdrawal of Hizbollah to the north of the Litani

River, and the co-deployment of Lebanese and UNIFIL forces in the south (UNSC, 2006b). The resolution also imposed an arms embargo on non-state groups in Lebanon (see Box 10.2).

Hizbollah supporters during a 'victory over Israel' rally in the suburbs of Beirut, 22 September 2006. © Hussein Malla/ AP Photo

Despite the end of open warfare, the factors that led to conflict persist, including disputes over territory and the involvement and interests of foreign supporters. Both Hizbollah and Israel continue to be in violation of UN Security Council resolutions. The Israeli government has claimed its right to continue to collect reconnaissance from fly-overs and has threatened overwhelming retaliation for any further attacks on its territory. At the same time, Hizbollah has reportedly embarked on a 'massive, unprecedented recruitment, training, and rearmament campaign' in preparation for what it expects to be the inevitable next military engagement with Israel (Blanford, 2008).

For these reasons the post-conflict label is hard to apply to Southern Lebanon. Both parties remain in a state of high readiness, have suggested that future conflict is likely, and continue to call for the destruction or elimination of one another. There is no 'peace process' to serve as a guide for conflict resolution, generally a prerequisite for moving from war to peace. While several countries, led by the United States, have begun to support the reform of Lebanon's state security apparatus as a means of counter-balancing Hizbollah's semi-autonomy (Worth and Lipton, 2008), it is not clear how this effort will play out in the south of the country.

THE SOUTHERN LEBANON ARMED VIOLENCE ASSESSMENT

To understand both the immediate and the ongoing effects of the 2006 war on Southern Lebanese civilians, a representative sample of households in Southern Lebanon[2] was surveyed about their experiences during and after the war. Civilians often bear the brunt of armed conflict in ways that leave lasting personal, economic, educational, and psychological effects. An attempt was made to assess some of these impacts using standardized survey tools in the hope that the findings could be used to raise awareness about the current needs of the South Lebanese population. Box 10.3 describes the survey methodology while Box 10.4 discusses the sample demographics.

Study findings

The following sections present some of the principal findings of the Southern Lebanon Armed Violence Assessment. The chapter focuses on arms and security issues, including public attitudes towards gun ownership and the government regulation of civilian weapons and non-state armed groups.

Box 10.3 Survey methodology[3]

Sampling

This survey utilizes a modified cluster sampling methodology. Cluster sampling is typically used to identify clusters of households within towns and villages, but here it was used to identify the towns and villages themselves. Various techniques, including random sampling, were employed to select households within each town or village. This method helped overcome the lack of accurate demographic and population data for Southern Lebanon.

The sampling method involved four distinct stages:

- *Stage one:* The first stage entailed the selection of towns. Southern Lebanon's three largest towns–Tyre, Marjayoun, and Bint Jbeil–were automatically included, and 50 other smaller towns were added using a probability proportional to size (PPS) sampling method. The PPS determinations employed pre-2006 geo-coded digital satellite maps[4] and the most recent electoral rolls as a proxy for population distribution.[5]
- *Stage two:* The towns were demarcated using Global Positioning System (GPS) boundaries with random GPS points generated within them. If a GPS point coincided with a building containing a household, that building was automatically selected for the study.
- *Stage three:* If the GPS point did not coincide with a building containing a household, all buildings within a 20-metre radius of the GPS point were counted and one selected randomly. When a GPS location was not within 20 metres of a building, that point was removed from the sample. If a multi-household building (e.g. apartment block) was identified, the interviewer determined the number of households in the building and randomly selected one using prepared sets of random numbers. If a targeted dwelling was unoccupied, interviewers attempted to locate the former residents.[6]
- *Stage four:* A primary respondent was selected within each household. All adults in the household had an equal probability of being selected. The interviewer recorded the total number of adults aged 18 and over living in the household on 11 July 2006, when the Israel-Hizbollah war began, and chose the person with the most recent birthday (at the date of the interview). If the selected adult was not present, attempts were made to interview that person at a later date.

Sample size

Based on population estimates generated by electoral roll data, a sample of 400 households was sought for the town of Tyre, and 200 each for Marjayoun and Bint Jbeil. For each of the smaller towns the figure was 16. This approach yielded a total of 1,600 locations in the sample. Nevertheless, Hizbollah security personnel prevented interviewers from conducting the survey in Bint Jbeil and El Khyiam, which brought the total number of households surveyed to 1,388.[7]

The study primarily sought to identify the proportion of people suffering some impact from the 2006 war. It was expected, conservatively, that this would be 20 per cent of those surveyed. Given these expectations, a +/– 2 per cent confidence interval (CI) was calculated based on a confidence level of 95 per cent. In an effort to obtain a conservative sample size, it was assumed that the intraclass correlation coefficient was 1 (i.e. if a house is bombed, all members are affected). Then, using the standard formula

$$SE(p) = \sqrt{\frac{p(1-p)}{n}}$$

and assuming the observed proportion of a variable would be roughly 20 per cent, with a sample size of 1,600 households, the standard error (SE(p)) would be 1 per cent for a completely random sample, and the 95 per cent CI would be +/– 2 per cent. The precise impacts of the multi-stage sampling method and the clustering effects of selecting all members of a household were not known beforehand. In order to take account of these uncertainties, the CI was doubled to +/– 4 per cent.

Interviewers and questionnaire

Arabic-speaking interview teams with at least one year paid interviewing experience were dispatched to the selected households. The primary respondent answered a series of questions on his (or her) own behalf and that of household members. Another set of questions, including psychometric assessments to measure symptoms of post-traumatic stress disorder, were asked only of this adult.

The survey instrument (questionnaire) had six distinct sections: household demographics, experiences during and after wartime, history of human rights violations, gun ownership and attitudes, a screening for post-traumatic stress disorder, and a quality of life assessment. Interviews began on 13 March 2008 and concluded on 16 May 2008.

▶

The first section of the questionnaire reviewed the demographic characteristics of the household. It used a series of questions from the household survey that the International Labour Organization employs as part of its International Programme on the Elimination of Child Labour, one of two standardized surveys used to assess child labour practices.[8] The second section was taken directly from the Harvard Trauma Questionnaire, a checklist developed by the Harvard Program in Refugee Trauma for purposes of measuring the impacts of an earlier traumatic event.[9] The next section of the survey was designed to establish the human rights history of the respondent and other household members. The questions that appeared here were taken directly from the Port-au-Prince Human Rights study used by the authors in 2005 to assess eight types of human rights violations, including murders, physical assaults, sexual assaults, illegal detentions, property crimes, death threats, and threats of physical injury or sexual assault (Kolbe and Hutson, 2006). Many of the questions in the section on gun ownership and attitudes were adapted from the Middle East North Africa Action Network on Small Arms (MENAANSA) survey regarding weapons and community security in Gaza, Lebanon, the West Bank, and Sudan (MENAANSA, 2006).

Death and injury

More than half of survey respondents reported human rights abuses and other traumatic events during the war; 17.9 per cent stated that they had been in a life or death situation. Fifteen respondents (1.2 per cent) said that someone in their family had been killed, while 3.4 per cent said they themselves had been seriously injured in the war. IDF actions were blamed for all war-related deaths (11 of the 23 deaths that were reported).[10] Based on these results, it is estimated that 1,000 (+/- 600) individuals were killed in Southern Lebanon as a result of the 2006 war. This figure is in the range of previous estimates from NGOs, the media, and the Lebanese government. It does not include war-related deaths that occurred elsewhere in Lebanon.

Only one respondent disclosed being raped and only two individuals reported incidents of physical assault not associated with bombings, one by the IDF and one by 'an old husband'. There may have been under-reporting of sexual assault given that all of the female interviewers resigned during the first week of interviews due to their husbands' concerns about security, and so participants were interviewed by all-male research teams. Moreover, the literature indicates that victims of sexual abuse are routinely reluctant to disclose such violations, even when interviewed by women (Lunde and Ortmann, 1992).

Injury as a result of the war was more common. Survey results indicate that 0.9 per cent of all individuals suffered significant physical harm as a result of the war, representing 4.7 per cent of total households. It is estimated, therefore, that 5,800 (+/- 1,400) people were injured as a direct result of the war.[11] Estimates of the number of war casualties are probably too low, however, as interview teams were not allowed to enter Bint Jbeil, reportedly a hard-hit location.

A woman mourns for family members killed as a result of the 2006 war, Harees, August 2006. © Zohra Bensemra/Reuters

Box 10.4 Demographics of the sample

Of all primary respondents, 93.6 per cent identified themselves as Lebanese, while 4.6 per cent stated they were Palestinian and 1.6 per cent 'other'. The remaining 0.2 per cent refused to respond. There were 4.6 people per household in the study sample, with a standard deviation (SD) of 1.9. The average age of all household members was 30.5 years (SD 20.1), although the median age was 27 years, and 25 per cent of the sample was under 14 years of age, with 25 per cent over 46 years of age. Among primary respondents, 43.9 per cent were male and 56.1 per cent were female (compared to 47.8 per cent male and 52.2 per cent female for all adult household members).[12] The average age of men sampled was 30.1 years (SD 20.9) with a median age of 25 years. Women's average age was 31 (SD 19.3) with a median of 28 years.

Among primary respondents 25 years and older, 58.7 per cent had less than 12 years' education, 41.2 per cent had a Lebanese baccalaureate, and 15.9 per cent a bachelor's degree in arts or science. Of those interviewed, 3.6 per cent were illiterate.

The combined median income of surveyed households was USD 600 per month.[13] The monthly per capita income of these households averaged USD 189 (SD USD 163) with a median of USD 150. Slightly less than 8 (7.7) per cent of all households had received money from relatives living abroad in the preceding month, while 3.4 per cent had received some kind of financial assistance from non-relatives.[14]

The religious affiliation of primary respondents was: Shi'ite (84.8 per cent), Sunni (9.5 per cent), Maronite (3.3 per cent), Catholic (1.6 per cent), Greek Orthodox (0.6 per cent), Druze (less than 0.1 per cent), and other (0.2 per cent). Of those surveyed, 0.6 per cent refused to answer this question.

Property damage

One problem that was widely covered by the media during the war was the bombing of private homes. Since the advent of the war, 21.9 per cent of surveyed households reported being homeless for a period of time.[15] More than half of the households surveyed, 57 per cent, reported some form of property damage or loss. Of the 807 incidents disclosed during the interviews, 97 per cent were attributed to actions by the IDF (80 per cent of total incidents were caused by bombs or missiles). The survey results also reveal that 3.3 per cent of households suffered property damage as a result of earthquakes. It is estimated that 69,000 homes (+/- 3,700) were damaged or destroyed because of the war.

After the war, financial assistance was provided by government agencies, NGOs, and political organizations. Of those households in the study that reported property damage, 81 per cent said they received compensation for their loss. Of these, 71 per cent received money from the Amal-affiliated Council of the South (Majlis al-Janoub), while 39 per cent received funds from Hizbollah or Jihad al-Binaa, Hizbollah's reconstruction arm.[16]

Residents of the Haret Harek neighbourhood in Beirut return after the ceasefire to find their homes and businesses reduced to rubble, 14 August 2006. © Tanya Habjouqa/WPN

Political party and militia support

Although Hizbollah and allied parties (the March 8 political coalition) have dominated recent elections in the south, it is unclear how much popular support the various political parties have in the region. Elections are not a valid indicator of support in any part of the country since Lebanese electoral law and administrative rules restrict people from changing their voting district from where they were born to where they currently reside (Salamey and Tabar, 2008). In addition, political polls have generally relied only on registered voters, not the population at large, excluding certain groups that are, in effect, disenfranchised (e.g. Palestinian refugees and undocumented workers).[17] Lebanese political parties have a vested interest in claiming they have strong popular support. Lebanon has a confessional government, much like the power-sharing arrangement in Northern Ireland. If political parties can demonstrate that they are popular, they can claim a greater share of political power (e.g. ministerial posts) and government resources.

When asked whether they identified with or supported a particular political party, respondents were allowed to state any political party or organization without being prompted; this was an open-ended question, specifically designed to avoid guiding the respondent in his or her response. Less than 2 per cent of households refused to answer when asked their political affiliation. Just over 60 per cent of respondents stated that their household was not affiliated with a political party at all. Of the 40 per cent who reported supporting a political party, slightly more than 80 per cent supported 'the resistance', Hizbollah, or 'opposition parties'. Just over ten per cent supported Amal. The term 'resistance' refers to the defence of Lebanese interests against Israel, including the return of disputed border territory (Shaba Farms); it often means Hizbollah, which has been closely associated with the resistance in recent years.

Some caveats in interpreting survey results in this area are required. First, as noted earlier, interview teams were not allowed to enter Bint Jbeil and El Khyiam. Both of these towns are considered Hizbollah strongholds, so the study's estimates of support for the party are probably biased downwards. Secondly, Hizbollah and its allies may enjoy a degree of support for certain actions the party (or its militia wing) undertakes, such as resistance against Israel, that is not expressed as support for the party. Strong support for Hizbollah's social services arm may also affect responses to the question of political affiliation. Hizbollah's invasion of West Beirut in May 2008, criticized by many across Lebanon's political spectrum, appears to have had minimal influence on study findings as almost all of the interviews had been completed by the time the violence erupted.

Just over 60 per cent of households reported no affiliation with a political party.

Post-traumatic stress and quality of life

Only the primary respondent was given the Harvard Trauma Questionnaire. Of particular note, nearly 60 per cent of primary respondents stated that they experienced a recurrent thought or memory of a hurtful or terrifying event related to the conflict either 'sometimes' or 'a lot'. Also of particular concern, 3.5 per cent said they had difficulty performing work or daily tasks either 'sometimes' or 'a lot'.

The quality-of-life findings suggest that survey respondents were relatively satisfied with most aspects of their day-to-day lives. Particularly surprising was that, despite the recent war, most responded positively regarding their current sense of safety: only 3 per cent were unhappy or extremely unhappy in this regard. Safety was 'very' or 'extremely important' to 94.3 per cent of respondents. There appears to be a significant gap between the insecurity that Southern Lebanese, as a whole, have experienced in the recent past and their individual perceptions of insecurity in 2008. The rearming of Hizbollah and continuing tensions with Israel do not seem to have affected their opinion of the current security situation.

Security

Attitudes towards security varied according to the question but showed a strong preference for state security institutions. With respect to local security and crime, survey respondents indicated they were most likely to turn to the Lebanese police for assistance. As shown in Table 10.1, 91.5 per cent of respondents said the Lebanese army should, ideally, be responsible for security. Almost 90 per cent felt that improving the capacity of the police or other government security services would make their community safer. By contrast, only 23.6 per cent thought that expanding UNIFIL's presence on Lebanon's border with Israel would enhance community safety.

Political beliefs did not strongly alter attitudes on security. Of those supporting a political party, 89.9 per cent stated that the army should be responsible for overall security, compared to 92.4 per cent of those who were not affiliated with a party. There was a somewhat greater difference of opinion between supporters and non-supporters with regard to local security and crime. If personally threatened with violence, 85.4 per cent of party supporters stated that they would go to the police, compared to 92.7 per cent of non-supporters. In relation to stolen property, these tendencies were reversed, with 82.4 per cent of party supporters, versus 68.2 per cent of non-supporters, indicating they would seek police assistance.

Table 10.1 Security and gun control: responses

Question	Response	Party supporters	Non-party supporters	Total*
First person you address/call if an important asset of yours is robbed.	Police	82.4%	68.2%	73.6%
	Other	17.0%	31.8%	26.1%
First person you address/call if someone threatened to hurt or kill you.	Police	85.4%	92.7%	89.9%
	Other	14.0%	7.2%	9.8%
First person you address/call if someone threatened to hurt or kill you.	Community elders	13.0%	1.8%	6.1%
	Other	86.4%	98.1%	93.6%
Ideally, who do you think should be responsible for security?	Army	89.9%	92.4%	91.5%
	Other	6.3%	4.3%	5.0%
Are you for or against stricter government control on civilian weapons?**	For	16.1%	41.7%	33.2%
	Against	34.7%	29.4%	31.2%
Improving the capacity of police/security services would make my community safer.	Agree	88.3%	90.6%	89.7%
	Disagree	0.6%	0.4%	0.5%
Increased UN presence monitoring the border with Israel would make my community safer.	Agree	8.3%	32.7%	23.6%
	Disagree	63.5%	38.4%	47.7%
If Palestinian refugees left Lebanon, it would make my community safer.	Agree	37.5%	67.3%	56.5%
	Disagree	17.9%	12.6%	14.5%
Permanent peace agreements between Israel and Lebanon would make my community safer.	Agree	4.6%	4.2%	4.4%
	Disagree	91.9%	81.3%	85.4%

Notes:

* Percentages may not total 100 because responses such as 'I don't know' and 'I refuse to answer' were excluded.

** Note that 49.2 per cent of party supporters either 'did not know' or 'did not care' about this issue. Of the non-party supporters, 28.8 per cent expressed such sentiments.

Table 10.2 Security and gun control: odds ratios

	Response	Odds ratio	95 per cent CI	p
First person you address/call if an important asset of yours is robbed.	Police	2.266	2.232-2.301	<0.01
First person you address/call if someone threatened to hurt or kill you.	Police	0.480	0.470-0.490	<0.01
	Community elders	8.138	7.882-8.402	<0.01
Ideally, who do you think should be responsible for security?	Army	0.664	0.646-0.683	<0.01
Are you for or against stricter government control on civilian weapons?	Not for	3.049	2.989-3.111	<0.01
Improving the capacity of police/security services would make my community safer.	Disagree	1.208	1.107-1.317	<0.01
Increased UN presence monitoring the border with Israel would make my community safer.	Disagree	6.485	6.353-6.620	<0.01
If Palestinian refugees left Lebanon, it would make my community safer.	Disagree	2.543	2.495-2.592	<0.01
Permanent peace agreements between Israel and Lebanon would make my community safer.	Disagree	1.032	1.002-1.064	0.038

Notes: Odds ratio values greater than 1.0 indicate a greater probability among party supporters, while values less than 1.0 indicate a greater probability among non-party supporters. In calculating odds ratios, 'refuse to reply' and 'don't know' responses where excluded.

The odds ratios presented in Table 10.2 illustrate some important differences between party and non-party supporters in relation to security. For example, as just noted, both groups, by large margins, said they would first seek assistance from the police if threatened with injury or death. Nevertheless, party supporters were more than eight times more likely than non-supporters to indicate that they would first turn to community elders. In essence, while both supporters and non-supporters heavily favour the police in such situations, party supporters are much more likely, when selecting another actor, to choose community elders.

Of all respondents, 56.5 per cent agreed that the departure of Palestinian refugees from the country would make them safer. Survey respondents, by an overwhelming margin, did not think that a comprehensive peace agreement with Israel would improve their security (4.4 per cent asserting it would versus 85.4 per cent stating it would not). There was little difference between party supporters and non-supporters in this regard (4.6 per cent and 4.2 per cent agreement, respectively).

Gun ownership/policy

When asked if they thought owning a weapon would make their family safer, 41.9 per cent of respondents stated it would make them either 'much safer' or 'a little bit safer'. Despite this, when asked a series of questions about their personal gun ownership, only 4.7 per cent admitted to owning a weapon. Many survey participants were evidently reluctant to disclose such information. In several cases, guns were visible in the home during the interview, but the respondent insisted that they did not have any weapons.

Anecdotal evidence such as this, coupled with other research,[18] suggests that the survey findings are probably a gross undercount of gun ownership. South Lebanese consider the topic of guns and gun ownership politically sensitive and, with some exceptions,[19] are reluctant to discuss it with others. Among the respondents who did admit to owning a weapon, only 26.4 per cent stated that they had an arms licence. Among those who said they did not own a weapon, 50.2 per cent stated they did not need one, with 21.7 per cent stating that they did not like guns (multiple responses were allowed). Most respondents said they would not know where to acquire a weapon if they wanted one. The second-most common response was 'the black market', with 5.0 per cent stating this source.

Responses to questions on gun policy were mixed. Of the respondents, 47.1 per cent said they thought greater control over legal firearms licences would make their communities safer. When asked about collecting illegal guns, 42.0 per cent agreed that this, too, would enhance community safety. Overall, a significant percentage of individuals said that security could be improved by outlawing armed militias, enforcing gun regulations, and pursuing other arms control initiatives among civilians. If their satisfaction with their safety is as high as they claim, most respondents ought not to view such changes as potentially important to their overall safety. That they do may mean that political considerations are at play. Supporters of opposition parties are significantly less likely to back gun control efforts, with non-aligned and pro-government respondents viewing such initiatives much more positively.

A significant percentage of survey respondents backed civilian arms control.

Support or non-support for any political party also appears to influence attitudes regarding guns and gun regulation, with non-party supporters far more likely to favour regulation. Of those who did not identify with a specific party, more than half (55.4 per cent) 'strongly agreed' or 'agreed' that greater control of legal firearms licences would make their communities safer; only about one-third (32.0 per cent) of party supporters held the same view. When asked whether harsher punishment for illegal weapons possession would improve community safety, non-party supporters were much more likely to 'strongly agree' or 'agree' (55.7 per cent vs. 35.1 per cent of those who supported a party). Non-party supporters were also more likely to agree that collecting illegal guns from their owners would make communities safer (50.3 per cent vs. 27.8 per cent). When asked whether outlawing armed groups would enhance community safety, 46.2 per cent of non-supporters concurred, compared to 25.1 per cent of party supporters (19.9 per cent of non-supporters strongly agreed with this statement against only 2.5 per cent of party supporters).

DISCUSSION

In highly politicized environments it is often difficult for outsiders, or even insiders, to acquire a clear understanding of public opinion. Election results tell only part of the story, while political polls may not represent the population as a whole. Regardless of whether it is intentional, the misrepresentation of public attitudes by political actors is common and can soon take on the quality of received wisdom. Unquestioned assumptions about public attitudes towards security may, in turn, inform policies and actions that have harmful consequences for stakeholders—or that can backfire on security actors.

Based on direct contact with the public under controlled conditions, household surveys provide one means of clarifying the views of community members about their own security, their trust in state and non-state actors, and their outlook for the future. The results of such studies sometimes call for a reassessment of prior assumptions. The Southern Lebanon Armed Violence Assessment gave the people of the region an opportunity to speak on matters of direct consequence to them. What they said suggests that some correctives to widely held beliefs may be warranted.

Security and armed groups

Shortly after the Southern Lebanon Armed Violence Assessment had been completed, a second study sought to gauge opinion on arms and security issues in Lebanon. This study, conducted by Charney Research in July 2008 for the International Peace Institute (IPI), assessed attitudes in the whole country, not just Southern Lebanon. Participants rated Hizbollah's ability to provide security much lower than that of the Lebanese government. Almost two-thirds of respondents (65 per cent) thought that the Lebanese government could 'provide security and stability in [their] neighborhood', while only 34 per cent believed that Hizbollah could. The figure for the Lebanese army was 93 per cent. In addition, more than three-quarters (76 per cent) believed that only the army, 'not any of the non-governmental groups', should bear arms. The occupation of West Beirut by Hizbollah and its allies in May 2008 appeared to have had a negative effect on public attitudes towards the group, with 58 per cent stating that it was unjustified, compared to 40 per cent in favour. Fifty-nine per cent said they thought the events of May 2008 had weakened Hizbollah's political popularity (Charney Research, n.d.).

Given strong Shi'ite representation in the south, one would have expected the attitudes towards security and armed groups expressed in the Southern Lebanon Assessment to have differed from those of the IPI survey. Shi'ites were thought more supportive of 'armed resistance' against Israel. Because active participation in the resistance generally entails gun ownership and—in the current situation—a relationship with Hizbollah, it was believed that Shi'ite southerners would be less inclined to support the intervention of governmental institutions in security matters. In addition, Southern Lebanese generally have more direct contact with UNIFIL and more experience with Israeli bombardment; it was expected that both these factors would influence attitudes about security provision.

In fact, the results of the Southern Lebanon Assessment show some remarkable similarities to those of the country-wide IPI survey. In particular, the people of the south stated a strong preference for state security institutions, with the Lebanese army and police consistently cited as preferred security providers. This was true irrespective of the respondent's political affiliation. On one point, however, there is a marked difference between the two studies. Most of those interviewed for the Southern Lebanon Assessment appeared quite sceptical of UNIFIL's peacekeeping potential, indicating, by a margin of two to one, that they did not think that an increased UN presence on the border with Israel would improve community safety. The IPI study, by contrast, showed 80 per cent support for the UN peacekeeping force (Charney Research, n.d.).

Most of those interviewed appeared quite sceptical of UNIFIL's peacekeeping potential.

The Southern Lebanon Assessment challenges another common belief. Although it is often assumed Hizbollah is broadly popular among southerners, it appears that support for non-state armed groups in general—and Hizbollah in particular—is at least partially overestimated. The actions of Hizbollah or other non-state armed groups in the region may not reflect the will of most southerners.

Gun ownership and use

The ownership of small arms in Lebanon, and Southern Lebanon in particular, has a long history. Political instability over the course of many generations, with its attendant violence, has fostered a lingering perception of insecurity in the Lebanese population. The Lebanese civil war of 1975–90, the inability of the Lebanese state to protect its citizens, and the persistence of militias in the region have all encouraged individuals to hold arms for protection. As described elsewhere in this chapter, violence remains a feature of the Lebanese political landscape, fuelling arms acquisition by private citizens and militias. Media reports in the run-up to the 2007 presidential election, for example, indicated that arms purchases had risen sharply amidst increasing sectarian tensions (Blanford, 2007).

It seems likely that the weapons ownership rate of 4.7 per cent, measured in the Southern Lebanon Assessment, is a substantial underestimate. This figure contrasts with the 37.5 per cent of MENAANSA focus group participants who said that their household owned one or more guns (MENAANSA, 2006, p. 53).[20] It is also at odds with observations made during the Southern Lebanon study of (unacknowledged) weapons in the home. While the Southern Lebanon Assessment does not cast much light on levels of gun ownership in the south, it does reveal significant support for stricter government control of civilian weapons, as well as the outlawing of non-state armed groups. Responses to questions on gun policy varied according to the question and the political affiliation of the respondent. Supporters of opposition parties were the least likely to back gun control efforts, with non-aligned and pro-government respondents viewing them much more favourably. Similar divisions were found between supporters of any political party and non-supporters, with the first group expressing the greatest scepticism. Both sets of respondents agreed, however, that strengthening the Lebanese police and other security institutions would improve the security of their communities.

The reluctance of many opposition supporters to embrace the regulation of civilian weapons or the prohibition of non-state militias reflects political divisions in the south and the country as a whole. Hizbollah, whose flag features a Kalashnikov, has long argued that its independent military capacity is essential to the armed struggle against Israel. It has consistently stated that it intends to keep its weapons and, moreover, launched its takeover of West Beirut in May 2008 in response to government moves to shut down its military communications network.

In this context, one surprising—and important—finding of the study is that, whatever their political inclinations, the people of Southern Lebanon express strong support for government security institutions. That would suggest that additional support for Lebanese security institutions is warranted. At the same time, the population's doubts regarding UNIFIL's relevance to regional security suggests that the international community's faith in peacekeeping may, in this case, be misplaced. Nevertheless, the contrasting views on weapons regulation underline a critical fact of Lebanese life, namely that the country remains prey to political instability. Until the root causes of political violence are addressed, many in Southern Lebanon appear reluctant to submit their weapons to governmental control. For the moment, the declared faith in public security providers has its limits.

CONCLUSION

The people of Southern Lebanon have survived protracted sectarian conflict, Israeli occupation, and, in the summer of 2006, a devastating war. Independent reports of widespread property damage and some 1,000 deaths in the south are supported by the findings of the Southern Lebanon Armed Violence Assessment. The study also helps to shed light on shared views on arms and security. Hizbollah remains a defining element in this equation, but the Southern Lebanon Assessment reveals that the opinions and experiences of the people of the region are somewhat more diverse than previously assumed.

While survey respondents reported, as of May 2008, high levels of satisfaction with their quality of life and sense of personal safety, as a group they were cautious on the question of government gun control, including the prohibition of non-state militias. Many pro-government and non-aligned participants said they supported such measures; among adherents of opposition parties, including Hizbollah, this was more exceptional. For now, many southerners appear to favour minimal interference from government in the private ownership of arms. Yet at the same time, whatever their political inclinations, survey respondents indicated they looked primarily to government security institutions, specifically the Lebanese army and police, to provide security. This support came at the expense of non-government militias, including Hizbollah's military wing, and the international peacekeeping force UNIFIL. Although Southern Lebanon has long been characterized as a Hizbollah stronghold, its people appear to have more confidence in state security institutions than previously believed.

Notwithstanding widely held beliefs about their popularity among the people of the south, the study also reveals that the support enjoyed by armed non-state actors, most importantly Hizbollah, is probably overestimated. The extent of the party's influence over the social, economic, and political life of Southern Lebanon should not be underestimated, but it cannot be assumed that its actions reflect the will of most southerners.

The people of Southern Lebanon stand at a critical juncture. Despite recent upheavals, many in the region support the regulation of civilian gun ownership and the banning of non-state armed groups. There is even greater—almost unanimous—support for state security institutions, including the Lebanese army and police. Aspirations, perhaps, for a better future, one in which the Lebanese state can provide security for all its citizens. As of early 2009, Lebanon was calm, yet pro-government and opposition forces remained at odds. Tensions with Israel also persisted, fuelled by reports that Hizbollah has rearmed since the 2006 war. In Lebanon, as in so many 'post-conflict' countries, insecurity clouds the horizon. ■

LIST OF ABBREVIATIONS

CI	Confidence interval
GPS	Global Positioning System
IDF	Israel Defense Forces
IPI	International Peace Institute
LAF	Lebanese Armed Forces
MENAANSA	Middle East North Africa Action Network on Small Arms
PLO	Palestine Liberation Organization
SD	Standard deviation
UNIFIL	United Nations Interim Force in Lebanon

ENDNOTES

1 See UNSC (2004a; 2006a).

2 The study was conducted in the Bint Jbeil, Marjeyoun, and Tyre districts.

3 For a complete account of the methodology, sampling, and calculations, along with the full text of the questionnaire, contact author Royce Hutson at <roycehutson@wayne.edu>.

4 Maps were provided by Google Earth Plus and MAPS Geosystems, Inc.

5 Voter rolls in Lebanon are based on place of birth, not current place of residence. It was assumed that any error this generated would be variable across all towns, rather than systematic, and thus was not considered to present significant bias.

6 In this way, the researchers sought to control for sampling bias that would arise if displaced families were systematically excluded from the study. In the event, attempts to make contact with former residents proved unsuccessful; 43 of the targeted households were unoccupied.

7 Target sample sizes did not always match actual sample sizes. In a number of smaller towns, interviews were conducted with fewer than 16 households; in others, more than 16 were surveyed. The final n (sample size) was 1,355 as data gathered from 33 households was considered unreliable.

8 For more on sampling techniques for household-based child labour surveys, see ILO (2008).

9 For more on the Harvard Trauma Questionnaire, see HPRT (n.d.).

10 A total of 15 respondents stated that a family member had been killed in the war, but 4 of these were eliminated because they did not seem to be war-related. The non-war deaths were caused by accident or illness unrelated to the war.

11 The Lebanese government's Higher Relief Council estimates that there were 4,409 injuries for all of Lebanon in 2006 (LHRC, 2006).

12 There was a slight oversampling of women; they were ten per cent more likely to be primary respondents (p=0.001).

13 For the purpose of reporting household income, Lebanese pounds have been converted into US dollars (using the exchange rate of LBP 1,500 = USD 1).

14 During 2006, Lebanese citizens received USD 5.7 billion in remittances, making up 25.2 per cent of the gross domestic product (IFAD, 2007, p. 16).

15 In the Southern Lebanon Armed Violence Assessment, respondents defined 'homelessness' for themselves. No estimate of the number of internally displaced families in Southern Lebanon exists; however, the Lebanon Higher Relief Council estimates that during the war about 974,000 individuals were displaced throughout the country (LHRC, 2009).

16 The percentages add up to more than 100 per cent as many households (36 per cent) received money from more than one donor.

17 For an example of one such poll, see the results of the *Fifth Survey of Lebanese Public Opinion* (LOAC, 2008). This survey found only modest support overall for Hizbollah, even among Shi'ites, 50 per cent of whom stated that Hizbollah best represented them, 22 per cent of whom indicated that Amal best represented them, and 17 per cent of whom identified 'no one'.

18 See MENAANSA (2006, p. 53).

19 See MENAANSA (2006, p. 34).

20 Participants in the study comprised residents of Beirut, the Beka'a Valley, and Southern Lebanon. See MENAANSA (2006, pp. 33–34).

BIBLIOGRAPHY

AI (Amnesty International). 2006. 'Israel/Lebanon: Deliberate Destruction or "Collateral Damage"? Israeli Attacks on Civilian Infrastructure.' August. <http://www.amnesty.org/en/library/info/MDE18/007/2006>

AP (Associated Press). 2007. 'Lebanese Military Analyst: Hezbollah Possess Sophisticated Weapons.' 15 August. <http://www.iht.com/articles/ap/2007/08/15/africa/ME-GEN-Lebanon-Hezbollah.php>

Bazzi, Mohamad. 2006. 'Hezbollah's Arsenal Inflicting Heavy Toll.' *Newsday*. 10 August. <http://www.newsday.com/news/nationworld/world/ny-womiss104846398aug10,0,2488200.story>

BBC (British Broadcasting Corporation). 2008. 'Lebanon Rivals Agree Crisis Deal.' 21 May. <http://news.bbc.co.uk/2/hi/middle_east/7411835.stm>

Blanford, Nicholas. 2007. 'Lebanon's Militias Rearm before Vote.' *Christian Science Monitor*. 7 November. <http://www.csmonitor.com/2007/1107/p06s01-wome.html>

—. 2008. 'UN Resolution 1701: A View from Lebanon.' *Policy Watch*, No. 1414. Washington, DC: The Washington Institute for Near East Policy. 21 October. <http://www.washingtoninstitute.org/templateC05.php?CID=2940>

Butler, Linda. 2006. 'Hizballah through the Fog of the Lebanon War: An Interview with Augustus Richard Norton.' *Journal of Palestine Studies*, Vol. XXXVI, No. 1, pp. 54–70. <http://people.bu.edu/arn/JPS3601_05_Norton_054_070%5B1%5D.pdf>

Charney Research. n.d. *Lebanon Public Opinion Survey*. New York: International Peace Institute. <http://www.ipacademy.org/asset/file/377/lebanese.pdf>

Cobban, Helena. 1984. *The Palestinian Liberation Organisation: People, Power and Politics*. Cambridge: Cambridge University Press.

Collelo, Thomas, ed. 1989. *A Country Study: Lebanon*. Washington, DC: US Federal Research Division, Library of Congress. <http://lcweb2.loc.gov/frd/cs/lbtoc.html>

—. 2003. 'Lebanon: A Country Study.' In John Rolland, ed. *Lebanon: Current Issues and Background*. Hauppauge, NY: Nova Scientific Publishers.

Fishman, Alex. 2008. 'Assessment: Beersheba Also in Rocket Range.' *Yedi'ot Aharonot* (Tel Aviv, in Hebrew). 27 November, p. 12.

Hizbollah. 1985. 'Open Letter to the Downtrodden.' <http://www.foia.cia.gov/browse_docs.asp?doc_no=0000361273>

Hoge, Warren. 2006. 'Syria Agrees to Lebanon Arms Embargo.' *New York Times*. 2 September. <http://travel2.nytimes.com/2006/09/02/world/middleeast/02nations.htm>

HPRT (Harvard Program in Refugee Trauma). *Harvard Trauma Questionnaire*. <http://www.hprt-cambridge.org/Layer3.asp?page_id=9>

HRW (Human Rights Watch). 2007. 'Why They Died: Civilian Casualties in Lebanon during the 2006 War.' <http://hrw.org/reports/2007/lebanon0907>

ICG (International Crisis Group). 2006. 'Conflict History: Lebanon.' <http://www.crisisgroup.org/home/index.cfm?action=conflict_search&l=1&t=1&c_country=62>

IFAD (International Fund for Agricultural Development). 2007. *Sending Money Home: Worldwide Remittance Flows to Developing and Transition Countries.* <http://www.ifad.org/events/remittances/maps/brochure.pdf>

ILO (International Labour Organization). 2008. *Sampling for Household-based Surveys of Child Labour.* <http://www.ilo.org/ipecinfo/product/viewProduct.do?productId=8770>

Kolbe, Athena and Royce Hutson. 2006. 'Human Rights Abuse and other Criminal Violations in Port-au-Prince, Haiti: A Random Survey of Households.' *The Lancet,* Vol. 368, Iss. 9538, pp. 864–73. <http://www.thelancet.com/journals/lancet/article/PIIS0140-6736(06)69211-8/abstract>

LHRC (Lebanon Higher Relief Council). 2009. 'Lebanon Under Siege.' Accessed 25 February 2009. <http://www.lebanonundersiege.gov.lb/english/F/Main/index.asp>

LOAC (Lebanese Opinion Advisory Committee). 2008. 'LOAC Releases Fifth Survey of Lebanese Public Opinion.' <http://www.lebaneseopinion.org/upload/iri-poll5.pdf>

Lunde, Inge and Jørgen Ortmann. 1992. 'Sexual Torture and the Treatment of Its Consequences.' In Metin Başoğlu, ed. *Torture and Its Consequences: Current Treatment Approaches.* Cambridge: Cambridge University Press.

MENAANSA (Middle East North Africa Action Network on Small Arms). 2006. *Public Perceptions of Small Arms and Light Weapons and Community Security in the Middle East.* Amman: MENAANSA and Quaker Service–American Friends Service Committee. February. <http://www.smallarmssurvey.org/files/portal/spotlight/country/nafr_pdf/mideast-leb-pales-sudan-2006_en.pdf>

Nerguizian, Aram. 2009. 'The Lebanese Armed Forces: Challenges and Opportunities in Post-Syria Lebanon.' Working draft. Washington, DC: Center for Strategic and International Studies. <http://www.csis.org/component/option,com_csis_pubs/task,view/id,5275/>

Norton, Augustus Richard. 2000. 'Lebanon's Malaise.' *Survival,* Vol. 42, No. 4. Winter 2000–01, pp. 35–50. <http://web.austin.utexas.edu/chenry/global/coursemats/2006/Norton2.pdf>

Prier, Pierre. 2008. 'Comment le Hezbollah impose sa loi au Liban.' *Le Figaro.* 30 May. <http://www.lefigaro.fr/international/2008/05/31/01003-20080531ARTFIG00042-comment-le-hezbollah-impose-sa-loi-au-liban.php>

Rabinovich, Itamar. 1985. *The War for Lebanon, 1970–1985.* Ithaca: Cornell University Press.

Rao, Prashant. 2006. 'Experts Reckon Shiite Muslim Group Has Strong Capabilities and Determination to Fight Israel.' Agence France-Presse. 18 July. <http://www.middle-east-online.com/english/?id=17002>

Rubin, Uzi. 2007. 'The Rocket Campaign against Israel during the 2006 Lebanon War.' *Mideast Security and Policy Studies,* No. 71. Ramat-Gan: The Begin–Sadat Center for Strategic Studies, Bar-Ilan University. June. <http://www.biu.ac.il/SOC/besa/docs/MSPS71.pdf>

Salamey, Imad and Frederic Pearson. 2007. 'Hezbollah: A Proletarian Party with an Islamic Manifesto: A Sociopolitical Analysis of Islamist Populism in Lebanon and the Middle East.' *Small Wars & Insurgencies,* Vol. 18, Iss. 3, pp. 416–38.

— and Paul Tabar. 2008. 'Consociational Democracy and Urban Sustainability: Transforming the Confessional Divides in Beirut.' *Ethnopolitics,* Vol. 7, Nos. 2–3. June–September, pp. 239–63.

Ta'if Agreement (Document of National Accord). 1989. <http://www.al-bab.com/arab/docs/lebanon/taif.htm>

UNDPKO (United Nations Department of Peacekeeping Operations). 2006. *United Nations Interim Force in Lebanon: Background.* Accessed March 2009. <http://www.un.org/Depts/dpko/missions/unifil/background.html>

UNSC (United Nations Security Council). 1978a. Resolution 425 (1978) of 19 March. <http://www.un.org/documents/sc/res/1978/scres78.htm>

—. 1978b. Resolution 426 (1978) of 19 March. <http://www.un.org/documents/sc/res/1978/scres78.htm>

—. 1978c. Resolution 427 (1978) of 3 May. <http://www.un.org/documents/sc/res/1978/scres78.htm>

—. 2004a. Resolution 1559 (2004) of 2 September. S/RES/1559 (2004) of 2 September. <http://www.un.org/Docs/sc/unsc_resolutions04.html>

—. 2004b. *Report of the Secretary-General Pursuant to Security Council Resolution 1559 (2004).* S/2004/777 of 1 October. <http://www.un.org/Docs/sc/sgrep04.html>

—. 2006a. Resolution 1680 (2006) of 17 May. S/RES/1680 (2006) of 17 May. <http://www.un.org/Docs/sc/unsc_resolutions06.htm>

—. 2006b. Resolution 1701 (2006) of 11 August. S/RES/1701 (2006) of 11 August. <http://www.un.org/Docs/sc/unsc_resolutions06.htm>

Worth, Robert and Eric Lipton. 2008. 'U.S. Resupplies Lebanon Military to Stabilize Ally.' *New York Times.* 25 October. <http://www.nytimes.com/2008/10/26/world/middleeast/26lebanon.html>

ACKNOWLEDGEMENTS

Principal authors

Royce Hutson, Athena Kolbe, Bernadette Stringer, Ted Haines, Harry Shannon, Imad Salamey

INDEX

G

H

I

O

P

Q

R

S

V

W

Y

Z